THE INTERNATIONAL LESSON ANNUAL 1988–89

September–August

A Comprehensive Commentary on
the International Sunday School Lessons
Uniform Series

Edited and with
Introductions by
HORACE R. WEAVER

Lesson Analysis by
WILLIAM H. WILLIMON
and
PAT McGEACHY

ABINGDON PRESS
Nashville

THE INTERNATIONAL LESSON ANNUAL—1988-89

Copyright © 1988 by Abingdon Press

ISBN 0-687-19152-1

Library of Congress ISSN 0074-6770

Lessons based on International Sunday School Lessons; the International Lessons for
Christian Teaching copyright © 1982 by the Committee on the Uniform Series, and
used by permission.

Scripture quotations marked KJV are from the King James, or Authorized, Version
of the Bible.

Scripture quotations marked "Moffatt" are from *The Bible: A New Translation* by James
Moffatt. Copyright © 1935 by Harper & Row, Publishers, Inc. Courtesy of the
publisher.

Scripture quotations marked NEB are from *The New English Bible*. Copyright © the
Delegates of the Oxford University Press and The Syndics of the Cambridge
University Press 1961, 1970. Reprinted by permission.

Scripture quotations marked RSV are from the Revised Standard Version of the
Bible, copyrighted 1946, 1952, © 1971, 1973 by the Division of Christian Education
of the National Council of the Churches of Christ in the U.S.A., and are used by
permission.

MANUFACTURED BY THE PARTHENON PRESS AT
NASHVILLE, TENNESSEE, UNITED STATES OF AMERICA

Editor's Preface

With this issue of *The International Lesson Annual* we begin the third year of the 1986–1991 cycle of the uniform lessons. We are proud of the interdenominational stance of the outlines for biblical studies, which were produced through the work of representatives of thirty-five denominations. We are also pleased that many denominations are represented among the thousands of teachers using this Annual. The *ILA* itself has been written by a team of interdenominational writers, whose names and religious affiliations are listed in the introduction of each quarter.

We are living in an age of expanding terrorism. We do not trust the people of other nations. We tremble at the thought of how easily an angry nationalistic leader can destroy all flora and fauna (including human life) on our planet. Our only real hope is in God. And even some persons of faith wonder if God can or will save humankind!

Now, more than at any other time in history, we face the theological question of how God will save his people from a universal holocaust. Two basic opinions are prevalent: (1) God, seeing the desperation of our time, will descend from heaven to earth to bring judgment on the evil and save the "remnant" of those who have been loyal; (2) God, who is not so much "up there in heaven" as close and aware of our terrible predicament, yearns for persons who will prophetically work with God to see that justice, mercy, kindness, love (good will), and honesty prevail in their individual and social lives. The second view is synergistic—that is, God yearns and looks for dedicated, Christ-like persons who will live the life-style that reflects spiritual kinship with God. God wants persons who will offer their lives to the doing of God's will. This is costly!

This Annual is designed to help teachers in presenting the good news to their students. Each lesson has five sections. The first section, "The Main Question," raises the basic question with which each lesson is concerned. The second section, "As You Read the Scripture," exegetically explores the Scripture passages being studied. The third section prints the passage from both the King James and Revised Standard versions. The fourth section, "The Scripture and the Main Question," contains expositions of the lessons' themes. The fifth section, "Helping Adults Become Involved," offers a step-by-step teaching plan. Topics under this latter heading include "Preparing to Teach," "Introducing the Main Question," "Developing the Lesson," "Helping Class Members Act," and "Planning for Next Sunday." In addition to these five helpful teacher sections, special articles deal with the Suffering Servant, Luke, and death and mourning.

An order blank for additional copies is included in the back of this book.

Horace R. Weaver, *Editor*

CYCLE OF 1986–1992—PLAN II
Arrangement of Quarters According to the
Church School Year, September Through August

	1986-1987	1987-1988	1988-1989	1989-1990	1990-1991	1991-1992
Sept. Oct. Nov.	Beginning of a Covenant People (Old Testament survey) (13)*	Creation Is a Continuing Event (Genesis) (13)	Through Suffering to Hope (Job, Isaiah, Jeremiah) (13)	Visions of God's Rule (Ezekiel, Daniel, 1 & 2 Thessalonians, Revelations) (13)	Prophets, Priests, and Kings (conflicts & concerns) Amos/Amaziah, Elijah/Ahab, David/Nathan, Isaiah/Ahaz, etc. (13)	From the Damascus Road to Rome (life of Paul—primarily Acts) (13)
Dec. Jan. Feb.	The Arrival of a New Age (New Testament survey) (12)	The Call to Discipleship (Matthew—emphasis on Sermon on the Mount)	Scenes of Love and Compassion (Luke) (13)	Lord of Life (the Gospel of John)	Stories Jesus Told (emphasis on parables from the Gospels) (13)	Songs & Prayers of the Bible (Song of Solomon, Psalms, the Magnificat, etc.) (13)
Mar. Apr. May	Undaunted love (the passion narratives of Luke) (9) Easter-Apr. 19 (8) ———— Hosea (5)	(19) Easter-Apr. 3 ———— Look Forward in Faith (Hebrews) (7)	Letters From Prison (Philemon, Colossians, Philippians, Ephesians) Easter-Mar. 26 (4) (13)	(20) Easter-Apr. 15 ———— Abiding in Love (1, 2, 3 John) (6)	Counsel for a Church in Crisis (1 & 2 Corinthians) Easter-Mar. 31 (5) (13)	The Strong Son of God (The Gospel) Of Mark) (8) Easter-Apr. 19 (8) ———— God's People in the World (1 & 2 Peter) (6)
June July Aug.	The Righteousness of God (Romans) (13)	Moses and His Mission (Exodus, Numbers, Deuteronomy) (13)	Conquest and Challenge (Joshua, Judges, Ruth) (13)	Wisdom as a Way of Life (Ecclesiastes, Proverbs, some Psalms, James) (13)	After the Exile (Ezra, Nehemiah, appropriate prophets) (13)	God's Judgment & Mercy (Neglected minor prophets: Nahum, Jonah, Obadiah, Habbakuk, Zephaniah) (7) Organizing for Ministry (Pastoral Epistles) (6)

*Parenthetical numerals indicate number of sessions.

Contents

FIRST QUARTER

Through Suffering to Hope

UNIT I: JOB—PROBING THE MEANING OF SUFFERING (SEPT. 4–25)

LESSON   PAGE

Introduction.. 11

1. When Suffering Comes... 12
   Sept. 4—*Job 1:1–2:10*
2. Helping People Who Hurt.....................................20
   Sept. 11—*Job 2:11-13; 4:1-9; 8:1-10; 11; 13:1-12*
3. Asking God Why...27
   Sept. 18—*Job 29:1–30:27*
4. Overcoming Through Faith....................................35
   Sept. 25—*Job 38:1-7; 40:1-9; 42*

UNIT II: ISAIAH—INTERPRETING A NATION'S SUFFERING (OCT. 2–30)

Introduction.. 42

5. Disappointing to God... 43
   Oct. 2—*Isaiah 5:1-25*
6. A Willing Volunteer... 50
   Oct. 9—*Isaiah 6*
7. A Comforting Word.. 58
   Oct. 16—*Isaiah 40*
   Spiritual Enrichment Articles:
   The Pain and Anguish of God
   Chester E. Custer...65
   Jesus' Model of the Messiah: The Suffering Servant
   Eldrich C. Campbell.. 68
8. The Suffering Savior...71
   Oct. 23—*Isaiah 52:13–53:12*
9. A Better Day.. 78
   Oct. 30—*Isaiah 65:8-25*

UNIT III: JEREMIAH—LOOKING FOR A NEW DAY (NOV. 6–27)

Introduction.. 86

10. Responding to God's Call.....................................87
    Nov. 6—*Jeremiah 1*
11. Hiding Behind Religion.. 94
    Nov. 13—*Jeremiah 7*
12. Suffering for Truth.. 102
    Nov. 20—*Jeremiah 37:1–38:13*
13. A New Covenant... 110
    Nov. 27—*Jeremiah 31:27-34*

SECOND QUARTER
Scenes of Love and Compassion

UNIT I: PROMISE AND EXPECTATION (DEC. 4–25)

LESSON   PAGE

Introduction 118
Spiritual Enrichment Article:
  The Unique Gentile Writer: Luke
  Horace R. Weaver   118
1.   Doubting God's Promise 124
    Dec. 4—*Luke 1:1-25, 57-80*
2.   Accepting God's Promise 131
    Dec. 11—*Luke 1:26-56*
3.   Rejoicing in God's Greatness 139
    Dec. 18—*Luke 2:1-20*
4.   Celebrating the Savior's Birth 147
    Dec. 25—*Luke 2:21-40*

UNIT II: PROCLAMATION AND MINISTRY (JAN. 1–29)

Introduction 155
5.   Anointed to Preach the Good News 155
    Jan. 1—*Luke 4:14-44*
6.   Accepting Our Mission 163
    Jan. 8—*Luke 5:1-11*
7.   Healing and Forgiveness 170
    Jan. 15—*Luke 5:12-26*
8.   Forgiveness: A Measure of Love 178
    Jan. 22—*Luke 7:36-50*
9.   Touch: A Step Toward Wholeness 186
    Jan. 29—*Luke 8:1-3, 40-56*

UNIT III: RESPONSE AND RESPONSIBILITY (FEB. 5–26)

Introduction 194
10.   Seeking God's Kingdom 194
    Feb. 5—*Luke 12:13-34*
11.   Expressing Gratitude 202
    Feb. 12—*Leviticus 13:9-17, 45-46; Luke 17:11-19*
12.   Responding to God's Call 210
    Feb. 19—*Luke 18:18-30*
13.   Becoming a Believer 217
    Feb. 26—*Luke 19:1-10*

THIRD QUARTER

Letters from Prison

UNIT I: PHILEMON—AN APPEAL FOR ACCEPTANCE (MAR. 5)

LESSON   PAGE

      Introduction.. 225

1.   An Appeal for Acceptance.....................................225
      Mar. 5—*Philemon*

UNIT II: COLOSSIANS—CHRIST THE LORD (MAR. 12–26)

      Introduction.. 233

2.   Citizens of a New Kingdom......................................234
      Mar. 12—*Colossians 1:1-14*

3.   Remedy for False Teaching....................................... 242
      Mar. 19—*Colossians 2:6-23*
      Spiritual Enrichment Article:
      On Facing Death
      Herbert H. Lambert.. 250

4.   Risen with Christ...252
      Mar. 26—*Luke 24:1-7; Colossians 1:15-29; 3:1-4*

UNIT III: PHILIPPIANS—LIFE IN CHRIST (APR. 2–23)

      Introduction.. 261

5.   To Live Is Christ... 261
      Apr. 2—*Philippians 1:1-26*

6.   Serving as Christ Served.. 269
      Apr. 9—*Philippians 1:27–2:30*

7.   Pressing On in Christ.. 277
      Apr. 16—*Philippians 3*

8.   Rejoicing in Christ.. 285
      Apr. 23—*Philippians 4*

UNIT IV: EPHESIANS—THE CHRISTIAN CALLING
(APR. 30–MAY 28)

      Introduction.. 292

9.   The Blessings of Being a Christian....................................293
      Apr. 30—*Ephesians 1:1-14*

10.   Peace with God and One Another.................................... 301
      May 7—*Ephesians 2*

11.   Building Up the Body of Christ..308
      May 14—*Ephesians 4:1-16*

12.   Called to New Life...316
      May 21—*Ephesians 4:17–5:20*

13.   Guidelines for Family Life... 324
      May 28—*Ephesians 5:21–6:4*

FOURTH QUARTER
Conquest and Challenge

UNIT I: JOSHUA—A TIME OF CONQUEST AND SETTLEMENT
(JUNE 4–25)

LESSON   PAGE

Introduction...333

1.   Stones for Remembering...334
        June 4—*Joshua 1–4*

2.   God Gives Victory...342
        June 11—*Joshua 6*

3.   Settlement of the Promised Land...............................351
        June 18—*Joshua 18:1-10; 21:43–22:6*

4.   Life Is Shaped by Choices..359
        June 25—*Joshua 24*

UNIT II: JUDGES—A TIME OF CONFLICT AND ADJUSTMENT
(JULY 2–AUG. 6)

Introduction...367

5.   Dealing with a Nation's Sins...................................367
        July 2—*Judges 1–2*

6.   Working Together for Justice....................................375
        July 9—*Judges 4–5*

7.   Gideon: Reluctant Leader..383
        July 16—*Judges 6*

8.   Gideon: Relying on God's Power................................392
        July 23—*Judges 7*

9.   Choosing Trustworthy Leaders..................................400
        July 30—*Judges 8:22–9*

10.   Samson: Man of Weakness and Strength......................408
        Aug. 6—*Judges 16*

UNIT III: RUTH—A RECORD OF COMMITMENT AND HOPE
(AUG. 13–27)

Introduction...416

11.   Courageous Choices...417
        Aug. 13—*Ruth 1*

12.   The Compassion of Boaz...425
        Aug. 20—*Ruth 2–3; Deuteronomy 24:19-21*

13.   The Fulfillment of Hope..433
        Aug. 27—*Ruth 4*

Through Suffering to Hope

UNIT I: JOB—PROBING THE MEANING OF SUFFERING
Horace R. Weaver

FOUR LESSONS   SEPTEMBER 4–25

This quarter's study of Job, Isaiah, and Jeremiah provides insight into the struggle that accompanied the individual and national suffering of the Hebrews. Each of these three persons suffered in significantly different ways. Job's sufferings were of a physical and theological sort; Isaiah suffered mental and social pain due to the denunciation of his religious insights by fellow Jews; Jeremiah's suffering arose from the psychological and social pain he felt when he had to renounce the Deuteronomic Reform of 621 B.C., having decided it could not change human life, and also when he prophesied doom to the exiled Jewish leaders in Babylon. Each, in their own way, learned the absolute value of dependence on the presence of God in their lives.

There are three units of study in this quarter: unit I, "Job—Probing the Meaning of Suffering"; unit II, "Isaiah—Interpreting a Nation's Suffering"; unit III, "Jeremiah—Looking for a New Day."

"Job—Probing the Meaning of Suffering" is a study of Job's struggle with the traditional Hebrew belief that suffering is the result of sin and prosperity is the result of righteous, religious living. The individual lessons are as follows: "When Suffering Comes," September 4, which focuses on Satan's being allowed to tempt Job; "Helping People Who Hurt," September 11, shows Job's endurance of the well-intentioned but insensitive ministry of three of his friends; "Asking God Why," September 18, tells how Job takes his case to God, stating his distress)and sense of alienation from God; "Overcoming Through Faith," September 25, tells of God's revelation to Job of how little Job understands life.

Contributors to the first quarter:

Eldrich C. Campbell, pastor, United Methodist Churches on Long Beach Island, New Jersey.

Chester E. Custer, executive secretary, director of Older Adult Ministry, Board of Discipleship, The United Methodist Church, Nashville, Tennessee.

Lynne Deming, responsible for planning curriculum for children, youth, and adults, Curriculum Resources Committee of the Board of Discipleship, The United Methodist Church, Nashville, Tennessee.

Horace R. Weaver, Ph.D in biblical literature; retired editor of adult publications, Curriculum Resources Committee of the Board of Discipleship, The United Methodist Church, Nashville, Tennessee.

William H. Willimon, minister to the university, Duke University, Durham, North Carolina.

Leonard T. Wolcott, retired professor of New Testament studies, Scarritt College, Nashville, Tennessee.

When Suffering Comes

Background Scripture: Job 1:1–2:10

The Main Question—William H. Willimon

Into one man's life there comes a shadowy, threatening figure. This one is called Satan, literally translated "the Accuser" or "Questioner." Who is this Satan? He is depicted as the one who raises questions about our firm beliefs. He is the one who attempts to undermine the certainty of our cherished assumptions.

In your own life, what is for you the major test of faith? Do you think the discoveries of science offer the greatest test of Christian belief. How is it possible to believe that a Divine Being has created and still cares for our world when science reveals to us that our world is only an infinitesimal speck within a vast universe?

Or do you believe that the everyday tragedies of life are the greatest test of faith? Perhaps you have known someone like Job whose faith was tested and eventually undermined because of seemingly pointless tragedy afflicting his or her life.

"God never puts more upon us than we can bear" is what people sometimes say. But I have noted as a pastor that there are times when life seems to hit us with so much misfortune that our once firm faith is gradually chipped away, until we have little that we believe in or hope for. The result of such "testing" is not a sure faith but rather a devastated one. In such times of testing, we fear because we know that we could go either way—toward stronger faith or toward a loss of faith. Which shall it be for Job? Which shall it be for us? What can we do to strengthen our faith in such times of testing?

Selected Scripture

King James Version	Revised Standard Version
Job 1:1-3, 8-11, 20-21	*Job 1:1-3, 8-11, 20-21*
1 There was a man in the land of Uz, whose name *was* Job; and that man was perfect and upright, and one that feared God, and eschewed evil.	1 There was a man in the land of Uz, whose name was Job; and that man was blameless and upright, one who feared God, and turned away from evil. 2 There were born to him seven sons and three daughters. 3 He had seven thousand sheep, three thousand camels, five hundred yoke of oxen, and five hundred she-asses, and very many servants; so that this man was the greatest of all the people of the east.
2 And there were born unto him seven sons and three daughters.	
3 His substance also was seven thousand sheep, and three thousand camels, and five hundred yoke of oxen, and five hundred she asses, and a very great household; so that this man was the greatest of all the men of the east.	
....	....
8 And the Lord said unto Satan,	8 And the Lord said to Satan,

hast thou considered my servant Job, that there is none like him in the earth, a perfect and an upright man, one that feareth God, and escheweth evil?

9 Then Satan answered the Lord, and said, Doth Job fear God for nought?

10 Hast not thou made a hedge about him, and about his house, and about all that he hath on every side? thou hast blessed the work of his hands, and his substance is increased in the land.

11 But put forth thine hand now, and touch all that he hath, and he will curse thee to thy face.

....

20 Then Job arose, and rent his mantle, and shaved his head, and fell down upon the ground, and worshipped,

21 And said, Naked came I out of my mother's womb, and naked shall I return thither: the Lord gave, and the Lord hath taken away; blessed be the name of the Lord.

Job 2:4-6, 9-10

4 And Satan answered the Lord, and said, Skin for skin, yea, all that a man hath will he give for his life.

5 But put forth thine hand now, and touch his bone and his flesh, and he will curse thee to thy face.

6 And the Lord said unto Satan, Behold, he *is* in thine hand; but save his life.

....

9 Then said his wife unto him, Dost thou still retain thine integrity? curse God, and die.

10 But he said unto her, Thou speakest as one of the foolish women speaketh. What? shall we receive good at the hand of God, and shall we not receive evil? In this Job did not sin with his lips.

Key Verse: **The Lord gave, and the Lord hath taken away; blessed be the name of the Lord. (Job 1:21)**

"Have you considered my servant Job, that there is none like him on the earth, a blameless and upright man, who fears God and turns away from evil?" 9 Then Satan answered the Lord, "Does Job fear God for nought? 10 Hast thou not put a hedge about him and his house and all that he has, on every side? Thou hast blessed the work of his hands, and his possessions have increased in the land. 11 But put forth thy hand now, and touch all that he has, and he will curse thee to thy face."

....

20 Then Job arose, and rent his robe, and shaved his head, and fell upon the ground, and worshiped. 21 And he said, "Naked I came from my mother's womb, and naked shall I return; the Lord gave, and the Lord has taken away; blessed be the name of the Lord."

Job 2:4-6, 9-10

4 Then Satan answered the Lord, "Skin for skin! All that a man has he will give for his life. 5 But put forth thy hand now, and touch his bone and his flesh, and he will curse thee to thy face." 6 And the Lord said to Satan, "Behold, he is in your power; only spare his life."

....

9 Then his wife said to him, "Do you still hold fast your integrity? Curse God, and die."[10] But he said to her, "You speak as one of the foolish women would speak. Shall we receive good at the hand of God, and shall we not receive evil?" In all this Job did not sin with his lips.

Key Verse: **The Lord gave, and the Lord has taken away; blessed be the name of the Lord. (Job 1:21)**

As You Read the Scripture—Lynne Deming

Job 1–2. As a whole these chapters form what is often called the prologue to the book of Job. Chapters 1–2 introduce us to the character of Job, portraying a man who is patient and remains calm no matter what happens to him. Originally the prologue in these two chapters and the epilogue in Chapter 42 were probably an independent story that formed part of the regional oral tradition in the area, long before the time Israel was established as a nation.

Job 1:1. Here we learn the basics about the main character. His name was Job, which means either "hostile" or "penitent." He was "blameless and upright," which is important to remember as we learn about what happened to him. The fact that he "feared God and turned away from evil" makes us wonder all the more how and why he endured everything that was laid on him.

We also read in this verse that Job came from the land of Uz. Two main possibilities exist for the location of Uz: It was either in Edom, a territory southeast of Israel between Israel and Egypt, or in Haran, which is far north of Israel. These two suggestions are based on verses in the Bible (such as Genesis 36:28 and 22:21) that mention the name Uz in connection with a particular location.

Verse 2. The fact that Job had ten children testifies to his righteousness, for in ancient times many offspring were considered to be a sign of righteous living and obedience to God.

Verse 8. To whom is God speaking? Satan is used here as a title, not a name. The word "satan" in verse 6 is better translated "the adversary." This figure is one of the members of the divine court, who came along with others to "present themselves before the Lord" (verse 6).

God's question, "Have you considered my servant Job?" means something like, "Have you thought about him at all?" If Satan has a pessimistic view of what persons on earth are like, he might pay attention to this Job, who is blameless and upright.

Verses 9-11. Here is Satan's answer to God's question of verse 8. First, Satan answers by asking a rhetorical question to which he assumes the answer is no: "Does Job fear God for nought?" Doesn't Job live a righteous life because his rewards are great? This question is the key to what happens to Job from now on.

Verse 20. Job stands up and tears his clothing when he hears what has happened to his children. In the ancient world, tearing one's garments was a visible sign of intense grief. In Genesis 37:34, Joseph's father Jacob tears his garments after learning that Joseph is missing and presumed dead.

Verse 21. Job's response is a pessimistic view of what life is all about.

Job 2:4. After God points out that Job has still maintained his integrity despite what has happened so far, Satan answers "Skin for skin." This proverbial expression is explained in the next sentence. Whatever one owns will be given up in exchange for one's life. The proverb may have originally been used by traders who dealt in animal hides.

Verses 5-6. Satan continues the challenge by saying that Job will surely curse God if he is physically harmed. God specifies that Job's life must be spared if the challenge is to continue.

Verse 9. Job's wife here advises him to give in, to give up his integrity. "Curse God and die," she says. Fortunately, Job does not follow her advice.

Verse 10. After all that has happened, Job still does not curse God "with his lips." In other words, Job does not curse God as his wife thinks he should do.

The Scripture and the Main Question—William H. Willimon

There Was a Man Named Job

The book of Job is one of the most loved books of the Bible. Its penetrating look at the problem of God's relationship to human suffering is unsurpassed in both poetic beauty and sheer honesty.

Satan, the Accuser, speaks the question which sets the tone for the rest of the book: "Does Job fear God for nought?" (1:9). In other words, does Job love and worship God simply because God is God, or because he hopes to obtain special favor and protection from God? Satan asks, "Hast thou not put a hedge about him and his house and all that he has, on every side? Thou hast blessed the work of his hands, and his possessions have increased in the land. But put forth thy hand now, and touch all that he has, and he will curse thee to thy face" (1:10-11).

The argument of the Accuser is a familiar one: When things are going great in life and everything is going our way, it is fine to love and worship God. But just let the going get rough, and we will desert God.

In my church, people who are going through times of trouble sometimes say, "God never puts more on us than we can bear." But I have not always found this saying to be true. Sometimes misfortune strengthens us; sometimes it crushes us. For every one who found his or her faith strengthened during time of crisis, there is someone else who lost his or her faith during similar situations. This is the Accuser's argument: Job will forsake God as soon as fortune forsakes him. All of Job's pious blessings will turn to hateful curses once pain comes.

The Lord Gave and the Lord Has Taken Away

Of course, suffering always comes. One doesn't have to live this life very long before one realizes that suffering "comes with the territory." What does it mean to suffer? When we speak of suffering we mean that we are in pain. But in itself, pain cannot be regarded as unmitigated evil. Pain is part of life, human life or any other. The dead cannot feel pain. Without pain, human beings would self-destruct. A parent protects a child from serious burns by holding the child's hand near a hot stove and saying, "Hurt!" The child, feeling the sensation of heat, makes the connection and avoids contact with the stove.

"Where does it hurt?" the doctor asks. Pain is a valuable diagnostic tool. A person who feels no physical pain is in a dangerous condition. Also, pain helps to immobilize the body during periods of serious illness, so that the body's curative processes can work to restore health.

Pain can also function to awaken our compassion. We feel the suffering of others as if it were our own. Empathy is somewhat selfish, since the pain we are feeling is the result of putting ourselves in the place of another. We hurt more at the thought of our pain than at the thought of the other person's affliction. But such empathy sometimes mobilizes us to find cures for dreaded illness, for instance, to avoid similar pain.

Life is pain. We come into the world through the pain of our mothers and we depart through suffering of our bodies. Today there is resentment toward pain in our culture. We have so many new methods of alleviating pain. Our medical establishment has, even if unintentionally, led us to believe that all pain can be eradicated and, by implication, that any pain is unjustified and without any benefit.

Yet we cannot regard all pain as an unmitigated evil. Without pain, how could humanity have developed and progressed? Imagine what sort of society would develop in a world without the pain of hunger, or excessive heat and cold. The human creativity exercised in farming, building, and hunting, by which we fend off painful conditions, would be pointless. There would be no need for exertion, cooperation, and ingenuity in a painless paradise. An anesthetic world without pain would leave little room for the development of all those qualities which make human life *human*.

Yet let us not be too positive about pain. When confronted with sickness and pain, Jesus did not simply philosophize about the pain as evidence of the way the world was wisely constructed; rather, he charged that the illness was the work of Satan (Luke 13:16). Paul fervently prayed that his "thorn in the flesh" would be removed (II Corinthians 12:7-9), knowing that he could do more for God if he were healthy than if he were sick.

Certainly, pain helps us to adapt. But some suffering is in no way proportional to the gravity of the danger—a toothache, for instance. Job's suffering is depicted as being so terrible, so utterly overwhelming and devastating, that no one could have told him that the pain would be worth it in the long run, that it would help him learn something that would make all of the suffering seem justified.

Thus we are struck by a cruel paradox: Pain is part of animal life, human or otherwise; yet pain, particularly chronic, excessive pain such as Job suffered, is evil. One person's pain from cancer causes her to feel self-pity, resentment toward others, cynicism. Another person's cancer mobilizes her to form the first cancer support group in her community, to seek out other victims, and to encourage them not to lose hope. What is the difference?

Blessed Be the Name of the Lord

Part of the difference between pain that edifies and pain that crushes must be in the way we experience pain. Two people suffer the same pain, yet one is able to endure, even to triumph, another is utterly crushed. Why?

In his autobiography, *Once to Every Man*, William Sloane Coffin recalls attending the funeral of a fellow classmate at Yale who had been killed in an accident. Coffin said that he sat there before the funeral in anger and cynicism, thinking about how unfair it is that things like this should happen in the world, how disgusting that people should worship a God who allows terrible tragedies like this to happen.

The service began with a priest moving down the aisle intoning the familiar words from Job, "The Lord gave, and the Lord has taken away; blessed be the name of the Lord."

Coffin said it was as if he heard a voice asking him, "Which part do you object to? The giving? The taking?"

Then he realized that it is all too easy for us to curse God when we experience suffering and loss, without remembering that the things and the people we hold so dear are themselves given to us be a loving God. In our pain, we forget that gift and focus only upon the loss, denying the goodness of the Giver of all good gifts.

Job, even in his time of suffering, was able to remember the gift and the Giver. In our times of suffering, which come in every life, let us pray that we will be able to remember.

Helping Adults Become Involved—Leonard T. Wolcott

Preparing to Teach

This lesson tells how to deal with suffering, through the story of Job. Read the printed resources. There is an excellent discussion of the meaning of Job in the introduction to Archibald MacLeish's play *J.B.*, which you might also want to read.

Use the following outline to organize the lesson:

     I.   Review the drama of Job.
    II. Note different reactions to suffering.
  III. Explore the meaning of suffering.
  IV. Examine personal responses to suffering, in light of
          our goals and our faith.
    V. Conclusion.

Read carefully "The Scripture and the Main Question" and "As You Read the Scripture." These form the heart of the lesson. The ideas, insights, and suggestions in these sections should be reflected continually in your lesson plan.

As you use the suggested outline, you may want to either quote or paraphrase ideas. You might like to jot in the margin of your outline the page number and paragraph being referred to. For example, you could write a reference to page 65, paragraph 3, as 65-3.

There should be a Bible for each class member. To make the story vivid, plan to tell the story of Job 1:1–2:10 as a play. Write up the dialogue and make copies for class members. For example:

Narrator: Job was blameless and upright, one who feared God, and turned away from evil. He had seven sons and three daughters, seven thousand sheep, three thousand camels, five hundred she-asses, and very many servants, so that he was the greatest of all the people of the East. His sons used to hold feasts and invite their sisters to eat and drink with them. When the days of the feasts had run their course, Job would send and sanctify his children, and he would rise early in the morning and offer burnt offerings for them, for he feared that they might have sinned in their hearts. Thus, Job did continually.

             Now there was a day when the sons of God came to present themselves before the Lord, and Satan also came.

The Lord: Whence have you come, Satan?

Satan: From going to and fro on the earth, and from walking up and down in it.

The Lord: Have you considered my servant Job?

Continue in this way, reading the several parts in the Bible. Print questions for discussion on newsprint or the chalkboard: Why do the righteous suffer? Is suffering God's punishment for evildoing? If we live a good life, tithe, and go to church, are we sure to prosper? Do pain and sickness make it easier or harder to believe in God's caring?

Introducing the Main Question

Basic and helpful ideas are presented in the section "The Main Question." These ideas are essential in helping to identify the purpose of the lesson.

"The Main Question" reviews problems we all have. Some class members will have more intense experiences of suffering than others. Human suffering may consist of the loss of possessions or loved ones. It may be experienced as physical pain, personal anxiety, frustration, tension in human relations, and, in some places, even as oppression. When it strikes, we try to cope with it by taking something that will relieve us, such as pain killers, or by escaping it, or by blaming others for it, or by trying to understand it.

I was called to counsel with Dan. Dan is the kind of young man old novels would call "clean-cut." But Dan is in prison. He is trying, however, to improve his life, to keep prison rules, to suppress his temper. He seeks advice from his counselor and chaplain. He studies the Bible and tries to follow Jesus' teaching.

A prison guard goaded him, then reported him, exaggerating minor infractions, and Dan was disciplined. Merits gained toward release and privileges earned, such as a private cell, were taken away. He was beginning at the bottom again. He was resentful. He prayed but never felt that God was hearing him or caring. Dan's thoughts were circling in despair.

Will Willimon states it well: There are times when life seems to hit us with so much tragedy and misfortune that our once firm faith is gradually chipped away, until we have little that we believe in or hope for. What can we do to strengthen our faith in such times of testing?

Developing the Lesson

I. Review the drama of Job.

Read aloud the printed scripture telling of Job's story. Explain the background as given in your resources. It begins as a folk-drama. It attacks the problem of suffering from a greater than common understanding of God. In the drama, God is holding court. Satan, a courtier, is the "adversary," cynical about the possibility of righteousness among human beings. God calls his attention to Job, pointing out his irreproachable piety. The cynical Satan questions Job's motives. God has confidence in Job's integrity. Satan does not, so he is given free reign to test Job.

There are seven sections in this passage: (1) The righteous, prosperous Job is introduced (1:1-5); (2) Job is discussed in a heavenly court scene (1:6-12); (3) Job is tested—he loses all his property and his children (1:13-21); (4) Job remains faithful (1:22); (5) at a second court scene in heaven, Satan is allowed still further testing (2:1-6); (6) Job is afflicted with a miserable sickness (2:7-9); (7) Job continues to respond with faith (2:10).

One way for the class to vividly grasp the story is for them to read it as a drama. If you have divided the passage 1:1–2:10 into speaking parts, distribute them now and assign parts. Or, the drama may be read directly from the Bible, with class members reading the different parts.

II. Note different reactions to suffering.

Let the class share stories of people who have suffered. How did they respond their suffering? Note the point Dr. Willimon makes in "The Scripture and the Main Question": "Suffering can lead to different consequences, depending on the sufferer's reaction."

III. Explore the meaning of suffering.

When things go well we say, "I must have been living right." When a good person suffers we ask, "Why do bad things happen to good people?" Do we really suppose that in the scheme of creation good behavior is rewarded with well-being and prosperity, and bad behavior with suffering? If we have compassion and do not want people we love to suffer, how could a compassionate God allow it?

Use these and the other questions you have listed, for class discussion.

IV. Examine personal responses to suffering, in light of our goals and our faith.

Ask: Are we frustrated at suffering because it interferes with the good life? What are our goals? Happiness? Success? Good health? Prosperity? If suffering spoils our goals are we angry with God? Some people stop going to church or say they no longer believe in God when they suffer or when their plans are frustrated. Their response is like that of a pouting child. Others blame someone else for their suffering. Legal suits are brought by people who have found someone to blame for their misfortunes.

V. Conclusion.

Come back to Job's response to his suffering. Satan was wrong. Job did not worship God for the divine protection he could get out of it (1:9-11). He worshiped God for God alone. Ask: Is Job's attitude toward God ours? Some tell us that God will help us win, become prosperous, have great health. Does this mean that if we do not win, are not prosperous, and do not have great health, that we are not properly serving God? Or can we have a vital, buoyant faith, even when we suffer?

Job was grieved at the loss of his children, yet he said, "the Lord gave and the Lord has taken away" (1:21). Was this fatalism? No, it was a recognition that all he had was due to the goodness of God. Read from 2:10: "Shall we receive good at the hand of God and shall we not receive evil?"

Helping Class Members Act

Ask the class to suggest ways to face suffering. Close by reading Job 1:22 and 2:10, and praying for courage to trust in God.

Planning for Next Sunday

Ask class members to think about how to be a friend to those who suffer. Ask them to read Job 2–3.

Helping People Who Hurt

Background Scripture: Job 2:11-13, 4:1-9; 8:1-10; 11; 13:1-12

The Main Question—William H. Willimon

My God, Why? is the engaging title of a book by Professor Frederick Sontag. In the book, Sontag examines various examples of human pain and suffering and various attempts to explain them. Eventually, he finds that most philosophical and theological explanations for suffering are inadequate. This leaves us, he says, with a gigantic "Why?" as we look at much undeserved suffering within the world.

Perhaps, some people say, we should not ask such questions. We should accept whatever pain and suffering we find in life as "God's will," and go on about our business. It is not for us humans to know the reasons for everything that goes on in the world, and besides, is it not bordering on sacrilege to demand explanations of God?

What does God do with our deepest questioning about the way the world works? What does God do with Job and his question? Is God offended that, in times of pain, suffering, and tragedy, we clench our fists and scream out, "Why?" Should we simply suffer in silence, enclosed in our shells, and "accept it all on faith"? Job's faith in God was so strong that he did not hesitate to question the workings of God. He was so convinced that God is just and good that he could afford to be angry, to shout out in rage at the misfortune which had befallen him in life, to demand of God explanations.

Job's ravings and questions could be seen as a mark of insufferable impudence toward the Creator. Or they could be seen as a sign in his own life that reasons lie behind the workings of the universe and that, ultimately, God wills good for his creatures. How can faith deal with this issue? As with Job, let us wrestle with the alternatives.

Selected Scripture

King James Version	Revised Standard Version
Job 4:1, 7-8	*Job 4:1, 7-8*
1 Then El'i-phaz the Te'man-ite answered and said,	1 Then Eli'phaz the Te'manite answered:
....	....
7 Remember, I pray thee, who *ever* perished, being innocent? or where were the righteous cut off?	7 "Think now, who that was innocent ever perished? Or where were the upright cut off?
8 Even as I have seen, they that plow iniquity, and sow wickedness, reap the same.	8 As I have seen, those who plow iniquity and sow trouble reap the same."

Job 8:1, 5-7

1 Then answered Bildad the Shu'hite, and said,

....

5 If thou wouldest seek unto God betimes, and make thy supplication to the Almighty;

6 If thou *wert* pure and upright; surely now he would awake for thee, and make the habitation of thy righteousness prosperous.

7 Though thy beginning was small, yet thy latter end should greatly increase.

Job 11:1, 4-6

1 Then answered Zo'phar the Na'a-ma-thite', and said,

....

4 For thou hast said, My doctrine *is* pure, and I am clean in thine eyes.

5 But oh that God would speak, and open his lips against thee;

6 And that he would show thee the secrets of wisdom, that *they are* double to that which is! Know therefore that God exacteth of thee *less* than thine iniquity *deserveth*.

Job 13:1-5

1 Lo, mine eye hath seen all *this*, mine ear hath heard and understood it.

2 What ye know, *the same* do I know also: I *am* not inferior unto you.

3 Surely I would speak to the Almighty, and I desire to reason with God.

4 But ye *are* forgers of lies, ye *are* all physicians of no value.

5 Oh that ye would altogether hold your peace! and it should be your wisdom.

Key Verse: **To him that is afflicted pity should be shewed from his friend; but he forsaketh the fear of the Almighty. (Job 6:14)**

Job 8:1, 5-7

1 Then Bildad the Shuhite answered:

....

5 "If you will seek God
and make supplication to the Almighty,

6 If you are pure and upright,
surely then he will rouse himself for you
and reward you with a rightful habitation.

7 And though your beginning was small,
your latter days will be very great."

Job 11:1, 4-6

1 Then Zophar the Na'amathite answered:

....

4 "For you say, 'My doctrine is pure,
and I am clean in God's eyes.'

5 But oh, that God would speak, and open his lips to you,

6 and that he would tell you the secrets of wisdom!
For he is manifold in understanding.
Know then that God exacts of you less than your guilt deserves."

Job 13:1-5

1 "Lo, my eye has seen all this, my ear has heard and understood it.

2 What you know, I also know;
I am not inferior to you.

3 But I would speak to the Al- mighty.
and I desire to argue my case with God.

4. As for you, you whitewash with lies;
worthless physicians are you all.

5 Oh that you would keep silent, and it would be your wisdom!"

Key Verse: **He who withholds kindness from a friend forsakes the fear of the Almighty. (Job 6:14)**

FIRST QUARTER

As You Read the Scripture—Lynne Deming

Job 4:1. This verse tells us who is speaking in the next two chapters. Eliphaz the Temanite is the first one of Job's three friends to speak to him concerning his fate. From this point on, the book is a series of speeches by the various persons involved. The friends each speak several times, Job answers each one, and finally God speaks to Job at the end of the book. The speeches of Job's friends portray various points of view coming from traditional wisdom circles in ancient Israel.

Verses 7-8. The question of Eliphaz, posed in verse 7, represents an understanding of retribution common in ancient Israel. Those who do evil ("plow iniquity") are punished in evil ways ("reap the same"). It is one possible explanation for why Job is suffering—he must have done something for which he is now being punished.

Job 8:1. This verse introduces us to the second of Job's friends, Bildad the Shuhite.

Verses 5-7. Bildad advises Job that even if he has not sinned, he should appeal to God as though he had, and God will restore him to his original situation. ("Rightful habitation" means the circumstances Job was in before his afflictions began.)

The promise Bildad makes to Job in verse 7 echoes the words of Eliphaz in his first speech to Job (5:23-36). The words promise a happy ending for Job if he will only appeal to God's mercy.

Job 11:1. In chapter 11 we hear from Job's third friend, Zophar the Naamathite.

Verse 4. Zophar repeats words he has heard Job speak when protesting his innocence. The word "doctrine" is difficult to understand, and the Hebrew might have originally read "conduct." Although Job frequently claims that his conduct is pure (see 9:20; 10:7), he never really says his doctrine is pure.

Verse 5. Zophar wishes aloud that God would appear and explain what Job has done to bring this punishment upon himself. Then, according to Zophar, Job's circumstances would make sense to everyone.

Verse 6. Here Zophar is direct and to the point. Despite the severity of Job's punishment, it is still not as bad as it would be if God were to punish Job for the full extent of his guilt. What Job really deserves is a lot worse, according to Zophar.

The Revised Standard Version notes mention that the meaning of the phrase "manifold in understanding" is unclear. In Hebrew, the word translated "manifold" really means "double." Perhaps Zophar is telling Job that God knows both sides of every situation, what is hidden and what is obvious. So God could reveal what is now unknown if Job would just ask God to do so.

Job 13. This chapter comes in the middle of a long speech by Job that begins at 12:1 and concludes at the end of chapter 14. In the first few verses of the chapter, Job is arguing that his friends are not perfect and have no right to judge him.

Verse 2. Here Job asserts that his friends are no better than he is. They know no more than he knows. They are not his superiors. The latter idea is expressed in exactly the same words in 12:3.

Verse 3. Job says he wishes to "argue my case with God." The Hebrew word for "argue my case" is used in legal situations when accused persons defend themselves before a judge.

Verse 4. In this verse we see some of Job's frustration with his friends and the advice they offer him. They are no help at all to Job; instead, they are "worthless physicians." They can offer no cure for Job's afflictions.

Verse 5. Job's plea that his friends keep their wisdom to themselves reminds us of ancient proverbs such as the one in Proverbs 17:28.

The Scripture and the Main Question—William H. Willimon

Who That Was Innocent?

The epithet has become a part of our language: "Job's Comforter." It means someone who presumes to offer comfort but only makes matters worse.

Some years ago I had pneumonia. My wife was teaching the third grade in a local elementary school. Because I had often helped with the class, they sent me their handmade get-well cards. One said: "Dear Mr. Willimon, I hope that you are feeling better. My grandfather had newmonia and died."

With friends like the ones who come to comfort Job, Job certainly needs no enemies! In the place of sympathy and understanding, they offer Job self-righteous, smug, calloused moralizing and scolding. Surely, they say, you must have done something terrible, to deserve the state you are in.

All of us have suffered the abuse of Job's Comforters from time to time. As a pastor, I am sometimes shocked to hear people say things to grieving people that only make the pain worse. Of course, they don't mean to hurt these people, but they don't think how their words sound to someone who is going through grief. I'm thinking of those people who say, "Didn't you ever encourage him to see a doctor? I'm sure that you could see something was wrong with his health." Or, "I suppose that my child could have ended up like yours if I had not been a strict disciplinarian." Or, "Did you ever think about taking her to a specialist? Our local doctors don't always know what they are doing." These are the people who say to a parent whose child has just been struck down by a speeding auto, "God must have wanted him more in heaven than down here with us," or who assuage a person's grief with, "There are reasons why God sends pain our way; we just have to accept it on faith."

Perhaps a fear of being a Job's Comforter keeps some people from reaching out to those who hurt. Time and again, when someone in the congregation is in pain, I have heard other members say, "I haven't said anything to them for fear of making matters worse." With models like Eliphaz, Bildad, and Zophar before us, no wonder we are hesitant to speak! None of us wants to be like them. In the face of their friend's terrible suffering and misfortune, all those three have to offer are religious platitudes and smug clichés.

I Would Speak to the Almighty

It is difficult to be compassionate until we know how pain feels. "Sympathy" means literally to "feel with" someone.

"You don't know what I'm going through," sufferers sometimes tell us. Their words fly in the face of cheap, superficial attempts at consolation. Of course, if this were completely true, then human existence would be sad isolation. No one could relate to anyone else unless he or she had had exactly the same experience as the other.

So many times we avoid the sufferer, saying, "I didn't know what to say. I didn't want to make her feel worse." Let us honestly admit that sometimes we say this because of our own vulnerability. Our own fear of mortality, our own feeling that "There, but for the grace of God, go I," leads us to avoid contact with the sufferer lest we "catch" what afflicts him—namely, awareness of finitude, vulnerability, and dependency.

As Christians, we "love as he loved us," namely, by *being there*.

Being there, sharing in the grief, facing the pain and the anguish are consoling. Whenever anyone says to me, "I want to say something to Jane. I know that she is going through a terrible time, but I just don't know what to say," then I always say, "*Go*, say anything to Jane, or say nothing at all, but go."

As a pastor, I have rarely heard suffering people criticize others for showing too much interest in their pain. Rather, I have heard, time and again, people in pain say, "I was going through a terrible time in my life and no one cared, no one visited, no one spoke to me about it." I try to assure these people that their fellow church members and friends do care but that they don't know how to care. So, in cases of pain, the main thing is to be with the person.

In our pain, such as that which Job suffered, we do not so much want answers as presence, the presence of our loving friends who are there, daring to expose themselves to our hurt and anger and questions, daring to be with us even in times of hurt. That presence is the real ministry of compassion that we have to offer hurting people.

Helping the Hurt

Every time we pray, "Thy kingdom come, thy will be done," we do so out of the knowledge that God does care and act. Each Sunday, as we intercede for sufferers in prayer, we name those before God whom Jesus knows as his beloved brothers and sisters in pain. The church that intercedes for the cancer victim is also the church that supplies the hot meals and changes the bandages.

In the book of Job we see that one of the great contributions of the Hebrew religion is the belief that God not only speaks, but that God also listens. God is in conversation with his creation. God hears our cries of pain. Jesus is the supreme communicative event of this dialogue. In his story is our hope, a confidence that in spite of our suffering, "in everything God works for good, with those who love him" (Romans 8:28) and that even on our crosses of pain "we are more than conquerors through him who loved us" (Romans 8:37).

Helping Adults Become Involved—Leonard T. Wolcott

Preparing to Teach

This lesson is about being a friend to those who suffer. The outline follows the Bible narrative:

I. Friends come to counsel Job.
II. Job complains about his suffering.
III. Job reacts to his comforters.
IV. Job places his confidence in God.

Read carefully "The Scripture and the Main Question" and "As You Read the Scripture." These form the heart of the lesson. The ideas, insights, and suggestions in these sections should be reflected continually in your lesson plan.

As you use the suggested outline, you may want to either quote or paraphrase ideas. You might like to jot in the margin of your outline the page number and paragraph being referred to. For example, you could write a reference to page 65, paragraph 3, as 65-3.

Have a Bible for each class member, chalk and chalkboard or markers and newsprint, and paper and pencils for class members. Post on the wall the key verses, Job 6:14 and Romans 8:38, 39.

Introducing the Main Question

Basic and helpful ideas are presented in the section "The Main Question." These ideas are essential in helping to identify the purpose of the lesson.

Because everyone experiences suffering, you and class members may share accounts of persons who agonize over the question, Why? or, Why me? After the saturation bombing of Hamburg, Germany, near the end of World War II, masses of unidentified dead were gathered in a common grave. The stone set above the grave carries the one word: *Warum?* ("Why?"). A missionary mother's son dies of polio. "I gave my life to serve God," she cried, "how could God take away my son?" A brilliant pianist lost both arms in a car accident. No one could diminish her bitterness. Logical answers bring no comfort and may carry no meaning to the one who is in the midst of personal agony.

Developing the Lesson

I. Friends come to counsel Job.

Illustrations of poor comforters are found in Dr. Willimon's "The Scripture and the Main Question." The Bible passages for today tell about Job's three friends and how they tried to handle the question of his suffering. All tried to give Job what they felt to be the religious, moral explanation of his suffering. All reacted to Job's questioning with shock. They came to God's defense.

For Eliphaz (Job 4:6-8), God metes out punishment in this life according to our behavior. If you "sow trouble" you will "reap the same." Eliphaz has fixed ideas about cause and effect. The righteous reap good, the wicked, evil. God prospers the righteous. He ruins the unrighteous. At this point you can read aloud Psalm 18:20-26. Do we sometimes oversimplify by applying scriptures without truly understanding a suffering friend's predicament?

Bildad feels that he has to defend God against Job's complaints (Job 8:1, 5-7). Here, then, is the second proposition, like the first but turned around: You suffer because you have sinned. Bildad's simple notion of God and life is typical of many people's. He interprets God's justice from a human idea of what is good and bad for the individual. He tells Job to confess that he is a sinner, and then God will forgive and prosper him.

Zophar, the third friend, is infuriated at Job's insistence on his own integrity (Job 11:1, 4-6). God has punished you, he is telling Job, so just submit. You are in no position to question God. Do not try to understand why you suffer. God knows what he is doing. He has let you off lightly. You probably deserve more punishment.

II. Job complains about his suffering.

Job continues to protest his innocence. He turns on his friends (Job 12–14). They have judged him unfairly.

III. Job reacts to his comforters.

Job says to his friends, "I know as much about this as you do. Don't talk down to me" (13:2). Do we counsel those who suffer as though we knew more about their problem than they do? Job said to his friends, "You whitewash with lies" (13:4). Whitewash covers up dirt, but the dirt is still there. To sufferers we mouth platitudes that fail to address their needs. As Shakespeare says in *The Tempest*, "You rub the sore when you should bring the plaster." Job says, "Worthless physicians are you all." Friends who really do not understand what another is going through cannot relieve suffering.

So what should friends do? Stay away? No, stay, but stay silent, says Job: "Oh that you would keep silent" (13:5). When a Burmese family is in sorrow, a priest comes to quote Pali scriptures that remind them that all life is suffering and fleeting. Contrast this to the helpfulness of Christian neighbors and friends in Africa, where they come to sit with a bereaved person—to sit all night, all day, maybe bringing a little food, maybe singing a few hymns, but mostly sitting silently by, bringing the presence of love.

We do need friends in our times of suffering. Read the key verse, Job 6:14. We need friends who will not preach to us, but who show they care.

IV. Job places his confidence in God.

Most important is Job's understanding of God: (1) He wants to argue his case with God (13:3), because he is confident that God is just. (2) Job feels free to cry out to God all the misery he feels, because he is confident that God listens. His friends talked but they did not listen. When people tell their tales of woe, they are glad to have a listener. (3) Job knows that God is always there. The New Testament expression of this is found in Romans 8:38-39: Nothing can separate us from God's love.

Helping Class Members Act

Ask class members what they would want most if they were suffering. Needs may differ. Some may prefer silence, and some may want people around, talking. Others may ask for scripture passages. List the needs on the chalkboard or newsprint. Usually, it is not an explanation we need so much in times of crisis as presence, the assurance that those who care are near us.

You may ask: How do you feel about God when you suffer? Can you cry out to him, talk to him? Do you sense he cares, understands?

Distribute paper and pencils. Ask the class to think about and jot down answers to two questions you may write on the chalkboard or newsprint: (1) How would I react to suffering? (2) Do I know anyone who is suffering now, and what can I do to show that I care? Call for silent prayer, asking for God's help in times of suffering and the wisdom to know how to comfort others. Read aloud Romans 8:37-39.

Planning for Next Sunday

Next Sunday's lesson faces the issue of our relationship with God in time of suffering. Ask the class to read Job 29-30. This passage reflects the way many feel about past happiness and present sorrow. Invite class members to bring poems or prose passages that have helped them face distress.

Asking God Why

Background Scripture: Job 29:1-30:27

The Main Question—William H. Willimon

"It was the best, worst experience I have ever had," she said to me, of a year she had spent working with the Peace Corps in Central America. I think I knew what she was describing. Do you? She was talking about an experience that was very difficult to live through, very painful, but in the end, looking back, an experience that was ultimately educational and worthwhile. Of course, we would be foolish to seek out such experiences—a painful illness, the loss of a job, a marital separation, a rebellious child. But the truth is, we do not have to seek out such experiences in life; they have a way of coming to us, whether we ask for them or not!

The key factor is, What do we make out of such experiences? Do they defeat us or strengthen us? I think it was G. K. Chesterton who once said, "Mankind can learn a great deal from history. Unfortunately, what we usually do when we encounter history is simply to pick ourselves up, brush ourselves off, and continue in the same direction."

Job had just lived through some of the most traumatic and tragic experiences that could ever befall a human being. What will these experiences do to him? Will they shake his confidence in God? Is he doomed to spend the rest of his life confused, wandering and befuddled by life? Or will this be for him a turning point in his faith? Will he be able to look back on these experiences and, while admitting their pain, tragedy, and senselessness, be able to say that he was transformed by them into a more faithful person?

FIRST QUARTER

Selected Scripture

King James Version	Revised Standard Version

Job 29:1-6

1 Moreover Job continued his parable, and said,

2 Oh that I were as *in* months past, as *in* the says *when* God preserved me;

3 When his candle shined upon my head, *and when* by his light I walked *through* darkness;

4 As I was in the days of my youth, when the secret of God *was* upon my tabernacle;

5 When the Almighty *was* yet with me, *when* my children *were* about me;

6 When I washed my steps with butter, and the rock poured me out rivers of oil;

Job 30:19-26

19 He hath cast me into the mire, and I am become like dust and ashes.

20 I cry unto thee, and thou dost not hear me: I stand up, and thou regardest me *not*.

21 Thou art become cruel to me: with thy strong hand thou opposest thyself against me.

22 Thou liftest me up to the wind; thou causest me to ride *upon it*, and dissolvest my substance.

23 For I know *that* thou wilt bring me *to* death, and *to* the house appointed for all living.

24. Howbeit he will not stretch out *his* hand to the grave, though they cry in his destruction.

25 Did not I weep for him that was in trouble? was *not* my soul grieved for the poor?

Job 29:1-6

1 And Job again took up his discourse, and said:

2 "Oh, that I were as in the months of old,
as in the days when God watched over me;

3 when his lamp shone upon my head,
and by his light I walked through darkness;

4 as I was in my autumn days,
when the friendship of God was upon my tent;

5 when the Almighty was yet with me,
when my children were about me;

6 when my steps were washed with milk,
and the rock poured out for me streams of oil!"

Job 30:19-26

19 "God has cast me into the mire, and I have become like dust and ashes.

20 I cry to thee and thou dost not answer me;
I stand, and thou dost not heed me.

21 Thou hast turned cruel to me;
with the might of thy hand thou dost persecute me.

22 Thou liftest me up on the wind, thou makest me ride on it,
and thou tossest me about in the roar of the storm.

23 Yea, I know that thou wilt bring me to death,
and to the house appointed for all living.

24 "Yet does not one in a heap of ruins stretch out his hand,
and in his disaster cry for help?

25 Did not I weep for him whose day was hard?
Was not my soul grieved for the poor?

26 When I looked for good, then evil came *unto me*: and when I waited for light, there came darkness.

26 But when I looked for good, evil came;
  and when I waited for light, darkness came."

Key Verse: **Wherefore hidst thou thy face, and holdest me for thine enemy? (Job 13:24)**

Key Verse: **Why dost thou hide thy face and count me as thy enemy? (Job 13:24)**

As You Read the Scripture—Lynne Deming

Job 29. This chapter begins Job's final speech, which ends at the conclusion of chapter 31. In chapter 29, Job looks back and reminisces about his happy past.

Verse 1. This speech of Job is introduced with the same words as the last speech, which began at 26:1.

Verse 2. The image of God watching over persons is common in the Old Testament. (See, for example, Numbers 6:24; Psalm 16:1; 91:11; 121:7-8.)

Verse 3. Again, a well-known image describes Job's happy past. He remembers a time when God provided light for his journeys through darkness. Isaiah 50:10 and Micah 7:8 also speak of God's light shining in the darkness.

Verse 4. Here Job speaks of his "autumn days." We usually think of the autumn years as later in life, but this reference is to a time of harvest. Literally, the Hebrew says "in the days of fruit gathering." So here, autumn symbolizes a time of prosperity in Job's past.

Verse 5. Job's statement about his children reminds us that they were taken from him, according to chapter 1 of the book. So Job looks back longingly upon a time when his children were still alive. In ancient Israel, children were a sign of one's prosperity, success, and happiness. Psalm 127:3-5 makes this clear.

Verse 6. Oil and milk were both symbols of prosperity and well-being.

Job 30. In contrast to chapter 29, where Job looks back on a happy past, in chapter 30 Job describes in detail his present misery. In parts of this chapter, including verses 19-26, we see clearly that Job is speaking directly to God.

Verse 19. Here Job complains that God has cast him into the mud so that he has "become like dust and ashes." Job had already accused God of casting him into a pit (see 9:31).

Verse 20. Job's statement reminds us of Psalm 130, which begins by stating, "Out of the depths I cry to thee." This is not the first time Job has complained that God does not heed his cries (see Job 19:7).

Verse 22. We can imagine Job's terror if we think of ourselves being carried by the wind through a violent storm.

Verse 23. Here Job expresses his certainty that he will die as a result of his afflictions. The "house appointed for all living" is a reference to the inevitability of death for everyone, including Job.

Verse 24. The Hebrew for this verse is quite difficult to translate, so we cannot be certain exactly what the verse means. The image is of a person in the midst of a heap of ruins, stretching out his hand and crying for someone to come and pull him out. Job is implying that although he has been crying to God for help, God has not answered his pleas.

Verse 25. In this verse, Job poses a rhetorical question. Speaking to God, he says "After all, didn't I have compassion on others who were having a hard time? Of course I did! So why, God, can't you have the same kind of compassion for me and help me out of this situation?"

Verse 26. Job continues by lamenting the fact that God did not rescue him from his misery. Instead, darkness came when Job asked for light, and evil came to Job when he sought good.

The Scripture and the Main Question—William H. Willimon

In the Days When God Watched Over Me

You know the old saying, "There are no atheists in foxholes." When the going gets rough and the bombs are falling, everyone turns to God. A billboard outside my town had big letters printed on it reading "TRY GOD," the implication being that, after one has tried everything, then try the one last resort—God.

What do you think about the use of God in this way? Undoubtedly, the adults who attend your class are much more than "foxhole Christians," people who only think about God when the going gets rough. They are here on Sunday to deepen their faith and to praise the God whom they love. Yet it is only natural, even fitting, that we should turn to God in times of trouble. After all, we know that God cares about us and for us.

In his time of deep trouble, Job turns to God, remembering "the months of old . . . when God watched over me" (29:2). To Job it seems as if God has forsaken him, so he cries out.

Even Jesus had his times when God seemed far from him. "My God, my God, why hast thou forsaken me?" he asked as he hung in agony on the cross. If even one as close to God as Jesus could feel this way, should we be surprised when we feel lost, alone, and forsaken? We may believe that God never forsakes us, but sometimes it *feels* as if we have been forsaken.

Are you shocked by Job's pleadings? Some people feel that religious people are those who never question anything, who always feel happy and close to God. These people must have never read the Bible! The Bible tells of many occasions—Job on his ash heap, Jesus on the cross—when people felt hurt, baffled, and forsaken, by the absence of God.

I remember visiting a woman whose husband had recently died in a tragic accident. I suggested to her that she was probably feeling some anger at God for what had happened.

"Anger? Why should I be angry with God?" she asked defensively.

"Well, even though I might know in my head that God had nothing to do with all this, I still might wonder why God had not stepped in to stop this terrible tragedy friom happening. Why did God create a world where tragedies like this are even possible?" I mused.

"But it would not be nice to be angry with God," she said.

In reading the story of Job, particularly this week's passages, I am impressed with Job's ability to feel anger, hurt, and resentment at the strange ways of the world, and to ask God, "Why?" When you think about it, it takes a great deal of faith to be bold enough to ask such questions of God.

You know that there are friendships where everything is kept on a superficial level. Neither person questions the other. No anger is expressed. Everything is smiles and sweetness.

But there are other friendships which are so deep, so secure, so utterly sure of mutual love, that the friends are free to express their true feelings, to talk about whatever is on their minds. Job seems to have this sort of friendship with God. So secure is his relationship to his Creator, so sure is he that God is love, that Job dares to question the actions of God, confident that God will not destroy him simply because he does not understand.

Thou Dost Not Answer Me

God has cast me into the mire,
    and I have become like dust and ashes.
I cry to thee and thou dost not answer me.
                    (30:19-20*a*)

Thus Job continues his long lament. Perhaps you are troubled by Job's declaration that God has intentionally placed him in his tragic situation. Can it be that the same loving God whom we have experienced in Jesus could actually be killing a man's sons and daughters and destroying his material possessions in order to punish him for some sin?

As Christians, when we think about misfortune, we should remember a number of things about our relationship with God. You remember the time they brought the blind man to Jesus, asking, "Who sinned in order to make this man blind? His parents? His grandparents?" Jesus did not respond to their questions but rather reached out and healed the poor man, thus demonstrating that God's will lay in restoration of the man's sight rather than in such calloused discussions of human tragedy. I find it difficult that the same God who wants our health deliberately brings sickness.

When we are in times of deep trouble, it is only natural for us to cry out in anguish. We feel hurt, abandoned, lost, alone. We love health. We feel that God has created us for more than suffering and heartache. So we cry out. And this is natural. Our very crying out is testimony to our awareness that something isn't right in this tragedy, that this is against all goodness, against the very will of God for his creatures.

So we should be honest about the pain, forthright about our hurt, even as Job honestly cried out in his suffering. God is not offended by our cries; God listens to us, particularly in our despair.

This doesn't mean that we will receive easy, simple answers to our cries, for we are asking some of the deepest questions about life when we inquire into the mystery of pain and suffering. But it is fair to ask the questions and fair to freely cry out.

Admittedly, we do bring much suffering upon ourselves. The person who smokes two packs of cigarettes each day need not cry out and blame God if he or she contracts lung cancer. Abuse of body has led to illness. God was not the cause.

Yet you know that all sickness is not so easily dismissed. Some sickness comes upon us whether we care for our bodies or not. Some people's children cause heartache whether they are conscientious parents are not. Some people lose their jobs and are unemployed whether they work hard or not. Life involves a good deal of unearned, unmerited pain.

I Looked for Good

Behind Job's honest cries for answers lay a more profound search. Job was crying out not simply for rational, satisfactory answers to the great mystery of life; Job was crying out for God. His anguish and pain had cut him off from the God whom he loved. Alone, bereft, suffering, Job was in an intolerable situation.

Job did not know Jesus. But we Christians cannot read the tragic tale of Job without thinking of the Christ. There, on the cross of Jesus, though we heard no answer to the question of pain, we saw God. God came and hung on a cross, suffering more than most of us will ever suffer, willing to be with us, even in the very darkest times of life. That is the Christian response to life's most perplexing question, Why?

Helping Adults Become Involved—Leonard T. Wolcott

Preparing to Teach

This lesson encourages class members to ask honest questions and to penetrate beyond the superficial phrases people use in the face of grief, pain, and affliction.

Use the following outline to prepare the lesson:

I. We look back with nostalgia to happier days, which seem blessed by God.

II. We are to bring to the surface the feelings we really have when we suffer.

III. We are to accept the fact of despair and yet reach out to God in hope.

Read carefully "The Scripture and the Main Question" and "As You Read the Scripture." These form the heart of the lesson. The ideas, insights, and suggestions in these sections should be reflected continually in your lesson plan.

As you use the suggested outline, you may want to either quote or paraphrase ideas. You might like to jot in the margin of your outline the page number and paragraph being referred to. For example, you could write a reference to page 65, paragraph 3, as 65-3.

Before class time, write on a chalkboard or newsprint these key points for lecture and discussion:

good times: happy memories
hard times: honest questions
you, suffering, and God

Think about clichés people use in the face of suffering, such as "Hope for the best!" "It could be worse"; "Grin and bear it"; "That's life for you"; "Well, it must be God's will"; "It'll all come out right" and such. Job's wife said, "Curse God and die."

Introducing the Main Question

Basic and helpful ideas are presented in the section "The Main Question." These ideas are essential in helping to identify the purpose of the lesson.

Begin with the main question, What kind of persons do we become as the result of our experiences? Think of a time of trouble you have gone through. What did it do to you? Did it change you and your attitudes? How did it affect you? Did it transform your life?

Developing the Lesson

I. We look back with nostalgia to happier days, which seem blessed by God.

Share happy memories of good times—maybe when you were a child and won commendation from your teacher, or beat up a bully who picked on you, or were taken to the circus with the gang. Or maybe in your youth you won a contest or were part of a winning team. Class members will enjoy telling about any memory about the "good old days" that stands out for them. Many are too busy living today to think about their yesterdays. A friend's grandfather lived vigorously every day as a respected editor and community leader in his home town. When incapacitating illness struck him, confining him to his house, he was soon forgotten. Then his mind turned to pleasant memories of his past honor and success. It was that way with Job.

Sharing memories will help prepare the class for a review of Job 29. Call attention to the kinds of things Job recalled with pleasure: a happy family, well-being, his children about him (verse 5); milk and oil aplenty, that is, prosperity (verse 6).

To know the appreciation and respect of others is a large part of happiness. Job remembered that he had been respected (verses 8, 9, 10), that people had approved of him (verse 11), that he had been benevolent (verses 12, 13, 15, 16), that he had seen to it that justice prevailed (verses 14, 17), that he had had a rich heritage to pass on to others (verses 18-20), and that people had accepted, believed in, and followed his leadership (verses 21-25).

II. We are to bring to the surface the feelings we really have when we suffer.

You may ask the class to sugggest phrases people repeat to others who suffer. You may write these on the chalkboard or newsprint. Do these common phrases evade the real questions about suffering?

Among the many questions Job asks, this lesson focuses on those that contrast with his memories of the good days of the past: What is harder to bear than total disrespect, especially from the meanest of people? (Job 30:1-10). But it is just as hard to be tormented by worthless people (30:12-14), and physical pain makes it worse (30:16-18). No one comes to help (30:24-28), not even those whom he had once helped (verses 25, 26), so there is mental anguish (30:27) and destitution (30:29). The horribleness of these days is, for Job, an indication that God has cut him off (30:19-23).

III. We are to accept the fact of despair and yet reach out to God in hope.

Ask the class: Are prosperity and happiness always a sign that God is with us, blessing us? The playwright Ibsen has the rascally Peer Gynt thank God for prospering him, although he abandoned his wife and grew rich in the slave trade.

Another question: Is suffering an indication that God has abandoned us? That he does not hear our prayers for relief? Even if we do believe that God is not punishing us, it is not easy to think he is near or cares, when we are in agony. Even Jesus cried out on the cross, "My God, why hast thou forsaken me?" (Mark 15:34).

Job, remembering his past faithfulness to God and his kindness to the poor, does not understand why he should suffer so in disgrace and indignity.

There may be many timid souls who rush from pain into deadening narcotics and never ask these questions. There may be secular people for whom God is not real, who live and die without asking these questions. There may be religious people who never ask these questions, like the woman of whom Dr. Willimon speaks, who said, "It would not be nice to be angry with God.

People who live fully and deeply often cry out when they are stopped by suffering, Why? When pain or grief is intense, when we know we cannot escape into the happy past and we cannot fantasize a happy future, then we ask the seemingly unanswerable questions. The biographer of a great missionary wrote, "Everyone knows that life promises more than it fulfills."

And still we ask, we hope. Job cries, "Yet does not one in a heap of ruins [as in quicksand] stretch out his hand" (30:24). In our misery we, like Job, turn in on ourselves. Nevertheless, in our misery, because we believe in God, we still turn to him. No genuine hope is centered in self. Our hope is centered in God. God may not relieve us from our pain, but he lifts us up above our pain. The very uncertainty and unreality of our existence finds hope in the reality of God's being.

Helping Class Members Act

Ask class members to share any poems, prose passages, or other resources that have helped them face the question of suffering. Also, ask them to tell of anyone they have visited (or written to) as a result of last week's commitment.

Ask for the names of persons in need of prayer in their present suffering. Pray for them and for all class members, that they may have strength for times of suffering.

Planning for Next Sunday

This lesson has been about Job's questioning of God. Next Sunday's is about God's answer to Job's questions. Ask class members to read Job 38–42 before next Sunday and to think of lessons they have learned from their own experiences of suffering.

Overcoming Through Faith

Background Scripture: Job 38:1-7; 40:1-9; 42

The Main Question—William H. Willimon

What is two plus two? Where is the capital of North Dakota located? How many books are there in the Bible?

Life is full of questions. Of course, all would be well if the questions life puts to us were as simple to answer as these questions. You have lived long enough to know that life puts forward questions to which there are no easy answers.

Recently, I heard a distinguished philosopher comment on the nature of philosophical study. He said, "Philosophy deals with basically two kinds of questions: We deal with questions to which people already know the answers and with questions which everyone knows have no answers!"

One of the frustrating things about religion is that it deals, like philosophy, mostly with questions of the latter type. We long for an easy, objective, scientific answer to the questions which plague us. When none is forthcoming, we become frustrated and angry.

Throughout out study of the book of Job, we have heard Job raise some of the deepest questions men or women ever ask. There have been questions about suffering, pain, the rewards of goodness, and the justice of God.

At last, in today's lesson, God strides upon the scene of Job's questions and answers. Will we at last get some answers to these questions? Or will we be filled with even deeper ones? These are some of the questions that lie behind God's answers to Job.

Selected Scripture

King James Version

Job 38:1-7

1 Then the Lord answered Job out of the whirlwind, and said,

2 Who *is* this that darkeneth counsel by words without knowledge?

3 Gird up now thy loins like a man; for I will demand of thee, and answer thou me.

4 Where wast thou when I laid the foundations of the earth? declare, if thou hast understanding.

5 Who hath laid the measures thereof, if thou knowest? or who hath stretched the line upon it?

Revised Standard Version

Job 38:1-7

1 Then the Lord answered Job out of the whirlwind:

2 "Who is this that darkens counsel by words without knowledge?

3 Gird up your loins like a man,
   I will question you, and you shall declare to me."

4 "Where were you when I laid the foundation of the earth?
   Tell me, if you have understanding.

5 Who determined its measurements—surely you know!
   Or who stretched the line upon it?

6 Whereupon are the foundations thereof fastened? or who laid the corner stone thereof;

7 When the morning stars sang together, and all the sons of God shouted for joy?

Job 40:3-5

3 Then Job answered the Lord, and said,

4 Behold, I am vile; what shall I answer thee? I will lay mine hand upon my mouth.

5 Once have I spoken; but I will not answer: yea, twice; but I will proceed no further.

Job 42:1-6, 10

1 Then Job answered the Lord, and said,

2 I know that thou canst do every *thing*, and *that* no thought can be withholden from thee.

3 Who *is* he that hideth counsel without knowledge? therefore have I uttered that I understood not; things too wonderful for me, which I knew not.

4 Hear, I beseech thee, and I will speak: I will demand of thee, and declare thou unto me.

5 I have heard of thee by the hearing of the ear; but now mine eye seeth thee:

6 Wherefore I abhor *myself*, and repent in dust and ashes.

. . . .

10 And the Lord turned the captivity of Job, when he prayed for his friends: also the Lord gave Job twice as much as he had before.

Key Verse: I have heard of thee by the hearing of the ear; but now mine eye seeth thee. (Job 42:5)

6 On what were its bases sunk,
   or who laid its cornerstone,

7 when the morning stars sang together,
   and all the sons of God shouted for joy?"

Job 40:3-5

3 Then Job answered the Lord:

4 "Behold, I am of small account;
   what shall I answer thee?
   I lay my hand on my mouth.

5 I have spoken once, and I will not answer;
   twice, but I will proceed no further."

Job 42:1-6, 10

1 Then Job answered the Lord:

2 "I know that thou canst do all things,
   and that no purpose of thine can be thwarted.

3 'Who is this that hides counsel without knowledge?'
Therefore I have uttered what I did not understand,
   things too wonderful for me, which I did not know.

4 'Hear, and I will speak;
   I will question you, and you declare to me.'

5 I had heard of thee by the hearing of the ear,
   but now my eye sees thee;

6 therefore I despise myself,
   and repent in dust and ashes."

. . . .

10 And the Lord restored the fortunes of Job, when he had prayed for his friends; and the Lord gave Job twice as much as he had before.

Key Verse: I have heard of thee by the hearing of the ear, but now my eye sees thee. (Job 42:5)

As You Read the Scripture—Lynne Deming

Job 38. This chapter begins a long speech from God to Job which ends at verse 6 of chapter 42. Throughout the book, Job has been pleading his case with God and asking God for a response. We have heard lengthy responses by Job's friends. Now at last we hear what God has to say about Job's situation.

Verse 1. God answers Job "out of the whirlwind." The whirlwind is often the location of God in the Old Testament (see also Psalm 50:3; Zechariah 9:14).

Verse 2. God accuses Job of "darkening his counsel." In other words, Job has been obscuring God's ways and workings in the world. "Words without knowledge" were also ascribed to Job by Elihu, in 34:35.

Verse 3. Girding one's loins means preparing oneself for an important event. God is asking Job to prepare himself for an important dialogue. Job has been wanting to question God for some time, but God has something different in mind. As God tells Job, "I'm going to ask *you* questions, and you are going to answer me."

Verses 4-7. This section is the first in a long series of questions that God asks Job. These questions are designed to show how little Job really knows about the workings of God in nature.

In ancient times, the world was thought to have been built on a large foundation. God had specific specifications to follow for constructing the earth and used a measuring line to make certain all was in order. When God was finished with this task, there was much rejoicing. This event was heralded by the singing of the morning stars together.

Job 40. God starts a new speech at the beginning of this chapter, and Job now has a chance to respond. But his response is quite short (verses 3-5), at which time God resumes the questioning.

Verse 3. This is the first time Job attempts to answer God's questioning.

Verse 4. In this verse we realize that although he has a chance to speak directly to God, which is what he has asked for all along, Job now declines God's offer. He lays his hand upon his mouth, a phrase also found in Job 21:5 and 29:9. God's questions in the previous two chapters were designed to show Job's ignorance, and they apparently have done so.

Verse 5. Speaking "in one way and then two" is Job's way of saying that he has already said everything he wants to say on the subject.

Job 42. In this chapter Job gets another chance to speak directly to God. Unlike the last time, Job now decides to speak his mind.

Verse 2. This verse is the heart of the message of Job. Job concludes that the ways of God are all-powerful and not to be understood by human beings.

Verse 3. Here Job quotes a question posed to him earlier by God (see 38:2). Job seems to be saying that God was correct to accuse him earlier of concealing God's work and purpose in the world.

Verse 4. Again Job is quoting God's earlier words to him in 40:7. This quote introduces Job's answer in the following two verses.

Verse 5. Job responds to God and to all that has happened to him by saying that before he had only heard about God secondhand, but now he sees God face to face. God has come to Job personally, a humbling experience for Job.

Verse 6. The Hebrew word translated in the Revised Standard Version as

"I despise myself" is difficult to decipher. Job is probably responding out of his humility caused by God's intimate attention to his situation. His repentance in dust and ashes reminds us of the beginning of the book, when Job sits in ashes and scrapes his sores with a potsherd (see 2:8).

Verse 10. Here we read that Job's fortunes are restored, and he receives twice as much as he lost. Job's restoration occurs in the context of God's dealings with Job's friends (Job prays for them), not directly following Job's response in verses 5 and 6.

The Scripture and the Main Question—William H. Willimon

Then the Lord Answered Job

There are a number of ways to live the life of faith. One is to simply take life as it comes, accept things as they are, and ask as few questions as possible. "You must simply accept this on faith," people sometimes advise us; "there are just some things that we are not meant to understand." Life is a mystery and remains a mystery. The ways of God are so far above and beyond our ways that there is little use in trying to figure things out. This approach protects one from the anguish of not finding good answers to our tough questions. It also protects us from the possibility of receiving the wrong answers to our questions!

There is another way, the path of questions. It is the path which our friend Job seems to have taken. In this approach we try to be honest about our doubts, our frustrations, our questions. We believe that God has created a good, predictable world, so when bad, unpredictable, strange things happen, we ask, "Why?"

The second approach is risky, as Job himself discovered. When we ask questions we risk finding out things we might have avoided. We risk being confronted with friends such as those who troubled Job! We risk having our questions open up even more troublesome questions.

However, the second approach can also lead us to a deeper, surer faith. Our doubts can move us forward beyond doubt to greater certainty. This appears to be the case with Job, as God finally strides upon the scene and responds to Job's deep questions.

I Will Question You

Throughout the thirty-seven chapters of Job, our protagonist has been questioning the workings of providence. Yet when here in chapter 38 God finally comes on the scene, what Job gets are not answers but more questions! If we were anticipating that Job's questions would at last yield a simple, straightforward response from the Creator, we are to be disappointed.

God says to Job the questioner:

> Gird up your loins like a man,
>   I will question you, and you shall declare to me.
>
> Where were you when I laid the foundation of the earth?
>   Tell me, if you have understanding.
> Who determined its measurements—surely you know!
>
>   (38:3-5a)

In one of the longest speeches in the Bible, a speech that explodes with striking images of the vast, wondrous, awe-inspiring creation, Job hears God thunder forth. In so many words, God asks Job who he thinks he is, anyway. The writer depicts God as saying that to explain the kind of things Job wants explained would be like trying to teach algebra to a flounder!

In his best-selling book *When Bad Things Happen to Good People*, Rabbi Harold Kushner writes that when God speaks to Job, God says, "Job, I'm truly sorry about what's happening. It tears me up as much as it does you. But you know, of course, that I had nothing to do with the way things turned out. You know that I would love to help, but I can't."

I do not believe that's what God says to Job in the story. What we hear in this speech in chapters 38 and 39 is not impotence and kindhearted empathy, but rather the potent, all-embracing force of the God who made heaven and earth and all the creatures therein. If we are going to think about why bad things happen to good people, the story of Job suggests that we must use terms that describe someone other than Kushner's kindly but essentially limited and impotent God.

Do you think that God's answer to Job is much of an answer? What does all this raving about the morning stars (38:7) and the ostrich (39:13), the horse (39:19) and the mountain goat (39:1), have to do with an answer to Job's questions about unmerited suffering?

Perhaps by pointing out to Job the majesty and overpowering grandeur and complexity of creation, God is responding to Job's question with the only true response possible: This is a complex, mysterious world. You and your troubles are only one small part of the whole picture. There are some things for which there are no humanly understandable answers. Trust me, the God who made all of this, to know what I am doing.

A friend of mine told me about a terrible time she went through in her life. She lost her job; her health was poor. It seemed as if the whole world was caving in on her. She was filled with self-pity and deep remorse. Then one Sunday afternoon she took a drive along a mountain road overlooking her city. She stopped her car, got out, and sat for a while looking across the mountain valleys, seeing the high peaks in the distance.

"Suddenly," she said, "it occurred to me that me and my problems were only one small part of the whole picture. These hills had been here for millions of years. My lifetime, even at the longest, would occupy no more than one tiny dot in the history of this landscape. I was just one tiny little part of the whole picture."

She was filled with a sense of humility and awe. She felt strangely reassured by this vision of grandeur. I think that something very similar happened to Job as he listened to God's great speech in defense of his creation. He realized his own limitations in ever fully answering such difficult questions. From his own ego-centeredness, he was drawn toward the majesty of God and his creation.

> I know that thou canst do all things,
> and that no purpose of thine can be thwarted.
> ....
> Therefore I have uttered what I did not understand,
> things too wonderful for me, which I did not know.
> ....
> I had heard of thee by the hearing of the ear,
> but now my eye sees thee.
>
> (42:2, 3*b*, 5)

Job is restored in a new way. He feels the presence of God as never before, thus his faith is deepened in spite of the terrible things he has been through.

The story of Job reminds us that God does not change the rules just to suit us. God is not some sort of puppet who can be manipulated by pulling the right strings. This may seem a harsh theology. But the story of Job is not the only story. There is also the story of the Good Shepherd, the loving Father who waits for the prodigal son, the healing Savior who reaches out in love to all the sick and hurting. When the story of Job is put alongside these stories, we are given hope and help for even the darkest and most difficult times which we may encounter in life.

Helping Adults Become Involved—Leonard T. Wolcott

Preparing to Teach

This lesson can help class members consider how they let their troubles affect them. The Bible content of this lesson can be organized as follows:

    I. God's response to Job's complaints and questions.
    II. Job's reaction to God's response.
    III. God restores Job to health and prosperity.

Read carefully "The Scripture and the Main Question" and "As You Read the Scripture." These form the heart of the lesson. The ideas, insights, and suggestions in these sections should be reflected continually in your lesson plan.

As you use the suggested outline, you may want to either quote or paraphrase ideas. You might like to jot in the margin of your outline the page number and paragraph being referred to. For example, you could write a reference to page 65, paragraph 3, as 65-3.

Read the Bible passages with a commentary, if possible. If you have a devotional book that discusses how Christians deal with suffering, read it. Recall your own knowledge of how different persons have met suffering.

The conclusion should apply God's answers to Job, plus the New Testament understanding of God's love, to class members' experiences of suffering. You may print questions on newsprint or chalkboard to guide the class's thinking. (See the four questions under "Helping Class Members Act.")

Be sure there are enough Bibles, pencils, and paper for all.

Introducing the Main Question

Basic and helpful ideas are presented in the section "The Main Question." These ideas are essential in helping to identify the purpose of the lesson.

Will Willimon writes: For several seeks we have been listening to Job's friends, then Job, discuss the issue of why persons suffer. In this chapter, God speaks! In the dramatic moment God strides upon the scene of their questions and answers. Will we at last get answers to these questions? Or will we be filled with even deeper questions? This lesson says: Listen to God's answers to Job.

If your class begins with a hymn, one appropriate to the subject would be "How Great Thou Art."

Developing the Lesson

I. God's response to Job's complaints and questions.

See Dr. Willimon's story of the woman who, looking over mountain valleys at distant peaks, saw the smallness of her problems and found release from self-pity. As Dr. Willimon says, God does not change to suit us.

There is a pause in God's response. Job, who had boldly challenged God, is now speechless when God says, "He who argues with God, let him answer." Job can say no more than, "Look, I am of small account; what shall I answer you?" In chapters 40–41, we have more questions from God.

II. Job's reaction to God's response.

At last, in 42:3, 5, 6, we have Job's reaction. Three things happen to Job. (1) He is humbled: "I have uttered what I did not understand, things too wonderful for me, which I did not know." Read Psalm 8:1-4, which views man from the perspective of God's universe. (2) Job senses the presence of God as never before: "I had heard of thee by the hearing of the ear, but now my eye sees thee." He had argued with a belief in God that was a fundamental part of his heritage. But only now does God's presence become real. (3) Job is therefore brought to repentance: "I despise myself, and repent in dust and ashes." Job was too strong a personality to give in to the scolding of his friends. True repentance comes only when he is confronted by God.

III. God restores Job to health and prosperity.

What happens to Job as a result of his experience is partly God's doing. God restores Job to prosperity and respect. Thre are four necessary elements here: (1) Job has genuinely repented; (2) His friends acknowledge their error by accepting God's order to expiate their sins with a sacrifice—a typical old Hebrew practice; (3) Job prays for them, becoming their solicitor before God, and God hears his prayer and forgives; (4) Job accepts his new prosperity with a humble awareness of God.

Helping Class Members Act

The lesson is learned that suffering may come to people who have done no wrong, as well as to the wrongdoer, and that prosperity is not a sure indication of right-doing. Why then, is prosperity restored to Job as though it were a reward for his faithfulness? It is the writer's way of saying that Job now has a new life, one blessed by a new relationship with God. This new life is a symbol that (a) God is in charge, and (b) God knows the faithfulness of his servants.

Apply this lesson to Christian experience. Christians do not need a material reward for faithfulness. We have assurance of God's continuing love. We have, as Dr. Willimon points out, the stories of the good shepherd and the prodigal son, stories of God's seeking love for us. There is another consequence of suffering for Christians—we understand better the suffering of others. In coming into a closer relationship with God, we become partners with God in his ministry of love. A widow who suffered the loss of her husband made her home a haven for women who had suffered similar losses. Here they found supporting love to start a new life. Pastor Song of Korea overcame his grief at the murder of his two sons by a

Communist youth by taking the young Communist into his home and introducing him to Christ. Another man came through the barrenness of life after his divorce by committing himself to teach and guide youth in Africa. Class members may have similar stories to share.

Ask class members to take two or three minutes to think about the questions you have printed on the newsprint: (1) What kind of a person am I as a result of my experiences of suffering? (2) Have I become aware of the greatness of God and the wonder of his presence? (3) Am I listening to what God is saying in my life? (4) What can I do to be an agent of God's restoring love, for people who have suffered?

Ask the class to write on three-by-five-inch cards, if they like, an answer to the last question and to place the cards on a table in the classroom. Ask God's guidance and blessing on their commitment.

Planning for Next Sunday

Explain that the next five lessons are on Isaiah and deal with the suffering and hope of a nation. Ask class members to read Isaiah 5 and to bring newspaper or magazine clippings which show how far our society has strayed from the righteousness of God.

UNIT II: ISAIAH—INTERPRETING A NATION'S SUFFERING
Horace R. Weaver

FIVE LESSONS   **OCTOBER 2–30**

Scholars have helped us understand that the book of Isaiah is actually composed of three "books," each written in a different time and setting. The first book (chapters 1–39) was written by the prophet Isaiah, who lived in Jerusalem and ministered to his people about 740 to 687 B.C. The second book was written by an unknown writer who lived with the former leaders of Jerusalem in exile in Babylon, around 598 to 540 B.C. A brilliant theologian and writer, he is often referred to as Second Isaiah or Isaiah of Babylon, and his messages are found in Isaiah 40–55. The third book was written by a disciple of Second Isaiah and includes chapters 56–66. The five lessons drawn from Isaiah 1–66 include the messages of the above three prophets—creative, loving, helpful, and dedicated men of God.

Unit II is composed of five lessons: "Disappointing to God," October 2, is a study of the Song of the Vineyard; "A Willing Volunteer," October 9, considers the experience of Isaiah's call to be a prophet in Jerusalem; "A Comforting Word," October 16, examines Isaiah of Babylon's words of hope for the people in exile in Babylon; "The Suffering Savior," October 23, looks at the work of God's Suffering Servant; "A Better Day," October 30, deals with the ultimate restoration of God's people to joyful, peaceful relationships.

Disappointing to God

Background Scripture: Isaiah 5:1-25

The Main Question—William H. Willimon

Why Do Bad Things Happen to Good People? That was the title of a best-selling book a few years ago. In the book, Rabbi Harold Kushner explored the mystery of why suffering and pain often afflict innocent people. Undeserved suffering is one of the greatest challenges to faith. But the Bible also honestly confesses that sometimes the pain and suffering that come to people are the results of their own sinful actions.

In our better moments, we know this to be true. Lung cancer is one of the major causes of death in the United States today. Of course, the major cause of lung cancer is no great mystery. We have mountains of solid evidence proving that smoking is directly related to lung cancer. If you or I smoke and contract this dread disease, our suffering and pain would be a real tragedy. But perhaps an even greater tragedy would be that we brought this suffering upon ourselves through our own bad habits.

I think it is fair to say that in the Bible, a major issue is not why bad things happen to good people, but rather the tragic story of the expected bad consequences which befall bad people! Such is the case within our scripture today. Isaiah the prophet had the unpleasant task of announcing God's judgment upon a wayward Israel. To do so, he uses the now famous parable of the vineyard. Bad things are going to happen to a bad nation.

Why do bad things happen to good people? Why do bad things happen to *bad* people? These are the questions behind today's scripture.

Selected Scripture

King James Version	Revised Standard Version
Isaiah 5:1-7, 22-23	*Isaiah 5:1-7, 22-23*
1 Now will I sing to my well-beloved a song of my beloved touching his vineyard. My well-beloved hath a vineyard in a very fruitful hill:	1 Let me sing for my beloved a love song concerning his vineyard: My beloved had a vineyard on a very fertile hill.
2 And he fenced it, and gathered out the stones thereof and planted it with the choicest vine, and built a tower in the midst of it, and also made a wine-press therein: and he looked that it should bring forth grapes, and it brought forth wild grapes.	2 He digged it and cleared it of stones, and planted it with choice vines; he built a watchtower in the midst of it. and hewed out a wine vat in it; and he looked for it to yield grapes, but it yielded wild grapes.

3 And now, O inhabitants of Jerusalem, and men of Judah, judge, I pray you, betwixt me and my vineyard.

4 What could have been done more to my vineyard, that I have not done in it? wherefore, when I looked that it should bring forth grapes, brought it forth wild grapes?

5 And now go to; I will tell you what I will do to my vineyard: I will take away the hedge thereof, and it shall be eaten up; *and* break down the wall thereof, and it shall be trodden down:

6 And I will lay it waste: it shall not be pruned nor digged; but there shall come up briers and thorns: I will also command the clouds that they rain no rain upon it.

7 For the vineyard of the Lord of hosts is the house of Is'ra-el, and the men of Judah his pleasant plant: and he looked for judgment, but behold oppression; for righteousness, but behold a cry.

....

22 Woe unto *them that are* mighty to drink wine, and men of strength to mingle strong drink:

23 Which justify the wicked for reward, and take away the righteousness of the righteous from him!

Key Verse: **He looked for judgment, but behold oppression, for righteousness, but behold a cry. (Isaiah 5:7)**

3 And now, O inhabitants of Jerusalem
    and men of Judah,
  judge, I pray you, between me
    and my vineyard.

4 What more was there to do for my vineyard,
    that I have not done in it?
  When I looked for it to yield grapes,
    why did it yield wild grapes?

5 And now I will tell you
    what I will do to my vineyard.
  I will remove its hedge,
    and it shall be devoured;
  I will break down its wall,
    and it shall be trampled down.

6 I will make it a waste;
    it shall not be pruned or hoed,
    and briers and thorns shall grow up;
  I will also command the clouds
    that they rain no rain upon it.

7 For the vineyard of the Lord of hosts
    is the house of Israel,
  and the men of Judah
    are his pleasant planting;
  and he looked for justice,
    but behold, bloodshed;
  for righteousness,
    but behold, a cry!

....

22 Woe to those who are heroes at drinking wine,
    and valiant men in mixing strong drink,

23 who acquit the guilty for a bribe, and deprive the innocent of his right!

Key Verse: **He looked for justice, but behold, bloodshed; for righteousness, but behold, a cry! (Isaiah 5:7)**

As You Read the Scripture—Lynne Deming

Isaiah 5. This is a very famous chapter in the book of Isaiah. It paints a picture in poetry of the prophet trying to get the audience's attention by telling a story. Once their attention is fixed on the speaker, he announces a prophecy of doom for the nation of Israel.

Verse 1. The word translated "beloved" in the Revised Standard Version is probably better translated "friend." Who this friend is will not be made clear until the end of the poem. We can imagine the prophet standing in the midst of the inhabitants of Judah (verse 3), trying to focus attention on himself and his message by saying in a loud voice, "Let me sing for my friend a love song concerning his vineyard."

Verse 2. Before planting his vineyard, this friend did the hard work of digging up the soil and clearing the stones away. The stones were then used to build a tower in the midst of the vineyard, so it could be guarded against intruders. After all this preparation, however, he was greatly disappointed. The choice vines that had been planted in this well-prepared location should have produced large, juicy grapes. Instead, they brought forth wild grapes, which were small, hard, and had a sour taste.

Verses 3-4. Here the prophet reminds us again of the audience: inhabitants of Jerusalem and men of Judah—two ways of saying the same thing. Now, however, it is not the storyteller speaking. In this verse, the owner of the vineyard speaks, who is the friend, or beloved, of the prophet. The vineyard owner asks the persons hearing the story to judge whether or not he was at fault. After all, he had made the best preparations possible. What went wrong? What could he have done differently?

By now the hearers may have begun to realize that the story is making a point with larger implications than the failure of a vineyard to produce bountiful grapes. When asked to judge between the vineyard and its owner, the hearers of the story would have judged against the vineyard. The owner had done everything possible to ensure its success. In the same way, God had done everything possible on behalf of the people of Israel. But like the vineyard, the people did not respond.

Verse 5. The owner of the vineyard continues to speak and tells the hearers what is planned for the vineyard. If the hearers have realized the point of the story, they will understand that the judgment and punishment are intended for them. The owner will tear down the protection that has been provided for the vineyard (the hedge and the wall). In other words, God will no longer protect the people of Israel from their enemies.

Verse 6. The owner will no longer prune or hoe the vineyard. He will let briers and thistles grow inside it. The hearers understood that promise to mean that God's nurture and care of the people will be taken away. God will withhold nurture from the people, just as rain will not fall upon the vineyard to nourish it.

Verse 7. This verse makes clear the point of the story, in case the hearers have not understood it yet. The vineyard in the story represents the people of Israel, the hearers of the parable. God is the owner of the vineyard, who is displeased with its performance. God's disappointment in the people is graphically described in this verse: God looked for justice but found bloodshed instead. God looked for righteousness but received cries of oppression.

FIRST QUARTER

The Scripture and the Main Question—William H. Willimon

My Beloved Had a Vineyard

In scripture we find a wide array of literary types, all in the service of communication of God's truth. There are history lessons, stories, parables, fables, poems, songs, and lists of ethical injunctions. Biblical writers skillfully utilized different types of literature in order to communicate different things to readers.

A wise communicator knows that sometimes he or she must employ different kinds of literature in order to enable people to hear. The parables of Jesus are good examples of skillful application of literary technique. Instead of saying to people, "God sometimes makes people like you angry by loving those whom you despise," a statement which would elicit only anger, Jesus tells stories about a shepherd who goes looking for the one lost sheep and a woman who turns her house upside down looking for a lost coin. We listen to these parables, drawn into them by their narrative action, and suddenly, with our defenses down, we are enabled to hear things we could not have otherwise heard.

Today we begin a study of Isaiah the prophet. Who is a prophet? Some have the notion that a prophet is someone who can predict the future. Some prophets in Israel did foretell events that were going to happen to the nation. But that was never their main function. Prophets are "forthtellers," those who tell forth the messages of God. In order to do this, the prophets, like all good communicators, carefully choose their means of communication.

In the fifth chapter of Isaiah, the prophet tells a memorable story, a poem of a farmer who planted a disappointing vineyard. This is an allegory, a story in which the various elements of the story stand for other meanings. In this allegory, the Lord of Israel is compared to a farmer who lovingly plants a new vineyard, even as God has made a new nation out of those who were once Egyptian slaves.

> My beloved had a vineyard
> on a very fertile hill.
> He digged it and cleared it of stones,
> and planted it with choice vines.
> (5:1b, 2a)

In spite of the farmer's hard work, the vineyard yielded wild grapes (5:4). The farmer tells what he will do to his vineyard: "remove its hedge, . . . break down its wall, and it shall be trampled upon" (5:5).

The ruined vineyard is the house of Israel (5:7). Through the allegory, the nation is asked to pronounce judgment on itself. This technique is reminiscent of the prophet Nathan's parable before King David (II Samuel 12:1-12), a little story about a rich man who killed a poor man's lamb and served it up to his cronies. David was enraged by the tale, crying out for punishment of the arrogant rich man. "Thou art the man!" said Nathan to a stunned King David.

Which people is this who shall suffer ruin and devastation? Thou art the nation! says the prophet.

46

The Vineyard of the Lord of Hosts

What has happened in Israel is so typical of the dynamic of human history, even of our personal stories. Obviously, from the reproaches we read in Isaiah 5, Israel and Judah have prospered. We are not reading about wandering nomads. The nation is established in the land of promise. During this time of economic prosperity, the people have drifted away from their roots. The originating vision which once gave the young nation its vitality has become blurred. A people who were once unified in their common struggle have become divided between the insensitive rich and the oppressed poor. Does any of this sound familiar?

The first generation knows what real struggle and deprivation look like. It feels a sense of humility and gratitude for its blessings. But the second and following generations have known little of the struggle. In the eyes of later generations, material blessings seem more like rights than blessings, just deserts rather than divine gifts. This is the situation that Isaiah confronts. Do you see parallels between this situation and our own? How ironic it is that the affluence we enjoy, the material blessings of food, drink, homes, fellowship, should be among the factors which cheapen our lives and divide us.

I remember my mother noting that in the Great Depression of the 1930s, there seemed to be a spirit of unity and cooperation which does not exist in more prosperous times. During those difficult days, nearly everyone was struggling to survive. People shared from the little that they had.

Today, we have isolated poverty into certain segments of our society. The poor are sealed off in inner city ghettos or isolated rural areas. The rest of us go about our lives with little thought for the less fortunate among us. The reproaches of Isaiah 5 sound hauntingly appropriate to our own situation. Even as the hearers of the parable of the vineyard heard a little story turned upon them and their unfaithful ways, so you and I, in reading this ancient text of Isaiah 5, may feel that this old story has become our own:

> Woe to those who are wise in their own eyes.
> ....
> Woe to those who are heroes at drinking wine.
> ....
> who acquit the guilty for a bribe,
>   and deprive the innocent of his right!
>   (5:21-23)

Woe to Those Who Call Evil Good and Good Evil

Note that the prophet makes little distinction between personal and social evil. The personal sins of alcohol abuse and dishonesty, greed and pride, are set alongside the social sins of injustice, violence, and political corruption. We often differentiate between the personal and the social in our ethics and our religious life. But not God's prophet. Our sin is all of one piece, and there shall be consequences for it.

Actions have consequences. The evils that come to God's chosen ones are not simply the result of God's wrath; they are the result of the nation's moral decay. We sow what we reap. It is the prophet's sad duty to tell the nation that a bitter harvest is coming. The once beloved and manicured vineyard is going to be overcome with woe.

Of course, we don't like to think about such things. We prefer to think about happy things, enjoying today with little thought for tomorrow. This little story of the vineyard provokes profound self-examination.

Helping Adults Become Involved—Leonard T. Wolcott

Preparing to Teach

The last four lessons dealt with suffering that comes to good people. How, those lessons asked, are we to understand and respond to such suffering? The next five lessons deal with the suffering of a nation. Today's lesson is concerned with the suffering that a people brings upon itself.

The content of the lesson can be organized as follows:

I. Introduction
II. The Song of the Vineyard (verses 1-7)
III. The judgment on Judah (verses 8-25)

Read carefully "The Scripture and the Main Question" and "As You Read the Scripture." These form the heart of the lesson. The ideas, insights, and suggestions in these sections should be reflected continually in your lesson plan.

As you use the suggested outline, you may want to either quote or paraphrase ideas. You might like to jot in the margin of your outline the page number and paragraph being referred to. For example, you could write a reference to page 65, paragraph 3, as 65-3.

Read the allegory in Isaiah 5, with the aid of the lesson helps provided. Bring newspaper or magazine clippings of stories that illustrate the social sins of which Isaiah speaks. Type and duplicate copies of Isaiah 1:36, 37; Psalm 51:10; and a prayer of confession. You will need chalk and chalkboard or marker and newsprint.

Introducing the Main Question

Basic and helpful ideas are presented in the section "The Main Question." These ideas are essential in helping to identify the purpose of the lesson.

"Bad things happen to bad people." Using Dr. Willimon's "The Main Question," you will help class members see the orientation of the next five lessons. Remind them that individuals as well as societies often do suffer because they have ignored the rules of life God has structured into his universe, and his demands for righteousness in human relations.

A fundamental message of the Bible and of the church is that we are sinners, and as such under God's judgment, and this we must recognize.

Developing the Lesson

I. Introduction

Sometimes a factory, a farm, or business enterprise may fail because it is not productive. It may be due to bad management or to staff or workers who do not take responsibility for their work. Some class members may have personal knowledge of such failures. Students of history know of many nations and entire societies that collapsed when there was no responsible moral leadership.

II. The Song of the Vineyard (verses 1-7)

This passage is a parable (or better, an allegory) of such a failure. Read it aloud.

The farmer has worked hard to produce good grapes. He is, therefore, keenly disappointed in the results. Read verses 3 and 4 to the class. Class members may have had disappointments over failures after hard work. Ask: Is God ever disappointed in humanity? In Christians? In us?

Call attention to the use of parables, as explained in "As You Read the Scripture." Jesus used parables as a means of getting people's attention (and at the same time of getting his message across).

Point out that the people are asked to judge between the vineyard and the farmer (verses 3, 4) and in doing so they judge themselves. Call attention to Jesus' similar parable of a vineyard (Matthew 21:33-41).

The vineyard is judged and destroyed. Read verses 5 and 6.

III. The judgment on Judah (verses 8-25)

"For the vineyard of the Lord of hosts is the house of Israel, and the men of Judah . . . " Here comes the connection, and the disappointment of the Lord. Read verse 7. Here come the judgment and the woes.

The people, in their prosperity and affluence, have ignored God and righteousness. Note what Dr. Willimon says under "The Vineyard of the Lord of Hosts" in "The Scripture and the Main Question" about a people forgetting their roots. "Pride goes before destruction" (Proverbs 16:18). Apparently some people of Judah were surprised by what Isaiah said. Why, they wondered, were they condemned? They were condemned (1) for the unjust greed of the ruling classes (verse 8); (2) for their profligate living, drinking, banqueting, carousing, and bravado (verses 11, 12, 22); (3) for their brazen irreligiousness, making light of God (verses 12, 18-19); (4) for falsifying truth: calling "evil good and good evil" (verse 20); (5) for corruption in the system of justice (verse 23).

In a devastating statement, verse 7 sums it up:

> . . . he looked for justice,
> but behold, bloodshed;
> for righteousness,
> but behold, a cry!

God, the righteous defender of the underprivileged, is bitter at his people's failure to produce good fruit.

Suffering is the consequence:

> But they do not regard the deeds of the Lord,
> or see the work of his hands.
> Therefore my people go into exile
> for want of knowledge.
>
> (5:12, 13)

It is a matter of cause and effect, and the rest of the chapter details the effects. An analysis of the career of Adolf Hitler shows that his destruction was inevitable. As Victor Hugo said of Napoleon, he was destroyed "because of God." He transgressed against God's moral order.

FIRST QUARTER

God is the measure. In Job, human self-pity was measured against the greatness of God. Here, human pride and injustice are measured against the righteousness of God. "The Lord of hosts is exalted in justice" (verse 16.)

Helping Class Members Act

Is God disappointed in us? If you use the discussion method, get class members to respond to this question.

We resist self-condemnation. We like people who make us happy. We tend to vote for candidates who tell us we are doing just fine. In the annals of Israel's history, it is frequently noted that the kings listened to prophets who told them what they wanted to hear—and they suffered for it.

As Christians, however, we are called on to bring ourselves, our motives, our actions, our nation before God, to be measured by his demand for righteousness. Refer to the news stories and magazine articles brought in by the class, which show wrongdoing in society today. Let class members report similar stories. On the chalkboard or newsprint, record the kinds of wrongdoing reported on: political corruption, drug traffic, injustice, etc.

Where we have gone wrong, we are to repent. True repentance is the acknowledgment of God's greatness and justice (verse 16) and the confession of our own failure. Read, or distribute to class members, typed copies of Isaiah 1:16-17; Psalm 51:10; and a prayer of confession.

Planning for Next Sunday

Next Sunday's lesson is about Isaiah's call. Ask the class to read Isaiah 6:1-8 and Matthew 4:17-22. Assign one person to read and report on Jeremiah 1:4-10 and another to report on Ezekiel 1:26—2:3. Many short biographies of famous Christians, ancient and modern, are available. You might ask a class member to read one and report to the class on the manner of that person's call to enter Christian service.

LESSON 6   OCTOBER 9

A Willing Volunteer

Background Scripture: Isaiah 6

The Main Question—William H. Willimon

Today's scripture is one of the most familiar passages of the Hebrew Scriptures. If I remember correctly, this passage was always used at youth rallies, youth religious-emphasis weeks, and other occasions when the church stressed the value of "full-time church-related vocations." Invariably the preacher would take as his text this passage from Isaiah, which speaks of the dramatic call of Isaiah to be a prophet.

50

One wonders if the sense of vocation is out of fashion these days. When we speak of the work that people go into, we usually use the word "profession" or "career," or simply, "job." How many people today think of their job as their Christian vocation? Alas, for most of us, a job is simply a way of making a living, "bringing home the bacon" and little more.

The account of the call of Isaiah stirs us because it is thrilling to see someone so dramatically caught up in the purposes of God. And yet God's purposes are not limited to the "full-time church-related professional." One does not have to be a priest, a pastor, or a nun to serve God. God expects us to be of service in whatever vocation we follow, including those vocations which are outside of the church.

The Christian sense of vocation stems from a conviction that one's work, whatever it may be, is somehow caught up within God's work.

One day while worshiping in the temple, young Isaiah was caught up into the purposes of God. How do our lives become caught up in God's plans for the world? How can we sense the call of God upon our lives, so that we, with Isaiah, are able to say, "Here am I, send me"?

Selected Scripture

King James Version

Isaiah 6:1-8

1 In the year that king Uz-zi′ah died I saw also the Lord sitting upon a throne, high and lifted up, and his train filled the temple.

2 Above it stood the seraphim: each one had six wings; with twain he covered his face, and with twain he covered his feet, and with twain he did fly.

3 And one cried unto another, and said, Holy, holy, holy, *is* the Lord of hosts: the whole earth *is* full of his glory.

4 And the posts of the door moved at the voice of him that cried, and the house was filled with smoke.

5 Then said I, Woe *is* me! for I am undone; because I *am* a man of unclean lips, and I dwell in the midst of a people of unclean lips: for mine eyes have seen the King, the Lord of hosts.

6 Then flew one of the seraphim unto me, having a live coal in his hand, *which* he had taken with the tongs from off the altar:

7 And he laid *it* upon my mouth, and said, Lo, this hath touched thy lips; and thine iniquity is taken away, and thy sin purged.

Revised Standard Version

Isaiah 6:1-8

1 In the year that King Uzzi′ah died I saw the Lord sitting upon a throne, high and lifted up; and his train filled the temple. 2 Above him stood the seraphim; each had six wings: with two he covered his face, and with two he covered his feet, and with two he flew. 3 And one called to another and said:

"Holy, holy, holy is the Lord of hosts;
the whole earth is full of his glory."

4 And the foundations of the thresholds shook at the voice of him who called, and the house was filled with smoke. 5 And I said: "Woe is me! For I am lost; for I am a man of unclean lips, and I dwell in the midst of a people of unclean lips; for my eyes have seen the King, the Lord of hosts!"

6 Then flew one of the seraphim to me, having in his hand a burning coal which he had taken with tongs from the altar. 7 And he touched my mouth, and said: "Behold, this has touched your lips; your guilt is taken away, and your sin forgiven."

8 Also I heard the voice of the Lord, saying, Whom shall I send, and who will go for us? Then said I, Here *am* I; send me.

8 And I heard the voice of the Lord saying, "Whom shall I send, and who will go for us?" Then I said, "Here am I! Send me."

Key Verse: **I heard the voice of the Lord, saying, Whom shall I send, and who will go for us? Then said I, Here am I; send me. (Isaiah 6:8)**

Key Verse: **I heard the voice of the Lord saying, "Whom shall I send, and who will go for us?" Then I said, "Here am I! Send me." (Isaiah 6:8)**

As You Read the Scripture—Lynne Deming

Isaiah 6. This chapter gives us a first-person account of the call of the prophet Isaiah. Isaiah was in the temple in Jerusalem when he was commissioned by God to prophesy to the people of Israel.

Verse 1. This verse tells us exactly when and where Isaiah's call took place. "In the year that King Uzziah died" tells us that Isaiah was called in the year 742 B.C. His ministry lasted until the year 687 B.C., a total of fifty-five years. These particular years were important ones in Israel's history, since during this time the northern kingdom fell (721 B.C.), and the southern kingdom was none too stable.

Isaiah says he saw God sitting on a throne, "high and lifted up." The word "throne" refers to the ark of the covenant, the object traditionally thought to house the Deity. However, the prophet tells us nothing about the appearance of the throne, nor does he describe what God looks like. Isaiah's very brief description stands in contrast to the words of the prophet Ezekiel, who gives us a vivid description of the throne and the Deity.

Verse 2. Here the prophet describes the seraphim that hover above God's throne. We do not know how many seraphim are there, but each has six wings: Two cover his face, two cover his feet, and two are used in flying.

Verse 3. Now we also learn that these seraphim can speak, at least to each other. In Hebrew, repetition of words is often used for the purpose of extra emphasis. The holiness of God is the special point of emphasis here. God as the Holy One is a common image in the book of Isaiah (see 1:4, for example).

This short song of praise from the mouth of one of the seraphim tells us two main things about God. First, God is holy among all "the hosts," that is, God is most holy in the heavenly realm. Second, God's holiness pervades the earthly realm as well ("the whole earth is full of his glory"). This latter phrase reminds us of the prayer that concludes Psalm 72 (72:19).

Verse 4. The shaking of the foundations comes as a direct result of the words of the song in verse 3. The message is literally an earthshaking one. The image of thresholds shaking is repeated in the last vision of the prophet Amos.

This verse also tells us that the house, meaning the temple, was filled with smoke. The smoke signifies two things. First, it indicates the presence of God. Thunder, lightning, smoke, and loud noises all are common occurrences when God is present, which is termed a "theophany." Second, it provides a screen between God and the others present. Elsewhere the Old Testament tells us that no one should ever see God face to face (see Exodus 19:21, for example).

Verse 5. Now the prophet responds to what he has experienced. His first response is not one of joy, but rather a combination of dismay, awe, anxiety, and fear. He is prevented from being joyful by his current situation—he is a man of unclean lips living among people who are also unclean. His anxiety is also caused by the fact that he stands in the presence of God.

Verses 6-7. God now responds to the prophet's anxiety and to his hesitation to accept the call. His unclean lips are cleansed by the burning coal in the hand of one of the seraphim. The seraph makes clear the function of the burning coal. The prophet, forgiven and cleansed, can now accept God's commission to prophesy.

Verse 8. This verse contains the formal commission, or call. It comes from God in the form of two related questions: "Whom shall I send?" and "Who will go for us?" Isaiah, without further hesitation, answers "I am the one." He can now perform the task that God called him to do—speak on behalf of God to the hearts of the people of Israel.

The Scripture and the Main Question—William H. Willimon

In the Year That King Uzziah Died

"In the year that King Uzziah died I saw the Lord" (6:1). Thus begins the stirring account of Isaiah's call. The year is around 742 B.C. The youth Isaiah (who is possibly Uzziah's nephew) is confronting the dissolution of the old order, upon the death of the king. "The year that King Uzziah died" can be any time when things begin to fall apart for us. Where were you when you heard that John Kennedy had been shot, or that Martin Luther King, Jr., was dead? You can probably recount exactly where you were at that moment and can still feel the shock and horror, the fear for the future, that swept over you at that moment. In such times we know that a chapter in our lives is closing and another is being opened.

That was the way it was for young Isaiah. In this time of personal turmoil brought about by national events, the young man entered the temple to worship. Although I was too young to remember, I have seen newsreels of people flocking to church on the day after the end of World War II to give thanks for national victory. When Americans were being held hostage in Iran a number of years ago, many churches had special services to pray for the release of the captives. Perhaps Isaiah was in a similar frame of mind when he entered the temple. There he received a vision of God and felt the dramatic call of God upon his life.

During times when the old world is crumbling, we can have faith that God is bringing some new world into being. We should be alert and watchful for what God may be leading us toward.

I Heard the Voice of the Lord

It was in this dramatic event at the temple that Isaiah heard the very voice of God calling him by name. Although you and I may never have had so dramatic an encounter with the voice of God, we can affirm that we have had moments when we felt the sure tug of God upon our lives.

Recently, I heard an interview with a woman in New England who felt the call of God upon her life. For many years Gladys had suffered from emotional problems and alcoholism. After a terrible bout of depression and

53

excessive drinking, she was institutionalized for many months. When she was finally released from the hospital, she was sober but also terribly alone and terribly frightened. She went back to her mobile home to sit in despair. Without a job or friends, with nowhere to go and nothing to do, she knew that it would only be a matter of time before she would be worse off than before.

"I was sitting on the side of my bed, praying," said Gladys. "Then the keys to my old car just jumped off the dresser and fell at my feet. At that moment I knew that God was trying to tell me what to do. I said, 'I'll drive a taxi.' "

Gladys organized a taxi service for the people in the little towns near her. There was no public transportation available, and many people, particularly the sick and the elderly, had no way to get around. Her taxi service developed into a fleet of old but reliable cars driven by people much like Gladys. The taxis would pick up prescriptions at the pharmacist and deliver them, take people to and from senior citizens' meetings, and enable many to travel who before could only sit at home.

Of course, you may have your doubts about those car keys jumping off the dresser and falling at Gladys' feet. But the real miracle, the most wondrous thing about it, was not the flight of those keys but the voice Gladys heard, lifting her out of despair and confusion into the good purposes of God. That is the real story.

Gladys reminds us that God is still speaking to us in much the same what that God spoke to Isaiah in the temple, in the year that King Uzziah died. In such holy moments, ordinary individuals like you and me hear our names called, and our lives are given purpose and direction—not of our own doing, but out of God's doing.

Here Am I! Send Me!

Most of us are confronted almost daily with various claims upon our lives. People come to us wanting us to volunteer to help with the church clothes closet, the annual bazaar for the needy, the latest collection of signatures for ending apartheid in South Africa. Few of us are able to respond to everything. Life involves sorting out all the voices and appeals and deciding which ones are best directed toward us and our talents. Not every appeal to us is the voice of God.

In the year that King Uzziah died, some young men in Israel may have been asked to enter the government and serve in that capacity. Other young people may have been asked to stay home and raise good families for the future. Isaiah was asked to go be a spokesperson for God. Each of us has to decide what God wants us to do, based upon an assessment of our own abilities, the needs of the world, our intuitions, and past experience.

The main thing is that we listen, that we are always attentive to the possibility of the call of God, particularly in those times when everything seems to be falling apart for us. Often what appears to be only meaningless chaos is an opportunity for change and renewal. Sometimes our lives are disrupted and we are thrown off balance, so that we may be better able to move to some new state of existence. That was what Isaiah found out in the temple during the year that King Uzziah died. Today you will go to worship in your church. You will sing the hymns, participate in the prayers, move with other worshipers before the throne of God. Like Isaiah, you are entering the church to worship. Will your name be called today? Will this time of worship be transformed into a time of vocation? And what will be your response?

Here am I, send me!

Helping Adults Become Involved—Leonard T. Wolcott

Preparing to Teach

This lesson should inspire class members to allow themselves to be caught up in God's purposes and to respond to his call. It will follow the development in Isaiah 6:1-8.

The scripture passage may be divided into the following six points:

    I. Introduction
   II. In the temple of the Lord
  III. Awareness of God's presence
  IV. Awareness of personal uncleanness before God
   V. God's forgiving and cleansing
  VI. God's call

Read carefully "The Scripture and the Main Question" and "As You Read the Scripture." These form the heart of the lesson. The ideas, insights, and suggestions in these sections should be reflected continually in your lesson plan.

As you use the suggested outline, you may want to either quote or paraphrase ideas. You might like to jot in the margin of your outline the page number and paragraph being referred to. For example, you could write a reference to page 65, paragraph 3, as 65-3.

Read Isaiah 6:1-8 with "As You Read the Scripture" for background, then the rest of Isaiah 6. This will relate Isaiah's call to what he is called to do. Read Matthew 4:17-22.

Have available chalkboard and chalk or newsprint and marker, to record main points. A chart can help class members visualize the subject. Draw a vertical line to make two columns. Write "Human Need" in the left-hand column and "Christian Response" in the right-hand one. At the top of the chart write "Awareness of God: Repentance, commitment, commission."

Introducing the Main Question

Basic and helpful ideas are presented in the section "The Main Question." These ideas are essential in helping to identify the purpose of the lesson.

How can we sense the call of God upon our lives so that we, with Isaiah, are able to say, "Here am I, send me"? Read to your class the last paragraph of Dr. Willimon's section, "The Main Question."

Dr. Willimon provides illustrations of ways in which people of any age or at any place can respond to God's call.

If you asked someone to prepare a brief report on a famous Christian's call to service, ask that person to tell the class what he or she learned. Or, you can add to this any illustrations from stories you have read. Popular religious magazines, such as *Guideposts*, tell of persons who through some experience, often a painful one, responded to God's call on their lives.

Developing the Lesson

I. Introduction

Give background for the account in Isaiah 6. Isaiah, a statesman-priest, was concerned about his country's affairs and aware of Israel's God. The date is the end of the prosperous reign of King Uzziah (about 740 B.C.).

II. In the temple of the Lord

This setting is important. God, the people believed, dwelt in the temple to protect and inspire them. Isaiah had his experience at the time of worship. We go to church to worship, to praise God, to express our love to God, and to listen to what God may be saying to us. Isaiah was not startled out of boredom. In true worship there is a sense of expectancy. Since the entire Bible is about the actions of God for righteousness, the worship of God is a response to his activity.

III. Awareness of God's presence

The vision is an expression of the force of God's presence on Isaiah's awareness. How real is God to each class member?

Holiness is as much the attribute of God as righteousness. A holy God can be approached only in deep reverence and wonder. Awareness of God changes our life-direction. It comes in different ways. For Martin Luther, it was in a thunderstorm. John R. Mott became aware of God and of the world's need for Christ as he worshiped with students from many countries.

God speaks. The threshold shakes. Have we so shut out the voice of God by our noisy modern society, by our busyness, that we do not hear it, and so do not react?

IV. Awareness of personal uncleanness before God

A floor in shadows may not seem dirty, especially if it is regularly swept. But in a bright light the spots show up. Isaiah was not wicked by civilized standards. But he became conscious of his sins in the presence of God's holiness. We cannot be satisfied with ourselves when we are confronted by God. Isaiah was unnerved by the experience. Would we be? Ask anyone in the class who has had such an experience to share it.

V. God's forgiving and cleansing

If holy righteousness convicts of sin, it also forgives.

Holiness touches uncleanness: the divine touches the human. It is a change no person can effect for himself. God can and does come to the penitent believer.

The penitent psalmist cried: "Purge me with hyssop and I shall be clean; Wash me and I shall be whiter than snow" (Psalm 51:7). There is no one without some guilt, some wrong to self, to others, to God. But God will forgive our sins—no sin is so bad it cannot be forgiven.

The significance of God's forgiveness is restoration of a relationship with God, that we may be and do what God intended for us.

Only when forgiven was Isaiah ready to respond to God's call. Only when they had responded to Jesus' call to repentance were people ready to be chosen disciples.

VI. God's call

Ask the class to read together Matthew 4:17-22, about Jesus calling the disciples. Those assigned to investigate Jeremiah 1:4-10 and Ezekiel 1:26–2:3 may give their reports. Or read these scriptures aloud and ask the class what common elements they see in all these calls. Isaiah 6 repeats God's "voice" and the man's "lips." In Ezekiel, "voice" and "speak" are repeated. In Jeremiah the words are "Word of the Lord" and "speak," and it was "the man's mouth" which the Lord touched. The common emphasis is on communication from God through the prophets. The voice asks, "Whom shall I send . . . ?" The need for sending is found in the following passages: the inattention of "this people" to God. In all these passages the prophet, the disciple, the listener to God, is the connection, sent to make clear God's purpose to the people, to meet their needs, to bring them into God's will.

Note that calls come in different ways. Dr. Willimon has given some helpful examples. All biblical calls, such as Isaiah's, are a divine commission to respond to human need in God's way. A biblical calling is not just a job, but a carrying out of God's will. A call may involve going to a people far away, or to people nearby. It may mean leaving the work you are now doing for a special mission, or using your job to fulfill God's purpose.

Helping Class Members Act

Isaiah, in the temple experience, became involved in God's great purpose. Obedience to God means taking part in his work. Isaiah's response to God was unhesitating and firm; not simply, "I am willing to go," but, "Send me!" To firm commitment there comes clear direction. God says, "Go, and say . . . "

If you have made the suggested chart, use it here. God is concerned about human suffering. He wills goodness for his people. Class members can suggest what to write under "Human Need," on the left side of the chart. On the right side point out the conditions for Christian response to God's concern and purpose. Ask class members in a closing period of silence to consider: (1) Am I listening to God? (2) Am I aware of human need? and (3) Is God calling me to do something for him? For others? Am I saying "Here am I, send me"?

Planning for Next Sunday

Next Sunday's lesson is on words of hope. Ask class members to think about personal hopes they would like to come true. Ask them to read Isaiah 40.

A Comforting Word

Background Scripture: Isaiah 40

The Main Question—William H. Willimon

Reading the words of the prophets of the Hebrew Scriptures, one wonders how we ever came upon our image of a "True Prophet." Recently, I heard about a young preacher who was forced out of a church because his sermons had infuriated so many of his members. A bishop, commenting on the young man's plight, said, "He has suffered because he is a true prophet."

What do you think of when the word "prophet" comes to mind? You may think of a seer or a fortune teller. Scholars tell us that these are inaccurate representations of the prophets. The prophets did not foretell future events, but mostly concerned themselves with "forthtelling" the words of God.

What were the words of God which they spoke? Were they always words of fire, judgment, and condemnation? That is usually our image of "prophetic preaching." When I was in seminary, I remember a professor asking my class, "Do you intend to be a loving pastor or a truthful prophet? You need to decide now what sort of preacher you will be." Evidently, the professor thought that one could not be a truthful prophet and a loving pastor at the same time.

Today we read again the words of the prophet Isaiah, some of the most beautiful words of hope ever spoken. Like all true prophets of God, he speaks not always words of threat, fire, and judgment, but also, particularly in the worst of times for God's people, stirring words of genuine hope.

Selected Scripture

King James Version	Revised Standard Version
Isaiah 40:1-5, 9-11	*Isaiah 40:1-5, 9-11*
1 Comfort ye, comfort ye my people saith your God.	1 Comfort, comfort my people, says your God.
2 Speak ye comfortably to Jerusalem, and cry unto her, that her warfare is accomplished, that her iniquity is pardoned: for she hath received of the Lord's hand double for all her sins.	2 Speak tenderly to Jerusalem, and cry to her that her warfare is ended, that her iniquity is pardoned, that she has received from the Lord's hand double for all her sins.
3 The voice of him that crieth in the wilderness, Prepare ye the way of the Lord, make straight in the desert a highway for our God.	3 A voice cries: "In the wilderness prepare the way of the Lord. make straight in the desert a highway for our God.

58

4 Every valley shall be exalted, and every mountain and hill shall be made low: and the crooked shall be made straight, and the rough places plain:

5 And the glory of the Lord shall be revealed, and all flesh shall see *it* together: for the mouth of the Lord hath spoken *it*.

....

9 O Zion, that bringest good tidings, get thee up into the high mountain; O Jerusalem, that bringest good tidings, lift up thy voice with strength; lift *it* up, be not afraid; say unto the cities of Ju'dah, Behold your God!

10 Behold, the Lord God will come with strong *hand*, and his arm shall rule for him: behold, his reward *is* with him and his work before him.

11 He shall feed his flock like a shepherd: he shall gather the lambs with his arm, and carry *them* in his bosom, *and* shall gently lead those that are with young.

4 Every valley shall be lifted up,
    and every mountain and hill be
      made low;
  the uneven ground shall become
      level,
    and the rough places a plain.
5 And the glory of the Lord shall be
      revealed,
    and all flesh shall see it together,
  for the mouth of the Lord has
      spoken."

....

9 Get you up to a high mountain,
    O Zion, herald of good tidings;
  lift up your voice with strength,
    O Jerusalem, herald of good
      tidings,
  lift it up, fear not;
  say to the cities of Judah,
    "Behold your God!"
10 Behold, the Lord God comes
      with might,
    and his arm rules for him;
  behold, his reward is with him,
    and his recompense before
      him.
11 He will feed his flock like a
      shepherd,
  he will gather the lambs in his
      arms,
  he will carry them in his bosom,
    and gently lead those that are
      with young.

Key Verse: **And the glory of the Lord shall be revealed, and all flesh shall see it together: for the mouth of the Lord hath spoken it. (Isaiah 40:5)**

Key Verse: **And the glory of the Lord shall be revealed, and all flesh shall see it together, for the mouth of the Lord has spoken. (Isaiah 40:5)**

As You Read the Scripture—Lynne Deming

Isaiah 40. Isaiah 40 is the first chapter in what is often called "the book of the Consolation of Israel" (Isaiah 40–55). These sixteen chapters provided comforting words for the people of Israel who had been taken into exile, words of promise that they would be returning home before very long.

Verse 1. This verse introduces the theme of the next sixteen chapters: "Comfort, comfort my people." Usually, in the Old Testament the word "comfort" is used to describe what one person does for another. But here and elsewhere in this part of Isaiah, God is the one who comforts (see also Isaiah 49:13; 51:3, 12; 52:9).

Verse 2. God is putting words into the prophet's mouth. The prophet is instructed to tell the people that their "warfare" is ended. Another way to translate "warfare" is "time of service." God is conveying the message to Israel that her exile is coming to an end. "Her warfare is ended" and "her iniquity is pardoned" are two ways of saying the same thing. Israel has been punished long enough.

In this verse the prophet wants us to understand that Israel is in exile as punishment for her sins. The prophet places himself in the tradition of the prophets of judgment by saying that disobedience causes punishment. But he also introduces himself as a prophet of salvation by saying that God forgives, and that punishment is coming to an end.

Verse 3. We are not told whose voice is crying the famous words that follow. The voice could be God's voice, the voice of some invisible being, or perhaps a voice belonging to some member of God's court. However, the message of the voice is clear, and it continues through the end of verse 5.

Verses 3-5. We can tell from the message in these verses that God's command in verse 1 has been heard. The voice proclaims that the way of the Lord is being prepared, so that the people of Israel may return home. The first part of verse 3 reads: "In the wilderness prepare the way of the Lord." This same phrase is quoted in Luke 3:4, and in the other three Gospels as well (see Matthew 3:3; Mark 1:3; and John 1:23). The wording of this phrase differs in all the Gospel versions from the way it reads in Isaiah 40:3. The Gospel versions all indicate that the phrase "in the wilderness" refers to the location of the one whose voice is crying: "The voice of the one crying in the wilderness: Prepare the way of the Lord" (Luke 3:3). Our passage in Isaiah indicates, on the other hand, that "in the wilderness" refers to the place where the way of the Lord will be prepared. This difference in interpretation indicates that the Old Testament image has taken on a new meaning through several centuries of Christian tradition and interpretation.

The way of the Lord is a common image in this part of the book of Isaiah (see also Isaiah 42:16; 43:16, 19; 48:17; 49:11; 51:10).

Verses 3-5 conclude with the statement that the glory of the Lord will be revealed when the way of the Lord has been prepared. The glory of the Lord is a common image in the book of Ezekiel (see 1:28, for example), which was written about the same time as chapters 40–55 in Isaiah.

Verse 9. This verse introduces a section addressed to Zion (also called Jerusalem). The speaker commands Zion/Jerusalem to go up on a high mountain and proclaim the good news of God's coming. But who is Zion/Jerusalem?

Zion is called "herald of good tidings" in verse 9. The herald is to announce to the people in the cities of Judah, "Behold your God." What follows in the rest of this section tells us more about the twofold nature of God, who is coming to lead the people out of exile. God is mighty yet compassionate. At the same time, God's arm will rule in strength and will enfold the people as they are carried out of exile and led home to Judah.

The Scripture and the Main Question—William H. Willimon

Comfort, Comfort My People

One of the most stirring passages in Handel's immortal *Messiah* is the tenor solo, which pierces the air with these beautiful words, "Comfort ye, comfort ye my people, saith your God. Speak ye comfortably to Jerusalem" (Isaiah 40:1-2). These are fitting words to be spoken at either Easter or Christmas, when the *Messiah* is usually performed. Both Easter and Christmas speak to us the comforting word that our God has not left us to our own devices. Our God has come among us—"Emmanuel."

Perhaps that is why the Gospels depict Isaiah as Jesus' favorite prophet. Jesus quotes from Isaiah more than any other prophet of Israel. We began this study of Isaiah with the Song of the Vineyard, in which the prophet bitterly denounces the apostasy and infidelity of God's people. Jesus also had some harsh words for God's people, the people to whom so much had been given by God, but who had betrayed God through so much of their lives.

Yet, like Isaiah, Jesus also spoke words of hope and comfort. He sought to, in the words of the old saw, "Comfort the afflicted and afflict the comfortable". Through words and deeds of compassion, Jesus demonstrated the reality of the promise of Isaiah that

> . . . the glory of the Lord shall be revealed,
> and all flesh shall see it together,
> for the mouth of the Lord has spoken.
> (Isaiah 40:5)

How fitting, then, that in most of the Gospels the words of John the Baptist, the forerunner of Jesus, echo the words of Isaiah in announcing the arrival of God's great Messiah: "Prepare the way of the Lord, make straight in the desert a highway for our God" (Isaiah 40:3).

Herald of Good Tidings

Sometimes you hear people in the church say, "The Old Testament is a book of wrath and judgment; the New Testament is a book of grace and love." The presumption is that the Old Testament contains a fearful image of a God of wrath, but the New Testament describes a loving and compassionate Christ.

I hope you see that today's scripture from Isaiah disproves this simplistic picture. There is judgment in the New Testament: "Woe unto you, scribes and Pharisees!" There is also compassion in the Old Testament: "Comfort ye my people." Today's scripture comes toward the end of Israel's long and painful exile. The hard times are coming to a close. Performing the ministry of encouragement, God's prophet at last offers a message of hope. The glory of the Lord will at last return to the house of Israel. These are the "good tidings" the prophet is to herald. Good tidings, of course, is the meaning of our familiar Christian word, "gospel." The gospel is the good tidings about Jesus. Thus, there is gospel in the Old Testament as well as the New: the glad tidings and good news that our God does not abandon us.

This good news is at the very heart of our faith. Everyone, believer and non-believer alike, goes through times of distress. The difference between the person of faith and the person without faith is how they respond to the distress. "Pull yourself up by your bootstraps," "think positive," "every cloud has a silver lining," "things will probably get worse before they get better" are some of the many clichés and slogans people use to respond to distress. These sayings may contain some good insights, but none are specifically Christian.

The specifically Christian affirmation in time of trouble is similar to that of Isaiah, chapter 40: Our hope is in the God who loves us and will not let us go, even in our distress. This is the God of whom it can be said,

> He will feed his flock like a shepherd,
> he will gather the lambs in his arms,
> he will carry them in his bosom,
> and gently lead those that are with young.
> (40:11)

These beautiful images portray the tender love of our God. God is like a herald who brings good news (40:3-5), a good shepherd (40:11), a mighty creator (40:12), or a skilled artisan (40:18-20). This God is the one who "gives power to the faint, and to him who has no might he increases strength" (40:29). In times of distress, we believe that we are not left to our own devices. We do not rise or fall alone. Rather, our God holds us "in the hollow of his hand" (40:12).

Whether we are going through a time of national calamity, such as afflicted Isaiah's nation, or through periods of personal distress such as you and I must go through from time to time, this message of hope is the word of good tidings which keeps us going.

Behold, the Lord God Comes

Jane had been having a terrible time in her life. Ten years ago her husband had walked out on her and their children, leaving Jane with two young children to raise. Since she had no marketable job skills, she was forced to take a very menial job at a local factory. With the demands of her job, she had little time to be with her children. This conspired with the children's own hurt because of their father's desertion, and they grew to be difficult, rebellious teenagers. One left home in her early teens; the other was arrested for a minor offense and sent to a youth correctional institution.

This was more than Jane could handle. At her lowest ebb, she tossed and turned all night in her bed. In utter despair, she wandered into her kitchen in the middle of the night, shut all the doors, and turned on the gas of her stove, deciding to end her miserable life. She sat at her kitchen table, waiting for the gas to take effect and the end to come.

Looking out of her kitchen window, she saw the first rays of dawn. The rising sun was turning the whole sky a brilliant red. For Jane, it was a revelation. The rising sun seemed to say to her, "Tomorrow will come, tomorrow, more beautiful than today. Life is worth living. The world still belongs to God—so do you."

She rushed to the stove and turned off the gas. Hope filled her soul with the rising sun. When morning came and the sun was high in the sky, Jane left for work, confident that a new day could dawn in her life.

As for Jane, our "herald of good tidings" may come in many different forms: words of Scripture, the kind thoughts of a friend, the rising sun. In so many ways, our God comes to us to bring us hope and comfort.

Helping Adults Become Involved—Leonard T. Wolcott

Preparing to Teach

In this lesson you can share with the class the glory first felt when the prophet uttered the song in Isaiah 40. It is known to many through Handel's *Messiah*.

Use the following outline to organize the lesson:

    I.   Introduction
    II. God's judgment and human punishment
    III. God's might and human frailty, and God's triumph
         as the source of hope
    IV. God's caring and human comfort

Read carefully "The Scripture and the Main Question" and "As You Read the Scripture." These form the heart of the lesson. The ideas, insights, and suggestions in these sections should be reflected continually in your lesson plan.

As you use the suggested outline, you may want to either quote or paraphrase ideas. You might like to jot in the margin of your outline the page number and paragraph being referred to. For example, you could write a reference to page 65, paragraph 3, as 65-3.

Read Isaiah 40 several times. Read other commentaries to enrich your presentation.

Have available Bibles and chalk and chalkboard, or markers and newsprint, on which to write the elements of your outline.

Introducing the Main Question

Basic and helpful ideas are presented in the section "The Main Question." These ideas are essential in helping to identify the purpose of the lesson.

What is the source of your hope? What is God's word of hope for us? The prophet tells the people that they will find in God the fulfillment of hope, salvation from sin, comfort in distress. The people are in exile. But God's might and goodness are so great that they can already feel the joy of their promised return to Jerusalem. The object of the lesson is for us to be able to share in the same joy. If you can get a recording of Handel's *Messiah*, play the tenor solo, "Comfort Ye My People."

Developing the Lesson

I. Introduction

Give the background for this chapter using your commentary resources, "As You Read the Scripture" and "The Scripture and the Main Question."

The people are in exile in Babylon. Read aloud of their sorrow and longing for Jerusalem, in Psalm 137. The prophet speaks to this longing. Looming in the east is the rising Persian Empire which will free them.

Kingdoms rise and fall. All human powers fail, only God and God's plan are victorious in the end. Read aloud Psalm 2, which echoes this awareness.

II. God's judgment and human punishment

This prophet is not a sentimental dreamer. God does not wink at or excuse sin. Sinners will be punished. The prophet accepts the fact that exile was a deserved punishment. The Judeo-Christian message cannot be understood apart from the recognition that we are sinners. For example, a man fell to robbery to support his drug habit. Arrested, imprisoned, he eagerly studied the Bible. He said in his heart, "I have done wrong. I have wronged people. I belong in prison. But, oh, I want to change. I want to be delivered from my habit. Please God, help me." He hopes. He trusts. A time will come for his restoration.

Hosea 14 is a delightful invitation from God to his people to return. Read it aloud to the class. Isaiah 40:1-2 is the promise that punishment is over. It will be as though the whole land were smoothed out, the difficulties and distress banished (verses 3, 4). Ask the class: What is your wildneress? Describe Jane's wilderness as discussed in "The Scripture and the Main Question." We all, sometime in our lives, are in a wilderness, whether from our own misdoing or our inability to cope with change and tragedy. For the early Christians it was persecution for the faith. But there was the assurance that "in all these things we are more than conquerors through him who loved us" (Romans 8:37). The righteous God redeems his people.

III. God's might and human frailty, and God's triumphs as the source of hope

As in Job, we see here an emphasis on God's greatness and human frailty. In fact, the rest of Isaiah 40 after verse 11 reminds us of the questions God asked of Job, which show the impotence of man in contrast to God. Read aloud Isaiah 40:5 about the glory of God, and continue with verses 6-7. The brevity of human life and actions must be acknowledged if salvation is to take place.

Salvation comes with complete trust and dependence on God. A missionary, Helen Rosser, was captured by communists in the Korean war. She was held in a miserable concentration camp along with many captured soldiers. Her assurance in God's ultimate power gave her resilience. Many soldiers who had no faith to fall back on died; the combination of suffering with the constant "brain washing" by the communists was too much for them.

Viktor Frankl, the Viennese psychiatrist, suffered in Nazi concentration camps. He observed that only people who believed in a meaning for life, beyond having material things, were able to endure. They had faith and they held on.

That is what the prophet was telling his fellow Judeans. "Hold on. God is in charge of history. He will restore the right. He will redeem his people."

You may ask the class at this point, What do we depend on? What does our society depend on? Do you think the future will be better? Worse? Ask class members to state their major personal hopes. What would they like to see come true? What is the hope of the world? Of our country? For the prophet, the triumph of God is our hope.

IV. God's caring and human comfort

Sometimes people talk about being comfortable with themselves. The people of whom the prophet spoke were not comfortable with themselves. That is how they were able to recover and respond to God's comfort. In contrast, "All flesh is grass. . . . The grass withers, the flower fades but the word of our God will stand forever" (40:6, 8). Read with this Psalm 146:5-6. This happy psalm finds comfort in God's creative power and trustworthiness.

Ask someone to read aloud Psalm 138.

Our hope is in God. The power and the presence of God is the comfort and the joy of Christians.

Helping Class Members Act

God's comfort and care for his people are tied in with heralding the good tidings. Read aloud verses 9-11. What has happened in Zion, God's redemption of his people, itself becomes the herald of the good news. It is good news for all people.

It is good news for us. The experience of God's salvation becomes the experience of sharing it, sharing the source of our hope. So we tell it to others. We pass it on. The wonder of God's actions cannot be hidden from the world. Read, or let the class read together, the key verse, Isaiah 40:5.

Close with prayers in which as many as wish may say a few words, asking that God's wonder and glory be revealed to others through our lives.

Does your class sing hymns? Then close with "O Zion, Haste," a hymn based on this passage.

Planning for Next Sunday

Next Sunday's session reviews another of Isaiah's most famous passages, Isaiah 53. Ask class members to read it prayerfully and to discover what it tells about God's caring and purpose for us, his people.

The Pain and Anguish of God
CHESTER E. CUSTER

We sing of the glory of God, hear sermons on the love of God, read about the righteousness of God, and contemplate the power of God. But seldom do we speak of the pain and anguish of God. Yet the suffering and anguish of God are also very much a part of our Christian understanding of the Eternal. We immediately think of Jesus in Gethsemane and of the Cross, which is our foremost witness to the suffering love of God.

The anguish of God must surely be a counterpart of God's love. We understand something of this when we look into our own hearts, knowing that love is frequently called upon to suffer. We anguish *with*, anguish *because of*, anguish *over* both individuals and situations. The father's anguish over his prodigal son, and over his older son's critical attitude, was an expression of seeking and suffering love (Luke 15:11-32). It was one of Jesus' parables to illustrate God's own love and concern. The anguish of Mary, the mother of Jesus, at the crucifixion, was the other side of love.

During this writing assignment, word has been received of a tragic accident that has befallen a young family. The father and the mother, who was soon to give birth to their second child, were both killed in a head-on car collision. Their two-year-old son was critically injured. Anguish is the broken heart of love.

We often think of the transcendence of God, of God's omnipotence, of God as the "Holy Other." But this is only one aspect of our understanding of the Eternal. God is also immanent, near-at-hand, ever present. The naming of the Christ Child is a continual reminder of God's presence with us: "His name shall be called Emmanuel, which means 'God with us' " (Matthew 1:23). God enters into the pain and agonies of life and death with us. In fact, the term "agony" comes from the Greek *agonia*, meaning "to struggle." Rather than being far removed from us, on the sidelines as it were, detached from the uncertainties and troubles we encounter, God struggles and agonizes with us.

Sometimes the pain of God is understood most clearly in light of our own spiritual agony. Job cried in his distress, "O that I knew where I might find him" (Job 23:3). And Jesus prayed that the cup of suffering might pass from him in Gethsemane. The anguish of the dark night of the soul needs to be seen within the larger context of God's grace. It seems providential that in the arrangement of the Psalms, Psalm 22 begins with the words later uttered by Jesus in the garden, "My God, my God, why hast thou forsaken me," only to be immediately followed by, "The Lord is my shepherd, I shall not want" in Psalm 23. Furthermore, Jesus' anguished cry in Gethsemane was followed by, "Father, into thy hands I commit my spirit!" (Luke 23:46). From our own spiritual pain and agony, when God seems far away and "not there," we begin to understand the anguish of God who seeks *us* and cannot find us, who calls but receives no answer, who invites but gets no response. The depth of God's anguish can, to a limited degree, be understood from the human side of isolation.

The prophet Isaiah depicted the Messiah as one who bears our griefs and carries our sorrows (Isaiah 53:4). Among the various images of Christ is that of the Suffering Servant. Pascal wrote that "Jesus will be in agony until the end of the world." Two powerful symbols remind us of an eternal truth. The cross *with* the figure of Christ—the crucifix—reminds us of the agony of Christ suffering on our behalf. The cross *without* the figure of Christ—the empty cross—reminds us of the empty tomb and the risen Christ. These symbols, taken together—agony and resurrection—point us to a renewed and quickened life arising out of suffering love. We read in First Peter that "Christ also suffered for you, leaving you an example" (I Peter 2:21).

The anguish and pain of God are to be understood not only in terms of our own heartbreak and suffering, but also in light of our failure to live in terms of the divine will. God's purpose and will are often frustrated and thwarted by our self-centeredness and disobedience. Edwin Lewis writes that God makes it possible for us to be sinners, but it is not on that account that we were created. Rather, God created us to be saints, even though our sinfulness has to be endured by God as a condition of our sainthood (*The Creator and the Adversary* [Nashville: Abingdon-Cokesbury, 1948], p. 150). God agonizes over my sin and yours, over our blindness and unconcern. God agonizes when we pass by on the other side of human need. "God is forever clinging to our indifference in the hope that someday our needs, or at least our tragedies will waken us to respond to his advances" (Albert Edward Day, *The Captivating Presence*, quoted in Rueben P. Job and Norman

Shawchuck, *A Guide to Prayer for Ministers and Other Servants* [Nashville: The Upper Room, 1983], p. 33). We pray with John Baillie: "Holy God, to whose service I long ago dedicated my soul and life, I grieve and lament before thee that I am still so prone to sin and so little inclined to obedience. . . . O merciful heart of God, grant me yet again thy forgiveness" (*A Diary of Private Prayer* [New York: Charles Scribner's Sons, 1949], p. 107). Yes, we understand something of the pain and anguish of God when we pray, "Thy kingdom come, thy will be done," yet give little or no attention to making it so.

Does God also anguish over the church that is called to faithfulness and servanthood in the name of Christ? Anguish over our having settled down and settled in, having lost our passion for sharing the good news of the gospel? Anguish over our irrelevance as preachers, teachers, and daily disciples? Anguish over our limited outreach as a church in mission? Anguish over our timid response to the command "to do justice, and to love kindness, and to walk humbly with . . . God"? (Micah 6:8). God forbid that the message from on high in Hosea's day should be ours as well, when God said:

> "The more I called [Israel],
>   the more they went from me
> . . . .
> My people are bent on turning away from me
> . . . .
> How can I give you up, O Ephraim!
>   How can I hand you over, O Israel!
> . . . .
> My heart recoils within me."
>   (Hosea 11:2, 7-8)

God's suffering love extends to the entire family of nations. Who can deny both the human and divine anguish, when we contemplate the massive starvation in Africa, the war-torn people of the Middle East, the militarism that stalks the nations of the world, the walls and embargoes that divide people from one another. Just as God grieved over a disobedient Israel, so does the All-Righteous One grieve over our nations today. Christ still weeps over our Jerusalems!

Not long ago my wife and I visited Buchenwald in the German Democratic Republic—that ghastly place where at least 56,500 people were tortured and put to death. Coming to the barracks where Polish prisoners had been kept came also a group of people from Poland, bearing flowers. They placed the flowers on the memorial plaque, weeping. And this was fifty years after the Holocaust! Anguish and pain? We did not question the agony of the world and the anguish of God in the presence of what we saw there!

We cannot help but believe that God suffers with those who are discriminated against, with those who seek to work but who cannot find a job, with those who are forced off their farms because of misplaced government priorities, and with many others who live a precarious, day to day existence. Our Christian faith teaches us that we are co-laborers with God. If we are co-workers with God, then we are also co-agonizers with God, sharing together the burdens of those for whom Christ died. Dietrich Bonhoeffer, knowing he faced suffering, anguish, and eventual death at the hands of the Nazis, wrote, "It is not some religious act which makes a Christian what he is, but participation in the suffering of God in the life of the world" (William Kuhns, *In Pursuit of Dietrich Bonhoeffer* [Dayton, Oh.: Pflaum Press, 1967], p. 212).

Participating in the pain and anguish of God, taking upon ourselves the hurts of others, is really what it means to take up our crosses and follow Christ. Voluntarily bearing the burden of someone else, taking up a just cause, means that we not only take up and bear a cross, we share a cross. A young father said: "There have been far too many crosses that I have dropped along the way. I need someone to help me *share* the cross." God calls the church to share some crosses too heavy for one individual to bear alone.

The call to be attentive to the cries of other human beings and the world, and the call to be sensitive to the anguish of God, was a driving force in the life of Kagawa, the great social reformer of Japan. He wrote: "Oh, my soul! My soul! . . . Do you hear God's pain-pitched cry as He suffers because of the world's sore distress? God dwells among the lowliest of men. He sits on the dust heap among the prison convicts. With juvenile delinquents He stands at the door, begging bread. He throngs with the beggars at the place of alms. He is among the sick. He stands in line with the unemployed. Therefore, let him who would meet God visit the prison cell before going to the temple. Before he goes to church let him visit the hospital. Before he reads the Bible let him help the beggar standing at his door!" (Robert M. Bartlett, *They Dared to Live* [New York: Association Press, 1943), pp. 111-12).

Let us respond to the cries we hear and "not grieve the Holy Spirit of God" (Ephesians 4:30).

Jesus' Model of the Messiah: The Suffering Servant

ELDRICH C. CAMPBELL

There were two popular messianic expectations current in Jesus' day. The first centered around the coming of a prophet like Moses (Deuteronomy 18:15-19). That was why some people thought Jesus was "one of the prophets" (Luke 9:19; John 6:14).

The second expectation was that the Messiah would be a king like David (Daniel 7:13ff.). Such a Messiah would play the role of political liberator and world conqueror (Matthew 21:1-11).

The term Messiah, "the Anointed One," is found only twice in the Old Testament and is used by Jesus of himself only once (John 4:25-26). Jesus preferred the title "Son of man," so that he could define his understanding of messiahship in terms of service, sacrifice, and suffering.

The Pharisees wanted their Messiah to be a legalist, the Sadducees a *status quo* liturgist, the people a political leader, and the Essenes one who would bring the end of time. Jesus did not fit any of the above expectations. He was what God wanted him to be.

Jesus: The Suffering Servant

Jesus understood that his mission and work would be accomplished through obedience, suffering, and death; he was the fulfillment of the servant prophecies of Isaiah. In this way he freed messiahship from its this-worldly political associations and reinterpreted it in terms of the Old Testament concept of God's mighty act of salvation (Luke 19:10, 20-22).

The Servant Songs

There are four passages of scripture in Isaiah that are collectively called "the Servant Songs": 42:1-4; 49:1-6; 50:4-11; 52:13–53:12. As these passages are read we discover that the Servant's life is his real work; in fact, the climax of his vocation comes when he no longer proclaims a message, but remains silent (Isaiah 53:7; Matthew 27:14).

For our purposes the fourth Servant Song (52:13–53:12) is central:

1. *52:13-15.* God announces that in the end, "my servant shall prosper" and be "exalted and lifted up." At that time the world will find out who the Servant really is.
2. *53:1-3.* No one will believe the report about who this miserable person actually is. How could anyone with such an unpromising career be chosen by God?
3. *53:4-6.* The peoples of the world witness to a great truth revealed to them: The Servant has not suffered for his own sins, but for theirs. In his sufferings the Servant was actually making "an offering for sin" and thus "made intercession for the transgressors." Those who accept this sin-offering from themselves are reconciled to God and find pardon and peace.
4. *53:10-12.* God then announces the resurrection and glorification of the Servant. Since these events are a part of God's plan of salvation, they take place within "the will of the Lord."

The Servant's sufferings are effective only when they move persons to confession. It is not magic, controlling the will of the gods, but the avenue God provides for mankind to approach him (Hebrews 4:16).

Jesus' Suffering

It is the affirmation of the church that Jesus was God incarnate—a human being of flesh and blood in whom God fully dwelt (John 1:1, 14). He did not merely "appear" a man; he became one (Philippians 2:5-9). As a human being he experienced all the physical and mental pain and suffering common to all persons.

Jesus' sufferings were not just physical, nor were they confined to his three-hour experience on the cross. His family "did not believe him" (John 7:5); some said, "He is leading the people astray" (John 7:12); the religious leaders (John 11:4) rejected him (John 10:39; 18:3); the crowds who had flocked to him ended up crying "Crucify, crucify him!" (Luke 23:21).

His friends said, "He is beside himself [insane]" (Mark 3:21); his family (Mark 3:31) came to take him home, and others said, "He has a demon, and he is mad" (John 10:20). When the going got tough some of his disciples "drew back and no longer went about with him" (John 6:66). The hostility became so bad that he had to leave Israel "because the Jews sought to kill him" (John 7:1).

Following his betrayal and arrest (see Isaiah 53:8*a*), he was placed in a dungeon in Caiaphas' house overnight. He was tried for blasphemy (Mark 14:61f.) by the Jews and for treason by Pilate (Luke 23:1ff.), and denied by Peter.

At his trial he was humiliated and "scourged" by the soldiers (Matthew 27:26-31). This meant that whips were used to flog him. The whips would have been made of several strips of leather with lumps of lead or pieces of bone tied on, which would open large gashes on the back.

He was then taken to Golgotha and hung upon the cross, the ultimate humiliation and punishment, for "a hanged man is accursed by God" (Deuteronomy 21:22-23; Galatians 3:13).

Jesus' ministry was filled with suffering and anguish; yet he healed, forgave, cleansed, loved, reached out to the unlovable, and gave a thief the promise of paradise. The Servant's life was his real work.

Love Is a Verb

Jesus' exemplary life reveals that love is a way of living, a life-style, not a romantic emotion. Love is something we are supposed to be and do. Love *(agape)* is an activity of good intentions (will). His followers are to model their lives after his life, and to "love one another; even as [he has] loved [us]" (John 13:34). This kind of love wants the best for the other, even if that means sacrificing and/or suffering ourselves, so that the other might receive the best.

The Role of Suffering

From a practical point of view, I would never vote to suffer! But suffering, disappointment, and tribulation are part of the fabric of life. We are going to lose loved ones to death. Accidents and disease will affect us either directly or indirectly. The question is not, Will I suffer? but, How can Jesus use my suffering when it comes?

What is to be my witness in the midst of all this? Faith! Faith that witnesses: God is with me, "Emmanuel." Faith that witnesses: "In everything God works for good with those who love him" (Romans 8:28). Faith that witnesses: "We are more than conquerors through him who loved us" (Romans 8:37).

This is the example Jesus gave to the world through his suffering, and it is the witness we are called upon to give (John 20:21). It's not easy—but it's effective.

Jesus began his ministry by reading Isaiah 61:1-2 (Luke 4:18-19) and declaring, "Today this scripture has been fulfilled in your hearing." This text described Jesus' understanding of the role of every Spirit-filled Christian and reveals to us that we are to do the Christian thing even though the other may not respond.

The Suffering Savior

Background Scripture: Isaiah 52:13–53:12

The Main Question—William H. Willimon

Today's lesson contains two words which are not at all popular in today's world: "suffering" and "service." Of course, no one likes to suffer. Whether we are speaking of physical pain or emotional anguish, suffering is bad. But many of us moderns have come to think of suffering as completely unnecessary and always unfair.

"Life is suffering," said the Buddha. If you live very long you know that suffering is a part of life, particularly any life which accomplishes much. There is a certain amount of suffering involved in any attempt to do much in school. Achievement requires hard work, and hard work often entails suffering. A woman must suffer when she gives birth to a baby. Parents must sometimes suffer with wayward children. Can it be said that all of this suffering is unfair and senseless? Can we envision someone who achieves very much in life without any suffering, inconvenience, or pain?

If "suffering" is an unpopular word, "servant" is equally repugnant to our modern sensibilities. We live in an age of liberation, empowerment, and autonomy. The word "servant" carries connotations of impotency, dependency, and lowliness. Jesus' admonitions to the contrary, few of us see ourselves primarily in service to others. We want to stand on our own two feet and be responsible for ourselves, not humiliated by the demands of others.

The striking thing about today's scripture is that it puts these two unpopular words together—"suffering" and "servant"—and says that this is a primary image for God's love of Israel. In a world where everybody wants to be served, God serves us.

The question is, What does the image of the "Suffering Servant" tell us about the nature of God's love and our response to that love?

Selected Scripture

King James Version	Revised Standard Version
Isaiah 53:4-11	*Isaiah 53:4-11*
4 Surely he hath borne our griefs, and carried our sorrows: yet we did esteem him stricken, smitten of God, and afflicted.	4 Surely he has borne our griefs and carried our sorrows; yet we esteemed him stricken, smitten by God, and afflicted.
5 But he *was* wounded for our transgressions, *he was* bruised for our iniquities: the chastisement of our peace *was* upon him; and with his stripes we are healed.	5 But he was wounded for our transgressions, he was bruised for our iniquities; upon him was the chastisement that made us whole, and with his stripes we are healed.

6 All we like sheep have gone astray; we have turned every one to his own way; and the Lord hath laid on him the iniquity of us all.

7 He was oppressed, and he was afflicted, yet he opened not his mouth: he is brought as a lamb to the slaughter, and as a sheep before her shearers is dumb, so he openeth not his mouth.

8 He was taken from prison and from judgment: and who shall declare his generation? for he was cut off out of the land of the living: for the transgressions of my people was he stricken.

9 And he made his grave with the wicked, and with the rich in his death; because he had done no violence, neither *was any* deceit in his mouth.

10 Yet it pleased the Lord to bruise him; he hath put *him* to grief: when thou shalt make his soul an offering for sin, he shall see *his* seed, he shall prolong *his* days, and the pleasure of the Lord shall prosper in his hand.

11 He shall see of the travail of his soul, *and* shall be satisfied: by his knowledge shall my righteous servant justify many; for he shall bear their iniquities.

Key Verse: **He was wounded for our transgressions, he was bruised for our iniquities: the chastisement of our peace was upon him; and with his stripes we are healed. (Isaiah 53:5)**

6 All we like sheep have gone astray;
   we have turned every one to his own way;
  and the Lord has laid on him
   the iniquity of us all.

7 He was oppressed, and he was afflicted,
   yet he opened not his mouth;
  like a lamb that is led to the slaughter,
   and like a sheep that before its shearers is dumb,
   so he opened not his mouth.

8 By oppression and judgment he was taken away;
   and as for his generation, who considered
  that he was cut off out of the land of the living,
   stricken for the transgression of my people?

9 And they made his grave with the wicked
   and with a rich man in his death,
  although he had done no violence,
   and there was no deceit in his mouth.

10 Yet it was the will of the Lord to bruise him;
   he has put him to grief;
  when he makes himself an offering for sin,
   he shall see his offspring, he shall prolong his days;
  the will of the Lord shall prosper in his hand;

11 he shall see the fruit of the travail of his soul and be satisfied;
  by his knowledge shall the righteous one, my servant,
   make many to be accounted righteous;
  and he shall bear their iniquities.

Key Verse: **He was wounded for our transgressions, he was bruised for our iniquities; upon him was the chastisement that made us whole, and with his stripes we are healed. (Isaiah 53:5)**

As You Read the Scripture—Lynne Deming

Isaiah 53. This chapter contains most of what is called the fourth Servant Song in the book of Isaiah. The first three songs are found in Isaiah 42:1-4; 49:1-6; and 50:4-11. The fourth song begins at 52:13 and ends at 53:12.

Verse 4. The words "griefs" and "sorrows" used in the Revised Standard Version are difficult to translate. Another possibile translation is, "Surely he has borne our sicknesses and carried our pains." Even though we cannot be certain exactly what the words mean, we can understand in general what the verse is saying. The Servant is suffering on behalf of all the people, for the purpose of restoring them to a right relationship to God.

As in the previous three verses, the persons speaking are not identified. In verses 1-3, these unnamed speakers described the physical attributes of the Servant. In verses 4-6, they interrupt their description to speak about the burdens the Servant is carrying and how the Servant's suffering will affect the rest of the people.

Verse 5. Here the speakers say that by the chastisement of the Servant they have been made whole. Here the word "whole" indicates a general sense of peace or well-being.

Verse 6. In this verse the speakers indicate how they have been changed through what has happened to the Servant. The verse reads like many of the prayers of confession that are part of our worship services. Healing and peace have come to these persons, though they have gone astray, on account of the suffering of the Servant.

Verse 7. This verse states that the Servant suffered in silence. Unlike Job, who "cursed the day of his birth" (Job 3:1), the Servant "opened not his mouth." This verse continues the description of what happened to the Servant, which was interrupted by the confession of the speakers, in verses 4-6.

Verse 8. The first part of verse 8 is difficult to translate and to understand. The Revised Standard Version reads "By oppression and judgment he was taken away." Other possibilities include "He was carried off from prison and judgment," or "He was taken away from protection." Whatever the exact translation, we can be certain that the verse is speaking of some kind of violence and injustice that was inflicted on the Servant.

The second part of this verse tells us what finally happened to the Servant: He was "cut off out the land of the living." The phrase "stricken for the transgression of my people" is a parallel to the phrase that indicates the Servant's death. A better translation might be "stricken to death because of our sins."

Verse 9. This verse describes the Servant's burial. Shame is part of the Servant's death, just as it was part of his life. He is buried along with the wicked. The Revised Standard Version translates the second phrase in verse 9 "and with a rich man in his death." Other possible translations include "and [they made] his place of burial with evildoers." Like many other places in this chapter, the words used are uncommon and the grammar is extremely difficult to follow.

The last phrase in this verse repeats the idea that no matter what befell him, the Servant suffered in silence.

Verse 10. Here we are told that in spite of everything that has happened, God has all along been on the side of the Servant. "The will of the Lord" was that the Servant should suffer. The Revised Standard Version says God "has put him to grief"; another possible translation is "God has made him sick."

Verses 10-11. The second half of verse 10 and the first half of verse 11 list the reward that will come to the Servant after he is restored by God. He will live long enough to see his offspring, God's purposes will prosper in his hand, he will see the rewards of his work and be satisfied, and he will bring righteousness to many.

The Scripture and the Main Question—William H. Willimon

He Has Borne Our Griefs

When we Christians read Isaiah 52 and 53, we think of Christ. These beautiful words were first applied to Christ by the Gospel writers, and we continue to do so today. Christ is like the Suffering Servant about whom Isaiah speaks. Whether Isaiah had in mind the long-awaited Messiah who we see in Christ or not, it is fair for us to think of Jesus as the prime example of the one who saves through suffering.

For most of us, suffering seems to be one of the worst aspects of human life. Through the centuries, human beings have made great advances in the alleviation of human suffering. Suffering always seems harsh, cruel, and unfair. A missionary, recently returned from the scene of a tragic earthquake in Colombia, showed me a photograph of a little baby in a Colombian hospital. The child's head is bandaged. It had been pulled from the rubble of its destroyed house. Its parents and brothers and sisters were all killed in the earthquake. The little baby holds out its bandaged arms, crying for someone to reach out and help it. This picture is one of the most moving, devastating depictions of human misery and suffering I have ever seen. I plan to tack the photograph on my congregation's bulletin board as a reminder of how our brothers and sisters suffer around the world. A major part of the church's work is to assist in the alleviation of human suffering.

He Was Wounded for Our Transgressions

In *Man's Search for Meaning*, Viktor Frankl noted that "suffering ceases to be suffering in some way the moment it finds meaning." Christians claim that our suffering has meaning only as we enter into our pain as Christ entered into his. The story of Christ gives significance to our stories of suffering. Watching Christ hanging on the cross, blessing thieves, forgiving his tormentors, we note he suffered without regard for himself, in contrast to the way our suffering often drives us deeper into ourselves.

When the doctor tells us that we are suffering from heart disease, we ask, Why did this happen to me? without a thought for all the sufferers who have preceded and will follow us in this illness. And this is natural.

Natural too is the way we live our lives so as to maximize our pleasure and minimize our pain. We avoid commitments to others for fear that they will betray our trust and cause us anguish. We keep silent and play along with the crowd rather than risk public disapproval. We stand by and watch injustice, lest we become its next victim. Most of us are practical hedonists, and this is natural.

Utterly unnatural is the response of our God to suffering. Isaiah says that

God, and those who would be servants of God, enter suffering, bear the griefs and sorrows of others, and feel the same pain that sufferers feel. The story of Jesus himself is the story of one who engages the suffering of others not with philosophical argument or pious platitudes, but with active rebuke and firm compassion. Jesus enjoyed suffering no more than we. He wept and recoiled; he asked to be delivered from suffering three times. Feeling alienated, he cried out.

Lepers, the sick, the poor, and the oppressed crowded around him. He touched them, healed them, promised them a place in the kingdom. Ultimately, he did more than touch them in their pain—*He became one of them*. Here was a Messiah who saved through suffering.

> Surely he has borne our griefs
> and carried our sorrows,
> ....
> he was wounded for our transgressions,
> he was bruised for our iniquities
> (53:4-5)

That Made Us Whole

Early in its history, the church had to fight a heresy with a long name and dangerous implications: Patripassianism. This heresy stated that the great God almighty could not really suffer, as Jesus suffered on the cross. The Patripassians believed that it was an indignity to God to assert that God can feel the same pain as we humans can. The church fought the Patripassians and asserted that the Scriptures teach, as far back as the words from the prophet Isaiah, that this God hurts when his beloved creatures hurt. God is a Father who knows when even a sparrow falls to the ground, who feels pain and has pity. This God hurts.

Christianity, like Judaism before it, has no interesting philosophical answer for the mystery of human pain and anguish. All we have is a practical, concrete way of dealing with suffering. This faith neither denies pain, explains it away, nor accepts it with Stoic indifference. The cross is the sign of what God does with suffering. God answers the problem of human pain by *being there*.

"Where was God when my son was killed?" a mother asked. Her pastor answered, "Just where he was when his own Son was killed."

To say that "in Christ God was reconciling the world to himself" (II Corinthians 5:19) is to say that God has willingly invaded our history, taking upon himself, as a suffering servant, our dilemma. In the words of the old spiritual, "Nobody knows the troubles I've seen,/Nobody knows but Jesus,/Nobody knows the troubles I've seen,/Glory Hallelujah." You and I are called to "Love one another as I have loved you." That is a big order, when we have been loved by one who was willing to go to a cross to love us. It means that we are to be willing to be the same sort of suffering servant for one another that he has been for us:

—She changes a neighbor's bedclothes every day because there is no one else to do it.
—He retired from a prestigious executive job and now goes every day to the local elementary school to tutor disadvantaged students in math.
—They give up their vacation every year to go to their church's mission in Haiti, to do whatever needs doing for the poor there.

Who are these people? Isaiah predicted the arrival of a Suffering Servant who would heal the hurts of others by his own willingness to suffer their pain. I tell you, his prediction has come true. There are suffering servants all around us, healing the world the same way that God heals.

Helping Adults Become Involved—Leonard T. Wolcott

Preparing to Teach

This lesson helps us get in touch with God's entrance into human suffering. This is not just suffering, but suffering service! There are two kinds of suffering: the unavoidable and the volunteered.

The Bible passage for this lesson is about volunteered suffering. It tells how the Suffering Servant bears our burdens, the way he suffers, and the results of his suffering.

The Christian sees this Suffering Servant as Christ, suffering for and with man. God suffers for his people. Your aim for this lesson is to help class members recognize the love of God in suffering for individuals, and learn to express that love through taking on the sufferings of others.

    I.   Introduction.
   II.   What the Suffering Servant does for us (verses 4-5).
  III.   Why does the Servant suffer? (verses 5-6).
   IV.   How does the Servant suffer? (verses 7-9).
    V.   God's part in willing, approving, and rewarding what the Servant does (verses 10-11).
   VI.   Conclusion.

Read carefully "The Scripture and the Main Question" and "As You Read the Scripture." These form the heart of the lesson. The ideas, insights, and suggestions in these sections should be reflected continually in your lesson plan.

As you use the suggested outline, you may want to either quote or paraphrase ideas. You might like to jot in the margin of your outline the page number and paragraph being referred to. For example, you would write a reference to page 65, paragraph 3, as 65-3.

Find, or make and bring to class, a crude wooden cross with nails in it, to illustrate the difference between unavoidable suffering and a cross of self-giving for others. Prayerfully study the text. Prepare to write on chalkboard or newsprint the questions you find in the text below.

Introducing the Main Question

Basic and helpful ideas are presented in the section "The Main Question." These ideas are essential in helping to identify the purpose of the lesson.

Christians often say, "Christ died on the cross for me." Yes, that is what Isaiah 53 has always meant to the Christian: Christ's suffering in our behalf, to save us. We tend to forget, however, that Jesus repeatedly said to his disciples: "Take up your cross and follow me." "Go where I go." "Do what I do."

Dr. Willimon has illustrated the point with stories of persons who gave up vacation, a good job, or time to help others. You may cite other examples of self-sacrificing people to illustrate the servanthood. Make it clear that the cross of suffering for others is a choice of love. A mother, for example, may have a great opportunity in her profession to promote her own prestige, leadership, or salary. At that point her child may come down with a serious illness. The mother makes a choice to stay up all night with the child, to suffer with the child and risk losing that opportunity she has been working for.

Developing the Lesson

I. Introduction.

Focus on the words "suffering" and "service." Use Dr. Willimon's paragraphs in "The Main Question" about these two words, which he says "are not at all popular in today's world."

II. What the Suffering Servant does for us (verses 4-5).

"As You Read the Scripture" sums up the significance of verses 4 and 5, that "the Servant is suffering on behalf of all the people." (See "He Has Borne Our Grief" in "The Scripture and the Main Question.")

Ask the class: What are some other kinds of suffering? (Grief, pain, crippling disease, catastrophe, a natural disaster) Ask: Does God care when we suffer? How does he care? Read aloud verse 4. Dr. Willimon discusses this under "That Made Us Whole" in "The Scripture and the Main Question."

Ask: How do we bear suffering? In lecturing you may use Dr. Willimon's paragraphs under "He Was Wounded for Our Transgressions" in "The Scripture and the Main Question."

III. Why does the Servant suffer? (verses 5-6).

Did we cause the Servant's suffering? Verses 5 and 6 say that our transgressions, iniquities, and waywardness are responsible for causing him to suffer.

What is the result of the Servant's suffering? How are we made whole? Point out that suffering while being aware of God's love leads to a deeper relationship with God. The words "made whole" in verse 6 can be translated "leads to our peace." Our wholeness is related to God's wholeness.

IV. How does the Servant suffer? (verses 7-9).

We often suffer for our own wrongdoing. The righteous Servant, however, is suffers unjustly, as verses 8 and 9 point out.

We tend to meet suffering with complaint, with fighting back, with bitterness. The Servant, however, suffers in silence (verse 7). Read aloud here I Peter 2:23-25.

V. God's part in willing, approving, and rewarding what the Servant does (verses 10-11).

Where is God when there is suffering? See Dr. Willimon's story about the mother who asked this question. The answer is, "God is with us as he was with his Son, our Lord."

The suffering of Christ was God's will (verse 10). He invaded our history, taking on himself our dilemmas (verse 10).

God supported his Servant both against those who caused him to suffer and, yet, for them in his suffering.

God rewards his Servant. The reward is the effectiveness of his act in suffering for others.

VI. Conclusion.

Does God expect us to suffer? Here is the substance of this lesson: that what God was doing through his Servant, he will do through us if we, too, are willing to do his will as his servants. Christ "was reconciling the world to himself . . . and entrusting to us the message of reconciliation" and "God is making his appeal through us" (II Corinthians 5:19-20). This is Jesus' challenge to his disciples—that we take up our crosses and follow him (Matthew 16:24) at any cost.

Helping Class Members Act

Are Christians to participate in the task of the Suffering Servant? The church, the body of Christ, is to fulfill Christ's task. This is the essence of its ministry; its servanthood in the world.

Probably most class members give time and money to serve others through the church. Ask them to consider in what specific way God may be calling them to service. Discuss some project in which the class can jointly be a servant. Choose something that will involve more than donations to a cause, that will require time and effort from class members.

Planning for Next Sunday

Next Sunday's lesson is the last of three lessons on Isaiah. Ask class members to read Isaiah 65:8-25 in preparation. Ask them to draw up two lists, one about the ways in which we, collectively or individually, are unfaithful to God, and one about the ways God is faithful to us. Ask all to read Zephaniah 3:14-20 during the week.

LESSON 9   **OCTOBER 30**

A Better Day

Background Scripture: Isaiah 65:8-25

The Main Question—William H. Willimon

In a sense, we can read the story of Israel in two ways. From one point of view, it is the story of a wayward people who constantly fall away from the commandments of God through their idolatry, infidelity, and rebellion. The story of Israel is therefore the sad tale that is human history in general. In spite of all of God's efforts, we continually go our own way and forsake his love.

Of course, the story of Israel is also the tale of God's fidelity. In spite of all the ways in which Israel is unfaithful, God continues to be faithful to his promises. God refuses to wash his hands of the whole matter of Israel. Thus, the dark tale of our unfaithfulness is overshadowed by the bright gleam of God's faithfulness.

Fortunately for God's people, whether we speak of Israel or the church, the outcome of the story is not left up to us. We will not write the final chapter of this tale. The last chapter will be written by God. God is determined to have the last word here, and that last word will be a word of love.

Isaiah the prophet has chronicled the story of Israel's unfaithfulness. But in today's lesson, Isaiah announces the triumph of the love of God. God will not yet let go of his people. He will restore them and continue to enable them to be the key to the accomplishment of his divine purposes.

There is a word of hope here for us, as we read this message to Israel. That word of hope lies in the answer to this question: Will God continue to be faithful to his people in spite of our shortcomings and infidelity?

Selected Scripture

King James Version

Isaiah 65:17-25
17 For, behold, I create new heavens and a new earth: and the former shall not be remembered, nor come into mind.

18 But be ye glad and rejoice for ever *in that* which I create: for, behold, I create Jerusalem a rejoicing, and her people a joy.

19 And I will rejoice in Jerusalem, and joy in my people: and the voice of weeping shall be no more heard in her, nor the voice of crying.

20 There shall be no more thence an infant of days, nor an old man that hath not filled his days: for the child shall die a hundred years old; but the sinner *being* a hundred years old shall be accursed.

21 And they shall build houses, and inhabit *them*; and they shall plant vineyards, and eat the fruit of them.

Revised Standard Version

Isaiah 65:17-25
17 For behold, I create new heavens and a new earth;
and the former things shall not be remembered
or come into mind.

18 But be glad and rejoice for ever in that which I create;
for behold, I create Jerusalem a rejoicing,
and her people a joy.

19 I will rejoice in Jerusalem,
and be glad in my people;
no more shall be heard in it the sound of weeping
and the cry of distress.

20 No more shall there be in it an infant that lives but a few days,
or an old man who does not fill out his days,
for the child shall die a hundred years old,
and the sinner a hundred years old shall be accursed.

21 They shall build houses and inhabit them:
they shall plant vineyards and eat their fruit.

22 They shall not build, and another inhabit; they shall not plant, and another eat: for as the days of a tree *are* the days of my people, and mine elect shall long enjoy the work of their hands.

23 They shall not labor in vain, nor bring forth for trouble; for they *are* the seed of the blessed of the Lord, and their offspring with them.

24 And it shall come to pass, that before they call, I will answer; and while they are yet speaking, I will hear.

25 The wolf and the lamb shall feed together, and the lion shall eat straw like the bullock: and dust *shall be* the serpent's meat. They shall not hurt nor destroy in all my holy mountain, saith the Lord.

22 They shall not build and another inhabit;
  they shall not plant and another eat;
for like the days of a tree shall the days of my people be,
  and my chosen shall long enjoy the work of their hands.

23 They shall not labor in vain,
  or bear children for calamity;
for they shall be the offspring of the blessed of the Lord,
  and their children with them.

24 Before they call I will answer,
  while they are yet speaking I will hear.

25 The wolf and the lamb shall feed together,
  the lion shall eat straw like the ox;
  and dust shall be the serpent's food.
They shall not hurt or destroy
  in all my holy mountain,
    says the Lord.

Key Verse: **For, behold, I create new heavens and a new earth: and the former shall not be remembered, nor come into mind. (Isaiah 65:17)**

Key Verse: **For behold, I create new heavens and a new earth; and the former things shall not be remembered or come into mind. (Isaiah 65:17)**

As You Read the Scripture—Lynne Deming

Isaiah 65. In this chapter God answers the prophet's plea for restoration of the people to a right relationship with God. The chapter describes what the restored community will be like.

Verse 17. The phrase "new heavens and a new earth" reminds us of Revelation 21:1. Here in Isaiah, God is promising the transformation of heaven and earth in the restored community. The theme of God as Creator runs through the second half of the book of Isaiah. (See also Isaiah 41:20 and 66:22.) Because the earth will be restored, or renewed, people are to forget the "former things" that were part of the past. The prophet gives the same advice in Isaiah 43:18.

Verse 19. Here we read that God will rejoice along with Jerusalem at the news of her restoration. This same thought is expressed in Isaiah 62:5.

God continues the promise by saying thar weeping will no longer be heard in the streets of Jerusalem. This promise is a direct contrast to Jeremiah's pre-exilic prophecy that God "will make to cease from the cities of Judah and from the streets of Jersusalem the voice of mirth and the voice of gladness" (Jeremiah 7:34).

Verse 20. In the Old Testament view, living an abundant life meant living a long and full life. So the prophet pictures the restored community as a place where no one dies prematurely. Children will live to be a hundred years old in the new community God has created.

Verses 21-22. These verses contain a number of examples to show that peace and security will reign in this new situation. Work will not be in vain: Houses built will be lived in; planting vineyards will result in fruit to eat. A similar promise is given in Isaiah 62:8-9.

Verse 22 says, "Like the days of a tree shall the days of my people be." In other words, the poeple will live long lives. Jeremiah expresses a similar thought in 17:8.

Verse 23. This verse continues God's promise that no labor will be in vain in the restored community. Women will not labor in vain when they bear children. The Revised Standard Version says they will not "bear children for calamity"; another possible translation is "for sudden terror." Either way, the mesage is that mothers will not have to be concerned about the fate of their children. Why? Because their children will be among the blessed of the Lord, as will their children's children.

Verse 24. This verse tells us exactly why existence in the new community will be so peaceful and secure. Security will result directly from the relationship that will be established and maintained between God and persons. God will understand persons so well that before they even call, God will answer them. And God will continue to listen the entire time they are speaking. This prophet has alluded earlier to this special relationship between God and the chosen people in the restored community (see Isaiah 58:9).

Verse 25. This verse sounds similar to Isaiah 11:6-9, and it may have been taken directly from this earlier prophecy. This concluding statement takes the idea of peaceful existence one step further into the animal world. The restored community will be so peaceful and harmonious that wolves and sheep (two natural enemies) will live happily side by side.

The Scripture and the Main Question—William H. Willimon

There Is a Blessing in It

In a recent public opinion poll, Americans were asked, "Do you think things are getting better or worse?"

Nearly two-thirds of those polled said they believed that the future looks worse than the present.

This is a striking contrast to the public's response to the same question just two decades ago. "What does it mean," the pollster asked, "for the future of our country, when so many of us believe that the future is so bleak?"

Not long ago, in a discussion with students on the campus where I work, one student remarked, "What's the difference anyway? The Russians will probably drop the bomb before long and we'll all be reduced to ashes."

I shudder at the thought of a whole generation of students growing into adulthood firmly convinced that nuclear war is unavoidable and that there is little hope for a lasting or good future. What does such despair do to a people?

Of course, we do live in a world with massive problems and great challenges: overpopulation, nuclear proliferation, war, economic conflict, racial unrest—the list is endless. It should be noted that the world has always had severe problems. For instance, imagine all of the problems besetting the people in Isaiah's world. Israel had been forced into exile. A whole nation had been transported to serve as slaves for another nation. Even in the best of times, the people lived under the constant threat of famine. They were utterly defenseless against even the simplest illnesses. There were no hospitals, no Red Cross Centers, no antibiotics. The average person lived a life of unrelenting toil and misery and could expect to die at an early age. Perhaps we feel so depressed about our world because we know so little history. We fail to claim the real advances we have made in the betterment of human life.

Yet none of this denies that we really do have our problems. A world that lives under the constant threat of nuclear annihilation has its problems! The crucial thing may not be simply that we have our problems, but the manner in which we deal with those problems. Do we face the threats that come our way with despair or with hope?

I was a student during the 1960s. We were the student generation that participated in the civil rights and the anti-war movements. It was the dawning of the Age of Aquarius, when love, peace, and harmony would come to pass. Of course, we were naive and simplistic. As it turned out, the problems we sought to solve were a good deal more difficult and complex than we anticipated. But at least we were convinced that change was possible and that we had a responsibility to participate in that change.

As I work among students today, I find that this is a major difference between my student days and theirs. We really believed we could change the world for the better. They aren't so sure. Cynical about the political system, unsure what ought to be done about the complex issues which confront them, they withdraw into the personal confines of selfish ambitions and personal projects. After all, if the future of the world is bleak and hopeless, why not simply "eat, drink, and be merry, for tomorrow. . ."?

I Will Do for My Servant's Sake

It was just this sort of bleak, unpromising future which Isaiah spoke to in chapter 66. The words we study today were addressed to a people in exile, a people on the very edge of national and spiritual annihilation. You know from your study of previous lessons on the book of Isaiah that the prophet in no way denies the tragedy of what has happened to Israel. The pain is real, and there is plenty to weep about.

But there is also something to sing about. "Thus says the Lord," thunders forth the prophet. Will we hear the usual prophetic message of threat and judgment? No, we hear the prophetic message of hope and promise:

> For behold, I create new heavens
>   and a new earth;
> and the former things shall not be remembered
>   or come to mind.
> But be glad and rejoice for ever
>   in that which I create;
> for behold, I create Jerusalem a rejoicing,
>   and her people a joy.

(65:17-18)

The vision here is a bold one. Isaiah sees God doing cosmic work, turning the very heavens and earth upside down. Everything shall be made over and made new. Of course, this work is so grand that only the grand images of poetry can convey the promise. But, however it is done, Isaiah is clear about who shall do these wonderful works: the God of Israel. Even as God created the very first heavens and earth, God shall re-create. If God was able to create the first world, then why should God be unable to create a second and better one?

You cannot understand the message of Isaiah's hope without knowing the story of the creation. The story of Genesis precedes those words in Isaiah! Here is a hope based not upon the power of positive thinking or some wish that everything might work out all right. Here is a solid hope based upon what Israel already knows about the good and potent creativity of God.

Be Glad and Rejoice

> They shall not labor in vain,
>   or bear children for calamity;
> for they shall be the offspring of the blessed of the Lord,
>   and their children with them.
>
>   (65:23)

Imagine what these words meant to people who had seen their own children die of starvation and disease, or at the hands of cruel taskmasters in Babylonia. Their children shall live and prosper. Israel shall have a future!

There are some religions that teach that "whatever will be, will be." Everything that happens in the world, for good or ill, is exactly as God intends it. "It is just God's will," the Hindu would say.

The Judeo-Christian vision is quite different. We believe that there is good and there is evil. Everything that happens does not happen because God wants it that way. God is busy continually creating and re-creating. We are also called to be part of that process. Isaiah saw not only God creating a new world, but also saw God's people planning vineyards, having children, building houses (65:21-23)—in other words, God's people are also called to create a new world.

Helping Adults Become Involved—Leonard T. Wolcott

Preparing to Teach

This lesson is about God's promise of a new age of peace and well-being. The class is to face the question of its relevance to them, who live in a world of much suffering and evil.

The lesson can be organized as follows:

  I.   Introduction
  II. The human desire for a better world
  III. The problem of achieving a better world
  IV. The new heavens and new earth

Read carefully "The Scripture and the Main Question" and "As You Read the Scripture." These form the heart of the lesson. The ideas, insights, and suggestions in these sections should be reflected continually in your lesson plan.

As you use the suggested outline, you may want to either quote or paraphrase ideas. You might like to jot in the margin of your outline the page number and paragraph being referred to. For example, you could write a reference to page 65, paragraph 3, as 65-3.

Begin your preparation by reading Zephaniah 3:14-20. Notice its bright promise follows the judgment of people and nations who behave unjustly. Then read Isaiah 65:1-25 with the help of Dr. Deming's "As You Read the Scripture" and a commentary. These give background for your presentation.

A chart of parallels, listing the promises in Isaiah 65 over against apparent realities in the world will help the class face the issue of this chapter's message:

Joy	Weeping
Long, full life	Infant mortality
	Restricted old age
Happy homes	Refugees, homeless
Productive vineyard	Tenant farming
Peace, harmony	War, quarrels
God's answers	God's absence

See that the classroom has Bibles and chalk and chalkboard or markers and newsprint.

Introducing the Main Question

Basic and helpful ideas are presented in the section "The Main Question." These ideas are essential in helping to identify the purpose of the lesson.

"Will God continue to be faithful to his people in spite of our shortcomings and infidelity?" This question is asked by Dr. Willimon in "The Main Question." The scriptural word of hope, he says, lies in the answer to that question.

Developing the Lesson

I. Introduction

Isaiah 65 is a promise of a new age. The prophet speaks for God, in knowledge of the fact that many have not listened to God and have been rebelling against God's righteousness.

As in previous passages studied, the emphasis is on God the Creator. His people want restoration and more: a better life in the homeland. The problem is that some have been faithless. In the Zephaniah passage you can see that God makes clear his rejection of peoples who have rejected his purposes. Read aloud Zephaniah 3:6-8. In Isaiah 65 a glorious new age is promised, but some people will be left out. Read aloud Isaiah 65:13-14.

II. The human desire for a better world

Throughout history, people have dreamed of a better world. Many have told stories of a fantasized, perfect, happy age of the past. Others have looked forward to a better future. Writers have given us many blueprints for utopia.

Modern nations write ideals into their constitutions. The United Nations charter and its Declaration of Human Rights set up ideals for global harmony.

III. The problem of acheiving a better world

How can God help a secular, that is, God-ignoring people? Isaiah calls them a "rebellious people" (verses 1-15). Faithless, they come under judgment and are cursed. To be cursed means to be "cut off." They have alienated themselves from God's people by their own choice. They will not share in the good things of the new age. God wills to help them; he says, "Here am I! Here am I!" but they do not listen (verse 1). Read aloud verse 12.

Class members may make and read lists of signs of individual and collective unfaithfulness to God, and of God's faithfulness to us.

A better world is a possibility for the God-listening people. They are faithful because they listen. They are God's servants, described in contrast to the faithless in verses 8-16. They are like a cluster of good grapes holding promise of rich wine. These people hold promise of a better world. They are the seed of God's planned new age.

IV. The new heavens and new earth

The new heavens and the new earth are described in verses 17-25. This will be a place of well-being shared by a God-centered people. You may ask the class to repeat with you the key verse, 65:17: "For behold, I create new heavens and a new earth." In the new kingdom, "the former things shall not be remembered or come into mind." Ask someone to read aloud II Corinthians 5:17 and Philippians 3:13-14, Paul's restatements of the message of Isaiah 65:17 in Christian terms.

The essence of this new life will be a close relationship with God. Read Isaiah 64:24 aloud.

Helping Class Members Act

What does the new age mean to us? Discussion may help the class come to grips with the question, Is a new age really possible?

If you have made the chart suggested in "Preparing to Teach," show it at this point. The ideal in Isaiah 65 here contrasts with the actualities of our world.

Does this mean that "the new heavens and the new earth" is a figure for life after death? Will it be a future that God will bring through some cataclysmic chance? Refer to Revelation 21:1. Will the new age be something that the faithful people of God can build on earth?

It is clear in Isaiah 65 that the "new heavens and the new earth" stand for a relationship with God in which he is ever ready to hear us and shares our joy in his presence. This we can have now, if we will listen to God.

Ask for thoughtful, silent meditation, as you repeat, with pauses between, the following five questions:

1. Are we listening to God?
2. Do we have faith that God is listening to us?
3. Are we eager and ready to live in a new age—a God-centered life?
4. How do we live the new age? Are we sharing its benefits?
5. Have we come during this study of Isaiah to have a greater sense of being God's people, of answering his call?

Planning for Next Sunday

Next Sunday begins a unit in which, through the prophet Jeremiah, we continue to look at the biblical hope for a new day. We begin with Jeremiah's call. Ask class members to read Jeremiah 1 and John 1:43-51. Ask them to think about how God calls people today. Suggest that some class members look up in a Bible concordance the meaning and different uses of the phrases "the Word of the Lord" and "I am with you."

UNIT III: JEREMIAH—LOOKING FOR A NEW DAY
Horace R. Weaver

FOUR LESSONS   NOVEMBER 6–27

Unit III, "Jeremiah—Looking for a New Day," is based on the work of the prophet Jeremiah, who forsaw the consequences of Judah's denial of the prophetic demands of God: to do justice, love mercy, and walk humbly with God (as Micah summarized the messages of Amos, Hosea, and Isaiah). Refusal to be obedient to God's moral covenant had created hatred, jealousy, dishonesty, disloyalty, and ill will toward fellow Jews, which attitudes soon were applied to all foreigners and their nations. The causes of war were multiple; the universal principles of morality that make for peace were refused.

The lessons deal with the following: "Responding to God's Call," November 6, examines the twofold call from God; "Hiding Behind Religion," November 13, describes and evaluates the prophet's temple sermon in which he declares that war is inevitable, peace impossible; "Suffering for Truth," November 20, explores the prophet's willingness to assume personal suffering in the hope of changing the minds of his fellowmen; "A New Covenant," November 27, demonstrates the prophet's confidence and hope for a new covenant of the heart (of intentions, attitudes, and personal moral and religious commitments), which God yearns for human beings to adopt.

Responding to God's Call

Background Scripture: Jeremiah 1

The Main Question—William H. Willimon

In a recent lesson we studied Isaiah's dramatic call to become a prophet of God. Today's lesson concerns itself with another prophetic call, this time not to a person engaged in temple worship but an inexperienced youth. When the young Jeremiah heard the call of God, he felt he did not have the proper personal requisites to fulfill the commission of God.

How does God call people today? For many in your adult class, the notion of being called by God may seem far away and remote, an impossibility in today's world. Perhaps the notion of God calling each of us by name, giving us specific tasks to do, seems so impossible because we are not listening!

Jeremiah resisted the call of God. He had a number of reasons why God could not possibly be interested in someone like him. You and I also have ways that we resist the call of God. Perhaps the principal way is to reassure ourselves that God doesn't call people this way anymore. God talked to people long ago and asked them to do things, but that is not the case today.

How does God call people? That is the question lying behind our attempt to hear the Word of God in the scripture that begins our study of the prophet Jeremiah.

Selected Scripture

King James Version	Revised Standard Version
Jeremiah 1:4-10, 17-19	*Jeremiah 1:4-10, 17-19*
4 Then the word of the Lord came unto me, saying,	4 Now the word of the Lord came to me saying,
5 Before I formed thee in the belly I knew thee; and before thou camest forth out of the womb I sanctified thee, *and* I ordained thee a prophet unto the nations.	5 "Before I formed you in the womb I knew you, and before you were born I consecrated you; I appointed you a prophet to the nations."
6 Then said I, Ah, Lord God! behold, I cannot speak: for I *am* a child.	6 Then I said, "Ah, Lord God! Behold, I do not know how to speak, for I am only a youth." 7 But the Lord said to me,
7 But the Lord said unto me, Say not, I *am* a child: for thou shalt go to all that I shall send thee, and whatsoever I command thee thou shalt speak.	"Do not say, 'I am only a youth'; for to all to whom I send you you shall go, and whatever I command you you shall speak.

8 Be not afraid of their faces: for I *am* with thee to deliver thee, saith the Lord.

9 Then the Lord put forth his hand, and touched my mouth. And the Lord said unto me, Behold, I have put my words in thy mouth.

10 See, I have this day set thee over the nations and over the kingdoms, to root out, and to pull down, and to destroy, and to throw down, to build, and to plant.

....

17 Thou therefore gird up thy loins, and arise, and speak unto them all that I command thee: be not dismayed at their faces, lest I confound thee before them.

18 For, behold, I have made thee this day a defensed city, and an iron pillar, and brazen walls against the whole land, against the kings of Judah, against the princes thereof, against the priests thereof, and against the people of the land.

19 And they shall fight against thee; but they shall not prevail against thee; for I *am* with thee, saith the Lord, to deliver thee.

Key Verse: **The word of the Lord came unto me, saying, Before I formed thee in the bmlly I knew thee; and before thou camest forth out of the womb I sanctified thee, and I ordained thee a prophet unto the nations. (Jeremiah 1:4-5)**

8 Be not afraid of them,
for I am with you to deliver you,
says the Lord."

9 Then the Lord put forth his hand and touched my mouth; and the Lord said to me,
"Behold, I have put my words in your mouth.

10 See, I have set you this day over nations and over kingdoms,
to pluck up and to break down,
to destroy and to overthrow,
to build and to plant."

....

17 "But you, gird up your loins; arise, and say to them everything that I command you. Do not be dismayed by them, lest I dismay you before them.

18 And I, behold, I make you this day a fortified city, an iron pillar, and bronze walls, against the whole land, against the kings of Judah, its princes, its priests, and the people of the land. 19 They will fight against you; but they shall not prevail against you, for I am with you, says the Lord, to deliver you."

Key Verse: **The word of the Lord came to me saying, "Before I formed you in the womb I knew you, and before you were born I consecrated you; I appointed you a prophet to the nations." (Jeremiah 1:4-5)**

As You Read the Scripture—Lynne Deming

Jeremiah 1. Chapter one of the book of Jeremiah includes three elements: an introduction telling us about Jeremiah's circumstances (verses 1-3), Jeremiah's call to prophesy (verses 4-10), and visions related to his call (verses 11-19).

Verse 4. Here Jeremiah is speaking in the first person. The phrase "word of the Lord" is common in Jeremiah, since the prophet wants his audience to understand that he speaks on God's behalf.

Verse 5. Jeremiah is repeating God's words here, to the effect that God and Jeremiah have had a close relationship ever since (and even before) Jeremiah was born. The word "know" in Hebrew means more than just casual acquaintance.

Jeremiah's dialogue with God, beginning in verse 5, is similar to the calls of other prophets (Isaiah and Ezekiel, for example). However, we notice that God does not appear to Jeremiah. God only speaks to this prophet.

The last phrase in this verse ("I appointed you a prophet to the nations") gives us a clue about the nature of Jeremiah's prophecy. The oracles that make up the rest of the book are addressed to the nations of Judah, Egypt, Assyria, and Babylonia.

Verse 6. This verse tells us of Jeremiah's initial hesitation to answer God's call. Moses objected that he was slow of tongue. Isaiah said he was a man of unclean lips. Jeremiah objects here that he is only a youth, too young to speak for God.

Verses 7-8. God now answers Jeremiah's objection. God's answer is essentially a promise of support in whatever circumstances Jeremiah may find himself. God's support will be given mainly in the form of words to speak. This promise is probably the reason why the prophet emphasizes over and over again that he is speaking "the word of the Lord." In Jeremiah 23:16-22, Jeremiah compares his own prophecies to those of the false prophets. The main difference is that Jeremiah has received his words directly from God, and they have not.

Verse 9. This verse continues the image of God's Word coming through the mouth of the prophet. God actually touches Jeremiah's mouth, symbolizing the transference of God's words into the mouth of the prophet. This image reminds us of Isaiah's call, where one of the seraphim touches Isaiah's lips with a burning coal to cleanse them.

Verse 10. This verse concludes the call of Jeremiah, since it summarizes the message God wants Jeremiah to deliver to the people on God's behalf. The phrase "nations and kingdoms" indicates that Jeremiah was appointed as a "prophet to the nations" (verse 5). The message is active and not passive—it involves destruction, oppression, and restoration.

Verse 17. This verse and the two that follow it relate to what was discussed in verses 4-10. In between (verses 11-16) are two visions of Jeremiah: a rod of almond (verses 11-12) and a boiling pot (verses 13-16).

In verse 17 God is speaking to Jeremiah. God continues to emphasize that Jeremiah's task is to proclaim "the word of the Lord." Even though Jeremiah is only a youth (verse 6), he is to behave like a man. As in verse 8, God tells Jeremiah not to be afraid of the people who are to receive the message. Here God adds an additional warning. If Jeremiah cannot overcome his fear, God will make him even more afraid.

Verses 18-19. These two verses conclude the call of Jeremiah by elaborating on what his ministry will be like. The people of the land will not accept the message calmly. They will fight back. But God promises to fortify the prophet against their attacks. With God's support, Jeremiah will be strong enough to prevail against those unwilling to receive God's message. God's words here in this first chapter will serve Jeremiah well later in his ministry.

The Scripture and the Main Question—William H. Willimon

I Knew You

I must confess that Jeremiah 1 is one of my favorite passages of scripture. I love this image: "Before I formed you in the womb I knew you, and before you were born I consecrated you" (1:5). I am fascinated by the notion that God knows us and calls us, even before we are born.

This idea may seem a bit far-fetched. We like to think of ourselves as choosers—shapers of our own destinies, captains of our own fates, masters of our own souls. Much of modern life is consumed with making proper choices, with exercising our freedoms correctly. Presumably, a generation or two ago, people did not have so many choices. Young men grew up and went to work in the family business or followed the same trade as their fathers. If one's father was a farmer, more than likely you would be a farmer. For young women, there were even fewer choices.

Today, things are different. What should I do with my life? is a major question confronting our youth. There are so many possible paths and so many opportunities. I am told that over half of the jobs which will be in existence twenty years from now haven't even been created yet. Therefore, one must keep open to new opportunities, ready to make new choices for the future.

Yet today's text from Jeremiah suggests that, along with our choices for ourselves, God is also making choices. Along with our plans for our future, God is also making plans. I daresay few of us really consider this when we are living our lives. What does God want me to do with my life? is a question which many of us have put on the shelf. It has taken a back seat to questions like, Where can I make the most money for myself? What will make me most happy?

Should we wonder that the idea of the call of God seems far away and remote from us? The call of God may seem faint because we are not taking the time to listen! We are so busy listening to ourselves that we cannot hear the Holy One speak to us.

I Am with You

Even if we have difficulty understanding the reality of the call of God coming to someone with the directness that it came to Jeremiah, we should have little problem with Jeremiah's avoidance of that call. Now, the story in Jeremiah 1 becomes real for us. Jeremiah responds to God's word with, "Ah, Lord God! Behold, I do not know how to speak, for I am only a youth" (1:6).

In fairness to young Jeremiah, we must say that his is a most understandable response. He may be young, but he is wise enough to know that God's work is often difficult and demanding. He may know enough about prophets to know that they are often required to speak many unpopular words to people. He is unskilled and unlettered. Surely God's good work deserves someone who is much better qualified.

But no, he is the one God has chosen from the very first, even before he was born, for this task. Jeremiah's response reminds one of Moses', when he was called to be a liberator of his people. You will remember that Moses also had his reservations—he also didn't know how to speak in public. But God wanted Moses.

One thing which both Jeremiah and Moses overlooked: God would give them what they needed to respond to his call. To Jeremiah God says, "Behold, I have put my words in your mouth" (1:9). Jeremiah will not be out there on his own, left to his own skills and devices. God will be with him, giving him the authority he needs to do the work.

I am sure that there are people in your class who can relate to this story of Jeremiah's call. There are many in the church who can testify to the reality that, when God calls us, God empowers us to do the job.

God's call is always a mystery. One of the greatest mysteries is why God would choose this person and not some other. We don't know why. All we can do is listen for the call and be bold enough to say, as Jeremiah must have said, "I don't know why you asked me, but here I am, use me as you will."

I Am with You to Deliver You

Bessie Parker was my wife's step-grandmother, and my friend. She married my wife's grandfather many years ago, after his first wife died. The Reverend Mr. Parker served churches throughout low-country South Carolina and met Bessie in one of those churches. A few years after they were married, he contracted cancer. Gradually, it grew worse. On some Sundays, Mr. Parker was too ill to get out of bed and make the rounds of the little churches to preach to them. Bessie couldn't stand the thought that these little churches would be without a sermon on those days, so on more than one Sunday, she would get her Bible and drive to the churches, apologizing to them about being forced to hear a "substitute preacher."

The Sundays when Mr. Parker was disabled became more frequent. Eventually, he died. When he died, the bishop told the churches that he would be appointing them a new minister, but they all said with one voice, "We want Bessie to be our pastor. She *is* our pastor."

The bishop replied that women had not been used in Methodist pulpits except in the most unusual circumstances, that Bessie had not studied theology, and that it was all very unusual.

The little churches would not be deterred. They were thoroughly convinced that Bessie was the pastor they needed and deserved. They had felt the power of God coming through to them in her preaching and pastoral care.

Bessie herself objected. By now she was middle-aged. The thought of going back to school, of launching out in such a risky, new way, troubled her. But she felt that God was calling her. The bishop consented to let her serve "on a trial basis." She went back to school at Duke University and completed the Ministerial Course of Study. Eventually, she was ordained a deacon and spent thirty years serving United Methodist churches in South Carolina, retiring from a church of over a thousand members.

Bessie Parker's life reminds us that, like Jeremiah, God continues to call us by name, each in our very own way, to do his work in the world.

We need to listen. We need to be ready to lay our doubts and misgivings aside and "Go and proclaim" (Jeremiah 2:2) in word and deed the great, good deeds of God.

Helping Adults Become Involved—Leonard T. Wolcott

Preparing to Teach

The aim of this lesson is to help class members see how God chooses, uses, strengthens, and encourages persons as instruments of his word. The priority of God's action and word are basic to the lesson. Your presentation can be developed under these headings:

FIRST QUARTER

  I. Introduction.
 II. God chooses us.
III. God's presence and power are with us.
 IV. God speaks through us.
  V. Conclusion.

Read carefully "The Scripture and the Main Question" and "As You Read the Scripture." These form the heart of the lesson. The ideas, insights, and suggestions in these sections should be reflected continually in your lesson plan.

As you use the suggested outline, you may want to either quote or paraphrase ideas. You might like to jot in the margin of your outline the page number and paragraph being referred to. For example, you could write a reference to page 65, paragraph 3, as 65-3.

Have Bibles in the classroom, and chalk and chalkboard or markers and newsprint.

Introducing the Main Question

Basic and helpful ideas are presented in the section "The Main Question." These ideas are essential in helping to identify the purpose of the lesson.

Every member of the class must face these questions: Has God called me? Is God calling me? Has God chosen me for a special task? Have I made excuses not to do it? Do I feel inadequate to do what I feel God would have me do? Can I trust God to give me the strength to do it? Do I have courage to do what may go against the approval of even my friends, if God leads me to do it? These questions you will want to bring up through today's presentation. Help class members realize that their lives can be important in God's service.

Developing the Lesson

I. Introduction.

Give background information for the story of Jeremiah's call. Descendant of an ancient Hebrew family, he must have been an unusually thoughtful boy. Most people see only the immediacy and expediency of current events. Jeremiah's thoughts penetrated beyond and brought him to conclusions quite different from those of his contemporaries. Especially strong in his mind was the reality of God and his Word. The Word of the Lord seems to have come to him when he was a young man. Although the conviction of God's call was strong, he felt unequal to the task of being "a prophet to the nations" (verse 5). He felt unprepared, too young.

II. God chooses us.

God is the chooser. Call attention to John 1:43-51. Jesus chose Nathaniel before he had seen Jesus. God had known Jeremiah, that is, had chosen him, consecrated him, appointed him from before his birth. Refer here to Dr. Willimon's remarks in "The Scripture and the Main Question" about our making choices as to what we will do with our lives. Making great amounts of money or making a name for oneself has no major place in a Christian's decision as to what to do with his or her life. Talk with the class about persons you or they know who feel impelled to do what they do. We have no choice when God chooses us.

We hesitate (verse 6). Like Moses, like Jeremiah, we make excuses. We may think we lack the ability for what we know God wants us to do. Ask class members, Have you ever made excuses when a call on your time has come? Most of us have.

God commands (verse 7); "You shall go. . . .You shall speak" is God's reply to Jeremiah's attempt to beg off. It is a folly to evade God's commission. The book of Jonah contains the famous story of one man who tried to run away. When God calls, we have no choice. That is the way one translation puts Paul (II Corinthians 5:14): "The love of Christ leaves us no choice. . . . His purpose in dying for all was that men . . . should cease to live for themselves, and should live for him." God "sent" Jeremiah (verse 7). God "sent" Isaiah (Isaiah 6:8). Jesus "sent" the seventy disciples. God sends us into our world to do his will.

III. God's presence and power are with us.

God is present with us as we do his will. "I am with you," God said to Jeremiah. (Read Exodus 33:15-18 to the class.) This promise appears frequently in the Bible.

Ask the class to discuss the ways in which this promise is used in the Bible. (Look up the name "Emmanuel" in a concordance.)

After a bloody riot in Calcutta, India, no one ventured out into the streets except police constables, who stayed together in groups. Certainly no one dared go into the back alleys. A certain missionary, however, knowing some village Christians were stranded in those back alleys, went to see them. Ordinarily, this would have been foolhardy. He knew, however, that he was needed. He felt calm as he went, sensing that God was with him.

God empowers us, when we do his will, to do what we otherwise might not be able to do. God fortified Jeremiah (verses 9, 17). Tell the class Dr. Willimon's story about Bessie Parker, who was enabled to do what she could not have done on her own. Some class members may have had a similar experience of being given extra strength to meet some need or call. Recall what the Lord said to Paul: "My power is made perfect in weakness" (II Corinthians 12:9).

God will give us courage, as it was given to Jeremiah (verse 17). Of course we must make a determined effort, which is the meaning of "gird up your loins."

IV. God speaks through us.

This is a mystery to many whom God can use. Even a young Jeremiah! Even us! We are surprised at what God can do with people. The people of Nazareth were surprised when Jesus first spoke in their synagogue. Read Luke 4:22. Of him it was said "the very stone which the builders rejected has become the head of the corner" (I Peter 2:7).

The Inn of the Sixth Happiness is a movie about the true story of an uneducated London servant girl. She was sure God had called her to be a missionary. She was rejected by all the mission boards. She had no money. Yet, she managed to cross Siberia to become an effective representative of Christ in northern China.

How God uses us is another mystery. We do the unexpected through his direction. Against great odds (described in verses 17-19), God made Jeremiah into a prophet to the nations. Verse 10 describes the message God entrusted to him, a message of judgment and hope.

V. Conclusion.

The Word of the Lord is a powerful concept. It means that God, the all-powerful Creator, says to the people what he does and does what he says. A class member who looked up the phrases "the Word of the Lord" and "I am with you" can report on their meanings and uses in various contexts. This Word of the Lord was put into Jeremiah's mouth. To speak for God is not always easy. Verses 17-19 describe the nature of Jeremiah's prophetic task.

Helping Class Members Act

Use questions from the paragraphs under "Introducing the Main Question," above. You may lead a discussion on how Christians respond to God's call. One pastor of my acquaintance has said: "We have a call from God. But instead of obeying God's call, we have been leaving to secular agencies the personal and spiritual problems of the people. Every Christian can share the gospel with others." You may discuss with the class God's call to witness. Close with prayer, asking God to help us hear and respond to his call.

Planning for Next Sunday

In next Sunday's lesson Jeremiah exhorts the people to amend their ways. Ask class members to read Jeremiah 7. Ask them to bring to class clippings of current news items that show the life of the nation.

LESSON 11   NOVEMBER 13

Hiding Behind Religion

Background Scripture: Jeremiah 7

The Main Question—William H. Willimon

In a few weeks those of us in the United States will be celebrating Thanksgiving. This is a traditional national holiday, when we pause to give thanks. My children are currently preparing for a Thanksgiving pageant at their school. For the past few weeks they have been making cardboard turkeys, Pilgrim hats, and Indian costumes. Their pageant will recall the memories of the Pilgrim Fathers and Mothers who gave thanks that God has preserved their lives in a hostile new world. Thanksgiving is also a time to remember the blessings of food, freedom, and life.

How often the prophets of Israel called Israel to remember the past. Today we shall read Jeremiah's judgments against Israel. In the prophet's words, Israel has forgotten its past. It has forgotten that its national blessings are gifts from God.

We celebrate a day of thanksgiving in remembrance of the Pilgrims, who believed it was fitting to thank God for preserving them in the wilderness. This year, when we celebrate Thanksgiving, will we be remembering the same things? Will the average American have any real awareness that we are where we are today because of the grace and providence of God? Or do we find ourselves in much the same situation as Israel before us—have we forgotten our history and our purpose?

Selected Scripture

King James Version

Jeremiah 7:1-15

1 The word that came to Jer'e-mi'ah from the Lord, saying,

2 Stand in the gate of the Lord's house, and proclaim there this word, and say, Hear the word of the Lord, all *ye* of Ju'dah, that enter in at these gates to worship the Lord.

3 Thus saith the Lord of hosts, the God of Israel, Amend your ways and your doings, and I will cause you to dwell in this place.

4 Trust ye not in lying words, saying, The temple of the Lord, The temple of the Lord, The temple of the Lord, *are* these.

5 For if ye throughly amend your ways and your doings; if ye throughly execute judgment between a man and his neighbour;

6 *If* ye oppress not the stranger, the fatherless, and the widow, and shed not innocent blood in this place, neither walk after other gods to your hurt:

7 Then will I cause you to dwell in this place, in the land that I gave to your fathers, for ever and ever.

8 Behold, ye trust in lying words, that cannot profit.

9 Will ye steal, murder, and commit adultery, and swear falsely, and burn incense unto Ba'al, and walk after other gods whom ye know not;

10 And come and stand before me in this house, which is called by my name, and say, We are delivered to do all these abominations?

Revised Standard Version

Jeremiah 7:1-15

1 The word that came to Jeremiah from the Lord: 2 "Stand in the gate of the Lord's house, and proclaim there this word, and say, Hear the word of the Lord, all you men of Judah who enter these gates to worship the Lord. 3 Thus says the Lord of hosts, the God of Israel, Amend your ways and your doings, and I will let you dwell in this place. 4 Do not trust in these deceptive words: 'This is the temple of the Lord, the temple of the Lord, the temple of the Lord.'

5 "For if you truly amend your ways and your doings, if you truly execute justice one with another, 6 if you do not oppress the alien, the fatherless or the widow, or shed innocent blood in this place, and if you do not go after other gods to your own hurt, 7 then I will let you dwell in this place, in the land that I gave of old to your fathers for ever.

8 "Behold, you trust in deceptive words to no avail. 9 Will you steal, murder, commit adultery, swear falsely, burn incense to Ba'al, and go after other gods that you have not known, 10 and then come and stand before me in this house, which is called by my name, and say, 'We are delivered!'—only to go on doing all these abominations? 11 Has this house, which is called by my name,

11 Is this house, which is called by my name, become a den of robbers in your eyes? Behold, even I have seen *it*, saith the Lord.

12 But go ye not unto my place which *was* in Shi'loh, where I set my name at the first, and see what I did to it for the wickedness of my people Israel.

13 And now, because ye have done all these works, saith the Lord, and I spake unto you, rising up early and speaking, but ye heard not; and I called you, but ye answered not;

14 Therefore will I do unto *this* house, which is called by my name, wherein ye trust, and unto the place which I gave to you and to your fathers, as I have done to Shi'loh.

15 And I will cast you out of my sight, as I have cast out all your brethren, *even* the whole seed of E'phra-im.

become a den of robbers in your eyes? Behold, I myself have seen it, says the Lord. 12 Go now to my place that was in Shiloh, where I made my name dwell at first, and see what I did to it for the wickedness of my people Israel. 13 And now, because you have done all these things, says the Lord, and when I spoke to persistently you did not listen, and when I called you, you did not answer, 14 therefore I will do to the house which is called by my name, and in which you trust, and to the place which I gave to you and to your fathers, as I did to Shiloh. 15 And I will cast you out of my sight, as I cast out all your kinsmen, all the offspring of E'phraim."

Key Verse: **This is a nation that obeyeth not the voice of the Lord their God, nor receiveth correction: truth is perished and is cut off from their mouth. (Jeremiah 7:28)**

Key Verse: **This is the nation that did not obey the voice of the Lord their God, and did not accept discipline; truth has perished; it is cut off from their lips. (Jeremiah 7:28)**

As You Read the Scripture—Lynne Deming

Jeremiah 7. The first fifteen verses of chapter 7 contain Jeremiah's well-known temple sermon. This sermon was delivered by the prophet in the year 609 B.C., just after Johoiakim took the throne in Judah. We know from the writings of Baruch that Jeremiah was told by God to preach in the temple "in the beginning of the reign of Jehoiakim the son of Josiah (see Jeremiah 26:1-2). In fact, Jeremiah 26 repeats much of what is found in 7:1-15.

Verse 1. The chapter opens with what is a common phrase in the book of Jeremiah: "the word that came to Jeremiah from the Lord." The fact that God continually supports Jeremiah in his ministry by giving him the words to say is an important theological statement made from the beginning to the end of the book.

Verse 2. The first half of this verse continues the introduction of the sermon that begins in verse 1. Then in the middle of this verse (beginning with "Hear the word of the Lord") the actual sermon begins.

Verse 3. Again we see the assurance from Jeremiah that his words are spoken on behalf of God. God promises that if the people will change their ways, God will let them dwell "in this place." We can tell from reading verse 12 of this chapter that "this place" refers to the temple where God also dwells. (See also I Kings 8:29.)

Verse 4. This verse is difficult to understand. God is telling the people, through the mouth of Jeremiah, not to trust in the saying, "This is the temple of the Lord." Apparently, many persons thought that the fact that the temple was in Jerusalem guaranteed the continual presence of God with the people. It is true that God was considered as dwelling within the temple, but evidently the people had become complacent about God's protection. Jeremiah is here advising them that they need to "amend their ways" or God's protection will be taken away from them.

The fact that the phrase "the temple of the Lord" is repeated three times in a row gives it special emphasis. We saw this same kind of repetition for emphasis in the seraph's words spoken during the call of Isaiah (6:3).

Verses 5-6. These verses outline the changes that God required from the people. Mending their ways was going to involve working justice, ceasing to oppress others, and worshiping God alone.

Verse 7. Here is God's promise. Again the phrase "let you dwell in this place" is used. But here the prophet specifies that "place" means the land that had been occupied by the people of Israel ever since the days of Joshua.

Verses 8-9. The prophet makes more specific the sins the people have committed. Jeremiah is accusing them of violating several of the Ten Commandments—the eighth, sixth, seventh, ninth, first, and second commandments are mentioned. Jeremiah is making serious accusations.

Verse 10. God is asking, How can you commit all these sins, break all these commandments, and then come to the temple as though nothing is wrong and assume that I will protect you? You have broken your side of the covenant. What makes you think I won't do the same?

Verse 11. God compares the people to burglars who hide in the shadows (the temple) until the coast is clear, then go out and resume their activities.

Verse 12. God commands the people to go to Shiloh where the temple ("my place") used to be. They are to witness what God did to the temple there, to punish the people for their abominations. We know that the temple at Shiloh was destroyed by the Philistines during the time of Samuel (about 1050 B.C.). The battle is described in I Samuel 4. Shiloh was located in the territory of Ephraim, about twenty miles north of Jerusalem.

Verses 13-15. These verses restate the promise of punishment. Because they have broken the commandments, and because they have not heeded the warnings they were given to change their evil ways, the people will lose their temple and will be cast out of the sight of God. Chapter 26 of Jeremiah indicates that soon after Jeremiah spoke these words he was arrested.

The Scripture and the Main Question—William H. Willimon

Hear the Word of the Lord

It was a memorable sermon that Jeremiah preached that day in the temple. "Stand in the gate of the Lord's house, and proclaim there this word, and say, Hear the word of the Lord, all you men of Judah who enter these gates to worship the Lord" (7:2). Jeremiah's words were similar to those of New England Puritan Jonathan Edward's sermon, "Sinners in the Hands of an Angry God." They were like Martin Luther King, Jr.'s "I Have A Dream" speech, delivered on the steps of the Lincoln Monument in Washington. Here, in this temple sermon, Jeremiah calls a nation to task. Martin Luther King, Jr., said to an America in the grip of racial strife, "You have said that you honor freedom, brotherhood, and democracy—now will you live on the basis of your affirmations or not?" Like Martin Luther King, Jr., Jeremiah says, in effect, "You have said that you honor the Lord and his commandments—now will you live this way or not?"

Huddled there in the temple, the people believed they were hiding in the protective arms of God. But Jeremiah rebuked this mistaken notion, telling Israel that God would not protect them from the fruits of their sin and injustice.

Later Jesus would declare that "not everyone who says to me, 'Lord, Lord,' shall enter the kingdom"—only those who put actual deeds alongside their pious words.

Here is the great danger of our religion, the danger of coming to church this Sunday morning, the danger of studying the Bible in your adult class: that we will be tricked into thinking that it is enough for us to simply come to worship or open the Bible, that we do not have to fashion our lives to be congruent with our prayers and beliefs. It is so easy for our "religion" to become an escape from true religion. That is what Jeremiah accuses his people of—deluding themselves into thinking that they can reap the benefits of God's love without obeying God's will.

There may be religions in which it is enough to simply pray or sing, without regard for the conducts of one's daily life. But Judaism, and Christianity after it, is not one of those religions! Here, ethics and worship are one.

This is an appropriate thought for us at this time of the year, when we Americans move toward our annual celebration of national thanksgiving. Too often this celebration is a time for pious phrases about how thankful we are, how grateful we are for all the goodness we have received in this country. But do our deeds match our words? Do we actually conduct our lives in such a way that it is apparent that we regard our blessings as undeserved gifts of a good God, or do we act as if these things are our own achievements?

— An American Secretary of Agriculture speaks of food as a "weapon in our foreign policy arsenal"—food we have grown on the good soil God has given us!

— A politician declares, "I would rather bring down the whole world in nuclear war than yield one inch of soil that is rightfully ours."

— A congregation in a relatively affluent neighborhood struggles to meet its yearly budget, a budget that requires an annual gift to the church of only a couple of hundred dollars per year from every family, if it is to be met.

In the face of such realities, our great songs and declarations of thanksgiving and gratitude sound rather hollow.

Amend Your Ways

Jeremiah's name has found its way into our language. The word "jeremiad" has come to denote a condemnatory diatribe. There is good reason for associating Jeremiah with this sort of speaking, because much of this book consists of this sort of language, including the passages which we read for today.

Of course, you know that such harsh preaching can have its pitfalls. "You really stepped on our toes today, preacher," people sometimes comment on their way out of church, after hearing a "jeremiad." As a young preacher, I often wondered why people would say this with such apparent delight. Why would anybody enjoy having someone step on their toes? Then it occurred to me that with a preacher standing on your toes, telling you what to do, making you feel bad, you can't move anywhere or do anything. All you can do is to stand there and feel bad.

"You really stepped on our toes," is a complement to the preacher—you made us feel bad without enabling us to do anything about it! Thus, for many, going to church is a matter being subjected to advice on what they should be doing, then going home, eating a big dinner, and forgetting all about it! Feeling bad becomes a substitute for doing good.

In Jeremiah's tough temple sermon, he is very careful to say that God wants the people to "amend your ways and your doings": "If you truly execute justice one with another, if you do not oppress the alien, the fatherless or the widow . . . then I will let you dwell in this place" (7:5-7).

As Christians, we say much about the undeserved, unmerited grace of God, which saves us not on the basis of what we do but on the basis of what God has done in Jesus Christ. I sometimes express this grace by saying, "God loves us with no 'ifs' at all."

But Jeremiah's sermon reminds us that, while God loves us and chooses us without merit or condition, this love and choice place great responsibility upon us. We are God's people because of God's grace, but we cannot remain so without our response. *If* we truly love God, we will show it, not simply by our worship, but also by our work.

Imagine a marriage in which a couple had a big, lovely wedding, declared their love for one another, then they went off and never saw each other again. We would hardly call that a marriage. And yet, that is much the same way that many of us conduct our relationship with God. This will not do, says Jeremiah. There are conditions.

In the Land That I Gave You

It may be enough for other nations to persecute the homeless and to work injustice against the poor. But it is not enough for Israel. Israel has been bought with a price. Israel has a special claim upon its national life, which entails special obligations. A nation is chosen, not simply for special favors, but also for special responsibilities. Thus, injustice deserves a fierce rebuke when it is committed by a people who have been blessed so much.

Helping Adults Become Involved—Leonard T. Wolcott

Preparing to Teach

This lesson looks at the connection between religion and the conduct of human relations in a nation.

Organize the topics as follows:

    I.   The Word of God.
   II.   The sins of the people.
 III.   The people's false security.
 IV.   "Amend your ways."
  V.   The consequence of not listening to God.

FIRST QUARTER

Read carefully "The Scripture and the Main Question" and "As You Read the Scripture." These form the heart of the lesson. The ideas, insights, and suggestions in these sections should be reflected continually in your lesson plan.

As you use the suggested outline, you may want to either quote or paraphrase ideas. You might like to jot in the margin of your outline the page number and paragraph being referred to. For example, you could write a reference to page 65, paragraph 3, as 65-3.

Read Jeremiah 2:4-13. Make a list of current events which illustrate both the sins and the faith of people in today's world. Make a checklist of the sins mentioned in Jeremiah 7—for example, verse 6: oppression of aliens, orphans, widows, shedding innocent blood, false gods. Have Bibles available, also chalk and chalkboard or markers and newsprint.

Introducing the Main Question

Basic and helpful ideas are presented in the section "The Main Question." These ideas are essential in helping to identify the purpose of the lesson.

Are we true to our heritage of faith? Or are we, like ancient Judah, forgetting our history and purpose? What does it mean to obey the voice of God? Where does our security lie? How does a nation amend its ways?

Developing the Lesson

If class members have brought news items with them, display them on a wall or a table.

I. The Word of God.

This passage is called Jeremiah's Temple Sermon. It was delivered at the temple gate, where people thronged. His listeners were hardly in the mood for a scolding. A new young king, Jehoiakim, was reigning and things looked well for Judah's future, or so the people thought. The presence of the temple reassured them of their prospects.

How can the church get its message across to the passing throng? Refer to Dr. Willimon's section, which mentions Jonathan Edwards and Martin Luther King, Jr., speaking to America in their times. How and where do we get the Word of the Lord to the people today?

The Word of the Lord remains the key to all of Jeremiah, and to today's lesson. The Word of the Lord does not adjust to human selfishness or national interest.

II. The sins of the people.

The people were forgetting God—that was the problem. Read aloud Jeremiah 2:4-13. They still performed the prescribed rituals and sacrifices, but they were practicing religion without commitment, without spirit. They had put God in a box—the temple. When they were away from the temple, they acted as though they were away from God.

Forgetting God, the people acted on the basis of selfish interest and passion, using one another. The nature of society was sinful. Use your checklist here. Class members may call attention to news items that recall the sins of Judah as listed in Jeremiah 7, all violations of the Ten Commandments:

— Verse 6: oppression of strangers (taking advantage of aliens), of orphans (child neglect), of widows (battered) women, shedding innocent blood (technological warfare), idolatry (substitutes for God).
— Verse 8: trust in deceptive words (slogans, catch-phrases).
— Verse 9: murder, adultery, falsely swearing, worship of other gods.

III. The people's false security.

The people felt secure because they had the temple. Other nations had temples to house idols, but the Judean people considered that their temple housed God. In a sense, the temple kept God in Jerusalem. God was their national talisman for safety. As long as they performed the right ceremonies, God, they thought, would be satisfied. They would remain successful and affluent.

Jeremiah reminded them of Shiloh, where, in ancient times, God was supposed to dwell and where rituals took place. It had become desolate because of the sins of the people. Shiloh had not protected them. When they were not in the temple, the people acted as though they were away from God. They went after other gods and defrauded one another. To God, the worshipers assembled in the temple were no better than a group of robbers (verses 10-11).

What about us? An early church leader said that to be an atheist is better than to be one who pretends to be religious but lives a godless life. Dr. Willimon asks us to consider this Thanksgiving if we are being true to God. Do we accept leaders who mouth religous words but whose attitudes and actions run counter to the Word of the Lord? Do we keep the Bible in the house like a protective talisman, without knowing what it says? Do we think that so long as we believe the correct theology, our behavior does not matter? When we travel away from home, do we leave our morals behind? Security forces at Singapore have to be doubled when luxury ships arrive with tourists!

The Word of the Lord asks us, Are we substituting trust in the temple for obedience to God?

IV. "Amend your ways."

To the temple-goers Jeremiah says: God did not command correct temple rites, but obedience to his voice. This involves not just belief, but treating fellow human beings justly (verse 6).

Dr. Willimon asks us to imagine a big wedding, after which the couple parts, never to see each other again. A covenant relationship supposes a desire to be with one another. God covenanted with persons to "go with," to live continually in the presence and purposes of God. Obedience includes going with God.

It is not our destination that counts, but the destiny God plans for us.

The nation is chosen by God, says Jeremiah, to be responsible to his righteousness. God's love for us places responsibility on us to live out his will.

V. The consequence of not listening to God.

The Word of the Lord is to be listened to. In many languages, including those in which the Bible was written, the word for listening is related to the word for obeying. Not listening is disobedience. Read aloud the key verse (28): "This is the nation that did not obey the voice of the Lord." Jeremiah feared his nation to be hopelessly apostate. Read verses 27-29. The prophet felt, as many preachers do today, that the people were not taking him seriously. They neither repented nor changed.

Consequences are unavoidable: God will cast them out (verses 8-15). "And now, because you have done all these things, says the Lord, and when I spoke to you persistently you did not listen" (verse 13), they will be abandoned to their idolatry (verses 30-34).

Helping Class Members Act

Help the class to face the questions asked above under topic II. Are we, like the people of Judah, guilty of superficial religion? Are we, Christ's church, seeking to bring our nation to a faith that is obedient to God's commands? Lead the class in a few minutes of thoughtful prayers of confession. Ask class members, in a moment of quiet, to choose one wrong in the nation to become concerned about.

Planning for Next Sunday

Next Sunday's lesson takes up a different kind of suffering—suffering for the truth. Ask the class to read Jeremiah 37:1–38:13 and to think about what they can do as Christians about social wrongs that concern them.

LESSON 12   NOVEMBER 20

Suffering for Truth

Background Scripture: Jeremiah 37:1–38:13

"The truth hurts," people sometimes say. How true is that statement about the truth! History is the long record of how those who spoke the truth were often persecuted for their truth-telling. Even a cursory reading of the Old Testament reveals that few of God's prophets were accepted for their truth-telling.

Luke tells of the day that Jesus stood up in his hometown synagogue in Nazareth (Luke 4). There he took the scroll of one of the prophets and read it. When Jesus began interpreting the beloved text, trouble started, for he reminded people that God's prophets often behaved in unexpected ways. They behaved unexpectedly because we are unaccustomed to hearing the truth. He recalled how Elijah and Elisha went to outsiders with God's acts of compassion, rather than to insiders. Well, the rest is history. You remember the violent reaction Jesus' presentation of the truth received. On his way out the door, Jesus remarked that "No prophet is acceptable in his own country" (Luke 4:24). No real prophet is treated kindly.

Today we continue our study of the prophet Jeremiah. It comes as no surprise to us that Jeremiah's harsh words have brought him into conflict with the powers that be. He will pay dearly for his truthful presentation of God's word.

Sometimes we are called to suffer for the truth. How do we respond in such circumstances? Should we take the easy way out and avoid such unpleasantness? Those are some of the issues we shall be confronting in this week's lesson on truth and suffering.

Selected Scripture

King James Version

Revised Standard Version

Jeremiah 38:4-13

4 Therefore the princes said unto the king, We beseech thee, let this man be put to death: for thus he weakeneth the hands of the men of war that remain in this city, and the hands of all the people, in speaking such words unto them: for this man seeketh not the welfare of this people, but the hurt.

5 Then Zed′e-ki′ah the king said, behold, he *is* in your hand: for the king *is* not *he that* can do *any* thing against you.

6 Then took they Jeremiah, and cast him into the dungeon of Malchi′ah the son of Ham′me-lech, that *was* in the court of the prison: and they let down Jeremiah with cords. And in the dungeon *there was* no water, but mire: so Jeremiah sunk in the mire.

7 Now when E′bed-me′lech the Ethiopian, one of the eunuchs which was in the king's house, heard that they had put Jeremiah in the dungeon; the king then sitting in the gate of Benjamin;

8 E′bed-me′lech went forth out of the king's house, and spake to the king saying,

9 My lord the king, these men have done evil in all that they have done to Jeremiah the prophet, whom they have cast into the dungeon; and he is like to die for hunger in the place where he is: for *there is* no more bread in the city.

10 Then the king commanded E′bed-me′lech the Ethiopian, saying, Take from hence thirty men with thee, and take up Jeremiah the

Jeremiah 38:4-13

4 Then the princes said to the king, "Let this man be put to death, for he is weakening the hands of the soldiers who are left in this city, and the hands of all the people, by speaking such words to them. For this man is not seeking the welfare of this people, but their harm." 5 King Zedeki′ah said, "Behold, he is in your hands; for the king can do nothing against you." 6 So they took Jeremiah and cast him into the cistern of Malchi′ah, the king's son, which was in the court of the guard, letting Jeremiah down by ropes. And there was no water in the cistern, but only mire, and Jeremiah sank in the mire.

7 When E′bed-mel′ech the Ethiopian, a eunuch, who was in the king's house, heard that they had put Jeremiah into the cistern—the king was sitting in the Benjamin Gate—8 E′bed-mel′ech went from the king's house and said to the king, 9 "My lord the king, these men have done evil in all that they did to Jeremiah the prophet by casting him into the cistern, and he will die there of hunger, for there is no bread left in the city." 10 Then the king commanded E′bed-mel′ech, the Ethiopian, "Take three men with you from here, and lift Jeremiah the prophet out of the cistern before he dies." 11 So E′bed-mel′ech took the men with him and went to the house of the king, to a

prophet out of the dungeon, before he die.

11 So E'bed-me'lech took the men with him, and went into the house of the king under the treasury, and took thence old cast clouts and old rotten rags, and let them down by cords into the dungeon to Jeremiah.

12 And E'bed-me'lech the Ethiopian said unto Jeremiah, Put now *these* old cast clouts and rotten rags under thine armholes under the cords. And Jeremiah did so.

13 So they drew up Jeremiah with cords, and took him up out of the dungeon: and Jeremiah remained in the court of the prison.

wardrobe of the storehouse, and took from there old rags and worn-out clothes, which he let down to Jeremiah in the cistern by ropes. 12 Then E'bed-mel'ech the Ethiopian said to Jeremiah, "Put the rags and clothes between your armpits and the ropes." Jeremiah did so. 13 Then they drew Jeremiah up with ropes and lifted him out of the cistern. And Jeremiah remained in the court of the guard.

Key Verse: **Blessed are they which are persecuted for righteousness' sake. (Matthew 5:10)**

Key Verse: **Blessed are those who are persecuted for righteousness' sake. (Matthew 5:10)**

As You Read the Scripture—Lynne Deming

Jeremiah 38. This chapter forms part of a longer narrative section that begins at 37:1 and ends at 38:28. The narrative gives us the history of Judah during the time the Babylonians besieged Jerusalem. Jeremiah had been thrown into prison for trying to leave the city (37:11-15). The first thirteen verses in chapter 38 describe the punishment of Jeremiah and the intervention of King Zedekiah to save him.

Verse 4. This verse mentions the "princes" of the king. Verse 1 tells us that these princes are Sephatiah, Gedaliah, Jucal, and Pashhur. These princes advise the king that Jeremiah should be put to death. Why? Because he is "weakening the hands" (morale) of the people in Jersualem. By counseling the king to surrender to the Babylonian king Nebuchadrezzar, Jeremiah was being disloyal to his country's cause.

Verse 5. King Zedekiah is easily persuaded and hands Jeremiah over to the princes who wish for his death. This statement by the king supports his reputation as a weakling. Zedekiah certainly respected Jeremiah and the counsel he offered. He even took the prophet from a dungeon to ask his advice (37:17). When it came to supporting Jeremiah when confronted by his princes, however, the king was not able to stand up for the prophet.

Verse 6. Jeremiah is cast into a cistern that belonged to the king's son. Fortunately for Jeremiah, the cistern contained no water. It did, however, contain a lot of mud at the bottom.

Verses 7-9. Here we are introduced to another character in Jeremiah's story—Ebed-melech, an Ethiopian eunuch in the house of King Zedekiah. Eunuchs were a kind of palace officer, as we can see in 29:2, where they are listed among the persons in the palace who were taken into exile.

Ebed-melech went to the king, who was sitting at the Benjamin Gate. The Benjamin Gate was also the place where Jeremiah had been arrested while trying to leave the city (37:11-15). The king was seated there to hear court cases and make judgments on them. Since Ebed-melech was a court official, he had easy access to the king. He took that opportunity to give the king his opinion about what had happened to Jeremiah. Earlier the king had given the princes permission to do with Jeremiah whatever they thought necessary. But he was evidently unaware that the prophet had ended up in a filthy cistern, left there to starve to death in the mud.

Verse 10. The king is moved by the Ebed-melech's plea on Jeremiah's behalf. He reverses his earlier decision to put Jeremiah's fate in the hands of the princes. The king directs three men to lift Jeremiah out of the cistern. The original Hebrew says the king sent thirty men, but the Revised Standard Version and most other translations have changed it to three, thinking that thirty was probably a mistake. It would not take thirty men to lift Jeremiah out of the well. The difference between the Hebrew words for thirty and three is very slight. It is possible, though, that the king sent thirty men as a bodyguard, to protect Jeremiah.

Verses 11-12. Here we see the resourcefulness of Ebed-melech, as he finds a way to lift Jeremiah up. As he was let down by ropes, he will be lifted up by ropes, too. Ebed-melech makes special provision for Jeremiah's comfort. He gathers worn-out rags and old clothes for Jeremiah to place under his arms, between his armpits and the ropes. That way the ropes will not cut into Jeremiah's skin as he is being lifted up.

Verse 13. This verse concludes this part of the story. The rescue of Jeremiah is successful, and the prophet remains in the court of the guard. The same phrase is used to summarize the previous episode in Jeremiah's story (37:21).

The Scripture and the Main Question—William H. Willimon

Let Us Put This Man to Death

"Blessed are those who are persecuted for righteousness' sake" (Matthew 5:10). In this Beatitude, Jesus pronounces blessings on those whom the world curses—the ones who suffer persecution in the service of the truth.

In today's lesson we read of the sorry dealings in the court of the weak and vacillating King Zedekiah. The city of Jerusalem is under siege, and everyone is in a panic. Through an unholy alliance with Egypt, the king hopes to avert calamity at the hands of Nebuchadrezzar. Jeremiah refuses to say what the king and his pro-Egyptian advisors want to hear, and for that refusal the prophet's life is threatened.

This is an oft-repeated tale of conflict between men and women of God and political powers. A number of years ago, an American president had the idea of having private church services in the White House rather than going out to church. He had attended church on one occasion and had been treated to a blistering sermon on his international policies! So in the safe confines of the White House, he hoped to be spared such embarassment. Prominent clergy were invited to speak; all were asked to submit advance copies of their sermons to the president's counselors, who would check their "suitability." The president and his counselors were surprised that many of the invited preachers declined the invitation!

People in power often forget that prophets of God feel that there is a higher law to which everyone, no matter how powerful, must submit. Too often, influential people feel that the rules are made for other people, not for them. Kings and prophets inevitably clash.

This is exactly what has happened to Jeremiah. The king wants a happy report on how successful his administration is. What he gets from the prophet is a harsh and pessimistic rebuke. Why can't the prophet be patriotic? Let's all rally behind the administration and show them our support! Let's all be good, loyal citizens! Wave the flag!

Jeremiah is accused of treason. The royal advisors charge, "Let this man be put to death, for he is weakening the hands of the soldiers who are left in this city . . . by speaking such words to them. For this man is not seeking the welfare of this people, but their harm" (38:4).

These Men Have Done Evil

Ironically, it is a foreigner, an Ethiopian, who saves Jeremiah's life by interceding on his behalf before the angry king. His own people have rejected the prophet; it is up to a foreigner, an outsider, a nonbeliever, to save God's spokesperson.

The story raises all sorts of questions about patriotism, love of country, and loyalty to God. "My country, right or wrong" is not the attitude of Jeremiah. A prophet like Jeremiah may love his country, but he loves his country at its best, when it is living up to all that God intends it to be, not when it is cowering and scheming like Judah under Zedekiah.

While segregationists despised Martin Luther King, Jr.'s prophetic challenge to the injustice of racism, most Americans saw him as a national leader and a loyal American. He was simply trying to get certain Americans to live up to the promises of the Constitution. Yet when Dr. King began to criticize our involvement in the Vietnam War, he was fiercely condemned. King was told by many of his civil rights colleagues to refrain from criticism of the war, for fear that his pronouncements would gain the enmity of politicians, which would damage the gains of the civil rights movement. But Dr. King felt that he must speak out against wrong and injustice wherever he encountered it. He linked racism at home with violence in Southeast Asia and called for an end of the war. You know the end result of the work of this prophet, who dared to speak unpopular ideas.

Love of country is a fine thing. But often love of country comes into conflict with obedience to God. What then? As Paul told the governing authorities of his day, "We must obey God rather than men."

Are we as Christians prepared to take a stand against the popular wisdom of our day, even if it means that we must go against some of the policies of our own beloved country? Too often we think that because we live in a democracy, being Christian will pose no real problem for us. If we lived in a communist, totalitarian state, then we could expect conflict. But history teaches that democracies are as capable of injustice as other forms of government. We celebrate the freedoms we enjoy under our form of government, but we know that our country, even at its best, is far from perfect, far from the visions which God may have for us.

In God's eyes, lines between foreigners and insiders, loyal patriots and devoted Christians, do not exist, because God's standards are higher then even the highest of ours. Conflict is inevitable, and so is suffering.

Blessed Are the Persecuted

Even though we American Christians may not be persecuted as Jeremiah was, we must remind ourselves that many of our Christian brothers and sisters in other countries, countries which may be allies of the United States, are suffering terrible persecution. We American Christians should not be too smug about our avoidance of suffering. Perhaps our witness is so tame and accomodated that we offer no threat to the forces of evil. Are there issues that the American church has simply chosen to avoid or adjust to rather than to challenge?

The absence of persecution of a church or of an individual does not mean that either is guilty of infidelity. But we should not be surprised when, going about our Christian witness, we come into conflict with the governing authorities. Jeremiah did—so may we.

At the United States Naval Academy at Annapolis, the flag of the United States is carried in during the processional of the choir in the Sunday service in the chapel there. As the flag is brought in, it is carried before the cross and dipped down in reverence. This is a symbol of the relationship of our loyalties to God and to country. For a Christian, loyalty to God demands our greatest allegiance, even if that allegiance should cause us to suffer.

Helping Adults Become Involved—Leonard T. Wolcott

Preparing to Teach

Jeremiah could have avoided suffering by ignoring the truth or by keeping quiet. Jesus could have avoided the cross, as his struggle in Gethsemane shows (Luke 22:42-44).

Use this outline to organize the lesson:

      I. Telling the story
     II. Speaking the truth
    III. Shutting off the truth
     IV. Taking the prophet's side
      V. Sticking by the truth

Read carefully "The Scripture and the Main Question" and "As You Read the Scripture." These form the heart of the lesson. The ideas, insights, and suggestions in these sections should be reflected continually in your lesson plan.

As you use the suggested outline, you may want to either quote or paraphrase ideas. You might like to jot in the margin of your outline the page number and paragraph being referred to. For example, you could write a reference to page 65, paragraph 3, as 65-3.

Study Jeremiah chapters 37–38 and a map of Jerusalem. Visualize King Zedekiah sitting at the gate in the north wall, or Babylonian forces surrounding the city. Make a poster listing the elements of the story in these two chapters, as shown below. Do not write down the information in the parentheses, which will be added during the class session.

FIRST QUARTER

1. *Cast of Characters:*
   Hero: (Jeremiah, or the princes)
   Villain: (the princes, or Jeremiah)
   Man on the fence: (King Zedekiah)
   Defender of the prophet: (Ebed-Melech, Ethiopian employee in the palace)
   Soldiers and other patriots siding with the princes: (unknown)
   Those who realized the truth but did not speak out: (also unknown)
2. *Plot:* (Conflict between the pro-Egyptian patriot princes, on the one hand, and unyielding prophet of the Word of the Lord on the other. In between: a vacillating king.)
3. *Setting:* (The army of Babylon at the gates. The army withdraws, then returns and takes the city.)
4. *Action:* (Jeremiah advises surrender to Babylonian forces. Princes, whose personal interests lie with Egypt, condemn him for weakening the morale of the defenders. Weak king allows princes to throw Jeremiah into a cistern—deep, empty, but thick with mud. Ethiopian, with king's permission, rescues Jeremiah. Jeremiah assures king there will be no harm to him and city if he surrenders. Unsure, the king does not surrender. Babylonian army takes the city, enslaves the people, punishes Zedekiah.)

Introducing the Main Question

Basic and helpful ideas are presented in the section "The Main Question." These ideas are essential in helping to identify the purpose of the lesson.

At times Christians are called on to suffer for the truth. The question to be faced is, Are we willing to speak up and to suffer for the truth, or do we prefer to avoid all unpleasantness?

Developing the Lesson

I. Telling the story

If you have made the poster, fill in the appropriate information with the class's help, as suggested above. The identity of the hero and the villain depend on one's point of view. The princes presented themselves as patriotic heroes and Jeremiah as the villain who sympathized with the enemy. "Man on the fence" characterizes the king, an individual who is afraid to take a stand.

II. Speaking the truth

Read Jeremiah 38:1-3. Decision-makers always have advisers (asked and unasked), consultants, and lobbyists.

The Bible and secular history have many stories of false advisers. Through ignorance, self-interest, fear, or desire to please rulers, many advise wrongly. Rehoboam, King Solomon's successor, by following the advice of his jaunty young counsellors lost most of his kingdom (I Kings 12:1-20).

True advisers are those who speak honestly, without ignorance, self-interest, fear, or favor. Truth sometimes hurts, but is always for the best in terms of God's righteousness. It never is based on expediency, nor does it support power or privilege. It is often unpopular.

III. Shutting off the truth

Read verses 4-7. Naturally, people become angry when their nation is condemned for wrongdoing, or advised to take action contrary to immediate self-interest or national pride. They will try to shut off the truth-speaker whom they consider false. The princes felt justified in condemning Jeremiah. His recommendation to surrender was hurting the morale of an army roused for battle.

Ask the class to read aloud the key verse, Matthew 5:10: "Blessed are those who are persecuted for righteousness' sake." Ask: Does this mean that to speak for righteousness always means persecution? Dr. Willimon, in "The Main Question," remarks that most prophets, and Jesus too, found that their truth-telling was unacceptable. Throughout history we have persecuted those who make us uncomfortable. Savonarola fearlessly condemned the sins of his city's leadership in Florence, Italy, in the fifteenth century. They burned him to death. In the twentieth century, a fellow Hindu killed Gandhi for advising goodwill toward Muslims. Martin Luther King, Jr., was killed for counseling brotherhood of the races. In the early days of Communist China, outspoken Christian leaders were imprisoned for "unpatriotic activities."

IV. Taking the prophet's side

Read verses 7-13. We may not all be capable of speaking out individually against the abuse of righteousness, but we can stand by those who do. Mention the courage of Ebed-Melech. He was an alien in the employ of the king. By taking Jeremiah's side he risked his own life. What might the princes do to him? But he was quick to speak, lest Jeremiah die in the mud of the cistern. He was wise, prompt, and considerate in the way he rescued Jeremiah. We may thank God for the Ebed-Melechs among us.

V. Sticking by the truth

Read verses 14-18. Still under arrest, shaken and weak, facing the possibility of death by starvation, Jeremiah stuck by his truth-telling to the king.

In speaking the truth we must be clear and sure. Reformer Martin Luther, standing condemned by church leaders at the Diet of Worms, boldly spoke the truth he believed in and said: "Here I stand. I cannot do otherwise. God help me."

Truth is obedience to God, read verse 20. We have the authority to say, "Obey God!" to kings, dictators, and presidents—or else! Read verse 21. Do not be afraid of honest assertion. There is evil consequence in disobeying God.

Helping Class Members Act

Ask the class to agree on one concern they would like to address as a class. Depending on their selection, they may want to write a letter to key persons. As a Christian group, your class letter will not be simply "for" or "against." Keep it from sounding religiously arrogant or preachy. But, like Jeremiah, make no compromise of truth. Try to help the persons you write to understand the application of God's righteousness to whatever social problem you are writing about.

Close with guided prayer, asking: Are you willing to sacrifice your personal interest and even the approval of friends and the public, if need be, for the sake of truth? Pray for God's guidance in his truth.

Planning for Next Sunday

Next Sunday's lesson is based on the most celebrated passage in Jeremiah—31:27-34. Ask all to read it carefully and jot down any questions they may have about it, or any question they feel has been unanswered in this thirteen-week series on suffering and hope.

LESSON 13   NOVEMBER 27

A New Covenant

Background Scripture: Jeremiah 31:27-34

The Main Question—William H. Willimon

This Sunday is the first one in the Christian season of Advent. Advent is a time of expectancy, when the church prepares itself for the arrival of the Christ-child at Bethlehem. During this period our hearts are filled with longing, as we wait with Israel for the long-promised Messiah and examine our lives, that we may be better prepared for him.

For whom are we awaiting? The Hebrew Scriptures contain the long record of Israel's difficulties in living up to God's covenant with Israel, first promised to Abraham, father of the nation. Jeremiah has joined with Israel's other prophets in speaking a word of judgment upon the sins of Israel. Time and again God restored his promises to Israel, only to have the nation fall away. We observe in Israel's national life what you and I have also seen in our personal lives. We want to do right. We make our New Year's resolutions, but though we start out afresh with new resolve, it never seems to work out the way we want. Old habits, old thoughts return, and we stay in the same old rut. What hope is there for us?

These are some of the questions bringing us to the end of our study of the prophet Jeremiah. In the midst of the tragic desolation of Israel, Jeremiah looks forward to a new day. Even as we find ourselves, here on the first Sunday of Advent, awaiting some new and fresh act of deliverance in our lives, so Jeremiah looks forward to the day when there will be a new covenant ratified upon the very hearts of the people through the gracious actions of God.

Selected Scripture

King James Version	Revised Standard Version

Jeremiah 31:27-34

27 Behold, the days come, saith the Lord, that I will sow the house of Is′ra-el and the house of Judah with the seed of man, and with the seed of beast.

28 And it shall come to pass, *that* like as I have watched over them, to pluck up, and to break down, and to throw down, and to destroy, and to afflict; so will I watch over them, to build, and to plant, saith the Lord.

29 In those days they shall say no more, The fathers have eaten a sour grape, and the children's teeth are set on edge.

30 But every one shall die for his own iniquity: every man that eateth the sour grape, his teeth shall be set on edge.

31 Behold, the days come, saith the Lord, that I will make a new covenant with the house of Is′ra-el, and with the house of Judah:

32 Not according to the covenant that I made with their fathers, in the day *that* I took them by the hand to bring them out of the land of Egypt; which my covenant they brake, although I was a husband unto them, saith the Lord:

33 But this *shall be* the covenant that I will make with the house of Is′ra-el; After those days, saith the Lord, I will put my law in their inward parts, and write it in their hearts; and will be their God, and they shall be my people.

34 And they shall teach no more every man his neighbor, and every man his brother, saying, Know the Lord: for they shall all know me, from the least of them unto the greatest of them, saith the Lord: for I will forgive their iniquity, and I will remember their sin no more.

Jeremiah 31:27-34

27 "Behold, the days are coming, says the Lord, when I will sow the house of Israel and the house of Judah with the seed of man and the seed of beast. 28 And it shall come to pass that as I have watched over them to pluck up and break down, to overthrow, destroy, and bring evil, so I will watch over them to build and to plant, says the Lord. 29 In those days they shall no longer say:

'The fathers have eaten sour grapes,
and the children's teeth are set on edge.'

30 But every one shall die for his own sin; each man who eats sour grapes, his teeth shall be set on edge.

31 "Behold, the days are coming, says the Lord, when I will make a new covenant with the house of Israel and the house of Judah, 32 not like the covenant which I made with their fathers when I took them by the hand to bring them out of the land of Egypt, my covenant which they broke, though I was their husband, says the Lord. 33 But this is the covenant which I will make with the house of Israel after those days, says the Lord: I will put my law within them, and I will write it upon their hearts; and I will be their God, and they shall be my people. 34 And no longer shall each man teach his neighbor and each his brother, saying, 'Know the Lord,' for they shall all know me, from the least of them to the greatest, says the Lord; for I will forgive their iniquity, and I will remember their sin no more."

Key Verse: **I will put my law in their inward parts, and write it in their hearts; and will be their God, and they shall be my people. (Jeremiah 31:33)**

Key Verse: **I will put my law within them, and I will write it upon their hearts; and I will be their God, and they shall be my people. (Jeremiah 31:33)**

As You Read the Scripture—Lynne Deming

Jeremiah 31. This chapter forms part of a longer section that includes oracles about the future restoration of Israel. The prophet describes what life will be like when restoration is complete. The verses covered in today's lesson are well known for their description of the "new covenant."

Verse 27. God promises to plant "the seed of man and the seed of beast" in Judah and in Israel. In other words, God will repopulate the cities that were vacated when the people were taken into exile.

Verse 28. In the past, there has been much destruction in the land. The words "pluck up," "break down," "overthrow," and "destroy" remind us of the oracle that introduces the book of Jeremiah (see 1:10). What God promised in the beginning of Jeremiah's ministry has now come to pass. The land has been destroyed. Now, however, God is promising to reverse the trend of destruction.

Verses 29-30. Again speaking of the future, God promises that judgment and punishment will no longer be passed down from generation to generation. This is a major theological statement. Up to now, the view has been that each generation suffers for sins committed by previous generations. That view is reflected in the saying, which must have been well known in Jeremiah's time, "The fathers have eaten sour grapes, and the children's teeth are set on edge." In verse 30, we see an indication that this view is no longer tenable. The people are to understand that judgment and punishment are for their own sins, and not for the sins of previous generations. This belief holds true for individuals as well as the people as a whole. This same view is expressed in Ezekiel 18, where the prophet also discusses the saying about sour grapes.

Verse 31. The introduction repeats the one found at the beginning of verse 27. Here God promises to make a new covenant with the people of Israel and Judah. The Hebrew says, literally, "I will cut a new covenant." This language picks up the term used in the very earliest covenants in the book of Genesis.

Verse 32. Here we are told why the covenant will be called "new." It will be unlike covenants made in Israel's early history. Specifically, the covenant at Sinai is mentioned, which was made when God led the people out of Egypt. God goes on to remind the people here that they broke the earlier covenant. Presumably, this new covenant will be unlike the earlier covenants because the people will not break it.

In this verse the people are reminded that God was their "husband" in those early days. The book of Jeremiah, like the book of Hosea, uses the image of God as husband (see Jeremiah 3).

Verse 33. Instead of being inscribed on tablets of stone, as the Sinai covenant was, this new covenant will be written on the hearts of individuals. By hearts the prophet means minds, wills, and intentions. The people will obey this new law, or covenant, not because of outer motivation. The motivation for obedience will come from within. As in previous covenants,

God promises, "I will be your God, and you will be my people." This same promise is made in the book of Ezekiel (see 11:20, for example).

Verse 34. God's reputation will spread from person to person and from nation to nation. Here the prophet gives us a vision that is universal in scope. The covenant will involve knowledge of and obedience to the Lord. But it will also involve God's forgiveness of the sins of the people. Verses 33 and 34 are quoted directly in the book of Hebrews (see 8:8-12). The fact that the writer of Hebrews uses Jeremiah's prophecy to illustrate the power of the covenant attests to the importance of these words in Jeremiah.

The Scripture and the Main Question—William H. Willimon

Behold, the Days Are Coming

We have followed Jeremiah through his harsh condemnation of Israel. We have seen the prophet condemn the nation's armies, king, laws, even its worship in the temple, as apostate and an insult to God.

Amidst this bad news, in today's scripture we hear a note of good news, a note not unfitting for this first Sunday in the Christian season of Advent.

Using the old term "to cut a covenant," an expression relating to the time when Moses went up on Sinai to cut in stone a covenant between Israel and its God, Jeremiah foretells a day when an entirely new covenant shall be cut, not in tablets of stone, but in the very hearts of all the people (31:31f.).

The law of God, which formerly came to the people as a set of external demands, will be transformed into internal desire. No longer will the knowledge of God be something extrinsic to us; it will arise out of our inmost selves. "I will forgive their iniquity, and I will remember their sin no more" (31:34). This is the blessed day to which the prophet points the nation.

Out of harsh and unrelenting rebuke comes a sure promise of divine forgiveness and restoration. This God has not given up on his people, despite the greatness of their sins. God will continue to love and forgive. This is the promise which enables our relationship with God to exist—God forgives. Without this promise, we would be hopeless.

I Will Put My Law Within Them

I sometimes tell couples who are preparing for marriage that one benefit of marriage is that it gives one lots of opportunity to forgive and to be forgiven. It may be even harder to accept forgiveness from a spouse than to give it.

One of the reasons that the church asks couples to make a public profession in order to marry is that the church is convinced there is no way for a man and a woman to live together without the public promise to love. There are just too many opportunities to wound one another for a marriage to survive without a promise.

I use marriage as a sort of analogy for the relationship all of us enjoy with God. The Old Testament depicts God as willing to enter into a promise with us: I will be your God, you will be my people. This is what happened to Israel on Mount Sinai. This is the commitment, the covenant, that makes relationship possible. Jeremiah now sees that this promise will become part of the very soul of the people. What God previously wrote on stone, he will now write on their hearts.

Today, are people as willing to make commitments? Modern life seems so transient and mobile. The best-selling book *Passages* describes how most modern people view their lives: a long series of passages from one stage to another, an endless progression through different needs, ideas, life-styles. Who would be so reckless as to make a binding promise to another, when there will be so many changes in life's journey? Better to remain unattached, uncommitted, free, open to new possibilities, than to yoke oneself to another for life.

Ironically, the very mobility and transience of modern life may be the reason why commitments are so important. In times of great social dislocation and rootlessness, it is good for human beings to be able to count on a few things through the vicissitudes of life. There has to be a center, somewhere we know we belong, someone to count on. Promises, whether the promises of marriage or any other sort, help make the world a dependable, predictable place. They let us know that there are others who are committed to us, no matter what comes our way. Through promises, relationships are given time to grow and deepen. Life is transformed from a mere series of momentary, haphazard encounters into something rich, deep, and enduring.

We human beings are too fragile, too dependent upon one another, to leave our relationships to chance. Therefore we make promises to one another, showing ourselves to be responsible, committed, dependable persons. My life is built upon the promises I have made, the promises I am keeping, and promises of others to me.

One of the reasons marriage is so important to the church is that it reminds all of us, whether we happen to be married or not, of the sanctity of promises. When someone joins a church, we ask for promises. When parents bring a child for baptism, they are asked to make promises. Promises are the glue holding people together, the stuff out of which true community is formed. When you think about it, much Christian education, preaching, teaching, and life together is a life-long training in how to be faithful, dependable human beings capable of making and keeping promises.

I Will Make a New Covenant

All of this human promise-keeping is based upon the claim that God has also made and kept promises with us. The story of Israel begins with promises made to Noah, to Abraham, to Israel, and to Moses. There were many tragic wrong turns in the nation's journey, when Israel strayed from its part of the promise. Jeremiah had much to say about the infidelity of his people. But God continually acted to restore the relationship through forgiveness. God was determined that the promise would not perish.

Anytime in a human relationship that we are forced to forgive someone for a wrong they have done us, we are mirroring the constant forgiveness God has had to show us. It is important for us to retell this old story of divine forgiveness of human error, such as we hear it from the prophet Jeremiah, because we are called to live the very same story in our lives with one another. We love because he first loved us. We forgive because, again and again, God has forgiven us.

When promises and commitments are broken, we feel betrayed; anger and hurt rises within us. But we must remember that we feel the same way that God feels when we, in thought and deed, betray him. Any response we make, in keeping our commitments or in forgiving those who break commitments to us, is based on our experience of God's commitment to us.

"How can you possibly forgive your husband for being so unfaithful to you?" I asked a woman.

"How could God possibly forgive me for being unfaithful?" she asked me back.

Helping Adults Become Involved—Leonard T. Wolcott

Preparing to Teach

The lessons of suffering and hope culminate in this one, on the promise of a new covenant. The messages of Job and of the prophets Isaiah and Jeremiah build toward the ultimate message of Jesus Christ. Dr. Willimon, in "The Scripture and the Main Question," stresses two themes, promise and forgiveness, which will be the lesson's focus.

Organize the lesson according to this outline:

   I.   God changes a negative past to a positive future.
  II.   Sin is the responsibility only of the individual who commits sin.
 III.   A new covenant is given.
 IV.   The new covenant means that through forgiveness, a new relationship is established between God and his people.
  V.   Conclusion.

Read carefully "The Scripture and the Main Question" and "As You Read the Scripture." These form the heart of the lesson. The ideas, insights, and suggestions in these sections should be reflected continually in your lesson plan.

As you use the suggested outline, you may want to either quote or paraphrase ideas. You might like to jot in the margin of your outline the page number and paragraph being referred to. For example, you could write a reference to page 65, paragraph 3, as 65-3.

Read the background scripture; Psalm 30:5; Ezekiel 18:26-28; Hosea 2; and I Corinthians 11:25. Have three-by-five-inch cards ready to distribute. Type and duplicate copies of the following questionnaire. Leave three blank spaces under each question.

1.   What have I learned about God?
2.   What have I learned that will help me in my suffering?
3.   What have I learned about being a good friend to sufferers?
4.   What have I learned about hope?
5.   What have I learned about prayer?
6.   What have I learned about what sin is and does to a person?
7.   What have I learned about being a part of God's people?
8.   What is the new covenant?
9.   This is my call and commitment:

FIRST QUARTER

Introducing the Main Question

Basic and helpful ideas are presented in the section "The Main Question." These ideas are essential in helping to identify the purpose of the lesson.

The aim of the lesson is to help class members understand, look forward to, and appropriate the new covenant.

Ask: On Thanksgiving Day, did you give thanks for the joy of fellowship with God? Often our sins and selfishness spoil that fellowship. Can we have hope for a restored, lasting fellowship of faith?

Developing the Lesson

I. God changes a negative past to a positive future.

The great exchange is depicted in Jeremiah 31:28. Read it aloud. As God has plucked up and broken down Judah because of its sinfulness, now he will "build and plant." Ask class members to compare their feelings about seeing an old shack being destroyed and a new house being built, or a withered plant being cut down and a fresh green plant growing in spring. In both cases, the old is exchanged for the new. Read Ezekiel 18:26-28. Here is a sad promise to the righteous man who exchanges goodness for iniquity, but a glad promise to the wicked man who turns to goodness. In Jeremiah 31:28 God is making the latter promise: good to all who repent and exchange their evil ways for God's goodness.

II. Sin is the responsibility only of the individual who commits sin.

For another change, read aloud Jeremiah 31:29-30. The Israelites believed that generations of people must suffer for the wrongs done by their ancestors. During the time of Jeremiah, children were growing up in an exile for which they were not responsible. But in the coming days, says the prophet, nations and individuals will be responsible for their own sins (read Ezekiel 18). And God's offer of mercy is renewed to every generation and to every person.

III. A new covenant is given.

Ask the class to repeat together with you the chorus of this passage: "Behold, the days are coming." Try it again, making it loud and joyful. Then read verses 31-32. Explain that to the Israelites a covenant was not just a contract but a sacred agreement.

The old covenant was engraved in stone at Sinai. The people had been unfaithful to their part of it. Note the close family love implied by the word "husband." Summarize the theme of Hosea 2, where a husband takes back a faithless wife. In fact, as in Isaiah 65, which we studied several weeks ago, the contrast here is between the people's infidelity to God and God's continuing fidelity to them.

A faithful God is renewing his covenant with his people. God is always near. He does not cast us off forever. He is waiting, looking for our return, like the father in Jesus' story of the prodigal son.

IV. The new covenant means that through forgiveness, a new relationship is established between God and his people.

Read aloud verses 33-34. This new covenant will be more enduring, because it will be engraved on the people's hearts. The heart is the seat of one's will, conscience, purposes, and attitude. God will write his covenant into the very motivations of our lives. Faith will no longer be an externally stated creed to be learned (and forgotten), or a theology to be subscribed to (and neglected). Faith will be a living experience that we will not have to ask about or be taught.

The essence of this faith experience is communion of God's people with the people's God. To know God is to have a conscious relationship with him, one of love.

V. Conclusion.

How can this be? Repeat the end of verse 34: "For I will forgive their iniquity, and I will remember their sin no more." Forgiveness! A young man told me, "I prayed. I said to God, 'How can you forgive the great wrong I did against you?' And God answered, 'What wrong?'" God forgives and forgets it. Only his love remains. In Christ the Christian finds the new covenant experience. Read to the class Jesus' words at the Last Supper (I Corinthians 11:25). This bond is universal. It is offered to *all* people, and we can share it with *all* people. It is God's forgiving love for all humanity.

Helping Class Members Act

Distribute three-by-five-inch cards. Ask members to write on one side three words that have meant the most to them during the last three months of this study. You may write suggestions on the chalkboard or newsprint, such as covenant, forgiveness, repentance, promise, sins, new, suffering, hope, servant, call, restoration, creator, prayer.

After a few minutes ask the class to pray about and then write on the reverse side of the card their personal response to God's offer of a new covenant. When they have finished writing, suggest they keep the card in their Bibles and review it from time to time.

The last thirteen lessons have looked at Job, Isaiah, and Jeremiah on the subject, "Through Suffering to Hope." Distribute the questionnaire you have prepared. Ask the class to answer as many questions as they like. Names are not necessary on papers.

Planning for Next Sunday

The title of the next quarter's studies is "Scenes of Love and Compassion." This quarter is a study of the Gospel of Luke. It would be helpful to read the entire Gospel of Luke prior to studying the individual lessons.

The next lesson deals with the birth of John the Baptist. Ask for three volunteers to prepare a three- to five-minute skit on the scripture. One volunteer will play a news reporter interviewing the other two actors, playing Zechariah and Elizabeth, about their experience. Their answers, based on the first chapter of Luke, will seek to convey how the first-century couple felt about the unexpected events. Encourage the actors to carefully read the scripture lesson, to do a little research, and to use their imaginations to fill in details.

Scenes of Love and Compassion

UNIT I: PROMISE AND EXPECTATION
Horace R. Weaver

FOUR LESSONS   DECEMBER 4–25

The lessons for this quarter are based on selected passages from Luke's Gospel. Earlier in the cycle (March–May 1987) passages from the Passion narrative in Luke were studied; later (December 1990–February 1991) many of Luke's parables will be studied. Also excluded from this quarter are passages having parallels in Matthew, which were studied from December 1987 to February 1988.

The themes for each of the three units of this quarter are as follows: unit I, "Promise and Expectation"; unit II, "Proclamation and Ministry"; unit III, "Response and Responsibility."

Unit I, "Promise and Expectation," based on portions of Luke's birth narrative, is scheduled for the Christmas season. The titles for each of the four lessons in this unit are as follows: "Doubting God's Promise," December 4, is based on the priest (Zechariah) who doubted the angel's announcement that he and his wife (Elizabeth) would have a child. "Accepting God's Promise," December 11, reviews Mary's experience of God's announcement that she would bear a son who would be above all other persons. "Rejoicing in God's Greatness," December 18, describes the events that took place in Bethlehem ("house of bread"), where Jesus, the bread of life, was born. "Celebrating the Savior's Birth," December 25, is based on the events at Herod's temple when the baby Jesus was dedicated to God and his work for humankind.

Contributors to the second quarter:
Boyce Bowden, Board of Communications, The United Methodist Church, Oklahoma Conference, Oklahoma City, Oklahoma.
Horace R. Weaver.
William H. Willimon.
Mike Winters, pastor of Presbyterian Church of Berwyn, Chicago, Illinois.

———————

The Unique Gentile Writer: Luke

Horace R. Weaver

In studying the Gospel According to Luke, it is good to be aware that he was not a Jew. Some of the Jewish content of Matthew and Mark do not appear in Luke's Gospel. Many times Luke includes data not found in the other Gospels. It is helpful to ask why he does so; what was this Gentile writer trying to say that was different from the other Gospels? We will list these differences as headings and discuss them separately.

Luke Dedicated His Gospel to a Person

Luke is the only writer in the New Testament who dedicated his work to a distinct person. Being a Gentile and a Greek, Luke used the customary Greek method of dedicating his writing to a specific person—Theophilus. A dedication implied a purpose for his writing to that person.

In this introduction, Luke tells Theophilus about his method of writing. Luke states that he has "compiled" (not composed) "a narrative of the things which have been accomplished among us, just as they were delivered to us by those who from the beginning were eyewitnesses and ministers of the word" (1:1-2). Luke is suggesting that he had talked to those who had experienced many of the events in Jesus' ministry—teachings, healings, conversations, intimate moments of self-disclosure to loved ones, the crucifixion, the resurrection, and post-resurrection meetings (for forty days! [Acts 1:3] with his apostles and disciples.

Luke wants Theophilus to know that he had "followed all things closely for some time past" in order "to write an orderly account for you, most excellent Theophilus, that you may know the truth concerning the things of which you have been informed." Obviously he is writing not only to inform Theophilus, but also in hopes of winning him to Luke's convictions and style of life as found in Jesus, the Messiah ("Christ," in Greek).

Who Was Theophilus?

There are several suggestions as to whom Luke dedicated his Gospel. Theophilus may be any person who loves God. It is a fascinating possibility. Luke certainly would have welcomed all lovers of God to read his carefully "compiled" Gospel. Another view suggests that he was dedicating his book to a specific person who, if converted, would have tremendous influence in the spread of the Gospel. Perhaps Luke dedicated his book to a Roman official, such as a governor or procurator (for Luke's use of "most excellent," see Acts 23:26; 24:2; 26:25). Another intriguing theory is that Theophilus was the secret name by which the Roman church knew the cousin of Emperor Domitian, T. Flavius Clemens, whose wife Domitilla was a member of the church. He may have received some catechetic instructions in the Christian faith. For some unknown reason, T. Flavius Clemens (a possible heir to the Roman throne) was exiled to Gaul for life. (Speculate a bit on what it would have meant if he had become the Roman emperor.) It could be that Luke had heard that Theophilus had received hostile reports of the Christians. (See the discussion in *The Interpreter's Dictionary of the Bible,* vol. R–Z, p. 620.)

Luke Claims Jesus, Not the Caesars, Is Savior of the World

Luke was apparently well trained in Greek thought and Roman politics, as well as in medicine. Luke dates events in the life of Jesus by reference to the Roman emperors and procurators, the ruling tetrarchs and kings, the ruling High Priest, and the leading theologians (rabbinical leaders of the two "seminaries").

The Roman emperor in the days of Jesus' birth and childhood was Augustus Caesar (27 B.C.–A.D. 14). It was he who ordered the edict of registration that caused Jesus to be born not in Nazareth but in Bethlehem (which suggests that Joseph must have owned some property there, since he was to pay taxes on property in Bethlehem).

Caesar was the family name of the emperors of this era. There were Gaius Julius Caesar, his grandnephew Octavian (who was later adopted and ruled as Augustus Caesar), and three emperors to whom Luke also refers: Tiberius Caesar, Claudius Caesar, and Nero Caesar. We are interested at this point with Octavian Augustus Caesar. His leadership brought in the amazing Pax Romana ("Peace of Rome"), which brought peace to land and sea. (For example, piracy was outlawed by force.) For his efforts the Roman senate erected an altar to Pax Augusta (still existent in the Campus Martius of Rome) called the Ara Pacis Augustae. It was January 16, 25 B.C., when the senate gave him the title Augustus ("divine") Caesar.

In various areas of the Mediterranean he was hailed as "savior of the whole world" (*sotera tou sympantos kosmos*); he was also called "God" in many Greek inscriptions. The Roman senate celebrated the occasion of his birthday by declaring, "The birthday of the god has marked the beginning of the good news through him for the world" (Priene inscription). In the angel's speech to the shepherds, Luke is making the not-so-subtle claim that Jesus is Savior and Son of God (which title had been given to Octavian years earlier!) and that the good news (*evangelion*) of Caesar did not mark the beginning of peace to the world, but rather the birth of the Babe in Bethlehem. The real bearer of peace and salvation to all the world was not the person elected by the Roman senate but him who was born in Bethlehem. It was in the birth of Jesus that the peace of the world would come, not in the birth of Pax Augusta. The truth was heralded not by the choirs within the senate but by angelic ("messenger") choirs: "Glory to God in the highest, and on earth peace among men with good will." Luke shows little interest here or elsewhere in the pomp and circumstance of a Davidic Messiah; he emphasizes the Lowly One who comes in the kingdom of God. (Read Acts 1:1-6 where Jesus differentiates betweeen the kingdom of Israel and the kingdom of God.)

The Coming of the Holy Spirit

During the boyhood days of John (son of Zechariah and Elizabeth and Jesus' second cousin) and Jesus there was a spiritual drought that hovered over the "Chosen People." After Ezra had read the Torah and the people had adopted it as their Scripture, and after the elders of the synagogues had adopted the Prophets (around 200 B.C.), an unexpected attitude toward their Scriptures arose to plague the Israelites. The voice of prophecy died at that time. If anyone wanted to know the will of God, they were to go to the sacred books of the Torah and Prophets. They were not to ask, What does a modern prophet say is the will and purpose of God? They were to ask a rabbi or priest to interpret the Scriptures for their modern times. They soon learned that when God speaks only through the written page, the voice of God in the inner conscience dies out—not because God doesn't want to speak but because the one praying doesn't expect God to speak now. As the writer of Psalm 74 laments, "There is no longer any prophet" (verse 9). They listened only to the historical voice of the Deity, as found on vellum and papyrus. Little wonder unwritten (oral) laws were developed by pious rabbis. Yet, these were not the Word of God but the opinions of pious men.

Luke felt the power of new life surging through the inner lives of both Jews and Gentiles. He had felt it himself! He writes in both his Gospel and in the Acts of the Apostles that a new day has come for humankind. The Spirit of God has become vocal. God is no longer silent. (Perhaps it is really that human beings are finally realizing that God is seeking to speak to them. Listen!)

So it is that Elizabeth is told she will soon bear a baby, though she is past menopause. Her husband is confident God has spoken a word of assurance, and the baby's name will be Johannan (John). Mary in Nazareth knows the silence of God is broken! She is to bear a son who will be named after the great Joshua (Jeshua in Hebrew, Jesus in English, Jesu in Latin). Aged Simeon and a friend, Anna, see and hold the baby Jesus in their arms and declare that he is the Messiah. They laugh and perhaps dance in joy, for the living God is making their hopes come alive. They are learning to feel and listen.

Luke tells how the Spirit of God, heretofore not felt for the past four hundred years, moves in the life of John's cousin, Jesus of Nazareth. Luke tells that Jesus heard the voice of the Holy Spirit say: "You are my beloved Son. You are my long-awaited Messiah. In you I am well pleased." The Spirit "drove him into the desert" until he worked through the meaning of messiahship. First he learned what it was not: the messianic dreams of the priests, the Pharisees, the Essenes (with their apocalyptic military hopes), the Zealots, or the Herodians. Jesus made the meaning of the Messiahship clear when he modeled it on the Suffering Servant of Isaiah of Babylon (chapters 53–53 of Isaiah).

Then the Spirit moved Jesus to go to Capernaum, where he called two of his cousins (James and John) and certain friends (such as Andrew, who had introduced his brother Peter to Jesus while in Jerusalem, according to John's Gospel). Then Jesus visited his native synagogue in Nazareth, where he was invited to teach. He turned to the lectionary reading for the day from the Prophets (Isaiah 61) and declared that he knew he was God's chosen Messiah, and what message and actions would direct his messiahship:

> The Spirit of the Lord God is upon me,
>   because the Lord has anointed me
> to bring good tidings to the afflicted;
>   he has sent me to bind up the brokenhearted,
> to proclaim liberty to the captives,
>   and the opening of the prison to those who are bound;
> to proclaim the year of the Lord's favor.
>
> (Isaiah 61:1-2a)

(Note that Luke omits the last line: "and the day of vengeance of our God.")

The congregation of men (and the women behind the latticework) should have shouted for joy; God, after four hundred years of silence, is speaking to his people again. Hallelujah! (Praise ye the Lord!)

Luke declares in many ways that the Holy Spirit has come into the life of Jesus, by showing Jesus' miracles of physical healing and restoration of sanity, his awareness of God ("Emmanuel"), his requests for forgiveness by God and persons, his mending of broken human relationships, and so on, ad infinitum, including the clear activity of the Holy Spirit throughout the book of Acts.

SECOND QUARTER

Jesus' Amazing Grace Toward Outcasts

Luke offers a unique service in telling of Jesus' amazing grace toward outcasts, the unfortunates of society. We note several instances:

1. Luke records that Jesus said, "Blessed are you poor" (Matthew's Gospel says "Blessed are the poor in Spirit").
2. Luke shows Jesus honoring the Gentile woman of Zarephath and the Gentile man (Naaman) of Syria, both of whom were considered unclean (Luke 4:25-27).
3. The gospel is for all persons, including the loathed Samaritans, as shown in Luke 9:51-56.
4. Luke portrays Jesus as the friend of sinners, for Luke alone tells of the woman who anointed Jesus' feet, bathed them with her tears, and wiped them with her hair (Luke 7:36-50).
5. Jesus praises the faith of a Roman centurion in Luke 7:9.
6. Matthew tells how Jesus sent his disciples out to preach, but told them not to go to the Samaritans or Gentiles (Matthew 10:5). Luke omits that statement!
7. When the message of John the Baptist is stated, all four Gospels quote Isaiah 40: "Prepare the way of the Lord; make straight in the desert the highway of our God." But only Luke continues that verse with "And all flesh shall see the salvation of God" (Luke 3:6).

Add to the above Lukan interpretations of Jesus' message the following examples of what is often called Luke's Gospel of the Outcasts (chapters 15–19): a stray sheep (15:3-7), a lost coin (15:8-10), a prodigal son (15:11-32), a sick beggar (16:19-31), a Samaritan leper (17:11-19), a mistreated widow (18:1-8), a despised publican (18:9-14), a blind beggar (18:35-43), and a chief tax collector (19:1-10).

The above sixteen examples illustrate well the unique concern of Luke for the lost, the despised, the poor, the sick, and the unclean.

Luke would have gladly supported Fabor's hymn:

> There's a wideness in God's mercy,
>   Like the wideness of the sea;
> There's a kindness in His justice,
>   Which is more than liberty.
>
> For the love of God is broader
>   Than the measure of man's mind;
> And the heart of the Eternal
>   Is most wonderfully kind.

Luke's Unique Openness to the Mission of Women

In the first letter to the Corinthians, 9:5, Paul states that the twelve apostles were married, and that theoretically he has such a right to a wife also. Furthermore, the wives traveled with their apostolic husbands on their various missions. Peter and his wife went to Bithynia to carry the good news of Jesus, the Christ. All the other apostles' wives were with their husbands on similar missions. We wish Paul had said something about the contributions of these wives to their husbands' work. Luke sensed this lack of appreciation for women. Remember, Paul and Luke traveled hundreds of miles together and valued one another highly. He wonder if Luke raised questions about women's rights.

Luke, Paul's "beloved doctor," probably came from Macedonia, where women enjoyed a more emancipated position than in any other country at the time (so William Barclay, *The Gospel of Luke,* The Daily Study Bible [Philadelphia: Westminster, 1953], p. xvi). This may help account for the unique acceptance and honored place of women in his writing. Several times he refers to the fact that Jesus broke with the traditions of the Jews by teaching women as well as men.

Luke helps us see Jesus' use of twin parables: Jesus told the men a parable about a man who lost one of his hundred sheep and searched till he found it; then he told the women a parable about a woman who lost one of her ten silver coins (10 percent of her social security!) and how she frantically searched till she found it and rejoiced. So God rejoices when anyone (male or female) who is lost, is found.

A number of women from Galilee followed Jesus and his disciples and ministered to them. Joanna, whose husband was Chuza, a (financial?) steward to Herod Antipas, may well have financed their religious campaigns on a number of occasions. It was women who came to minister to Jesus after his crucifixion: Mary of Magdala, Joanna, and Mary, the mother of James the Less and his brother Joseph). Mark adds the name of Salome (mother of James and John Zebedee) and "also many other women who came up with him to Jerusalem" (Mark 15:40-41).

Earlier in his Gospel, Luke refers to mothers of the faith: Mary, Elizabeth, and Anna (a saint from the temple). Soon were added women like Mary Magdalene, Aunt Salome, Joanna, Mary, Martha, and of course Mary the mother of Jesus. We think of Mary teaching her son his first prayer, which he prayed every night: "Into thy hands I commit my spirit; thou has redeemed me, O Lord, faithful God" (Psalm 31:5). Imagine the pain within the heart of Mary as she heard that same prayer come from her son's lips as the last words of his physical life!

It is not surprising that those women who "watched from afar" as their beloved Master (Luke's Greek word for the Hebrew "rabbi") hung on the cross were the first to come to his tomb to embalm his body. Women, whose hearts had been pierced by daggers of hate, injustice, dishonesty, and brutality, came to the tomb and learned that he was not here—he had risen. These same women told the men who had gathered together in a meeting place to mourn and search for meaning and hope that Jesus had been raised by God from the dead. And soon they knew it was so, and their hearts burned within them as they felt his presence there.

Not too long after this experience of the risen Lord, Christians became aware that the walls of hostility between men and women, Jew and Gentile, had been destroyed. Jesus' experiences with God produced the dynamics that, as Paul would write in Ephesians 2:14-16, have broken down the physical walls of the temple separating men from women, and the mental and spiritual walls separating Gentiles from Jews. In Christ, all stand equal before God, a unity which can be experienced by those who accept the faith of and in Jesus Christ their Lord.

Doubting God's Promise

Background Scripture: Luke 1:1-25, 57-80

The Main Question—William H. Willimon

Today we begin a series of lessons on the birth of Jesus. We shall study the early chapters of Luke's Gospel. In these chapters, Luke wants to make clear that the coming of Jesus was something strange and unexpected—beyond the imaginations of people, even very devout religious people. Of course, it may not seem strange to you that devout and religious people (perhaps *especially* the devout) should lack imagination.

Often people tell us, "You have simply got to accept the facts." In saying this, they are implying that we live in a fantasy world of unrealistic expectations. Undoubtedly, many people outside the church feel that religion has a tendency to lead people into false expectations. Karl Marx once called religion "the opiate of the masses." In Marx's opinion, religion had a narcotic effect upon people. It kept them sedated and chained to the status quo.

What do you think? All of us need hope for the future. When we face the problems and challenges of modern life, the desperate situations that confront us all, we need to have some vision of God that enables us to live in the future. In this world, with its many problems, set backs, and tragedies, all there is? Or is it possible that God is active, creating for us a world infinitely better than we could have created on our own?

Luke says that Jesus was born to a people who had for centuries rehearsed the promises of God. But what happens when those promises are fulfilled? An aging man and woman are told, quite inconceivably, that they are to conceive a child. Their disbelieving response is quite believable. In fact, it reminds us of our responses to similar circumstances. The question for today is, Are the promises of God dependable and trustworthy?

Selected Scripture

King James Version

Luke 1:5-13, 18-20, 24-25

5 There was in the days of Her'-od, the king of Ju-dae'-a, a certain priest named Zach'-a-ri'-as, of the course of A-bi'-a: and his wife *was* of the daughters of Aa'-ron, and her name *was* E-lis'-a-beth.

6 And they were both righteous before God, walking in all the commandments and ordinances of the Lord blameless.

7 And they had no child, because that E-lis'-a-beth was barren, and they both were *now* well stricken in years.

Revised Standard Version

Luke 1:5-13, 18-20, 24-25

5 In the days of Herod, king of Judea, there was a priest named Zechari'ah, of the division of Abi'jah; and he had a wife of the daughters of Aaron and her name was Elizabeth. 6 And they were both righteous before God, walking in all the commandments and ordinances of the Lord blameless. 7 But they had no child, because Elizabeth was barren, and both were advanced in years.

8 And it came to pass, that while he executed the priest's office before God in the order of his course.

9 According to the custom of the priest's office, his lot was to burn incense when he went into the temple of the Lord.

10 And the whole multitude of the people were praying without at the time of incense.

11 And there appeared unto him an angel of the Lord standing on the right side of the altar of incense.

12 And when Zach'-a-ri'-as saw *him*, he was troubled, and fear fell upon him.

13 But the angel said unto him, Fear not, Zach'-a-ri'-as: for thy prayer is heard; and thy wife E-lis'-a-beth shall bear thee a son, and thou shalt call his name John.

....

18 And Zach'-a-ri'-as said unto the angel, Whereby shall I know this? for I am an old man, and my wife well stricken in years.

19 And the angel answering said unto him, I am Ga'-bri-el, that stand in the presence of God; and am sent to speak unto thee, and to shew thee these glad tidings.

20 And, behold, thou shalt be dumb, and not able to speak, until the day that these things shall be performed, because thou believest not my words, which shall be fulfilled in their season.

....

24 And after those days his wife E-lis'-a-beth conceived, and hid herself five months, saying,

25 Thus hath the Lord dealt with me in the days wherein he looked on *me*, to take away my reproach among men.

Key Verse: The angel said unto him, Fear not, Zacharias: for thy prayer is heard; and thy wife Elisabeth shall bear thee a son, and thou shalt call his name John. (Luke 1:13)

8 Now while he was serving as priest before God when his division was on duty, 9 according to the custom of the priesthood, it fell to him by lot to enter the temple of the Lord and burn incense. 10 And the whole multitude of the people were praying outside at the hour of incense. 11 And there appeared to him an angel of the Lord standing on the right side of the altar of incense. 12 And Zechari'ah was troubled when he saw him, and fear fell upon him. 13 But the angel said to him, "Do not be afraid, Zechari'ah, for your prayer is heard, and your wife Elizabeth will bear you a son, and you shall call his name John."

....

18 And Zechari'ah said to the angel, "How shall I know this? For I am an old man, and my wife is advanced in years." 19 And the angel answered him, "I am Gabriel, who stand in the presence of God; and I was sent to speak to you, and to bring you this good news. 20 And behold, you will be silent and unable to speak until the day that these things come to pass, because you did not believe my words, which will be fulfilled in their time."

....

24 After these days his wife Elizabeth conceived, and for five months she hid herself, saying, 25 "Thus the Lord has done to me in the days when he looked on me, to take away my reproach among men."

Key Verse: The angel said to him, "Do not be afraid Zechariah, for your prayer is heard, and your wife Elizabeth will bear you a son, and you shall call his name John." (Luke 1:13)

SECOND QUARTER

As You Read the Scripture—Mike Winters

Luke 1:1-4. The Gospel begins with a salutation to one called Theophilus (see Acts 1:1). The title "most excellent" in verse 3 may indicate that Theophilus was a civic or government official. The purpose of the Gospel may have been to further instruct Theophilus, already a believer. Or it may have been written to Theophilus as a defense of a defamed Christianity.

Verse 5. The setting in time of the angel's appearance to Zechariah to announce the conception of John was the reign of Herod. Though Herod reigned for thirty-three years B.C., the probable date here was approximately 6 B.C. Abijah was a descendant of Aaron. During the time of David, the priests were divided into twenty-four courses. The division of Abijah was the eighth course (I Chronicles 24:10). It is more likely, however, that Zechariah was a descendant of another Abijah, a chief priest during Jerusalem's reconstruction who returned to Jerusalem from Babylon with Zerubbabel (Nehemiah 12: 4, 7).

Verses 6-7. Childlessness in Jewish culture was a sign of God's disfavor and displeasure (Luke 1:25). Aged Zechariah and Elizabeth, however, were "righteous before God, walking in all the commandments and ordinances of the Lord blameless." Even so, they would have experienced the birth of a child, especially a son, as a sign of God favor.

Verses 8-9. King Hezekiah appointed the divisions of the priests "for burnt offerings and peace offerings, to minister in the gates of the camp of the Lord and to give thanks and praise" (II Chronicles 31:2). Zechariah's turn came by a chance selection. This indicates that he probably did not have a turn at regular intervals. More than likely, his selection for duty was rare. It was considered an honor. Incense was burned on an altar of acacia wood. Burning incense was to be a perpetual ritual (Exodus 30:1, 8).

Verse 10. Incense was burned every morning and evening (Exodus 30:7-8). Thus, the people were gathered outside for prayer twice a day.

Verses 11-12. When the angel appeared to Zechariah, he was afraid. His fear was probably not unlike Mary's fear (Luke 1:29) or the shepherds' fear (Luke 2:9) when "the glory of the Lord shone around them." In Isaiah's vision of the "Lord sitting upon a throne, high and lifted up," his first words were, "Woe is me!" (Isaiah 6:1, 5).

Verse 13. Zechariah had no need to fear, for he was blameless. The angel brought the good news that Zechariah's secret, lifelong petition was to be answered. His wife would conceive a son, who would be called John. The name John means "God is gracious."

Verse 18. The announcement of his wife's conception of a son was bewildering. Zechariah confronted the biological facts of life: He was an elderly man and his wife was past menopause. His response may have been a request for a sign, a confirmation, of this good news.

Verse 19. Gabriel, one of the seven archangels (in Jewish angelology) also appeared to Mary to announce to her the miraculous conception of a son (Luke 1:31). Angels were God's messengers.

Verse 20. The very sign for which Zechariah asked would be his loss of the power of speech—his punishment for doubting the angel's credibility. When Zechariah's son was born, he wrote a note explaining to his relatives that the child's name was John, and then he was able to speak again!

The Scripture and the Main Question—William H. Willimon

Great Needs Require Great Deeds

In his book on Christian-Jewish relations, *Christians and Jews, Getting Our Stories Straight*, Rabbi Michael Goldberg notes that the Jewish "master story" portrays God's salvation of his people a bit differently from the Christian understanding.

In the Exodus account, the Hebrews languish in Egyptian slavery. "I have heard the cry of my people," God says, "and am come to deliver them." In order to deliver them, God appears to a Hebrew living in Egypt, a man named Moses. Appearing to Moses in the burning bush, God tells Moses that he has been selected as a liberator of the Chosen People. When Moses is reluctant, God continues to press him, even enlisting Moses' brother Aaron as his spokesman. Goldberg notes that throughout the Exodus story it is clear that God intends to use these people to help accomplish the liberation of his people from slavery. God helps them through numerous signs and wonders, but we have the sense that the liberation would not have happened were it not for cooperative leaders like Moses, Aaron, and Miriam.

Goldberg contrasts the role of humans in the Exodus account with their roles in the account of the coming of Christ. Once again, God's Chosen People are enslaved, this time to the forces of Rome. Once again, the advent of God among them is announced by strange and wondrous events. This story of deliverance opens not with a burning bush but with accounts of strange births to unlikely parents.

Of course, old Elizabeth and Zechariah are participants in God's work. Whatever God has in mind for the salvation of his people, it will not be the proverbial one-man show. A variety of unlikely actors are enlisted for the drama. But they are enlisted in a way that makes it quite clear, right at the beginning, that the "show" God wants to present will be so strange, so utterly beyond the bounds of human imagination, that only God could pull it off.

People like old Elizabeth and Zechariah are not heroes who receive a nudge here and there from God; rather, they are the confused, surprised, often unwilling vessels that God uses to accomplish a mighty work of deliverance.

Behind their story is the evangelist Luke saying that the good that needs doing, the salvation required, is so great, so far-reaching, that only God can bring it about. Therefore, the role of men and women in this story, if they are to be part of God's saving work, will not be to take matters into their own hands but rather to trust God and allow their lives to be taken into *God's hands.*

How Can This Be?

In the story of Elizabeth and Zechariah, Luke gives us a foretaste, a preview, of the story of Jesus. When God moves to save, the ways of God's movement will be strange and mysterious. We can expect to be dumbfounded, even as Zechariah was.

Our conventional belief that "God helps those who help themselves" crumbles when we are faced with the really great problems of life. We

SECOND QUARTER

Americans tend to be a pragmatic people, thinking of ourselves as doers, achievers, and problem-solvers. Our amazing advances in technology have led us to believe that we can solve any problem we set our minds to, given enough money, energy, and commitment. This mindset has led to great achievements.

But it has also led to much frustration. Many of life's great problems seem insoluble through technology. We have learned to cure many illnesses, but we still die. Massive hunger and starvation, political injustice, and the threat of nuclear war continue to plague us. Many modern people feel that their lives are out of control and beyond human help. Tens of thousands are cynical, disillusioned, fearful. What is there to hope for if we cannot hope in our technology and our competence?

This great question lies behind today's little story of Elizabeth and Zechariah. Like thousands of their fellow Jews, they were people without hope, because no merely human resources could change their situation for the better.

They were then confronted with divine resourcefulness, a love and power so beyond their imaginations that they were dumbfounded. We are so accustomed to presuming that hope for the future depends upon our taking matters into our own hands that we are as surprised and unbelieving as Elizabeth and Zechariah when God comes to us promising to take matters into his hands.

God doesn't deal in trifles. If we have reached the point, as many of us suspect, that many of our greatest fears and most of our difficult problems are insoluble with human resources, then we should not be surprised by our disbelief when confronted by God's point of view. How can this be? we ask. How can it be that "peace on earth, goodwill toward all people" is promised? How can it be that good shall triumph and evil shall be defeated? Our surprise knows no bounds because, judged on the basis of this strange beginning of the story of Jesus, God's resourcefulness knows no bounds.

Surprising Salvation

The first act of the drama of Jesus' advent opens with the spotlight falling on two unlikely characters. Elizabeth, advanced in years and childless, is told that she will be part of God's promise to save. Already we sense that God will move in an unexpected way. Luke's culture must have looked upon Elizabeth—an old, "barren" woman—with the same contempt that we now bestow on all elderly people. She reminds one, in her age and situation, of the first recipient of a divine promise of pregnancy—Sarah.

Think about your life and your world. What problems and situations do you regard as the most hopeless and terrible? God has promised to make our causes his own, to bring all things unto himself. For us, the birth of John was the preview of the birth of Jesus, who embodied the fullness of God's faithfulness. So we retell this story, impressed by its strangeness, its surprise. Then we look back over aspects of our lives that seem so hopeless and we remember: As long as God is faithful and busy, there is always reason to expect the unexpected, to believe his promise of love, and to hope.

Helping Adults Become Involved—Boyce A. Bowdon

Preparing to Teach

With this lesson we begin a new quarter of study entitled "Scenes of Love and Compassion."

Lessons for this quarter are based on selected passages from Luke's Gospel of key scenes in the story of Jesus.

To prepare yourself for teaching this quarter, read a good introduction to Luke's Gospel, such as the one found in *The Interpreter's Bible*, volume 8. Then read the Gospel of Luke in its entirety, preferably at one setting.

While reviewing Luke, jot down notes. Prepare a five-minute report to share with your class. Include such basic information as when Luke was written, by whom, for whom, and how it is like and how it is unlike Matthew and Mark.

As you read Luke 1, the scripture for this lesson, try to put yourself in the place of Zechariah and Elizabeth.

In Mike Winters's exegesis, you will find helpful information and insights about the historical setting. For example, Winters points out that childlessness in Jewish culture was a sign of God's disfavor and displeasure. This explains why Zechariah and Elizabeth were so confused and disturbed. Both of them were "righteous before God, walking in all the commandments and ordinances of the Lord blameless" (Luke 1:6). Naturally, they couldn't understand why God had deprived them of children. Have there been times when you have wondered why God was depriving you of something you wanted and deserved? When? What were the circumstances? Reflecting on those questions will help you identify with Zechariah and Elizabeth.

After completing your reading and research, reflect upon what you have learned. With the concerns and interests of your class members in mind, write down two goals that you hope to accomplish in this lesson, such as to help class members become more aware that (1) God often fulfills our wishes and dreams in ways that we never expected, and (2) our usefulness in God's service extends far beyond the time when society labels us obsolete and useless.

If you follow the suggestions presented below, you will need a supply of Bibles, pencils, and paper to distribute to your class, and newsprint and markers or a chalkboard and chalk.

Here is one way to outline this lesson:

> I. The scene of love and compassion
> II. Questions raised by the scene
> III. Message of the scene for us

Read carefully "The Scripture and the Main Question" and "As You Read the Scripture." These form the heart of the lesson. The ideas, insights, and suggestions in these sections should be reflected continually in your lesson plan.

As you use the suggested outline, you may want to either quote or paraphrase ideas. You might like to jot in the margin of your outline the page number and paragraph being referred to. For example, you could write a reference to page 65, paragraph 3, as 65-3.

SECOND QUARTER

Introducing the Main Question

Basic and helpful ideas are presented in the section "The Main Question." These ideas are essential in helping to identify the purpose of the lesson.

To get your class members' attention and to help them see immediately that this lesson deals with real-life issues, you may want to begin this session by asking the following questions:

Have you ever encountered disappointments that seemed undeserved?

Have your sometimes been inhibited by fear of the unexpected?

Have you ever discovered new opportunities in unexpected situations?

Have you ever been confused when your wishes and dreams were fulfilled?

Have you ever felt that you have passed the time of your usefulness?

After asking the questions, you might say, "If you answered yes to any of these questions, you should find it easy to identify with Zechariah and Elizabeth, the couple featured in this scripture lesson."

Developing the Lesson

I. The scene of love and compassion

Have last week's volunteers present their skit. Afterward, give class members time to react to the story. Ask them what message they found in the story.

II. Questions raised by the scene

Ask: What do we have in common with Zechariah and Elizabeth? To stimulate discussion, you may want to refer to the questions you used in introducing the lesson.

God communicated his promise to Zechariah and Elizabeth by sending the angel Gabriel to them. How does God communicate his promises to us?

God promised the couple that Elizabeth would give birth to a son. What has God promised us? Out of wishful thinking, we sometimes assume God has made promises that he has not made.

Here's an activity that should be helpful. Divide your class into four research teams. Assign team one the Gospel of Matthew, team two the Gospel of Mark, team three the Gospel of Luke, and team four the Gospel of John. Have each team check its respective Gospel for promises that Jesus made. Give them ten minutes to complete their research and then have a spokesperson from each team report to the total group. Have someone record the findings on newsprint or a chalkboard. After all four teams have reported, lead the class in briefly discussing each of the promises.

Helping Class Members Act

III. Message of the scene for us

In his introduction to this lesson, Dr. Willimon observes that "the question for today is, Are the promises of God dependable and trustworthy?"

That question is not just one for theologians to discuss and speculate about in academic debate. Like Zechariah and Elizabeth, we are inclined to ask, Can I count on God's promises?

Ask the class: Why do we sometimes doubt God's promises?

Zechariah paid a price for doubting God's promise to him. What price do we pay when we doubt his promises to us? You may want to share some of the helpful observations that Dr. Willimon makes on this in his exegesis.

Zechariah and Elizabeth were surprised when God's promise to them was fulfilled. Perhaps some member of the class would like to share an experience in which she or he was surprised when a promise from God was fulfilled.

Planning for Next Week

Next week's lesson will focus on Mary, the mother of Jesus, and her encounter with the angel Gabriel. Select two class members to re-create that encounter in a three-minute skit based on Luke 1:26-38. Ask the other class members to read Luke 1:26-56.

Accepting God's Promise

Background Scripture: Luke 1:26-56

The Main Question—William H. Willimon

Many things have changed in American religious life in my own lifetime. Particularly remarkable changes have occurred among Protestants and Catholics. I can still remember a man coming to our church when I was a young boy and speaking on the evils of Catholicism, how the Catholics were working to take over our country and how Protestants always needed to be vigilant in order to keep Catholics from getting too far ahead.

When asked about major differences between Protestant and Catholic beliefs, one significant example was our beliefs about Mary. Catholics, we were told, venerated Mary, gave her great prominence in their religion, and treated her almost equal with Jesus himself. Protestants, we were told, regarded Mary as a rather minor figure of the gospel.

This is most unfortunate, particularly for Protestants, because it taught us to push Mary into the the background of the gospel. Today's scripture reminds us that when Jesus was born, Mary moved to a central place in the story. In fact, biblical scholar Raymond Brown calls Mary, "the first and foremost disciple." There is no way to read the story of Jesus, particularly as Luke tells it, without seeing the central place this young woman occupies in the narrative of God's salvation.

The promise of God confronts a young peasant woman in a little town named Nazareth. Her dilemma, as well as her response, becomes a model of discipleship; you and I can see our own struggles with the promises of God reflected in her. What does this young woman have to teach us about the path of discipleship?

Selected Scripture

King James Version

Revised Standard Version

Luke 1:26-38

26 And in the sixth month the angel Ga'-bri-el was sent from God unto a city of Gal'-i-lee, named Naz'-a-reth,

27 To a virgin espoused to a man whose name was Jo'-seph, of the house of Da'-vid; and the virgin's name *was* Mar'-y.

28 And the angel came in unto her, and said, Hail, *thou that art* highly favoured, the Lord *is* with thee: blessed *art* thou among women.

29 And when she saw *him*, she was troubled at his saying, and cast in her mind what manner of salutation this should be.

30 And the angel said unto her, Fear not, Mar'-y: for thou hast found favour with God.

31 And, behold, thou shalt conveive in thy womb, and bring forth a son, and shalt call his name JE'-SUS.

32 He shall be great, and shall be called the Son of the Highest: and the Lord God shall give unto him the throne of his father Da'-vid:

33 And he shall reign over the house of Ja'-cob for ever; and of his kingdom there shall be no end.

34 Then said Mar'-y unto the angel, How shall this be, seeing I know not a man?

35 And the angel answered and said unto her, The Holy Ghost shall come upon thee, and the power of the Highest shall overshadow thee: therefore also that holy thing which shall be born of thee shall be called the Son of God.

36 And, behold, thy cousin E-lis'-a-beth, she hath also conceived a son in her old age: and this is the sixth

Luke 1:26-38

26 In the sixth month the angel Gabriel was sent from God to a city of Galilee named Nazareth, 27 to a virgin betrothed to a man whose name was Joseph, of the house of David; and the virgin's name was Mary. 28 And he came to her and said, "Hail, O favored one, the Lord is with you!" 29 But she was greatly troubled at the saying, and considered in her mind what sort of greeting this might be. 30 And the angel said to her, "Do not be afraid, Mary, for you have found favor with God. 31 And behold, you will conceive in your womb and bear a son, and you shall call his name Jesus.

32 He will be great, and will be called the Son of the Most High;
  and the Lord God will give to him the throne of his father David,

33 and he will reign over the house of Jacob for ever;
  and of his kingdom there will be no end."

34 And Mary said to the angel, "How can this be, since I have no husband?"

35 And the angel said to her,
  "The Holy Spirit will come upon you,
  and the power of the Most High will overshadow you;
  therefore the child to be born will be called holy,
  the Son of God.

36 And behold, your kinswoman Elizabeth in her old age has also conceived a son; and this is the sixth

month with her, who was called barren.

37 For with God nothing shall be impossible.

38 And Mar'-y said, Behold the handmaid of the Lord; be it unto me according to thy word. And the angel departed from her.

Key Verse: **Mary said, Behold the handmaid of the Lord; be it unto me according to thy word. (Luke 1:38)**

month with her who was called barren. 37 For with God nothing will be impossible." 38 And Mary said, "Behold, I am the handmaid of the Lord; let it be to me according to your word." And the angel departed from her.

Key Verse: **Mary said, "Behold, I am the handmaid of the Lord; let it be to me according to your word." (Luke 1:38)**

As You Read the Scripture—Mike Winters

Luke 1:26-38. The narrative includes the Annunciation, the archangel Gabriel's announcement of God's incarnation in Jesus.

Verse 26. The sixth month indicates the progress of Elizabeth's pregnancy with John rather than the time of year. The feast of the Annunciation is celebrated on March 25 in some Christian traditions. Galilee was a province in Palestine just north of Judea and west of the Sea of Galilee. Nazareth was one of seven cities of Galilee mentioned in the New Testament.

Verse 27. The virgin's name is Mary, it is discovered at the very end of the verse. In the phrase before her identity is revealed, her existence and identity are defined in terms of the man to whom she is betrothed. For a twentieth-century thinker, this is a foreign concept indeed. We affirm as modern people that each person's worth and dignity is his or hers alone, independent of any other person. The real surprise in this verse, to first-century people, is that God chose young, betrothed Mary, a woman, solely on her merits and her worth and without consulting the men in her life. Identifying Mary as a virgin may be simply a way of saying that this conceived child was special. And indeed the child conceived was the incarnate God. Very little is said, however, about the conception of Jesus in Scripture. This paragraph beginning with verse 26, in 3:23 where Jesus is said to be the "son (as was supposed) of Joseph" (the parenthesis being Luke's), and Matthew 1 are the only places in Scripture where evidence of Mary's special conception is found. The story is certainly important for its theological value, proclaiming this conceived child "Son of the Most High," but it should never become Christianity's acid test. The story is valuable because it says that this conceived child, though like all of us, is yet very unlike any of us. It is God.

Verse 28. The KJV adds to this verse, "Blessed art thou among women." This phrase was probably borrowed from verse 42.

Verse 29. Mary is afraid. She is troubled by the meaning of Gabriel's words to her. When Gabriel appeared to Zechariah, he too had been afraid. His fear, unlike Mary's, was of the angel's presence.

Verse 30. In verse 28 Mary is addressed as "O favored one." In this verse her favor with God is repeated

Verse 31. In Matthew 1:21 the announcement is made to Joseph in a dream. Here it is made to Mary.

Verses 32-33. Jesus will be in the messianic tradition of David. The Davidic dynasty transmitted the messianic hope. God's promise to David, who wished to build a temple for God, was instead to build David's dynasty into an everlasting kingdom (II Samuel 7:13-16). In that hope, each successive king (there was but one queen—Athalia; see II Kings 11) was anointed. Each monarch of that dynasty was the people's symbol of hope for a just, God-like rule on earth.

Verse 34. Mary understood the biology of conception quite well. Not at all unlike aged Zechariah, who pondered how his postmenopausal wife was to conceive, Mary asks in light of her virginity, "How can this be?" Note that Zechariah's incredulous "How?" resulted in a punishment, but Mary's inquiry results in an explanation of her conception and a confirming sign.

Verse 35. The angel explains to Mary the birds and bees of theological conception. The description of Mary's conception is not at all unlike the way Jesus is conceived in all of us; we call it faith. The idea that Christians are pregnant with Christ is a hopeful and intriguing image.

Verses 36-37. The confirming sign for Mary is the conception of her ancient, barren kinswoman, Elizabeth. These verses are the only ones that indicate Jesus' blood relationship to John.

Verse 38. This is Mary's "Ah ha!" experience. She understands what has happened and what is required of her.

The Scripture and the Main Question—William H. Willimon

The Promise of Salvation

Holding my child in my arms for the first time, I looked into his little face and wondered what this boy might become. Where will he go, what will he do? How high will he climb in his life? How low will he sink?

Any parent looking into the face of a newborn child must wonder the same things. As adults, we know how life can be. Life has its joys, yes. But it can also have its sadnesses, and they can be devastating.

What did Mary feel when she looked into the face of her newborn son? Simeon had told her that "a sword will pierce through your own soul also." Surely Mary knew enough to know that if this child was indeed God's Messiah, she had good reason to fear what the future might hold for him. What did it mean for Mary to hear the promise of God and say yes?

Time and again in the story of Israel, the Lord is depicted as the one who promises to save his people in their times of trouble. Noah was saved from the devastating flood. Jacob was preserved in Egypt. When they were in slavery, the Lord heard the cries of the oppressed people and led them to freedom through the work of Moses. When they were starving in the wilderness, the Lord gave his people manna and water from the rock. This is a God who hears and delivers.

Isaiah tells of the birth of a child who shall be named "Wonderful Counselor, Mighty God, Everlasting Father, Prince of Peace" (9:6). Whether or not Isaiah was thinking of Jesus, Christians immediately took these words and applied them to Jesus of Nazareth, who was their Counselor, Father, and Prince of Peace.

And the Virgin's Name Was Mary

When we have a good piece of news, it is natural for us to want to share that news with those who are closest to us. We carefully decided which close friends to share it with first, so they can join us in our celebration.

Luke says that when the time was right for God's Anointed One to be born, that news was carefully announced to certain privileged people. It is important for us to note who those chosen few were.

They are not the people one might have expected. The birth of the Messiah was not announced to the biblical scholars; in fact, they seem to have missed the whole thing! It was not announced to the priests in the temple or to the politicians in the statehouse. None of these high and mighty ones got the news.

The news comes first "to a virgin betrothed to a man whose name was Joseph, of the house of David; and the virgin's name was Mary" (1:27).

It might not shock us that Mary was the first to get the news; after all, she was the mother-to-be of the child. But to an early hearer of this story, living in second-century Palestine, this might seem a strange story indeed. In that part of the world, in that day, women were considered second-class citizens at best. Women were on the bottom of society, the virtual property of their husbands.

Not only are we told that Mary was a woman, but she was an unmarried woman. Women's only hope then was for a good marriage. As an unmarried woman, this Mary could have had no property or status. As an unmarried pregnant woman—well, you can imagine her difficult situation.

And yet it was to this person that the angel Gabriel first told the news, along with aging Zechariah and Elizabeth, who were also thought to be lowly, for other reasons.

Even in today's society, where advances have been made in social justice, women and the aging are often relegated to second-class status. These two groups are often on the poverty level. They are not traditionally thought to be among the powerful and influential. So we are able to sense some of the surprise and shock of this story of deliverance.

To this unmarried woman Gabriel says, "Hail! O favored one, the Lord is with you" (1:28).

The Favored One

From the way the story of the Annunciation reads, Mary was evidently frightened by the arrival of Gabriel. And why not? It is always a frightening thing to find oneself face-to-face with the purposes of God and to find out that you are chosen to be part of those purposes.

Perhaps Mary felt like her old kinswoman Sarah (wife of the father of their faith, Abraham), who was also told that she was to bear a child into the world. Sarah had laughed because it seemed impossible for a woman her age to give birth to a child. Mary did not laugh, but she was certainly frightened by the prospect of it all.

Mary was in an embarassing situation. Like Sarah before her, she felt herself out of place in the way the world judges right and wrong. She felt that she was the wrong person, and that it was the wrong time and the wrong place. But unlike Sarah, Mary responded not with a laugh but with "Behold, I am the handmaid of the Lord; let it be to me according to your word" (1:38).

135

In her response, Mary becomes a model for discipleship. In fact, Mary is often called the first disciple since she is the first in the story of Jesus to respond affirmatively to the call of God and to place her life at God's disposal.

"I am the handmaid of the Lord," she says. She is God's assistant, a co-worker with God in bringing about the deliverance of the people who sit in darkness.

Do you know any Marys in your church—people who are approached by God for some surprising, difficult, unexpected work of deliverance and who say yes?

When God's messengers come into your life, asking you to be God's assistant, will you be able to respond as Mary? Will you be able to see God working out salvation for the world through you?

Sweet Little Jesus Boy

One of our most provocative Christmas songs comes from black American Christians: "Sweet little Jesus boy, and we didn't know who you was."

Mary seems to have questioned who exactly her son was, when he took his bar mitzvah at the age of twelve. He and his cousin John (who would be called the Baptist, or baptizer) would have become sons of the covenant together, being the same age. Each boy probably asked questions that the priests and rabbis found difficult to answer.

When Mary and Joseph left Jerusalem for Nazareth, Jesus did not accompany them. When his parents finally found him at the great temple, he replied to their anxious questions, "Did you not know that I would be at my Father's?" (Luke 22:49. Note that the Greek omits the noun after "Father's." Did Jesus say, "At my Father's *house*?" *"business?" "concerns?"*) Mary was mystified by his response.

Later, Mary and her three other sons and daughters sought Jesus because he seemed to be "beside himself"—losing his mind. Having done those things that the Messiah was expected to do, she looked at her "sweet little Jesus boy," and wasn't sure who he was. So also wondered many a priest, rabbi, Pharisee, member of the Sanhedrin, procurator, and others. Who is this sweet little Jesus boy? Mary was not always as confident in later years as she was when he was a little baby boy. And Mary remembered those early years when Simeon had blessed her and said to her, "A sword will pierce through your own soul also." Who is this manger-born Jesus boy?

Helping Adults Become Involved—Boyce A. Bowdon

Preparing to Teach

Read Isaiah 9:2-7 and Luke 2:1-20.

Set an objective for the lesson, such as to remind class members that God calls to service all kinds of people, including some who are ordinary by society's standards.

Here is one way to outline the lesson:

     I.   The scene of love and compassion
    II.   Questions raised by the scene
   III.   Message of the scene for us

Read carefully "The Scripture and the Main Question" and "As You Read the Scripture." These form the heart of the lesson. The ideas, insights, and suggestions in these sections should be reflected continually in your lesson plan.

As you use the suggested outline, you may want to either quote or paraphrase ideas. You might like to jot in the margin of your outline the page number and paragraph being referred to. For example, you could write a reference to page 65, paragraph 3, as 65-3.

Introducing the Main Question

Basic and helpful ideas are presented in the section "The Main Question." These ideas are essential in helping to identify the purpose of the lesson.

Developing the Lesson

I. The scene of love and compassion

Present the role-play of Mary and the angel Gabriel, which was assigned to two class members at the end of last week's lesson.

Remind the class that last week's lesson was also about the announcement by the angel Gabriel of an approaching birth. In that lesson the mother-to-be was Elizabeth, a woman who was beyond the age for child bearing.

Ask the class to compare Mary's visit with Gabriel to Zechariah's visit with Gabriel. In what ways were the two visits similar? How did the responses of Zechariah and Elizabeth differ?

II. Questions raised by the scene

The passage we are studying in this lesson is one of two in the Gospels making reference to the virgin birth. Have someone read aloud the other one—Matthew 1:18-25—and ask the class to compare it to the Luke version.

The virgin birth issue is not one of the major concerns of this lesson. If you spend much time speculating and debating about it, you will not have time to accomplish your other goals. However, if some members of your class are disturbed and confused about the virgin birth issue, you probably should devote a few minutes to it.

You might point out that the virgin birth apparently was not a major concern of biblical writers. The Gospel of Mark makes no mention of a virgin birth. While the Gospel of John refers to the Word becoming flesh, it does not mention a virgin birth, and neither do the writings of Paul.

Paul and the early Christians were far more concerned about the life and ministry of Jesus, and for them what really mattered was his death and resurrection.

You might find it helpful to quote the following statement from Mike Winters's exegesis: "The story is certainly important for its theological value, proclaiming this conceived child 'Son of the Most High', but it should never become Christianity's acid test."

Dr. Winters observes that the point of the story is that even though Jesus was like us, he was not like us. He was the incarnate God.

Discuss God's choice of Mary as the mother of Jesus.

If you have a recording of the Magnificat, this would be an excellent time to play it for the class. If you don't have the recording, have someone read aloud Luke 1:46-55.

Draw attention to Luke 1:48, in which Mary praises God for "regarding the low estate of his handmaiden."

Acknowledge to the class that God does use wealthy, talented, educated, beautiful, gifted people in his work. You might list a few examples. But God also uses people who are ordinary by the standards of society, and even some who are often considered undesirable.

Read to your class the following quotation from Dr. Willimon's exposition: "The birth of the Messiah was not announced to the biblical scholars; in fact, they seem to have missed the whole thing! It was not announced to the priests in the temple or to the politicians in the statehouse. None of these high and mighty ones got the news. The news came first 'to a virgin betrothed to a man whose name was Joseph, of the house of David; and the virgin's name was Mary.' "

Ask the class to cite examples of "ordinary people" who played major roles in the ministry of Jesus and in the early years of the church. While the examples are being given, have someone list the persons named on newsprint. The list could be quite lengthy. Make sure it includes shepherds, fishermen, people like Peter and Andrew, and the other disciples.

Now focus on the present day. Ask the class: Is God still using ordinary people for extraordinary tasks? Ask for specific examples. Have these names listed on newsprint, too.

Helping Class Members Act

III. Message of the scene for us

Ask your class the question that Dr. Willimon poses in his exposition: "What did it mean for Mary to hear the promise of God and say yes?"

Dr. Willimon identifies Mary as "a model of discipleship" in whom "you and I can see our own struggles with the promises of God reflected." He asks the following main question, which you may ask your class: "What does this young woman have to teach us about the path of discipleship?"

After the class has had ample opportunity to express their views on this key question, you might focus attention on Luke 1:38. Read the passage aloud. Point out that Mary referred to herself as "the handmaid of the Lord." Since a handmaid was a servant, evidently she saw her mission not in terms of being served, but in terms of serving. That's one thing we can learn from Mary about being a disciple of Christ.

Make this point: Mary knew God was not choosing her because of her goodness; God was choosing her because of God's goodness. God was taking the initiative, just as he did when he chose Abraham, Moses, and others for special missions.

The Magnificat reflects a humble spirit. Mary praised God for mighty things he had done for her; she did not praise God for making a wise choice when he picked her.

How about us? How do we respond when God calls us to a mission?

Lead your class in reflecting upon the first statement the angel Gabriel made when he appeared to Mary: "Hail, O favored one, the Lord is with you!" Ask this question: In what sense was Mary a "favored one"? Allow ample time for discussion. Make sure this point is made: Mary was not favored in the sense that she was insulated from physical pain, mental anguish, or spiritual struggle. Ask for examples of the hardships Mary experienced.

Point out that those whom God calls to special missions today are also "favored people." But being favored is no guarantee of good health and prosperity.

Read to the class the last paragraph of Dr. Willimon's exposition: "When God's messengers come into your life, asking you to be God's assistant, will you be able to respond as Mary? Will you be able to see God working out salvation for the world through you?"

Planning for Next Sunday

Ask class members to read Luke 2:1-20.

Rejoicing in God's Greatness

Background Scripture: Luke 2:1-20

The Main Question—William H. Willimon

In the past couple of lessons we have been talking about the promises of God. Earlier we noted that as one looks across the headlines in this morning's newspaper, it is sometimes most difficult to believe that God is at work in today's events. Can you see any events in today's newspaper which suggest that even today the promises of God are being worked out among us?

Perhaps our problem is that it is always difficult to look at the "news" of the day and discern the "good news" (gospel) behind the headlines.

A number of years ago archeologists discovered a library of clay tablets in Egypt. Here were the records of the pharaohs of fourteen centuries before the birth of Jesus. Undoubtedly, they were looking at the library of the one who was the pharaoh just before the time of Moses and the Exodus. They found records listing how much wheat was bought and sold each year in Egypt, records that counted the number of cows and other livestock, records of every detail of Egyptian life.

In all these records there was not one mention of the thousands of Hebrew slaves who won their freedom from the pharaoh. The event that is, for those of us in the Judeo-Christian tradition, the key one of the period is not even mentioned! It is enough to make one wonder: Are there promises of God being fulfilled today which we are unable to see because of our lack of faith? Luke says that when Jesus was born, many failed to grasp the significance of his advent. They failed to rejoice at the promise fulfilled, because they were unable to see. How can we see?

SECOND QUARTER

Selected Scripture

King James Version

Luke 2:1-16

1 And it came to pass in those days, that there went out a decree from Cae'-sar Au-gus'-us that all the world should be taxed.

2 (*And* this taxing was first made when Cy-re'-ni-us was governor of Syr'-i-a.)

3 And all went to be taxed, every one into his own city.

4 And Jo'-seph also went up from Gal'-i-lee, out of the city of Naz'-a-reth, into Ju-dae'-a, unto the city of Da'-vid, which is called Beth'-le-hem; (because he was of the house and lineage of Da'-vid:)

5 To be taxed with Mar'-y his espoused wife, being great with child.

6 And so it was, that, while they were there, the days were accomplished that she should be delivered.

7 And she brought forth her firstborn son, and wrapped him in swaddling clothes, and laid him in a manger; because there was no room for them in the inn.

8 And there were in the same country shepherds abiding in the field, keeping watch over their flock by night.

9 And, lo, the angel of the Lord came upon them, and the glory of the Lord shone round about them: and they were sore afraid.

10 And the angel said unto them, Fear not: for, behold, I bring you good tidings of great joy, which shall be to all people.

11 For unto you is born this day in the city of Da'-vid a Saviour, which is Christ the Lord.

12 And this *shall be* a sign unto you; Ye shall find the babe wrapped in swaddling clothes, lying in a manger.

13 And suddenly there was with

Revised Standard Version

Luke 2:1-16

1 In those days a decree went out from Caesar Augustus that all the world should be enrolled. 2 This was the first enrollment, when Quirin'i-us was governor of Syria. 3 And all went to be enrolled, each to his own city. 4 And Joseph also went up from Galilee, from the city of Nazareth, to Judea, to the city of David, which is called Bethlehem, because he was of the house and lineage of David, 5 to be enrolled with Mary his betrothed, who was with child. 6 And while they were there, the time came for her to be delivered. 7 And she gave birth to her first-born son and wrapped him in swaddling cloths, and laid him in a manger, because there was no place for them in the inn.

8 And in that region there were shepherds out in the field, keeping watch over their flock by night. 9 And an angel of the Lord appeared to them, and the glory of the Lord shone around them, and they were filled with fear. 10 And the angel said to them, "Be not afraid; for behold, I bring you good news of a great joy which will come to all the people; 11 for to you is born this day in the city of David a Savior, who is Christ the Lord. 12 And this will be a sign for you: you will find a babe wrapped in swaddling cloths and lying in a manger." 13 And suddenly there was with the angel a multitude of the heavenly host praising God and saying,

"Glory to God in the highest,

140

the angel a multitude of the heavenly host praising God, and saying,

14 Glory to God in the highest, and on earth peace, good will toward men.

15 And it came to pass, as the angels were gone away from them into heaven, the shepherds said one to another. Let us now go even unto Beth'-le-hem, and see this thing which is come to pass, which the Lord hath made known unto us.

16 And they came with haste, and found Mar'-y, and Jo'-seph, and the babe lying in a manger.

Key Verse: **She brought forth her firstborn son, and wrapped him in swaddling clothes, and laid him in a manger; because there was no room for them in the inn. (Luke 2:7)**

and on earth peace among men with whom he is pleased!"

15 When the angels went away from them into heaven, the shepherds said to one another, "Let us go over to Bethlehem and see this thing that has happened, which the Lord has made known to us." 16 And they went with haste, and found Mary and Joseph, and the babe lying in a manger.

Key Verse: **She gave birth to her first-born son and wrapped him in swaddling cloths, and laid him in a manger, because there was no place for them in the inn. (Luke 2:7)**

As You Read the Scripture—Mike Winters

Luke 2:1-16. In Luke's Gospel the birth narrative is given more detail than in Matthew's Gospel. Luke tells how it happened that Jesus was born in Bethlehem of Judea to homeless and displaced parents and that shepherds, aglow from the angels' visitation, herded their sheep to Bethlehem so they could "see this thing that has happened." In Matthew's Gospel, Jesus is named at the announcement of his birth (Matthew 1:25). In Luke's account, however, Jesus is not named until eight days later, at his circumcision (Luke 2:21).

Verse 1. Caesar Augustus was emperor of Rome from 27 B.C.–A.D. 14. The phrase "that all the world should be enrolled" no doubt refers only to the Roman Empire.

Verse 2. The historian Josephus referred to a census during the time when Quirinius was governor of Syria, which he calls "the first enrollment." The date of this census was twelve or thirteen years after Jesus' birth. There is no other historical mention of a census at this time. The census that Josephus mentions was noteworthy to him because the order resulted in unrest in the Galilean provinces.

Verses 3-4. That everyone "went to be enrolled, each to his own city" seems a curious mandate indeed, especially since the Roman government cared nothing about Jewish lineage. The result, however, for Luke was to move Mary and Joseph from a Nazareth to a Bethlehem setting. This was, perhaps, to fulfill a messianic promise (Micah 5:2). Luke traces Jesus' genealogy back to David through his "supposed" father, Joseph (3:23-31).

Verse 5. One's "betrothed" is the person to whom one is engaged. Its Middle English root is "troth." "Troth" is the word a person uses to "enter a covenant with another, a pledge to engage in a . . . relationship forged of trust and faith in the face of unknowable risks" (Parker Palmer, *To Know As*

SECOND QUARTER

We Are Known: A Spirituality of Education. [San Francisco: Harper and Row, 1983] p. 31). Joseph and Mary were facing unknowable risks, for messianic promises, though full of hope, are full of uncertainty.

Verses 6-7. Jesus was the first-born son of Joseph and Mary (see Luke 8:19). Jesus had at least four brothers and two sisters (Mark 6:3). The term "brother" in Semitic usage may also refer to other blood relationships. "Swaddling cloths" were simply strips of cloth wrapped around newborns. A "manger" is a feeding trough for livestock.

Verse 8. Luke's Gospel tells us that Jesus was born at night during the season of the year when sheep were kept in fields. If this is so, Jesus' birth was between April and November.

Verse 9. It is significant that Luke records the angels' appearing to shepherds rather than to people of power, position, or wealth. The whole point of the incarnation is that God took on a humble form. The shepherds' fear might best be understood as awe.

Verses 10-12. The good news announced to the shepherds was good news for *all people.* Can it be a message of hope even for unbelievers? The news was the announcement of a Savior, one who cares about a person's character and well-being, both spiritual and physical. It was an announcement of the Christ, the one who will fulfill messianic expectations. It was an announcement of the Lord, one who is sovereign, the creator, the victor over death. Zechariah's angelic sign was to be struck mute (Luke 1:20). Mary's sign was old and barren Elizabeth's pregnancy (Luke 1:36). The shepherds' sign was a baby "wrapped in swaddling cloths and lying in a manger."

Verses 13-14. Here is the announcement of a new day of peace, in the sense of "shalom." This Hebrew word means health, wholeness, justice—when everything is right. It expresses a world view. The Greek word for peace is a rather negative term indicating merely the absence of conflict or war. The passage may also be rendered to express more inclusiveness, as in the KJV.

Verses 15-16. There is always a response to good news. The shepherds responded by going "to Bethlehem to see [witness or confirm] this thing." Our response to God's grace is an act of confirmation of God's love. It is our witness.

The Scripture and the Main Question—William H. Willimon

Seeing, They Do Not See

Probably, you have seen the little visual puzzle. Someone presents you with a card printed with some black splotches. What is it? you are asked. You look at it carefully. It's the face of a cow—yes, that's what it is, a photograph of a Guernsey cow. Then the person points out to you a beard, the eyes, the hair. It is a picture of Christ!

It all depends on your point of view—what you are looking for, your perspective. Once you see it, you wonder how you could have missed it. It all seems so clear, so obvious. Once it's pointed out to you, you see it well. Before, you saw nothing.

In a way, that's how Luke presents this story of the birth of Jesus. To him, it seems incredible that so many who waited for so long for the arrival of the

142

Messiah were so blind to the reality of his advent. Everyone waited, but not all were able to see. Why?

Sometimes we don't see because we're looking for the wrong thing or looking in the wrong direction. A few years ago, I spent a number of frustrating hours searching in vain for Halley's Comet. A friend of mine, an amateur astronomer, was ecstatic about his sighting. Even with my borrowed sky maps and small telescope, I couldn't tell what I was looking for.

When Jesus was born, many missed him because they were looking in the wrong direction. When the Messiah came, they thought, he would appear to the powerful, people like King Herod in his great palace. If the Messiah were coming to liberate the oppressed from the yoke of Roman occupation, then he would be found among the armed Zealots in the Judean hills waiting for a chance to attack the Romans and put them in their place. Or surely the Messiah is to be found among those who revere and love God's word—the scholars in the temple who have devoted every moment of their lives to the study of the Scriptures.

But no, the Messiah slips into human history quietly, unexpectedly, born to a poor young woman and her carpenter husband in a manger in Bethlehem.

You and I ought to have more sympathy than scorn for all those who failed to see the Christ's arrival, for we know that we also tend to look in wrong places for the works of God. Our newspaper headlines are filled with politics, power, prestige, and possessions. Our newsmakers are not carpenters or poor outcasts in backwater towns like Bethlehem. The television news commentators rarely travel to cow stables for material for the six-thirty news report!

In Those Days There Went Out a Decree from Caesar

Centuries before that memorable night in Bethlehem, a melancholy man named Job sat dejected and cried out, "God, where are you? Why do you not show yourself?" It is the cry of the suffering and dejected of every age.

A young man named Elihu took Job's cry as a challenge to the goodness of God. Attempting to defend God's seeming absence, he retorted:

> Why do you contend against him,
>   Saying, "He will answer none of my words"?
> For God speaks in one way,
>   and in two, though man does not perceive it.
>   (Job 33:13-14)

In his misery, Job could not see that God could be near him.

The biblical record is replete with illustrations of God reaching out to people in ways and times they could not imagine: Jacob wrestling at midnight on the banks of the river Jabbok, Moses before the strange fiery bush while he tended his father-in-law's sheep, Isaiah at the temple in the year that King Uzziah died, old Zechariah and Elizabeth childless for so long. But all of these visitations pale before the wonder of "the Word made flesh" in a stable in a little town called Bethlehem.

God promises to come among us. But will our eyes be open to God's advent? So many of the blinders—cultural, psychological, spiritual, political—that kept them from seeing the Babe at Bethlehem as God's Messiah also keep us from seeing.

"In those days a decree went out from Caesar Augustus that all the world should be taxed" (Luke 2:1). Has it ever struck you what a strange way this is to begin the story of Jesus' nativity? Even though this is a story about Jesus, we are accustomed to reading our history from the viewpoint of world leaders and esteemed politicians. "During the Eisenhower Administration," we say. "While Elizabeth reigned over England." "During the regime of Fidel Castro in Cuba."

Usually, when you study history in high school or college you spend most of your time learning the names and dates of people like Augustus Caesar—important, powerful people who shook and ruled the world. These are the people we read of in history books and newspapers.

But when Luke mentions such once-famous politicians as Augustus, Quirinius, and Herod, we note a strange irony. Luke never sticks in a detail like this unless he has some theological purpose in mind. Is Luke attempting to say more with this mention of these distinguished Romans than merely to give us the dates of Jesus' Nativity? Yes, more than the date, he is giving us insight into the *meaning* of the Nativity!

For by the time Luke wrote his Gospel, no one save a few historians remembered Augustus, much less Quirinius. These men, once so powerful, whose word could once spell death to thousands, so feared and hated or admired in their own day, were now dead and gone. At one time, Augustus could send out a decree and command poor Jewish families like Jesus' to journey many miles just to be enrolled (so he could keep track of his Jewish subjects). But where is he now?

And where is that poor, homeless baby born that night to Mary and Joseph in Bethlehem? The one for whom there was no room, the one who the newspapers ignored and the Roman historians forgot; this little baby has now turned Caesar's world upside down. Caesar's mighty legions could not stop the spread of his truth and his light.

Therein, says Luke, is the irony. What the world considers important and noteworthy often fades into insignificance. And what the world ignores or relegates to some forgotten cow stable is often the key to the world's future. Because God doesn't always work in the way that we think.

Search the starlit December skies for a sign, look into the secret places of your own heart for a word, come to church this Sunday anticipating a vision, for now, even as then, God is moving among us, coming close to us and we, looking in the wrong places, often miss the whole thing. Watch.

Helping Adults Become Involved—Boyce A. Bowden

Preparing to Teach

With Christmas only a week away, the scripture passage in this lesson is certainly timely. It is the beloved Nativity story that most of us have been hearing every Christmas for as long as we can remember.

The familiarity of the passage can create a problem. We hear the words, "In those days a decree went out from Caesar Augustus that all the world should be taxed," and immediately we tend to stop listening closely. Why? Because we know what is coming next. The trouble is, even though we have heard the passage many times, we may have never examined it carefully.

In *Overhearing the Gospel* (Nashville: Abingdon, 1978), Fred Craddock asks how we can teach people who already know the story, or preach to people who have already heard it.

Craddock points out that some Christians are "so well wadded . . . that when the sermon begins they tend to tune out and turn off the old, old story." He observes that some "who say, 'Here we go again' have not in fact ever gone before" (pp. 26-27).

Without questioning their sincerity, the same observation could be made about many persons in Sunday school classes. Many of us have overheard more than we have understood. Therefore, one objective for this lesson might be to help class members find a fresh message in this familiar passage.

Here is one way to outline the lesson:

    I.   The scene of love and compassion
   II. Questions raised by the scene
  III. Message of the scene for us

Read carefully "The Scripture and the Main Question" and "As You Read the Scripture." These form the heart of the lesson. The ideas, insights, and suggestions in these sections should be reflected continually in your lesson plan.

As you use the suggested outline, you may want to either quote or paraphrase ideas. You might like to jot in the margin of your outline the page number and paragraph being referred to. For example, you could write a reference to page 65, paragraph 3, as 65-3.

Have Bibles, paper, and pencils available for all. Provide a selection of Bible commentaries and dictionaries.

Introducing the Main Question

Basic and helpful ideas are presented in the section "The Main Question." These ideas are essential in helping to identify the purpose of the lesson.

Explore with the class Dr. Willimon's main question: Are there promises of God being fulfilled today that we are unable to see because of our lack of faith?

I. The scene of love and compassion

Have someone read aloud Luke 2:1-20.

How can you make this dramatic scene come alive? Paraphrasing could be one of the most effective methods of helping your class take a fresh look at the passage.

Distribute Bibles, paper, and pencils. Ask each person to rewrite Luke 2:1-20, using as few of the original words in the text as possible. Invite the class to consult a Bible commentary or dictionary. Limit the time for rewriting to about ten minutes.

Ask for volunteers to read their versions. Take time to examine interesting insights and interpretations. Pass along several of the most creative and insightful versions to your pastor; he or she might want to use them in worship sessions, in church newsletters, or elsewhere.

II. Questions raised by the scene

In each of the two previous lessons, an angel has appeared; first to

Zechariah and then to Mary. It happens again in this lesson. This time an angel appears to the shepherds. Ask the class to compare the three encounters. What do they have in common? Make sure these similarities are included: In each case, (1) the initial reaction of the one to whom the angel appears is fear, (2) a message is given, and (3) a sign is offered.

All Luke reports is that the baby Jesus is "wrapped in swaddling clothes and lying in a manger." Ask this question: Why does Luke's announcement of the birth of Jesus tell us so much about the shepherds and so little about the baby and his parents? There is no mention of the size, the appearance, or the temperament of the child.

Point out to the class that shepherds were common people. To care properly for their flocks, they could not always observe ceremonial niceties. Consequently, they were despised by the religiously orthodox.

Read to the class the following statement contained in Mike Winters' exegesis: "It is significant that Luke records the angels' appearing to shepherds rather than to people of power, position, or wealth. The whole point of the incarnation is that God took on a humble form."

Ask this question: What difference does it make that God took on a humble form? What if he had taken the form of a military hero, as the Jews were expecting? Would it have made a difference? Why?

In "The Scripture and The Main Question," Will Willimon points out that many people missed Jesus when he was born because they were looking in the wrong direction. They expected the Messiah to be seen among the powerful, such as Herod in his great palace, or among the armed Zealots in the Judean hills waiting for a chance to attack the Romans, or among the scholars in the temple who devoted almost every moment of their lives to studying the Scriptures.

He concludes by saying: "You and I ought to have more sympathy than scorn for all those who failed to see the Christ's arrival, for we know that we also tend to look in the wrong places for the works of God."

Ask class members if they agree that we tend to look in the wrong places for the works of God. Where do we look? Where should we look?

Read this quote from Dr. Willimon to the class: "The biblical record is replete with illustrations of God reaching out to people in ways and times they could not imagine."

Ask your class members to divide into small groups of no more than three or four people and to share with one another, if they would like, personal experiences that illustrate how God reaches out to people in surprising ways and at strange times.

After this time of sharing, invite anyone who would like to do so to share his or her story with the entire class.

While the class is still divided into small groups, read this quote from Dr. Willimon: "What the world considers important and noteworthy often fades into insignificance. And what the world ignores or relegates to some forgotten cow stable is often the key to the world's future. Because God doesn't always work in the way that we think."

Ask class members who want to do so to share experiences from their own lives when God worked in ways they were not expecting.

Helping Class Members Act

III. Message of the scene for us

Ask class members to act on what they have learned today by resolving during the coming week to do the following:

— Spend a few minutes each day pondering the meaning of the birth of Jesus. What difference does it really make that God came to earth in the form of a child?
— Reflect a few minutes each day about how God is working in unexpected ways in your life.
— Take advantage of every opportunity to share with another person what you believe to be the real meaning of Christmas.
— Rejoice in God's greatness each day and help others to rejoice, too.

Planning for Next Sunday

Ask class members to read Isaiah 35 and Luke 2:21-40. Ask for a volunteer to prepare a ten-minute report on Jewish messianic expectations at the time of Christ. *The Interpreter's Dictionary of the Bible*, volume 3, pages 360-65, containing a good discussion of the topic.

LESSON 4   DECEMBER 25

Celebrating the Savior's Birth

Background Scripture: Luke 2:21-40

The Main Question—William H. Willimon

A few years ago, the last time that Christmas fell on a Sunday, our church's Council on Ministries was discussing plans for celebrating Advent and Christmas. "We have a big problem this year," one man said.

"What is the problem?" another asked.

"Haven't you looked at the calendar? This year Christmas falls on Sunday. Will we have church that Sunday or simply call things off? Everybody will probably be out of town. I am sure that people are not planning on coming to church on Christmas Day with all the other things they have to do."

Is this finally what has happened to Christmas? Have we so misplaced our priorities, allowed the unimportant things to crowd out the important, that on the occasion when Christmas falls on a Sunday, this is a problem for us rather than a glorious opportunity?

What better way to celebrate the arrival of Christ into this waiting world? What better time to gather at church and celebrate Sunday within the context of the fulfillment of our hope?

So often Sunday morning is a reminder of everything that isn't right with our world. We meet and look with discouragement on the size of the congregation gathered there that day. "Where is everybody else?" we ask.

This Sunday, of all Sundays, ought to be different. This Sunday the scripture is not about waiting and expectation, as are so many of the scriptures we study. Today's scripture is about *fulfillment*. The people who have sat waiting in darkness have seen light.

For what are you waiting? For what good are you standing on tiptoes in expectation?

The main question is: What are the hopes that sustained Simeon and Anna and many of their Jewish contemporaries, and that sustain us too?

Selected Scripture

King James Version	Revised Standard Version

Luke 2:25-38

25 And, behold, there was a man in Je-ru'-sa-lem, whose name *was* Sim'-e-on; and the same man *was* just and devout, waiting for the consolation of Is'-ra-el: and the Holy Ghost was upon him.

26 And it was revealed unto him by the Holy Ghost, that he should not see death, before he had seen the Lord's Christ.

27 And he came by the Spirit into the temple: and when the parents brought in the child Je'-sus, to do for him after the custom of the law,

28 Then took he him up in his arms, and blessed God, and said,

29 Lord, now lettest thou thy servant depart in peace, according to thy word:

30 For mine eyes have seen thy salvation,

31 Which thou hast prepared before the face of all people;

32 A light to lighten the Gen'-tiles, and the glory of thy people Is'-ra-el.

33 And Jo'seph and his mother marvelled at those things which were spoken of him.

34 And Sim'-e-on blessed them, and said unto Mar'-y his mother, Behold, this *child* is set for the fall and rising again of many in Is'-ra-el; and for a sign which shall be spoken against;

35 (Yea, a sword shall pierce through thy own soul also,) that the thoughts of many hearts may be revealed.

Luke 2:25-38

25 Now there was a man in Jerusalem, whose name was Simeon, and this man was righteous and devout, looking for the consolation of Israel, and the Holy Spirit was upon him. 26 And it had been revealed to him by the Holy Spirit that he should not see death before he had seen the Lord's Christ. 27 And inspired by the Spirit he came into the temple; and when the parents brought in the child Jesus, to do for him according to the custom of the law, 28 he took him up in his arms and blessed God and said,

29 "Lord, now lettest thou thy
    servant depart in peace,
  according to thy word;
30 for mine eyes have seen thy
    salvation
31 which thou hast prepared in the
    presence of all peoples,
32 a light for revelation to the
    Gentiles,
  and for glory to thy people Isra-
    el."

And his father and his mother marveled at what was said about him; 34 and Simeon blessed them and said to Mary his mother,

  "Behold, this child is set for the
    fall and rising of many in
    Israel,
  and for a sign that is spoken
    against
35 (and a sword will pierce through
    your own soul also),
  that thoughts out of many hearts
    may be revealed."

36 And there was one An'-na, a prophetess, the daughter of Pha-nu'-el, of the tribe of A'-ser: she was of a great age, and had lived with an husband seven years from her virginity;

37 And she *was* a widow of about fourscore and four years, which departed not from the temple, but served *God* with fastings and prayers night and day.

38 And she coming in that instant gave thanks likewise unto the Lord, and spake of him to all them that looked for redemption in Je-ru'-sa-lem.

36 And there was a prophetess, Anna, the daughter of Phan'u-el, of the tribe of Asher; she was of a great age, having lived with her husband seven years from her virginity, 37 and as a widow till she was eighty-four. She did not depart from the temple, worshiping with fasting and prayer night and day. 38 And coming up at that very hour she gave thanks to God, and spoke of him to all who were looking for the redemption of Jerusalem.

Key Verse: **Mine eyes have seen thy salvation, which thou hast prepared before the face of all people. (Luke 2:30-31)**

Key Verse: **Mine eyes have seen thy salvation which thou hast prepared in the presence of all peoples. (Luke 2:30-31)**

As You Read the Scripture—Mike Winters

Luke 2:21-40. Eight days after Jesus' birth, he was circumcised and named. The name Jesus means "savior." After a period of forty days, Mary and Joseph went to Jerusalem for the ritual of purification. Leviticus 12: 6-8 describes the ritual for a woman's purification after she has given childbirth. In the RSV, verse 22 indicates that Joseph also participated in the ritual, which is not indicated in the KJV. It is while Mary, Joseph, and the baby Jesus are in Jerusalem for this ritual that Luke introduces the holy man Simeon and the prophetess Anna.

Verse 25. Simeon's name was a common one among Jews. His life was lived expecting the fulfilment of God's messianic promises, "looking for the consolation of Israel." "The Holy Spirit was upon him" is Luke's way of saying that Simeon has something very special to say (see Luke 4:18 for comparison).

Verse 26. The Holy Spirit revealed to Simeon that he would see the "Lord's Christ" in his own lifetime. The word "Christ" is the Greek translation of the Hebrew word "Messiah," meaning "the Anointed." All of Judah's and Israel's monarchs were anointed in this same messianic promise. Jesus' disciples proclaim Jesus the Christ in Luke 9:20; there, Peter professes Jesus as "the Christ of God."

Verse 27. Luke's narrative confuses the custom of presenting an infant in the temple with rite of purification. The rite of purification did not require the presence of the infant. The timing of Simeon's presence in the temple was providential, inspired. At the right moment he was there to see Jesus. The promise made to him was thus fulfilled.

Verse 28. In the spirit, Simeon entered the temple and took Jesus in his arms. Simeon blessed God. Our prayers today usually ask for God's blessing, a significant departure from Simeon's style, who instead "blessed God."

Verses 29-32. These verses are called the Nunc Dimittis. The name is from the Latin translation of the first words in verse 29. Its theme is the salvation of *all* people. The readers of Luke cannot easily dismiss universalism, the concept that all will be saved.

Verse 29. Simeon acknowledged the fulfillment of the promise in verse 26. He announced that he has fulfilled his purpose in life. The imagery from the words "lettest thou thy servant depart in peace" depicts the freeing of a slave.

Verse 30. The salvation of God was a messianic hope. The idea of seeing salvation is a way of describing its relevation, of understanding it (Luke 3:6).

Verse 31. The hope of salvation is "prepared in the presence of all people," where it can be seen and grasped and understood.

Verse 32. Salvation as Israel's "glory" and the Gentiles' "light" was a theme of God's covenant promises. Abraham's descendants were blessed to be a blessing to the nations (Genesis 12:2, especially Isaiah 42:6).

Verse 33. Gabriel's appearance to Mary (1:26), the shepherds' confirmation (2:15-17), and now Simeon's prophecy compounded Mary's and Joseph's wonder. For Jews, every firstborn son was conceived into the messianic promise, but there was only one Messiah. The marvel was the independent confirmations of this hope in the child, Jesus.

Verse 34. The rise and fall of many refers to the judgment separating the righteous from the unrighteous.

Verse 35. Jesus will be a source of grief for Mary.

Verses 36-38. Under circumstances similar to Simeon's, the prophetess Anna meets the baby Jesus and thanks God. She too saw in Jesus his messianic future. Like Simeon's "consolation of Israel" (verse 25), Anna's "redemption of Jerusalem" alludes to the promised Messiah. Anna's life was dedicated to service in the temple. There were, of course, restrictions on that service, because she was a woman.

The Scripture and the Main Question—William H. Willimon

Mine Eyes Have Seen Thy Salvation

I suppose if we took our cue from the Christmas angels, we should be beside ourselves with joy as we at last come to the long-awaited Christmas Day. We should be running about to tell someone the good news of the birth of Christ.

The word "angel" comes from the Greek word for "messenger." Our word "evangelism" comes from a similar root. It means "good messages" or "good news." An evangelist is someone who tells the good news of Jesus Christ to others.

When Jesus was born, says Luke, his family, being devout Jews, took him to the temple for the ritual of purification. There, an old man named Simeon, "righteous and devout, looking for the consolation of Israel," saw who the child was and praised God (Luke 2:25).

In bringing old Simeon center stage, Luke again, in his subtle and skillful way, impresses us that Jesus—the Messiah born among the poor and lowly, to an unmarried mother, announced to poor shepherds—was sent to those on the fringes of society. Alas, in Jesus' society, even as in our own, older people were often pushed to the periphery of things. When people become nonproductive in our society, we tend to think of them as insignificant. So we put our older citizens away in nursing homes or centers for the elderly.

Luke doesn't want us to miss the fact that it was to an old man that the truth of the Christ appeared. When even his own parents could see little more than a charming baby boy, this old man could see that this child is nothing less than "thy salvation which thou hast prepared in the presence of all peoples" (Luke 2:30-31).

He Blessed God

Someone has just been to the doctor for a test. The lump that has been growing on the back of the neck looks suspicious. Is it malignant? There is the anxious waiting, the unknowing. Then at last, the results come back. Praise God! The test is negative. No problem, no problem at all.

Who will she tell the good news to first? Who will be the privileged one? Watch carefully, for the one she selects to tell first will be that person who means the most to her, her closest friend and confidant. So as we continue to study the story of the good news of Jesus' birth, let us note to whom the good news is revealed, for that will tell us much about the nature of the good news.

In previous lessons we noted how curiously the birth of Jesus is reported by Luke. Caesar requires all the world to be taxed. Yet moving in silently, in the form of a baby, is the Son of God. Caesar, so powerful in the world's eyes, will be defeated by this little baby, before the story is over.

Then Luke turns our attention away from the manger toward the fields outside Bethlehem. There, keeping watch over their flocks, are shepherds—among the lowest orders of Near Eastern society. Their work was regarded as menial and demeaning. Yet it was to these poor, lowly people that God's angel came to give the good news.

Had not Mary sung, when she was told she was to give birth to Jesus:

> He has put down the mighty from their thrones,
> and exalted those of low degree;
> he has filled the hungry with good things,
> and the rich he has sent empty away.
> (Luke 1:52-53)

Mary sings of a Messiah who comes to save the poor and the oppressed, to liberate the downtrodden. That Messiah's appearance is confirmed by the angel's song to the shepherds. Now, in today's scripture, an old man named Simeon is doing the singing.

No wonder that singing is such an important part of our Christmas celebrations. In the opening chapters of Luke's Gospel, everyone does seem to be singing—Mary, Zechariah, the angels, Simeon. There are moments in life when prose just will not do, when only poetry can express our deepest feelings. There are times when we need music in order to adequately express our joy.

The birth of Jesus is recorded by Luke as an occasion of that kind. It is as if the whole world were breaking into song. Little wonder that when you and I think of the miracle of Christmas, we find that we must do so through Christmas carols and poetry.

Here is a preview of the sort of ministry Jesus will undertake when he becomes an adult. He will not save by lording over people, by using force

151

and power. That is the world's way. Rather, he will yoke himself in solidarity with those he comes to save. He will become one of them, stand beside them, suffer as they suffer, and die as they die.

Other religions speak of salvation by the gods whom they worship. But only Christianity makes this bold affirmation of a God who loves so much that he dares to become a human being—not only that, but dares to become an *infant* human being, a *poor* infant human being. This is the miracle of the incarnation, which separates Christianity from the rest of the world's great faiths.

The Danish philosopher Søren Kierkegaard tells the parable of the king who wished to tell his subjects how much he loved and cared for them. How could he tell them? A royal decree? No, that was too cold, too aloof. "What does a king really know about us?" they would ask.

He could come among them in his royal robes with his soldiers and an impressive entourage, but that would be too grand. They would all bow down before him, not out of love but out of fear. That was not what he wanted.

So he decided to come among them dressed in rags, as some of them dressed. He would live where they lived and thereby would show them the way to a more abundant life. His love would be demonstrated by his presence as one of them.

Ironically, the people's reaction, when the king in rags revealed who he really was, was anything but admiration.

"This man can't be our king," they shouted. "Kings are high and lifted up, not like us. Kings are all-powerful, not lowly. We will not have this poor man for our king!"

It would be wonderful to remain in the warm glow of the manger, to stay in perpetual adoration before the infant Christ. But no, we must go back home, back to the fields or the office, the classroom or the nursing home. There is where the battle must be fought, there is where the message and mission of Christ rises or falls. It is there that the real Christmas song must be sung.

Can we leave church this morning singing as did Simeon, confident that God is moving in this child to bring salvation to all? Let us then join our voices with his:

> Lord, now lettest thou thy servant depart in peace,
> according to thy word;
> for mine eyes have seen thy salvation
> which thou hast prepared in the presence of all peoples.
> (Luke 2:29-31)

Helping Adults Become Involved—Boyce A. Bowdon

Preparing to Teach

Read Isaiah 35, Luke 2:21-40, and, if possible, *The Interpreter's Bible,* volume 8, pages 59-66.

With the needs and concerns of your class members in mind, set some objectives for this lesson. For example, your objectives might be to help class members become more aware of the importance of hope in their lives, and to affirm to them that our only basis of hope is in God.

The lesson should help class members better understand the hopes for a Messiah that sustained Simeon and Anna and many of their Jewish contemporaries, and ourselves as well.

If you have followed the suggestions offered in the three previous lessons of this unit, you have used several role-plays. The effectiveness of this teaching method may be diminishing, but if you think your group would enjoy and profit from one more, then try this: Enlist players to assume the roles of Mary, Joseph, Simeon, and Anna, and have them prepare a short portrayal of the scene described in Luke 2:21-40.

Here is one way to outline the lesson:

I.   The scene of love and compassion
II. Questions raised by the scene
III. Message of the scene for us

Read carefully "The Scripture and the Main Question" and "As You Read the Scripture." These form the heart of the lesson. The ideas, insights, and suggestions in these sections should be reflected continually in your lesson plan.

As you use the suggested outline, you may want to either quote or paraphrase ideas. You might like to jot in the margin of your outline the page number and paragraph being referred to. For example, you could write a reference to page 65, paragraph 3, as 65-3.

Have available pencils, paper, and newsprint and markers or a chalkboard and chalk.

Introducing the Main Question

Basic and helpful ideas are presented in the section "The Main Question." These ideas are essential in helping to identify the purpose of the lesson.

William Willimon refers to a church member who was wondering if church should be called off on Sunday because it would be Christmas Day and people would have too many other things to do to attend services.

You might want to read that section to your class or tell it in your own words. Then ask class members how they felt about coming to church today. What are the advantages to Christmas's falling on Sunday? What are the disadvantages?

A good way to introduce the lesson on this Christmas Sunday would be to focus attention for a few moments on last week's assigned scripture reading, which is an expression of the Christmas promise.

Have a class member read the passage aloud. Then point out that Isaiah 35:1-10 reflects the spirit of the prophet Isaiah even though it may have been written centuries after Isaiah's death.

Point out that this was a message of hope for people who had no visible reason to hope. The ground for their hope was not in themselves, because they were powerless. Their hope was in God, because God was all-powerful and would come and save the faithful remnant.

Developing the Lesson

I. The scene of love and compassion

Have someone distribute pencils and paper to the class. Have last week's volunteer present the report on the Messianic expectation, or present it yourself if necessary. Tell the class to write down characteristics the Messiah was expected to possess, as they are mentioned during the report.

Spend a few minutes discussing the report. Ask class members to share their lists of the characteristics of the Messiah; write these on newsprint. Display the newsprint in a prominent place for review during the remainder of the class session.

Lead the class in a careful examination of the scripture for this lesson, Luke 2:21-40. A good way to do this is to share insights from Mike Winters' exegesis that you think might help your class gain a better understanding of Simeon and Anna. Present the role-play of the meeting of Mary, Joseph, Anna, and Simeon, and discuss it.

II. Questions raised by the scene

Dr. Willimon explains in his exposition that older people in the days of Jesus were pushed to the periphery of things, just as they are today, because of declining ability to produce. He observes that "Luke doesn't want us to miss the fact that it was to an old man that the truth of the Christ appeared."

As a means of reviewing the previous lessons of this unit, ask the class to cite other examples of "common people" who played key roles in Luke's story of the birth of Jesus.

Share with your class the following statement by Dr. Willimon: "Other religions speak of salvation by the gods whom they worship. But only Christianity makes this bold affirmation of a God who loves so much that he dares to become a human being—not only that, but dares to become an *infant* human being, a poor infant human being. This is the miracle of the incarnation, which separates Christianity from the rest of the world's great faiths."

In your own words, tell the class about Søren Kierkegaard's parable of the king, which Dr. Willimon includes in his exposition.

Helping Class Members Act

III. Message of the scene for us

Focus the attention of the class on the fact that Simeon and Anna kept their expectations and faith alive and strong long after they had lost their youth. Ask: What can we do to keep our expectations and faith alive and strong as long as we live? See if your class can come up with ten suggestions. Have someone write them on newsprint.

Ask class members to reflect silently for a moment on what they have been studying in this unit on portions of Luke's birth narrative. Then ask: What makes Christmas important for you? Have the class write their answers. Invite those who would like to share what they have written to read their statements to the class.

You might pass along some of the best statements to the editor of your church newsletter, for publication. Or you might give them to your pastor; he or she might want to include them in a message.

Close the session by reading aloud the following question posed by Dr. Willimon: "Can we leave church this morning singing as did Simeon, confident that God is moving in this child to bring salvation to all?"

Planning for Next Sunday

Ask class members to read Isaiah 61:1-4, 10-11 and Luke 4:14-44. Isaiah 61:1-2 is basic for understanding Jesus' interpretation of the meaning of messiahship. Jesus identifies with the prophetic concept of the "anointed of God" as being one who loves all persons—sick or well, hurt or healthy, blind or whole, imprisoned by evil acts or by the consequences of hate, greed jealousy, dishonesty, and selfishness. Jesus' understanding of what God wants from his Messiah is clearly articulated in Isaiah 61:1-2. These verses are the touchstone of Christian faith.

UNIT II: PROCLAMATION AND MINISTRY
Horace R. Weaver

FIVE LESSONS   **JANUARY 1–29**

Unit II, "Proclamation and Ministry," focuses on Jesus' ministry to people. The keynote to his ministry was presented in his sermon in Nazareth. Here he identified how he knew he was called to be God's Messiah ("The Spirit of the Lord is upon me because . . ."), which call was based on Isaiah 61:1-2. God's intention for messiahship is clearly stated in these verses.

The focus of this unit is seen in its lessons. "Anointed to Preach the Good News," January 1, states clearly Jesus' commitment to a prophetic ministry of faith and action. In "Accepting Our Mission," January 8, Jesus challenges three men: "Do not be ordinary fishermen; come and let me make you fishers of men." "Healing and Forgiveness," January 15, tells of Jesus having touched and healed a leper, after which (having broken the Law) he withdrew to the desert, apparently to think about the consequences of his compassionate action. "Forgiveness: A Measure of Love," January 22, describes Jesus' eagerness to offer new life to any and all sinners. "Touch: A Step Toward Wholeness," January 29, describes a woman's desperate efforts to touch Jesus, that she might be healed by his power ("energy").

LESSON 5   **JANUARY 1**

Anointed to Preach the Good News

Background Scripture: Luke 4:14-44

The Main Question—William H. Willimon

Some years ago the top Broadway show of the season was *Mass Appeal*. It was a play about an aging priest who was given the tough job of supervising a young seminarian on his way into the priesthood. I particularly remember the notorious scene when the young priest preached his first sermon. The older priest had built most of his ministry on flattering the people. His sermons were witty, charming, and never offensive.

But the young priest had decidedly different ideas about preaching. He began his sermon, "God doesn't care about all of your mink coats, fancy clothes, and expensive cars!"

The older priest was horrified, and the congregation was angered. How dare this upstart young man preach like this? On Monday morning, the older priest got many telephone calls urging him to "Teach him how to preach."

Of course, the scene in the play touches off our memories of Jesus' first sermon in his hometown synagogue in Nazareth. As we begin a new year, we study this story today. Right at the beginning, Luke shows us some of the many reasons why Jesus eventually paid for his preaching with his life.

Having celebrated with joy the arrival of Jesus at Christmas, now we are confronted with harsh reality: This Jesus will not be one who flatters, compliments, and soothes us. He comes to confront and challenge us. What will be our response to the Babe of Bethlehem when he grows up and becomes a young preacher? That is the question which guides today's lesson.

Selected Scripture

King James Version

Revised Standard Version

Luke 4:16-21, 40-43

16 And he came to Naz'-a-reth, where he had been brought up: and, as his custom was, he went into the synagogue on the Sabbath day, and stood up for to read.

17 And there was delivered unto him the book of the prophet E-Sai'-as. And when he had opened the book, he found the place where it was written,

18 The Spirit of the Lord *is* upon me, because he hath anointed me to preach the gospel to the poor; he hath sent me to heal the broken-hearted, to preach deliverance to the captives, and recovering of sight to the blind, to set at liberty them that are bruised.

19 To preach the acceptable year of the Lord.

20 And he closed the book, and he gave *it* again to the minister, and sat down. And the eyes of all them that were in the synagogue were fastened on him.

21 And he began to say unto them, This day is this scripture fulfilled in your ears.

....

40 Now when the sun was setting,

Luke 4:16-21, 40-43

16 And he came to Nazareth, where he had been brought up; and he went to the synagogue, as his custom was, on the sabbath day. And he stood up to read; 17 and there was given to him the book of the prophet Isaiah. He opened the book and found the place where it was written,

18 "The Spirit of the Lord is upon me,
because he has anointed me to preach good news to the poor.
He has sent me to proclaim release to the captives
and recovering of sight to the blind,
to set at liberty those who are oppressed,
19 to proclaim the acceptable year of the Lord."

20 And he closed the book, and gave it back to the attendant, and sat down; and the eyes of all in the synagogue were fixed on him. 21 And he began to say to them, "Today this scripture has been fulfilled in your hearing."

....

40 Now when the sun was setting,

all they that had any sick with divers diseases brought them unto him; and he laid his hands on every one of them, and healed them.

41 And devils also came out of many, crying out, and saying, Thou art Christ the Son of God. And he rebuking *them* suffered them not to speak: for they knew that he was Christ.

42 And when it was day, he departed and went into a desert place: and the people sought him, and came unto him, and stayed him, that he should not depart from them.

43 And he said unto them, I must preach the kingdom of God to other cities also: for therefore am I sent.

Key Verse: **The Spirit of the Lord is upon me, because he hath anointed me to preach the gospel to the poor. (Luke 4:18)**

all those who had any that were sick with various diseases brought them to him; and he laid his hands on every one of them and healed them.

41 And demons also came out of many, crying, "You are the Son of God!" But he rebuked them, and would not allow them to speak, because they knew that he was the Christ.

42 And when it was day he departed and went into a lonely place. And the people sought him and came to him, and would have kept him from leaving them; 43 but he said to them, "I must preach the good news of the kingdom of God to the other cities also; for I was sent for this purpose."

Key Verse: **The Spirit of the Lord is upon me, because he has anointed me to preach good news to the poor. (Luke 4:18)**

As You Read the Scripture—Mike Winters

Luke 4:14-44. The baptism of Jesus (Luke 3:21) was a symbol of his messianic anointment. All the kings of Judah were anointed and thus considered "messianic."

In the Holy Spirit that descended on him at his baptism, Jesus was led into the wilderness, where he was tempted by the devil. The temptation story (Luke 4:1-13) reveals how Jesus rejected the common, but incorrect, ideas of the Messiah. First, Jesus rejected the idea that the Messiah would symbolize or prefigure the wealth of the Jewish nation. Second, Jesus refused an imperial kingdom. And third, Jesus showed that the messianic promise was lodged in a faithful, trustworthy God.

After the wilderness experience, Jesus visited Nazareth on the Sabbath. As his custom was, he went to the synagogue. There he read Isaiah 61:1-2, then sat down to preach, clarifying his messianic mission. The mood of the people shifted from pride to anger to open hostility. This was the inaugural address of Jesus, as he began his public ministry. It outlined his mission: preach good news to the poor; proclaim release to the captives and restored sight to the blind; proclaim the acceptable year of the Lord.

Verses 16-17, 20. Much has been made about Jesus' custom of faithful attendance at synagogue. There were other synagogues in Nazareth, the city where Jesus grew up. This synagogue, however, was one where Jesus' family was known (verse 22). The customary service in the synagogue consisted of reciting the Shema (Deuteronomy 6:4-5), prayers, a reading from the Law, a reading from the Prophets, a sermon (seated), and a blessing. Jesus read from the prophet Isaiah and sat down, a way of saying he was going to preach.

Verses 18-19. This is Isaiah 61:1-2. When you look at that passage, you will see that Luke omitted the second half of verse 2. These verses were written during the Babylonian Exile, at some time when the Jews either anticipated release or were already free. Babylon was falling; the Persian Empire was rising. The Persian king, Cyrus, allowed the Jews to return to their homeland to rebuild the walls and temple of Jerusalem (read Isaiah 61:1-4).

Verse 19 is a formula that announced the Year of Jubilee (Leviticus 25:10). Keeping the historical context of Isaiah 61 in mind, the Jews' release from captivity to return to their homeland was clearly a Jubilee idea. What was the Year of Jubilee? Every seventh year was called a Sabbath year. Agricultural activities were suspended, and the land rested. After seven Sabbath years, the fiftieth year was called the Year of Jubilee. The Year of Jubilee was a plan to ensure that poor, landless, and enslaved people would not be so forever.

Jesus used these verses to clarify his mission as the Messiah. His message would not be to the wealthy, as was supposed, but to the poor. The promise was not that the nation would be an imperial empire like Rome, but a hope for the oppressed, that they might be free. Jesus announced the messianic age in terms of the Year of Jubilee.

Verse 40. In the Spirit of the Lord (Luke 3:22; 4:1,18), Jesus began his public ministry by healing, through the laying on of hands. "Laying on hands" in our tradition symbolizes the power of the Holy Spirit to heal (Acts 4:30), one's call to service (Acts 6:6), and the call to faith (Acts 8:16-17).

Verse 41. Simeon knew the infant Jesus was the Christ (Luke 2:26), and so did the demons.

Verse 42. The rigors of public life are tiring. Jesus often sought a lonely place to pray and rest. But there was no rest.

Verse 43. Jesus' plan was to declare "the acceptable year of the Lord," the Year of Jubilee, to all cities—to Jews first, then to the Gentiles.

The Scripture and the Main Question—William H. Willimon

The Spirit of the Lord Is Upon Me

With all the odd, unfamiliar passages in Scripture, it's good to begin this new year studying one with which we are familiar: Luke 4:14-30. We have been over this ground dozens of times—Jesus in the pulpit at Nazareth, putting it to the homefolks and raising their anger. Put it to them, Jesus, we know who you *really* are, Son of God, Lord of Lords. It's a pity about those in Nazareth who didn't know.

We wonder how they could have been so intractably ignorant. Jesus is in the very bosom of Judaism, in Nazareth where he was brought up. There he had been circumcised and dedicated. He is in the synagogue, "as his custom was," says Luke. His chosen text, words from the prophet Isaiah, was as familiar to them as Luke 4:16-30 is to us. Here is no outsider or rebel, but one of their own. The congregation exclaims, "Is not this the carpenter's son?" There is nothing in the story to indicate that they are sneering or expressing contempt. They are perhaps expressing delight: Here is one of our own, reading so well texts of our own! Jesus, yes, young Jesus, Joseph's and Mary's boy, home from school for midwinter break. It's good to have him back home. We've heard of his accomplishments in Capernaum. We know him.

We wish we could have been there that Sabbath in Nazareth. Sure, we know this story of the hometown sermon by heart, but wouldn't it have been good to be there as eyewitnesses? Then we could have seen Jesus firsthand, without having to hear the story secondhand. Haven't you sometimes thought to yourself, "Oh, if I could only have been there and seen a miracle or two for myself."

We presume that believing would be easier if we were there. We must base our belief on secondhand hearsay. But if we could have been there, belief would be a cinch. Here we are in our time, and there, two thousand years away, is Jesus. "How can an event, once significant in its time, be significant for all time?" asked Lessing. Belief would be easier if just for a moment we could climb aboard our time machine and be there.

Yet, if mere time were the problem, why did the folk at Nazareth not see? Why didn't they know him?

They didn't know him because they knew him.

When people are new, unfamiliar, strange, we react with excitement. "How odd," we say, "how utterly fascinating! I've never thought about it that way before. Yes, I shall have to go home and think this one over." And we so like it when the preacher tells us something that we can go home and think over.

It was the ministers' Monday morning coffee hour, and one of the brothers was bragging about a visiting preacher he had at his church. "You should hear him," he said, "his style, his illustrations, his power—he is wonderful."

"Joe, you ought to hear me three hundred miles from home," said another. "I'm downright brilliant."

Luke wants it well understood: The problem with Jesus is not between the new and the old, between the known and the unknown, but between the people of God *and their own memories*—between the known and the known.

I preached in Canada last summer, preceded by a two hundred-voice choir and a five-minute introduction by a bishop telling everyone how lucky they were to have me. I couldn't fail.

But I stand up on a typical Sunday in Duke Chapel preceded by, "Oh its him again. Nobody special."

He Has Anointed Me to Preach Good News

Jesus, hometown boy, Joe and Mary's son, addressed Israel from her own Scripture, her own past, her own authoritative texts, with a reading from the familiar prophets, a text they already knew.

"The Day of the Lord is here!" he announced. "Amen!" they shouted. There was an excited stirring among the Chosen People of the Lord at Nazareth. "Amen!" All of our waiting for deliverance is over at last. The Lord is coming! At last he is coming to redeem his own! People lifted themselves up on their crutches; old men wept for joy; the oppressed looked up, their faces filled with hopeful expectation. "Amen!"

"When the Lord came earlier, there were lots of poor hungry women in Israel, but God chose to help a foreign widow instead. You know that story," said Jesus. There was silence.

"And speaking of old, familiar stories," continued Jesus, "you all remember the one about how Elisha healed an army officer, a *Syrian*, rather than all those poor deserving lepers in Israel." The congregation was silent.

"When the Lord came to deliver us," Jesus said, "remember that he answered the human needs of many more than just the Chosen. It's in the Bible." Jesus said. "You know the story of Isaiah, Elijah, Elisha." And a chorus of "Amens" becomes a thunder of silence. It is that silence of judgment when an exciting new sermon is suddenly recognized as nothing but an old story we already know and wish to God we could forget.

The church, which like the synagogue before also stands judged by our own, familiar stories, should listen carefully.

Proximity to and familiarity with the persons, texts, and ideas of religion is a privilege that also blinds, dulls, and impedes. Isn't this the carpenter's son? We know him.

"Yes," says Jesus, continuing the sermon (later, in Luke 11:29-32), "pagan Ninevah will get to judge this place, because Ninevah repented when Jonah preached to them. The Queen of Sheba ventured across the world to hear Solomon, and yet here among you is one greater than either Jonah or Solomon. At the judgment, you will claim your privilege to free passes, recalling the evening you had dinner with Jesus or when he preached in your town (Luke 13:26-27), but to no avail. Judgment begins with God's own house."

When someone in his audience blessed Jesus' mother, Jesus countered, "Blessing belongs only to those who hear and keep the word" (11:27-28). It doesn't even pay to be a relative.

The church should listen, for like the good synagogue-going folk of Nazareth, we can be sure that privilege continues to be perilous. We know, and sometimes our knowing is our undoing. This familiar biblical pattern of going to one's own people, preaching, being rejected, and then going elsewhere, is repeated many times in Jesus' and Paul's ministries and is even repeated in the church today.

"I wish I knew the Bible better," she said. It is possible to know the Bible too well. Having Scripture, knowing it, owning it, may be the most dangerous kind of knowledge.

Helping Adults Become Involved—Boyce A. Bowden

Preparing to Teach

The scripture for this lesson includes what Mike Winters calls "the inaugural address of Jesus, as he began his public ministry." It will be worth your time to read what *The Interpreter's Bible* says about this passage; see volume 8, especially pages 88-93.

To help your class get in mind the context for today's lesson, prepare a brief report—three minutes should be enough—on the experiences of Jesus in the wilderness, where he thought through his mission and the method he would use to pursue it. *The Interpreter's Bible* will help you with this.

Here is one good way to help class members grasp the meaning of Luke 4:14-44 and apply it to their own lives: Devote a substantial portion of the session to a sub-group study of portions of the passage.

To prepare for this activity, you will need to write out assignments on index cards for distribution to the study teams. Give one card to each team.

Obviously, the size of your class will determine the number of teams you have and the number of cards you need to make. Try to limit the teams to no more than five members. Have more than one team working on each question, if that is what it takes to keep teams small.

The assignments to be written are as follows:

Group 1. "He has anointed me to preach good news to the poor" (Luke 4:18).
    a. What does it mean to be poor? Name some different kinds of poverty.
    b. Find examples in Matthew, Mark, Luke, or John that demonstrate how Jesus preached good news to the poor.
    c. In what ways does your church preach good news to the poor?
    d. In what ways can you as a Christian individual preach good news to the poor?

Group 2: "He has sent me to proclaim release to the captives" (Luke 4:18).
    a. What does it mean to be a captive? Name some different kinds of captivity.
    b. Find examples in Matthew, Mark, Luke, or John that demonstrate how Jesus preached deliverance to the captives.
    c. In what ways does your church deliver captives?
    d. In what ways can you as an individual Christian deliver captives?

Group 3: "He has sent me to proclaim . . . recovering of sight to the blind" (Luke 4:18).
    a. What does it mean to be blind? Name some different kinds of blindness.
    b. Find examples in Matthew, Mark, Luke, or John that demonstrate how Jesus enabled the blind to see.
    c. In what ways does your church help the blind see?
    d. In what ways can you as an individual Christian help the blind see?

Group 4: "He has sent me to . . . set at liberty those who are oppressed" (Luke 4:18).
    a. What does it mean to be oppressed? Name some different kinds of oppression.
    b. Find examples in Matthew, Mark, Luke, or John that demonstrate how Jesus set at liberty those who were oppressed.
    c. In what ways does your local church free the oppressed?
    d. In what ways can you as an individual Christian free the oppressed?

Here are some objectives you might pursue in this lesson: to encourage class members to take a fresh look at the mission of Jesus, as he perceived it; to stimulate class members to examine their own views of Jesus; to motivate class members to think about the mission of the church and of Christian individuals in today's world.

One way to outline the lesson is:

      I. The scene
     II. Questions raised by the scene
   III. Message of the scene for us

Read carefully "The Scripture and the Main Question" and "As You Read the Scripture." These form the heart of the lesson. The ideas, insights, and suggestions in these sections should be reflected continually in your lesson plan.

As you use the suggested outline, you may want to either quote or paraphrase ideas. You might like to jot in the margin of your outline the

page number and paragraph being referred to. For example, you could write a reference to page 65, paragraph 3, as 65-3.

Have a supply of paper, pencils, Bibles, and Bible commentaries available.

Introducing the Main Question

Basic and helpful ideas are presented in the section "The Main Question." These ideas are essential in helping to identify the purpose of the lesson.

Developing the Lesson

I. The scene

To refresh the class members' memories of the context for today's lesson, give your report on the wilderness experience of Jesus.

II. Questions raised by the scene

Read aloud the beginning of Luke 4:18, "The Spirit of the Lord is upon me, because the Lord has anointed me . . ."

Ask the class to discuss the following questions: (1) In what sense was the Spirit of the Lord on Jesus? (2) Can the Spirit of the Lord also be on us? If so, how can we tell when it is? What are the consequences of the Spirit of the Lord being on us? (3) What does it mean to be anointed by the Lord to do a task? Does God anoint us to do tasks? How can we tell when God has anointed us?

The "Preparing to Teach" section suggested that you form four study teams to explore in depth the meaning of Luke 4:18. If you plan to do this, now is an appropriate time to form the teams and distribute the assignments.

Ask the class members to count off from one through four and to form into groups. Distribute to each group one of the cards you have prepared and ask its members to spend ten minutes answering the questions on their card and preparing a three-minute report for the class.

After the teams have completed their assignments, have them report to the total class. Allow time after each report for other class members to respond and to offer their insights.

Helping Class Members Act

III. Message of the scene for us

Have someone read aloud Luke 4:20-30. Point out that the people were impressed with Jesus' gracious words until verse 23. Then they were filled with wrath and tried to kill him.

Ask: Why were the hometown folks angry? The answer, obviously, is that Jesus challenged their restricted view of the Messiah's mission. Ask: How do we sometimes try to force Jesus to be the kind of Messiah we want him to be?

Dr. Willimon says the folk at Nazareth didn't know Jesus "because they knew him." What does that mean? Are we sometimes guilty of this same tendency?

Dr. Willimon writes: "Having Scripture, knowing it, owning it, may be the most dangerous kind of knowledge." Ask class members to respond to that observation.

Read aloud this statement that Dr. Willimon makes: "Having celebrated with joy the arrival of Jesus at Christmas, now we are confronted with a harsh reality: This Jesus will not be one who flatters, compliments, and soothes us. He comes to confront and challenge us. What will be our response to the Babe of Bethlehem when he grows up and becomes a young preacher?"

Silence can be golden, even in a Sunday school class. Give the class a couple of minutes to quietly reflect on today's session. Then close with a prayer appropriate for the beginning of a new year.

Planning for Next Sunday

Ask class members to read Luke 5:1-11.

Accepting Our Mission

Background Scripture: Luke 5:1-11

The Main Question—William H. Willimon

I preach each Sunday in a glorious setting: a beautiful Gothic chapel at the center of Duke University. I enjoy watching people enter this building. If they are here for the first time, I like to watch their eyes turn upward and their mouths drop open, overwhelmed by the glory and majesty of the place. And that's exactly what the architect intended—that these soaring arches and brilliant windows should overwhelm us with the glory of God. It's an emotion one doesn't have too often in contemporary religion, with our prefab, multipurpose gymnasium churches, where everything is scaled down to fit the needs of covered-dish suppers.

But to be here beneath the monumental glory of it all—vast building, great choir—is to want to cry out as Jacob did when heaven's ladder was brought down to him, "Surely the Lord is in this place!" Simon Peter must have had a similar experience the day he let Jesus use his (and his brother Andrew's) fishing boat. Jesus had sat down and taught the people. After teaching he ordered Peter to lower his nets—and their nets were filled. Peter reacted in two ways: He called Jesus Lord, recognizing him as the Messiah, and he fell to his knees in repentance, for he was a sinful man. In response to Peter's reactions, Jesus declared that he would henceforth be "catching men." And when they brought the boats of the partners (Peter and Andrew, and James and John), "they left everything and followed him."

The main question is twofold: What does it mean to stand before and gaze upon the faces of God and Jesus, who are both loving, judging, and holy; and what are the consequences of taking Jesus seriously?

163

Selected Scripture

King James Version

Luke 5:1-11

1 And it came to pass, that, as the people pressed upon him to hear the word of God, he stood by the lake of Gen-nes'-a-ret,

2 And saw two ships standing by the lake: but the fishermen were gone out of them, and were washing *their* nets.

3 And he entered into one of the ships, which was Si'-mon's and prayed him that he would thrust out a little from the land. And he sat down, and taught the people out of the ship.

4 Now, when he had left speaking, he said unto Si'-mon, Launch out into the deep, and let down your nets for a draught.

5 And Si'-mon answering said unto him, Master, we have toiled all the night, and have taken nothing: nevertheless at thy word I will let down the net.

6 And when they had this done, they inclosed a great multitude of fishes: and their net brake.

7 And they beckoned unto *their* partners, which were in the other ship, that they should come and help them. And they came, and filled both the ships, so that they began to sink.

8 When Si'-mon Pe'-ter saw *it*, he fell down at Je'-sus knees, saying, Depart from me; for I am a sinful man, O Lord.

9 For he was astonished, and all that were with him, at the draught of the fishes which they had taken:

10 And so *was* also James, and John, the sons of Zeb'-e-dee, which were partners with Si'-mon. And Je'-sus said unto Si'-mon, Fear not; from henceforth thou shalt catch men.

11 And when they had brought their ships to land, they forsook all,

Revised Standard Version

Luke 5:1-11

1 While the people pressed upon him to hear the word of God, he was standing by the lake of Gennes'-aret. 2 And he saw two boats by the lake; but the fishermen had gone out of them and were washing their nets. 3 Getting into one of the boats, which was Simon's, he asked him to put out a little from the land. And he sat down and taught the people from the boat. 4 And when he had ceased speaking, he said to Simon, "Put out into the deep and let down your nets for a catch." 5 And Simon answered, "Master, we toiled all night and took nothing! But at your word I will let down the nets." 6 And when they had done this, they enclosed a great shoal of fish; and as their nets were breaking, 7 they beckoned to their partners in the other boat to come and help them. And they came and filled both the boats, so that they began to sink. 8 But when Simon Peter saw it, he fell down at Jesus' knees, saying "Depart from me, for I am a sinful man, O Lord." 9 For he was astonished, and all that were with him, at the catch of fish which they had taken; 10 and so also were James and John, sons of Zeb'edee, who were partners with Simon. And Jesus said to Simon, "Do not be afraid; henceforth you will be catching men." 11 And when they had brought their boats to land, they left everything and followed him.

and followed him.

Key Verse: **When they had brought their ships to land, they forsook all, and followed him. (Luke 5:11)**

Key Verse: **When they had brought their boats to land, they left everything and followed him. (Luke 5:11)**

As You Read the Scripture—Mike Winters

Luke 5:1. In Nazareth, at the beginning of Jesus' public ministry, the people would have thrown him headlong down the brow of the hill (Luke 4:29). But in Capernaum, the people were astonished at his teachings (4:32). The people sought Jesus, even in the lonely places (4:42) where he rested and prayed. Building on Jesus' rise to popularity, Luke writes that the people pressed upon him. They wedged him against the shore of the sea. Lake Gennesaret is the Sea of Galilee. The setting is probably near the plain of Gennesaret, southwest of Capernaum.

Verses 2, 10a. The fishing partners were Simon, Andrew, and James and John, the sons of Zebedee. Their method of fishing required two boats, which would deploy a large net in a circle. After a night of fishing in which they caught nothing (verse 5), they beached their boats and began washing and mending their nets. Their work day was nearly ended.

Verse 3. This becomes Simon's story. Simon, seated in the boat-become-lectern, became Jesus' captive audience. One can almost imagine Simon, chin resting in hands, listening to Jesus speak to the crowd near by.

Verses 4-5. Simon indicated that further fishing at that particular moment would be fruitless. He and his partners had been fishing the same waters all night and had caught nothing. But something in Jesus' teaching told Simon that Jesus was special. Whatever it was that Simon, a fishing expert, saw in Jesus, a fishing novice, at this point was unexpressible. Obviously, Simon recognized some authority in Jesus.

Verses 6-7. If they were using their great dragnets, Simon and his partners would have had to be working together. This story of a great haul of fish is similar to the one in the post-resurrection story in John 21:4-14. There is surprise here. Was Jesus a miracle worker? Or was Jesus Lord?

Verses 8-9a. This is the only place in Luke where Simon is called Simon Peter. Simon Peter was in awe. He humbled himself before Jesus. He confessed his sins. He acknowledged Jesus' lordship. This is only the second time in Luke that the term "Lord" is applied to Jesus. The first time was the angel's announcement to the shepherds of Jesus' birth. "Lord" is God's title (Luke 1:68). Although the word "Lord" appears many times in Luke up to this point, all of its uses except in these two cases apply only to God.

Verses 9b-10a. This became James's and John's story as well. They too were awed by Jesus.

Verse 10b. This story is the story of Simon's call to Jesus' ministry. The call came after a series of events. First, Simon heard Jesus' teaching. Second, Simon witnessed Jesus' mighty acts. Third, Simon confessed his sins. Fourth, Simon affirmed Jesus as Lord. Fifth, Jesus dispels Simon's awe and calls him to a new kind of fishing. Can these events leading up to Simon's call instruct the church today in the form of valid calls to ministry?

Verse 11. Apparently, James and John, the sons of Zebedee, also responded to the call. "They left everything"—that phrase by itself doesn't betray the emotional struggle such a decision would require. The emotional struggle to leave everything was even more heightened for Simon, James, and John, because they left it after a successful fishing venture, rather than after a night of fruitless toil.

The Scripture and the Main Question—William H. Willimon

The People Pressed in upon Him

Luke enjoys contrasting the acceptance of the good news by some of its hearers and the rejection of the same good news by others. One person's good news may be another's bad news. You will undoubtedly recall the episode in Luke 4, where an admiring congregation turned into an angry, homicidal mob when Jesus preached.

But here, in chapter five of Luke, the situation appears different. Jesus, having been refused acceptance by the synagogue at Nazareth, decides to preach in an "open air" synagogue. Luke portrays Jesus preaching by the Lake of Gennesaret. Jesus was so cramped by the crowd of listeners pressing upon him that he did an unprecedented thing: He got into a nearby boat (which belonged to Simon and Andrew) and had it moved a little bit from the shore. This gave him a new platform to preach from. Jesus has become a celebrity, a notable person able to attract a crowd. One can visualize the fascinated, admiring followers all pressing in upon him, all eager to hear him speak.

But when Jesus speaks directly to the fisherman named Simon, Simon's response is quite the opposite from that of the crowd. "Depart from me, for I am a sinful man, O Lord," says Simon, when he is confronted by the miraculous catch of fish (5:8).

It is one thing to be a distant admirer of Jesus, and it is another thing to be confronted by Jesus and his power directly, as he calls your very own name and asks you to be part of his mission.

"Christ has many admirers," observed the Danish Christian philosopher Kierkegaard, "but he wants not admirers but followers."

Too much modern religion displays a kind of "chumminess" with the living God, which Peter would not have known. As he falls to his knees, we know that we are seeing a man confronting the vast distance between his life and the ways and will of God. Peter's exclamation of humility is the cry of a person who has come into the presence of the living God and been humbled in the process.

It was at this event of the draught of two boatloads of fish that Jesus called Peter to be an apostle, and Peter discovered his Lord.

Read John 1:35-42, which tells how Peter and Andrew had been disciples of John the Baptist, but asked Jesus if they might follow him instead. So it seems probable that when Jesus saw these brothers in Bethany, beyond the Jordan, he called them to become his apostles. Peter and Andrew, James and John, responded affirmatively to their new Messiah, Jesus.

Depart from Me

Peter's "Depart from me, for I am a sinful man!" has little to do with our conventional definitions of sin. The sin being confessed here has not to do with the occasional picadillo, what Mommy told you not to do, but rather with the gaping chasm between who you are and who God is. We have counselors and therapists to help us handle sin as misdeed. But what if our sin (with a capital *S*), our real uncleanness, is the gap between ourselves and God?

Freud noted that we project our parents onto God. It's natural for us to think of God as the big Mommy-Daddy in the sky—making a list, checking it twice. But what if you come to your church to worship and find, to your terror, that God isn't like that at all, that God is that great other, that over-againstness, which Peter saw that day when he looked into the eyes of Jesus. God's love is the searing light that penetrates our facade.

What if God, the one Peter saw projected back at him in the eyes of the Rabbi (Jesus), is like a mirror of truth and self-knowledge that you are made to gaze upon? There you see reflected every moment of your life, every secret thought, all the good little things you have done for bad little reasons, the way you live, every second, for you and you alone. My God, to be made to look upon that mirror, even for an instant, who could endure it?

God's holiness is the mirror through which our pretentious goodness is seen for what it really is. We catch just a glimpse of God and get more than we wanted and cry, "Depart from me!"

"It is a fearful thing to fall into the hands of the living God." Why could he not leave Peter with his nets, fishing? Why could he not let *us* be, content with our little lies, masks fixed firmly in place, quite happy to play our games?

They Followed Him

But you know, he never does. Across the gap between him and us, he reaches in love. He is no mere cold mirror of judgment but a living God of grace. Jesus calls Peter to be a disciple, promising to teach him to catch more than fish. Refusing to leave this sinful man, he forgives him even when Peter denies him three times at the cross—he forgives him! Because once the living God gets a grasp on you, he doesn't let go.

As a young priest, Martin Luther was so anxious when he led his first Mass that he was physically ill. Luther felt so unworthy—like Peter. Why would Jesus want someone like Peter to assist in his holy mission?

We don't know. All we know is that he chooses even us, even Peter, to be part of his saving work.

Part of the holiness and awe we feel when face to face with our God is the awesomeness of God's love and mercy. In the parables of Jesus—the prodigal son, the laborers in the vineyard, the lost sheep—we see how God's love is forever reaching out across our inadequacies and shortcomings to embrace us.

God is holy, but also loving. Although Peter has many faults, Jesus gives him a mission. Through Peter, many people will accept the good news.

Before you end today's lesson, read Acts 2. Can it be that the dumbfounded, undependable, confused fishermen that we read about in the Gospels are the same who now boldly preach the gospel?

Helping Adults Become Involved—Boyce A. Bowdon

Preparing to Teach

It alway helps to have clearly defined objectives. Here are two you might consider for this lesson: to help class members become more aware that God has a mission for each of us, and to encourage class members to seek that mission and to give themselves to its fulfillment.

Here's one way to outline the lesson:

     I. The scene: Jesus calls his apostles.
    II. Questions raised by the scene.
   III. Message of the scene for us.

Read carefully "The Scripture and the Main Question" and "As You Read the Scripture." These form the heart of the lesson. The ideas, insights, and suggestions in these sections should be reflected continually in your lesson plan.

As you use the suggested outline, you may want to either quote or paraphrase ideas. You might like to jot in the margin of your outline the page number and paragraph being referred to. For example, you could write a reference to page 65, paragraph 3, as 65-3.

Introducing the Main Question

Basic and helpful ideas are presented in the section "The Main Question." These ideas are essential in helping to identify the purpose of the lesson.

The main question is twofold: What does it mean to stand before and gaze upon the face of God and Jesus, who are both loving, judging, and holy? What are the consequences of taking Jesus seriously?

Briefly review last week's lesson, pointing out that Jesus disturbed the people of Nazareth, his hometown, when he challenged their preconceived notions about the mission and methods of the Messiah. They attempted to kill him and would have thrown him over a cliff.

Point out that Jesus attracted large crowds in his ministry along the Sea of Galilee, where he spent much time. Luke 4:37 says "reports of him went out into every place in the surrounding region." It's easy to understand why. He was meeting the real needs of people—teaching with authority, casting out demons, healing the sick, and giving hope to the hopeless.

Developing the Lesson

I. The scene: Jesus calls his apostles.

Devote a few minutes to helping class members zero in on the setting for Peter's, James's, and John's dramatic call to mission. Paint a word picture of the scene portrayed in Luke 5:1-11. Mike Winters' exegesis contains helpful information that will help you describe the setting. Have someone read aloud Luke 5:1-11.

Point out that Simon, James, and John were professional fishermen. They had been fishing all night without any success, as Luke 5:5 reports. Ask class members to put themselves in the boat with Simon. How would they have felt if they had been there?

II. Questions raised by the scene.

Ask: Why do you think Simon and his partners bothered to let down their nets when Jesus told them to do so? Follow that question with this one: Have there been times when you felt God was asking you to do something that went against your better judgment? Ask each class member to discuss that question with someone seated near him or her.

In his exegesis, Mike Winters observes that Simon's call came after the following series of events: Simon heard Jesus' teaching, witnessed Jesus' mighty acts, and confessed his sins. Then Jesus dispelled Simon's awe and called him to a new kind of fishing.

After reviewing with your class this sequence of events, ask the question that Dr. Winters poses: Can these events leading up to Simon's call instruct the church today about valid calls to ministry?

Dr. Willimon observes in his exposition that today's lesson is not about the joy of being in the presence of God but rather the terror. Ask: How do you feel when you are conscious of being in God's presence?

Back in the 1960s, a Hollywood movie star described God as "a living doll." We may not share so casual and cozy an attitude toward the Almighty, but all too often we do think of God as a Super-Santa, the "Man Upstairs." The Heavenly Father has given way to the "Heavenly Pop," or just "Daddy."

Ask class members if they agree that we lack a sense of awe. Ask them to suggest what we can do to regain an awareness of the majesty of God. Can the recent discoveries in space open our eyes to God's greatness?

Read aloud the following statement that Dr. Willimon made in another setting: "Worship is not only a place to dream and envision a 'new heaven and a new earth' where the deaf hear, the blind see, and outcasts come to a feast; worship is also a time set apart to focus our attention on and attach ourselves to something and someone outside ourselves" (*The Service of God* [Nashville: Abingdon, 1983], p. 140).

Ask the class to respond to Dr. Willimon's statement. What risks do we take when we worship God in genuine reverence?

Allow class members to express their views and listen carefully to what they say. Then you might share an observation Dr. Willimon once made about what happens when we come face to face with the living God. He said we see ourselves as we really are. "I believe that the Bible says that the experience of coming face-to-face with the living God may be a pleasant or an unpleasant experience. It may provoke love or fear. One may wish to draw near or to run away" (*Worship as Pastoral Care* [Nashville: Abingdon, 1979], p. 97). Ask the class to discuss this question: What does it mean to be a sinner? You will find some helpful insights in Dr. Willimon's exposition, under the subhead, "Depart From Me!"

One of the most important points to make in this lesson is that Jesus did not leave Simon, even when Simon asked him to depart. Jesus instead called Simon to enter into his service and promised to teach him to catch more than fish.

Many adults—lay people as well as clergy—have had religious experiences that have completely changed their lives. Ask class members to pair off and share briefly with one another an occasion when they felt God was calling them to a mission.

Helping Class Members Act

III. Message of the scene for us.

In closing today's lesson, you might read aloud the following statement that Dr. Willimon makes in his exposition: "It is a fearful thing to fall into the hands of the living God. Why could he not leave Peter with his nets, fishing? Why could he not let us be, content with our little lies, masks fixed firmly in place, quite happy to play our games."

Now ask: To what mission is God calling us today, as a church? As a Sunday school class? As individuals? Allow a few minutes for discussion of how these missions can be discovered, accepted, and fulfilled.

Planning for Next Sunday

Ask class members to read Psalm 103:1-13 and Luke 5:12-26.

LESSON 7   JANUARY 15

Healing and Forgiveness

Background Scripture: Luke 5:12-26

The Main Question—William H. Willimon

"Lord, if you will, you can make me clean" (Luke 5:12). This is what the man suffering from leprosy cried out to Jesus. Of course, today none of us think that a disease like leprosy signifies that one is "unclean." Through the advances of modern medical science, we have learned that disease is caused by bacteria or viruses, not by sin or divine displeasure. We can imagine the immense suffering that was caused sick people in the past because of misconceptions about the nature of illness. Not only did their illness bring them pain and suffering but it also brought the additional anguish of social ostracism and censure, because many were convinced that sick people, or their parents or even grandparents, had committed some sin that had led to the sickness.

And yet, before we pat ourselves on the back, we must also admit that there is still a certain amount of social stigma attached to sickness. Part of the horror of AIDS lies in the social ostracism that accompanies the disease. Victims are put in isolation and avoided.

There are less dramatic but no less painful examples. Anyone afflicted with sickness may feel left out of the mainstream of society. People who are suffering through a long or disfiguring illness often report that they feel they are being put on the shelf and forgotten. How do you feel when you are ill? Do any of these same feelings of separation and isolation infect you? If so, pay attention to today's lesson. For today's lesson depicts Jesus as one who reaches out to people in their illness to embrace them, heal them, and make them his followers.

Selected Scripture

| King James Version | Revised Standard Version |

Luke 5:17-26

17 And it came to pass on a certain day, as he was teaching, that there were Phar'-i-sees and doctors of the law sitting by, which were come out of every town of Gal'-i-lee, and Ju-dae'-a, and Je-ru'sa-lem: and the power of the Lord was *present* to heal them.

18 And, behold, men brought in a bed a man which was taken with a palsy: and they sought *means* to bring him in, and to lay *him* before him.

19 And when they could not find by what *way* they might bring him in because of the multitude, they went upon the housetop, and let him down through the tiling with *his* couch into the midst before Je'-sus.

20 And when he saw their faith, he said unto him, Man, thy sins are forgiven thee.

21 And the scribes and the Phar'-i-sees began to reason, saying, Who is this which speaketh blasphemies? Who can forgive sins, but God alone?

22 But when Je'-sus perceived their thoughts, he answering said unto them, What reason ye in your hearts?

23 Whether is easier, to say, Thy sins be forgiven thee; or to say, Rise up and walk?

24 But that ye may know that the Son of man hath power upon earth to forgive sins (he said unto the sick of the palsy,) I say unto thee, Arise, and take up thy couch, and go into thine house.

25 And immediately he rose up before them, and took up that whereon he lay, and departed to his own house, glorifying God.

26 And they were all amazed, and they glorified God, and were filled with fear, saying, We have seen

Luke 5:17-26

17 On one of those days, as he was teaching, there were Pharisees and teachers of the law sitting by, who had come from every village of Galilee and Judea and from Jerusalem; and the power of the Lord was with him to heal. 18 And behold, men were bringing on a bed a man who was paralyzed, and they sought to bring him in and lay him before Jesus; 19 but finding no way to bring him in, because of the crowd, they went up on the roof and let him down with his bed through the tiles into the midst before Jesus. 20 And when he saw their faith he said, "Man, your sins are forgiven you." 21 And the scribes and the Pharisees began to question, saying, "Who is this that speaks blasphemies? Who can forgive sins but God only?" 22 When Jesus perceived their questionings, he answered them, "Why do you question in your hearts? 23 Which is easier, to say, 'Your sins are forgiven you,' or to say, 'Rise and walk'? 24 But that you may know that the Son of man has authority on earth to forgive sins"—he said to the man who was paralyzed—"I say to you, rise, take up you bed and go home." 25 And immediately he rose before them, and took up that on which he lay, and went home, glorifying God. 26 And amazement seized them all, and they glorified God and were filled with awe, saying, "We have seen strange things today."

strange things to day.

Key Verse: **They were all amazed and they glorified God, and were filled with fear, saying we have seen strange things today. (Luke 5:26)**

Key Verse: **Amazement seized them all and they glorified God and were filled with awe, saying, "We have seen strange things today." (Luke 5:26)**

As You Read the Scripture—Mike Winters

Luke 5:17. This is the first time Luke mentions the Pharisees in his Gospel. The Pharisees called themselves "associates" or "companions" of the Law of Moses. The term "Pharisee" means "segregationist." They separated themselves from everything outside the Law. To insure compliance with the Law they developed a so called "hedge around the Law." They hoped to provide a safety net of sorts against sin. For example, if the Law said, "Drive fifty-five miles per hour," the Pharisees would drive fifty.

"Teachers of the law" is what Luke calls the scribes. They were the legal experts.

The power of Jesus was from God. At least one variant text of this passage emphasizes that the power to heal was God's; it reads, "the power of the Lord was present to heal them." In this power, Jesus taught (Luke 4:14) and healed. As a result of his teaching and healing activities, the Pharisees and scribes came from all of Galilee and Judea. Thus, Luke reports the development of opposition against Jesus.

Verse 18. The paralytic's bed was a stretcher of sorts.

Verse 19. Because the crowd was so thick, the paralytic's friends decided to enter the home through the roof. In Mark 2: 4, the type of roofing is not specified. Since it was probably a Palestinian house, it would have had a thatch roof. Luke describes the house as having the tile roof typical of Roman structures.

Verse 20. Jesus responded to the faith of the paralytic's friends. Jesus' forgiveness was based on the faith of those who exerted this unusual effort, rather than the faith of the paralytic. This statement challenges the Christian model of forgiveness, which is based on the sinner's confession and contrition.

Jesus' statement to the paralytic does not necessarily mean that the paralysis was a result of sin.

Verse 21. It is true that only God can forgive sins. But God decides how sins are forgiven. The prophets warned Israel about their blind insistence that *correct forms* of worship would save them. God despises worship when it is empty of humility, kindness, and justice (Amos 5:21-24). It is possible that God's way may differ from what God's people think it is. God's plan was to delegate the power to forgive sins to Jesus. The Pharisees and scribes were wrong to accuse Jesus of blasphemy. The real blasphemy was that they failed to see God's purposes being fulfilled through Jesus (read Isaiah 61:1-2).

Verses 22-23. The questions are rhetorical. The point that Jesus is making is that whether the act is healing a paralytic or forgiving a paralytic's sin, it is God who does it. Healing and forgiveness were of the power of the Lord (verse 17).

Verse 24. In Luke, the title "Son of Man" was the term Jesus used to refer to himself. Jesus could have meant a couple of different things by the title. One idea the title conveys is simply Jesus' humanity; indeed, Jesus was human. But the title was also the name of the coming Messiah (Daniel 7:13-14). Jesus was both human and Messianic. Or to say it in the ancient formula of the Nicene Creed, Jesus was "God of God . . . and was made man." He was one and both, human and divine, at the same time. Luke uses the term in its messianic meaning.

Verses 25-26. The people acknowledged God's mighty work. God was glorified by all. The paralytic rose and walked home. The Pharisees and scribes and others were seized with amazement. The healing was an experience everyone remembered and pondered. For some, this would be the point at which their opposition to Jesus was set. For others, it would be the point of choosing new life.

The Scripture and the Main Question—William H. Willimon

There Were Teachers of the Law Sitting By

Undoubtedly many of the people in your adult group remember this story fondly from their childhood. We all remember the dramatic scene of the paralyzed man whose friends so desperately wanted him to be healed that they cut a hole in the roof and let him down through it. I can vividly remember from children's church school classes the arguments we had over what the owner of the house thought about this large hole being cut in his roof!

Luke puts these details in his story of the paralyzed man because he wants us to note the depth of caring of the man's friends. They were willing to tackle any obstacle in order to get their friend close to Jesus and his healing touch.

Luke, a dramatic writer who always has a sense for irony, also wants us to compare the man's friends to the "Pharisees and teachers of the law sitting by" (5:17). Can you visualize them in your own mind? Here were the scholars, the religious experts and leaders, "sitting by." Jesus is busy teaching, and the multitudes are pressing upon him. But the religious leaders, arms folded, are sitting by with scorn and contempt on their faces, listening to this rural rabbi teach.

Let us ponder this image. Do we have here a vivid and sad picture of the state of organized religion when confronted by human need? The people are hurting. They will do almost anything to get close to the sources of healing and compassion. But those who bear the promises of God sit by in scorn with their arms folded. It is all too easy for us to watch Sunday morning television shows and be filled with scorn for the strutting faith healers and television evangelists. But are we able to look beyond them to their audiences? Here are people who obviously have great need. You and I may have questions about faith healers and their ability to meet these people's need, but what is our church doing in response?

The history of the church is full of times when the church was too concerned about its own religious and social respectability to reach out to human need. For instance, John Wesley was brought up as a proper Oxford scholar and establishment theologian. But when he saw the wretchedness of the Kingswood coal miners, Wesley reached out to them, even though it meant going to the coal fields and preaching to them in the open air.

SECOND QUARTER

Your Sins Are Forgiven

When the sick man is brought to Jesus, Jesus' response is somewhat surprising. He does not at first say, "Rise and walk," but rather, "Your sins are forgiven you" (5:20-21). Of course, people in Jesus' day believed that there was a direct link between sin and disease. In our day, we tend to think of illness as a result of bacterial or viral infection or physical harm. And yet, there is a tendency to think of sick people as having done something to deserve their illness. We wonder if they ate the right food or got enough sleep or took care of themselves properly.

Of course, we must be honest and admit that sometimes sickness is the result of bad behavior. The person who smokes a pack of cigarettes for thirty years should not be surprised if lung cancer or heart disease strikes. We know that obesity is a cause of many different health disorders. A physician once told me that he estimated that at least two-thirds of the people in the hospital at any given moment were there due to alcohol-related problems.

Yet let us note that Jesus is not speculating on what the man's sin might be. The Bible says that *all* of us are sinners. You and I know that there is a definite connection between our spiritual and our physical well-being. Jesus does not speculate on the man's moral state, He does not lecture or condemn him. Rather, he reaches out and heals him by forgiving him. To be forgiven is to be healed of spiritual wretchedness.

Upon hearing Jesus forgive the man's sins, the religious teachers and experts who have been sitting by are enraged. "Who is this that speaks blasphemies?" they ask (5:21).

Don't you find their response interesting? Here a pitiful man has been healed of his paralysis. But what are the religious leaders doing? Are they praising God for such a wonder? Are they congratulating Jesus on being able to minister to his spiritual and physical condition? No, they see this act of compassion as a theological scandal.

I can almost see the poor man becoming used to his new legs—standing erect for the first time perhaps in his whole life, walking about, enjoying his blessed freedom. But the teachers of the Law ignore him and choose instead to argue with Jesus about theology!

They Glorified God and Were Filled with Awe

"And amazement seized them all, and they glorified God and were filled with awe, saying, 'We have seen strange things today'" (5:26). Thus the crowd responds to the miraculous work of Jesus. Which do you think was a greater scandal, that Jesus healed people or that he forgave their sins? Is it even possible to make a distinction between our physical well-being and our spiritual health? Jesus appears to see our spiritual and our physical well-being as a unity. And the point behind this story is that he cares about both. He reaches out to human need, whether spiritual or physical, in compassion and love. In so doing, he puts himself on a collision course with the religious establishment and shows that he will reach out beyond our pettiness to touch those who suffer.

Think about the program of your church. In what ways, revealed in the program, mission, and budget of your congregation, does it seem that the present day church is "sitting by"? On the other hand, in what ways do you see your church reaching out across boundaries to heal those who suffer spiritually and physically? The church exists not simply to minister to spiritual needs—our guilt, our loneliness, our quest for meaning. The church is also called to minister to physical needs as well—the material needs of the poor and the sick and suffering persons in our community and around the world. How well do we model Jesus' concern for the healing and forgiveness of the world? It all depends upon where we see ourselves in the story.

Helping Adults Become Involved—Boyce A. Bowdon

Preparing to Teach

After some preparatory study, jot down a few teaching objectives, such as these: (1) to help class members become more aware of what Jesus' contemporaries thought about the relationship between sin and sickness, forgiveness and healing; (2) to stimulate class members to think about how their spiritual health affects their physical health; (3) to help class members become more aware of the views Jesus' contemporaries had of him, and the views Jesus had of himself; (4) to reassure class members that Jesus (as Dr. Willimon writes) "reaches out to people in their illness to embrace them, heal them, and make them his followers"; (5) to challenge class members to be instruments of healing by following the example set by the paralyzed man's friends.

Here's one way you might outline the lesson:

      I.   People involved in the scene
           A. The paralytic
           B. The paralytic's friends
           C. Jesus
           D. The Pharisees
           E. The crowd
     II. Key issues in the scene
           A. Forgiveness and healing
           B. Jesus' authority and power
    III. Message of the scene for us

Read carefully "The Scripture and the Main Question" and "As You Read the Scripture." These form the heart of the lesson. The ideas, insights, and suggestions in these sections should be reflected continually in your lesson plan.

As you use the suggested outline, you may want to either quote or paraphrase ideas. You might like to jot in the margin of your outline the page number and paragraph being referred to. For example, you could write a reference to page 65, paragraph 3, as 65-3.

Introducing the Main Question

Basic and helpful ideas are presented in the section "The Main Question." These ideas are essential in helping to identify the purpose of the lesson.

To introduce this lesson, share the following story with your class. An

SECOND QUARTER

Oklahoma City minister received a phone call about two o'clock one morning from a nurse at a hospital. The nurse told him that a young mother whose infant was at the point of death was asking for a minister to come and pray with her.

Within fifteen minutes, the minister was at the hospital, visiting with the distraught mother. Her story slowly came out. During the early months of pregnancy, she had been using heroin, and her baby had been born an addict. "God is punishing me and my baby for what I did," she kept saying over and over. "Please help me get forgiveness so my baby will be all right."

The minister prayed with her, read passages from the Bible, and did everything he could to comfort the woman and to assure her of God's love. But before morning, her baby died.

"God hasn't forgiven me, and he never will. And I hate him," the woman screamed.

Ask the class members to keep this story in their minds. We will come back to it later.

Developing the Lesson

Have someone read Luke 5:17-26. And then ask the class to take a closer look at the people involved in the healing.

I. People involved in the scene
A. The paralytic
We don't know his name, age, or the particulars of his illness. He may have suffered from a neurosis brought on by an overwhelming sense of guilt. At any rate, he was helpless and hopeless. Ask: In what ways are we like the paralytic?

B. The paralytic's friends
Obviously, they were deeply concerned about him. Perhaps they had heard that Jesus had healed many people suffering from a variety of physical conditions. They may have witnessed some of his miracles. At any rate, they were convinced Jesus could help. As Dr. Willimon writes, "They were willing to tackle any obstacle in order to get their friend close to Jesus and his healing touch."

Ask: What can we learn from the friends of the paralytic that will enable us to be agents of God's healing?

C. Jesus
The faith these men demonstrated in Jews and the love they demonstrated for their friend made an impact on Jesus. In response, he forgave the paralytic's sins and enabled him to walk again. Ask: By forgiving and healing the paralytic, and by his conversation with the Pharisees, what did Jesus reveal about himself?

D. The Pharisees
For a good description of the Pharisees, read page 105 of *The Interpreter's Bible*, volume 8. It points out that these religious leaders were not essentially bad. They had originally set out to preserve what they believed to be the authorized commandments and codes for religious speech and conduct. But they had lost their sensitivity to new ideas. They were disturbed by the reports about what Jesus was saying and doing. His popularity was becoming a threat to them. Some had come long distances in hopes of discrediting him. Rather than mix with the ordinary people who crowded

around Peter's house, the heresy hunters sat together at a distance and waited for Jesus to say or do something they could use to condemn him. When Jesus healed the paralyzed man, it didn't matter to them that a man who had been lame was now walking. It did matter to them that Jesus had blasphemed. They didn't see the miracle Jesus had performed; they only saw the violation of orthodoxy he had committed.

Ask: The Pharisees were blind to the miracles of God and felt threatened by new and different religious expressions. How can we avoid making these same mistakes?

E. The crowd

People who had witnessed the dramatic healing and had heard the tense exchange between Jesus and the Pharisees were amazed. Filled with awe, they glorified God, saying "We have seen strange things today." Ask: If you had been present, how do you think your life would have been influenced by this event?

II. Key issues in the scene
A. Forgiveness and healing

It was commonly assumed during the days of Jesus' earthly ministry that sickness and other misfortunes were caused immediately or ultimately by an evil spirit, sometimes sent by God as punishment for sin.

The book of Job attacked the popular assumption that all misfortune is related to sin, and Jesus attacked that view occasionally, too. Have someone read aloud John 9:1-3, as an example.

However, Jesus acknowledged the connection between physical well-being and spirutal health. Luke 5:17-16 is a good example of how he sometimes related sin and sickness, forgiveness and health.

Ask your class to express their views on this question: What is the relationship between spiritual health and physical health? Take into consideration the insights of contemporary thinkers.

B. Jesus' authority and power
Ask: What does Luke 5:17-26 reveal about the authority and power of Jesus?

Helping Class Members Act

III. Message of the scene for us

Direct the attention of the class back to the story you used to introduce this lesson. Ask them to put themselves in the position of the minister. In light of Luke 5:17-26, what would they have said to the distraught mother? You might set up a role-play. Ask several class members to take turns counseling with the mother.

Close the session by challenging class members to be instruments of healing by following the example set by the friends of the paralyzed man.

Planning for Next Sunday

Ask class members to read Romans 5:1-11 and Luke 7:36-50.

Forgiveness: A Measure of Love

Background Scripture: Luke 7:36-50

The Main Question—William H. Willimon

"Forgive those who persecute you." "Forgive someone seventy times seven times."

Of all the sayings of Jesus, I find his sayings about forgiveness the most difficult. Every Sunday, when we pray the Lord's Prayer and we must say "Forgive us our trespasses as we forgive those who trespass against us," I always cringe, because I know how often I fail to do just that. Why should it be so hard to forgive people?

Surely part of the problem is that in forgiving someone, I must admit that this person whom I regard as so vile and evil because he or she has wronged me is actually very much like myself. When I am asked to forgive the trespasses of others as my own have been forgiven, I am admitting that the only reason I have a relationship with God is because of God's willingness to forgive all the evil, vile things I have done against God.

Thus forgiveness is a rather humbling experience. You and I enjoy drawing lines across the world between the good and the bad, the just and the unjust, the forgiveable and the unforgiveable.

In today's scripture, Jesus cuts across the lines of judgment we draw and reaches out to a sinner. Speaking of a common harlot, he says, "Her sins, which are many, are forgiven, for she loved much; but he who is forgiven little, loves little."

"Who is this who even forgives sins?" they ask of Jesus. Knowing how difficult forgiveness is for us in everyday life, you and I ought to be particularly attentive to Jesus' gift of forgiveness as it is portrayed in today's lesson.

Selected Scripture

King James Version

Revised Standard Version

Luke 7:36-50

36 And one of the Pharisees desired him that he would eat with him. And he went into the Pharisee's house, and sat down to meat.

37 And, behold, a woman in the city, which was a sinner, when she knew that *Jesus* sat at meat in the Pharisee's house, brought an alabaster box of ointment.

38 And stood at his feet behind *him* weeping, and began to wash his

Luke 7:36-50

36 One of the Pharisees asked him to eat with him, and he went into the Pharisee's house, and took his place at table. 37 And behold, a woman of the city, who was a sinner, when she learned that he was at table in the Pharisee's house, brought an alabaster flask of ointment, 38 and standing behind him at his feet, weeping, she began to wet his feet with her tears, and

feet with tears, and did wipe *them* with the hairs of her head, and kissed his feet and anointed *them* with the ointment.

39 Now when the Pharisee which had bidden him saw *it*, he spake within himself, saying, This man, if he were a prophet, would have known who and what manner of woman *this is* that toucheth him: for she is a sinner.

40 And Jesus answering said unto him, Simon, I have somewhat to say unto thee. And he saith, Master, say on.

41 There was a certain creditor which had two debtors: the one owned five hundred pence, and other fifty.

42 And when they had nothing to pay, he frankly forgave them both. Tell me therefore, which of them will love him most?

43 Simon answered and said, I suppose that *he*, to whom he forgave most. And he said unto him, Thou hast rightly judged.

44 And he turned to the woman, and said unto Simon, Seest thou this woman? I entered into thine house, thou gavest me no water for my feet: but she hath washed my feet with tears, and wiped *them* with the hairs of her head.

45 Thou gavest me no kiss: but this woman since the time I came in hath not ceased to kiss my feet.

46 My head with oil thou didst not anoint: but this woman hath anointed my feet with ointment.

47 Wherefore I say unto thee, Her sins, which are many, are forgiven: for she loved much: but to whom little is forgiven, the *same* loveth little.

48 And he said unto her, Thy sins are forgiven.

49 And they that sat at meat with him began to say within themselves, Who is this that forgiveth sins also?

50 And he said to the woman, Thy faith hath saved thee; go in peace.

wiped them with the hair of her head, and kissed his feet, and anointed them with the ointment. 39 Now when the Pharisee who had invited him saw it, he said to himself, "If this man were a prophet, he would have known who and what sort of woman this is who is touching him, for she is a sinner." 40 And Jesus answering said to him, "Simon, I have something to say to you." And he answered, "What is it, Teacher?" 41 "A certain creditor had two debtors; one owed five hundred denarii, and the other fifty. 42 When they could not pay, he forgave them both. Now which of them will love him more?" 43 Simon answered, "The one, I suppose, to whom he forgave more." And he said to him, "You have judged rightly." 44 Then turning toward the woman he said to Simon, "Do you see this woman? I entered your house, you gave me no water for my feet, but she has wet my feet with her tears and wiped them with her hair. 45 You gave me no kiss, but from the time I came in she has not ceased to kiss my feet. 46 You did not anoint my head with oil, but she has anointed my feet with ointment. 47 Therefore I tell you, her sins, which are many, are forgiven, for she loved much; but he who is forgiven little, loves little." 48 And he said to her, "Your sins are forgiven." 49 Then those who were at table with him began to say among themselves, "Who is this, who even forgives sins?" 50 And he said to the woman, "Your faith has saved you; go in peace."

SECOND QUARTER

Key Verse: He said to the woman, "Your faith has saved you; go in peace." (Luke 7:50)

Key Verse: He said to the woman, Thy faith hath saved thee; go in peace. (Luke 7:50)

As You Read the Scripture—Mike Winters

Luke 7:36. The Pharisee's name was Simon (verse 40). Jesus was a dinner guest of Pharisees on at least two other occasions (Luke 11:37; 14:1). Simon apparently had some interest in Jesus. He thought Jesus might be a prophet (verse 39). He acknowledged Jesus as a teacher, or rabbi (verse 40). Yet Simon did not offer the warmth or the customary rituals associated with an invitation to dinner (verses 44-46).

At the table, Simon and his guests actually reclined on couches. Their feet would have been away from the table, their sandals left at the door.

Verse 37. The woman may have been a prostitute. That conclusion is drawn from the phrase "who was a sinner." The phrase "woman of the city" is not to be understood the same way we would understand the modern phrase "woman of the night." She was from the city, perhaps Capernaum.

The alabaster jar was filled with an oil for the ritual anointment of the head (compare Mark 14:3).

Though the setting seems to be a private dinner, the presence of uninvited guests signaled no concern. On other occasions in Jesus' ministry the masses pressed at the doors of private homes (Mark 1:33).

Verse 38. There is no indication that Jesus and this woman had ever met. Yet her sense of humility and gratitude seem to build on some experience. Anointing Jesus' feet with an ointment meant for the head must have been extravagant.

Verse 39. Simon believed that his own faith was a prophetic one. Apparently he believed that the prophets believed as he did. He knew the woman was a sinner, and he avoided all contact with sinners. Jesus did not. Thus Simon could no longer believe Jesus to be a prophet. Jesus' association with sinners and unclean people was a major source of friction between him and the Pharisees (Luke 5: 29-30; Mark 1:41).

Verses 40-43. This parable teaches about forgiveness. The lesson is that the one who is forgiven the greater debt will love the creditor more than the one forgiven a lesser debt. The parable may not have been in this story, originally.

Verse 41. A denarius was worth about twenty cents and represented a day's wage (Matthew 20:2). Five hundred denarii were equal to about $100 (equal to five hundred days' labor).

Verses 42-43. When the debtors were forgiven, Jesus asked, "Which will love [the creditor] more?" Love, indeed, is a response to the experience of forgiveness.

Verses 44-46. These verses indict Simon for his less than adequate welcome. Simon kept Jesus at arm's length, to critically analyze the truth of Jesus. The woman, with no discretion or pride, threw caution to the wind and lavished on Jesus a touching moment of love.

Verse 47. Her love was not the work that resulted in her forgiveness. Rather, her love was a response to her forgiveness. Jesus noted that "she loved much," which was proof to him that she had experienced much forgiveness.

Verses 48-50. The issue raised in these verses is a familiar controversy (Luke 5:20-25).

Verses 48-49. When Jesus said, "Your sins are forgiven," Simon's and his other guests' "teeth were set on edge." For the Pharisees, this was a sour declaration (Luke 5:21). The Pharisees believed that only God could forgive sins. The woman, a sinner, knew something about Jesus that Simon and his ritually righteous friends did not. In Jesus was the power of God.

Verse 50. Her faith saved her. Because she believed, she was made righteous (Romans 1:17). The woman was sent with the blessing of peace. "Go in peace" is an ancient blessing (I Samuel 1:17). In Jesus' mind is the idea of "shalom." It is the quality of being well, of being right with God.

The Bible and the Main Question—William H. Willimon

A Woman Who Was a Sinner

One of the designations by which people addressed Jesus was "rabbi," which means in Hebrew "teacher." Jesus taught people about the kingdom of God.

In this series of lessons, we've spoken of various memorable stories about Jesus. In today's scripture, Jesus functions as a teacher—a teacher whose subject matter was no less than God.

Socrates was not only a great philosopher but also a superb teacher. He taught people mainly by asking them questions. "What is truth?" Socrates would ask.

"Truth is whatever the elders tell us," his students would reply.

"Really?" said Socrates. "You have found that everything the elders tell you is true?"

"Well, no, not exactly," they would say, and the learning would begin. Have you ever had a teacher who taught you by this "Socratic method" of instruction?

Sometimes Jesus used questions to instruct. "What does it profit a person to gain the whole world yet lose his soul?" he once asked. "Who do you think was a neighbor to the wounded man in the ditch: the priest, the person who passed by on the other side of the road, or the despised Samaritan who helped the man?" Good teachers challenge us through their probing questions.

But the teaching of Jesus is most noted for its use of stories, parables, and little narratives from everyday human experiences, which help us to see deep matters in new ways. Today we shall focus upon a memorable story of Jesus.

Do You See This Woman?

Why did Jesus use stories to communicate his truth? What are we supposed to learn from these stories about the matter at hand—forgiveness as a measure of love?

One day Jesus was eating at the home of a Pharisee (Luke 7:36-50). The Pharisees are often presented by the Gospel writers as self-righteous religious snobs who lord their rules-and-regulations religion over everyone else. Well, while Jesus eats at the Pharisee's table, a weeping, penitent woman (described as "a sinner") enters.

The woman stands behind Jesus, wets his feet with tears, washes them, and pours ointment upon him. This is more than the smug Pharisee can take. He says to himself (just loud enough for everyone at the table to hear), "Ha! They call this man Jesus a prophet. If he were a real prophet he would be able to see what sort of woman this is who behaves so unseemly towards him."

After all, he seems to imply, the real work of a prophet is to be able to tell sinners from the righteous and to know how to avoid sinners. But this man Jesus allows a sinner to touch him (the word "touch" here in the Greek can mean "caress," "fondle," or "stroke"). Is this any way for a true prophet, a truly godly person, to be carrying on?

Jesus responds with a story: A creditor had two debtors. One debtor owed him a thousand dollars, another owed him five dollars. The creditor, in a great act of generosity, wiped out both debts. Think hard now, which one do you believe would be the most grateful?

The Pharisee replies, "Well, I suppose the one who owed him more."

"Right!" says Jesus. "You showed me no love because you have nothing for which to be forgiven. But this woman, whose sins are many, has been forgiven much, therefore she is very grateful."

Probably, the Pharisee got the point of the little story. His smug self-righteousness shows that he is a man who thinks he has no needs; therefore he will receive very little. Only those who know they have great needs are given much; only they will be grateful.

Of course, the implication is that BOTH the woman and the Pharisee are sinners, though she is a knowing sinner and he is unknowing, which is a rather great difference as far as Jesus is concerned. One knows she has been forgiven by God, the other doesn't.

Who Is This Who Even Forgives Sins?

Perhaps one reason we find it so difficult to have pity on people like this weeping, pentitent woman is that we basically consider ourselves good, decent people. After all, we are here in church, aren't we? We find it difficult to feel forgiveness for her because we do not feel in need of forgiveness ourselves.

If Jesus had responded directly to the Pharisees' criticism with "You religious snobs, you ought to be ashamed of yourselves! Why do you begrudge the grace and forgiveness of God? I am befriending these people because God loves them," what do you think their response would have been?

Instead, he says, in effect, "Let me tell you a little story about some people." We find outselves becoming involved in the story, and we let our defenses down. After all, we are simply hearing a little story about some other people. By the end of the story, though, we gasp, "Oh no! This is a story about ME! I am the stuffy older brother who could not accept his father's inclusive love. I am the pious and uncaring priest who passes by the wounded man lying in the ditch. I am the ungrateful debtor."

Jesus is not simply a wise philosopher who wants to communicate a few abstract ideas for our intellectual consideration. He is a Savior, a Messiah who wants not simply intellectual assent but also discipleship. He wants followers, not admirers, people who learn to respond to the world as he does.

His parables engage us to the depths of our being. We put ourselves in the places of the people in the stories, and that is exactly what he wants us to do. We are to see our faces among the faces of his parables, until we recognize with shock and surprise, "That's me; that's how it is in my life."

Thus, in listening to the parables we are faced with an either/or situation. Either we must turn toward this Savior and change our lives accordingly, or we must reject him and turn away. In this way, his teaching style matches the desired outcome. He is not simply conveying facts or interesting information. He is talking about our becoming part of a new world, citizens of a new kingdom made of people who look at the world in a very different sort of way. Therefore his parables are a perfect way to talk about this truth.

The great theologian Karl Barth once said that when he read the Bible, he saw his face on all its pages. The trouble is, sometimes it's hard to know which face in the story is your face. I confess that I am usually that good little bad boy who comes humbly back home, never that stick-in-the-mud older brother. I am the good Samaritan who takes time to help the man in the ditch, not those busy self-satisfied people who passed by on the other side.

Where is your face in this story of the Pharisees and the penitent woman? Where are you seated around the table with Jesus?

Helping Adults Become Involved—Boyce A. Bowdon

Preparing to Teach

Many people, perhaps some in your class, have difficulty confessing mistakes and shortcomings, even though they fell guilty and strongly desire to be forgiven. And, of course, many people tend to misjudge others, to be unduly critical and unforgiving. This lesson can truly make a difference in the lives of your class members.

Your objectives for this lesson should be to remind class members that (1) God's forgiveness is a consequence of God's love; (2) love is an expression of gratitude for forgiveness; (3) all of us, as long as we live, need to receive God's forgiveness; (4) with God's help we are capable of making changes in our life-styles; (5) we should express our gratitude for God's forgiveness by actions as well as by words; and that (6) following the example of Jesus, we should be open to all people and willing to forgive everyone for anything.

Read Luke 7:36-50 and, if possible, *The Interpreter's Bible*, volume 8, pages 141-46.

Here is one way you might outline the lesson:

I. The scene: Jesus visits Simon.
   A. The scene reported by Luke 7:36-50.
   B. Examination of Luke 7:36-50.
II. People in the scene.
   A. Simon the Pharisee.
   B. The repentant woman.
   C. Jesus.
III. Issues raised in the scene.
   A. Conditions for forgiveness.
   B. Consequences of forgiveness.
IV. The scene's message for us.

SECOND QUARTER

Read carefully "The Scripture and the Main Question" and "As You Read the Lesson." The ideas, insights, and suggestions in these sections should be reflected continually in your lesson plan.

As you use the suggested outline, you may want to either quote or paraphrase ideas. You might like to jot in the margin of your outline the page number and paragraph being referred to. For example, you could write a reference to page 65, paragraph 3, as 65-3.

Have either newsprint and markers or chalkboard and chalk available.

Introducing the Main Question

Basic and helpful ideas are presented in the section "The Main Question." These ideas are essential in helping to identify the purpose of the lesson.

A third grade Sunday school teacher asked her class, "What is the first thing we must do before we can receive God's forgiveness for our sins?" An eager youngster who always had an answer shouted out, "Sin." And he was right.

Todays' scripture lesson tells about two people. One knew she had taken the first step toward forgiveness. The other didn't.

Developing the Lesson

I. The scene: Jesus visits Simon.
   A. The scene reported by Luke 7:36-50.

Have someone read the passage aloud. Ask other class members to try to visualize the scene being described.

   B. Examination of Luke 7:36-50.

To help class members better understand the scripture lesson, share with them information contained in Dr. Winters' exegesis. Be sure to include the following: (1) Jesus was a dinner guest of Pharisees on at least two other occasions; (2) at the table, Simon and his guests actually reclined on couches. Their feet would have been away from the table, their sandals left at the door; (3) it was not unusual for uninvited guests to drop in at a private dinner in Palestine.

II. People in the scene.
   A. Simon the Pharisee.

Why did Simon invite Jesus to eat with him? After the class has had an opportunity to respond to the question, make sure the following point is made before moving on: We can only speculate about Simon's motive for inviting Jesus. He may have had genuine interest in him, thinking he might be a prophet. He may have just been curious. He may have felt obligated to show courtesy. Or he may have had ulterior motives—hoping that Jesus would let his defenses down in this relaxed setting and further incriminate himself with heretical statements.

Simon was critical of the way Jesus responded to the woman. He said to himself, "If this man were a prophet, he would have known who and what sort of woman this is who is touching him, for she is a sinner." The Greek word for "touching" that Luke uses here could also mean "caress," "fondle," or "stroke." Was this any way for a truly godly person to carry on? Ask the class: If you had been present, how would you have reacted to the way Jesus responded to the woman?

184

B. *The repentant woman.*

She may have been a prostitute. At least she had "many sins," according to Jesus. Her actions reveal that she was painfully aware of her sins. She is described as a weeping, penitent woman.

C. *Jesus.*

Ask: Why did Jesus accept Simon's invitation for dinner? Make sure this point is made: While Jesus frequently associated with social and religious outcasts, he also was eager to be with members of the social and religious establishment. He did not exclude anyone, not even his outspoken critics. He accepted Simon's invitation even though he knew Simon might have ulterior motives for inviting him. He must have recognized that while going to Simon's home could be risky, this was an opportunity to reach someone, to demonstrate God's love. Ask: What did Jesus reveal about God when he accepted Simon's invitation to go to his home?

III. *Issues raised in the scene.*

A. *Conditions for forgiveness.*

Ask the class to compare Simon's attitude toward Jesus with the attitude of the repentant woman toward hm. Make sure these points are made: (1) The woman and Simon had at least one thing in common—both were sinners; (2) the woman was aware of her sins; Simon was not. She was humble; he was self-righteous.

Ask class members to list conditions for forgiveness. Have someone write the list on newsprint or a chalkboard.

B. *Consequences of forgiveness.*

The woman, having experienced God's forgiveness, went out of her way to demonstrate her love for Jesus. Simon, not having experienced forgiveness or even a need for it, failed to extend even the common courtesies that were always shown to guests. The woman's love for Jesus was a consequence, not a condition, of forgiveness. Name some other consequences of forgiveness. Have the list written on newsprint or chalkboard. Make sure that the ability to forgive others is included in the list.

You might also want to share with the class what Will Willimon says about forgiving others. He points out that forgiving others is a "humbling experience," partly because when we forgive others we admit that they are very much like ourselves. When we pray the Lord's Prayer, asking God to forgive us as we forgive others, we are admitting that the only reason we have a relationship with God is because God is willing to forgive all the evil and vile things we have done against God.

Helping Class Members Act

IV. *The scene's message for us.*

Ask class members to reflect silently on a question that Dr. Willimon asks: "Where is your face in this story of the Pharisees and the penitent woman? Where are you seated around the table with Jesus?"

Planning for Next Sunday

Ask the class to read Psalm 116:1-10; Matthew 21:21-22; Luke 8:1-2, 40-56.

Touch: A Step Toward Wholeness

Background Scripture: Luke 8:1-3, 40-56

The Main Question—William H. Willimon

Life involves coming up against the limits of life. In every person's life, there are boundaries, walls that we can't get over, locked doors that cannot be opened. We spend much of our lives attempting to scale the walls, pushing at the doors, rattling the locks. Sometimes we succeed. But often we fail, and life becomes a process either of learning to live with the boundary or of raging in cynical despair against the imposed limits.

In your mind, what are the most troubling boundaries we face in life? Many people face the boundary of prejudice. It is a horrible thing to be judged by someone on the basis of your sex, the color of your skin, or your economic status in life. It seems so terribly unfair because someone is putting us down on the basis of some external characteristic, before we have a chance to prove ourselves or before they have a chance to really get to know us.

Illness is also a boundary. When we are incapacitated, left to suffer as the world goes by, it is easy to sink into self-pity and misery. But what can we do? Without health, there are few options for us.

Death is the ultimate boundary. It is the end of all of our striving, all of our possibilities. In fact, the other boundaries we encounter in life are like little deaths. Our feelings about every other boundary hint at what it is like to face the greatest boundary of all—death.

In today's scripture Jesus confronts all of the boundaries human society sets up before us. What is his response? How might you and I learn from Jesus' response to the boundary situations in life, as we face them ourselves.?

Selected Scripture

King James Version	Revised Standard Version
Luke 8:41-55	*Luke 8:41-55*
41 And behold, there came a man named Ja-i'-rus, and he was a ruler of the synagogue: and he fell down at Je'-sus' feet, and besought him that he would come into his house:	41 And there came a man named Ja'-irus, who was a ruler of the synagogue; and falling at Jesus' feet he besought him to come to his house, 42 for he had an only daughter, about twelve years of age, and she was dying.
42 For he had one only daughter, about twelve years of age, and she lay a dying. But as he went the people thronged him.	As he went, the people pressed round him. 43 And a woman who had had a flow of blood for twelve
43 And a woman having an issue of blood twelve years, which had	years and could not be healed by any

spent all her living upon physicians, neither could be healed of any,

44 Came behind *him*, and touched the border of his garment: and immediately her issue of blood stanched.

45 And Je'-sus said, Who touched me? When all denied, Pe'-ter and they that were with him said, Master, the multitude throng thee and press *thee*, and sayest thou, Who touched me?

46 And Je'-sus said, Somebody hath touched me: for I perceive that virtue is gone out of me.

47 And when the woman saw that she was not hid, she came trembling, and falling down before him, she declared unto him before all the people for what cause she had touched him, and how she was healed immediately.

48 And he said unto her, Daughter, be of good comfort: thy faith hath made thee whole; go in peace.

49 While he yet spake, there cometh one from the ruler of the synagogue's *house*, saying to him, Thy daugher is dead; trouble not the Master.

50 But when Je'-sus heard *it*, he answered him saying, Fear not: believe only, and she shall be made whole.

51 And when he came into the house, he suffered no man to go in, save Pe'-ter, and James, and John, and the father and mother of the maiden.

52 And all wept, and bewailed her: but he said, Weep not; she is not dead, but sleepeth.

53 And they laughed him to scorn, knowing that she was dead.

54 And he put them all out, and took her by the hand, and called, saying, Maid, arise.

55 And her spirit came again, and she arose straightway: and he commanded to give her meat.

one, 44 came up behind him, and touched the fringe of his garment; and immediately her flow of blood ceased. 45 And Jesus said, "Who was it that touched me?" When all denied it, Peter said, "Master, the multitudes surround you and press upon you!" 46 But Jesus said, "Some one touched me; for I perceive that power has gone forth from me." 47 And when the woman saw that she was not hidden, she came trembling, and falling down before him declared in the presence of all the people why she had touched him, and how she had been immediately healed. 48 And he said to her, "Daughter, your faith has made you well; go in peace."

49 While he was still speaking, a man from the ruler's house came and said, "Your daughter is dead; do not trouble the Teacher any more." 50 But Jesus on hearing this answered him, "Do not fear; only believe, and she shall be well." 51 And when he came to the house, he permitted no one to enter with him, except Peter and John and James, and the father and mother of the child. 52 And all were weeping and bewailing her; but he said, "Do not weep; for she is not dead but sleeping." 53 And they laughed at him, knowing that she was dead. 54 But taking her by the hand he called, saying, "Child arise." 55 And her spirit returned, and she got up at once; and he directed that something should be given her to eat.

Key Verse: He . . . took her by the hand, and called saying, maid, arise. (Luke 8:54)

Key Verse: Taking her by the hand he called, saying, "Child, arise." (Luke 8:54)

As You Read the Scripture—Mike Winters

Luke 8:40-56. Jesus continued to preach, teach, and heal throughout the Galilean region, even to the country of the Gerasenes. There Jesus cast out demons. Returning to Galilee, probably to the city of Capernaum, Jesus encountered Jairus and a hemorrhaging woman. Jesus resurrected Jairus's dead daughter and healed the woman.

Verse 41. Jairus was a ruler of the synagogue. He was one of the leaders of the council of elders. His responsibilty was the supervision of worship in the synagogue (Acts 13:15).

In oriental custom there are three degrees of bowing when meeting a person. The first is a slight nodding motion. The second, showing a greater degree of respect, is a waist bow. The third degree is full prostration, showing total respect. One would have guessed, by virtue of Jairus's synagogue responsibilities, that his loyalties would have been with Jesus' opposition. It must have been a surprise, indeed, that Jairus would have prostrated himself at Jesus' feet.

Verse 42. Jairus's daughter was twelve years old. In ancient Semitic culture she had come of age. Though she was still a child, socially she had completed adolescence. Whereas Mark referred to the child as Jairus's little daughter (Mark 5:23), Luke say she was Jairus's only daughter.

Verse 49. Jesus overheard the comment made to Jairus, that his daughter was dead.

Verse 50. Here and in verse 48, the Greek phrases translated "shall be well" and "made you well" have a special meaning. The phrases means freedom from oppression or rescue from destruction. Also, here as in verse 48, faith and healing are linked. This is characteristic in Luke (verse 17:19, 18:42). Also, in verse 7:50, Luke linked faith and salvation. In the doctrine of justification by faith, the faithful are saved by the power of God. Faith is not the saving power. In the same way, Luke taught that healing is by God's power. Faith is not the power that healed. Faith must always be understood as a response to God's healing and saving power. Both Jairus and the hemorrhaging woman came to Jesus in response to God's healing and saving power.

Verses 51-53. The professional mourners, including flute players (Matthew 9:23), were already weeping and wailing at Jairus's door. They laughed at Jesus' naiveté. Everyone knew the girl was dead. As on the Mount of Transfiguration (Luke 9:28), Jesus invited only Peter, James, and John into the dead girl's room with Jairus and his wife.

Verses 54-55. The girl was resurrected by the word of God's power, "Child, arise." As a sign that she was really alive, Jesus ordered them to give her some food. (The resurrected Jesus ate with his disciples as a sign of his resurrection, Luke 24:41-43.)

The resurrection of the girl, however, is different from Jesus' and from the resurrection of which the apostle Paul spoke in I Corinthians 15. Although the girl's restoration to life was apparently more than a resuscitation (meaning she was really dead), her resurrected form was not changed. The bodily form of the resurrected Jesus was veiled. He was finally recognized while eating (Luke 24:30-31). In Paul's writings the mortal body and the resurrected body are compared to the seed and the emerging sprout.

Verse 43. The woman's disease was "menorrhagia," continuous menstruation. Even worse than the disease itself was that it made her perpetually ritually unclean. She had had the disease for twelve years. Jairus' daughter was twelve years old.

The RSV omits the phrase "and had spent all her living upon physicians." The idea that Luke was a physician is based on this phrase, which remains in some of the ancient texts. The logic is, a good physician might be sensitive to medical fraud.

Verse 44. The woman touched the fringe on Jesus garment. The fringe was called the "sacred tassel" (Numbers 15:38-39). When she touched the sacred tassel, God healed the woman. (See also Acts 19:12.)

Verses 45-48. Jesus sought the face of the one who had touched him. We can only imagine the woman's fear. She had made Jesus unclean by her touching. But she came forward, thus professing her faith. She believed. She touched. She was healed. She was sent away in peace.

The Scripture and the Main Question—William H. Willimon

The People Pressed Around Him

The scene is a typical one in all of the Gospels—crowds of sick people pressing in on Jesus. There is the pitiful sight of the man named Jairus, a high official in the synagogue, reduced to nothing because "he had an only daughter, about twelve years of age, and she was dying" (Luke 8:42). No sooner had Jairus come before Jesus than there appeared in the crowd a woman who had had "a flow of blood for twelve years and could not be healed by anyone" (8:43). We are told that Jairus was an important and influential man. We are told little about the woman. We can surmise that because she was not only a woman, but a woman who had been ill for a long time, she was probably very poor. But any distinctions their society may have made between Jairus and this woman crumbled, because they were both laid low by illness. As the old medicine advertisement used to say, "When you've got your health, you have everything." And when you don't have your health, you have very little.

When you read the Bible, it is amazing how much of it is consumed with questions on illness. Particularly in the psalms, there is great concern about the anguish one suffers when one is sick. There are continual pleas to God to reach out to help the suffering. In our own day, though we have made many strides in the treatment of illness, illness still consumes a major portion of our national budget.

We can imagine how Jairus must have felt. Although he might have had prestige, great learning, and influence, with his only daughter seriously ill nothing was important to him except her recovery. When a family member experiences serious illness, all family activities stop. Everything focuses on the sick person and his or her recovery. Illness has a way of taking over every other concern.

It is important to note first that Jesus is in the midst of the suffering. He is not meditating on a mountain top, serene and aloof. He wades into the midst of the suffering. He reaches out and touches those who hurt. Thus we see that Jesus not only preached compassion, he lived it. He became the very embodiment of compassion. Today's scripture is not unusual, because there are many instances of Jesus' healing sick people. And that is part of its significance—it is not unusual. It is very typical of Jesus to reach out to those who hurt.

She Had Been Immediately Healed

Some time ago a friend told me about an experience he had while he was working as an orderly in a Chicago inner city hospital. To work his way through college, he took this rather menial job of emptying bed pans, bathing patients, and doing other duties in the rooms. Each evening he noticed an older man working as a volunteer orderly. He worked alongside the man and was most impressed by the man's dedication to his work and his sensitivity to the needs of the patients. He wondered how this man could give himself so unselfishly.

Later, he was amazed to find out that this man was the head of a major corporation in the city. And yet two nights a week he worked in the hospital until midnight as a volunteer orderly. My friend wondered what motivated him to do this, so he asked him one night.

"Oh I just feel if there is something that I can do for those who are less fortunate than I am, I ought to do it," the man replied.

"I don't mean to be rude or impertinent," my friend said. "But I wonder why you don't just donate the money it would take to hire another orderly here at the hospital. I'm sure that it wouldn't cost you that much to pay the entire salary of a full-time orderly here rather than come over here a couple of nights a week yourself."

The man replied, "That's just the point. I could give the money, and it would cost me very little. I have more money than time. By coming over a couple of nights a week, it really does cost me something. Besides, I am giving these people the personal touch—something they couldn't get if I just sent money over here to hire someone else to do it. I don't think that anything can beat the personal touch."

My friend was so impressed by the man's response that he has never forgotten him. To this day, that man's emphasis on the "personal touch" has been for my friend the very model of love and compassion.

When I was growing up, our church school class always took baskets of food to poor people on holidays like Thanksgiving and Christmas. These food baskets have been much ridiculed over the years as being paternalistic and demeaning. Today the emphasis is on social programs and other governmental means of alleviating the plight of the poor. And yet, as I look back on those experiences, I must say that those baskets of food at least ensured that our compassion would have the "personal touch." It forced us not only to give some food but also to come into personal contact with the victims of poverty. I can still remember the vivid impression that visiting those poorly heated, bad houses made upon me.

Personally, I think that our charity has lost something, now that our concern for the poor is measured mainly in taxes, government programs, and other anonymous, impersonal ways. Nothing is so powerful as the personal touch.

Do Not Fear . . . She Shall Be Well

"Reach out and touch someone" was the slogan of a popular advertisement for long distance telephone service a few years ago. Christians are called to follow Jesus's example and reach out and touch those whom the world often considers untouchable. When we are ill, our sickness often produces terrible feelings of isolation. We feel cast upon life's sidelines, far from the action of everyday life. Through visitation, sending get-well cards, and willingness to run errands, dress bandages, do housework, and more, we show in tangible ways our solidarity with those who suffer and our compassion for their needs. It is a relatively easy thing for us to reach out to someone who suffers and say, "I love you." It is much more costly to show our love through acts of compassion, even as Jesus reached out and touched.

In Jesus' day, sick people were considered unclean. They had no knowledge about how germs cause sickness, but they still felt that sick people should be isolated from those who are well. In our own day, our knowledge of the communicability of disease through germs and viruses makes us continue to treat the sick as untouchable.

It cost Jesus to show compassion. It may also cost us. We are called to reach out and touch people in body and in spirit, so that we might be full participants in God's continuing work to bring people to fullness and abundance of life.

Helping Adults Become Involved—Boyce A. Bowdon

Preparing to Teach

With the concerns and needs of your class members in mind, set a couple of objectives for this session. You might choose from these: (1) to raise the awareness of class members about the anguish that sickness caused during the days of Jesus, and still causes today; (2) to reassure class members that God has provided and continues to provide healing; (4) to remind class members that in a sense all healing is divine healing; (5) to affirm the significance of touch as a means of transmitting to others feelings that words can not express.

Here is one way to outline the lesson:

     I.   The scene.
         A. Scripture reading.
         B. Explanation of scripture.
    II.   People in the scene.
         A. Jairus.
         B. The woman with the hemor-rhage.
         C. Jesus.
   III.   Issues raised in the scene.
         A. The prevalence of illness.
         B. God is the source of all healing.
         C. The healing touch.
   IV.   Message of the scene for us.

SECOND QUARTER

Read carefully "The Scripture and the Main Question" and "As You Read the Scripture." These form the heart of the lesson. The ideas, insights, and suggestions in these sections should be reflected continually in your lesson plan.

As you use the suggested outline, you may want to either quote or paraphrase ideas. You might like to jot in the margin of your outline the page number and paragraph being referred to. For example, you could write a reference to page 65, paragraph 3, as 65-3.

Be sure that Bibles, pencils, paper, and either newsprint and markers or a chalkboard and chalk are available.

Introducing the Main Question

Basic and helpful ideas are presented in the section "The Main Question." These ideas are essential in helping to identify the purpose of the lesson.

You might begin this session by reading (or putting in your own words) the following statement that Dr. Willimon makes in his introduction to the main question:

> Life involves coming up against the limits of life. In every person's life, there are boundaries, walls that we can't get over, locked doors that cannot be opened. We spend much of our lives attempting to scale the walls, pushing at the doors, rattling the locks. Sometimes we succeed. But often we fail, and life becomes a process of either learning to live with the boundary or raging in cynical despair against the imposed limits.

Today's lesson is about two people who reached their limit and found help from a power beyond themselves.

Developing the Lesson

I. The scene.
  A. Scripture reading.
Ask someone who is a dramatic reader to read aloud Luke 8:41-55, while class members try to visualize the scene.
  B. Explanation of scripture.
Share with your class insights from Dr. Winter's exegesis that you think might promote understanding of this scripture. Be sure to include his discussion of the oriental custom of bowing when meeting a person. Emphasize that when Jairus fell prostrate at Jesus' feet, he was making a statement about his respect for Jesus.

II. People in the scene.
  A. Jairus.
As one of the leaders of the council of elders, Jairus was one of ten men responsible for the supervision of worship in the synagogue. One would have guessed, by virtue of his position, that he would have opposed Jesus. Why do you think he ran to Jesus for help when his daughter was critically ill?
  B. The woman with the hemorrhage.
The woman with the hemorrhage apparently suffered from menorrha-

192

gia, a continuous menstruation. In addition to what this condition did to her physically, it left her ceremonially unclean. She was not permitted to enter the temple or synagogue or to socialize with others. To help the class realize the penalty that the woman faced for being unclean, have someone read aloud Numbers 5:2-4.

   C. Jesus.

When the woman with the discharge touched the fringe of Jesus' garment, she made him ceremonially unclean too.

How did Jesus react? Was he angry? No, he told the woman, "Daughter, your faith has made you well; go in peace."

Read to the class the following statement that Dr. Willimon makes in his exposition: "Jesus is . . . in the midst of the suffering. He is not meditating on a mountain top, serene and aloof . . . . He reaches out and touches those who hurt. Thus we see that Jesus not only preached compassion, he lived it. He became the very embodiment of compassion."

Ask the class: What does Jesus' response to Jairus and his daughter, to the woman with the hemorrhage, and to other sick people reveal about the nature of God?

III. Issues raised in the scene.
   A. *The prevalence of illness.*

Divide the class into Bible research teams of three people each. Have the teams compete to see which one can find the most references to sickness in Matthew, Mark, Luke, and John. Allow five minutes or so for the search, then compare findings. This activity should make your class more aware than ever that the Bible contains many references to sickness and the anguish it causes victims and loved ones.

Ask class members to discuss in the same groups of three the following questions, in light of personal experience: What's it like to have a severe illness? What does it do to the family?
   B. *God is the source of all healing.*

Throughout the centuries, sick people and others facing problems that defy human solutions have discovered a power beyond themselves that has made a vital difference in their ability to cope. As an example of the help that troubled people have found, have someone read aloud Psalm 116:1-10.

Faith does not heal. God heals. Faith is a response to God's healing and saving power.

Ask the class: What channels of healing does God use today? While the class is responding, have someone make a list on newsprint or the chalkboard. Invite members of the class to share how faith in God's healing power has helped them cope with sickness or other anguish.
   C. *The healing touch.*

Ask these questions and give class members an opportunity to respond briefly: Is there such a thing as a healing touch? Has the touch of another person ever brought comfort or healing to you? If so, what were the circumstances?

Helping Class Members Act

IV. Message of the scene for us.

How can a Christian of today be an "embodiment of compassion"? Share with the class the story that Dr. Willimon tells about the head of a major corporation who volunteered as an orderly in a Chicago hospital, so he could give patients the "personal touch."

Read to the class this statement made by Dr. Willimon: "We are called to reach out and touch people in body and in spirit, so that we might be full participants in God's continuing work to bring people to fullness and abundance of life."

Ask these questions: As a church, how can we reach out to people and give a personal touch? How can we do this as a church school class? As individuals?

Planning for Next Sunday

Ask class members to read Matthew 13:31-33, 44-48 and Luke 12:13-34.

UNIT III: RESPONSE AND RESPONSIBILITY
Horace R. Weaver

FOUR LESSONS   **FEBRUARY 5–26**

Unit III, "Response and Responsibility," notes various ways that persons responded to Jesus and his call. He calls for a new attitude toward possessions, a sense of joyful gratitude to God, a total commitment to Jesus and his self-giving way, and an openness to God and other people.

The major emphases of the lessons are as follows: "Seeking God's Kingdom," February 5, distinguishes the important from the unimportant things in life. "Expressing Gratitude," February 12, discusses how only one of the ten lepers was made "whole"; nine were still self-centered and ungrateful. "Responding to God's Call," February 19, declares that all persons may hear God's call and make a decision for or against it. "Becoming a Believer," February 26, illustrates the need not only to believe (even the Devil believes in God) but also to make amends for intentionally committed wrongs.

LESSON 10   **FEBRUARY 5**

Seeking God's Kingdom

Background Scripture: Luke 12:13-34

The Main Question—William H. Willimon

In my last church, a church school class for young couples began a study developed by my denominaton, entitled "Television and Human Values." At first, I wondered if studying television was an appropriate topic for an adult church school class. I was surprised when the class studied the material for over thirteen weeks! I was even more surprised when I heard that the size of their group nearly doubled during that period.

What was going on here? I had to ask myself.

Television has been called by some "the idiot box." This class discovered that television can be more appropriately called "the ideology box." As we watch television for hours daily, we are being subjected to an ideology that may be alien to the Christian faith. In all sorts of subtle ways we imbibe values and principles that may be explicitly un-Christian. I saw recently that the average American child watches television for twenty hours per week! What is this doing to our children? We can be sure that television is forming them into certain sorts of people who respond to the world in certain sorts of ways, many of which may be decidely un-Christian.

Among the evils that television is fostering is increased materialism. We are bombarded with advertisements telling us to buy this, seek this, try that. In today's scripture, Jesus confronts our anxiety about things. What word is Jesus offering us in our struggle to keep material possessions in their place? The main question of this lesson is, What really matters most in life?

Selected Scripture

King James Version

Revised Standard Version

Luke 12:13-15, 22-34

13 And one of the company said unto him, Master, speak to my brother, that he divide the inheritance with me.

14 And he said unto him, Man, who made me a judge or a divider over you?

15 And he said unto them, Take heed, and beware of covetousness: for a man's life consisteth not in the abundance of the things which he possesseth.

....

22 And he said unto his disciples, Therefore I say unto you, Take no thought for your life, what ye shall eat; neither for the body, what ye shall put on.

23 The life is more than meat, and the body is *more* than raiment.

24 Consider the ravens: for they neither sow nor reap; which neither have storehouse nor barn; and God feedeth them: how much more are ye better than the fowls?

25 And which of you with taking thought can add to his stature one cubit?

Luke 12:13-15, 22-34

13 One of the multitude said to him, "Teacher, bid my brother divide the inheritance with me." 14 But he said to him, "Man, who made me a judge or divider over you?" 15 And he said to them, "Take heed, and beware of all covetousness; for a man's life does not consist in the abundance of his possessions."

....

22 And he said to his disciples, "Therefore I tell you, do not be anxious about your life, what you shall eat, nor about your body, what you shall put on. 23 For life is more than food, and the body more than clothing. 24 Consider the ravens: they neither sow nor reap, they have neither storehouse nor barn, and yet God feeds them. Of how much more value are you than the birds! 25 And which of you by being anxious can add a cubit to his span of life? 26 If then you are not able to do as small a thing as that, why are

26 If ye then be not able to do that thing which is least, why take ye thought for the rest?

27 Consider the lilies how they grow: they toil not, they spin not; and yet I say unto you, that Sol'-o-mon in all his glory was not arrayed like one of these.

28 If then God so clothe the grass, which is to day in the field and to morrow is cast into the oven; how much more *will he clothe* you, O ye of little faith?

29 And seek not ye what ye shall eat, or what ye shall drink, neither be ye of doubtful mind.

30 For all these things do the nations of the world seek after: and your Father knoweth that ye have need of these things.

31 But rather seek ye the kingdom of God; and all these things shall be added unto you.

32 Fear not, little flock; for it is your Father's good pleasure to give you the kingdom.

33 Sell that ye have, and give alms; provide yourselves bags which wax not old, a treasure in the heavens that faileth not, where no thief approacheth, neither moth corrupteth.

34 For where your treasure is, there will your heart be also.

Key Verse: **Seek ye the Kingdom of God; and all these things shall be added unto you. (Luke 12:31)**

you anxious about the rest? 27 Consider the lilies, how they grow; they neither toil nor spin; yet I tell you, even Solomon in all his glory was not arrayed like one of these. 28 But if God so clothes the grass which is alive in the field today and tomorrow is thrown into the oven, how much more will he clothe you, O men of little faith! 29 And do not seek what you are to eat and what you are to drink, nor be of anxious mind. 30 For all the nations of the world seek these things; and your Father knows that you need them. 31 Instead, seek his kingdom, and these things shall be yours as well.

32 "Fear not, little flock, for it is your Father's good pleasure to give you the kingdom. 33 Sell your possessions, and give alms; provide yourselves with purses that do not grow old, with a treasure in the heavens that does not fail, where no theif approaches and no moth destroys. 34 For where your treasure is, there will your heart be also."

Key Verse: **Seek [God's] kingdom, and these things shall be yours as well. (Luke 12:31)**

As You Read the Scripture—Mike Winters

Luke 12:13-15. Religious law, social law, personal morality, and ethics were confused in Jewish tradition. Theologically, it was a good idea. It demonstrated Israel's belief that God is sovereign over all things, religious and secular. It was only natural for someone with a civil complaint to seek counsel from a rabbi. Jesus, however, drew lines between civil and religious codes. Jesus' concern was for complete loyalty to the kingdom of God. Jesus' "otherworldliness" stood against the world of idolatrous worship, such as allegiance to states and accumulated wealth. Jesus would not allow himself to be drawn into an argument about inheritance. Such an argument can only be developed on a hope that inherited wealth can save. It cannot; only God can save. Paul warned against lawsuits in I Corinthians 6:6-8.

Verse 13. Deuteronomy 21:17 states that the firstborn son is to receive a double portion of his father's inheritance.

Verse 15. The warning concerning "covetousness" anticipates the story that follows. A fulfilled human life does not consist of being wealthy (I Timothy 6:6-10).

Verses 16-21. This story is about hoarding wealth to no end. Though the farmer in the story presented a prudent example, the truth is that the joy gained from this kind of security soon passes away. An even wiser and more prudent plan is implied. That plan is, lay up treasures in heaven.

Why is Jesus so "otherworldly"? Jesus' otherworldly ethics, such as "do not be anxious about your life" (verse 22) and "do not seek what you are to eat" (verse 29) are based on the belief that the kingdom of God, which will cancel the present age, is imminent. In other words, one might say that the kingdom of God is coming regardless of one's ethics, so be forewarned to live rightly. On the other hand, Jesus also believed that the kingdom of God was already present. This being the case, the ethics in these verses are the new law of the land. It is unfair to blend the "not yet" and the "present reality" of the kingdom of God. Christian ethics are developed in that tension.

Verse 22. The word "therefore" indicates that these verses are conclusions drawn from the previous story. The word "anxiety" conveys a sense of carelessness—*care less* about this life!

Verse 23. What is the purpose of life? It is not food and clothing (verse 15).

Verse 24. The birds are an example of perfect trust in God.

Verse 25. Psalm 39: 5 says, "Thou hast made my days a few handbreadths." The length of a cubit is the distance between the elbow and the extended finger tip. A cubit's length is relative here only as a figure of the measure of time.

Verse 26. Jesus has developed an argument based on the absurdity of worry over how long one lives. The conclusion is that all worry about life is equally absurd.

Verse 27. The lilies Jesus mentions are wildflowers. One source indicates that "toil" is a man's labor and "spin" is a woman's labor. They "neither spin nor weave" is a variant reading in the RSV margin.

Verse 28. Dried grass was used as fuel. "O men of little faith!" is Jesus' expression of frustration. The frustration is the way the worldly life distracts from the otherworldly life, from life in the kingdom of God.

Verses 29-30. God knows what is needed for human life (Matthew 6:8).

Verse 31. God's kingdom is even more important than food and water. Matthew 6:33 adds God's righteousness to the quest.

Verse 32. The "little flock" is the church.

Verses 33-34. Luke's rendering offers a more practical application of these teachings than does Matthew 6:19-21. Giving to the poor was an especially pious act (verse 18:22).

The conclusion of all of this is simple. In order to live in the world, people need food, water, and clothing. But these things are not to be the sole purpose of living. If they are, it is an idolatry, and their worship is anxiety. Instead, life's purpose is best spent in search of God's kingdom.

SECOND QUARTER

The Scripture and the Main Question—William H. Willimon

Seek First His Kingdom

In his book *Escape from Evil* (New York: Free Press, 1975) Ernest Becker argued that our natural and inevitable human urge to deny mortality is the root cause of human evil.

We humans are, first of all, animals. We may achieve many things in this life, but we never escape this primal fact. Because we are animals, the instinct for survival is strong. Like any other creature, we are driven by the will to consume, survive, and propagate life. And yet, unlike the other animals so far as we know, humanity is cursed with a unique characteristic—we are conscious that we shall die.

We know that we are terminal and cannot bear the thought. To the Creator, the psalmist could complain:

> Thou turnest man back to the dust,
> and sayest, "Turn back, O children of men!"
> For a thousand years in thy sight
> are but as yesterday when it is past,
> or as a watch in the night.
>
> Thou dost sweep men away; they are like a dream,
> like grass which is renewed in the morning:
> in the morning it flourishes and is renewed;
> in the evening it fades and withers.
>
> ....
>
> For all our days pass away under thy wrath,
> our years come to an end like a sigh.
> The years of our life are threescore and ten,
> or even by reason of strength fourscore;
> yet their span is but toil and trouble;
> they are soon gone, and we fly away.
>
> (Psalm 90)

Herein, Becker argues, lies the source of human evil. We strive to be something we are not, namely, immortal. Therefore we link our lives to institutions—colleges, churches, clubs, nations—all of which have an aura of immortality about them. We know that we shall die but our church, our school, our fraternity, our nation, will go on. Rather than stand alone, we huddle behind the flag or the president. Thus, the state became prominent in human history precisely at the time when the traditional consolations of religion seemed to be in decline. Nationalism became a major path to immortality. Hitler promised the Thousand Year Reich. We build bombs and do anything we think necessary for national defense, because the state, our way to immortality, must be preserved at all costs.

So-called primitive man attempted to control the life-threatening powers of nature through magic, ritual, and voodoo. It has never seemed right that human beings, as marvelous as we are, should be at the mercy of the elements. Magic gave us the possibility of control. Today the conceit continues, not through older forms of magic but through our closest approach to magic—money.

Beware of All Covetousness

Becker calls money "the new universal immortality ideology." How else does one explain the human drive since primitive times to accumulate more than we need, to amass useless goods and to display wealth?

Wealth becomes not a mechanism for brute survival of biological life but a mechanism for achieving immortality. Money became magic, sacred. The first banks were temples. Jesus noted a coin with Caesar's image stamped upon it and took this as a symbol of someone's religious commitment (Matthew 22:21). It was a false god, a competitor with the real God for human loyalty. "You cannot worship this god and the Lord," Jesus said.

Money not only gives us power while we live, it can be accumulated and passed on, so that its power endures even after death, giving one a semblance of immortality. People may die, but they can endow chairs with their names at universities or erect mausoleums, or commission great works of art. In short, they can use money to deny the determinism of nature.

But popular wisdom says, "You can't take it with you." This attempt to discredit our greed actually confirms it. We know in our heart of hearts that we can't take it with us, that we shall die. This knowledge is not an argument against greed but its justification. We shall die, yes, but our children will continue. We can at least pass the power on to them in our wills. Our names will live on in our sons and daughters, who build upon our accumulation and continue the family business after we have gone.

Socialists sometimes label capitalism "legalized greed." True, greed is a major manifestation of the capitalist malaise. But it could also be said that socialism is "legalized envy." The socialist is doubly outraged that some have more than others. Economic inequality seems patently unfair to the socialist because material possessions still seem the only means of immortality. Through governmental coercion, goods are redistributed. It seems clear, then, that at bottom, the capitalist and socialist are the same. Both rely upon wealth, however distributed, to provide them a sense of immortality.

Do Not Be Anxious About Your Life

Christianity is a threat to both capitalism and communism—at least when it takes its own message seriously. One reason that primitive Christians could part with material possessions, even life itself, so cheerfully was that they had their eyes fixed upon "the city which has foundations, whose builder and maker is God" (Hebrews 11:10). As Ernest Becker notes, "Primitive Christianity is one of the few ideologies that has kept alive the idea of the invisible dimension of nature and the priority of this dimension for assuring immortality" (p. 86). The only salvation worth having is salvation from our fear of death and our terror of insignificance. Christianity, historically, has offered this possibility. "He who finds his life will lose it, and he who loses his life for my sake will find it," says Christ (Matthew 10:39).

Christianity is subversive to any one-dimensional ideology that sees the world and people in only materialistic terms, to any ideology that reduces human beings to simple matters of race, class production, and consumption. By avoiding the Christian call to renounce possessions, class, race, gender, and all other materialistic, totemistic claims upon our lives, we deny the existence of any realm other than the material. We are thus free to

199

pursue wealth and its powers with a vengeance and wholehearted dedication unknown to our forebears. This is the situation for which today's scripture is both judgment and grace.

Helping Adults Become Involved—Boyce A. Bowdon

Preparing to Teach

With the concerns and needs of your class members in mind, jot down a few objectives for this lesson. Here are some you might consider: (1) to encourage class members to take an honest look at what matters most to them; (2) to remind class members of the folly of seeking to find a sense of self-worth, security, and immortality in material possessions; (3) to remind class members that all our possessions—including things accumulated as a result of hard work and good management—are gifts from God; (4) to remind class members that we are totally dependent upon God, regardless of how financially secure we may be; (5) to reassure class members that we should do the best we can and leave the rest with God, without worrying unduly; (6) to affirm that our major aim in life should be to seek everyday to find and to follow God's will for us—to let God's rule be real in our lives.

Read the devotional reading, Luke 12:13-34, and, if possible, *The Interpreter's Bible*, volume 8, pages 225-31.

Here is the way to outline the lesson:

> I.   Presenting the scripture.
>   A. Scripture reading.
>   B. Scripture background.
> II. The role of money.
>   A. Money matters.
>   B. Money isn't everything.
> III. Worry is useless.
> IV. Seek true security.
> V.   Message for us in the scripture.

Read carefully "The Scripture and the Main Question" and "As You Read the Scripture." These form the heart of the lesson. The ideas, insights, and suggestions in these sections should be reflected continually in your lesson plan.

As you use the suggested outline, you may want to either quote or paraphrase ideas. You might like to jot in the margin of your outline the page number and paragraph being referred to. For example, you could write a reference to page 65, paragraph 3, as 65-3.

Have available pencils, paper, and newsprint and markers or a chalkboard and chalk.

Introducing the Main Question

Basic and helpful ideas are presented in the section "The Main Question." These ideas are essential in helping to identify the purpose of the lesson.

To introduce this lesson, you might like to say something like this: People often were surprised by the response Jesus gave to questions he was asked.

Sometimes the questions were carefully worded to trick him into making a statement that could be used against him as evidence of blasphemy or some other violation of political or religious law. But Jesus was a master at using the critic's questions to his own advantage in making the point that needed to be made. Today's scripture lesson begins with a question posed to Jesus by a man who wanted him to help settle a dispute he was having with his brother concerning an inheritance.

Rabbis were often asked to rule in such cases, but Jesus had no intention of being pulled into this conflict. He recognized that the real problem was much deeper: It had to do with attitudes toward material possessions. And so Jesus got to the heart of the matter, as he always did. What he had to say, as a result of that man's efforts long ago to involve him in a family dispute, speaks to us today. Whether we are rich or poor or somewhere in between, there's a message in this scripture passage for us.

Developing the Lesson

I. Presenting the scripture.
  A. Scripture reading.
Have someone read aloud Luke 12:13-34, while other class members jot down on paper what they consider to be the scripture's most important ideas. After the scripture has been read, invite class members to read their lists. Have someone write the ideas on newsprint or the chalkboard, for reference during the session.
  B. Scripture background.
Share with the class insights from Dr. Winters's exegesis that might help them better understand the lesson.

II. The role of money.
  A. Money matters.
Jesus did not condemn the rich fool's hard work and good management. He made it clear on several occasions that his followers should invest their talents and be responsible stewards of their possessions.

John Wesley, one of the founders of Methodism, urged people to "earn all you can, save all you can, and give all you can."

Ask the class: Why does money matter? What are some of the good things it does? While class members call out their answers, have someone write them on newsprint or on the chalkboard.
  B. Money isn't everything.
Dr. Willimon, in his exposition, makes some interesting statements about money. Here's one you might read to the class: "So-called primitive man attempted to control the life-threatening powers of nature through magic, ritual, and voodoo. It has never seemed right that human beings, as marvelous as we are, should be at the mercy of the elements. Magic gave us the possibility of control. Today the conceit continues, not through older forms of magic but through our closest thing to magic—money."

Ask: What are some things money cannot provide? Again, while answers are being given, have someone write them on the chalkboard or newsprint.

Direct the attention of the class to the two lists showing what money can and can't do. Review the lists for a moment.

III. *Worry is useless.*

Not only does the scripture for this lesson contain a message for those who have more possessions than they need, it has a message for those who don't have enought to get by. Direct attention to Luke 12:22-30. What does Jesus mean when he says we should not be anxious?

IV. *Seek true security.*

Make this statement, or one like it, in your own words: The main point Jesus wanted to make by his parable of the rich fool was that material resources, even though they are very important, cannot provide true security. True security is found when we "seek first the kingdom of God."

Divide the class into four groups. Give the following assignments:

Group One: In what sense was the rich farmer a fool?

Group Two: What should a Christian's attitude be toward money?

Group Three: What is the kingdom of God?

Group Four: Name three specific ways that we can seek first the kingdom of God.

After the groups have had time to answer their questions, have them share their views with the whole class. Provide an opportunity for everyone to respond following each group's report.

Helping Class Members Act

V. *Message for us in the scripture.*

Will Willimon ends his introduction to this lesson with three questions that might stimulate class members to act. Present them for discussion: What word is Jesus offering us in our struggle to keep material possessions in their place? How can God help us overcome our greed? How can God give us something worth living for that is more important than a VCR, an automobile, or a mink coat?

Planning for Next Sunday

Ask class members to read Psalm 105:1-5; Leviticus 13:9-17; 45:46; and Luke 17:11-19.

LESSON 11   FEBRUARY 12

Expressing Gratitude

Background Scripture: Leviticus 13:9-17, 45-46; Luke 17:11-19

The Main Question—William H. Willimon

In our age, great emphasis has been put upon the rights of the individual citizen. The civil rights movement is one of the great social adventures of our time. Our United States Constitution is based upon the assumption that there are certain inalienable human rights. The Constitution exists to make sure that everyone has the same rights and freedoms.

The trouble is, with all of our interest in rights, there is little room left for the experience of gratitude. After all, if my food, shelter, clothing, and health are "my right," then why should I feel gratitude? I feel these are my just deserts, something I have a right to enjoy. In such a climate, it is difficult to feel grateful for having the necessities of life. In emphasizing human rights, we have made human gratitude problematic. When something is a right, then it is hard to be surprised by it or deeply grateful for it.

The Bible contends that gratitude is a quality that must be cultivated. We are not necessarily born feeling grateful. It is only our experience of the gracious love of God that moves us to see our lives and all those things that are most precious to us as gifts from a loving God.

The main question is, How is it possible to feel and express gratitude in our day and time?

Selected Scripture

King James Version

Revised Standard Version

Luke 17:11-19

11 And it came to pass, as he went to Je-ru'-sa-lem, that he passed through the midst of Sa-mar'-i-a and Gal'-i-lee.

12 And as he entered into a certain village, there met him ten men that were lepers, which stood afar off:

13 And they lifted up *their* voices, and said, Je'-sus, Master, have mercy on us.

14 And when he saw *them*, he said unto them, Go shew yourselves unto the priests. And it came to pass, that, as they went, they were cleansed.

15 And one of them, when he saw that he was healed, turned back, and with a loud voice glorified God,

16 And fell down on *his* face at his feet, giving him thanks: and he was a Sa-mar'-i-tan.

17 And Je'-sus answering said, Were there not ten cleansed? but where *are* the nine?

18 There are not found that returned to give glory to God, save this stranger.

19 And he said unto him, Arise, go thy way: thy faith hath made thee whole.

Luke 17:11-19

11 On the way to Jerusalem he was passing along between Samar'ia and Galilee. 12 And as he entered a village, he was met by ten lepers, who stood at a distance 13 and lifted up their voices and said, "Jesus, Master, have mercy on us." 14 When he saw them he said to them, "Go and show yourselves to the priests." And as they went they were cleansed. 15 Then one of them, when he saw that he was healed, turned back, praising God with a loud voice; 16 and he fell on his face at Jesus' feet, giving him thanks. Now he was a Samaritan. 17 Then said Jesus, "Were not ten cleansed? Where are the nine? 18 Was no one found to return and give praise to God except this foreigner?" 19 And he said to him, "Rise and go your way; your faith has made you well."

Key Verse: **When [the leper] saw that he was healed . . . [he] fell down on his face at his feet, giving him thanks. (Luke 17:15-16)**

Key Verse: **When [the leper] saw that he was healed . . . he fell on his face at Jesus' feet, giving him thanks. (Luke 17:15-16)**

As You Read the Scripture—Mike Winters

Luke 17:11. In verse 9:51, Luke's Gospel stops, then resumes. At that point the mood and intensity of the Gospel change. No longer is Jesus' ministry confined to the cities and country about the Sea of Galilee. Suddenly, it says Jesus "set his face to go to Jerusalem," where he was to suffer and die. Verse 11 reminds the reader of Jesus' purpose. He is *still* on his way to Jerusalem.

It appears, however, that Jesus' movement to Jerusalem was more general than direct. One stopover was in Samaria, sandwiched between the regions of Galilee and Judea.

Verse 12. Those who were diagnosed leprous may have actually had any number of skin diseases, from boils to rashes, including actual leprosy. The clinical name for leprosy is Hansen's Disease. The rules concerning the diagnosis of leprosy for Jesus' time are found in Leviticus 13:1-59.

Though leprosy was not in itself a fatal disease, some deaths were related to it. Anesthetic leprosy paralyzes the nerves of the affected limbs. Its victims injure those limbs with no sensation of pain, so they do not seek treatment. Often, injured limbs are lost.

The isolation imposed on the leper in Jesus' Palestine was as disastrous as the disease itself. Lepers lived in their own camps outside the city's walls. When they saw people approaching, they had to shout the warning, "Unclean! Unclean!" The story in II Kings 7:3-4 alludes to the suicidal despair lepers experienced. Indeed, many lepers would have preferred death over separation from everything familar and loved, including their families.

Earlier, Luke 5:12-14 records one leper's healing by Jesus. In that story, the leper dared to approach Jesus. Jesus actually touched him, against all prohibition. Here the lepers keep their required distance from Jesus.

Verse 13. There is a recognition factor here. Rather than shouting the warning, "Unclean!" the lepers shouted, "Jesus, Master, have mercy on us."

No acceptable treatment of their day had brought them any relief, so they were attempting an unorthodox treatment.

Verse 14. Jesus treated them with the command to present themselves to the priests in Jersusalem—the same despairing words they had heard time and again. They had been to the priests for examination and diagnosis, most certainly. But this time they were going not for diagnosis but for the ritual cleansing sacrifices. By the word of God's power in Jesus, they were healed. The ritual prescribed for lepers on the day of their cleansing was two days of offering, on the first and eighth days (Leviticus 14:1-57).

Verses 15-16. Only the Samaritan returned and prostrated himself at Jesus' feet and gave thanks. The Samaritan would have been suspicious of the rituals and sacrifices in Jerusalem. Insight into the conflict between the Samaritans and Jews can be found in the story of Jesus and the woman at the well. See John 4:19-26. In Jewish communities a Samaritan would have been despised, even without leprosy.

Verses 17-18. Do not judge the nine who did not return to give thanks.

Jesus' comment is not necessarily meant to be a lesson in thanksgiving, but a lesson in the inclusiveness of the kingdom of God.

Only the despised foreigner, a Samaritan, responded. As for the others, for years their necks had been under the foot of an oppressive disease. Thanklessly, they had followed the rules that kept them isolated. All they ever saw or heard of humanity was horror and shock and abusive language. No doubt they wondered if there was a just God. Now that they had been healed, one cannot imagine they were thankless, but one can understand their seemingly thankless response. For that reason, the real miracle was that even one returned, not as a matter of course but as a genuine, deliberate expression of thanks.

Verse 19. This is a familiar formula to Luke's readers. There is a difference between "healing" and "being made well." Ten were healed. One was made well. Wellness speaks of a holistic understanding of health.

The Scripture and the Main Question—William H. Willimon

He Saw That He Was Healed

On his way to Jerusalem, Jesus encountered some men suffering from leprosy. He healed all of them, but only one returned to give thanks.

It's easy for us to criticize those who did not return. We like to think we would have at least done that. But would we? We are dealing with people who suffered terribly for perhaps a very long time. They had already paid their dues. Some of them were probably bitter. They had already lost some of the best years of their lives. Now, they wanted to go show themselves to their friends, to take up where life left off. Can you blame them for not coming back and expressing gratitude? Gratitude is not as easy or natural an emotion as we may think.

Encounters with Gratitude

Frankly, I didn't care for him when we first met. He's not the sort of person that you warm up to, at first. You must get used to him. It takes time and life before he becomes part of you. You have to work at getting along with him.

It was my mother who kept trying to get us together.

"Say 'Thank you' to Uncle Henry for giving you the silver dollar," she said. From then on, he was always there, standing in the background all day long, pushing in at dinner time when she said, "I don't think I heard anyone say they enjoyed supper tonight." Then, before bedtime, after toys were put away and the blanket was pulled up around me snugly, when the light was turned out, there he was. "Thank you God for Mamma, and Daddy, and Bud, and Harry, and for the nice day, and for everyone. Amen."

And always, upon returning home, she asked, "Did you tell Uncle Charles how much you enjoyed going to the circus?" Yes, I told him, but he should have been able to look at me and tell how much I enjoyed it without having to bring him along. Just once I would have loved to go to the circus, or a football game, or get through one birthday party without him.

"He's part of the family," my mother said. "He was part of the home that I grew up in, so naturally, when I got married and began a home of my own, Gratitude came along to help us get started right. Why, I wouldn't think of serving a meal, or having a party, or a family reunion, or bringing in the vegetables from the garden, or even sitting on the porch in the evenings without Gratitude."

"But sometimes I just forget," I said.

"Yes, I know," she said. "That's why I'm here to make sure that you don't. One day, it will be natural for you, and you won't forget. One day, having him with you will be second nature. He'll be so much a part of you . . ."

So, good friend of the family, constant if sometimes awkward companion of my earliest years, he skipped along beside me when I started school in the fall of my sixth year.

"You'll be glad I'm with you," he said.

"I will?" I asked.

"Yes," he replied.

"Your teachers will be impressed that you know me."

It was Gratitude who helped me pack my suitcase for college when the time came for that big step. "You know, many people have brought you to this place in life," he told me as he folded another pair of socks.

"Yes, I know, but I don't have the words to tell them. I don't know what to say," I said.

"That's all right," he said. "You don't have to say anything to them. They have taught you and coached you, and your mother has sacrificed and saved for you, not expecting anything in return. The best way to tell them is just to go there and do the best you can."

"And if I fail?" I asked. "What then?"

"Then you give thanks for the experience and grow from it and try something else," he said.

"That's just what I would have expected you to say," I said. "Here, put in this Bible for good luck."

"Yeah," he said, "you'll need it where you're going!"

Whenever I look back on those years, I can't do so without Gratitude.

And, on that winter midnight in 1974, when we drove hurriedly through deserted streets of North Myrtle Beach and rushed into the labor room for our first child, guess who greeted us there?

"I didn't expect to see you out at this time of night, here," I said to him.

"Really?" asked Gratitude in amazement. "Typical of you to think that all it takes to have a baby is an obstetrician! I'm on duty down here at the delivery room full-time," he said.

When I held that small, squalling boy-child in my arms for the first time, wondering how on earth I could be so lucky, I was so glad that I knew Gratitude, and I was glad that he had been there with us for the delivery.

Which brings me to the strange side of Gratitude. I came to expect him to pop up at important times: my college graduation, the day I got married, when my children were born, when I came to Duke Chapel. Go through our family photograph album and you'll see his smiling face in the background, never one to miss a Christmas morning, or a family reunion, or a vacation at the beach. There he was.

But Paul says to us, "Always and for everything give thanks." When the call came, we were sitting with Gratitude in my den, having a party to celebrate my mother's recovery from surgery. The voice said, "We did all we could . . . pulmonary embolism, we think . . . She went quickly."

Through dark, cold, January Durham streets we drove in shock, in disbelief. Papers were signed, clothes and a few potted plants and get-well cards were collected, and back home we went.

I turned into the driveway. Walked up to my door, opened it. There he was. "Don't you think it's time for you to go?" I asked. "The party's over. You take the rest of the champagne with you, if you want. We'll call you after we get back from the funeral. Don't call us, we'll call you."

And Gratitude looked me straight in the eye and, with a voice that mimicked my mother's, said, "Say 'Thank you' to the nice God."

"Look, I don't think you're being very funny," I said.

But he didn't listen. No, he was already getting out the family photograph albums, at 2:00 A.M. no less, passing them around—pictures of my first steps on the lawn, my second Christmas, my first bicycle, my mother at my sister's wedding, my mother sending me on my trip to California, my mother rocking our children. And someone began to laugh about the time we were in a little town in England, and we were laughing and crying and then I understood.

"Don't go, Gratitude," I said. "Please stay. She would want you here. I was wrong. You do belong even now—especially now."

That night I knew Paul was right. It is not only possible, but even necessary that we should "always and for everything" give thanks. The presence of Gratitude transforms even the darkest nights into glorious days. For a Christian, Gratitude is the very key to life.

Helping Adults Become Involved—Boyce A. Bowdon

Preparing to Teach

What can this lesson accomplish? Here are some objectives you might consider: (1) to remind class members that all of us have reason to be grateful to God; (2) to stimulate class members to develop attitudes of gratitude; (3) to encourage class members to examine themselves, asking, "Do I show God I'm grateful?"

Here's an outline that you might adapt to fit your particular teaching situation.

I.   The scene: Ten lepers had a serious problem.
II. Issue raised by the scene: Why did only one leper express gratitude?
III. Benefits of expressing gratitude.
IV. Developing an attitude of gratitude.

Read carefully "The Scripture and the Main Question" and "As You Read the Scripture." These form the heart of the lesson. The ideas, insights, and suggestions in these sections should be reflected continually in your lesson plan.

As you use the suggested outline, you may want to either quote or paraphrase ideas. You might like to jot in the margin of your outline the page number and paragraph being referred to. For example, you could write a reference to page 65, paragraph 3, as 65-3.

Have available paper, pencils, and a chalkboard and chalk or newsprint and markers.

SECOND QUARTER

Introducing the Main Question

Basic and helpful ideas are presented in the section "The Main Question." These ideas are essential in helping to identify the purpose of the lesson.

You might want to introduce the lesson by sharing this story about my friend who received a thank you card from a nephew who had been visiting her family for a week. The young man told how grateful he was for the special effort that had gone into making his trip enjoyable. He bragged about the food, the entertainment, everything.

My friend was touched. "Getting that card really brightened my day," she said. "I wasn't expecting it. I've had nephews and nieces in my home dozens of times in the past five years and this is the first time one ever sent me a card."

Interesting, isn't it? Some people express their gratitude and others don't, even though they have just as much reason to be grateful. Why? It seems that some people take good health and good fortune and all other good things for granted. Others appreciate everything and show it. How do we account for the difference? How can we become more appreciative? We will examine those questions in this lesson.

Developing the Lesson

I. The scene: Ten lepers had a serious problem.

To help your class members become more aware of how devastating the diagnosis of leprosy was in the Jewish community, have someone read aloud Leviticus 13:9-17, 45-46.

After the passage from Leviticus has been read, share with the class the information about leprosy that Dr. Winters includes in "As You Read the Scripture." He points out that in Jesus' Palestine, a wide variety of skin diseases—everything from boils and rashes to actual leprosy—were diagnosed as leprosy. Leprosy was not fatal in itself, but some deaths were related to the disease. For example, anesthetic leprosy paralyzed the nerves of affected limbs. Since victims could not feel pain, they would not be aware of injuries, and sometimes the limbs would be lost due to lack of care.

The isolation imposed on the leper was as disastrous as the disease. Lepers lived in their own camps outside the city's walls and were required to shout "Unclean! Unclean!" when they saw people approaching.

To help class members sense how hopeless lepers often felt, have someone read aloud II Kings 7:3-4.

Have someone read aloud Luke 17:11-19. Ask other class members to try to visualize the scene being described in the passage. Share with the class the information that Dr. Winters gives in his comments about verses 14, 15, and 16.

II. Issue raised by the scene: Why did only one leper express gratitude?

All ten of the lepers had experienced the same miraculous healing. Ask the class to speculate why only one turned back and expressed gratitude. Have someone make a list on the chalkboard or on newsprint of "explanations" the other nine who were also healed might have given if they had been asked why they didn't show their appreciation to Jesus.

Give this question some thought before class and prepare your own list of their possible explanations. Your list might include:

—"He knew I was grateful. There was no reason for me to thank him."
—"How did I know the healing was going to last?"
—"I was just too excited. I wanted to get the priest to pronounce me clean so I could go share the good news with my family."
—"I didn't want to get myself obligated to him."

Direct attention to the list of possible explanations. Now ask: Do we use these same excuses to explain why we fail to express our gratitude to God for his blessings?

Ask your class these two questions: What causes people to express gratitude? What causes people not to express gratitude? Make a list of explanations given by the class on the chalkboard or newsprint.

Share with the class what William Willimon writes in "The Scripture and the Main Question" about his encounters with gratitude. You may want to read the entire section to the class. If not, tell the story in your own words. Ask: What does Dr. Willimon's story tell us about how the habit of expressing gratitude is developed?

III. Benefits of expressing gratitude.

Ask the class: How does expressing gratitude help the one who expresses it? How does expressing gratitude help the one to whom it is expressed?

Helping Class Members Act

IV. Developing an attitude of gratitude.

Distribute pencils and paper to the class. Ask class members to write down—for their eyes only—ten reasons they have for being grateful to God.

Ask: How can we express our gratitude to God? Again, have a list made on the chalkboard or newsprint.

After the class has finished, add to the list your suggestions. One might be: A good way for us to express gratitude to God is by being kind to God's children. List examples of such behavior.

To conclude the session, read this statement written by Dr. Willimon: "The presence of Gratitude transforms even the darkest nights into glorious days. For a Christian, Gratitude is the very key to life." Then read Psalm 105:1-5. Ask class members to make a conscious effort during the week ahead to "give thanks to the Lord, call on his name," and "make known his deeds among the peoples!"

Planning for Next Sunday

Ask class members to read James 3:1-13 and Luke 18:18-30.

Responding to God's Call

Background Scripture: Luke 18:18-30

The Main Question—William H. Willimon

When I was a youth I remember hearing a sermon in which a preacher stated, "In all the Bible, when God speaks to people, God calls them by their very own names."

I thought about the Bible stories I knew and decided that the preacher was right. Not only does God call people by their very own names, but God seems to speak to us in ways uniquely fitted to our needs. How unfortunate that many contemporary approaches to evangelism imply that God calls everyone the same way. Everyone is supposed to have an instantaneous and dramatic conversion experience. But since we are all different, it is reasonable to assume God calls us in different ways.

People are forever being tempted to change Jesus' call of the individual person into universal principles for everyone. He called upon some to leave their fishing nets and follow him, but not everyone. In today's scripture, Jesus calls a young man to go and sell everything that he has and give it to the poor. The story is noteworthy in part because Jesus did not demand this of everyone.

How does Jesus call people? How does he call you and me? In today's scripture study, we will ponder the nature of the call of God and our responses. We will be particularly concerned with how God speaks to us affluent, materially blessed Americans. How does God call *us*?

Selected Scripture

King James Version

Luke 18:18-30

18 And a certain ruler asked him, saying, Good Master, what shall I do to inherit eternal life?

19 And Je'-sus said unto him, Why callest thou me good? none *is* good, save one, *that is* God.

20 Thou knowest the commandments, Do not commit adultery, Do not kill, Do not steal, Do not bear false witness, Honour thy father and thy mother.

21 And he said, All these have I kept from my youth up.

22 Now when Je'-sus heard these things, he said unto him, Yet lackest thou one thing: sell all that thou

Revised Standard Version

Luke 18:18-30

18 And a ruler asked him, "Good Teacher, what shall I do to inherit eternal life?" 19 And Jesus said to him, "Why do you call me good? No one is good but God alone. 20 You know the commandments: 'Do not commit adultery, Do not kill, Do not steal, Do not bear false witness, Honor your father and mother.'" 21 And he said, "All these I have observed from my youth." 22 And when Jesus heard it, he said to him, "One thing you still lack. Sell all that you have and distribute to the poor, and you will have treasure in heaven; and come, follow me." 23 But

hast, and distribute unto the poor, and thou shalt have treasure in heaven: and come, follow me.

23 And when he heard this, he was very sorrowful: for he was very rich.

24 And when Je'-sus saw that he was very sorrowful, he said, How hardly shall they that have riches enter into the kingdom of God!

For it is easier for a camel to go through a needle's eye, than for a rich man to enter into the kingdom of God.

26 And they that heard *it* said, Who then can be saved?

27 And he said, The things which are impossible with men are possible with God.

28 Then Pe'-ter said, Lo, we have left all, and followed thee.

29 And he said unto them, Verily I say unto you, There is no man that hath left house, or parents, or brethren, or wife, or children, for the kingdom of God's sake,

30 Who shall not receive manifold more in this present time, and in the world to come life everlasting.

when he heard this he became sad, for he was very rich. 24 Jesus looking at him said, "How hard it is for those who have riches to enter the kingdom of God! 25 For it is easier for a camel to go through the eye of a needle than for a rich man to enter the kingdom of God." 26 Those who heard it said, "Then who can be saved?" 27 But he said, "What is impossible with men is possible with God." 28 And Peter said, "Lo, we have left our homes and followed you." 29 And he said to them, "Truly, I say to you, there is no man who has left house or wife or brothers or parents or children, for the sake of the kingdom of God, 30 who will not receive manifold more in this time, and in the age to come eternal life."

Key Verse: **Now when Jesus heard these things, he said unto him, Yet lackest thou one thing: Sell all that thou hast, and distribute unto the poor, and thou shalt have treasure in heaven; and come, follow me. (Luke 18:22)**

Key Verse: **And when Jesus heard it, he said to him, "One thing you still lack. Sell all that you have and distribute to the poor, and you will have treasure in heaven; and come, follow me." (Luke 18:22)**

As You Read the Scripture—Mike Winters

Luke 18:18-19. The rich ruler was an official of some synagogue. He called Jesus "Good Teacher." Yet he did not realize that Jesus really was good. He could not see God incarnate in Jesus.

"Only God is good" is an assertion seldom made today except by boys and girls when they pray at meals: "God is great, God is good." "God is good" is a difficult affirmation for those who assert the sovereignty of God as the first theological principle. Though God is sovereign, inevitably the question arises, How can a sovereign God who is good allow the world to suffer? If "God is good" is the first theological principle, then the world's suffering is not viewed as God's creation, but in opposition to God. Is God good? Or is God sovereign? Or is God both?

Eternal life is life in the kingdom of God.

Verse 20. Jesus names only half of the Ten Commandments, those that regulate behavior towards others. Missing, however, from these commandments is "Do not covet" (Exodus 20:17). Though it is missing, it seems to have special application to this story. There is a link between wealth and covetousness. The argument might go like this: Wealthy people simply buy whatever they covet, thus they buy their way out of that sin. They have put their trust in their purchasing power to save them. And their accumulations are their gods, or idols.

Verse 21. It was assumed by the rich ruler, and by other rabbis, that one could indeed meet the requirements of the Law.

Verses 22-23. Jesus' command to sell and give away all he had must have been an especially confusing mandate. The rich ruler, no doubt, had always believed that his wealth was a sure sign of God's blessing and God's call. Jesus' new commandment created for the rich ruler an insurmountable wall in the way of his entry into the kingdom of God. Unfortunately, he valued his possessions and wealth even more than he did the kingdom of God.

Verse 24. Accumulated possessions offer tangible security, which often becomes a barrier to God's security. If wealthy people feel especially judged by this, well they should. But the broader lesson is a word of warning to watch out for every and any thing that becomes the object of security and trust. This is a lesson for poor and rich alike. The special tragedy of the rich ruler was that he was betting on his material security to somehow assure him entry into the kingdom. The rich ruler's history of obedience is not really the issue here, though if Jesus had included "Do not covet," the rich man might have realized he wasn't so obedient after all.

Verse 25. The saying is only a figure of speech for something absolutely impossble.

Verses 26-27. The question here may reflect stunned amazement, because everyone believed what the rich ruler believed, mainly, that wealth is a sign of God's blessing and call. Their bewildered question reflected a new revelation that salvation must be impossible. And indeed salvation is impossible if one trusts in possessions, intellect, obedience, or anything else to save him or her. Salvation is God's work. God will work salvation only in those people who abandon the obstacles of this world's security (Romans 9:16).

Verse 28. Peter realized that he and his partners had given up everything (verse 5:11).

Verses 29-30. Jesus is not promising rewards to his disciples. Jesus' words of assurance point to a universal understanding of home, wife, brothers, parents, and children. Indeed, the kingdom of God is the family of God.

The Scripture and the Main Question—William H. Willimon

"Money, money, money makes the world go around," sings a character in a popular broadway musical. When one thinks of all the anxiety, grief, stress, and physical harm that are a direct result of our frantic pursuit for possessions, you must agree that it does indeed seem that money is the most important thing in the world.

Arguments about money are the primary cause of stress among married couples. Daily our newspapers tell of people who have killed for the smallest

sums of cash, to say nothing of those of us ⌐
ourselves in our harried rat race of achievem

Just because we are Christian doesn't mean
tensions about money. One of my parishione⌐
because he was ill. As he hunted among th⌐
worship service, he came on a television evange
for funds to build a hospital where Jesus ⌐
cancer—if viewers would send in twenty do⌐
evangelist needed funds to keep his new televisi⌐
money, money.

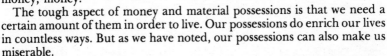

The tough aspect of money and material possessions is that we need a
certain amount of them in order to live. Our possessions do enrich our lives
in countless ways. But as we have noted, our possessions can also make us
miserable.

What makes the difference? That is the question behind today's scripture
concerning possessions.

Take Heed

If you were to chart human life, noting the predominant concerns at each
stage in life's pilgrimage, concern about material possessions would mark
each step along the way.

The little child begs for a dime for candy, and holds his breath, clenches
his teeth, and screams if Mommy doesn't hand it over.

The teenager, in a desperate attempt to be accepted as one of the crowd,
buys the special shoes and clothes that are "in" at the moment. Quality is not
the goal in these purchases; the main thing is to buy what will ensure
popularity. At an early age, we come to use possessions to win friends and to
achieve a sense of personal well-being.

The college student, while sometimes deriding his parents' preoccupation with house, car, job, and prestige, longs for the best car or the best
stereo in the dorm. She burns the midnight oil in hopes of getting the
grades to get a choice job. It's not desire for knowledge that motivates her.
It's a desire for a job bringing in enough income to meet her expectations.

A middle-aged couple neglect their children in order to fulfill the
children's every material desire. An older couple are filled with anxiety over
the future of a lifetime of accumulation. Is this life?

A young man comes to Jesus and asks him to settle an inheritance dispute.
But Jesus doesn't get involved in the brothers' squabble over the money.
Instead, he uses it as an occasion to warn everyone, "Take heed, and beware
of all covetousness; for a man's life does not consist in the abundance of his
possessions" (Luke 12:15).

Take heed, take heed, lest today's vain desires become tomorrow's
necessities. Take heed lest the worthless things in life crowd out the
worthwhile. That's often the way it is with money.

Here is a man whom we might call the epitome of success, of the
"American way." He has built his business up from nothing into a thriving,
prosperous venture. He sits upon the boards of two corporations and is a
trustee at a major university. We would call him a model citizen.

But God, as Jesus implies in the parable of the rich fool, might call him a
fool. All his financial achievements, his full barns, his stocks and bonds, his

counts, what good will they do him when the angel of death the shoulder and he breathes his last?

n who in the eyes of the world appears so wise is in reality very He foolishly thought his wealth could shield him from death. "So is o lays up treasure for himself, and is not rich toward God" (12:21).

We put our money into IRAs to insure us against poverty when we grow old. We install burglar alarm systems to protect our possessions. We build bigger houses, bigger warehouses, bigger savings accounts. We pass it on to our heirs so that they can build even bigger barns and savings accounts.

But when we are tapped on the shoulder by the angel of death, what then? "And the things you have prepared, whose will they be?" (12:20).

Where Your Treasure Is

"Consider the lilies," says Jesus. See their beauty, their luxuriance, yet what have they done to earn their beauty? Their glory comes as a gift from God. "Fear not," then, Jesus says (12:32).

But this is easier said than done. Anxiety over material things is a major source of emotional and physical health problems. Sometimes our anxiety is related to fears about obtaining just the basic necessities of life. Often it is related to fears about obtaining things that are in no way necessary for survival.

Recently Americans were asked by public opinion researchers, "Are you happier today than you were ten years ago?" A vast majority of those asked responded, "No." This is interesting since, even with inflation and unemployment, American's buying power in the 1980s has taken a sizable jump since the 1970s.

Why don't we *feel* happier and more financially prosperous? The reason, say psychologists, is what is called the "adaptation level phenomenon." This means that our levels of expectation in life adapt to our levels of achievement. Simply stated, the more we have, the more we want. Our incomes may have risen, but they never rise as fast as our expectations.

No wonder that when we attempt to "lay up treasure" for ourselves, we doom ourselves to perpetual unhappiness. We can never get as much as we want. We may get what we need, but what we want is another matter.

If God gives the lilies of the field—fragile plants that bloom and wither in a day—what they need, how much more will God supply our needs? But our wants are our big problem, not our needs.

There are those who try to present the Christian faith as being unconcerned with material things. Nothing could be further from the truth. Christianity is concerned with keeping our possessions in their place, so to speak.

While Jesus may have had no possessions of his own, he knew the power that material things can exercise over us. "For where your treasure is, there will your heart be also" (12:34). A persons' checkbook stubs can tell us as much about his or her heart as anything else.

Helping Adults Become Involved—Boyce A. Bowdon

Preparing to Teach

Here is one objective you might consider for this lesson: to remind class members that their relationship to God (their discipleship) is more important than any other relationship or any other resource, including wealth.

Read James 3:1-13, Luke 18:18-30, and, if possible, *The Interpreter's Bible*, volume 8, pages 312-16.

Here is one way to outline this lesson:

I. The scene: Jesus' encounter with the rich ruler.
II. Issue raised by the scene: What's wrong with being rich?
III. What does this scene reveal about God?
IV. What this scene reveal about the difficulty of entering the kingdom of God?

Read carefully "The Scripture and the Main Question" and "As You Read the Scripture." These form the heart of the lesson. The ideas, insights, and suggestions in these sections should be reflected continually in your lesson plan.

As you use the suggested outline, you may want to either quote or paraphrase ideas. You might like to jot in the margin of your outline the page number and paragraph being referred to. For example, you could write a reference to page 65, paragraph 3, as 65-3.

Be sure either markers and newsprint or a chalkboard and chalk is available.

Introducing the Main Question

Basic and helpful ideas are presented in the section "The Main Question." These ideas are essential in helping to identify the purpose of the lesson.

The story of the rich ruler featured in this lesson lends itself to role-playing. To help make the main question come alive, enlist one class member to play the part of Jesus and another to play the part of the rich ruler. Have them present their version of Luke 18:18-30.

Developing the Lesson

I. The scene: Jesus' encounter with the rich ruler.

Share with the class some of the basic information and key insights in Dr. Winters's examination of the scripture. Be sure to include that the rich ruler (apparently a synagogue official) was looking for inner satisfactions that he had not found, despite his success in keeping the commandments. Evidently he thought there was something more he should be doing. His question was, What more must I do? He seems to have been confident that he could meet whatever requirements were posted. His faith was in himself, not in God.

II. Issue raised by the scene: What's wrong with being rich?

Dr. Willimon writes that a chart of the predominant concerns at each stage of life would show concern about material possessions present in each step.

Read to the class or describe in your own words the observations Dr. Willimon makes about the materialistic preoccupations of the little child, the teenager, the college student, and the middle-aged couple. Ask the class to react. Do they agree?

Jesus said, "It is easier for a camel to go through the eye of a needle than for a rich man to enter the kingdom of God." Why is it difficult? Ask for class members' opinions.

Dr. Winters asserts that wealthy people are tempted to put their trust in their purchasing power to save them. Their accumulations are their gods, or idols. Ask the class: Do you agree that the tangible security of accumulated possessions often becomes a barrier to feeling God's security? Why?

The rich ruler probably assumed, as most rich rulers of the day would have, that wealth was a sure sign of God's approval and God's call. Do some people of today make the same assumption? Ask class members for their opinions. Dr. Winters writes, "The special tragedy of the rich ruler was that he was betting on his material security to somehow assure him entry into the kingdom."

Jesus told the rich ruler that if he wanted to have treasure in heaven he should go and sell everything he had and distribute the proceeds to the poor. But he made no such demands of another rich collector, Zacchaeus. Have someone read aloud Luke 19:1-10, which reports Jesus' encounter with Zacchaeus. Then ask the class: Why wasn't Jesus consistent? Why did he ask the rich ruler to give away his money, which he had apparently earned justly, while not demanding that Zacchaeus give away his money, much of which apparently had been obtained dishonestly?

After the class has had an opportunity to discuss the question, you might make this statement: Jesus saw that the rich ruler was turned in on himself rather than centering himself on God. He perceived that the man's possessions were more important to him than pleasing God. His property had become his idol, preventing him from placing his trust and commitment in the true God; that's why Jesus insisted that he give away all that he owned.

Ask the class: What problems are caused by the frantic pursuit of possessions? While the class is responding, have someone list the problems on newsprint or the chalkboard.

Dr. Winters points out in "As You Read the Scripture" that Jesus names only half of the Ten Commandments, the half that regulates human behavior toward others. Missing from that list is the commandment "Do not covet." Dr. Winters suggests that wealthy people can buy whatever they covet, thus avoiding the sin of coveting. Ask the class if they agree. While Jesus had a lot to say about people who made money their God, he also affirmed the importance of being industrious and good stewards of resources. What are some ways money can enrich life? Again, make a list.

III. What does this scene reveal about God?

Jesus said to the rich ruler, "Why do you call me good? No one is good but God alone." Ask class members what they think Jesus meant by that statement.

IV. What does this scene reveal about the difficulty of entering the kingdom of God?

If it is difficult for a rich person to enter the kingdom of God, is it any easier for a poor person? Why? Emphasize that it is impossible for anyone to enter the kingdom of God on the basis of possessions, intellect, obedience, or any other merit. Salvation is God's work.

Helping Class Members Act

Read this quotation from Dr. Willimon to your class: "Anxiety over material things is a major source of emotional and physical health problems. Sometimes our anxiety is related to fears about obtaining just the basic necessities of life. Often it is related to fears about obtaining things that are in no way necessary for survival."

Ask class members to think about their own anxieties related to money. Are those anxieties really necessary?

Dr. Willimon points out in his introduction to this lesson that God seems to speak to us in ways that respect our individuality. He asks, "How does God call *us*?" Ask class members to share their views on what God is demanding of affluent, materially blessed Americans.

Close the session by reading the following statement. William H. Willimon observes that a person's checkbook stubs can tell us as much about a person's heart as any document. What conclusion could someone reach about you and the values you live by if the only information available about you was your checkbook?

Planning for Next Sunday

Ask the class to read Psalm 68:19-20; Acts 9:10-12; and Luke 19:1-10.

_____

LESSON 13   FEBRUARY 26

Becoming a Believer

Background Scripture: Luke 19:1-10

_____

The Main Question—William H. Willimon

In last week's scripture we read about the call of Jesus to a wealthy young man, who went away sorrowful because he was unable to follow Jesus' strict demands. In today's scripture the situation is different. Jesus comes to someone, calls him to follow, and he responds, "Behold Lord, the half of my goods I give to the poor; and if I have defrauded any one of anything, I restore it fourfold" (Luke 19:8).

No wonder that this story of the call of Zacchaeus was one of the most beloved Bible stories from our childhood. The image of Zacchaeus being called down out of the tree to follow Jesus is one that sticks with you. I suggest that one reason the story of Zacchaeus still impresses us is that in this little story we see that dynamic call and wholehearted response that are the very core of the Christian faith. You and I see ourselves reflected in this picture of Zacchaeus. We do not always respond with such wholehearted commitment, but we know in the story of Zacchaeus that we see the path Jesus calls us to walk.

SECOND QUARTER

However God calls us, whatever God asks of us in our lives, we can be sure that once we have encountered God, or have been encountered by God in the person of Jesus Christ, we can never again be the same. What is the shape of the Christian response to the call of God in Jesus Christ? What does God expect from each of us? These are some of the questions we shall ponder in today's lesson—an old and familiar story with some eternal truths.

Selected Scripture

King James Version

Luke 19:1-10

1 And *Je'-sus* entered and passed through Jer'-i-cho.

2 And, behold, *there was* a man named Zac-chae'-us, which was the chief among the publicans, and he was rich.

3 And he sought to see Je'-sus who he was; and could not for the press, because he was little of stature.

4 And he ran before, and climbed up into a sycomore tree to see him: for he was to pass that *way*.

5 And when Je'-sus came to the place, he looked up, and saw him, and said unto him, Zac-chae'-us, make haste, and come down; for to day I must abide at thy house.

6 And he made haste, and came down, and received him joyfully.

7 And when they saw *it*, they all murmured, saying, That he was gone to be guest with a man that is a sinner.

8 And Zac-chae'-us stood, and said unto the Lord; Behold, Lord, the half of my goods I give to the poor; and if I have taken any thing from any man by false accusation, I restore *him* fourfold.

9 And Je'-sus said unto him, This day is salvation come to this house, forsomuch as he also is a son of A'-bra-ham.

10 For the Son of man is come to seek and to save that which was lost.

Revised Standard Version

Luke 19:1-10

1 He entered Jericho and was passing through. 2 And there was a man named Zacchae'us; he was a chief tax collector, and rich. 3 And he sought to see who Jesus was, but could not, on account of the crowd, because he was small of stature. 4 So he ran on ahead and climbed up into a sycamore tree to see him, for he was to pass that way. 5 And when Jesus came to the place, he looked up and said to him, "Zacchae'us, make haste and come down; for I must stay at your house today." 6 So he made haste and came down, and received him joyfully. 7 And when they saw it they all murmured, "He has gone in to be the guest of a man who is a sinner." 8 And Zacchae'us stood and said to the Lord, "Behold, Lord, the half of my goods I give to the poor; and if I have defrauded any one of anything, I restore it fourfold." 9 And Jesus said to him, "Today salvation has come to this house, since he also is a son of Abraham. 10 For the Son of man came to seek and to save the lost."

Key Verse: **Behold, Lord, the half of my goods I give to the poor; and**

Key Verse: **Behold, Lord, the half of my goods I give to the poor; and** if I have taken any thing from any man by false accusation, I restore him fourfold. (Luke 19:8)

if I have defrauded anyone of anything, I restore it fourfold. (Luke 19:8)

As You Read the Scripture—Mike Winters

Luke 19:1. "Passing through Jericho" is Luke's way of locating this story, but it also reminds the reader that Jesus was on his way to Jerusalem (Luke 9:51). An important center of trade, Jericho was on the main route for travelers between Galilee and Jerusalem.

Verse 2. Zacchaeus was a chief tax collector. He had a contract with the Roman government to collect revenues in Jericho, a lucrative position because of the importance of Jericho to trade. But however elevated Zacchaeus's position was, he was still viewed by the Jewish community as a collaborator with the Roman oppressor. Jewish tax collectors were despised by their own people and counted among sinners (verse 7).

In the story of the rich ruler (Luke 18:18-27), wealth stood in the way of entry into the kingdom of God. In constrast, the story of Zacchaeus depicts how a rich man achieved salvation.

Verses 3-4. Zacchaeus had heard of Jesus before. The rabbi Jesus was known as a friend of outcast, sinner, and tax collector alike (Luke 5:29-30). Indeed, Zacchaeus, the outcast, would have wanted to see this Jesus.

The sycamore was really a fig mulberry, the same tree that the prophet Amos cultivated (Amos 7:14).

Verse 5. Did Jesus go to Jericho to stay with Zacchaeus? Was this intentional? Or was this a spur-of-the-moment incident in the life of an all-knowing Messiah? Perhaps Zacchaeus's home was a preaching station for Jesus' disciples, a household that was open to their witness (Matthew 10:5-11, especially verse 11).

Verses 6-7. Zacchaeus's joy was that Jesus would risk associating with him, a tax collector. There is not doubt about the risks Jesus took in associating with sinners and outcasts.

Verse 8. Whereas the rich ruler could not follow Jesus because he was very rich (Luke 18:23), the rich Zacchaeus responded to Jesus by giving one-half of his goods to the poor. It is important to note that Zacchaeus's gift is a free response. Jesus did not command him as he did the rich ruler (Luke 18:22). Also Zacchaeus, by free response, promised to make reparations to everyone he had defrauded. The rules governing repayment for theft stated that the victim shall be repaid fourfold (Exodus 22:1), which was also the law of Rome.

Verse 9. Zacchaeus the tax collector had an experience that changed him. As a changed man, even if he continued as a tax collector, he would have had a new ethics. Genuine response to Jesus resulted in a dramatic change in his world view and morality. Zacchaeus's life became oriented to the kingdom of God. Zacchaeus exhibited the outward signs of the salvation of God he had received.

God made an everlasting covenant with Abraham and his descendants (Genesis 17:7) so that God would have a people who would be a blessing to the nations (Genesis 12:3). Not unlike that first covenant, God also made a covenant with Zacchaeus and his family. They were assured of salvation, but salvation is only a benefit of the covenant. God changed Zacchaeus from an unscrupulous tax collector into a man with a vision of the kingdom of God. The new question for Zacchaeus became, How does a tax collector live in the kingdom of God?

Verse 10. "Son of man" is the messianic title Jesus used of himself. The Son of man came to save sinners, heal the sick, and find the lost. In Luke 5:31 Jesus said, "Those who are well have no need of a physician." This statement would have been appropriate here. It would have been a biting criticism of the scribes and Pharisees and whoever else is self-righteous.

The Scripture and the Main Question—William H. Willimon

There Was a Man Named Zacchaeus

As we study this familiar story of Jesus and Zacchaeus, we must not allow our childhood fascination with this story to blur its original bite. The story opens with Luke making the scandalous observation that this man Zacchaeus was "a chief tax collector, and rich" (19:2). As a tax collector, Zacchaeus had made the decision to collaborate with the oppresive Roman overlords. How did Zacchaeus's neighbors feel about him? We have only to recall how the French felt about those who collaborated with the occupying Nazis, to understand.

Not only was he a collaborator with the Romans, but he grew rich through his crime. The Romans occupied foreign lands, milked them of their wealth, and sent it to Rome. Zacchaeus the tax collector was one of the agents of Roman theft. His job naturally presented many opportunities to grow rich. Some of his fellow countrymen would have bribed him to get a break on their taxes, and he would probably have skimmed off a good portion of the taxes for himself before turning them over to the Romans. Again and again in the Gospels, Jesus has stinging words for the rich. Throughout the New Testament those who became rich through ill-gotten gains are considered particularly despicable. Did not Jesus himself say that it is easier for a camel to get through the eye of a needle than for a rich person to enter the kingdom of God? Did he not say in the Beautitudes, "Woe to you who are rich?"

The story will be ruined for us if we conceive of Zacchaeus as basically a nice little man who was misunderstood, who down deep was basically good. By telling us that he was a tax collector and a rich man, Luke wants to put aside any such romantic niceties. Zacchaeus was a very low-type person, an outsider, an unworthy and bad man. This is the sort of man who climbed up into the sycamore tree to get a view of Jesus.

Jesus Looked Up and Said

It was this sort of low-life to whose houses Jesus invited himself to dinner. In the Near East, to eat with someone is considered a mark of strong friendship. Most of a person's income was consumed in buying food. When in the Twenty-third Psalm the psalmist declares, "Thou preparest a table for me in the presence of mine enemies," the psalmist is making a statement about deep friendship. The person who invites you to dinner is the one who will stand beside you through thick and thin. Thus, Jesus was not merely making a show of friendship toward Zacchaeus but was declaring the most intimate sort of association by agreeing to sit at his table.

Perhaps, in seeing Jesus go to Zacchaeus's house for dinner, you will recall how often Jesus gets into trouble for eating with sinners and outcasts. Time and again, particularly in the Gospel of Luke, Jesus is severely criticized for not honoring the proper boundaries separating the sinful from the righteous. Once again, in going to the house of Zacchaeus, Jesus has broken down boundaries in order to reach out to someone.

Now, it is fine for Jesus to reach out to those who are suffering and ill, as we have observed him doing in previous lessons. But here he is reaching out to someone who is neither suffering nor wretched, at least by our standards of wretchedness. He is reaching out to a man who is quite rich and secure. Thus, Luke again underlines the scandalousness of Jesus' love and compassion.

Salvation Has Come to This House

Because Jesus is willing to risk going to Zacchaeus's house, Zacchaeus becomes a believer. Jesus proudly declares, "Today salvation is come to this house, since he also is a son of Abraham. For the Son of man came to seek and to save the lost" (19:9-10). When criticized earlier for his fraternization with sinners, Jesus declared that "those who are sick have no need of a physician." Of course, behind this statement of Jesus' is the implication that sometimes the sickest people of all are those who don't know how sick they really are! Did Zacchaeus feel that something was missing in his life? Did he feel that even though he had great wealth, he still lacked some of the most basic things in life? We don't know.

What we do know is that often we believers, those of us on the inside, those of us who attend church and participate in adult church school classes, are most in danger of thinking that we are quite well. After all, we are not like Zacchaeus. Most of us are not very wealthy, nor have we collaborated with evil governments. We are here in church, and that must count for something. Where would Zacchaeus be located in your church?

What would be the response in your church if your minister showed up in your adult church school class this Sunday with a man who had been directing a prostitution ring in your community? "This is John Jones, who has become my friend, and I would like to introduce him to you. I am sure that he would enjoy being in your Sunday school class today, and I want all of you to make him feel very much at home." You can imagine the awkward, dumbfounded expressions of the people in your class. What would they say? Would they stand befuddled, as the crowd was when Jesus pulled Zacchaeus out of the tree and marched off to his home? Would your minister soon be moving from your church?

You probably know from personal experience that becoming a believer in Jesus Christ isn't always easy. There are great hurdles for you to overcome, great disciplines and risks to undertake. But sometimes the toughest part about becoming a believer in Jesus Christ is learning to accept his love for other people—people whom we neither accept nor like. After all, if Jesus can bring salvation into the life of one like Zacchaeus, who might be the next convert?

Helping Adults Become Involved—Boyce A. Bowdon

Preparing to Teach

This lesson brings to a close the thirteen-week unit "Scenes of Love and Compassion."

The scene we focus on this week will be familiar to you and your classmates. Many of us have childhood memories of Sunday school lessons about Zacchaeus, and we still know the song we learned in vacation Bible school about the little man in the tree whom Jesus told to come down. But, as Dr. Willimon observes, this old and familiar story contains some eternal truths.

With the interest and needs of class members in mind, set an objective for the lesson, such as to help class members become more aware of what is involved in becoming a believer.

To prepare yourself to teach, read Psalm 68:19-20; Acts 9:10-12; Luke 19:1-10; and, if possible, *The Interpreter's Bible*, volume 8, pages 320-27.

Here is one way to outline the lesson:

     I. The scene of love and compassion:
         Jesus encounters Zacchaeus.
         A. Presenting the scene.
         B. Scripture background.
    II. Persons portrayed in the scene.
         A. Zacchaeus.
         B. The crowd.
         C. Jesus.
   III. Issues raised in the scene.
         A. Conditions for salvation.
         B. Consequences of salvation.
   IV. The scene's message for us.
         A. Our response to "sinners."
         B. Making amends for our sins.
         C. Hearing God's call.

Read carefully "The Scripture and the Main Question" and "As You Read the Scripture." These form the heart of the lesson. The ideas, insights, and suggestions in these sections should be reflected continually in your lesson plan.

As you use the suggested outline, you may want to either quote or paraphrase ideas. You might like to jot in the margin of your outline the page number and paragraph being referred to. For example, you could write a reference to page 65, paragraph 3, as 65-3.

Introducing the Main Question

Basic and helpful ideas are presented in the section "The Main Question." These ideas are essential in helping to identify the purpose of the lesson.

Introduce the lesson by telling the story of the rich publican named Zacchaeus. Review Dr. Willimon's opening paragraphs in "The Main Question." Contrast the way the rich man in last Sunday's lesson refused

Jesus with Zacchaeus's ready response to Jesus' call. Describe what Zacchaeus declared he would do because he had met Jesus (Luke 19:8).

This introduces us to the main question: What is the shape of the Christian response to the call of God?

Developing the Lesson

I. The scene: Jesus encounters Zacchaeus.
  A. Presenting the scene.
Have someone read aloud Luke 19:1-10. Or, use a role-play to present the scene. Assign one person to be Zacchaeus, one to be Jesus, and have all the others be the crowd.
  B. Scripture background.
Share with the class information and insights contained in Dr. Winter's exegesis that might establish the setting and clarify the scripture. For example, these facts might be mentioned: (1) This incident occurred near the end of Jesus' ministry, when he was on his way to Jerusalem; (2) Jericho, located about twenty miles northeast of Jerusalem, was an important trade center in the days of Zacchaeus.

II. Persons portrayed in the scene.
  A. Zacchaeus.
To help your class clear up any glorified views they may have of Zacchaeus, read to them the following statement, made by Dr. Willimon: "The story will be ruined for us if we conceive of Zacchaeus as basically a nice little man who was misunderstood, who down deep was basically good. By telling us that he was a tax collector and a rich man, Luke wants to put aside any such romantic niceties. Zacchaeus is a very low-type person, an outsider, an unworthy and bad man."

Discuss how the Hebrews hated the occupying Roman army and despised the collaborating tax collectors. Explain how the tax collectors enriched themselves at the people's expense.

Ask the class: Why did Zacchaeus, one of the richest men in Jericho, want to see Jesus?
  B. The crowd.
The crowd murmured and said, "He has gone in to be the guest of a man who is a sinner." What did their reaction reveal about them? If you had been in the crowd that day, how do you think you would have felt?
  C. Jesus.
Jesus was making a statement when he invited Zacchaeus to spend the day with him. To eat with someone was considered to be a mark of friendship. The person who will invite you to dinner is the person who will stand beside you through thick and thin.

Instead of spending his time with the "good folks" of Jericho, Jesus went home with the town's worst sinner. What does this tell us about Jesus?

Jesus told the crowd, "Today salvation has come to this house, since he also is a son of Abraham. For the Son of man came to seek and to save the lost." What did Jesus reveal about his sense of identity and mission in this statement?

III. Issues raised in the scene.
  A. Conditions for salvation.
Discuss with the class how Zacchaeus's response to Jesus is a model of Christian conversion.

B. *Consequences of salvation.*

Zacchaeus said to Jesus and to the crowd, "Behold, Lord, the half of my goods I give to the poor; and if I have defrauded anyone of anything, I restore it fourfold."

Both Roman and Jewish law (see Exodus 22:1) required convicted thieves to pay back their victims fourfold. Zacchaeus promised to comply with that penalty and even to do more—to give half of his goods to the poor. What does this signify about how Zacchaeus's life changed as a result of his encounter with Jesus? Dr. Winters observes that God changed Zacchaeus from an unscrupulous tax collector into a man with his feet in the kingdom of God. The new question for Zacchaeus became, "How does a tax collector live in the kingdom of God?"

Helping Class Members Act

IV. *Message of the scene for us.*

A. *Our response to "sinners."*

How should we treat those we believe to be immoral or unethical?

Dr. Willimon poses an interesting question that you might ask your class members: "What would be the response in your church if your minister showed up in your adult church school class this Sunday with a man who had been directing a prostitution ring in your community?"

B. *Making amends for our sins.*

People who have experienced a spiritual awakening often seek to make restitution for wrongs they have done. Ask class members to reflect on their sins against others and to think of ways they might make restitution.

C. *Hearing God's call.*

To close this session, you might read the following statement that Dr. Willimon makes in his introduction to this lesson: "However God calls us, whatever God asks of us in our lives, we can be sure that once we have encountered God, or have been encountered by God in the person of Jesus Christ, we can never again be the same."

Ask class members to prayerfully reflect upon that statement and to answer for themselves this question: What is God calling me to do and to be?

Preparing for Next Sunday

Ask the class to read the letter of Paul to Philemon.

THIRD QUARTER

Letters from Prison

UNIT I: PHILEMON—AN APPEAL FOR ACCEPTANCE
Horace R. Weaver

ONE LESSON   MARCH 5

This quarter's four units are based on four letters traditionally referred to as Paul's prison letters: Unit I, "Philemon—An Appeal for Acceptance"; unit II, "Colossians—Christ the Lord"; unit III, "Philippians—Life in Christ"; unit IV, "Ephesians—The Christian Calling."

Unit I, "Philemon—An Appeal for Acceptance," is a one-lesson unit. The letter addresses three persons: Philemon, Apphia, and Archippus. Paul is apparently writing from Rome (though possibly from Ephesus) to encourage his spiritual son Philemon to accept Onesimus, Philemon's runaway slave, as a brother in Christ. Philemon sets the standard for treating runaway slaves as brothers.

Contributors to the third quarter:

Ralph Decker, retired professor of New Testament, Boston University School of Theology and Scarritt College; former member of the staff of the Board of Higher Education, The United Methodist Church, Nashville, Tennessee.

Herbert H. Lambert, general editor, Cooperative Uniform Series, Bethany Press, Christian Board of Education, St. Louis, Missouri.

Ronald E. Schlosser, director, American Baptist Films, Valley Forge, Pennsylvania.

Horace R. Weaver.

William H. Willimon.

LESSON 1   MARCH 5

An Appeal for Acceptance

Background Scripture: Philemon

The Main Question—William H. Willimon

One of the most beloved hymns of the church is the evangelical favorite, "Just As I Am." Nearly all of us can remember this hymn, commonly used at the altar call at Billy Graham Crusades. Dr. Graham gives the invitation to people to come down to the front and accept Christ. Then the choir softly sings, "Just as I am, without one plea . . . O Lamb of God, I come, I come."

It is a great comfort to know that God will indeed take us just as we are. If the salvation of any of us depended on our becoming perfect people, thoroughly good people, astutely believing people, who among us could be

225

saved? Fortunately, God is gracious. We are saved because God is willing to take us just as we are.

But let no one think that God leaves us just as we are. God's grace is transforming. The history of the church is full of dramatic examples of men and women who have been turned around, reborn, completely changed by the love of God in their lives.

Do you think that real change is possible in a person's life? Sometimes we become cynical about the ability of people to completely change their old ways and take on new ones.

Today's scripture tells about two people who made great changes in their lives because of their Christian commitment: Philemon and Onesimus. Will we similarly be able to respond to the changes that God is working in our lives? That is the question.

Selected Scripture

King James Version

Philemon 4-20

4 I thank my God, making mention of thee always in my prayers,

5 Hearing of thy love and faith, which thou hast toward the Lord Jesus, and toward all saints;

6 That the communication of thy faith may become effectual by the acknowledging of every good thing which is in you in Christ Jesus.

7 For we have great joy and consolation in thy love, because the bowels of the saints are refreshed by thee, brother.

8 Wherefore, though I might be much bold in Christ to enjoin thee that which is convenient,

9 Yet for love's sake I rather beseech *thee*, being such an one as Paul the aged, and now also a prisoner of Jesus Christ.

10 I beseech thee for my son O-nes'-i-mus, whom I have begotten in my bonds:

11 Which in time past was to thee unprofitable, but now profitable to thee and to me:

12 Whom I have sent again: thou therefore receive him, that is, mine own bowels:

13 Whom I would have retained with me, that in thy stead he might have ministered unto me in the bonds of the gospel:

Revised Standard Version

Philemon 4-20

4 I thank my God always when I remember you in my prayers, 5 because I hear of your love and of the faith which you have toward the Lord Jesus and all the saints, 6 and I pray that the sharing of your faith may promote the knowledge of all the good that is ours in Christ. 7 For I have derived much joy and comfort from your love, my brother, because the hearts of the saints have been refreshed through you.

8 Accordingly, though I am bold enough in Christ to command you to do what is required, 9 yet for love's sake I prefer to appeal to you—I, Paul, an ambassador and now a prisoner also for Christ Jesus—10 I appeal to you for my child, Ones'imus, whose father I have become in my imprisonment. 11 (Formerly he was useless to you, but now he is indeed useful to you and to me.) 12 I am sending him back to you, sending my very heart. 13 I would have been glad to keep him with me, in order that he might serve me on your behalf during my imprisonment for the gospel; 14 but I preferred to do nothing without your consent in order that your goodness might not be by compul-

14 But without thy mind would I do nothing; that thy benefit should not be as it were of necessity, but willingly.

15 For perhaps he therefore departed for a season, that thou shouldest receive him for ever;

16 Not now as a servant, but above a servant, a brother beloved, specially to me, but how much more unto thee, both in the flesh, and in the Lord?

17 If thou count me therefore a partner, receive him as myself.

18 If he hath wronged thee, or oweth *thee* ought, put that on mine account;

19 I Paul have written *it* with mine own hand, I will repay *it*: albeit I do not say to thee how thou owest unto me even thine own self besides.

20 Yea, brother, let me have joy of thee in the Lord: refresh my bowels in the Lord.

sion but of your own free will.

15 Perhaps this is why he was parted from you for a while, that you might have been back for ever, 16 no longer as a slave but more than a slave, as a beloved brother, especially to me but how much more to you, both in the flesh and in the Lord. 17 So if you consider me your partner, receive him as you would receive me. 18 If he has wronged you at all, or owes you anything, charge that to my account. 19 I, Paul, write this with my own hand, I will repay it—to say nothing of your owing me even your own self. 20 Yes, brother, I want some benefit from you in the Lord. Refresh my heart in Christ.

Key Verse: **Perhaps he therefore departed for a season, that thou shouldest receive him for ever . . . a brother beloved. (Philemon 15-16)**

Key Verse: **Perhaps this is why he was parted from you for a while, that you might have him back for ever . . . as a beloved brother. (Philemon 15-16)**

As You Read the Scripture—Ralph Decker

Philemon 4-7. This paragraph is a special preparation for the request Paul is about to make. Paul addresses Philemon as "my brother," praises his good deeds, and emphasizes his reputation for encouraging members of the faith.

Verse 4. As usual, Paul follows his salutation with a word of thanksgiving.

Verse 5. Paul's thanks are for the love that draws Philemon close to other Christians and the faith, that draws him close to Christ. "Saints" is Paul's usual term for Christians, which does not mean that they are perfect, but that they are sanctified, that is, set apart for the service of God.

Verse 6. The Greek for this verse is not clear. It may mean that by sharing, Paul and Philemon will enrich each other's spiritual life. More likely, it means that Philemon's shared love and faith will enrich the spiritual experiences of the Christian community.

Verse 7. The King James Version, following the Greek, uses "bowels" to refer to the seat of human emotions. The Revised Standard Version substitutes "heart," in accordance with present usage.

Philemon 8-20. The next two paragraphs set forth the purpose of the letter. Paul appeals for Onesimus, first, that he be allowed to return to his

(Paul's) service, and, second, that Philemon accept him as a brother in Christ. Paul is careful to make his appeal a request rather than a command.

Verse 8. He does point out that his position as an apostle would allow him to require Philemon to do what should be done.

Verse 9. But Paul makes love, rather than duty, the motive for the action requested. The Revised Standard Version reads "Paul, an ambassador" where the King James Version reads "Paul, the aged." This is because the Greek words for "old man" and "ambassador" differ by one letter and some manuscripts use one, some the other. The note of authority favors the translation "ambassador." An ambassador is a person with the power to speak and act for the one he or she represents. Paul represents Christ.

Verse 10. This verse may be taken to mean either that Paul is appealing on behalf of Onesimus or that he is asking Philemon to give Onesimus to him. Whichever may have been first in Paul's mind, both are involved. Paul is concerned for Onesimus's personal welfare (verse 17). He also wanted Onesimus with him (verses 13-14). The father-child relationship pictured was a spiritual, not a biological one. Paul had converted Onesimus and had been a prisoner when he did so. Acts 28:30-31 reports that Paul was allowed to have visitors and to teach while in prison.

Verse 11. This verse contains a play on words. The name "Onesimus" means "useful." Thus, Paul says, in effect, "Useful was useless but now he is useful again."

Verse 12. The deeply affectionate relationship between Paul and Onesimus is reflected in Paul's statement that in sending Onesimus home he is sending his very heart ("bowels").

Verse 13. Paul frankly states that he wants to keep Onesimus to help him during his imprisonment. He suggests that Onesimus would be acting in behalf of his master, Philemon.

Verse 14. Paul wished to avoid any appearance of infringing on Philemon's rights or of forcing him to act.

Verse 15. Paul suggests that divine providence was involved, opening the way for a new relationship between Philemon and Onesimus. A slave is a slave only during his lifetime; a brother is a brother forever.

Verse 17. "Partner" is a business term. Paul and Philemon are united in important work and must share everything.

Verse 18. It has been suggested that Onesimus stole from Philemon as he ran away. There is no evidence for this. Yet, Paul assumes responsibility for any debts or penalties incurred by Onesimus.

Verse 19. Paul makes his offer legally binding by putting it in his own handwriting. He reminds Philemon that he owes his introduction to Christ to him (Paul).

The Scripture and the Main Question—William H. Willimon

For Love's Sake

Today we Christians face many moral dilemmas. What shall we do about abortion, or nuclear arms, or atomic power? There are Christians on both sides of most of these issues. If someone asks, "What is the Christian point of view on this particular problem?" we may find ourselves hesitating, unsure of what to say because we know full well that sincere Christians may differ in their opinions.

Sometimes we imagine that ours is a particularly modern situation. We imagine that there was a time when the moral issues confronting the church were much simpler. Or at least, even if the issues were tough, Christians agreed about what ought to be done. Doesn't the book of Acts say of the early church that "all who believed were together and had all things in common"? (Acts 2:44).

But today's lesson from the little letter to Philemon should assure us that there was never a time when all Christians agreed on every issue. From the very earliest days of the church, there were disagreements among Christians over the exact contours of the Christian life.

Slavery was a fact of the Roman world. While we think of slavery as a horrible matter, many Romans saw it as an advance in civilization. Conquering Romans often made slaves of the defeated peoples in the countries they captured. This may seem barbaric to us, but there were worse options. In earlier centuries captured peoples had merely been slaughtered and their cities destroyed. While slavery is a terrible condition for a human being to be in, it was seen as better than death. Roman slaves often served as teachers, and became beloved family members and close friends of their masters.

And yet, slaves were still slaves—the property of their masters. A complex legal system protected the rights of masters. There were also some rights for slaves, but very few. In the letter to Philemon, we see two early Christians in a head-on collision with their culture's customs and traditions.

Onesimus was a runaway slave who had stolen something from his master. Somehow, he found his way to Paul and became a member of the church. Roman law was clear on what ought to be done to runaway slaves, particularly those who had defrauded or disobeyed their masters. Strict and cruel punishment awaited any slave who committed such crimes.

But what if this slave had become a Christian? Poor Philemon! When he became a Christian, how could he have possibly known that he would be asked to make such sacrifices, such radical changes in his behavior. His Christian friend Paul writes to ask him to be reconciled to this slave who has wronged him. Roman law declared that masters have absolute authority over the persons of their slaves. But now Philemon has himself come under the authority of a higher law. It is that law, the law of God, which Paul asks Philemon to accept.

My Child, Onesimus

I remember my surprise when a black friend of mine told me that he had always disliked Paul and his writing because he was offended by Paul's urging early Christian slaves to obey their masters.

I tried to convince him that Paul's words need to be interpreted in the light of attitudes of the day and in light of the situation as Paul saw it. Paul really believed that the world was quickly coming to an end, that Jesus would return any day, and thus that it was just as well for most social arrangements to remain as they were, since everything would end soon anyway.

But my friend was unmoved. His own great-grandparents had known the cruelty of American slavery, and he could not forgive Paul for not condemning the practice, even in ancient Rome.

I can understand my friend's sensitivity. But perhaps his opinion of Paul might have improved if he had weighed Paul's words to Philemon. Consider how radical and subversive Paul's appeal to Philemon would have seemed in that day. Paul asks Philemon to regard Onesimus as a brother in Christ. The one who was little more than property was now a brother. Paul speaks of this slave as "my very heart" (verse 12).

The late Dr. H. Shelton Smith, of Duke University, wrote an outstanding book that chronicled the history of the American church's relationship to the institution of American slavery. On the whole, it is a sad story, a story summarized in the title of Dr. Smith's book: *In His Image, But*. . . . The Bible clearly teaches that all of us have been created in the image of God. But we have not always related to every human being as if that person was God's image. White southern ministers argued that black people were not full human beings, that they were inherently inferior, and that the Bible supported slavery.

Fortunately, there was another side to the story. There were many Christians who were able to see that the Bible is also a foe of any system that would degrade human beings and cheat them of their God-given dignity. It is fine for me to look upon my brother as a piece of property. But what happens when that man becomes a Christian, when the same God who accepts me accepts him? That insight puts everything in a new light. The old social arrangements are turned on their heads, and everything is changed.

This is what happened to Philemon. Paul appeals to him to recognize the dramatic changes that have occurred in his life and in that of his former slave.

As someone who was born in the American South and who has spent nearly all of my life there, I can testify to the transformation that can occur in people and in their relationships with others, because of the love of Christ. I have seen people converted from hate, resentment, and racial prejudice, to being able to regard all people as brothers and sisters. Such transformation is virtually impossible to conceive of except as a miraculous result of the active love of Christ in their lives.

Confident of Your Obedience

You and I are now moving with Christ through the Christian season of Lent. During these forty days we focus upon the cross and the terrible price Christ paid for us.

Christianity also costs us something. Jesus promised us that we would also have crosses to bear. In your own life, what painful, surprising changes have you been required to make in your relations with other people, as a result of your relationship to Christ? What changes are yet to be made if your life would more closely resemble the way of life Christ calls each of us to follow?

Helping Adults Become Involved—Ronald E. Schlosser

Preparing to Teach

This week you will be starting a new quarter's study of four New Testament books traditionally referred to as the Prison Epistles. These letters belong to a time late in the apostle Paul's life and bring together a combination of Christian doctrine and Christian ethics that represents his most mature thought. They reveal much of Paul's personality, and through them we are able to come to know him more intimately.

We will begin with the shortest of the letters—the epistle to Philemon. Why do you suppose this letter was included in the Bible? It stands alone as a very personal document about a very private matter. Why was it preserved by the early church?

We can only guess at the reasons for its inclusion in the canon. For one thing, it provides a revealing look at the innermost thoughts of Paul, at his great sensitivity and warm heart. It is a model of Christian courtesy. No letter could be more courteous, more tactful, more loving. It is a heartfelt expression of Christian love and a testimony to the power of Christian conversion.

As you prepare your lesson plan, read the letter in several modern translations. Note that it has a number of things in common with Paul's letter to Colossians. Both mention Timothy as being with Paul at the time of writing; both contain expressions of thanksgiving and prayer for the recipients; both convey the greetings of the same Christians who were with Paul (Epaphras, Mark, Aristarchus, Demas, and Luke); and both were delivered by Tychicus (see Colossians 4:7-9). Indeed, the church at Colossae met in the home of Philemon (see verse 2 of Philemon). This may be another reason why the letter was preserved. Not only was Philemon an important member of the church, but later on, according to some scholars, Onesimus became the bishop of Ephesus. This personal epistle had strong historical appeal.

The session for today will focus on three goals: (1) to discern what Paul's letter to Philemon reveals about Philemon, Onesimus, and Paul; (2) to identify the decisions that these three faced; (3) to consider the changes that occur in one's life when one accepts Christ as Savior and Lord.

Use the following outline to organize the lesson:

      I.   Pose the question.
     II.   Study the letter to Philemon.
   III.   Summarize findings.
   IV.   Consider the issue of slavery.
    V.   Reflect on changes.

Read carefully "The Scripture and the Main Question" and "As You Read the Scripture." These form the heart of the lesson. The ideas, insights, and suggestions in these sections should be reflected continually in your lesson plan.

As you use the suggested outline, you may want to either quote or paraphrase ideas. You might like to jot in the margin of your outline the page number and paragraph being referred to. For example, you could write a reference to page 65, paragraph 3, as 65-3.

Have available in the classroom hymn books containing the hymn "Just As I Am," plus pencils and paper.

Introducing the Main Question

I. Pose the question.

Begin by asking the question raised by Dr. Willimon in his opening comments under "The Main Question": Do you think that real change is possible in a person's life? Can people have their lives completely changed if they become Christians?

Indicate that in today's lesson we are going to look at changes that needed to be made and that were made in the lives of some people in Paul's day. These were changes that represented ideas and actions requiring a radical departure from the norms of that day.

II. Study the letter to Philemon.

Briefly comment on the new study beginning today on the Prison Epistles. Then ask someone to read aloud the letter to Philemon, preferably from a modern translation. Following the reading, ask the class members to get together in pairs to discuss the following four questions (which you might write on the chalkboard or newsprint):

1. What does the letter reveal about Philemon?
2. What does the letter reveal about Onesimus?
3. How much pressure did Paul apply on Philemon to get him to take Onesimus back?
4. What does the letter reveal about Paul?

Allow about ten minutes for the members to work through the questions. Then discuss them as a total class.

Developing the Lesson

III. Summarize findings.

The comments by Dr. Decker ("As You Study the Scripture") and the discussion of slavery by Dr. Willimon ("The Scripture and the Main Question") should provide helpful background for dealing with the questions. The following comments are suggestive of the kinds of answers the class may give.

Philemon was an influential Christian who lived in Colossae. He must have been well-to-do, since he owned slaves and had a house large enough for the church to meet in. Philemon became a Christian through the ministry of Paul (verse 19). Paul considered him a partner and a fellow worker (verses 1, 17). Philemon was well loved by Paul and the other Christians (verses 5, 7).

Onesimus was Philemon's slave who had run away. In Rome he had met Paul and, like his master, had been converted by him. He was a great help to Paul; the name Onesimus means "useful." Paul made an interesting play on this word in his appeal to Philemon (see verse 11). Just as Paul thought of Timothy as his son, so too he considered Onesimus his child.

Paul asked Philemon to forgive his runaway slave and take him back. If we read between the lines, Paul may even have been hinting that Philemon should grant freedom to Onesimus and return him to Paul to continue as his helper (verses 12-14).

Paul appealed to Philemon on the basis of their common faith in Christ. Paul spoke to Philemon as a brother and urged him to accept his former slave as a brother also (verse 16). After all, Paul said, you "owe me" (verse 19).

Paul revealed a heart of love and compassion. Yet he did not hesitate to assert his authority in urging Philemon to do right by Onesimus. Four times Paul alluded to the fact that he was in prison (verses 1, 9, 13, 23)—an imprisonment for the cause of Christ.

IV. Consider the issue of slavery.

Look more closely at the issue of slavery: Was Paul condoning slavery by not speaking against it? Note Dr. Willimon's comments. Paul saw Onesimus no longer as a slave but as a brother in Christ. Refer to Galatians 3:28. Paul challenged the caste system in society.

Helping Class Members Act

V. Reflect on changes.

Refer to Dr. Willimon's comments about the hymn "Just As I Am" in his opening paragraphs under "The Main Question." Ask your class members to think about their own conversions. What were they like prior to conversion? What changes took place when they accepted Christ as their Savior and Lord? Perhaps some members would be willing to share their testimony aloud with the rest of the class. Don't push hard on this, but the atmosphere may be conducive to such a time of sharing.

After the sharing, pose these questions: What changes have taken place in your life from the time of your conversion until now? Have you had to make new friends or explain the change in your life to your old friends? How have your relations to other people changed? How have your actions changed? While these are mainly thought questions, some class members may wish to respond aloud.

Then ask: What changes may still need to be made in your life? Are there areas that have to be worked on so that you can be a better witness for Jesus Christ? Suggest that members write down one or two things they feel they should do to be better Christians.

Conclude by having the class sing prayerfully (or speak aloud in unison) the words of the hymn "Just As I Am."

Planning for Next Sunday

Suggest that during the week class members read the background scripture for next Sunday, Colossians 1:1-14. They should give some thought to what Protestant Christians believe about saints. Urge them to talk to their Catholic friends regarding ideas about saints.

UNIT II: COLOSSIANS—CHRIST THE LORD
Horace R. Weaver

THREE LESSONS   **MARCH 12–26**

In this unit we are made aware of the value of heresy! The Christians of Colossae were substituting a system of philosophy for Pauline beliefs. The system rested on several claims from astrology, such as the doctrine of angelic beings (called "the elementary spirits of the universe"), which were to be worshiped (Colossians 2:8, 18). The angels were thought to be well organized in a celestial hierarchy, which included titles to indicate their ranks: "thrones . . . dominions . . . principalities . . . authorities" (1:16).

These angels were thought to mediate between people and God and to offer redemption to humankind. That some of the beliefs of this doctrine derived from the mystery cults is attested in Colossians 1:26, where Paul speaks of Christian truth as the "mystery hidden for ages . . . but now made manifest to his saints." Various gnostic ["knowledge"] schools fed their students on the importance of mystery-revealed doctrines.

The heresies led Paul to show how Christ was superior to all "heavenly bodies," angelic beings, celestial hierarchies, and revelations of gnostic wisdom. Paul's writings are superb statements about the superiority of Jesus Christ in all of life.

Paul's convictions are found in the following lessons: "Citizens of a New Kingdom," March 12, portrays Paul's prayer that God would give the Colossian fellowship wisdom and insight in understanding the significance of Christ. "Remedy for False Teaching," March 19, discusses how Paul emphasized Christ's authority over all other other sources of authority. "Risen with Christ," March 26 (Easter celebration), proclaims Jesus the first fruits of the grave (that is, he was the first to be resurrected), a participant with God in creation, and the head of the church.

LESSON 2   MARCH 12

Citizens of a New Kingdom

Background Scripture: Colossians 1:1-14

The Main Question—William H. Willimon

I know a young woman who after a long struggle became a Christian. She was an actress, a beautiful woman who had begun an exciting career on the stage. But her new-found Christian faith was taking her on some unexpected journeys.

"The other day," she said, "the strangest thing happened. I began thinking about an ex-lover of mine. We lived together for about two or three years and then went our separate ways a few years ago. I had not thought of him until the other night. And that was just it. I had not thought of him, had not given him a moment's thought.

"When he came to mind, I was filled with a great sense of remorse and sadness. We had parted on reasonably friendly terms. But now I felt great sadness for what I had done to him. I know that I hurt and abused him. But until now, I did not care.

"Isn't it funny," she said. "Now that I'm a Christian, I am taking responsibility for all sorts of people I hardly even know. Now this stranger is my brother."

Of what new kingdom had this woman become a citizen? In what new and unexpected direction had her life turned?

Selected Scripture

King James Version

Colossians 1:1-14

1 Paul, an apostle of Jesus Christ by the will of God, and Ti-mo′-the-us *our* brother,

2 To the saints and faithful brethren in Christ which are at Co-los′-se: Grace *be* unto you, and peace, from God our Father and the Lord Jesus Christ.

3 We give thanks to God and the Father of our Lord Jesus Christ, praying always for you,

4 Since we heard of your faith in Christ Jesus, and of the love *which ye have* to all the saints,

5 For the hope which is laid up for you in heaven, whereof ye heard before in the word of the truth of the gospel;

6 Which is come unto you, as *it is* in all the world; and bringeth forth fruit, as *it doth* also in you, since the day ye heard *of it*, and knew the grace of God in truth:

7 As ye also learned of Ep′-a-phras our dear fellowservant, who is for you a faithful minister of Christ;

8 Who also declared unto us your love in the Spirit.

9 For this cause we also, since the day we heard *it*, do not cease to pray for you, and to desire that ye might be filled with the knowledge of his will in all wisdom and spiritual understanding;

10 That ye might walk worthy of the Lord unto all pleasing, being fruitful in every good work, and increasing in the knowledge of God;

11 Strengthened with all might, according to his glorious power, unto all patience and longsuffering with joyfulness;

12 Giving thanks unto the Father, which hath made us meet to be partakers of the inheritance of the saints in light:

13 Who hath delivered us from

Revised Standard Version

Colossians 1:1-14

1 Paul, an apostle of Christ Jesus by the will of God, and Timothy our brother,

2 To the saints and faithful brethren in Christ at Colos′sae:

Grace to you and peace from God our Father.

3 We always thank God, the Father of our Lord Jesus Christ, when we pray for you, 4 because we have heard of your faith in Christ Jesus and of the love which you have for all the saints, 5 because of the hope laid up for you in heaven. Of this you have heard before in the word of the truth, the gospel 6 which has come to you, as indeed in the whole world it is bearing fruit and growing—so among yourselves, from the day you heard and understood the grace of God in truth, 7 as you learned it from Ep′aphras our beloved fellow servant. He is a faithful minister of Christ on our behalf 8 and has made known to us your love in the Spirit.

9 And so, from the day we heard of it, we have not ceased to pray for you, asking that you may be filled with the knowledge of his will in all spiritual wisdom and understanding, 10 to lead a life worthy of the Lord, fully pleasing to him, bearing fruit in every good work and increasing in the knowledge of God. 11 May you be strengthened with all power, according to his glorious might, for all endurance and patience with joy, 12 giving thanks to the Father, who has qualified us to share in the inheritance of the saints in light. 13 He has delivered us from the dominion of darkness and transferred us to the kingdom of his beloved Son, 14 in whom we have redemption, the forgiveness of sins.

the power of darkness, and hath translated *us* into the kingdom of his dear Son:

14 In whom we have redemption through his blood, *even* the forgiveness of sins.

Key Verse: [God] hath delivered us from the power of darkness, and hath translated us into the kingdom of his dear Son: In whom we have redemption through his blood, even the forgiveness of sins. (Colossians 1:13-14)

Key Verse: [God] has delivered us from the dominion of darkness and transferred us to the kingdom of his beloved Son, in whom we have redemption, the forgiveness of sins. (Colossians 1:13-14)

As You Read the Scripture—Ralph Decker

Colossians 1:1-2. Paul opens this letter with the usual salutation. The words "and the Lord Jesus Christ" (King James Version) are omitted from the Revised Standard Version, because they do not appear in the best manuscripts and are regarded as a later addition. Paul's reference to himself as an apostle—a special, divinely appointed messenger—is a statement of his authority for writing to a church he had not founded or even visited.

Verse 1. Timothy was Paul's young assistant. He may have been converted during Paul's visit to Lystra in Asia Minor during the first missionary campaign. In any case, he joined Paul when he passed through Lystra on the second journey and became one of his most reliable helpers (Acts 16:1-4). He was probably not imprisoned but remained near Paul to minister to him.

Verse 2. Colossae was a small city on the Lycus River in southwestern Asia Minor. It was about a hundred miles east of Ephesus on the main east-west highway across Asia Minor.

Colossians 1:3-8. Paul's usual paragraph of thanksgiving gives the information that he was not personally acquainted with the Colossian church, but knew of it through Epaphras, a fellow-worker. Epaphras was a Colossian (4:12), and he may have founded the Colossian church.

Verse 4. Clearly, Paul had never been in Colossae, since he knew of the church's faith and problems only by hearing.

Verse 5. The designation of the gospel as "the word of truth" foreshadows Paul's attack on the false doctrine that had infiltrated the local church.

Verse 6. Paul related the faith of the Colossians to that of all other Christians and reported the rapid spread of the Christian movement.

Verse 7. Epaphras brought the gospel to Colossae under Paul's supervision. This could have taken place during Paul's third missionary campaign, during which he spent three years in Ephesus and "all the residents of Asia (the Roman province of Asia) heard the word of the Lord" (Acts 19:1-10).

Colossians 1:9-14. This prayer for the Colossians reflects several aspects of the heresy being promoted in their church, which emphasized knowledge (1:9-10) and worship of angels (1:13).

Verse 9. The prayer that the readers would "be filled with the knowledge of [God's] will" suggests the nature of the heresy Paul was combatting. The idea of fullness appears throughout the letter. This suggests that the false teachers claimed to offer "a full gospel," of which they said Epaphras had taught only the rudiments. Paul defines fullness not as special knowledge of spiritual mysteries, as did the heretics, but as direct knowledge of God's will.

Verse 10. Such knowledge results in a life that involves good works and spiritual growth and is worthy to be offered to the Lord.

Verse 11. Paul further prays that the Colossians will keep growing stronger through the gift of God's power. Thus, they will be able to remain steadfast.

Verse 12. Paul's final petition is that the Colossians will be moved to gratitude for God's unmerited goodness. It is not their own achievements but God's grace that has made them fit ("qualified") for a share in the destiny prepared for those set aside by and for God: "the hope which is laid up . . . in heaven" (1:5).

Verse 13. The Colossian Christians were mostly from Gentile backgrounds. Their experience in accepting Christ was like that of moving from one nation to another. God had taken them out of heathenism and placed them under the rule of his beloved Son.

Verse 14. The words "through his blood" (King James Version) are not in the best manuscripts and are regarded as a later addition. Basically, "redemption" meant the buying back of a person or thing held by another. Paul uses it as a word for spiritual deliverance through the forgiveness of sins.

The Scripture and the Main Question—William H. Willimon

The Saints in Christ at Colossae

Some years ago I was traveling in Yugoslavia. It was midsummer, the height of the tourist season there. We had paid for a ticket on the car ferry from Dubrovnik back to mainland of Greece. But when we arrived at the ferry landing, we found that the company had sold too many tickets and that there was no way to get our car on board.

All my protestations were to no avail. To make matters worse, the company refused to refund our money. I tried everything to reason with them. Then I finally said, "Look, I am a citizen of the United States. If you don't help me, I will contact my government for assistance in this matter."

Our money was refunded at last, and we were on our way.

There were numerous times when the apostle Paul would claim the benefits of his Roman citizenship. Although he was a Christian, he relied on the Roman system of justice for protection.

Of course, citizenship not only has privileges but also responsibilities. As an American, I vote, pay taxes, obey the laws, and work to make this a better country for all.

In writing to the church at Colossae, the writer uses the image of citizenship to talk about the privileges and responsibilities of the Christian faith. To be baptized into Christ is to become a citizen of a new kingdom and to follow the way of a new king. In speaking of this new relationship, the writer to the Colossians says, "[God] has delivered us from the dominion of darkness and transferred us to the kingdom of his beloved Son, in whom we have redemption, the forgiveness of sins" (1:13-14).

These new citizens are called "saints." In the New Testament, saints are the baptized, both living and dead, who are part of Christ's church. Saints are those who have "heard and understood the grace of God in truth" (1:6).

To Lead a Life Worthy of the Lord

You and I are now in the Christian season of Lent. This is the forty-day period before Easter. Historically, Lent was a time when people prepared for their baptism, for baptism was always done early on Easter morning, in the first light of dawn.

Baptism is a powerful symbol of the dramatic change required of those who would be citizens of this new kingdom of God. From the first, the church was concerned that converts should know that becoming a Christian involves a radical departure from their old way of life.

The ancient rite of baptism began with a dramatic renunciation of paganism and a confession of the Christian faith. One thus exchanged citizenship in one kingdom for another. The candidates for baptism disrobed, taking off all of their old clothing and jewelry so that, in the words of the baptismal liturgy, "nothing alien might go down into the water." Little from one's old existence was to be carried into the new.

Then the candidate was thrust into the water three times in the name of the Trinity and in remembrance of Jesus' three days in the tomb after his crucifixion. Even as Jesus had to die so that our salvation might be accomplished, so we must die to our old selves in order to be born to our new beings. Newly baptized persons were given a white robe to be worn at worship during the week following Easter. The sign of the cross was traced on the forehead in oil marking the baptized person for Christ, as a slave was branded for his owner or a soldier tatooed for the emperor.

This dramatic process had been preceded by as many as three years of intense instruction in the Christian faith. One had to know something to be a Christian; one had to be prepared for the shock of moral innovation, a shock so dramatically symbolized by the water of baptism.

This baptism process dramatically emphasized the transferral from one kingdom to another. In the Byzantine rite of baptism, this reorientation is dramatized by the *apotaxis* and *syntaxis* just before baptism: The candidate turns to face the west, the place of darkness, and curses Satan, and then turns east, toward the light, professing adherence to a new Lord.

As you read this account of early Christian baptism, you may be thinking to yourself that our present baptismal practices look rather weak and insipid by comparison. Perhaps that's why many contemporary Christians are weak and insipid when compared to our brave forebears in the faith!

We baptize by kissing on the cheek and handing them the right hand of fellowship and a pledge card. But here is a faith that might end up placing them on a cross. Do you think that the church could do a better job of initiating new converts, so that we make much clearer to them what is required of them in this new kingdom, with its new way of life?

A new seriousness about the church demands a new seriousness about baptism. Whether baptism of infants or adults is involved, we must examine our preparation for baptism as well as the way we celebrate it and ask ourselves if we are making the demands of discipleship clear enough.

If you are interested in learning more about early Christian baptism and the relevance of baptism for Christians today, you may be interested in my book, *Remember Who You Are: Baptism, a Model for Christian Life* (Nashville: The Upper Room).

There are those who believe that Colossians might have been an early Christian baptismal instruction sermon or lecture, since it has so many allusions to baptism. Whether it was an actual baptismal sermon or not, it provides us with an excellent opportunity to think about the significance of baptism. This is entirely appropriate to the season, since, from a very early date, the forty days of Lent were seen as a time for reflection upon baptism and rededication to the new kingdom whose citizens we become when we are baptized.

He Has Delivered Us

To be a Christian is to be a citizen of two kingdoms at one time. We are citizens of this world, with its many demands and allegiances, and we are also citizens of the kingdom of God. There will be conflict between our loyalties and commitments. Sometimes we will be faced with painful choices: What should I do about the military draft? Should I pay taxes that are used for war? What is the importance of material things in my life? Where is my primary citizenship? These are among the difficult questions which citizens of temporal kingdoms are called to answer. Though we may be tempted by these conflicts to settle down in the kingdom of the earth, we must keep our sights on that other kingdom in which we are citizens. To be a Christian is to hold residence in two places at one time.

Helping Adults Become Involved—Ronald R. Schlosser

Preparing to Teach

The focus for the next three weeks will be on Paul's letter to the church at Colossae. Colossae was a city near Laodicea in Asia Minor, approximately a hundred miles east of Ephesus. It was the home of Paul's friend and helper, Epaphras, who was a leader in the church there (Colossians 1:7-8; 4:12-13).

Paul had received word from Epaphras about the false teachings that were threatening the church. These teachings were probably an early form of Gnosticism, which became prominent in the second century. This heresy, among other things, denied that Jesus was part of the Godhead and taught that he was divine only from his baptism to his crucifixion. It further emphasized that only a chosen few received saving knowledge through special visions. Paul wrote his letter to warn the Colossians against such false doctrine and to commend them for their faith and love.

The learning goals for today's session are threefold: (1) to become familiar with background information on Paul's letter to the Colossians, including the reason it was written; (2) to weigh the demands of being citizens of two kingdoms; (3) to consider the privileges and responsibilities of our Christian citizenship.

Use the following outline to organize the lesson:

      I.   Consider the meaning of citizenship.
     II. Introduce the letter to the Colossians.
   III. Explore privileges and responsibilities.
        A. Being a Christian.

        B. Called to be saints.

        C. The imagery of baptism.

  IV. Make a commitment.

Read carefully "The Scripture and the Main Question" and "As You Read the Scripture." These form the heart of the lesson. The ideas, insights, and suggestions in these sections should be reflected continually in your lesson plan.

As you use the suggested outline, you may want to either quote or paraphrase ideas. You might like to jot in the margin of your outline the page number and paragraph being referred to. For example, you could write a reference to page 65, paragraph 3, as 65-3.

Have on hand for the session a supply of 3-by-5-inch index cards and pencils. A map of the Roman world at the time of Paul would also be useful to have in the classroom.

Introducing the Main Question

I. Consider the meaning of citizenship.

Begin by referring to Dr. Willimon's account of his experience in Yugoslavia, told in the opening paragraphs of "The Scripture and the Main Question." Note how he found it necessary to assert the fact that he was a United States citizen.

Discuss with the class the benefits of U. S. citizenship. Many native citizens take it for granted, but those who are foreign born and applying for citizenship do so for very significant reasons. What are some of them?

Pose the question: Is it possible to be citizens of two kingdoms at once? Refer to Dr. Willimon's comments about this under the subheading "He Has Delivered Us."

Developing the Lesson

II. Introduce the letter to the Colossians.

Note that in his letter to the believers at Colossae, the apostle Paul uses the image of citizenship to talk about the privileges and responsibilities of the Christian faith. Spend a few minutes talking about the church at Colossae. Locate the city on a map of the Roman world. Tell about Epaphras's relationship to the church and the threat posed by the false teachings creeping in (see Dr. Decker's comments). If you have access to a Bible commentary, look up additional background information. (Next week's lesson will focus specifically on the false teachings, so just a brief mention of them needs to be made today.)

III. Explore privileges and responsibilities.

  A. Being a Christian.

Return to the theme of citizenship. Indicate that even as there are privileges and responsibilities in being a citizen of the United States, so too there are privileges and responsibilities in being a citizen of God's kingdom. Divide the class into two groups. Have one group list the privileges of being a Christian and the other group list some of the responsibilities. After a few minutes of small group discussion, have the groups share their lists.

Next, have someone read aloud today's scripture, Colossians 1:1-14. Ask the class if this passage includes anything that can be added to either list. Note especially verses 9-12, which mention things Paul prays for the Colossians: (1) knowing God's will; (2) leading a life worthy of the Lord; (3) bearing fruit in every good work; (4) being strengthened with God's power to endure everything; (5) being thankful for God's grace.

B. Called to be saints.

Note in verse 12, as in verse 2, Paul refers to Christian believers as "saints." What is the class's understanding of this term? Who are saints, and should Christians be called saints today?

Some class members may have spoken to Catholic friends about their belief in saints, as suggested in last week's assignment. If so, let them share their findings. After talking about individual saints, point out that in the New Testament reference is always made (with one exception) to "saints"—plural. The one exception is found in Philippians 4:21, but there the reference is to each Christian as part of a group, not a person of supernatural holiness worthy of veneration.

"Saints"—the plural form—are mentioned some sixty times in the New Testament. They include such people as the poor at Jerusalem (Romans 15:26). According to Paul, all Christians are "called to be saints" (Romans 1:7). To be a saint, then, is both a privilege and a responsibility, a calling for every believer. It is a call to holiness, integrity, and devotion to Christ.

C. The imagery of baptism.

Refer to Dr. Willimon's description of baptism in the early church as symbolizing the spiritual transformation that takes place in the new-born believer—the citizen of a new kingdom. He also raises a question that you may wish to discuss with the class: "Do you think that the church could do a better job of initiating new converts, so that we make much clearer to them what is required of them in this new kingdom, with its new way of life?" Mention that in many overseas churches a period of probation—up to a year in some cases—is required of a person seeking membership, to ensure that the new convert truly understands and follows the demands of Christian discipleship. Would this be a good idea in our American churches?

Helping Class Members Act

IV. Make a commitment.

As Dr. Willimon points out, we are now in the Christian season of Lent. It might be a good time for class members to reflect on their Christian life and the degree of commitment they express in their walk with Christ. Suggest that class members think about what specific thing or things they can do during this Lenten season to strengthen their dedication to their Lord.

Distribute pencils and index cards to the class, and encourage the members to write down what they are willing to do between now and Easter to express their desire "to lead a life worthy of the Lord." It may be something profound, such as undertaking some regular disciplines like prayer and fasting to bring about spiritual renewal. It may be something as simple as giving up a favorite food for a time. Some persons may wish to consider becoming involved in some social action group working on poverty, military spending, the abortion issue, or the material excesses of the media and the market place.

In any case, the members should jot down on an index card what they intend to do, then take the card home with them to be a reminder of their commitment as a citizen of God's kingdom.

Close the session with a prayer for God's strength and blessing to carry out these promises during the coming weeks.

Planning for Next Sunday

In addition to reading the background scripture, Colossians 2:6-23, class members should draw up a list of what they feel are fundamental Christian beliefs.

LESSON 3   MARCH 19

Remedy for False Teaching

Background Scripture: Colossians 2:6-23

The Main Question—William H. Willimon

Jane's family had always been members of the little church. She had grown up in it and had attended the youth group's meetings from time to time.

After high school, Jane went away to college. There she encountered many experiences which caused her to question her faith. She realized that she had many questions about her beliefs. For the first time, she asked questions about many attitudes she had previously taken for granted.

Soon Jane felt as if she were adrift on a sea of uncertainty. She experimented with drugs. Her grades suffered, and her family became worried about her.

In such a state, Jane was a good target for a fringe religious group that operated on her campus. One night she went to one of their meetings, at which they focused on Jane, urging her to go with them on a retreat the next weekend. That weekend Jane was converted to their philosophy. In two weeks she had left college and was traveling with members of the group. Her parents did not know her whereabouts and the group refused to give them any information about her. Jane had become another victim of a cult.

Unfortunately, Jane's story is repeated by thousands of people every year. When our beliefs are fragile and we are unsure of our own values and commitments, we are easy prey to "philosophy and empty deceit," as the letter to the Colossians says (2:8).

How can we be sure that our beliefs are true and that they are strong enough to withstand the pressure of competing faiths? That is today's question.

Selected Scripture

King James Version	Revised Standard Version

Colossians 2:6-19

6 As ye have therefore received Christ Jesus the Lord, *so* walk ye in him:

7 Rooted and built up in him, and stablished in the faith, as ye have been taught, abounding therein with thanksgiving.

8 Beware lest any man spoil you through philosophy and vain deceit, after the tradition of men, after the rudiments of the world, and not after Christ.

9 For in him dwelleth all the fulness of the Godhead bodily.

10 And ye are complete in him, which is the head of all principality and power:

11 In whom also ye are circumcised with the circumcision made without hands, in putting off the body of the sins of the flesh by the circumcision of Christ:

12 Buried with him in baptism, wherein also ye are risen with *him* through the faith of the operation of God, who hath raised him from the dead.

13 And you, being dead in your sins and the uncircumcision of your flesh, hath he quickened together with him, having forgiven you all trespasses;

14 Blotting out the handwriting of ordinances that was against us, which was contrary to us, and took it out of the way, nailing it to his cross;

15 *And* having spoiled principalities and powers, he made a shew of them openly, triumphing over them in it.

16 Let no man therefore judge you in meat, or in drink, or in respect of an holyday, or of the new moon, or of the sabbath *days:*

17 Which are a shadow of things to come; but the body *is* of Christ.

18 Let no man beguile you of your

Colossians 2:6-19

6 As therefore you received Christ Jesus the Lord, so live in him, 7 rooted and built up in him and established in the faith, just as you were taught, abounding in thanksgiving.

8 See to it that no one makes a prey of you by philosophy and empty deceit, according to human tradition, according to the elemental spirits of the universe, and not according to Christ. 9 For in him the whole fulness of deity dwells bodily, 10 and you have come to fulness of life in him, who is the head of all rule and authority. 11 In him also you were circumcised with a circumcision made without hands, by putting off the body of flesh in the circumcision of Christ; 12 and you were buried with him in baptism, in which you were also raised with him through faith in the working of God, who raised him from the dead. 13 And you, who were dead in trespasses and the uncircumcision of your flesh, God made alive together with him, having forgiven us all our trespasses, 14 having canceled the bond which stood against us with its legal demands; this he set aside, nailing it to the cross. 15 He disarmed the principalities and powers and made a public example of them, triumphing over them in him.

16 Therefore let no one pass judgment on you in questions of food and drink or with regard to a festival or a new moon or a sabbath. 17 These are only a shadow of what is to come; but the substance belongs to Christ. 18 Let no one

reward in a voluntary humility and worshipping of angels, intruding into those things which he hath not seen, vainly puffed up by his fleshly mind,

19 And not holding the Head, from which all the body by joints and bands having nourishment ministered, and knit together, increaseth with the increase of God.

Key Verse: **As ye have therefore received Christ Jesus, the Lord, so walk ye in him: Rooted and built up in him, and stablished in the faith, as ye have been taught, abounding therein with thanksgiving. (Colossians 2:6-7)**

disqualify you, insisting on self-abasement and worship of angels, taking his stand on visions, puffed up without reason by his sensuous mind, 19 and not holding fast to the Head, from whom the whole body, nourished and knit together through its joints and ligaments, grows with a growth that is from God.

Key Verse: **As therefore you received Christ Jesus the Lord, so live in him, rooted and built up in him and established in the faith, just as you were taught, abounding in thanksgiving. (Colossians 2:6-7)**

As You Read the Scripture—Ralph Decker

Paul had made a statement on the person and work of Christ, declaring that the whole universe was centered in him and that all things, natural and supernatural, were created in and for him (Colossians 1:15-20). He had also declared that Christ, through suffering on the cross, had provided a way of reconciliation of man to God (1:21-23). Thus, he had prepared the way for his answer to the false teaching that had invaded the church at Colossae.

Colossians 2:6-7. Paul called on the Colossians to center their lives on Christ and to continue to believe and act "just as (they) were taught." This gives approval to the teaching of Epaphras (1:7) as being a full and complete gospel.

Verses 8-15. This paragraph deals with the errors of the heretics. It reads as if Paul is writing against a form of Gnosticism—a philosophical and religious movement widespread in the Greek and Roman world. Its name comes from the Greek word *gnosis*, which means "knowledge." Basically it taught that all matter is evil and that persons must secure release from matter through special knowledge and with the aid of a number of supernatural beings and powers. Many aspects of Gnosticism are reflected here.

Verse 8. The heretics were corrupting the gospel that a person is saved by the grace of God accepted by faith in Christ. They were adding a "philosophy," which Paul calls deceitful, that explained the nature of the universe. They also added "traditions," which may have been stories of what Jesus had taught his disciples in secret and which Paul calls human inventions. They also mixed in astrology and demonology through worship of "elemental spirits of the universe," all of which Paul says are subordinate to Christ.

Verses 9-10. These are key verses and their key word is "fulness." They teach that Christ is not, as the heretics had been teaching, a partial revelation of God. In Christ, God gives a complete revelation of himself. Believers have everything they need when they have Christ.

Verse 11. The heretics were requiring circumcision, a practice brought in from the Jewish religion. Paul answers that the real mark of belonging to God is in the spirit, not in the circumcised flesh. Gnosticism taught that the flesh was evil. Paul teaches that Christ's people have been freed from the domination of the flesh.

Verse 12. Paul uses baptism as a symbol that Christians have died to sin and the flesh. He saw baptism not as a cleansing but as a transformation from a life dominated by the flesh to a life dominated by the Spirit.

Verse 14. Paul changes his symbols here. He portrays sins as placing persons in debt to God. That debt is canceled by the power of the cross. Thus, the crucifixion has removed everything that stands between humankind and God.

Verse 15. The heretics taught and practiced the worship of angels and other superhuman powers. Paul says that all such beings are under Christ's control.

Verses 16-19. These verses deal with other practices of the heretics which Paul considers in error. They also seem to refer to some unnamed leader of the heresy who, puffed up by what he claims are special visions, was downgrading Christ and insisting on angel worship.

Verse 16. The mistaken practices included taboos on certain foods and drinks, similar to the Jewish dietary laws, and the observance of special days, similar to the Jewish seasonal holy days.

Verse 17. Paul says that Christians have been freed from those ritual practices, which had no real saving power.

Verse 18. This seems to again refer to a leader who claims special revelation.

Verse 19. That leader cannot contribute to spiritual growth because he has separated himself from Christ, who is the center of the universe and the source of power.

The Scripture and the Main Question—William H. Willimon

Established in the Faith

"It doesn't matter what you believe as long as you are sincere."

Have you heard that before? Such a statement assumes that feelings are more important than beliefs, that beliefs are an irrelevant "head trip" that do not relate to how we live. We can easily show that we act in certain ways becaue we believe in certain ways. I feel that stealing is wrong; I do not steal because I believe that people have a right to their own belongings. I feel that war is wrong; I do not participate in war because I believe that there are better ways to settle international disputes.

Or someone else may say, "I would rather see a sermon than hear one." This implies that sermons are dull theological lectures that only have importance as they are put into practice. "Actions speak louder than words" is how we sometimes say it. Action is the most important thing in life. Beliefs are just lots of irrelevant words. The important thing is the action.

But there are great dangers in making religion purely a matter of the heart ("it doesn't matter what you believe as long as you are sincere") or of the hands ("actions speak louder than words"). Thinking about our faith is also important.

Today's scripture shows an early Christian church struggling with the problem of belief. Evidently, these early Christians were convinced that correct doctrine and right belief were much more than an irrelevant "head trip." To them, it made all the difference in the world what one believed.

Chapter 2 of Colossians reminds us that it does matter what you believe. Sincerity has little to do with it. It is possible to be sincerely wrong. It is possible for people to believe in something, with all their hearts, and still believe something that is untrue, unfounded, and unrealistic. Down through the ages, all sorts of good, sincere people have done horrible things while sincerely believing they were doing right.

Be honest. Sometimes we say, "It doesn't matter what you believe as long as you are sincere," trying to remove belief from the level of rational examination. To some, it seems cold and cruel to criticize or rationally examine something that someone holds dear. But reason is one of the gifts God gives us, along with Scripture, the tradition of the church, and our own everyday human experience and common sense. When we use these gifts to examine what we believe, we are enabled to grow in faith and to deepen our grounding in faith. Growth in belief is important.

Once a mother asked me to talk to her daughter and "tell her what we believe so that her faith will not be destroyed when she goes off to college." Unfortunately, faith is not that kind of thing. If some pastor can talk a teenager into believing something, some professor can talk her out of believing it just as easily. Belief is not a matter of getting your head straight, then locking your brain into that position for the rest of your life. Our beliefs live and develop with our lives.

Rooted and Built Up in Him

From what I observe, neither professors in college, nor preachers, nor books and arguments make or break beliefs. Life is the toughest test of belief. Life and daily experiences constantly test your faith. New experiences challenge the way you always thought about things. So, you find yourself constantly having to rethink what you once firmly believed. You find yourself having to start all over again and think through what you believe and who you have faith in.

The best the church can give you to enable your faith to grow and to develop are the tools and skills, the guidelines and encouragement, you need to think these things through. In Colossians 2, we see the writer taking these new Christians back to the few bedrock essentials of their faith. He doesn't want to build the whole structure of faith for them. But he does want them to stand on a secure foundation.

No one can do our thinking for us. That's one reason why what you do each Sunday morning in your adult class is so important. Here, in the weekly give and take of your Bible study and discussions, all of you are being "rooted and built up in him and established in the faith, just as you were taught" (2:7).

Belief is never a purely personal, completely individual matter. One reason why some people may avoid attending your adult class is that they do not want to have their cherished beliefs and prejudices exposed to the scrutiny and the questions of fellow Christians. It is easier for them to stay home and think (if they think) and let think. But we are all in this together, and the questions and challenges of others are helpful to us in our own spiritual growth and development.

Beware of False Teaching

But do we have the right to say that a sincerely held belief is wrong? Some say, "Well, even though I do not agree with what they believe, they seem to be doing people a lot of good." But "doing people a lot of good" does not make something right. Infant sacrifice did the Canaanites "a lot of good," but the Hebrew prophets condemned it. Sacred prostitution and idol worship did the Colossians' pagan neighbors "a lot of good," but the writer of the letter to the Colossians condemned all paganism as leading nowhere.

Let's be honest. One reason why we humbly sit back and refuse to make judgments or to take a stand on some alien doctrine is that we are so unsure of ourselves and what we believe, so shallowly grounded in Scripture, that we dare not express an opinion on matters of belief.

A number of years ago, we were shocked by the revelation that eight hundred people had committed group suicide, and some murder, at Jonestown. These fanatic followers of Jim Jones were willing to take their own lives rather than to forsake their belief that Jim Jones was a new Messiah.

In the press accounts and editorials that followed the Jonestown tragedy, two explanations seemed to emerge: (1) These were mostly poor, oppressed, deprived people, who were easy victims for Jones's fanaticism. They killed themselves because they could do no better. (2) Jim Jones was a maniac whose madness led his followers into insanity. They killed themselves because they were crazy.

Many there were poor, and Jim Jones was probably crazy. But I think the real scandal of Jonestown is that even in the twentieth-century United States there are still people who are willing to die rather than forsake their beliefs.

We have devised a society that believes that a little religion can be a good thing—as long as we don't take our beliefs too far, with too much seriousness. Jonestown challenged this easy philosophy.

The history of the church is full of examples of those who felt that our beliefs are worth dying for. What we believe does make a difference.

Helping Adults Become Involved—Ronald E. Schlosser

Preparing to Teach

In Greek mythology we read about the sirens, a group of enchanting singers who lived on an island in the Mediterranean Sea. Their voices were so sweet and melodious that sailors passing by would be filled with a desperate longing to hear more. They would steer their ships shoreward, only to wreck their ships on the jagged rocks of the sirens' island. We also read how Orpheus snatched up his lyre when the Greek Argonauts approached the sirens' island and played a tune so clear and ringing that it drowned out the sound of those lovely, fatal voices.

Today there are many alluring voices that distract us on our journey through life. We are easily beguiled and tempted. The need has never been greater for Christians to immerse themselves in God's Word to drown out these enticing voices.

In today's session we will be considering some of the false beliefs that very subtly influence Christians to compromise their faith. The goals for the session are (1) to examine our beliefs and determine how firmly we believe them, (2) to identify the bedrock essentials of the Christian faith, and (3) to consider what measures to use to test our beliefs.

Use the following outline to organize the lesson:

    I.   Consider the strength of our beliefs.
   II.   Respond to an opinion poll.
  III.   Examine Paul's message for the Colossians.
       A. The troublesome heresy.
       B. The reaffirmation of Christian beliefs.
  IV.   Identify fundamentals of the faith.
   V.   Share struggles.

Read carefully "The Scripture and the Main Question" and "As You Read the Scripture." These form the heart of the lesson. The ideas, insights, and suggestions in these sections should be reflected continually in your lesson plan.

As you use the suggested outline, you may want to either quote or paraphrase ideas. You might like to jot in the margin of your outline the page number and paragraph being referred to. For example, you could write a reference to page 65, paragraph 3, as 65-3.

Prepare beforehand copies of the following opinion poll to distribute to the class during the session. If it is not possible to make a copy for each member, put the statements on the chalkboard or newsprint and have blank paper and pencils available.

Opinion Poll

After each statement, mark your opinion about it, whether you (1) strongly agree, (2) agree somewhat, (3) disagree somewhat, or (4) strongly disagree.

1. It doesn't matter what you believe as long as you are
     sincere.   1-2-3-4
2. Actions speak louder than words.   1-2-3-4
3. Even if I don't agree with what a person believes, I respect
     that person's right to believe it.   1-2-3-4
4. If what you believe produces good results, there must be some
     truth to it.   1-2-3-4
5. If you believe something strongly enough, you should be
     willing to die for it.   1-2-3-4

Introducing the Main Question

I. Consider the strength of our beliefs.

Refer to the story of Jane, which Dr. Willimon tells in the section "The Main Question." Ask the class his question about fragile beliefs.

II. Respond to an opinion poll.

Distribute the opinion poll you have prepared and ask the class to take a few minutes to respond to it. Then discuss each of the statements aloud, with the members voicing their opinions. There are no right or wrong answers, but Dr. Willimon comments on each of the ideas contained in the statements. Share his opinions with the class. Do the class members agree or disagree with him?

Developing the Lesson

III. Examine Paul's message for the Colossians.

A. The troublesome heresy.

Review the comments made last week about the purpose of Paul's writing to the church at Colossae. Recall the problem of the false teachings creeping into the church. Some scholars call it a "Judaic-Gnostic heresy," which included a denial of the preexistent deity of Christ, an emphasis on observing sacred days and religious rituals, some form of angel worship, a belief that all matter is evil and is in conflict with the spirit, and the existence of secret knowledge that only a select few obtained through special visions.

B. The reaffirmation of Christian beliefs.

Read aloud today's scripture text, Colossians 2:6-19. Note first the strong words in verses 6-7: "live," "rooted," "build up," "established." What images do these words convey?

Next look at verses 18-15. What do these verses say about who Jesus Christ is and what he has done? Paul asserts that the fullness of deity dwells in Christ. God is incarnate in him. All rule and authority rests in Christ. Believers in Christ have received the fullness of life. Their sins have been forgiven. The powers that would destroy believers have themselves been disarmed.

Share Dr. Decker's comments on these verses, which describe how Paul is addressing the false teachings of the day. Are there religious faiths today that deny or deemphasize the deity of Christ? How should Christians respond to them?

Now look at verses 16-19. What false teachings are alluded to here? See again Dr. Decker's comments. Paul uses the imagery of the church as a living body, whose health and growth comes from God.

IV. Identify fundamentals of the faith.

Move now to a consideration of what constitutes the bedrock essentials of the Christian faith. Refer to Dr. Willimon's comment near the end of the section "The Scripture and the Main Question," that many Christians are so unsure of themselves and what they believe that they dare not express an opinion on matters of belief. List on the chalkboard or newsprint what class members feel are the fundamental Christian beliefs. You may not be able to get consensus on every statement, but you should get a pretty basic listing of key Christian doctrines pertaining to the existence of God, the person and work of Jesus Christ, the authority of the Scriptures, the promise of eternal life, and the preeminence of love as the guide for Christian living.

Then raise the question, How do we test our beliefs? How can we know if what we believe is true or false? Dr. Willimon suggests several criteria: reason, Scripture, the tradition of the church, everyday human experience, and common sense. Are there others? "Life," says Dr. Willimon, "is the toughest test of all." Does your class agree or disagree? Why?

Helping Class Members Act

V. Share struggles.

Have class members reflect on the source of their beliefs. Where did they get them? What part did their parents, their families, and their upbringings play in forming their beliefs? What role did the church play? Do they find that they are still grappling with beliefs—discarding old ones, revising suspect ones, adopting new ones?

Perhaps a few of the members would be willing to share with the class some of the beliefs they are presently struggling with. It may be that by voicing aloud the things that concern them, other class members may be able to offer new insights or at least new approaches to dealing with them. Dr. Willimon observes that the church can help our faith to grow and develop by giving us "the tools and skills, the guidelines and encouragement" to think through our beliefs. Ths concluding activity might accomplish just this for some of your members.

Planning for Next Sunday

In addition to reading next week's background scripture (Luke 24:1-7; Colossians 1:15-29; 3:1-4), ask class members to think through what the Easter hope is for them personally. What does Easter really mean to them?

On Facing Death

HERBERT H. LAMBERT

Recently I had two successive encounters with death. The experience left me with a new attitude toward death and also toward life.

After having had influenza several days, I was taken to a hospital emergency room. I spent eleven days there with what the doctor called depletion of electrolytes—sodium, postassium, and calcium. During five of those days I was delirious, unable to recognize visitors or control my actions.

As I lay tossing on my bed, without books or glasses or dignity, I tried to recall appropriate scriptures. All I could think of was Psalm 42–43, with its repeated refrain:

> Why are you cast down, O my soul?
> And why are you disquieted within me?
> Hope in God; for I shall again praise him,
> my help and my God.

The psalmist was talking to himself, as though one part of him had more faith than another. That was true to my experience! One part of him was disquieted and cast down, because the world had come to an end. Another part of him still believed that God would give help, and that he would live to praise God. We do not know who won the argument, only that the argument continued. The greatest dream the psalmist had was that one day he would be able to return to God's house:

> Oh send out thy light and thy truth;
> let them lead me,
> let them bring me to thy holy hill
> and to thy dwelling!

But the argument with self continued, and a third time the psalmist repeated,

> Hope in God; for I shall again praise him,
> my help and my God.

When I finally began to awaken from my delirium, the doctor told me I had "knocked on the pearly gates." I believed him because, for several days, I had been fully convinced that I had died. I had pictured in my mind what life would be like for my wife Esther after my death.

I recall discussing my death with my son. We had recently purchased a word processor and had set it up in the basement. I told my son to remove it from the basement, now that I was dead, because of the danger of flooding.

My wife Esther helped me slowly come back to reality. I learned my letters all over again by watching "Sesame Street." I gradually came to look forward to returning home and going back to work.

One of the special places that Esther and I shared together was Forest Fawr, our hidden cabin in the woods. On the fourth day after I returned home, we went there. Esther stacked wood, while I sat on the deck and watched. I was able to walk with her into the woods, where we found some Dutchman's Breeches. We made note of the place so that she could come back later that day and transplant some of them.

We drove to a nearby town to get an ice cream treat. On our way back, we approached a blind curve. The next thing I knew I was lying in pain on an operating table, talking with a doctor. He told me there had been a collision and that my wife was in another hospital, not doing well. In a few moments he reported that she was dead.

I had encountered death the week before. I had prepared myself to depart this life and had contemplated what it would be like for Esther after I was gone. Now the roles were reversed. Esther was gone, and I remained behind. It was almost impossible for me to take up again the responsibilities and requirements of living. Time and again I cried out through my tears, "Esther, I don't want to go on living without you!"

Then I recalled what I had felt when I had been near death. I had accepted the fact that my wife would go on alone, without me. Now I had to live with the other possibility—going on without her. I would do it, I decided, with the same courage I had expected her to show as a widow.

Our marriage had always been a partnership. We both worked hard at our respective jobs. Esther was a psychiatric social worker in a hospital. It was not unusual for her to leave for work at 6:30 A.M., return home about 6:00 P.M., eat a quick bite, and then counsel a family for two hours or more in her office. She was dedicated to the needs of persons and to the ministry to which she had been ordained. Because she kept most of her work confidential, no one will ever know how many lives she touched or how many persons she helped.

When I think of Esther's single-minded dedication, I think of the remarkable self-taught scientist John Albert Brashear. On the door of his backyard laboratory was written: "Somewhere beneath the stars there is a task that only you can do. Never rest until you find it."

We visited the observatory Brashear built on a hill in Pittsburgh. We were surprised to find that he and his wife were buried near the telescope. Their epitaph is appropriate: "We have looked too long at the stars to be afraid of the night."

Esther devoted a big portion of her life to combatting depression. She had seen what it does to people, to their energy, to their happiness, to their will to live. She knew that depression cannot be dispelled by mere "positive thinking" or by empty platitudes. She knew that depressed people must be given an opportunity to talk about their concerns, real and imagined, with someone who understands and cares. Patiently she led many persons from despair and depression to hope.

Esther had admired Paul Tillich's little book *The Courage to Be* ever since its publication. She often quoted the last sentence in that book: "The courage to be is rooted in the God who appears when God disappears in the anxiety of doubt." Esther knew that anguish and anxiety are part of life. She did not seek to deny or avoid them but to deal with them in ways that would lead to faith and strength. If she has a message for me and for all who mourn her passing, it is a call to keep trying—no matter how difficult it seems.

Twenty years ago Esther founded and directed "The Threshold," a day-care center for emotionally disturbed adults. Once a month I went there with her to a social gathering. I always marveled at how hard it was to tell the doctors, therapists, and family members from the disturbed persons. It showed me that, given the right conditions, anyone can be a victim of mental illness.

Now Esther has passed over a threshold. I went with her to the door and then turned back. As I continue in this life, I cannot look at it as casually as I did before. I know now that death may be closer than any of us think. Things that once seemed important no longer seem so. I keep asking what really matters, what deserves my best efforts.

I know now that Esther had prepared for this transition. She had talked with several persons recently about the possibility of death. A few days before her accident she met with the elders of our congregation. Someone recalled that she read from *The Leaning Tree*, by Patrick Overton:

> When we walk to the edge of all the light we have and take a step into the darkness of the unknown, we must believe that one of two things will happen—
>> There will be something solid for us to stand on,
>> Or, we will be taught how to fly.

LESSON 4   MARCH 26

Risen with Christ

Background Scripture: Luke 24:1-7; Colossians 1:15-29; 3:1-4

The Main Question—William H. Willimon

This life, as good as it often is, is never quite enough. Things are going well for me today, the sun is shining, and I and my loved ones are in good health, but what about tomorrow? Even the good days are not quite as good as they might be when you realize that the good days never last forever. Everything ends.

Our life journeys do not go on forever. We grow, we mature, we age, we die. No institution, no nation, no person endures. This was the vision of the psalmist who cried,

> Thou turnest man back to the dust,
>   and sayest, "Turn back, O children of men!"
> For a thousand years in thy sight
>   are but as yesterday when it is past,
>   or as a watch in the night.
>
> Thou dost sweep men away; they are like a dream,
>   like grass which is renewed in the morning:
> in the morning it flourishes and is renewed;
>   in the evening it fades and withers.
> ....
>   our years come to an end like a sigh.
>   (Psalm 90:3-6, 9*b*)

What hope is there for us when everything and everyone we love keeps decaying, growing old, and dying?

Today's scripture is a response to this fundamental question. Because something has happened on this day to Christ, something has happened to you and me. Christ is raised! We are raised!

Selected Scripture

King James Version

Luke 24:1-7

1 Now upon the first *day* of the week, very early in the morning, they came unto the sepulchre, bringing the spices which they had prepared, and certain *others* with them.

2 And they found the stone rolled away from the sepulchre.

3 And they entered in, and found not the body of the Lord Jesus.

4 And it came to pass, as they were much perplexed thereabout, behold, two men stood by them in shining garments:

5 And as they were afraid, and bowed down *their* faces to the earth, they said unto them, Why seek ye the living among the dead?

6 He is not here, but is risen: remember how he spake unto you when he was yet in Galilee,

Revised Standard Version

Luke 24:1-7

1 But on the first day of the week, at early dawn, they went to the tomb, taking the spices which they had prepared. 2 And they found the stone rolled away from the tomb, 3 but when they went in they did not find the body. 4 While they were perplexed about this, behold, two men stood by them in dazzling apparel; 5 and as they were frightened and bowed their faces to the ground, the men said to them, "Why do you seek the living among the dead? 6 Remember how he told you, while he was still in Galilee, 7 that the Son of man must be delivered into the hands of sinful men, and be crucified, and on the third day rise."

7 Saying, the Son of man must be delivered into the hands of sinful men, and be crucified, and the third day rise again.

Colossians 1:15-20

15 Who is the image of the invisible God, the firstborn of every creature:

16 for by him were all things created, that are in heaven, and that are in earth, visible and invisible, whether *they be* thrones, or dominions, or principalities, or powers: all things were created by him, and for him:

17 And he is before all things, and by him all things consist.

18 And he is the head of the body, the church: who is the beginning, the firstborn from the dead; that in all *things* he might have the preeminence.

19 For it pleased *the Father* that in him should all fulness dwell;

20 And, having made peace through the blood of his cross, by him to reconcile all things unto himself; by him, I *say*, whether *they be* things in earth, or things in heaven.

Colossians 1:15-20

15 He is the image of the invisible God, the first-born of all creation; 16 for in him all things were created, in heaven and on earth, visible and invisible, whether thrones or dominions or principalities or authorities—all things were created through him and for him. 17 He is before all things, and in him all things hold together. 18 He is the head of the body, the church; he is the beginning, the first-born from the dead, that in everything he might be pre-eminent. 19 For in him all the fulness of God was pleased to dwell, 20 and through him to reconcile to himself all things, whether on earth or in heaven, making peace by the blood of his cross.

Colossians 3:1-4

1 If ye then be risen with Christ, seek those things which are above, where Christ sitteth on the right hand of God.

2 Set your affection on things above, not on things on the earth.

3 For ye are dead, and your life is hid with Christ in God.

4 When Christ, *who is* our life, shall appear, then shall ye also appear with him in glory.

Colossians 3:1-4

1 If then you have been raised with Christ, seek the things that are above, where Christ is, seated at the right hand of God. 2 Set your minds on things that are above, not on things that are on earth. 3 For you have died, and your life is hid with Christ in God. 4 When Christ who is our life appears, then you also will appear with him in glory.

Key Verse If ye then be risen with Christ, seek those things which are above, where Christ sitteth on the right hand of God. (Colossians 3:1)

Key Verse: If then you have been raised with Christ, seek the things that are above, where Christ is, seated at the right hand of God. (Colossians 3:1)

As You Read the Scripture—Ralph Decker

These scripture passages deal with two aspects of the resurrection: the empty tomb and the risen Christ. Luke, with the other Gospel writers, tells of the first. Paul makes not a single mention of it in his letters. His emphasis is upon the post-resurrection appearances (I Corinthians 15:3-8) and upon the exaltation of Christ to the right hand of God (Colossians 3:1). Because of the false teaching at Colossae, which placed Christ in a position subordinate to other spiritual beings, the letter to the Colossians is especially strong in asserting the primary position of Christ in all creation.

Luke 24:1-7. In Luke, as in all the Gospels, the experience of the resurrection began with the discovery that the tomb was empty. This was followed by angelic assurances that Jesus had risen and by experiences of his presence.

Verse 1. The "they" of this verse were "the women who had come with him from Galilee" (23:55-56). The body of the crucified Jesus had been hastily buried late on Friday. The Sabbath (Saturday), on which no work could be done, had passed. The first day of the week (Sunday) had begun at sunset on our Saturday. Next morning, as soon as it was light, the women went to the tomb to complete the embalming of the body.

Verse 2. The tomb was probably a cave, the opening of which had been closed with a large round boulder.

Verse 3. The King James Version, following some late manuscripts, adds the words "of the Lord Jesus" after the word "body." The Revised Standard Version omits them, because older and better manuscripts do not include them.

Verse 4. Luke treats the appearance of the two personages as supernatural. They appear suddenly to the women and are dressed in dazzling apparel. It is clear that Luke regarded them as angels. He records a similar appearance at the ascension of Jesus (Acts 1:10).

Verse 6. Jesus' Galilean prediction of his death can be found in Luke 9:22, paralleled in Matthew 16:21 and Mark 8:31.

Colossians 1:15-20. This is the heart of the letter. It is part of Paul's argument against the false doctrine of angelic mediators between God and humankind. Referred to as "the elemental spirits of the universe" (2:8), These celestial beings were worshiped (2:18), were said to be organized into ascending ranks with titles to denote their standing (1:16), and were supposed to offer redemption through special knowledge. Paul's position is that Christ is the sole mediator, that all created beings are subject to him, and that he alone brings redemption. Here Paul presents the risen and exalted Christ, preeminent in the universe (verses 15-17), in the church (verses 18-20), and in the lives of the Colossian believers (verses 21-23).

Verse 15. Christ has shown mankind what God is like. The same figure of the image of God is used in Hebrews 1:3. Christ is firstborn, not in the matter of time but in the matter of position.

Verse 16. He is the divine agent in the creation of all things. The same statement is found in John 1:3. Even the angels, listed here according to their ranks, were created through him and so are inferior to him.

Verse 17. The unity and order of the universe are due to his power and control.

Verse 18. He is the one head to which the church can look for guidance and redemption. He inaugurates a new life.

Verse 19. God's redemptive power resides in Christ. It is not distributed piecemeal throughout a series of angelic beings.

Verse 20. The one way to reconciliation and redemption has been opened by the sacrificial death on the cross.

Colossians 3:1-4. Through baptism, the believer participates in the death and resurrection of Christ—dying to sin and rising again into a new life. He or she must, then, focus the thoughts and desires on heaven, where Christ reigns.

The Scripture and the Main Question—William H. Willimon

The Firstborn from the Dead

Last year, after our Easter service in Duke Chapel—after the grand music, the anthems by the 150 voices of the chapel choir, the blasts from the orchestra, and the lovely melodies of the congregation accompanying the great Easter hymns of the church—I returned to my office and found this note on my desk: "Thank you for the service today. Our twelve-year-old son is in Duke Hospital, paralyzed, and we found the service such a comfort."

I was undone. What difference had this service made, as grand as it might have been, compared to the tragedy of a twelve-year-old paralytic? Or what difference for the child's pitiful parents?

So many Sundays we come to church, and the preacher urges us to do better in our lives. We are urged to give more to the church or to create better family life. We are counseled to read our Bibles daily or to be more faithful in our church attendance. Such exhortation is fine for those who are able-bodied, strong, and competent. Perhaps that's why we enjoy such preaching—because we like to think of ourselves as strong, capable people.

But what is the word of the church to those who are not well and strong? What is the word to that little child lying on a bed in Duke Hospital, or to his parents and family?

It could be argued that if the church has nothing to say to this child and his parents, the church has nothing to say to anyone. If it will not play in a cancer ward or a shoddy nursing home for the elderly, then whatever it is, it isn't good news.

Our little self-help, do-it-yourself religion is fine for most days in life. But on the darkest days, when our backs are against the wall and we have absolutely nowhere to turn to and there is absolutely nothing to be done, what then?

A friend of mine, Jim Wallis, is the director of the Sojourners Christian Community in Washington, D.C. A few years ago, when he was visiting with Coretta Scott King during a commemoration of the life and work of Dr. Martin Luther King, Jr., Jim was asked by Mrs. King to visit a young man who was on death row in the Georgia State Penitentiary. The young man had been there since he was sixteen, when he had killed a young woman. He was now nineteen and was scheduled to die in a few months in the electric chair.

Wallis said that when he came to the young man's cell, the young man looked through the bars and said, "Hey preacher, what is the good news?"

For one eternal moment, Jim said that he stood there, dumbfounded. What is the good news for a young man in this situation? Is there any news that can be called good for someone on death row, someone with his back against a wall?

If there is a word, it must not be a small one, petty and trivial. It must be a word cosmic in its scope, beyond the bounds of the wildest imagination, something eternal, far-reaching, stupendous.

That is the sort of word we hear when we read Colossians 1:15-29.

Not content to relegate Jesus to the level of a "great prophet," a fine "moral example," an "inspiring teacher," the writer makes the bold Easter claim that this Jesus, the one who was humiliated, suffered, and crucified, this Jesus is the very one in whom "all things were created, in heaven and on earth, visible and invisible, whether thrones or dominions or principalities or authorities—all things were created through him and for him" (1:16).

In other words, what the Bible says of God Almighty in Genesis 1 and 2, the writer of Colossians now says about Jesus. Even as the Creator holds the earth and its inhabitants in the very palm of his mighty hand, so Jesus now is the one in whom "all things hold together" (1:17).

He is the "first-born of all creation" (1:15), the first being of all creation, the one whose image sets its stamp on everything else. Now, in Easter, in his resurrection from the dead, we see that he is not only Lord of life but also Lord over death. All things are under his command and control, even that thing which you and I fear the most—death.

If You Have Been Raised with Christ

"If then you have been raised with Christ . . ." (3:1). There is no doubt expressed here; the first word of the sentence is perhaps better translated "since."

What happened to Jesus on Easter was not just for him, but for everyone. His power over life and death extends to us and our lives and deaths.

Because the Easter event is true, you and I do have something to say to the twelve-year-old child lying in the hospital. We do have a word of good news for the young man awaiting execution on death row. We have something cosmic, imaginative, and powerful to say to the child dying of starvation in East Africa, to the refugee mother in Palestine, to those suffering from terminal illnesses in hospitals.

We can say, with the writer of Colossians, that the same one who, just a few days ago, suffered horribly on the cross, is now the very one seated in heaven, holding all things in the palm of his hand. Knowing who is in charge makes a great deal of difference. Knowing the beginning and end of the whole story makes the temporary setbacks and confusing turns of plot more understandable. Because "Christ is seated at the right hand of God" (3:1), we are able to look at life and death in a very different way.

"Preach the great and grand themes of faith," the great British preacher, Henry Spurgeon, urged his students. It is clear that today's scripture from the letter to the Colossians deals with the very greatest of themes: the triumph of God's love and power over the bonds of death. In the church we must boldly proclaim this great truth, because when your back is against the wall and your future looks bleak, only the greatest of truths can help.

For You Have Died, and Your Life Is Hid with Christ

Many scholars believe that Colossians is an early baptismal sermon, or perhaps an early baptismal instruction book. It certainly contains many baptismal images.

In the early church, most baptisms took place on Easter, as the first rays of light dawned. Those who were to be baptized were brought in to the baptismal room, where they entered a pool and were thrust under the water three times in the name of the Father, the Son, and the Holy Spirit. This was also a reminder that, even as Christ was in the tomb for three days, so we also die and rise with him.

In other words, the church proclaimed that we go through the same movement from death to life that Jesus went through from Good Friday to Easter Sunday. To be a Christian is to be someone who has died, who has learned to let go of "the things that are on earth" (3:2) in order to set one's sights "on things that are above" (3:2).

This Easter, what is the good news?

Helping Adults Become Involved—Ronald E. Schlosser

Preparing to Teach

Picture in your mind two contrasting scenes. In the first scene, the streets of Jerusalem are dark and deserted. The only movement is that of Roman patrols moving about, making sure that there are no disturbances after what happened that day on a hill outside the city. Along a dark street there sits a house, quiet, lights out, locked shut. You knock and get no answer. If you listen carefully, you hear a muffled stirring inside and a whisper, "Let no one in." Plainly, there are frightened people inside. You sense that the fear gripping these people must be related in some way to the terrible events of the day.

Now imagine that it is three days later. You are on the same street and approach the same house. The lamps are burning brightly. The doors are wide open. You hear the sounds of singing and laughter. As you enter you are warmly welcomed. The room is filled with joy and confidence.

What made the difference? Just three words: "Jesus has risen!" They made the difference then, and they make the difference now.

On this Easter Sunday you will be leading your class toward three learning goals: (1) to appreciate anew the Easter event by considering its effect on those who were there; (2) to gain a better understanding of the nature of Jesus Christ as risen Savior and Lord; (3) to determine what is the good news that Christians can share with the weak, the sick, the imprisoned, and the dispossessed.

Use the following lesson outline:

    I.   Experience a mood.
   II. Discover new truths about the resurrection.
       A. The Easter hope.
       B. The risen Christ.
  III. Affirm good news to share.

Read carefully "The Scripture and the Main Question" and "As You Read the Scripture." These form the heart of the lesson. The ideas, insights, and suggestions in these sections should be reflected continually in your lesson plan.

As you use the suggested outline, you may want to either quote or paraphrase ideas. You might like to jot in the margin of your outline the

page number and paragraph being referred to. For example, you could write a reference to page 65, paragraph 3, as 65-3.

For this session you should have available hymnbooks containing the hymn "Christ the Lord Is Risen Today." You will also need pencils and paper.

Introducing the Main Question

I. Experience a mood.

The mood of darkness and hopelessness pictured in the first scene described above is the same mood Dr. Willimon conveys in "The Main Question." Set this mood, using your own words. Read aloud Psalm 90:3-10, as well as Ecclesiastes 1:2-9. Then tell the story of Jim Wallis and the boy in prison, which Dr. Willimon refers to in "The Scripture and the Main Question." Ask: What is the good news for such a person? What is the word of the church to those who have no hope?

Developing the Lesson

II. Discover new truths about the resurrection.

A. The Easter hope.

Of course, for Christians, there *is* hope because of the resurrection. This is the hope and confidence we affirm this Easter.

Distribute hymnbooks to the class, and ask the members to turn to the hymn "Christ the Lord Is Risen Today." Read aloud the words (or sing them, if you wish). What mood do they convey? How is hope expressed? Have the class members share their feelings.

B. The risen Christ.

Indicate that today's scripture includes three passages. Divide the class into three groups, and assign each group one of these passages: Luke 24:1-7; Colossians 1:15-20; Colossians 3:1-4. Distribute pencils and paper so class members can take notes.

Group 1, studying Luke 24:1-7, should discuss the emotions of the women when they arrive at the tomb, discover it empty, and return home.

Group 2, looking at Colossians 1:15-20, should discuss what this passage reveals about the nature of Christ. What are his attributes?

Group 3, examining Colossians 3:1-4, should discuss the new nature of the believer in Christ, what is expected of the believer here on earth, and what the believer can expect in the life hereafter. What are the "things that are on earth" and the "things that are above"?

Allow five to seven minutes for small group discussion, then come together as a class for reporting.

Luke 24:1-9. The progression of emotions that seems to have taken place in the women at the tomb might be characterized as follows:

1. *Expectancy (verse 1).* The women, most certainly downcast, came expecting to embalm Jesus' body.
2. *Discovery (verses 2-3).* We can imagine their surprise and bewilderment in finding the tomb empty.
3. *Confrontation (verses 4-5).* When the women saw the angels, they were frightened and bowed down.

4. *Remembrance (verses 6-8)*. At last things began to make sense, as they remembered what Jesus had told them earlier.
5. *Sharing (verse 9)*. Excited but perhaps not yet understanding the full implications, they returned to tell the disciples what had happened.

Colossians 1:15-20. The following attributes of Christ can be seen in this passage:

1. *Christ, the incarnate God (verses 1, 19)*. In Christ, God became flesh and dwelt among us. Christ is the perfect revelation of God to humankind.
2. *Christ, the unifying force (verses 16-17)*. Christ contains in himself the reason why creation exists (its cause) and the end toward which it is moving (its goal).
3. *Christ, the head of the body (verse 18)*. Paul uses this figure of speech elsewhere in his epistles (see I Corinthians 12:27; Ephesians 4:15; Colossians 2:19). Christ is the source from which the church derives its life and strength and power.
4. *Christ, the reconciler (verse 20)*. By his death on the cross Jesus fulfilled the ultimate purpose of God: to remove all barriers between the Creator and the creation.

Colossians 3:1-4. This passage speaks of three things:

1. *New life (verse 1)*. We have been "raised with Christ." Because Christ lives, we too shall live.
2. *New responsibilities (verse 2)*. We are to set our minds on and to seek "the things that are above." Our thoughts and values are to reflect our new natures. We are to put away those "things [of our old nature], that are on earth" (see Colossians 3:5-17).
3. *New hope (verses 3-4)*. One's new life in Christ brings its own glory on earth and the assurance of fellowship with him in the realm beyond.

Helping Class Members Act

III. Affirm good news to share.
    Dr. Willimon concludes his comments with this question: "This Easter, what is the good news [that we can share with others]?" Ask your class to think about the question and then to offer suggestions that you can list on the board. Here are some things that might be mentioned:

1. The good news of the resurrection is that God is in control. The world can and does make sense. In the struggle with evil, God's forces will ultimately triumph.
2. The good news of the resurrection is that we can live by the power of the risen Christ. The power that brought Jesus Christ from the dead is the power we can claim. It is a power that is present with us now, not simply a future hope.
3. The good news of the resurrection is that death is not the final fate awaiting us. We have eternal life, a quality of life that begins now when we accept Christ as our Savior and continues into eternity. This is the message and hope of Easter.

Planning for Next Sunday

The lesson for next week begins a new unit and the study of Paul's letter to the Philippians. Encourage your class members to read the entire letter in one sitting. During the week they should jot down on a piece of paper the kinds of decisions, both major and minor, they are called upon to make that week.

UNIT III: PHILIPPIANS—LIFE IN CHRIST
Horace R. Weaver

FOUR LESSONS   **APRIL 2–23**

The small city of Philippi received its name from Philip, the father of Alexander the Great. It received the rank of colony from Augustus Octavian Caesar. Paul introduced Christianity to this colony and thus to Europe. In Acts, Luke tells us of a vision in which Paul saw a man of Macedonia calling to him: "Come over and help us." The man was Luke, a physician whom Paul met at Troas, in northwestern Asia. Luke and Paul, in company with Silas and Timothy, sailed to Neapolis and walked the short distance to Philippi.

Unit III, "Philippians—Life in Christ," offers four lessons, as follows: "To Live Is Christ," April 2, focuses on Paul's understanding that the believer's life must be centered in Jesus Christ; "Serving as Christ Served," April 9, discusses how Jesus' way of self-giving love becomes a reality in the life of those who follow him; "Pressing On in Christ," April 16, reviews the experience of growing toward God's ultimate goal; "Rejoicing in Christ," April 23, encourages us to experience the joyful contentment, even amid distressing circumstances, that following Christ brings.

LESSON 5   **APRIL 2**

To Live Is Christ

Background Scripture: Philippians 1:1-26

The Main Question—William H. Willimon

"I really think that, in spite of all I have gone through, all of this has been for the best," she said.

I could be forgiven for being a bit skeptical of her claim, for she had been through some very difficult times. Her bout with cancer and her husband's illness and death were experiences that few could claim as good.

And yet, she was convinced that in spite of all the bad that had happened to her, much good had come out of it. She was a stronger person. Her faith had been tested, but she had emerged a stronger Christian because of, or at least in spite of, the testing.

Perhaps you have had experiences in your own life which, though they were difficult, did ultimately influence your life for the better.

Today's scripture was written by Paul when he was going through a terrible time in his life: He was in prison awaiting execution. Did this mean that all of his hard work on behalf of the gospel was in vain? How did he face the future—with hopelessness or with confidence?

You and I sometimes find ourselves trapped by the circumstances of our lives. How is it possible for us, and for Paul, to live in hope in spite of the circumstances?

Selected Scripture

King James Version

Philippians 1:12-26

12 But I would ye should understand, brethren, that the things *which happened* unto me have fallen out rather unto the furtherance of the gospel:

13 So that my bonds in Christ are manifest in all the palace, and in all other *places*;

14 And many of the brethren in the Lord, waxing confident by my bonds, are much more bold to speak the word without fear.

15 Some indeed preach Christ even of envy and strife; and some also of good will:

16 The one preach Christ of contention, not sincerely, supposing to add affliction to my bonds:

17 But the other of love, knowing that I am set for the defence of the gospel.

18 What then? notwithstanding, every way, whether in pretence, or in truth, Christ is preached; and I therein do rejoice, yea, and will rejoice.

19 For I know that this shall turn to my salvation through your prayer, and the supply of the Spirit of Jesus Christ,

Revised Standard Version

Philippians 1:12-26

12 I want you to know, brethren, that what has happened to me has really served to advance the gospel, 13 so that it has become known throughout the whole praetorian guard and to all the rest that my imprisonment is for Christ; 14 and most of the brethren have been made confident in the Lord because of my imprisonment, and are much more bold to speak the word of God without fear.

15 Some indeed preach Christ from envy and rivalry, but others from good will. 16 The latter do it out of love, knowing that I am put here for the defense of the gospel; 17 the former proclaim Christ out of partisanship, not sincerely but thinking to afflict me in my imprisonment. 18 What then? Only that in every way, whether in pretense or in truth, Christ is proclaimed; and in that I rejoice.

19 Yes, and I shall rejoice. For I know that through your prayers and the help of the Spirit of Jesus Christ this will turn out for my

20 According to my earnest expectation and *my* hope, that in nothing I shall be ashamed, but *that* with all boldness, as always, *so* now also Christ shall be magnified in my body, whether *it be* by life, or by death.

21 For to me to live *is* Christ, and to die *is* gain.

22 But if I live in the flesh, this *is* the fruit of my labour: yet what I shall choose I wot not.

23 For I am in a strait betwixt two, having a desire to depart, and to be with Christ; which is far better:

24 Nevertheless to abide in the flesh *is* more needful for you.

25 And having this confidence, I know that I shall abide and continue with you all for your futherance and joy of faith;

26 That your rejoicing may be more abundant in Jesus Christ for me by my coming to you again.

deliverance, 20 as it is my eager expectation and hope that I shall not be at all ashamed, but that with full courage now as always Christ will be honored in my body, whether by life or by death. 21 For to me to live is Christ, and to die is gain. 22 If it is to be life in the flesh, that means fruitful labor for me. Yet which I shall choose I cannot tell. 23 I am hard pressed between the two. My desire is to depart and be with Christ, for that is far better. 24 But to remain in the flesh is more necessary on your account. 25 Convinced of this, I know that I shall remain and continue with you all, for your progress and joy in the faith, 26 so that in me you may have ample cause to glory in Christ Jesus, because of my coming to you again.

***Key Verse:* For to me to live is Christ, and to die is gain. (Philippians 1:21)**

***Key Verse:* For to me to live is Christ, and to die is gain. (Philippians 1:21)**

As You Read the Scripture—Ralph Decker

The church at Philippi was the first established by Paul on what we now know as the European continent. About A.D. 48, during his second missionary campaign, Paul was led by a vision to cross the Aegean Sea from Asia Minor to Macedonia, the northern part of Greece. Philippi was the chief city of the area. Paul's first visit was shortened by persecution; he and Silas were imprisoned and asked to leave the city. They left behind a small but devoted group of converts (Acts 16:9-40). Paul revisited them a number of times and a special relationship developed. The Philippians formed a stable congregation noted for its generosity, especially in support of Paul's work. Although other dates and places have been suggested, it is generally believed that Paul wrote this letter while imprisoned in Rome (about A.D. 63–64). Its purpose is clear: Paul wrote to thank the Philippians for their financial support. In doing so, he praised their loyalty, gave them some guidelines for living, warned against false teachers, and called for unity within the church.

Philippians 1:12-15. After the usual salutation (1:1-2), thanks for the faith and loyalty of his readers (1:4-8), and a prayer for their growth in the faith (1:9-11), Paul reports that much good has resulted frm his imprisonment.

Verse 12. The phrase "what has happened" refers to Paul's imprisonment, which actually aided the spread of the gospel.

Verse 13. The praetorian guard may have been the special detachment of troops that guarded the emperor. As its members were assigned to guard Paul and were frequently changed, knowledge of him and his work would have spread quickly through the unit and beyond it. Paul apparently turned his prison cell into a chapel and converted his jailors and others ("the rest") as well.

Verse 14. The emboldened brethren were Paul's loyal associates, who were encouraged by this spread of knowledge about their leader and his message. It is clear that the reports spread among and by the soldiers were favorable.

Verses 15-18. The results of the imprisonment were not all good. Not only Paul's friends were emboldened. Rival evangelists took advantage of the situation. Paul treats their spirit of rivalry as of no importance, since they are preaching the gospel of Christ.

Verse 15. There were numerous traveling evangelists and preachers. Some were friendly toward Paul, some were envious.

Verse 16. Some of them, though not of Paul's party, realized that the gospel as well as Paul was on trial and did what they could to support him and his work.

Verse 17. Others, probably long-standing opponents of Paul who insisted that his gospel was incomplete because he did not require converts to be circumsized, as they did, used his situation to denounce him.

Verse 18. Edgar Goodspeed translated this verse as follows: "What difference does it make? All that matters is that . . . Christ is being made known."

Verses 19-26. These verses deal with Paul's inner struggle. He was now an old man (Philemon 9). He had worked hard (II Corinthians 11:23-28). His present imprisonment could end in either release or death. Which should he want?

Verse 19. Paul seems to expect release.

Verse 20. He does not rule out the possibility of being killed for his faith.

Verse 21. This is one of Paul's greatest statements of faith. His life, as long as he lives, will be used in the service of Christ. Death, because of his commitment, will be the high point of that service.

Verse 22. Elsewhere Paul wrote of death as a sleep from which all would waken in a general resurrection (I Corinthians 15:51-52; I Thessalonians 4:15-17). Here, facing the possibility of his own death, he sees it as immediate entry into the heavenly presence of Christ.

Verses 23-26. Paul was willing to postpone the joy of Christ's immediate presence if in doing so he could prepare others for it.

The Scripture and the Main Question—William H. Willimon

I Shall Rejoice

At first reading, we wonder if Paul is being honest with us. Here he is, languishing in jail. Knowing Paul's boundless energy and his total commitment to the spread of the gospel to all parts of the world, it is difficult to picture him a prisoner in a tiny cell. And yet, Paul makes the claim "that what has happened to me has really served to advance the gospel. . . . Yes, and I shall rejoice" (Philippians 1:12, 18).

Perhaps Paul is attempting to keep a stiff upper lip through all of his misfortunes. Or perhaps, out of concern for his struggling little congregations, he is attempting to reassure them, even though he is in great despair.

Paul's astounding affirmation of hope even in his hopeless circumstances arises from his conviction that "for me to live is Christ, and to die is gain. If it is to be life in the flesh, that means fruitful labor for me . . . [but] my desire is to depart and be with Christ, for that is far better" (1:21-23).

Paul's relationship with Christ enabled him to embrace both life and death. Whether life or death, Paul was able to take things as they came, confident that in life or in death he was secure in Christ's love.

If he were to live, that would enable Paul to continue to teach and to preach, to spread the good news of Christ into all the world. But if he were to die, it would mean complete nearness to Christ. Paul's confidence in the power of Christ's love enabled him to embrace either life or death with hope.

You and I listen to such words, for we know that sometimes life's circumstances make us feel trapped. Undoubtedly there were other prisoners who looked upon their imprisonment quite differently from Paul. Some blamed others for their fate and were filled with bitterness. Some sat in quiet despair. But Paul was able to see good even amid the bad. His vision was more than a mere belief that every cloud has a silver lining. Rather, it was based on his conviction that the same Lord who had preserved him in life would also preserve him in death. So whether it would be life or death for him, it would be life or death in the Lord.

To Live Is Christ

You and I live in a world that has given us so much choice, in the way our lives will go. A few generations ago, men and women had fewer options. If you were a man, more than likely you would go into the same trade your father followed. If you were a woman, your options were even more restricted.

But today, things are different. Young people agonize over the choice of their life work. There are so many possibilities. Many of tomorrow's jobs are not even in existence today. A person may follow many different careers in a single lifetime.

Here is my family on a Friday night outing. Where shall we go out to eat? Even in our relatively small city, we are able to enjoy French, Italian, Hungarian, Indonesian, Portuguese, Mexican, or German cuisine, all within a mile or so of our home. This is a wonderful array of culinary choice.

This is the situation of Paul, when he spoke of his own dilemma of choice: "For me to live is Christ, and to die is gain. If it is to be life in the flesh, that means fruitful labor for me. Yet which I shall choose I cannot tell. I am hard pressed between the two. My desire is to depart and be with Christ, for that is far better. But to remain in the flesh is more necessary on your account" (1:21-24).

Sometimes the multiple choices are a great problem. Many of us modern people resemble the man standing in front of a well-filled refrigerator, trying to decide about a midnight snack: "I'm hungry, but I don't know what I want to eat."

Too many choices can paralyze us. In *Future Shock*, Alvin Toffler speaks of the "peril of overchoice." Overchoice is that numbing modern sensation of having too many options, too many alternatives. We feel overwhelmed by the prospect. There is so much to do that we don't know what to do.

When our great-grandparents sat down to dinner, they were forced to eat whatever happened to be in season at that time of the year or those few foods that they were able to cure or can for themselves. We can sit down to a meal of oranges from Israel, pineapple from Hawaii, beef from Argentina, fish from Japan, or a host of other choices. Much of modern life is consumed with the dilemma of having to decide, having to choose between what we do and do not want.

But what do you do when there are no choices, or very few desirable choices?

The doctor comes in with the report from this year's physical. You can tell, from the look in her eyes, that the report is not good. When she finally says the word "cancer," you were expecting it. You then ask the questions: Can it be treated? How long do I have? What are my prospects for cure?

There is that day when your boss comes in and tells you the bad news. You had been expecting it, down deep, but you didn't want to admit it. You had heard the rumors that the boss was looking for younger people for the job. Now it has become official. They want you out—and at sixty-one! How can you hope to find another position at sixty-one?

So, after a couple of months of unfruitful searching, you settle down in a job—not much of a job by most people's standards, but the only one you can find at this stage in your life. There you are, trapped in this menial job until your retirement.

What do you do in situations like these? You can whine. You can let out a deep sigh and settle down to quiet hopelessness. Or you can become bitter, curse fate, rave about the injustice and unfairness of it all: What did I do to deserve this? Why did this happen to me?

All of those options were available to Paul, as he sat in his prison cell and contemplated his options. He was the prisoner of the Roman government. His fate was entirely in the hands of some petty Roman official. There he sat languishing, waiting for a word. What would it be? Death by the sword, or freedom?

With Full Courage

The story of Paul in jail at Rome reminds all of us, in our personal times of imprisonment, that there is a way to live in spite of the lack of choice. We are free to choose how we shall respond to our lack of choice. If we live or die, if we come out of this particular circumstance or not, we shall do so as those beloved and cared for by Christ.

There is a way even when there is no way.

Helping Adults Become Involved—Ronald E. Schlosser

Preparing to Teach

In his comments in "The Scripture and the Main Question," Dr. Willimon refers to Alvin Toffler's "peril of overchoice." Nowhere is this more in evidence now than in the television and video industry. For households having access to cable television, there are dozens and dozens of channels one can choose among when selecting programs to watch. If one has a videocassette recorder, the local video emporium, supermarket, or convenience store can provide hundreds of tape titles from which to choose.

How do you (or your family) decide what television programs to watch on a given evening? What criteria do you use? Do you consciously make choices, or do you just change channels until something interesting appears on the screen?

How to develop the ability to make wise decisions in all areas of life is what you will be helping your class explore in today's lesson. There are two primary learning goals: (1) to gain insight into the circumstances surrounding the writing of Paul's prison epistles, and of Philippians in particular; (2) to reflect on how we face decision-making situations.

Use the following lesson outline:

    I.   Consider decisions we make.
    II. Examine background information.
   III. Discern Paul's feelings and attitudes.
   IV. Identify and share insights.

Read carefully "The Scripture and the Main Question" and "As You Read the Scripture." These form the heart of the lesson. The ideas, insights, and suggestions in these sections should be reflected continually in your lesson plan.

As you use the suggested outline, you may want to either quote or paraphrase ideas. You might like to jot in the margin of your outline the page number and paragraph being referred to. For example, you could write a reference to page 65, paragraph 3, as 65-3.

Last Sunday you asked your class members to keep track of the kinds of decisions they were called upon to make during the week. You ought to do that yourself right now. Jot down some of these decisions—from deciding what to eat, what to wear, and what to do on a given day, to perhaps some larger decision that has long-term implications. What options were available, and what criteria did you use to decide on a course of action?

Prior to the lesson write on the chalkboard or newsprint the three questions you would like your class to discuss in section III.

Introducing the Main Question

I. Consider decisions we make.

Begin by talking about the many decisions, large and small, we all must make as we go about daily living. Refer to Dr. Willimon's comments about the multiple choices we have in our society.

Ask the class members to tell about the kinds of decisions they had to make during the week. To get the discussion going, you might share some of your own experiences.

Raise the question about what one does when there are few or no options in a decision-making situation. Dr. Willimon gives several examples, then refers to the situation Paul faced, as he sat in his prison cell near the end of his life. What might have been his attitude? What would have been your attitude?

Developing the Lesson

II. Examine background information.

To help the class understand the context of today's scripture passage, you need to give some background information about Paul's imprisonment, his writing of the Prison Epistles, and the letter he wrote to the church at Philippi. Dr. Decker notes that Paul wrote his letter to the Philippians while imprisoned in Rome about A.D. 63–64. From Acts 28:16-31 we learn that Paul was allowed to stay in his own hired house, though guarded, and that he had frequent visitors. His letter to the Philippians was probably written toward the close of his imprisonment. The tone of the letter suggests that he had been in Rome for some time and that he was expecting to be released so that he could visit his friends at Philippi (see Philippians 1:26; 2:23-24). Dr. Decker recalls how Paul first came to Philippi and began his work there (Acts 16:9-40). The Christians at Philippi loved Paul dearly, as he did them (see Philippians 1:3-11).

III. Discern Paul's feelings and attitudes.

Now turn to the passage for study. Read aloud Philippians 1:12-26, then note that in the Revised Standard Version this section is divided into three paragraphs: verses 12-14, 15-18, and 19-26. Ask the class members to pair themselves in twos to discuss these three questions, each pertaining to one of the paragraphs: (1) What effect did Paul's imprisonment have on him and on others around him? (verses 12-14). (2) How did Paul feel about the different motives for preaching? (verses 15-18). (3) What were Paul's hopes and desires? (verses 19-26).

Allow about five minutes for the pairs to discuss the questions, then call the class together for total group discussion. Encourage the members to share their insights, as you touch on each question. In addition to the summary statements below, refer to Dr. Decker's comments as he goes though the passage verse by verse.

Effects (verses 12-14). Paul is delighted that his imprisonment has had such good results. His guards have heard the gospel and have been telling others, and believers who had been holding back in proclaiming the gospel were now becoming more aggressive and confident in their witnessing.

Motives (verses 15-18). Paul realizes that some rival evangelists were using his imprisonment to promote their own particular beliefs. While he condemned their motives, he could rejoice that Christ was still being proclaimed. To him, after all, this was the most important thing.

Desires (verses 19-26). Paul's conflicting desires are expressed. He is ready and willing to die so that he can be with his Lord. Yet he feels he is still needed by the new believers to help them in their spiritual growth.

Helping Class Members Act

IV. Identify and share insights.

As Dr. Willimon points out, Paul's relationship with Christ enabled him to face both options—death and life—with confidence and even joy. What about your class members? Can they face important decisions with equal confidence? How should one deal with decisions about health, loss or change of job, divorce, care of failing parent or spouse, change of residence, retirement, and the like?

Encourage open sharing, but be sensitive to the very personal nature of some situations that might arise. Be supportive of those who do want to share some very real concerns and problems.

Here are some of the positive insights that might be mentioned: The prayers and support of Christian friends are redemptive; God can bring good out of seemingly bad circumstances; when we are in God's will, we can face anything with confidence; physical death is not the end—it ushers one into the immediate presence of Christ.

Close the session by referring to a promise found in Proverbs 3:5-6, which expresses good counsel for Christians seeking to know God's will in difficult situations.

Planning for Next Sunday

Ask the class to pay particular attention this coming week to television commercials and to advertisement in newspapers and magazines projecting certain images of success. In the eyes of our society, what is success? The background scripture for next week is Philippians 1:27–2:30. Urge class members to read it from at least two different versions or translations.

Serving as Christ Served

Background Scripture: Philippians 1:27–2:30

The Main Question—William H. Willimon

What are the images of success in our society? A good place to find some would be magazine advertisements and television commercials. Here we are told what we must buy if we are to be successful, as our society judges success. These commercials tell us that a successful person is one who has power and prestige. The successful man or woman is the one who steps out of a late model European sports car, dressed in the latest mode and wearing this or that fifty-dollar-a-bottle perfume.

I work on a university campus, and there are many competing images of success here. But nearly all of them imply that a successful person is one who has an advanced academic degree, extensive knowledge in some field of study, and other powers that can be translated into money in the "real world" outside the university. The successful person here is the scientist, the physician, the attorney, the business person who is able to "make it big" in the world.

But here we are on the third Sunday of Easter, coming to church to worship one who models a very different definition of success. Here was one who served with a basin and towel, who washed his disciples' feet and died for them on a cross.

What do his life and death tell us about success?

Selected Scripture

King James Version

Revised Standard Version

Philippians 1:27-30

27 Only let our conversation be as it becometh the gospel of Christ: that whether I come and see you, or else be absent, I may hear of your affairs, that ye stand fast in one spirit, with one mind striving together for the faith of the gospel;

28 And in nothing terrified by your adversaries: which is to them an evident token of perdition, but to you of salvation, and that of God.

29 For unto you it is given in the behalf of Christ not only to believe on him, but also to suffer for his sake;

30 Having the same conflict which ye saw in me, and now hear *to be* in me.

Philippians 2:1-11

1 If *there be* therefore any consolation in Christ, if any comfort of love, if any fellowship of the Spirit, if any bowels and mercies,

2 Fulfill ye my joy, that ye be like-minded, having the same love, *being* of one accord, of one mind.

3 *Let* nothing *be done* through strife or vainglory; but in lowliness of mind let each esteem other better than themselves.

4 Look not every man on his own things, but every man also on the things of others.

5 Let this mind be in you, which was also in Christ Jesus:

6 Who, being in the form of God, thought it not robbery to be equal with God:

7 But made himself of no reputation , and took upon him the form of a servant, and was made in the likeness of men:

8 And being found in fashion as a man, he humbled himself, and became obedient unto death, even the death of the cross.

Philippians 1:27-30

27 Only let your manner of life be worthy of the gospel of Christ, so that whether I come and see you or am absent, I may hear of you that you stand firm in the spirit, with one mind striving side by side for the faith of the gospel,

28 and not frightened in anything by your opponents. This is a clear omen to them of their destruction, but of your salvation, and that from God. 29 For it has been granted to you that for the sake of Christ you should not only believe in him but also suffer for his sake, 30 engaged in the same conflict which you saw and now hear to be mine.

Philippians 2:1-11

1 So if there is any encouragement in Christ, any incentive of love, any participation in the Spirit, any affection and sympathy, 2 complete my joy by being of the same mind, having the same love, being in full accord and of one mind. 3 Do nothing from selfishness or conceit, but in humility count others better than yourselves. 4 Let each of you look not only to his own interests, but also to the interests of others. 5 Have this mind among yourselves, which you have in Christ Jesus, 6 who, though he was in the form of God, did not count equality with God a thing to be grasped, 7 but emptied himself, taking the form of a servant, being born in the likeness of men. 8 And being found in human form he humbled himself and became obedient unto death, even death on a cross. 9 Therefore God has highly exalted him and bestowed on him the name which is above every name, 10 that at the name of Jesus every knee should

9 Wherefore God also hath highly exalted him, and given him a name which is above every name:

10 That at the name of Jesus every knee should bow, of *things* in heaven, and *things* in earth, and *things* under the earth;

11 And *that* every tongue should confess that Jesus Christ *is* Lord, to the glory of God the Father.

bow, in heaven and on earth and under the earth, 11 and every tongue confess that Jesus Christ is Lord, to the glory of God the Father.

Key Verse: **Let this mind be in you, which was also in Christ Jesus: Who . . . made himself of no reputation, and took upon him the form of a servant. (Philippians 2:5-7)**

Key Verse: **Have this mind among yourselves, which is yours in Christ Jesus, who . . . emptied himself, taking the form of a servant. (Philippians 2:5-7)**

As You Read the Scripture—Ralph Decker

Philippians 1:27-30. This paragraph introduces an exhortation that lasts through 2:18. It calls for a kind of congregational unity that would confound critics of the Christian faith.

Verse 27. The fourth word of this verse is rendered "conversation" in the King James Version, but "manner of life" in the Revised Standard Version. The difference in translation suggests we should take a look at the Greek original. Literally, the Greek verb means "to behave as a citizen." It is quite possible that Paul was here anticipating what he says later in the letter: "Our commonwealth is in heaven" (3:20). The New English Bible translates that statement as "We are citizens of heaven." Paul is calling for his readers to conduct themselves as worthy citizens of Christ's kingdom. Such conduct will result in unity of spirit and in united effort in the spread of the gospel.

Verse 28. The Philippian Christians had suffered or were facing persecution. Their adversaries are not named. They may have been either Jews who regarded Christianity as a heresy, or Jewish-Christians who insisted upon circumcision. Paul says that unity will show the opponents that God is on the side of the Christians and will save them.

Verse 29. For Paul, suffering was a part of the Christian life. Christ had suffered, and his followers will suffer. Suffering for Christ's sake is a privilege and a sign of God's favor, since it allows the suffering believer to share in the experience of Christ.

Verse 30. Paul offers his own life as an example. The Philippians had seen his sufferings when he was among them, and they had heard of his present sufferings in prison.

Philippians 2:1-4. Paul continues his call for unity and adds a call for humility.

Verses 1-2. Paul lists blessings he and the Philippians have shared, as a basis for his call for unity of mind, attitude, and purpose.

Verse 3. He warns against two attitudes that destroy unity—selfishness and conceit—and calls for humility. Humility is an attitude that enables one to regard others as equal to or better than oneself.

Verse 4. The combination of unity and humility will lead one to look after the interests of the group as well as one's own interests.

Verses 5-10. These verses contain one of the loftiest passages of all Paul's writings. The language, literary style, and thought are eloquent and elevated. The passage is so superior to the rest of the letter in these respects that some scholars believe that Paul has quoted an early Christian hymn to reinforce his appeal for humility. They argue that it breaks the flow of exhortation, is liturgical in style, and emphasizes the servanthood of Jesus in a way seldom found in Paul's letters. In any case, it is a profound theological statement, setting forth Paul's doctrine of the person and work of Christ.

Verse 5. The disposition that will enable the readers to act in unity and humility for the sake of all will come by sharing in the disposition of Christ.

Verse 6. Here are the origins of the doctrines of the deity and pre-existence of Christ. Before his incarnation he shared the very nature and being of God. He was, therefore, divine. He might have claimed for himself the honors due to God, but he refused to take what belonged to the Father.

Verse 7. According to Paul's doctrine of the incarnation and servanthood of Christ, Jesus surrendered his divine rank for that of a human and a servant.

Verse 8. His death on the cross was the supreme act of humility and service.

Verse 9. Paul's doctrine of the exaltation of Christ says that his self-denial won him a position higher than he had had before. The name above every name is given in the next sentence.

Verses 10-11. That name is "Lord." The words "Jesus Christ is Lord" formed the earliest creed of the Christian church. Paul quotes them three times in his letters (Romans 10:9; I Corinthians 12:3; and here).

The Scripture and the Main Question—William H. Willimon

Have This Mind Among Yourselves

Today's scripture is one of the most significant passages describing the nature of Christ. Philippians 2 is a doxology, that is, a hymn of praise to Christ. Some biblical scholars feel that Philippians was an early Christian hymn, perhaps used in early Christian baptismal liturgies. When the person was being baptized, perhaps the church stood by and sang this hymn.

The context is Paul's desire that the Christians at Philippi live in response to the gospel. "Do nothing from selfishness or conceit, but in humility count others better than yourselves. Let each of you look not only to his own interests, but also to the interests of others" (2:3-4).

How is such self-forgetful behavior possible? You and I come into this world looking out for Number One. When a newborn infant is hungry, it cries out. The infant does not know or care if its parents are asleep or engaged in some important business. The baby cries until its needs are met, until its parents drop everything and respond to its crying.

Of course, such behavior is "only natural" for the baby. If the baby were not "selfish" and did not cry out, it might perish. But this perfectly natural, perfectly understandable behavior will bring us to grief later in our lives. We come into life organizing the whole world around ourselves and our needs and wants. We continue this self-centeredness through the rest of our lives, a bit more skillfully and subtly than the crying baby, but nevertheless managing to let up a howl when we do not get our way.

It is this innate self-centeredness that Paul counters here in the second chapter of his letter to the Christians at Philippi.

How can we achieve unselfishness? For sure, not by some heroic act of will. Trying to be heroic only makes us more self-concerned. There is only one way, as Paul sees it. We must "have this mind among [ourselves], which is [ours] in Christ Jesus" (2:5).

"Though he was in the form of God, did not count equality with God a thing to be grasped, but emptied himself, taking the form of a servant, being born in the likeness of men. And being found in human form he humbled hmself and became obedient unto death, even death on a cross" (2:6-7).

Note the movement of ideas in this stirring passage. Rather than aspiring for, grasping, or reaching toward the divine, the way we normally conduct our lives, "he emptied himself, taking the form of a servant." Actually, the word "servant" here is a bit too polite a translation. The Greek word is *doulos*, which also means "slave." Christ was willing to be a slave for the cause of righteousness.

For Paul, Christ's mission involved "downward mobility." The Gospel of Mark, on the other hand, enjoys depicting Jesus as a miracle worker, someone even the wind and the seas obey. But Paul was impressed with the humiliation, weakness, and obedience that the Son displayed (see II Corinthians 8:9).

When people looked at Christ, they did not see God in the flesh, otherwise they would not have hung him up to die on a cross (I Corinthians 2:8). Here was a Messiah who won his victories through obedience to God, through self-emptying and suffering, not through miraculous powers. As is said elsewhere, "Although he was a Son, he learned obedience through what he suffered" (Hebrews 5:8).

He Emptied Himself

The first time we met Jesus, that day when he stood knee-deep in Jordan water at his baptism, we realized that we were dealing with a very different image of God. In the Jordan, with John the Baptist drenching him with water, we saw the beginning of the way that would eventually take him to the cross. His baptism intimated where it would finally end—our baptism does the same—no cross, no crown (Philippians 2:3-11).

Taking the Form of a Servant

What form do we take in our life together as Jesus' contemporary followers? When people look at our churches, what do they see? Let's take a moment and reflect on our churches' budgets. Where does the money go? How much is spent in saving our own lives, and how much is spent on emptying ourselves for the sake of others? Of course, the church has legitimate needs. We can't look after the needs of others if we don't have a building, if we don't educate and train our people. But few church budgets even approximate Jesus' own self-emptying stance.

How do we contemporary disciples compare when set alongside the image of our master? Our churches participate in the same extravagant monetary displays as other worldly powers. Grinning television evangelists present Christianity as the best deal a person ever had, a good way to make rich and happy people even richer and happier.

Church life becomes a self-serving matter of giving more time and money to the church to help the church preserve its own life, rather than lose it. The board meets not to agonize over how the church can better expend its resources in helping others but to discuss how to keep the neighborhood children from damaging the church's playground equipment.

In today's scripture, we are given a stunning image of the "downward mobility" of Christ. In our upward-mobility world, with its images of success based upon power and material advantage, today's scripture offers each of us a challenge and a cause for sober personal and church-wide self-examination.

Helping Adults Become Involved—Ronald E. Schlosser

Preparing to Teach

How do you feel about people who boast, "We're Number One"? Whether in reference to an athletic team or a government's military or space capability, such an attitude reflects the innate self-centeredness that characterizes much of our American way of life. Christians need to regularly examine their own behavior to see if it is self-giving or self-serving.

In today's session your class will be asked to do three things: (1) to compare the world's standards of success with the life-style exhibited by Jesus; (2) to reflect on the meaning of humility and servanthood; (3) to resolve to live as Jesus would, walking "in his name."

Use the following lesson outline:

    I.   Consider images of success.
    II. Explore the scripture.
        A. Small group study.
        B. Group reports and discussion.
        C. Further reflection.
   III. Consider implications.
        A. The church as servant.
        B. Worship.

Read carefully "The Scripture and the Main Question" and "As You Read the Scripture." These form the heart of the lesson. The ideas, insights, and suggestions in these sections should be reflected continually in your lesson plan.

As you use the suggested outline, you may want to either quote or paraphrase ideas. You might like to jot in the margin of your outline the page number and paragraph being referred to. For example, you could write a reference to page 65, paragraph 3, as 65-3.

As you prepare your lesson plan, try to think of hymns that speak about "the name of Jesus." Here are a few that may come quickly to mind: "Take the Name of Jesus with You," "How Sweet the Name of Jesus Sounds," "I Know of a Name," "There Is No Name So Sweet on Earth," and "O for a Thousand Tongues to Sing." Select one of these to use during a time of worship at the close of the session. Be sure there are hymnbooks available containing the hymn, or have the words duplicated for distribution to the class.

Prior to the session, cut out advertisements from magazines that illustrate contemporary images of success. Automobile and clothing ads are the most obvious ones, but any ads showing happy, prosperous people would be usable.

Introducing the Main Question

I. Consider images of success.

Begin by asking the main question posed by Dr. Willimon, "What are the images of success in our society?" Distribute the advertisements you have cut from magazines, asking the class to suggest what these ads say about society's image of success. What feelings do they try to elicit in the reader?

Talk about television commercials. Which ones say something about a successful or happy life-style? To what do these commercials appeal? Do they encourage self-centeredness?

Comment on the "We're Number One" philosophy mentioned above. How do class members feel about people who always want to be first? Does this just reflect a healthy competitive spirit, or is it symptomatic of something wrong with our society?

Developing the Lesson

II. Explore the scripture.
   A. Small group study.

Indicate that in today's scripture passage, Paul first describes the manner of life that should characterize Christian believers, and then he points to Jesus as the example whose life-style we should follow.

Divide your class into two groups (or if it is large, into a number of smaller groups). Ask one group to study Philippians 1:27–2:4 and discuss this question: What qualities does Paul say should characterize believers in Christ? Ask the other group to study Philippians 2:5-11 and discuss this question: How is Christ an example for Christians?

Allow about ten minutes for the small group discussion, then call the class together to report findings.

B. Group reports and discussion.
   Philippians 1:27–2:4. As class members report on the qualities that should characterize Christian believers, list them on the chalkboard or newsprint. Refer to Dr. Decker's comments on these verses. Your list might include
—Unity of spirit
—Unity of purpose
—Unity of action
—Freedom from fear
—Steadfast belief in Christ
—Willingness to suffer
—Unity of love
—Being in full accord
—Selflessness and humility
—Concern for others

Discuss the meaning of humility. Someone defined humility as "something that when you realize you have it, you've lost it." Ask the class to describe people they know whom they feel exemplify humility. Can one consciously acquire the attribute of humility?

Philippians 2:5-11. This eloquent passage is one of the most quoted passages in the New Testament. It is as profound in its theology as it is in its lyric beauty. The key word in the passage is "emptied" in verse 7. It refers to Christ's willingness to surrender his divine role and take on the status of a slave. Although Christ did not give up his *divine* nature, he did take on a human nature and lived as a servant among the people of his world. It was the supreme example of humility, for it led to his death on a cross, the cruelest and most degrading punishment one could experience. Yet in this act of extreme submission Christ was exalted to a position of glory and honor.

C. Further reflection.

Discuss with your class the idea of "downward mobility" mentioned by Dr. Willimon in his comments. What implications does this have for our Christian life-style and our Christian mission? If Christ came to be a servant, what do we need to do as his followers? Read Matthew 20:25-28. Note that greatness (success) is defined in terms of servanthood.

Helping Class Members Act

III. Consider implications.

A. *The church as servant.*

Move from a consideration of an individual Christian's call to be a servant to the church's call to be a servant. What effect does viewing "the church as servant" have on how the church ministers in the community? Refer to Dr. Willimon's questions under the subsection "Taking the Form of a Servant." Reflect on your church's budget. How much is expended self-centeredly and how much for others?

Spend some time brainstorming what could be done in your neighborhood or community if there were a change in priorities, if there were funds available, if there were volunteers willing to work, if there were leaders ready to organize and promote. How could existing church facilities be used in creative new ministries?

After writing down on the chalkboard or newsprint all the ideas suggested by the members, identify one or two that have real possibilities. What steps would be needed to set in motion plans to undertake such ministries? Challenge your class members to support the beginning of a new servant-ministry themselves.

B. *Worship.*

Close the session with a brief time of worship. Read aloud Philippians 2:10-11. Mention some of the hymns familiar to your class that speak of the name of Jesus. Select one to read or sing, such as "Take the Name of Jesus with You" or "O for a Thousand Tongues to Sing." Close with a prayer of thanks for Christ's willingness to become a servant and for calling us to follow in his footsteps. Challenge the class to "walk in Jesus name."

Planning for Next Sunday

Ask class members to skim through Charles M. Sheldon's book *In His*

Steps, if they have it or can find it in the library. Next week's scripture passage will be Philippians 3:7-21.

Pressing On in Christ

Background Scripture: Philippians 3

The Main Question—William H. Willimon

A few years ago, one of the top movies of the season was the film *Chariots of Fire*. This movie covered the long journey of two very different, yet surprisingly similar, young men to the Olympics. They were runners, and the story of their heroic efforts to become the world's best runners was a moving testimonial to the indomitable human spirit.

I'm sure that one reason athletics is so popular is that we see in the athlete's struggle and training human nature at its best. We see people who give their all to the game, who overcome all odds to triumph.

Athletes remind us that life consists of setting goals, of staying the course, of overcoming setbacks, and of keeping our determination. Many people who participated in athletics as children or youth in school credit their training with helping them to be successful in later life. It was on the playing field that they first learned the virtues of hard work, the endurance of pain and difficulty, and the thrill of victory.

In what ways do our lives as Christians resemble athletic competition? What is the race in which we are running? What is our common goal as Christians? These are among the questions of today's Bible study.

Selected Scripture

King James Version	Revised Standard Version
Philippians 3:7-21	*Philippians 3:7-21*
7 But what things were gain to me, those I counted loss for Christ.	7 But whatever gain I had, I counted as loss for the sake of Christ. 8 Indeed I count everything as loss because of the surpassing worth of knowing Christ Jesus my Lord. For his sake I have suffered the loss of all things, and count them as refuse, in order that I may gain Christ 9 and be found in him, not having a righteousness of my own, based on law, but that which is
8 Yea doubtless, and I count all things *but* loss for the excellency of the knowledge of Christ Jesus my Lord: for whom I have suffered the loss of all things, and do count them *but* dung, that I may win Christ,	
9 And be found in him, not having mine own righteousness, which is of the law, but that which is	

through the faith of Christ, the righteousness which is of God by faith:

10 That I may know him, and the power of his resurrection, and the fellowship of his sufferings, being made comformable unto his death;

11 If by any means I might attain unto the resurrection of the dead.

12 Not as though I had already attained, either were already perfect: but I follow after, if that I may apprehend that for which also I am apprehended of Christ Jesus.

13 Brethren, I count not myself to have apprehended: but *this* one thing I *do*, forgetting those things which are behind, and reaching forth unto those things which are before,

14 I press toward the mark for the prize of the high calling of God in Christ Jesus.

15 Let us therefore, as many as be perfect, be thus minded: and if in any thing ye be otherwise minded, God shall reveal even this unto you.

16 Nevertheless, whereto we have already attained, let us walk by the same rule, let us mind the same thing.

17 Brethren, be followers together of me, and mark them which walk so as ye have us for an ensample.

18 (For many walk, of whom I have told you often, and now tell you even weeping, *that they are* the enemies of the cross of Christ:

19 Whose end *is* destruction, whose God *is their* belly, and *whose* glory *is* in their shame, who mind earthly things.)

20 For our conversation is in heaven; from whence also we look for the Saviour, the Lord Jesus Christ:

21 Who shall change our vile body, that it may be fashioned like unto his glorious body, according to the working whereby he is able even to subdue all things unto himself.

through faith in Christ, the righteousness from God that depends on faith; 10 that I may know him and the power of his resurrection, and may share his sufferings, becoming like him in his death, 11 that if possible I may attain the resurrection from the dead.

12 Not that I have already obtained this or am already perfect; but I press on to make it my own, because Christ Jesus has made me his own. 13 Brethren, I do not consider that I have made it my own; but one thing I do, forgetting what lies behind and straining forward to what lies ahead, 14 I press on toward the goal for the prize of the upward call of God in Christ Jesus. 15 Let those of us who are mature be thus minded; and if in anything you are otherwise minded, God will reveal that also to you. 16 Only let us hold true to what we have attained.

17 Brethren, join in imitating me, and mark those who so live as you have an example in us. 18 For many, of whom I have often told you and now tell you even with tears, live as enemies of the cross of Christ. 19 Their end is destruction, their god is the belly, and they glory in their shame, with minds set on earthly things. 20 But our commonwealth is in heaven, and from it we await a Saviour, the Lord Jesus Christ, 21 who will change our lowly body to be like his glorious body, by the power which enables him even to subject all things to himself.

Key Verse: **Forgetting those things which are behind, and reaching forth unto those things which are before, I press toward the mark for the prize of the high calling of God in Christ Jesus. (Philippians 3:13-14)**

Key Verse: **Forgetting what lies behind and straining forward to what lies ahead, I press on toward the goal for the prize of the upward call of God in Christ Jesus. (Philippians 3:13-14)**

As You Read the Scripture—Ralph Decker

Philippians 3:7-21. Paul warns his readers against false teachers. Some of these were claiming superiority to Paul on the ground that Christianity was part of Judaism and that they were true to Judaism's teachings, while Paul was a renegade Jew who had deserted them. All through his ministry Paul had to contend with the "Judaizers": teachers who maintained that a Gentile must become a Jew before he could be a Christian. To do so he must be circumcized and keep the dietary and other laws of the Jewish faith. Paul was proud of his national and religious heritage, but he did not consider it essential to salvation. Nor did he consider his moral achievements to be complete. He was still pressing on toward the experience of complete union with Christ. He urges his readers to join in the quest.

Verse 7. In defending his position, Paul had set forth the extent and richness of his Jewish origins and moral attainments (verses 4*b*-6). From his new relationship with Christ he looks back and realizes that the things he thought were bringing him salvation had really stood in the way of it. He uses bookkeeping language to say that since he could place his union with Christ on the "profit" side of his life account, he had found his racial standing and his observance of the Jewish laws worthless. They were, therefore, moved to the "loss" column.

Verse 8. He goes beyond his heritage and record of good conduct to characterize all worldly advantages as worthless in comparison with the knowledge of Christ. Alongside that knowledge, everything else is as worthless as trash and is to be discarded, lest it stand in the way of gaining understanding. This passage echoes Jesus' parables of the treasure hidden in a field and the pearl of great price, in which the finders sold everything else in order to buy the most valuable thing (Matthew 13:44-46).

Verse 9. To "gain Christ and be found in him" is to attain righteousness, or a proper relationship with God. It cannot be attained by observing rules and regulations. It is a status conferred by God in response to faith in Christ.

Verses 10-11. Knowing Christ means more than being acquainted with him or knowing about him. It means experiencing his power by sharing in his sufferings and in his resurrection triumph.

Verse 12. Lest he be accused of boasting, Paul says that his own relationship with Christ is still far from perfect. Paul is striving to perfect it. His motivation for doing so comes from his Damascus road experience, in which Christ called him to be an apostle (Acts 26:12-18).

Verse 13. Paul had a single aim or purpose: to attain perfect union with Christ. He uses the metaphor of a race in which the runner dares not look back but uses every effort to reach the goal.

Verse 14. In the Greek and Roman games, it was the practice to set the prize or trophy at the place where the race was to end. The sight of what they were striving for inspired the contestants to do their best. For

Christians, the "prize" is "God's call to the life above, in Christ Jesus" (NEB). A similar reward is suggested in Jesus' parable of the talents: "Well done, good and faithful servant . . . enter into the joy of your master" (Matthew 25:21).

Verses 15-16. It is to mature Christians that Paul makes his appeal to join him in continuing to grow spiritually. He does not condemn those who differ but assures them that God will enlighten them if they are faithful to the truth they have.

Verses 17-21. Paul offers himself as an example of what a Christian should be. This was not egotistical. Early converts had no Christian Scriptures or traditions to guide them. They had to choose which church leaders to follow as their life-patterns.

The Scripture and the Main Question—William H. Willimon

The Worth of Knowing Jesus Christ as My Lord

Paul is in prison. From his jail cell he writes that, even in his tough present circumstances, he is able to say, "I count everything as loss because of the surpassing worth of knowing Christ Jesus my Lord. For his sake I have suffered the loss of all things, and count them as refuse, in order that I may gain Christ and be found in him, not having a righteousness of my own . . . but that which is through faith in Christ" (Philippians 3:8-9).

That is quite a testimonial to the goodness of life in Christ. Here is Paul, who has been forced to leave behind family, friends, and the traditions of his people and who now finally finds himself languishing in a Roman jail awaiting possible execution. And yet he is able to say that it has all been worthwhile.

In speaking of the Christian life, Paul frequently uses images from other aspects of life to illuminate aspects of what it is like to be a Christian. You may recall Paul's comparison of the church to a bride ('the bride of Christ') in Ephesians, or his comparison of the church to a living human body with its various members and limbs, in I Corinthians. Now, in his letter to the Philippians, Paul uses a sports metaphor, that of runners in the midst of a race, to talk about how it feels to live as a Christian.

As I write these words, the basketball team from my university is preparing to play in the national championship game in Dallas. I have watched these young men from their first days here at the university. Their first year of college basketball, when they were freshmen, was a virtual disaster. They won few games and many predicted that they would never develop into a first-class basketball team. A number of them were considered too short for college basketball. Those who were tall were considered too clumsy.

But observers only rated their physical characteristics. They overlooked the factor of the characters of these young men. In the summers, they practiced every day; they lifted weights and studied strategy. Each year they improved, until in their senior year they went virtually undefeated. They are now basking in the glory of the NCAA finals, in Dallas.

Many people, even those who are not part of our university, are pulling for them to win, because everyone likes the story of the underdog who rises to the top, the losers who become winners by virtue of their own hard work and dedication.

Straining Forward to What Lies Ahead

In comparing Christian life to running a race, Paul reminds us that being a Christian is no easy affair. There are too many factors working against us for it to be easy. We are not Christian by natural inclination. We are subject to all sorts of temptations. The world is not always on our side. There may be suffering and sacrifice.

Therefore we must respond to the demands of Christ as if we were athletes preparing for the big race. Long hours of training will be required. In fact, your presence in your adult class this Sunday morning might be looked upon as a training session, a work-out, a practice, a scrimmage, for the task of living as a Christian on Monday morning.

In this race, Paul has excelled. It has been tough for him, but it has also been a great adventure. How wonderful that he is able to say, even toward the end of his life and his career as the world's greatest missionary, that he is "forgetting what lies behind and straining forward to what lies ahead" (3:13).

You and I have encountered too many people who toward the end of their lives want only to ponder the "good old days" and lament the present state of affairs. They condemn the present and the future as confusing and bad. Only the past has any fascination for them. But not Paul. The joy with which he has run the race in the past enables him to look into the future with confidence. He knows that the same Lord who guided things in the past will be the Lord who will stride with his church into the future.

What factors enable an older person to age graciously and to face the future with confidence? How can we maintain our zest for life even as we age and enter years of declining health and productivity? Perhaps a key is in training. Studies show that our older years can be happier and healthier if we prepare by leading active, healthy lives now. Perhaps the same holds true for our spiritual lives. Paul was able to endure his present situation in prison because, in a sense, he had been training for such misfortune all along. He had gotten in shape for the demands of the future because he had spent his whole adult life "straining forward to what lies ahead . . . the goal for the prize of the upward call of God in Christ Jesus" (3:13-14).

The Power of His Resurrection

When he was a boy, Theodore Roosevelt was told that he would probably spend the rest of his life as an invalid. His constitution was too frail, his lungs too weak from asthma, to hope for much more. But Roosevelt's father would not accept this for his son. He installed a fully equipped gymnasium in their home and young Teddy worked out in the gym every day until he was transformed from a sickly child into a robust picture of health. This early training accounting for his lifetime of vitality and vigor.

Today there is much concern over proper diet and proper physical fitness and exercise. We have learned that there is a definite connection between such care of our bodies and our mental state in life.

Perhaps we should be equally concerned about our spiritual well-being. Life causes us to meet various challenges. We may never be required to suffer as Paul suffered for his faith, but we are still challenged. How we respond to these spiritual challenges will be determined, in no small way, by how well we have trained and prepared ourselves for them.

Let us run the race with preseverance, even as saints like Paul have run it before us.

Paul concludes this passage of scripture with the challenge: "Brethren [and sisters], join in imitating me, and mark those who so live as you have an example in us" (3:17). Paul had pressed on toward "the goal for the prize of the upward call of God," and welcomed all who would join him in the contest.

Helping Adults Become Involved—Ronald E. Schlosser

Preparing to Teach

In the early part of this century, a book appeared which, in less than three decades, became the world's best seller, second only to the Bible. It was translated into every major language of the earth, and it influenced millions of lives. The book was Charles M. Sheldon's *In His Steps*. It tells the story of a minister who had the inspiration one Sunday to challenge the members of his congregation to undertake a unique experiment. He asked for volunteers to join him for one year in trying to follow Jesus as closely as possible. They would not do anything without first asking this question: "What would Jesus do?"

Whatever your feeling is about the appropriateness of such an undertaking, in today's lesson your class will be exploring what it means to be like Christ. More specifically, the learning goals will be (1) to consider the personal implications of knowing and following Christ as Savior and Lord, and (2) to appreciate the importance of training—both physical and spiritual—to keep ourselves healthy, effective Christians.

Use the following lesson outline:

    I.   Reflect on sports activities.
   II.   Dig into the scripture text.
       A. The worth of knowing Christ (verses 7-11).
       B. The importance of a goal (verses 12-14).
       C. The need for Christ's mind (verses 15-16).
       D. The desire to follow Christ (verses 17-21).
  III.   Decide on courses of action.
       A. What would Jesus do?
       B. Resolve to train.

Read carefully "The Scripture and the Main Question" and "As You Read the Scripture." These form the heart of the lesson. The ideas, insights, and suggestions in these sections should be reflected continually in your lesson plan.

As you use the suggested outline, you may want to either quote or paraphrase ideas. You might like to jot in the margin of your outline the page number and paragraph being referred to. For example, you could write a reference to page 65, paragraph 3, as 65-3.

As you prepare your lesson plan, read the background scripture from several translations. Consider some of the areas in your own life in which you feel you need to grow as a Christian.

Bring to the session a supply of three-by-five-inch index cards and pencils. Also have available a number of different Bible translations.

Introducing the Main Question

I. Reflect on sports activities.

Refer to Dr. Willimon's comments about athletics in the section "The Main Question." Ask your class members how many participated in sports when they were younger, or perhaps still do? Have them share some stories of their athletic experiences. Discuss with them what is required of athletes in order to win. Words such as patience, discipline, consistency, and endurance might be mentioned. (See Dr. Willimon's comments about his university's basketball team.) Note that endurance produces character. Read Romans 5:3-5.

Developing the Lesson

II. Dig into the scripture text.

Ask someone to read aloud today's scripture passage, Philippians 3:7-21. Distribute various Bible translations and versions so that members can make comparisons as the passage is read. As you deal with the passage in a verse-by-verse manner, focusing on the phrases and words listed below, encourage the members to comment on the various ways that key words and phrases in the passage are rendered in their versions. Refer also to Dr. Decker's comments.

A. The worth of knowing Christ (verses 7-11).

"Loss." What are we willing to lose to follow Christ? What did Paul lose?

"Righteousness." What is righteousness and how can it be attained?

"Power of his resurrection." Why was knowing Christ and his resurrection power so important to Paul? Is it that important to us?

"Share his sufferings." Of what value is suffering? Refer again to Romans 5:3-5.

B. The importance of a goal (verses 12-14).

"I press on." Paul feels that he still needs to grow in Christ. He has not yet attained full Christian maturity. How do we feel about our own spiritual maturity?

"Toward the goal." Why are goals important? In business there is "management by objectives." In order to achieve, one must move toward well-defined goals. Likewise, to live a Christian life we must identify the standards and goals by which we will measure our growth.

C. The need for Christ's mind (verses 15-16).

"Mature" What is Christian maturity? Develop a definition.

"Be thus minded." Paul feels Christians should have the same mind (aim and purpose) as he has. By extension, he sees this as a reflection of the mind of Christ. We who would be mature should have Christ's mind in us. What kind of mind is this? (See Philippians 2:5-7; it is a servant's mind, a desire to give oneself to others. Refer to Mark 10:45.)

D. The desire to follow Christ (verses 17-21).

"Imitating me." Is Paul being egotistical in making this statement? (See Dr. Decker's comments.) Paul urged the early believers to imitate him because he strove to imitate Christ. Refer to I Corinthians 11:1 and Philippians 4:9. Jesus is our model. He is both our goal and our guide to full Christian maturity.

"Enemies of the cross." Who are these enemies? Verse 19 describes them as carnal, materialistic persons.

"*Our commonwealth.*" How do other versions translate this phrase? The King James Version uses the word "conversation." The same word "conversation" is used in Philippians 1:27 to mean "manner of life." The Greek words used in both verses have a common root. In essence Paul is saying, "Our lives must be lived as if governed by the laws and principles of God's kingdom. We must behave as heavenly citizens because we indeed are just that."

Helping Class Members Act

III. *Decide on courses of action.*
    A. *What would Jesus do?*

We are still faced with the thorny question, What would Christ have us do? Refer to the book *In His Steps*, mentioned above. Is this a legitimate approach to take in making decisions—asking, What would Jesus do? Discuss this with your class. (Because Jesus lived and acted in a culture much different from ours, it is difficult to know what Jesus would do if he were to face certain of the complex problems we face today. It might be better to consider what Jesus would *think* about the issues involved and then to act in a way that would be consistent with this thinking.)

    B. *Resolve to train.*

Refer to the story of Teddy Roosevelt that Dr. Willimon tells at the end of his comments. Distribute the index cards and ask class members to think of specific "exercises" they would be willing to do to improve their spiritual well-being. Although they may think first of spiritual exercises, such as setting aside a time each day for Bible study, prayer, and meditation, there might be some physical exercises they could do that would enhance their spiritual development. For example, a weight problem or poor eating habits may contribute to a poor self-image. By adopting some positive physical disciplines, their spiritual well-being might be nurtured. Perhaps the two kinds of exercises can be combined: talking with God as one takes a daily walk or run, or reading a Christian book or magazine while one peddles an exercise bike.

Encourage the members to write down one or two specific "exercises" they will do this week. They should take the cards home as reminders of their resolve.

Planning for Next Sunday

The passage for study next Sunday is Philippians 4:4-19. In addition to reading this, class members should skim through the whole book and count the number of times the words "joy" and "rejoice" appear.

Rejoicing in Christ

Background Scripture: Philippians 4

The Main Question—William H. Willimon

On Easter Sunday, in most of our churches, we pull out all the stops. We sing at the top of our voices that Jesus Christ has risen today, hallelujah! If there are youth in the church who play the trumpet or trombone, they may be asked to accompany the choir on Easter. The pews are packed with people, more people than on any other Sunday of the year, everybody here to sing at the top of their voices with joy at the wonderful thing that has happened.

But this Sunday, Easter is five weeks behind us. Do you find the same feeling within the congregation today, now that Easter is long past? To be honest, few of us feel the same joy that we felt on Easter. Joy is an emotion difficult to sustain over long periods of time. This doesn't mean that what we felt on Easter was not real; it just means that the emotion of joy is fragile. We Christians worship on Sunday because Sunday is the day of resurrection. Every Sunday is a "little Easter" for us. But making every Sunday a replay of Easter is difficult. The cares of the world, the little everyday problems of life, eat away at our joy. We are quickly brought low by the facts of life, in the days after Easter.

Paul wrote to the Philippians, "Rejoice in the Lord always" (Philippians 4:4). How is such a thing possible for us in these days after Easter?

Selected Scripture

King James Version	Revised Standard Version
Philippians 4:4-19	*Philippians 4:4-19*
4 Rejoice in the Lord alway: *and* again I say, Rejoice.	4 Rejoice in the Lord always: again I will say, Rejoice. 5 Let all men know your forbearance. The Lord is at hand. 6 Have no anxiety about anything, but in everything by prayer and supplication with thanksgiving let your requests be made known to God. 7 And the peace of God, which passes all understanding, will keep your hearts and your minds in Christ Jesus.
5 Let your moderation be known unto all men. The Lord *is* at hand.	
6 Be careful for nothing; but in every thing by prayer and supplication with thanksgiving let your requests be made known unto God.	
7 And the peace of God, which passeth all understanding, shall keep your hearts and minds through Christ Jesus.	
8 Finally, brethren, whatsoever things are true, whatsoever things *are* honest, whatsoever things *are* just, whatsoever things *are* pure, whatsoever things *are* lovely, what-	8 Finally, brethren, whatever is true, whatever is honorable, whatever is just, whatever is pure, whatever is lovely, whatever is gracious, if there is any excellence, if there is

soever things *are* of good report; if *there be* any virture, and if *there be* any praise, think on these things.

9 Those things, which ye have both learned, and received, and heard, and seen in me, do: and the God of peace shall be with you.

10 But I rejoiced in the Lord greatly, that now at the last your care of me hath flourished again; wherein ye were also careful, but ye lacked opportunity.

11 Not that I speak in respect of want: for I have learned, in whatsoever state I am, *therewith* to be content.

12 I know both how to be abased, and I know how to abound: everywhere and in all things I am instructed both to be full and to be hungry, both to abound and to suffer need.

13 I can do all things through Christ which strengtheneth me.

14 Notwithstanding ye have well done, that ye did communicate with my affliction.

15 Now ye Phil-lip'-pi-ans know also, that in the beginning of the gospel, when I departed from Macedonia, no church communicated with me as concerning giving and receiving, but ye only.

16 For even in Thes-sa-lo-ni'-ca ye sent once and again unto my necessity.

17 Not because I desire a gift: but I desire fruit that may abound to your account.

18 But I have all, and abound: I am full, having received of E-paph-ro-di'-tus the things *which were sent* from you, an odour of a sweet smell, a sacrifice acceptable, wellpleasing to God.

19 But my God shall supply all your need according to his riches in glory by Christ Jesus.

anything worthy of praise, think about these things. 9 What you have learned and received and heard and seen in me, do; and the God of peace will be with you.

10 I rejoice in the Lord greatly that now at length you have revived your concern for me; you were indeed concerned for me, but you had no opportunity. 11 Not that I complain of want; for I have learned, in whatever state I am, to be content.

12 I know how to be abased, and I know how to abound; in any and all circumstances I have learned the secret of facing plenty and hunger, abundance and want. 13 I can do all things in him who strengthens me.

14 Yet it was kind of you to share my trouble. 15 And you Philippians yourselves know that in the beginning of the gospel, when I left Macedo'nia, no church entered into partnership with me in giving and receiving except you only; 16 for even in Thessaloni'ca you sent me help once and again. 17 Not that I seek the gift; but I seek the fruit which increases to your credit. 18 I have received full payment, and more; I am filled having received from Epaphrodi'tus the gifts you sent, a fragrant offering, a sacrifice acceptable and pleasing to God. 19 And my God will supply every need of yours according to his riches in glory in Christ Jesus.

Key Verse: **Rejoice in the Lord alway: and again I say, Rejoice. (Philippians 4:4)**

Key Verse: **Rejoice in the Lord always; again I will say, Rejoice. (Philippians 4:4)**

As You Read the Scripture—Ralph Decker

Philippians 4:4-7. It should be remembered that Paul was in prison and facing the possibility of death when he wrote these words about patience, joy, and peace.

Verse 4. Paul had already mentioned joy and rejoicing a dozen times in this letter. Now, in closing it, he uses a word which combines his call to Christian joy with his farewell. The Greek word translated "rejoice" was commonly used as a way of saying "good-bye," similarly to our "be happy" or "have a good day." Paul had used it in 3:1, where he had started to close his letter. He had interrupted it to give a special warning against false teachers. Now, he picks up his earlier line of thought.

Verse 5. The word translated "forbearance" has given translators much concern as to its exact meaning. It seems to refer to a gentle, courteous life-style, rather than to patience. The Douay Version translates it "modesty." The phrase "the Lord is at hand" may mean either that he is always near to the faithful or that he is coming soon, probably the latter. Paul shared with the majority of early Christians the belief in an early return of their Lord. The hope was a source of joy and gave reason for gentle, courteous living in the face of derision and persecution.

Verse 6. This verse echoes part of Jesus' Sermon on the Mount: "Do not be anxious about your life" (Matthew 6:25-34). Constant prayer can prevent anxiety. True prayer includes thanksgiving for blessings received as well as requests for God's help on present needs.

Verse 7. Constant prayer and the power of God give the peace of God—a blessing that "surpasses all our dreams" (James Moffatt's translation). Joseph H. Thayer defines it as "the tranquil state of a soul assured of its salvation through Christ, and so fearing nothing from God and content with its earthly lot, of whatever sort that is" (Joseph H. Thayer, *A Greek-English Lexicon of the New Testament* [N.Y.: American Book Co., 1889], p. 182). In the word translated "keep" Paul likens the peace of God to a military guard protecting the hearts and minds of the faithful.

Verse 8. Persons become what they think about. Paul urges his reader to concentrate their thoughts on matters of excellence and worth in order to develop positive, life-enriching qualities in themselves. Paul goes beyond thinking. He calls for action governed by the values listed.

Verse 9. Again, Paul offers himself as a model. In the absence of Scriptures and well-formulated codes of conduct, living examples were the best guides. The phrase "the God of peace" was one of Paul's favorite terms for the deity (Romans 15:33; 16:20; II Corinthians 13:11; I Thessalonians 5:23).

Verses 10-19. This paragraph contains that for which the whole letter was written—thanks for a gift of money from the church at Philippi. Paul's thanks are an interesting expression of both his independence based on his ability to adjust to circumstances and his gratitude for the support of others. Very carefully, he makes it clear that the gift was not really needed but that it was appreciated and that the spirit behind it is a cause for rejoicing.

Verse 13. This is one of the great faith statements of Paul.

Verses 14-19. The church at Philippi was the only church from which Paul received and accepted gifts and financial support. He made it clear to other churches that he did not ask or accept funds from them (I Corinthians 9:3-14; I Thessalonians 2:9). He supported himself by his own handiwork.

However, after he left Philippi and had gone to Thessalonica (Acts 17:1-3), he had accepted at least two gifts from the Philippians to support his work (verse 16). The Philippians, after a long gap, had again sent financial support (verse 10). It was delivered by Epaphroditus (verse 18).

The Scripture and the Main Question—William H. Willimon

Rejoice

You and I, as Americans, live in a nation in which the pursuit of happiness is a cardinal principle. The pursuit of happiness is written into our Declaration of Independence. We believe that people ought to be free to pursue happiness—however they define it. And yet many Americans know that happiness is a most elusive virtue.

One of the reasons churches struggle with poor attendance on many Sunday mornings in the spring and the summer is that many church members are at the beach, or the lake, or the mountains, or the races, or the myriad of other recreational activities that occupy our weekends. Driving through my neighborhood the other day, I was astounded to note how many nearby families own expensive campers, motorcycles, and other vehicles which are exclusively devoted to weekend recreational use. A neighbor of mine was saying to me the other day, "A family's second home has became as important, if not more important, than its first home."

Is it any wonder that there are many Sundays when the preacher stands up in the pulpit and thinks to him or herself, "Where is everybody today?" Chances are that everybody is out "pursuing happiness." Our new American affluence has enabled many of us to have enough money to invest in possessions that are beyond life's basic necessities. But are we happier?

One of the problems of seeking happiness through the acquisition of material things is that there is a sort law of rising expectations. Simply translated, this means that the more we have, the more we want. A while back a man proudly showed me his new motor home. Eight people can sleep in the vehicle. It has a full kitchen and a full bathroom. He said to me, "It all started when we bought a small tent to take the boys camping on the weekends. From a tent we moved to a small camping trailer. And then from the trailer we moved to our first motor home—a simple affair which consisted of a few pull-down bunks and a small galley. Now we have ended up with this monster. Let me give you some advice. Don't ever get started on this camping thing unless you are willing to be bitten by the bug."

Years ago, when we bought our first stereo, the salesperson told us, "The trouble with owning a stereo is that every stereo is simply a first step on the way to another. There is always some component that you want that is a little bit better than what you have."

We think to ourselves, "If I can just get this thing, I will be happy." One thing only leads to another, and we cannot acquire things as fast as our expectations arise. Our lives are plagued by invidious comparisons with those around us. The "pursuit of happiness" becomes a materialistic treadmill, as our lives become frantic efforts to keep up with the Joneses.

Rejoice in the Lord

When Paul says "Rejoice in the Lord always," he is obviously speaking of much more than the superficial pursuit of happiness, as we usually define it.

He is speaking of a peculiar kind of joy that comes from one's relationship with Christ. Many people today will not find the happiness they seek, because they are attempting to base their happiness on things. When Paul wrote to the Philippians, he was probably addressing a church that had known first-hand persecution. The church at Philippi was a small, persecuted group of believers on the fringe of a vast pagan empire. And yet these were the people whom Paul urged to "rejoice always." How is such happiness possible?

Perhaps the most difficult thing about true happiness is that happiness cannot be an end in itself. One of the surest ways not to find happiness is to go out looking for it on its own terms. The couple who say to themselves, "Let's go out tonight and be happy," are setting themselves up for failure. The family that begins the first day of a vacation saying, "We are going to do everything we can to be happy this week," will probably come home disappointed.

Happiness seems to be one of those experiences in life that are byproducts of something else. Show me a couple who get married in order to "be happy" and I will show you a very unhappy couple a few years later. And yet there are many married couples who will tell you that they have achieved real and deep happiness in marriage—by not looking for only happiness. Many married couples can testify that they have experienced happiness in marriage by going through times of marital stress and difficulty. Happiness often arises out of those situations in which we sacrifice ourselves for some greater goal.

Any parent can probably point to times when he or she suffered greatly while raising children. Children often cause parents great sadness. However, looking back, the parent is able to say that being a parent did bring great joy. The joy came from a task well done, a job well performed, a commitment that was kept.

Perhaps this is why Paul could urge the Philippians to be joyful always. They had kept the faith. They had not wavered in their commitment to Christ. Therefore they truly did have much for which to be happy. Happiness is one of the things that makes life worth living. But we shall not have it if we seek it for itself. True joy must be based on something more substantial than momentary "highs." Therefore, Paul's urging of the Philippians to rejoice comes after his urging them to be faithful.

Our happiness comes much the same way.

Paul's magnificent statement in verses 7-8 may well close this lesson:

> And the peace of God will keep your hearts and minds in Christ Jesus. Finally, brethren, whatever is true, whatever is honorable, whatever is just, whatever is pure, whatever is lovely, whatever is gracious, if there is any excellence, if there is anything worthy of praise, think about these things.

Helping Adults Become Involved—Ronald E. Schlosser

Preparing to Teach

Read through today's scripture passage, Philippians 4:4-19, and note how many quotable verses it contains. Over the years people have selected some of them as their life verses, or have memorized them as a source of strength and affirmation for their lives:

— 4:4 has appeared as a motto on wall or desk plaques.
— 4:7 is often quoted as a benediction in a worship service.
— 4:8 is sometimes used as a memorization verse in church school.
— 4:11 has comforted many persons facing difficult situations.
— 4:13 often serves as a life verse for lay persons as well as clergy.
— 4:19 is an affirmation that has helped many get through tough times.

Which of these has special meaning for you? Perhaps you will wish to commit several of these verses to memory.

The word "joy" or "rejoice" is used fourteen times in Philippians (Revised Standard Version). Skim through the book and see if you can spot them. Circle them with a pen or pencil. You will be asking your class to do this early in the session.

In today's session you will be guiding your class to do at least two things: (1) to identify the components of joy and the difference between happiness and joy; (2) to consider why the Christian life brings joy to a person.

Use the following lesson outline:

I.   Share our ideas about joy.
II. Explore the biblical meaning of joy.
     A. Joy and happiness.
     B. Personal experiences.
     C. Paul's concluding affirmation.
III. Summarize learnings about joy.

Read carefully "The Scripture and the Main Question" and "As You Read the Scripture." These form the heart of the lesson. The ideas, insights, and suggestions in these sections should be reflected continually in your lesson plan.

As you use the suggested outline, you may want to either quote or paraphrase ideas. You might like to jot in the margin of your outline the page number and paragraph being referred to. For example, you could write a reference to page 65, paragraph 3, as 65-3.

Have available sheets of construction paper, colored marking pens, and a roll of masking tape.

Introducing the Main Question

I. Share our ideas about joy.
Dr. Willimon observes in his comments on the main question that "joy is a fragile emotion." Ask class members whether they agree or disagree with this observation. Encourage everyone to share an opinion, perhaps giving an example from life.

At the end of last week's session, you asked the class to skim through Philippians and count the number of times the word "joy" and "rejoice" appear. Did anyone do that? If not, allow a few minutes for the entire class to do it. To save time, divide the class into four sections, each taking a different chapter. Suggest that the members circle the words with a pen or pencil.

As each reference is given, have someone read the verse aloud. The references are 1:4; 1:18; 1:19; 1:25; 2:2; 2:17; 2:18; 2:28; 2:29; 3:1; 4:1; 4:4 (two references); 4:10.

Developing the Lesson

II. Explore the biblical meaning of joy.

Point out that Philippians 4:4 is today's key verse. It often appears as a motto on a wall or desk plaque. Share Dr. Decker's comments about this verse, then ask for insights or observations from class members. Why should Christians always rejoice? What are the components of joy, of rejoicing? Is joy something more than a momentary "high"?

Alan Richardson, in *A Theological Word Book of the Bible*, sees joy as a gift from God. It is "by the power of the Holy Spirit" that joy arises (Romans 15:13). It is a fruit of the Spirit (Galatians 5:22). When one experiences God's presence in one's life, joy becomes full. We sense Paul's joy in his affirmation that nothing can separate him from the love of God in Christ Jesus (Romans 8:39). Joy has an eternal dimension. In the wedding metaphor used in such passages as John 3:29 and Revelation 19:7, joy is pictured as the ultimate expression of those who worship in the presence of God. Joy, abiding joy, comes as one realizes that one's sins have been forgiven and that life eternal is possible through Jesus Christ. If Christians do not live a joyful life, it is because they are not appropriating all the available riches of grace in Christ Jesus.

A. Joy and happiness.

Ask: What is the difference between joy and happiness? The bulk of Dr. Willimon's comments in "The Scripture and the Main Question" deal with this question. Discuss with the class his observation that happiness usually comes to us as a byproduct of something else.

B. Personal experiences.

Read through the rest of the passage (verses 5-19), referring to Dr. Decker's comments on each verse as you go along. Give special attention to those verses identified earlier as favorite quotable verses (7, 8, 11, 13, 19). Encourage your class members to tell what these verses mean to them, particularly if any have chosen them as life verses. This time of sharing may be of more value to the class than any impersonal exposition of Scripture texts.

C. Paul's concluding affirmation.

Verse 19 might be better understood and appreciated if seen in its historical context. In the preceding verse, Paul speaks of having received gifts sent to him by the Philippian Christians through Epaphroditus. A reading of Philippians 2:25-30 will reveal that when the Philippians had heard of Paul's imprisonment, they sent one of their number, Epaphroditus, to Rome with provisions to minister to Paul's needs. While Epaphroditus was there, he became seriously ill. When his friends in Philippi heard of it, they became quite concerned. Epaphroditus was distressed that he had caused them grief. But he recovered, and Paul sent him back to Philippi with this letter of thanks. Thus Paul could speak from experience that "God will supply every need of yours." It was true for him, for Epaphroditus, and for all who put their trust in Christ Jesus.

Helping Class Members Act

III. Summarize learnings about joy.

As we read this letter of thanksgiving and joy, it is hard to believe that its author was a prisoner, poor and lonely and facing possible death. If anyone should have been depressed and despairing, it was Paul. Yet he was upbeat, exultant, triumphant. Why?

Dr. Willimon suggests that joy comes from a task well done, a job well performed, a commitment which was kept. Paul expresses as much in his second letter to Timothy. Read II Timothy 4:2-6.

As a way of pulling together and affirming the learnings from this lesson, ask the class members to think about how they would complete this sentence: "Joy comes from . . ." Distribute sheets of colored construction paper and marking pens and suggest that each member write out a response to the statement.

As the members complete their sentences, they should tape them to the wall or chalkboard at the front of the room. Have a roll of masking tape handy for them to use.

When all the sheets are posted, have the members in spontaneous fashion read aloud their sentences. Make this a time of joyous affirmation and testimony.

Close by repeating Paul's benediction in Philippians 4:7.

Planning for Next Sunday

A new book and a new unit of study will be introduced next week. The book is the letter to the Ephesians, and the unit of study will deal with the Christian calling. Ask class members to read Ephesians 1:3-14 and to think about blessings that they have received from God in recent weeks.

UNIT IV: EPHESIANS—THE CHRISTIAN CALLING
Horace R. Weaver

FIVE LESSONS   **APRIL 30–MAY 28**

F. W. Beare, exegete for the letter to Ephesians in *The Interpreter's Bible*, writes:

> In effect the epistle offers a Christian gnosis of redemption—a revealed knowledge of the ultimate meaning of the universe and of human destiny, and of the significance of Christ and the church in relation to the sum of things. The primitive eschatology is wholly abandoned: the thought of an imminent catastrophic end of the age and of the appearance of Christ in glory to execute judgment and to establish the kingdom of God upon earth is not so much as mentioned, and would indeed be utterly foreign to the writer's central doctrine. Our Lord is caled "the Messiah," as the fulfillment of Israel's ancient hope (1:12; 2:12; etc.); but the office of messiahship is no longer conceived in terms of one who shall come in the clouds of heaven to judge and to rule as king. As Messiah, our Lord is the integrating power of the universe—the living center of all history and all nature, to which all things are even now being gathered into one in keeping with the divine purpose in creation . . . [this] epistle is the first manifesto of Christian imperialism, exhibiting the church as the spiritual empire which must

grow until it unites all mankind under the glorious sovereignty of Christ the Lord. (vol. 10, p. 607)

Unit IV, "Ephesians—The Christian Calling," is divided into five lessons. "The Blessings of Being a Christian," April 30, focuses on Christians' call to praise God's great eternal purpose through their way of life. "Peace with God and One Another," May 7, expounds on God's call in Christ to heal the broken relationships that divide us from God and one another. "Building Up the Body of Christ," May 14, emphasizes Christ's command that Christians use their varying gifts for building up the church, the body of Christ. "Called to New Life," May 21, discusses how Christians are to discard their old life-styles and "put on the new nature, created after the likeness of God." "Guidelines for Family Life," May 28, teaches that the new Christ-like life-style must pervade all life, including family life.

The Blessings of Being a Christian

Background Scripture: Ephesians 1:1-14

The Main Question—William H. Willimon

It was my friend Clayton's fifth birthday. When Clayton's mother asked him what sort of birthday party he would like to have, he said, "I want a party where everybody will be a king or a queen."

His mother asked him, "You mean that you would like to be a king?"

Clayton said, "No, I mean that I want everyone there to be a king or a queen."

So they set to work. They made a dozen crowns out of cardboard and covered them with aluminum foil. They then made a dozen royal scepters from coat hangers, cardboard, and aluminum foil. They fashioned a dozen royal purple robes from crepe paper. Everything was in readiness.

When the guests arrived, each was surprised to be given a crown, a scepter, and a robe. It was a most royal affair. A dozen kings and queens paraded up the street to the end of the block and then back again. Everyone feasted on cake and ice cream and had a regal good time.

That night, when Clayton's mother was tucking him into bed and they were talking about what a good time he had had at his birthday party, he said, "I wish everyone could be a king or a queen—not just on my birthday but *every day.*"

Well, Clayton, something very much like that happened to all of us on a day a long time ago, at a place called Calvary. We, who were nobodies, became somebodies. We, who were orphans, became royalty.

What is the calling and royal destiny of those who have accepted Jesus Christ?

Selected Scripture

King James Version	Revised Standard Version

Ephesians 1:3-14

3 Blessed *be* the God and Father of our Lord Jesus Christ, who hath blessed us with all spiritual blessings in heavenly *places* in Christ:

4 According as he hath chosen us in him before the foundation of the world, that we should be holy and without blame before him in love:

5 Having predestinated us unto the adoption of children by Jesus Christ to himself, according to the good pleasure of his will,

6 To the praise of the glory of his grace, wherein he hath made us accepted in the beloved.

7 In whom we have redemption through his blood, the forgiveness of sins, according to the riches of his grace;

8 Wherein he hath abounded toward us in all wisdom and prudence;

9 Having made known unto us the mystery of his will, according to his good pleasure which he hath purposed in himself:

10 That in the dispensation of the fulness of times he might gather together in one all things in Christ, both which are in heaven, and which are on earth; *even* in him:

11 In whom also we have obtained an inheritance, being predestinated according to the purpose of him who worketh all things after the counsel of his own will:

12 That we should be to the praise of his glory, who first trusted in Christ.

13 In whom ye also *trusted*, after that ye heard the word of truth, the gospel of your salvation: in whom also after that ye believed, ye were sealed with that holy Spirit of promise,

14 Which is the earnest of our inheritance until the redemption of

Ephesians 1:3-14

3 Blessed be the God and Father of our Lord Jesus Christ, who has blessed us in Christ with every spiritual blessing in the heavenly places, 4 even as he chose us in him before the foundation of the world, that we should be holy and blameless before him. 5 He destined us in love to be his sons through Jesus Christ, according to the purpose of his will, 6 to the praise of his glorious grace which he freely bestowed on us in the Beloved. 7 In him we have redemption through his blood, the forgiveness of our trespasses, according to the riches of his grace 8 which he lavished upon us. 9 For he has made known to us in all wisdom and insight the mystery of his will, according to his purpose which he set forth in Christ 10 as a plan for the fulness of time, to unite all things in him, things in heaven and things on earth.

11 In him, according to the purpose of him who accomplishes all things according to the counsel of his will, 12 we who first hoped in Christ have been destined and appointed to live for the praise of his glory. 13 In him you also, who have heard the word of truth, the gospel of your salvation, and have believed in him, were sealed with the promised Holy Spirit, 14 which is the guarantee of our inheritance until we acquire possession of it, to the praise of his glory.

the purchased possession, unto the
praise of his glory.

Key Verse: **That we should be to
the praise of his glory, who first
trusted in Christ. (Ephesians 1:12)**

Key Verse: **We who first hoped in
Christ have been destined and
appointed to live for the praise of
his glory. (Ephesians 1:12)**

As You Read the Scripture—Ralph Decker

The theme of Ephesians is church unity. It recognizes the world as a place
of constant strife—between good and evil (6:12), between God and
rebellious humans (2:2), within the church (4:14), within the home
(5:21–6:9), and within individuals (4:22-23). Against that background it
proclaims that God intends unity, that Christ is God's agent of
reconciliation, and that the church is Christ's instrument for accomplishing
his mission. It teaches that unity within the church is basic to all other
unities.

The letter also presents some problems. The three oldest manuscripts do
not contain the phrase "to the Ephesians" (1:2). Accordingly, the Revised
Standard Version omits it. Some scholars believe that Ephesians was a
general letter circulated among the early churches and that the phrase was
added later. This would account for the formal tone and lack of personal
greetings and reference to local problems in a letter supposedly addressed
to a congregation to which Paul had ministered for three years. Indeed, the
language and style are so different from Paul's other letters than some
doubt that he was the author. They think it may have been written after
Paul's death by a devoted disciple who was steeped in Paul's language and
thought and who wrote a summary of his teaching in letter form. The
traditional view is that it was written by the apostle Paul about A.D. 61 from
his prison in Rome (Acts 28:30) to the church at Ephesus in Asia Minor.

In any case, it is agreed that the letter is Pauline in content and presents
the three main ideas of Paul's gospel: (1) the grace of God as the only means
of human salvation; (2) the preeminence of Christ and the unity of all things
in him; (3) the church as the body of Christ and the instrument for carrying
on his ministry.

Ephesians 1:3-14. As is usual in Paul's letters, the address and salutation
(verses 1-2) are followed by a prayer of thanksgiving. The other letters
express thanks for the personal blessings and experiences of the writer or
the readers. This prayer is different. It deals with cosmic and eternal
matters: the heavenly places (verse 3), the foundation of the world (verse 4),
the fullness of time (verse 10), the union of heaven and earth (verse 10). It is
a hymn of praise that blesses God for his plan of salvation implemented in
Christ and assured by the Holy Spirit.

Verse 3. The phrase "in Christ" is the keynote of the entire letter. Along
with the equivalents "in him" and "in whom," it appears more than thirty
times, eight of them in this paragraph. The thanks here are for spiritual
blessings, such as grace, hope, and love, which enrich the inner life and
show the recipient what heaven is like.

Verse 4. God's purpose to raise up holy and blameless human beings has
existed from the beginning of creation.

Verse 5. Human experience is used to illustrate the experience of salvation. "Adoption" (King James Version) suggests that entering a right relationship with God is like an orphan finding a home and family.

Verse 6. Those who have experienced salvation will praise God's grace—the unmerited goodness that God freely bestows and that surpasses anything humans can achieve or deserve.

Verse 7. "Redemption" is another word used to illustrate the experience of salvation. It is like that of a captive being bought out of slavery.

Verse 8. The grace of God is limitless. He lavishes it, giving it abundantly.

Verse 9. God's purpose is no mystery; it has been revealed in Christ.

Verse 10. God's purpose is to unite all things in him and through him to each other.

Verse 13. Sealing (branding) is applying a mark of ownership, which involves care and protection.

Verse 14. The word translated "guarantee" really means "down payment" or "first installment," something that has taken place. In experiencing the Holy Spirit, believers have begun to inherit God's ancient promises.

The Scripture and the Main Question—William H. Willimon

Absence and Presence

There is a kind of alternating rhythm in worship and in life between recognition of God's absence and experience of God's presence. We may not like to admit to the absence of God, yet it is as real as God's presence. In even the most saintly life, there are always spaces, vacant places of the heart when God seems far away. "Truly thou art a God who hidest thyself," says Isaiah. Even one so close to God as Jesus could cry out from the cross, "My God, my God, why hast thou forsaken me?"

In our church, our deeds, and our lives, God is often absent. Partly, this is so because of who God is—bigger than our concepts, institutions, ideals, or righteousness.

At other times God is absent because there are places God can't go. God is where justice is done; yet we tolerate injustice. God, the Babe at Bethlehem reminds us, is with the poor and outcast; yet we take the side of the rich and powerful.

The Work of Praise

But now, as you sing, it is time to celebrate God's presence.

So much of our time in church is spent discussing words like "should," "ought," and "must." Sunday is the day to heap on the burden of greater responsibility to be borne the rest of the week, the day when the preacher tells you what you ought to do.

Praise soars above this prosaic obedience, command, and obligation. Praise is an expression of abundance rather than need, a time when we are able to say with the psalmist, "My cup runneth over." Praise arises like laughter, spontaneously welling up within us until we can no longer sit and be silent. Without denying the reality of God's absence in much of our life, we can admit to the reality of God's presence.

What you are doing now is best described in the words of the old Westminster catechism, when it asks, "What is the chief end of man?" The response: "To glorify God and to enjoy him forever."

In praise, we are fulfilling our chief purpose in life, the main reason why the Creator has placed us upon this planet—not to obey or even to serve but rather to enjoy! Remember that one of the chief charges against Jesus was "This man is a glutton and drunkard." His critics were shocked by Jesus' enjoyment of God and people.

Our praise, our joy, is joy in response to the presence. The Lord is here, among us. Joy is invariably reflexive, responsive. You can't decide to be joyful. Joy is not something we do. It is rather the fitting response to the action of someone else upon us. When we praise we join "all the company of heaven" in their song of unending praise. We experience our chief purpose in life—to enjoy God forever. As C. S. Lewis says, "Joy is the serious business of heaven." Here, on Sunday morning, for moments within this hour of worship, we are rehearsing the parts we shall play in heaven, glorifying and enjoying God forever. Doxology is the serious business of the church.

Praise is best done as a hymn, an anthem, poetry, or music. That's why so much of today's scripture from Ephesians is poetic in nature. It is as if the writer cannot talk about the glory of God in any other way except through a song. Prose is usually too confining for the joyful business we are about here. We are, in this moment, in the words of the old hymn, "lost in wonder, love and praise." You may have come here this morning wondering, What does God want me to do with my life? What ought I to do tomorrow morning? How do I look, here in church? Now, all that is quite beside the point. Our gaze has been wrenched away from ourselves—our problems, our thoughts of ought and should and must. By adoration, we have moved beyond mere thinking, planning, evaluating, or self-conscious posturing. There is a sense that here, in praise, worship is really worship.

The beginnings of praise are present in most lives, implicitly and incipiently: The "ah" that rises from our lips when a skyrocket bursts in a July evening sky; the hush that comes over us when we stand on the summit and look across a hazy blue mountain valley; the tear that comes to our eyes when we hold our children for the first time in our arms. Praise, as we said, is being who we really are, fulfilling our chief end, our main purpose in life. It is as natural as breathing for a child to jump and shout for joy when it hears that a circus is coming to town. It is as natural as falling in love, walking on the beach at sunset, and embracing someone who is dear to us. Praise moves beyond words, quickly becoming music or dance.

Praise is a means of loving, an expression of what we value most and whom we love the most. Praise is a means to loving, a way of deepening our relationship to the One "in whom we live, and move, and have our being." We kiss because we are in love. We kiss in order to be in love. The act of affection both expresses where we are and moves us to where we wish to be. Praise is like that.

Life as Praise

Of course, there is always a danger that, in worship, our praise might become an end in itself. This is the danger when worship becomes the exuberant "high," a mere trip into some fantasy world that has nothing whatsoever to do with the real world. There are some styles of worship that are frankly escapist, pure ecstasy and little else. People come in to worship, get all happy, excited, and emotional, then put their coats and hats back on and reenter the real world.

THIRD QUARTER

In my Wesleyan tradition, we tend to be preoccupied with busyness, intercession, self-improvement, self-conscious activism, and breathless activity. Church is where you come not to praise God, to glorify and enjoy God, but to get your list of assignments for next week: work on improving your marriage, try to be kind to your business partners, get your social attitudes cleaned up.

Here, in this act of praise, is the antidote to this rather (if I may use such a strong phrase) a-theistic conception of Sunday worship. Praise is response to the loving presence of God. Without that presence, we might as well turn the church into a self-improvement class, a lecture on ancient religion, or a pep-rally for our latest social justice cause. Alas, this is what church has too often become for many of our people.

Our purpose is praise. We are, in the words of Paul, to present our bodies, our whole lives, to God as our gift (Romans 12:1). A Christian, in a sense, doesn't recognize the difference between life in church and life on the outside. All life, our worship or our work, is our attempt to praise God. Our ethics are similar to our singing—offering ourselves and our gifts to God.

Helping Adults Become Involved—Ronald E. Schlosser

Preparing to Teach

Today's lesson is the first of five that focus on the letter to the Ephesians. The lessons comprise a unit that looks at the Christian calling to live as God's people in a divided and broken world. The themes of unity and peace underlie the message of Ephesians.

Dr. Decker provides a brief overview of the book and introduces some questions about its authorship and intended readers. You may wish to do some additional study on this in a Bible commentary.

Recall what the situation in Ephesus was like in Paul's day. Living in the city were a good number of Jews, many of whom were Roman citizens. They worshiped in the synagogue there, where Paul preached during his brief first visit (Acts 18:19-21). When Paul later returned for a longer stay, he found so much Jewish opposition to his teachings that he moved to the school of Tyrannus (Acts 19:9). Forced to leave the city following a riot instigated by its silversmiths, Paul left Timothy behind to help the new church resist the false doctrine that was having a corrupting influence (I Timothy 1:3-7).

Refer to a Bible dictionary for more information about Ephesus. Locate the city on a Bible map; it is on the west coast of Asia Minor, almost directly east of Athens across the Aegean Sea.

The learning goals for the session will be (1) to discern the meaning of praise and how one can best praise God, and (2) to identify some of life's blessings and to praise God for them.

Use the following lesson outline:

       I. Review background information.
      II. Examine key words.
    III. Experience a time of sharing.
         A. Hymns of praise.
         B. Testimonies of praise.

Read carefully "The Scripture and the Main Question" and "As You Read the Scripture." These form the heart of the lesson. The ideas, insights, and suggestions in these sections should be reflected continually in your lesson plan.

As you use the suggested outline, you may want to either quote or paraphrase ideas. You might like to jot in the margin of your outline the page number and paragraph being referred to. For example, you could write a reference to page 65, paragraph 3, as 65-3.

Have hymnbooks available for the session, particularly ones containing the gospel song "Count Your Blessings."

Introducing the Main Question

I. Review background information.

Begin by noting that this is the beginning of a five-lesson unit based on Paul's letter to Ephesus. Ask class members to share what they know about the city of Ephesus. Locate it on a Bible map. Note that it was situated at the junction of natural trade routes, north and south, east and west. It was on the main route from Rome to the East. Also mention its fame as the home of the temple of Artemis (Diana). Refer to the account in Acts 19 of Paul's trouble with the silversmiths.

If you feel it would be helpful, raise the question of authorship (see Dr. Decker's comments). Whether or not Paul or a close student of his wrote the epistle, it does reflect Paul's teachings. Its purpose was to remind the readers, both Jews and Gentiles, that they had been united in the body of Christ and that they should guard against slipping back into their former practices. For today's session, the main question is, What is the calling and royal destiny of those who have accepted Jesus Christ?

Developing the Lesson

II. Examine key words.

Ask the class members to read Ephesians 1:3-14 silently and to pick out a key word or phrase in each verse. They should underline it or jot it down on a piece of paper. Allow about five minutes for this individual study. Then have a time of sharing. What ideas do the key words convey?

More than likely your class members will select different key words (particularly if they use different versions and translations). You ought to do this exercise yourself and share your own selections. The following is one set of possibilities. As you discuss each verse, refer to Dr. Decker's comments when appropriate.

Verse 3: "blessed," "blessing." What are some of the spiritual blessings we have received in Christ?

Verse 4: "holy," "blameless." Is it possible for sinful creatures such as we to ever achieve this calling?

Verse 5: "destined," "purpose." Can there be any doubt what God's will is for us?

Verse 6: "grace." See Ephesians 2:8.

Verse 7: "redemption," "forgiveness." A missionary, translating the word "redemption" into the language of the Bambaras of West Africa, used the phrase, "having your neck taken out." The Bambaras remembered stories of the great slave raids, when their people were captured and driven to the coast with heavy iron collars around their necks, chained to the slave ahead and to the one behind. Their only hope of escape from the pain of the collar and the life of slavery ahead was to be bought from the slave dealer and freed. Redemption was "having your neck taken out."

Verse 8: "lavished." Can your class think of a more descriptive word for God's generosity?

Verse 9: "wisdom," "insight." God's purpose was clearly stated in verse 5.

Verse 10: "unite." Christian unity is a theme of the letter to the Ephesians. In Christ we are united with Christians who have gone before us (past); with those who are living now, whatever their background, race, or nationality (present); and with those who will follow after us (future).

Verse 11: "purpose," "will." See verses 5 and 9.

Verse 12: "praise of his glory." This phrase is also used in verse 14. This is our destiny—to praise God and enjoy him forever. What does it mean to praise God? Refer to Dr. Willimon's comments on this in the subsection headed "The Work of Praise."

Verse 13: "word of truth," "gospel of your salvation," "believed in him," "sealed with the promised Holy Spirit." This verse is rich in spiritual truth.

Verse 14: "guarantee." The word refers to being "sealed" in the preceding verse. See II Corinthians 1:22. It is similar in concept to taking random samplings of grain being sold for market. The quality of the sample is a "guarantee" that the whole shipment is like that. Life in the Spirit now is a sample or guarantee of the fuller life to come.

Helping Class Members Act

III. *Experience a time of sharing.*
  A. *Hymns of praise.*
    In his comments on the nature of praise, Dr. Willimon states that "praise is best done as a hymn, an anthem, poetry, or music." Distribute hymnbooks to the class and ask the members to look for hymns that are good examples of "praise" hymns. Have them read aloud lines or verses from these hymns that are particularly expressive.
  B. *Testimonies of praise.*
    Although more accurately categorized as a gospel song than a hymn, "Count Your Blessings" is indirectly a call to praise God. (Read Ezekiel 34:25-26.) Suggest that your class members do just what the song calls for. Have them think of blessings they have received from God. These should be as specific as possible. You might start off by sharing aloud a blessing in your own life. After each person shares a blessing, the class might respond, "Praise the Lord!" or "May Jesus Christ be praised!" Make this a time of testimony and praise.
    Close with singing a hymn of praise, perhaps one of the hymns suggested earlier. "Joyful, Joyful, We Adore Thee" would be a good selection.

Planning for Next Sunday

The scripture for next week's lesson is Ephesians 2:8-22. Encourage your class to read the entire second chapter of Ephesians to see these verses in context. Also ask the members to think about some of the walls that separate people in our day.

Peace with God and One Another

Background Scripture: Ephesians 2

The Main Question—William H. Willimon

One of the major causes of war and international unrest is the separation of the various nations by boundaries. National boundaries may have been drawn up with little rationale behind them. But once they are fixed in place, each nation zealously guards its own territorial limits. Even as I write this lesson, there has been a violent confrontation between American and Libyan forces. The Libyans claim that their national boundaries were violated by American warships. The Americans claim that they were patrolling open seas. A few years ago, we had a memorial service here on campus for a Duke University student who was killed when the Soviets shot down a Korean passenger jet that had strayed into their territorial boundaries.

What is true of nations is also true of individuals. We draw boundaries around ourselves and dare anyone to cross them. Human beings are separated by racial, ethnic, and sexual lines. There are invisible walls between us—invisible but powerful walls.

"Good fences make good neighbors," is how the old adage goes. In our personal lives, we seem to believe this. Unfortunately, the old saying is not true. Big fences lead to big misunderstandings and enmity between people.

In writing to the Ephesians, Paul confronts a divided church. He says to them that Christ has broken down the walls we erect between one another. What are some of the walls that separate you from other people, and how has Christ enabled you to break them down and reach out to others?

Selected Scripture

King James Version	Revised Standard Version
Ephesians 2:8-22	*Ephesians 2:8-22*
8 For by grace are ye saved through faith; and that not of yourselves: *it is* the gift of God:	8 For by grace you have been saved through faith; and this is not your own doing, it is the gift of God—9 not because of works, lest any man should boast. 10 For we are
9 Not of works, lest any man should boast.	
10 For we are his workmanship, created in Christ Jesus unto good works, which God hath before ordained that we should walk in them.	his workmanship, created in Christ Jesus for good works, which God prepared beforehand, that we should walk in them.
11 Wherefore remember, that ye *being* in time past Gentiles in the flesh, who are called Uncircumcision by that which is called the Circumcision in the flesh made by hands;	11 Therefore remember that at one time you Gentiles in the flesh, called the uncircumcision by what is called the circumcision, which is made in the flesh by hands—12
12 That at that time ye were	remember that you were at that time separated from Christ, alienated

without Christ, being aliens from the commonwealth of Israel, and strangers from the covenants of promise, having no hope, and without God in the world:

13 But now in Christ Jesus ye who sometimes were far off are made nigh by the blood of Christ.

14 For he is our peace, who hath made both one, and hath broken down the middle wall of partition *between us*;

15 Having abolished in his flesh the enmity, *even* the law of commandments *contained* in ordinances; for to make in himself of twain one new man, *so* making peace;

16 And that he might reconcile both unto God in one body by the cross, having slain the enmity thereby:

17 And came and preached peace to you which were afar off, and to them that were nigh.

18 For through him we both have access by one Spirit unto the Father.

19 Now therefore ye are no more strangers and foreigners, but fellow-citizens with the saints, and of the household of God;

20 And are built upon the foundaton of the apostles and prophets, Jesus Christ himself being the chief corner *stone*;

21 In whom all the building fitly framed together groweth unto an holy temple in the Lord:

22 In whom ye also are builded together for an habitation of God through the Spirit.

from the commonwealth of Israel, and strangers to the covenants of promise, having no hope and without God in the world. 13 But now in Christ Jesus you who once were far off have been brought near in the blood of Christ. 14 For he is our peace, who has made us both one, and has broken down the dividing wall of hostility, 15 by abolishing in his flesh the law of commandments and ordinances, that he might create in himself one new man in place of the two, so making peace. 16 and might reconcile us both to God in one body through the cross, thereby bringing the hostility to an end. 17 And he came and preached peace to you who were far off and peace to those who were near; 18 for through him we both have access in one Spirit to the Father. 19 So then you are no longer strangers and sojourners, but you are fellow citizens with the saints and members of the household of God, 20 built upon the foundation of the apostles and prophets, Christ Jesus himself being the cornerstone, 21 in whom the whole structure is joined together and grows into a holy temple in the Lord; 22 in whom you also are built into it for a dwelling place of God in the Spirit.

Key Verse: **Now therefore ye are no more strangers and foreigners, but fellow citizens with the saints and of the household of God. (Ephesians 2:19)**

Key Verse: **So then you are no longer strangers and sojourners, but you are fellow citizens with the saints and members of the household of God. (Ephesians 2:19)**

As You Read the Scripture—Ralph Decker

Ephesians 2 teaches that the church is the unifying force that will bring humankind and eventually the entire universe into harmony. For Paul, separation from God could be described only as "death." So, a proper relationship with God is "life." The chapter opens with the statement that all persons—both Gentiles (the "you" in verse 1) and Jews (the "we" in verse 3)—were children of death before God provided life through Christ. The second paragraph deals with the uniting of Gentiles and Jews taking place within the church.

Ephesians 2:8. Salvation is a gift from God. It cannot be earned, even by faith. Faith is that through which one accepts what is freely given. Indeed, faith itself is a gift from God. It is not a good work, the result of decision and effort. God takes the initiative in generating faith.

Verse 9. If humans could earn salvation through good works, they would be sure to boast of that achievement, as they do of others. Paul knew that humans have no cause to boast (Romans 3:27–4:3).

Verse 10. Critics have sometimes said that Paul had no place for good works. This verse should correct that idea. It puts works in their proper place—the result of salvation, not its cause. Doing good works is a way of life for those who have been saved.

Verse 11. This and the following verse show that the letter was originally addressed to Christians who were mostly from Gentile backgrounds. Their separation from God's chosen people was clear. They lacked circumcision, the mark of membership in the covenant community.

Verse 12. Since both covenant and Christ came first to the Jews, the Gentiles were strangers to the promises of God. Paul saw them as without hope of resurrection and eternal life. The same sentiment appears in I Thessalonians 4:13.

Verse 13. Where non-Jews had formerly been regarded as separated from God by failure to observe the rules and rituals of Judaism, the way to nearness to God had been opened by the sacrificial death of Jesus on the cross. Now, God could be approached directly through faith in Christ.

Verse 14. Jews and Gentiles are reconciled to each other through Christ. Since both find peace in him they find peace with each other. The metaphor of the dividing wall was based on a barrier which actually existed in the temple at Jerusalem. Non-Jews were forbidden under penalty of death to pass a wall dividing the outer Court of the Gentiles from the inner courts of the Jews. This kept Gentiles (like Luke) from approaching the altar and the Holy of Holies, where persons came closest to God. There were no such barriers in the fellowship of Christ and his followers. All distinctions were erased. "There is neither Jew nor Greek . . . slave nor free . . . male nor female . . . all are one in Christ" (Galatians 3:28; compare Colossians 3:11).

Verses 15-16. Christ has abolished the Jewish law, with the rules and requirements that caused dissension between Jew and non-Jew. All through his ministry, Paul had to contend with those who claimed that Gentiles could become Christians only by becoming Jews first. This verse makes his position clear. No such step is necessary, since the world is no longer divided into Jews and Gentiles.

Verses 17-18. In Christ, the union of those who were near (the Jews) and those were far off (Gentiles) was complete.

Verse 19. The Gentiles were no longer strangers (visiting aliens with no rights in the community of faith) or sojourners (resident aliens with limited rights). They were full citizens of the kingdom.

Verse 20. In a metaphor drawn from architecture, the church is the dwelling of God, its foundations are the prophets and apostles, the chief cornerstone upon which all other building material must be aligned is Christ, and Christian believers are the material of which the church is built.

THIRD QUARTER

The Scripture and the Main Question—William H. Willimon

Separated from Christ

In writing to the church at Ephesus, Paul reminds them that they were once considered outside the realm of salvation. Because most of them were Gentiles, they had no claim whatsoever upon the sacred promises of Israel: "Remember that at one time you Gentiles in the flesh . . . were . . . separated from Christ, alienated from the commonwealth of Israel, and strangers to the covenants of promise, having no hope and without God in the world" (2:11-12).

Evidently, the church at Ephesus is having problems with divisions. Their members have come from various backgrounds and nationalities, but now they are to be one. Lest any of these new Christians should boast, Paul reminds them that if it were not for the generous, inclusive love of Christ, they wouldn't be here in the first place! "For he is our peace, who has made us both one, and has broken down the dividing wall of hostility" (2:14).

It is sad to note that even with these early Christians, even among those who only recently had been brought into the faith, there was factionalism and party strife. The same divisiveness continues in the church today. So many of our congregations are known more for their intrachurch squabbles than for their unity and community.

"You Methodists really have some fights, don't you?" commented a man to me after our last General Conference. This man is not a church member, and I shudder when I think of the sort of witness our church presented to him. There is little likelihood that he will be attracted to my church, after watching us fight it out with one another.

Ephesians makes the point that Christ is the great unifier, rather than the great divider. Christ is the one who in his words and work "has broken down the dividing wall of hostility" that divides us from one another. Perhaps you can recall numerous events in Scripture where Jesus is depicted as the one who brings people near to God and near to one another.

I am thinking of the episode of the Samaritan woman at the well, where a woman is surprised to find that Jesus dares to speak to her in spite of her race, her religion, and her sex. Jesus reached out to her, an action surely regarded as scandalous by many people in his day. He reached out to the despised little man in the sycamore tree. He told the story of the waiting father who embraced rather than chastised his returning prodigal son. Jesus was forever bringing people together, breaking down the walls we erect between ages, nations, races, sexes.

This is a thought found throughout the Bible. "God is not partial. He will not take a bribe," says Deuteronomy 10:17. In Galatians 2:6, when Paul is questioned about problems between slaves and masters in the church, Paul says, "God shows no partiality." God makes no distinction between slave or free, male or female, Jew or Greek. Or as Jesus said, "He makes his sun to rise on the good and the bad; his rain to fall upon the just and the unjust."

When Peter returned from his missionary journey, the elders at First Church Jerusalem were angry because it had been reported to them that Peter not only had been seen eating with Cornelius, a *Roman*, a Roman *Gentile*, a Roman Gentile *soldier*, but that Peter had dared to baptize Cornelius. Peter defends himself by saying, "Truly I perceive that God shows no partiality, but in every nation any one who fears him and does what is right is acceptable to him" (Acts 10:34).

I know of no sadder sights around the university where I live than those of the professor who plays favorites, the student who makes distinctions between his or her fellows of different colors, and the administrator who enforces the rules for some but not for all.

The Dividing Wall of Hostility

"Something there is that doesn't love a wall," writes Robert Frost. But life tells us that we ought to learn. So much of our life is spent living behind some sort of wall. Life is "intramural." There is a wall between East and West Berlin and between the Arabs and the Israelis. The way to live with the Soviets? Keep a good, high wall. Keep stacking up the bombs and missiles; match every bomb they put up with one of our own. "National defense" is a fancy way of saying, "Good fences make good neighbors."

Partition, partiality, apartheid—I'm sure that they all have the same linguistic derivation. In our distant past, somebody looked across the field at his neighbor. Their eyes met. And then he searched for a stone, and then another stone, inventing the wall even before the wheel. And we can paint it, fresco it, or graffiti it, but it is still a wall, a partition, a boundary. Walls do a good job of keeping our neighbor out but an even better job of keeping us in. For the thing about walls is, it's hard to know who is locked in and who is locked out. Once the thing is built, everybody is a prisoner.

"Well, you know her," he said of his fellow church member. "She's in the country club-sports car-fancy-clothes set." Case closed. We have that wall all in place. Everything is tied down and closed. We don't have to worry about getting to know a real, interesting, unique human being anymore, because there is now this wall between us.

According to Ephesians 2, Christ has kicked down all of our dividing walls and boundaries—the walls between God and us, the walls between ourselves and other people.

Perhaps we cannot take down the walls between us and other people until the wall between us and God is first dismantled. When we are unsure of our relationship to God, we see our brother or sister as a threat. We must convince ourselves that we are as good as they are, or better, that God loves us just a little more than God loves them. We must therefore label them as evil, unfaithful, ignorant, or demonic. We do this, like a jealous, insecure child, because we are threatened by the notion that God could love anyone else but us.

But once the wall between us and God is taken down—the wall of our guilt, our sin, our rebellion; the wall that Christ confronted at his death on the cross—then we are able to reach out to our neighbor. We come to see our neighbors not as competitors in the competition to be God's only begotten children but as brother and sisters who all stand under the grace and forgiveness of God (2:15-18).

"And he came and preached peace to you who were far off and peace to those who were near; for through him we both have access in one Spirit to the Father" (2:17).

I wonder: Perhaps we would have more unity in the church if we continually focused our thoughts upon the miracle that we, who were once so far off, have been brought close to God by the amazing grace of Christ. If I could better remember my own need for someone to reach out to me in love, then I might be better able to reach out in love to someone else.

THIRD QUARTER

Helping Adults Become Involved—Ronald E. Schlosser

Preparing to Teach

In his discussion of "The Main Question," Dr. Willimon refers to the adage "good fences make good neighbors." This saying is taken from Robert Frost's oft-quoted poem "Mending Wall." In the poem Frost observes, "Something there is that doesn't love a wall." There seems to be a natural tendency in people to want it down. A wall not only keeps intruders out but also keeps others in. The Berlin Wall is a stark example of this.

Yet Frost seems to think that at times walls have their place and their benefits. To know where boundaries are and to observe those boundaries may be good for individuals and society. Certainly we all benefit from the secure walls of our homes. And in localities where backyards become playgrounds for children and shortcuts for pets and stray animals, walls and fences sometimes can prevent strained neighborly relations.

In any case, in today's lesson your class will be discussing walls that are harmful. The learning goals are (1) to consider what are the walls that separate persons from one another and from God, and (2) to recognize how Christ breaks down the walls that separate people from each other and from God.

Use the following lesson outline:

> I. Explore dividing walls.
>   A. Experiences of separation.
>   B. Walls that separate.
> II. Consider the work of Christ.
> III. Resolve to heal divisions.

Read carefully "The Scripture and the Main Question" and "As You Read the Scripture." These form the heart of the lesson. The ideas, insights, and suggestions in these sections should be reflected continually in your lesson plan.

As you use the suggested outline, you may want to either quote or paraphrase ideas. You might like to jot in the margin of your outline the page number and paragraph being referred to. For example, you could write a reference to page 65, paragraph 3, as 65-3.

In addition to the background scripture (Ephesians 2), read the story of Jesus' encounter with the woman at the well in John 4 and with Zacchaeus in Luke 19. Consider what walls were broken down in each of these encounters.

Have pencils and paper on hand for use during the session.

Introducing the Main Question

I. Explore dividing walls.
  A. Experiences of separation.

Begin by asking the question, Have you ever felt left out, excluded, discriminated against? How did you feel? Some members may wish to share experiences aloud.

During the confirmation hearings for Chief Justic Rehnquist a few years back, the issue of "restrictive covenants" in property deeds came to light.

These exclusionary clauses, a common practice of a day long gone, prohibited certain minority groups from buying property in areas owners wished to keep exclusively for their "own kind." Now illegal, such covenants often go unnoticed when old deeds are transferred, and they prove an embarrassment when brought to light. Have any members of your class ever felt they were not wanted, either by neighbors where they lived or by groups they wished to join?

B. Walls that separate.

Refer to Robert Frost's poem "Mending Wall," from which the words "Good fences make good neighbors" are taken. Does the class agree or disagree with the statement? Share Dr. Willimon's coments on the subject and then ask: What are the walls that separate people from one another? Consider some of these:

1. Walls between nations. The Berlin Wall is a physical barrier that symbolizes a deeper philosophical division between East and West.

2. Social walls. Races, ethnic groups, and social and economic classes often are kept apart by walls of prejudice and discrimination.

3. Religious walls. Christians, Jews, and Muslims have long been involved in conflicts that shamefully sully the high ideals that would otherwise characterize their beliefs. There are doctrinal walls that separate those who identify themselves as liberal, conservative, or fundamentalist.

Note what Dr. Willimon says about such walls in his comments under the subheading, "The Dividing Wall of Hostility."

Developing the Lesson

II. Consider the work of Christ.

Move now to a study of Ephesians 2:8-22. Have the members pair up for this activity. On a piece of paper they should make two columns, one headed "What Jesus Did for Us" and the other, "What We Have Become Because of It" or "What We Are in Christ." After a time of two-by-two study, have the members share their findings. Jot them down on the chalkboard or newsprint. The list might include the following:

What Jesus Did

—Shed his blood on the cross
—Made us one with God
—Broke down the dividing wall of hostility
—Reconciled us to God in one body
—Preached peace to those far off and near
—Provided access to the Father
—Became the cornerstone of God's holy temple

What We Are in Christ

—Saved by grace through Christ
—God's workmanship
—Created for good works
—Brought near to God
—One people (believers of different backgrounds) in union
—Fellow citizens and members of God's household
—A dwelling place of God

As you discuss the items on the two lists, refer when appropriate to the comments by Dr. Decker. Also note Dr. Willimon's references to the woman at the well and to Zacchaeus, in his discussion of the dividing wall of hostility. What were the barriers that Jesus broke down in his encounter with each of these people? Use the story of Peter's meeting with and acceptance of Cornelius (Acts 10) to illustrate how the Christian gospel is for everyone and that God shows no partiality.

Helping Class Members Act

III. Resolve to heal divisions.

Review the kinds of walls people erect between people. Discuss ways that Christians can work to break down these walls. See if the members can find similar walls in the New Testament that were broken down by Christ, Paul, or the early Christians.

Focus on walls that might be erected in churches. What causes divisions within congregations? Recall some of the divisiveness that the apostle Paul faced in the churches he visited, most notably the church at Corinth. (See I Corinthians 3:3-4; 6:1-6; 8:7-9; 14:26-28.) How did he handle it and what can we learn from him? (See, as an example, his words to the Philippians concerning the disagreement between Euodia and Syntyche in chapter 4, verses 2-3. He felt it was the responsibility of the whole church to work together to restore harmony within the fellowship.)

Close the session with prayer, asking your members to pray for the Spirit of Christ to help them open themselves to God and to one another, that their fellowship might be "joined together" to grow "into a holy temple in the Lord."

Planning for Next Sunday

Ask for volunteers who would be willing to debate or discuss this statement, which Dr. Willimon makes in the next lesson: "A test for a true church is its ability to integrate a large variety of people into its life together." Look ahead to the resources for next week's lesson for background material to give to each side of the debate. The rest of the class should read Ephesians 4:1-16.

LESSON 11   MAY 14

Building Up the Body of Christ

Background Scripture: Ephesians 4:1-16

The Main Question—William H. Willimon

One of the best things about being in the Christian church is the opportunity to discover many gifts and talents of people within the church.

As far as I am concerned, a test for a true church is its ability to integrate a large variety of people into its life together.

So many times in life, when people are nonproductive because they are too ill, too young, or too old, they are cast aside by society. They feel useless and unwanted, because society has decided that they can make no positive contribution to the world. In the church, it ought to be different.

I had a woman in my church who had suffered a terrible illness that left her nearly totally paralyzed. But she was always wanting to do something for the church, even in her paralyzed condition. One day I asked her to do some telephoning for me, and because she enjoyed it so much, I regularly asked her to call members of various church committees and remind them about upcoming meetings. She did with joy and enthusiasm.

A funny thing happened. Attendance at all of our church meetings jumped to an all-time high. Why? Because this dear person was giving of her special ability to help others.

As one man said, "When you get home late in the afternoon and dread the thought of going to a church meeting, to receive a call from a paralyzed woman reminding you about the meeting is a powerful incentive!"

The body of Christ has some amazing members. We need all of them to make the church all that it can be. In today's lesson, we shall explore some of the ways in which the body of Christ integrates the many gifts and talents of the people whom Jesus has called to serve him.

Selected Scripture

King James Version

Ephesians 4:1-16

1 I therefore, the prisoner of the Lord, beseech you that ye walk worthy of the vocation wherewith ye are called,

2 With all lowliness and meekness, with longsuffering, forbearing one another in love;

3 Endeavouring to keep the unity of the Spirit in the bond of peace.

4 *There* is one body, and one Spirit, even as ye are called in one hope of your calling;

5 One Lord, one faith, one baptism,

6 One God and Father of all, who *is* above all, and through all, and in you all.

7 But unto every one of us is given grace according to the measure of the gift of Christ.

8 Wherefore he saith, When he ascended up on high, he led captivity captive, and gave gifts unto men.

9 (Now that he ascended, what is it

Revised Standard Version

Ephesians 4:1-16

1 I therefore, a prisoner for the Lord, beg you to lead a life worthy of the calling to which you have been called, 2 with all lowliness and meekness, with patience, forbearing one another in love, 3 eager to maintain the unity of the Spirit in the bond of peace. 4 There is one body and one Spirit, just as you were called to the one hope that belongs to your call, 5 one Lord, one faith, one baptism, 6 one God and Father of us all, who is above all and through all and in all. 7 But grace was given to each of us according to the measure of Christ's gift. 8 Therefore it is said,

"When he ascended on high he
led a host of captives,
and he gave gifts to men."

9 (In saying, "He ascended," what does it mean but that he had also descended into the lower parts of the earth? 10 He who descended is

but that he also descended first into the lower parts of the earth?

10 He that descended is the same also that ascended up far above all heavens, that he might fill all things.)

11 And he gave some, apostles; and some, prophets; and some, evangelists; and some, pastors and teachers;

12 For the perfecting of the saints, for the work of the ministry, for the edifying of the body of Christ:

13 Till we all come in the unity of the faith, and of the knowledge of the Son of God, unto a perfect man, unto the measure of the stature of the fulness of Christ:

14 That we *henceforth* be no more children, tossed to and fro, and carried about with every wind of doctrine, by the sleight of men, *and* cunning craftiness whereby they lie in wait to deceive;

15 But speaking the truth in love, may grow up into him in all things, which is the head, *even* Christ:

16 From whom the whole body fitly joined together and compacted by that which every joint supplieth, according to the effectual working in the measure of every part, maketh increase of the body unto the edifying of itself in love.

he who also ascended far above all the heavens, that he might fill all things.) 11 And his gifts were that some should be apostles, some prophets, some evangelists, some pastors and teachers, 12 for the equipment of the saints, for the work of ministry, for building up the body of Christ, 13 until we all attain to the unity of the faith and of the knowledge of the Son of God, to mature manhood, to the measure of the stature of the fulness of Christ; 14 so that we may no longer be children, tossed to and fro and carried about with every wind of doctrine, by the cunning of men, by their craftiness in deceitful wiles. 15 Rather, speaking the truth in love, we are to grow up in every way into him who is the head, into Christ, 16 from whom the whole body, joined and knit together by every joint with which is supplied, when each part is working properly, makes bodily growth and upbuilds itself in love.

Key Verse: **He gave some, apostles; and some, prophets; and some, evangelists; and some, pastors and teachers; For the perfecting of the saints, for the work of the ministry, for the edifying of the body of Christ. (Ephesians 4:11-12)**

Key Verse: **His gifts were that some should be apostles, some prophets, some evangelists, some pastors and teachers, to equip the saints for the work of ministry, for building up the body of Christ. (Ephesians 4:11-12)**

As You Read the Scripture—Ralph Decker

This chapter of Ephesians opens a section dealing with the impact upon daily life of the doctrine of Christian unity set forth in earlier chapters. This paragraph is a challenge to readers to demonstrate that unity by living in accord with God's purposes.

Verse 1. This verse, along with 3:1, forms the basis for counting Ephesians among the letters written by Paul while in prison (Philemon,

Colossians, Philippians, Ephesians). The phrase translated "of the Lord" in the King James Version and "for the Lord" in the Revised Standard Version should really read "in the Lord." Paul frequently spoke of his union with the Lord as being "in Christ." Here he is saying that the union has not been broken by imprisonment. The church and its members have been called to be the unifying force in the world. They must, therefore, cultivate qualities of peace and harmony.

Verse 2. Those qualities are listed. "Lowliness" may be understood as "humility" (Goodspeed) or "modesty" (Moffatt), "meekness" as "gentleness" (Confraternity Version). Love determines how the other qualities are to be practiced.

Verse 3. Christians are not to be passively peaceful, but to be eager and active in promoting unity and peace.

Ephesians 4:4-6. The church should be a place of unity. Despite its racial, national, and social diversity, its members agree on the fundamentals: body . . . Spirit . . . hope . . . Lord . . . faith . . . baptism . . . God.

It has been suggested that these verses may have been a creed used by the early church. The word "one," emphasizing unity, appears seven times in the three verses.

Verse 4. The church has already been called the body of Christ (1:23; 2:16).

Verse 5. The phrase "one baptism" refers to the meaning, not the method, of baptizing.

Verse 6. The God who is close enough to be called Father is also in control of the universe and everything in it.

Verse 7. Unity does not mean uniformity. Church members have various gifts. The limited talents of each are joined with those of all others in God's work.

Verse 8. The quotation is a free rendering of Psalm 68:18. The rabbis had applied it to Moses' ascent of Mount Sinai. Here, it is applied to Christ's ascent to the right hand of God. The "captives" were the evil forces from which Christ had freed humankind.

Verses 9-10. The discussion of gifts is interrupted by a discussion of Christ's incarnation, ascension, and exaltation. The mention of "lower parts of the earth" seems to be the earliest mention in Christian literature of the belief that Christ descended into hell. A later author said that he went to preach the gospel to the dead (I Peter 3:19; 4:6).

Verse 11. The matter of gifts is resumed with a listing of various kinds of ministry. A similar list is given in I Corinthians 12:28. Apostles were those sent out by Christ as his special representatives. Prophets were those who received and proclaimed revealed truths. Evangelists were missionaries who preached the good news to the unconverted. Pastors were those who provided spiritual care for the believers. Teachers were probably those who instructed new converts in Christian doctrine.

Verse 12. These various ministries are to serve one purpose: the strengthening of the church, the body of Christ.

Verse 13. That unity for which the letter has been appealing is to be found in a mature church, which resembles Christ in his fullness. This is the goal toward which the church must strive.

Verse 14. Even in its earliest days, the church was plagued by differences of opinion and disagreements on matters of faith and doctrine.

Verse 15. These differences can be resolved as the church grows more like Christ, its members speaking and acting from love, each contributing his or her gifts for the good of all.

The Scripture and the Main Question—William H. Willimon

These Were His Gifts

Those who study the dynamics of church growth agree: It is much easier to attract new members to congregations than to integrate them into the ongoing life of the congregation. As one church growth expert has put it, "We spend too much time worrying about how to get people in the front door, without taking notice of those who go out the back door."

As a parish pastor, I made evangelism and church growth a priority in my work. But I soon discovered that it was not enough simply to attract new people. We had to find places for them. If we didn't find them something to do within the congregation, some way to contribute and to feel responsible, we eventually lost them. People would look around six months after they joined and say, "Whatever happened to the Jones family?" The Joneses had left, because we had failed to integrate them.

Some church growth experts believe that a growing congregation should form at least one new small group every month in order to stay alive. People do not relate well to large groups of people. Therefore, small groups—Sunday school classes, a task force on some issue, a prayer and Bible study group—are important ways for people to achieve a face-to-face relationship with others in the church.

A congregation is a system in which interlocking parts work together. When one part is weak, the whole system suffers. This is the image of the church put forth in Ephesians 4. The writer to the Ephesians said that the church is like a body. All the members of the body must be healthy if the body as a whole is to be healthy. One of the tough parts about being a pastor is that you have to pay attention to all of the parts at once. And all of the parts are important.

But the writer says, "His gifts were that some should be apostles, some prophet, some evangelists, some pastors and teachers, to equip the saints for the work of ministry, for the building of the body of Christ" (Ephesians 4:11-12).

The church needs leaders and, according to the writer of Ephesians, God gives us leaders. From the beginning there were those who were needed to coordinate the work of the various parts of the body and to ensure that everyone had a place within the body. The work of the church requires a variety of gifts, and according to Ephesians, God gives us these gifts to do God's work.

Bible commentators have long discussed the proper place of the comma within Ephesians 4:11. In the original Greek, there are no commas. Does the passage read, "His gifts were that some should be . . . teachers to equip the saints . . . "? Or is it supposed to read, "His gifts were that some should be . . . teachers, to equip the saints . . . "? In other words, is equipping the saints for ministry the job of one special group of leaders—the clergy—or is it the responsibility of all leaders in the church? I prefer the latter interpretation. The job of the clergy is not to do all the work of the church. Rather, the job of the clergy is to "equip the saints for the work of ministry." All of us, by virtue of our baptism, share in Christ's call to Christian ministry. The unique vocation of the pastor is to be the one who equips the saints for the work of their ministry.

The pastor is the one who is to preach, teach, and counsel in such a way that the "saints" get the equipment through God's ministry within the world. In what ways does your pastor "equip the saints"? Do you see any tendencies within your own congregation to give over the work of ministry to the clergy and to rob the laity of their God-given responsibility?

To Equip the Saints for the Work of Ministry

Presumably, one of the reasons people have come to your church school class today is that they are seeking to be equipped for the work of ministry. As we go about our lives, Monday through Saturday, we are faced with many challenges. One reason we come to church on Sunday is to gain the skills, knowledge, and insights we need to be better witnesses for Christ within the world. Sometimes people use the analogy of a "filling station," in speaking about the church. They say that the church is where they come on Sunday morning to get "fueled up" for the responsibilities of the rest of the week. However, according to Ephesians 4, the better image of the church might be a garage! We come here and get the equipment we need in order to function well during the next week.

In my last church I discussed with our Pastoral Relations Committee the problems that arose because I was frequently out of town, due to my speaking and teaching responsibilities. I discussed with the committee whether or not the church ought to consider hiring an associate minister to assist me in my work and to make sure that the ministerial needs of the church were covered.

"I don't think that we ought to consider hiring another pastor here," said one man, "until we exhaust the ministerial possibilities within our own membership." The committee thought he was exactly right. There were many people within the congregation who were perfectly capable of visiting, teaching, and overseeing the various administrative responsibilities in the church. We therefore set about to identify these persons and to give them the equipment they needed to do this work. Through their efforts, whenever anyone in our congregation was in the hospital, that person was visited every day by someone in the congregation—not necessarily the pastor, but some skilled Christian who came to the hospital with words of compassion and concern.

As a pastor I wish I had more skills in equipping the saints for the work of ministry, rather than doing the work of ministry myself. Frankly, it sometimes takes a great deal more skill to enable someone else to minister than to do it yourself. But when we do it all ourselves, we rob the laity of wonderful opportunities to experience themselves as true ministers in Christ's name.

Take a moment and ask your class to reflect upon ways that your church could better "equip the saints."

Helping Adults Become Involved—Ronald E. Schlosser

Preparing to Teach

The term "church growth" was coined by Donald McGavran, a former Disciples of Christ missionary to India. He took two common words—

313

"church" and "growth"—and put them together in such a way as to bring into being a new concept and a new movement. The concept embraces both evangelism and discipleship. It involves not only bringing persons who do not have a personal relationship to Jesus Christ into fellowship with him, but also helping them become responsible church members.

The most controversial concept in the "church growth movement" is the one described as the principle of the homogeneous unit, or the "our kind of people" concept. This viewpoint states that people like to belong to a church of the same racial, linguistic, and class make-up. They like to feel comfortable together. They feel at home with others who share the same culture and life-style.

What do you think of this point of view? What do you suppose your class will think? Plan to begin the session with a debate or a discussion about this issue. Dr. Willimon makes the statement in "The Main Question" that "a test for a true church is its ability to integrate a large variety of people into its life together." Prior to the session, ask for at least two volunteers to defend this position and two to defend the "homogeneous unit" principle. If possible, provide this latter group with reference material found in such books as *Your Church Can Grow* by C. Peter Wagner (Ventura, Cal.: Regal Books, 1976) and *Understanding Church Growth* by Donald McGavran (Grand Rapids, Mich.: Eerdmans, 1970).

The learning goals for the session are threefold: (1) to sense the need and responsibility to grow as the Body of Christ; (2) to discern the variety of spiritual gifts and their purposes; (3) to consider what gifts God has given each of us.

Use the following lesson outline:

    I.   Consider signs of a vital church.
         A. The question of homogeneity.
         B. What people look for.
    II. Examine the nature of spiritual gifts.
         A. The Christian calling.
         B. The variety of gifts.
    III. Explore areas of ministry.
         A. Discovering one's gifts.
         B. The challenge of lay minstry.

Read carefully "The Scripture and the Main Question" and "As You Read the Scripture." These form the heart of the lesson. The ideas, insights, and suggestions in these sections should be reflected continually in your lesson plan.

As you use the suggested outline, you may want to either quote or paraphrase ideas. You might like to jot in the margin of your outline the page number and paragraph being referred to. For example, you could write a reference to page 65, paragraph 3, as 65-3.

Introducing the Main Question

I. Consider signs of a vital church.
  A. The question of homogeneity.
As suggested above, begin the session with a debate or discussion among several members regarding the test for a true church. Dr. Willimon states

that a variety of people need to be integrated into its life. Some leaders in the church growth movement believe that churches, to be effective and successful, must be made up of people having a like mind and culture. They point to missionaries and Christian leaders from other countries who accept the "homogeneous unit" principle almost as a given. They call attention to Hispanic churches, black churches, Oriental churches, and white churches in the United States that are strong, healthy, and thriving.

  B. *What people look for.*

After the debaters or discussion leaders have talked for about ten minutes on the question, open the discussion to the whole class. Then move on to consider this question: What do people look for in choosing a church? Refer to Dr. Willimon's comments about the importance of small groups in a church.

Developing the Lesson

II. Examine the nature of spiritual gifts.

  A. *The Christian calling.*

Can a church grow without the spiritual growth of its members? Point out that when we become Christians, God expects us to grow.

Have the class divide into small groups of three or four to study Ephesians 4:1-7. After reading the passage, the groups should write a one-sentence summary statement that lifts up an important truth they feel Paul is making. Allow time for the groups to do their work, then have them share their ideas. Use the following questions to get at the heart of the passage: What does it mean to lead a life worthy of God's calling? To what has God called us? What was the grace given us?

  B. *The variety of gifts.*

The class discussion should lead into a discussion of "gifts." As a total group, do a verse-by-verse study of Ephesians 4:11-16, noting the comments of Dr. Decker and Dr. Willimon on these verses. Additional comments and study suggestions follow.

Verse 11. Compare the list of gifts here with those listed in I Corinthians 12:28. Three are on both lists: apostles, prophets, and teachers. The other two in Ephesians 4 are evangelists and pastors. We can identify with these today, as we can with helpers and administrators, listed in I Corinthians 12. We know that differing conditions call forth differing gifts of ministry. We probably can add some today that Paul would list also if he lived in our times. What are they? (Media communicators, musicians, artists, writers, counselors, technicians, social service workers, etc.)

Verse 12. Remember that all these gifts of ministry are from Christ. Christ calls us to minister on his behalf to build up his body. Refer to Dr. Willimon's analogies of the church as a filling station and a garage. How do class members react to such analogies? Do they agree or disagree with them? Why?

Verse 13. This states the goal of growth. You might ask various members to read the verse from different versions.

Verse 14. Paul mentions two hindrances to growth: lack of strong roots and gullibility (being easily swayed by lies and trickery). Ask the class members to suggest other hindrances, such as selfishness, materialism, compromise, and conformity.

Verses 15-16. We are to be more than followers of Christ; we are to be the very fullness of Christ. The emphasis is on the *unity* of the body. The whole body—the church—is to grow. We are joined together to nourish one another and to build up Christ's whole body.

Helping Class Members Act

III. *Explore areas of ministry.*
  A. *Discovering one's gifts.*
  Ask the class: How can persons discover their spiritual gifts? Among the answers the members might give are these: (1) Consider the gifts mentioned in the Bible as well as others you think are useful. (2) Try out some of the gifts to see if they fit you. (3) Reflect on how you feel about the gifts and whether they work well for you. (4) Get feedback from other Christians as to the effectiveness of these gifts.
  Related to this last point, discuss with the class the ways a congregation can better equip its members. Dr. Willimon observes that it is the unique vocation of the pastor to be the one who equips the saints. What role do the members have in helping one another discover and develop their gifts?
  B. *The challenge of lay ministry.*
  If time allows, pursue the idea of lay ministry, as mentioned by Dr. Willimon toward the end of his comments. Is a church really helping its members grow by hiring "specialists" to do youth ministry, visitation, teaching, and community service? Challenge your class members to get involved in ministry—to discover their gifts, develop them, and use them to God's glory!

Planning for Next Sunday

Suggest that next week the members wear something "fashionable" to class. Or, as an alternative, they should bring in pictures of the latest spring and summer fashions. Also, in preparation for the session they should read Ephesians 4:22–5:20.

LESSON 12   MAY 21

Called to New Life

Background Scripture: Ephesians 4:17–5:20

The Main Question—William H. Willimon

The great Protestant reformer, Zwingli, once compared the Christian life to the robe that was given to the young novice when he joined a monastic order.

Since the order only had one size of robe for all the monks, the robe was always much too big for the novice. The arms were too long to fit the arms of the young boy and the bottom of the robe dragged the ground when he walked. But given time, as the young novice matured, he would eventually grow to fit the robe. There would come that day when the young monk would have grown up to the robe, and it would fit him perfectly.

Zwingli says that this is the way we grow as Christians. At first, when we are baptized, the designation "Christian" is far too big for us. It doesn't fit; we do not wear it well. But given time, through our continued attempts to be faithful and through the workings of God's grace in us, eventually there comes that day when it fits. No one could imagine us any other way.

When we are called to follow Christ, we are called to take upon ourselves a new way of life. The shape and meaning of that new life in Christ is the subject of today's scripture.

Selected Scripture

King James Version

Ephesians 4:22-32

22 That ye put off concerning the former conversation the old man, which is corrupt according to the deceitful lusts;

23 And be renewed in the spirit of your mind;

24 And that ye put on the new man, which after God is created in righteousness and true holiness.

25 Wherefore putting away lying, speak every man truth with his neighbour; for we are members one of another.

26 Be ye angry, and sin not: let not the sun go down upon your wrath:

27 Neither give place to the devil.

28 Let him that stole steal no more: but rather let him labour, working with *his* hands the thing which is good, that he may have to give to him that needeth.

29 Let no corrupt communication proceed out of your mouth, but that which is good to the use of edifying, that it may minister grace unto the hearers.

30 And grieve not the holy Spirit of God, whereby ye are sealed unto the day of redemption.

31 Let all bitterness, and wrath, and anger, and clamour, and evil speaking, be put away from you, with all malice:

Revised Standard Version

Ephesians 4:22-32

22 Put off your old nature which belongs to your former manner of life and is corrupt through deceitful lusts, 23 and be renewed in the spirit of your minds, 24 and put on the new nature, created after the likeness of God in true righteousness and holiness.

25 Therefore, putting away falsehood, let every one speak the truth with his neighbor, for we are members one of another. 26 Be angry but do not sin; do not let the sun go down on your anger, 27 and give no opportunity to the devil. 28 Let the thief no longer steal, but rather let him labor, doing honest work with his hands, so that he may be able to give to those in need. 29 Let no evil talk come out of your mouths, but only such as is good for edifying, as fits the occasion, that it may impart grace to those who hear. 30 And do not grieve the Holy Spirit of God, in whom you were sealed for the day of redemption. 31 Let all bitterness and wrath and anger and clamor and slander be put away from you, with all malice, 32 and be kind to one another, tenderhearted, forgiving one another, as God in Christ forgave you.

317

32 And be ye kind one to another, tenderhearted, forgiving one another, even as God for Christ's sake hath forgiven you.

Ephesians 5:1-4, 18-20
1 Be ye therefore followers of God as dear children:

2 And walk in love, as Christ also hath loved us, and hath given himself for us an offering and a sacrifice to God for a sweetsmelling savour.

3 But fornication, and all uncleanness, or covetousness, let it not be once named among you, as becometh saints;

4 Neither filthiness, nor foolish talking, nor jesting, which are not convenient: but rather giving of thanks.

....

18 And be not drunk with wine, wherein is excess; but be filled with the Spirit;

19 Speaking to yourselves in psalms and hymns and spiritual songs, singing and making melody in your heart to the Lord;

20 Giving thanks always for all things unto God and the Father in the name of our Lord Jesus Christ.

Key Verse: **Put on the new man, which after God is created in righteousness and true holiness. (Ephesians 4:24)**

Ephesians 5:1-4, 18-20
1 Therefore be imitators of God, as beloved children. 2 And walk in love, as Christ loved us and gave himself up for us, a fragrant offering and sacrifice to God.

3 But immorality and all impurity or covetousness must not even be named among you, as is fitting among saints. 4 Let there be no filthiness, nor silly talk, nor levity, which are not fitting; but instead let there be thanksgiving.

....

18 And do not get drunk with wine, for that is debauchery; but be filled with the Spirit, 19 addressing one another in psalms and hymns and spiritual songs, singing and making melody to the Lord with all your heart, 20 always and for everything giving thanks in the name of our Lord Jesus Christ to God the Father.

Key Verse: **Put on the new nature, created after the likeness of God in true righteousness and holiness. (Ephesians 4:24)**

As You Read the Scripture—Ralph Decker

Paul appeals for distinctive living on the part of the readers. He maintains that Christians should be noticeably different in conduct from the pagans around them. Converts from paganism are called upon to make a clean break from their former life-styles.

Ephesians 4:22. To make clear the change in character and conduct, Paul uses the metaphor of a change of clothing. The reference to a "former manner of life" shows that the letter's readers were Christians of non-Jewish backgrounds. They had already been referred to as "you Gentiles" (2:11; 3:1). The evils here were commonly practiced among the Gentiles but were condemned by the Jewish moral code. In the Greek, the verb translated "put off" indicates a once-for-all action.

Verse 23. On the other hand, the verb translated "be renewed" carries the idea of continuing activity: "keep being renewed." The same idea appears in II Corinthians 4:16: "Our inner nature is being renewed every day."

Verse 24. This verse contains one of Paul's favorite themes. When the Lordship of Christ is accepted, a person's old nature dies, and the person becomes a new creature of a higher nature. The new nature is marked by righteousness.

Ephesians 4:25–5:4. This section deals with the changes in conduct that result from the change in inner nature. It lists vices that will be dropped and virtues that will be cultivated.

Ephesians 4:25. Falsehood (lying and deceit) is to be avoided, because it destroys the unity of the Christian community, the body of Christ. Truth-speaking, on the other hand, strengthens unity.

Verses 26-27. Anger itself is not a sin. There is a place for righteous indignation, as in response to injustice or brutality. But anger that rises from ordinary irritation with others and is harbored and nursed, gives rise to such sins as hatred, slander, and injustice.

Verse 28. If we assume that verses 25-29 reflect the readers' "former manner of life," this verse indicates that the early church accepted professional criminals who had made their living by theft. They were welcomed as sinners and were expected to "put off" their old way of life and live by honest work. Paul's reason for persons earning an honest income is striking: It enables one to help others.

Verse 29. Few things reveal a person's inner nature more quickly than speech. The letter of James devotes much space to the dangers of an uncontrolled tongue (James 3:1-12). Speech can hurt, but it can also edify.

Verses 30-32. Sealing was a mark of ownership. The gift of the Spirit, or being baptized with the Spirit, was a sign that a person belonged to Christ and would be saved in the day of judgment. The Holy Spirit, which guides, comforts, and strengthens individual believers and the Christian community, is grieved by human misdeeds that destroy the unity of the church. Those practices of the old nature are to be replaced with kindness, warm-heartedness, and readiness to forgive.

Ephesians 5:1. Throughout the New Testament the relationship between God and humans is presented in terms of the family. John 8:14-44 makes it clear that Jesus said that true family membership depends not on biological descent but upon sharing family traits and ideals. According to Matthew 5:44-45, Jesus urged his hearers to become God-like.

Verse 2. Christ was God-like. Being Christ-like will make persons God-like.

Verses 3-4. Sins stand in the way of imitating Christ. They should not even be talked about. Talk arouses interest and interest leads to action.

Verse 4. All of this verse deals with speech. The word "levity" refers to lewdness rather than humor. Kenneth Taylor suggests the translation, "Let there be no dirty stories, foul talk, and coarse jokes."

Verses 18-20. In Paul's day, as in ours, drunkenness was a major social evil. Paul suggests that those who have been seeking comfort in alcohol can find joy from fellowship with the Holy Spirit.

THIRD QUARTER

The Scripture and the Main Question—William H. Willimon

Put on the New Nature

In the early church, a person being baptized was asked to remove all clothing and jewelry and don a white robe, so that "nothing alien might go down into the water." We human beings are accustomed to making distinctions between different classes of people on the basis of the clothes they wear. Young people may adopt a certain fashion of dress in order to show that they are different from their parents. People buy expensive jewelry and wear fashionable clothes in order to display their personal wealth and status.

In asking that all of this jewelry and clothing be removed, the early church was attempting to state, at the very beginning of the Christian life, that the Christian way demanded change in a person's values. One of the most important changes required was in one's attitude about distinctions about people. Whereas the world ranks people on the basis of money, status, and possessions, the church refuses to recognize such distinctions. Therefore every Christian was given a new white robe to signify equality with the church.

The white robe also relates to the words in the book of Revelation, in which God's saints are said to be dressed in pure white robes. The white robe symbolized purity and newness. Even as we are born from the wombs of our mothers into a new form of existence, the baptismal font was considered a womb from which we are born to the newness of the Christian life.

Created After the Likeness of God

Whatever the Christian life means, it is clear that it means change. In today's scripture from the letter to the Ephesians, a number of images are used to convey the radical change required when someone becomes a Christian. The first book of the Bible, Genesis, speaks of the dramatic creative work of God. Ephesians claims that God continues this creative work in us when we become disciples. The creative God is always busy bringing order out of chaos, life out of death. That's what is expected to happen to us as Christians. The chaos of our lives is organized into something new, orderly, clean, and beautiful. Before, we may have been the victims of every passing fad, conflicting philosophy, and competing claim. Now we are recreated as one of those who bear "the likeness of God." You will recall, in the book of Genesis, that God says he wishes to create humanity "in our own image."

The trouble is, we take on alien identities. The divine image becomes distorted as our lives fall victim to other allegiances. In Christ, we are reborn and recreated day by day into that image which God originally intended for us.

Even as people are able to recognize the handiwork of artists like Picasso or Cezanne by looking at their paintings, so God ought to be able to look at each of us and see his imprint on our lives.

Something is gained when we become Christian, but something is lost also. For instance, when Paul spoke of his own new life in Christ, he seemed to not know whether to speak of it as birth or death. Paul uses both birth and death images to describe what happened to him on the Damascus Road. We are born new creatures, but we must also die to old loyalties. To be a Christian means that we must put away the former life-styles and adopt new ones more pleasing to God. Ephesians 4 and 5 list some of the life-style changes required for Christians to better resemble "the likeness of God."

Are you surprised to read that Christians are not to lie or to steal? Perhaps you thought that only nice people were in the early church! No, people in the early church resemble many of the people in your church today. That is, they have not arrived yet; they are still on the way. Christians face the same temptations and commit many of the same sins as those who are not Christians.

The difference between Christians and non-Christians, as far as their life-styles go, is that Christians are on the way to somewhere else. We are those who have submitted ourselves to the sometimes painful work of rebirth. This work requires numerous changes in the way we live, relate to other people, spend our money, and spend our time.

Unless there is some break between the old and new, some pain, some reformation, we have not yet participated in the new life. Most of us are not Christians by natural inclination. As someone has said, "God has no grandchildren." Each generation must submit to conversion and to change. This change is why the Christian life can possibly be called "new."

In True Righteousness and Holiness

Do you think that the church today puts enough stress on the need for change and reformation of our life-styles, as Christians? Sometimes I think that we put too much emphasis on the benefits of the Christian life, and neglect the obligations. Preachers point out all the good things God does for us Christians, without stating the necessity of changing our lives in order to more closely resemble the pattern of Christ. Today's scripture reminds us that nothing less than imitation is required. We are to imitate the one whose life so closely resembled God's that people were able to look at him and see the very face of God.

In the early church, when people became Christian, they were required to change. Can people look at Christians today and see the mark of changed lives?

Helping Adults Become Involved—Ronald E. Schlosser

Preparing to Teach

Jakob Boehme, German philosopher and mystic (1574–1624), once said, "The exterior is the signature of the internal." By this he recognized an important truth—that through our outward actions we reveal our inner selves.

Jesus had said this centuries before; evil comes from within a person (see Mark 7:20-23). In his letter to the Romans, Paul lists all kinds of evil (1:29-31), and a similar list is found in today's background scripture from Ephesians. This evil is the signature of the old nature. However, also listed in Ephesians are the characteristics of the new nature that are embodied by a person who is "in Christ."

In today's lesson we will be looking at these two natures and considering what should be the signature of our own life-style as Christians and as members of the church, the body of Christ. The learning goals are (1) to identify the characteristics of a person's "old nature" and the "new nature" as a Christian, and (2) to discern the meaning and implications of living in the world as the body of Christ.

Use the following lesson outline:

     I.   Discuss the importance of outward appearance.
    II.   Examine the old and new natures.
       A. The old nature.
       B. The new nature.
       C. A childlike nature.
       D. A loving nature.
       E. A joyous nature.
   III.   Explore implications for the church.

Read carefully "The Scripture and the Main Question" and "As You Read the Scripture." These form the heart of the lesson. The ideas, insights, and suggestions in these sections should be reflected continually in your lesson plan.

As you use the suggested outline for "Helping Adults Become Involved," you may want to either quote or paraphrase ideas. You might like to jot in the margin of your outline the page number and paragraph being referred to. For example, you could write a reference to page 65, paragraph 3, as 65-3.

Last week you suggested that class members come today dressed in something fashionable or bring in pictures of the latest spring and summer fashions. If you yourself do not wish to "dress up," you should at least bring in magazines and newspapers containing clothing ads. Some of the ads could be cut out, mounted on construction paper, and hung around the room to provide atmosphere for the opening discussion.

A chalkboard or sheets of newsprint should also be available.

Introducing the Main Question

I. Discuss the importance of outward appearance.

Begin by referring to Dr. Willimon's comments about Zwingli's comparison of the Christian life to a monk's robe and the early church's practice regarding clothing at the time of a person's baptism. Because clothing very often provided the basis by which people judged one another, the early church had all candidates for baptism wear white robes, to signify equality and oneness.

Consider the importance people give to clothing in our day. Look at the clothing ads in newspapers and magazines. What are the latest fashions? What image do designer clothes give to people who wear them? Are any class members wearing something "fashionable"? How do such clothes and accessories make them feel? Do people tend to judge others by the clothes they wear?

Remind the class of what James says about treating others on the basis of the clothes they wear. Read James 2:2-4. What would happen in your church if someone in threadbare clothes, perhaps in need of a haircut or a bath, wandered in and sat in a front pew? Even if everyone was polite to the person, what would most *think*? Do we judge one another by outward appearance? Note what I Samuel 16:7 says.

Developing the Lesson

II. Examine the old and new natures.
  A. The old nature.
  Introduce today's scripture, Ephesians 4:22–5:4, 18-20. Indicate that the writer speaks of what a person does as a reflection of his or her "old" or "new" nature. Our outward actions reveal our inner selves. Ask the class to read the passage silently and to pick out all the references to one's old nature. List these characteristics in a column on the left side of the chalkboard or newsprint.
  Now ask half the class to read Mark 7:20-23 silently, and the other half to read Romans 1:29-31. Add the evils mentioned in these passages to those already listed. Head the column "Old Nature."
  B. The new nature.
  Point out that many Christians in the first century came out of a pagan background and needed to be warned against returning to their former ways (Ephesians 4:22). How many sins and vices listed in the "Old Nature" column are still prevalent in modern society? Human nature has not changed.
  Note that while Ephesians 4:22 speaks of our "old nature," 4:24 tells us to put on the "new nature," which is the nature of Christ. Look back over the entire passage again (4:22–5:4, 18-20) and identify the characteristics of this new nature. Record these in a column on the right side of the chalkboard or newsprint and head the column "New Nature." Particularly emphasize the qualities mentioned in 4:32. Discuss the place of forgiveness in a Christian's life. Is it easier to forgive someone or to ask someone for forgiveness?
  C. A childlike nature.
  Look more closely at Ephesians 5:1. Recall the comments in the lesson for April 16 about being imitators of Christ. Focus on the phrase "as beloved children." Refer to Dr. Decker's comments on this verse and also to Jesus' words in Matthew 18:3, "Unless you turn and become like children, you will never enter the kingdom of heaven." Ask the class to list the qualities of childlikeness that should characterize a Christian (trust, innocence, happiness, humbleness, imagination, energy, and so forth). Point out that there are also aspects of the "old nature" in children (self-centeredness, anger, irritability, and disobedience, among others.)
  D. A loving nature.
  Consider the phrase "walk in love" in Ephesians 5:2. Christ is our model. Our Christian life-style should be one of servanthood and sacrifice, patterned after Christ. Love is to be the rule and goal of the Christian life.
  E. A joyous nature.
  The final three verses in today's study, Ephesians 5:18-20, also contain a contrast between the old nature and the new nature. Paul alludes to the pagan practice of turning religious festivals into drunken orgies. Wine flowed freely, leading to debauchery. Instead of becoming filled with wine, Paul says Christians should be filled with the Spirit. The pagan songs should be replaced with spiritual songs. The sexual excesses should give way to a joyous expression of thanks to God in Jesus' name.

Helping Class Members Act

III. *Explore implications for the church.*

Up to this point, we have been interpreting the scripture passage in terms of individual behavior as Christians. Close the session by exploring with the class what this passage says about the behavior of Christians united as the body of Christ. Consider these questions: What do servanthood and sacrifice imply, as the church addresses important issues of our day? How can our congregation model the life-style of "walking in love"? Is temperance education something needed in our church? What place should music have in our worship and in our attitude toward one another?

Conclude with a time of silent meditation. Ask the class members to think about what changes may need to be made in their lives as individual Christians and in the life of the church as a whole, so that the "new nature" in Christ will shine through.

Planning for Next Sunday

Have the class think about and list the characteristics of a Christian marriage and a Christian family. The scripture for study will be Ephesians 5:21–6:4.

LESSON 13   MAY 28

Guidelines for Family Life

Background Scripture: Ephesians 5:21–6:4

The Main Question—William H. Willimon

I feel sure that if you ask most people in your church to name the major problems people in your church face today, marriage and family conflicts would be at the top of the list. Whether located in rural, suburban, or urban environments, few congregations are free of the agony of marriage and family problems. With the soaring divorce rate, tensions between parents and children, and the breakdown of traditional family values, many people are searching for a means of achieving a better family life. If you browse among the titles at your local bookstore, you will see scores of self-help books for parents, husbands, wives, and children, all purporting to answer the problems of marital and family stress.

But what is the Christian response? This is our main concern in today's lesson. Does the Bible offer us any specific guidance for ordering family life?

You and I are in the midst of a revolution in the relationship between men and women. In our lifetimes we have seen radical changes in the relationship between husbands and wives as a result of this revolution. Many of the changes between men and women have been most beneficial and represent significant advances in human relationships. And yet many of these changes have wrought great stress upon the institution of marriage.

Sometimes we accuse the Bible of not being related to the concerns of everyday life. But that is certainly not the case with today's scripture. Today we will be relating the Bible to one of the most pressing concerns of contemporary life: relationships between husbands and wives, parents and children.

Selected Scripture

King James Version

Ephesians 5:21-33

21 Submitting yourselves one to another in the fear of God.

22 Wives, submit yourselves unto your own husbands, as unto the Lord.

23 For the husband is the head of the wife, even as Christ is the head of the church: and he is the saviour of the body.

24 Therefore as the church is subject unto Christ, so *let* the wives *be* to their own husbands in every thing.

25 Husbands, love your wives, even as Christ also loved the church, and gave himself for it;

26 That he might sanctify and cleanse it with the washing of water by the word,

27 That he might present it to himself a glorious church, not having spot, or wrinkle, or any such thing; but that it should be holy and without blemish.

28 So ought men to love their wives as their own bodies. He that loveth his wife loveth himself.

29 For no man ever yet hated his own flesh; but nourisheth and cherisheth it, even as the Lord the church:

30 For we are members of his body, of his flesh, and of his bones.

31 For this cause shall a man leave his father and mother, and shall be joined unto his wife, and they two shall be one flesh.

Revised Standard Version

Ephesians 5:21-33

21 Be subject to one another out of reverence for Christ. 22 Wives, be subject to your husbands, as to the Lord. 23 For the husband is the head of the wife as Christ is the head of the church, his body, and is himself its Savior. 24 As the church is subject to Christ, so let wives also be subject in everything to their husbands. 25 Husbands, love your wives, as Christ loved the church and gave himself up for her, 26 that he might sanctify her, having cleansed her by the washing of water with the word, 27 that he might present the church to himself in splendor, without spot or wrinkle or any such thing, that she might be holy and without blemish. 28 Even so husbands should love their wives as their own bodies. He who loves his wife loves himself. 29 For no man ever hates his own flesh, but nourishes and cherishes it, as Christ does the church, 30 because we are members of this body. 31 "For this reason a man shall leave his father and mother and be joined to his wife, and the two shall become one." 32 This is a great mystery, and I take it to mean Christ and the church; 33 however, let each one of you love his wife as himself, and let the wife see that she respects her husband.

32 This is a great mystery: but I speak concerning Christ and the church.

33 Nevertheless let every one of you in particular so love his wife even as himself; and the wife *see* that she reverence *her* husband.

Ephesians 6:1-4

1 Children, obey your parents in the Lord: for this is right.

2 Honour thy father and mother; which is the first commandment with promise;

3 That it may be well with thee, and thou mayest live long on the earth.

4 And, ye fathers, provoke not your children to wrath: but bring them up in the nurture and admonition of the Lord.

Key Verse: **Submitting yourselves one to another in the fear of God. (Ephesians 5:21)**

Ephesians 6:1-4

1 Children, obey your parents in the Lord, for this is right. 2 "Honor your father and mother" (this is the first commandment with a promise), 3 "that it may be well with you and that you may live long on the earth." 4 Fathers, do not provoke your children to anger, but bring them up in the discipline and instruction of the Lord.

Key Verse: **Be subject to one another out of reverence for Christ. (Ephesians 5:21)**

As You Read the Scripture—Ralph Decker

In studying this part of Ephesians, which deals with personal relations and family life, it must be remembered that Paul was a child of his age. His society was male-dominated, and family relationships were often based on submission rather than on love.

Ephesians 5:21. The King James Version treats this verse as the last sentence of the preceding paragraph, as though it says that all believers should try to please each other. The Revised Standard Version treats it as the introduction to a discussion of ideal family relationships based on mutual respect and subordination of personal desires. The latter arrangement seems better, since this verse is the key to the rest of the letter. The contrast between the King James reading "fear of God" and the Revised Standard's "reverence for Christ" is due to differences among the manuscripts. Both phrases make it clear that proper family relationships are a duty to God and Christ.

Verse 22. This verse should not be read alone, but in conjunction with verses 21 and 25. The command of 21 includes husbands as well as wives. Verse 25 suggests that wives should submit to love, not tyranny. The comparison of the husband to Christ must not be pushed too far. A husband is a limited human being.

Verse 23. The head controls the body. Christ, as head of the church, controls its actions and destiny and in turn receives its obedience. The husband, as head of the family, has controlling authority and the right to be obeyed. Again, the analogy must not be pushed too far. The husband is not the savior of the wife, as Christ is of the church. The verse may mean that the husband is protector and preserver of the family, as Christ is sustainer of the church.

Verse 25. The Greek word here translated "love" is *agapao*, the verb from which comes the familiar noun *agape*. These words do not refer to selfish, possessive love. They stand for an unselfish concern for another person. They speak of devotion and commitment to one who is valued for himself or herself. The example of such love is Christ, who gave his life out of love for others.

Verses 26-27. The church is being prepared for complete union with Christ, as a bride is prepared for her wedding.

Ephesians 5:28-31. Self-love is offered as a reason for husbands to love their wives.

Verse 28. Behind this verse is the doctrine that in marriage husband and wife become one flesh (Genesis 2:24).

Verse 29. The husband who accepts this doctrine will care for his wife as he does for his own physical welfare. Just so, Christ cherishes and nourishes the church.

Verse 31. The quotation from Genesis emphasizes the completeness of the marriage union.

Verse 32. The mystery of what draws one person to another is recognized but not solved. That mystery is said to be symbolic of the mystery of what draws persons to Christ.

Verse 33. This is a good summary of 5:21-33. "However" says that regardless of analogies, mysteries, and symbols, the duty of husbands and wives is clear. Husbands must love their wives; wives must respect their husbands.

Ephesians 6:1-4. This short section deals with parent-child relationships. It is similar to Colossians 3:20-21 but more detailed.

Verse 1. The direct address to children suggests that children were present in the congregations to which this letter was read. The phrase "in the Lord" again sets Christ as a model for interpersonal relationships. These instructions are addressed to parents and children who are Christians. Since they are both "in Christ," there can be no conflict between them.

Verses 2-3. The readers are reminded of the fifth commandment (Exodus 20:12).

Verse 4. Parents are responsible for the instruction and discipline of their children. If this is handled in ways worthy of followers of Christ, there will be peace and harmony. However, unfair or harsh discipline can destroy a family as surely as disobedience can.

The Scripture and the Main Question—William H. Willimon

Be Subject to One Another

Each generation has its own vocabulary. For my generation it was "power to the people," "involvement," and "change." When someone looks back on the 1980s they will think of words like "upscale" and "Yuppie." But I suspect one word will be remembered as the key to the seventies and eighties—"liberation." Ours is an age of the liberation of just about everybody. First came black liberation, and then women's liberation; now there's men's liberation.

Our age has seen increasing independence from outworn social restraints, and liberation from stultifying prejudice. This is good.

Yet because today's word is "liberation," today's word from Scripture is all the more embarrassing. For today's word from Ephesians 5 is not freedom, independence, or liberation—words our generation loves—but rather the Bible word for today is *submission*—a word that we abhor.

"Wives, be subject to your husbands" is not one of the loftier biblical injunctions. No wonder that Ephesians 5 is one of the more unpopular pieces of scripture. Let us therefore be done with Ephesians 5, placing it on the junkheap along with those other biblical passages urging the bashing of little babies' heads against stones and the obedience of slaves to masters. Submission is not our word.

Yet before you jettison Ephesians 5, please note that commentators call this one of the most abused and misinterpreted passages in the whole Bible. How so?

Out of Reverence for Christ

I call your attention to four insights about this passage:

1. Paul probably borrowed this listing of marital duties from the conventional wisdom of his day. Hellenistic Judaism had many of these household codes. Most of this is not specifically Christian, but part of Greek culture. Paul merely took conventional household wisdom and put a Christian veneer over it.

2. Wives are instructed to "be subject to your husbands." Given the time and the place the Bible was written, there is nothing surprising here. Paul, like any Near Eastern person of the day, looked upon women as subservient to their husbands. No one is surprised that a biblical passage is conditioned by its time and place.

3. Yet here is the surprise: Not only are wives told to be submissive to their husbands (which wasn't news), but husbands are also enjoined to "love your wives" (verse 25). In fact, much more space is given to the duties of husbands than to those of wives. Evidently Paul feels that husbands need more instruction in how to behave in marriage. Whereas wives are asked to be subject to their husbands, husbands are told to love their wives "as Christ loved the church and gave himself up for her" (verse 25). How did Christ love the church? By giving up his life for the church's sake. That's how husbands are urged to love their wives. The complete, sacrificial, selfless love of Christ is the model.

4. The writer goes even further, saying that "husbands should love their wives as their own bodies" (verse 28). This is the Hebrew principle that one must love one's neighbor as oneself (Leviticus 19:18; Matthew 7:12).

Any use of this passage to justify feminine subjugation in marriage or anywhere else is a calloused misreading of the text. That's not what it says. Indeed, considered in its original context, Ephesians 5 is a quite radical statement, with its emphasis on the responsibility of husbands.

Admittedly, submission is being urged. Everything follows from the opening statement: Be subject to one another out of reverence for Christ. Submission is the guiding principle. But it is not the submission of a lowly wife, to her monarchical husband. It is *mutual* submission of husband and wife, because of their relationship to Christ, who subjected himself to the world in order to love the world. For Paul, the human relationship of marriage derives its form from the divine-human relationship of Christ to his church. Elsewhere Paul says, "Through love be servants of one another" (Galatians 5:13).

Granted, we're talking about *mutual* submission, but are we any less offended? Many find the language of submission and subordination offensive. To the extent that such scripture has been used to justify husbands' exploitation of their wives, we should be offended. But is there an even greater offense behind Ephesians 5?

Remember, our word is "liberation"—freedom, autonomy, independence—not service, interdependence, or submission (mutual or otherwise). Our world was built by cowboys, explorers, entrepreneurs. We are a nation of individuals, Lone Rangers and Annie Oakleys standing on our own two feet.

And yet, here is a scripture which says, like so many biblical passages, that you can't "find yourself" by looking inward. By concentrating only on *your* feelings, needs, wants, and desires, and by learning to assert them more freely, to be liberated, you do not become a more creative self; you become more self-centered, smaller, and isolated. You haven't grown; you have shrunk.

Even marriage, the most intimate of human relationships, is viewed by many as a contract negotiated for the mutual benefit of autonomous individuals who relentlessly scan their feelings.

I serve on the board of a small, church-related college. Not long ago we hired an outside consultant to study the college and its program and tell us what we were doing well and what we were doing poorly. In his final report to the board, the consultant said, "At these small colleges, you often get a large number of students who tend to be dependent. They're not seeking maturity; they're looking for *in loco parentis*. They want to be Mama-ed and Daddied while they're here. Then you get faculty who want to play Mama and Daddy. I think the college ought to work harder to help them grow up."

An old, worn-out preacher spoke up. "Well, I guess it all depends on your definition of an adult. How do you define being grown up?"

"You know what maturity looks like," responded the consultant. "An adult is someone who is independent, autonomous, liberated from dependencies on others, free."

"Well, I was thinking," said the old preacher, "every adult I know who believes that is in big trouble right now." Who are the mature? Those who think they stand alone, aloof, needing no one? Or those who have grown enough to know otherwise?

Is such submission out of date, passé, or is it only—difficult?

Karl Barth once said that the Bible becomes God's word when the words of Scripture become your word.

In your marriage, in ordering your family life, what is *your* word?

Helping Adults Become Involved—Ronald E. Schlosser

Preparing to Teach

The family has always been a concern of God's people. Throughout the Old and New Testaments the family is presented as the foundation of human society. The story of the Hebrew people is a story of families. Jesus was a member of a family. The households of the first believers came together to make up the early church.

THIRD QUARTER

The statements Paul makes in Ephesians about the family have been often misunderstood and misused by Christians. Paul has too frequently been accused of promoting male domination of the family and parents' arbitrary authority over their children.

Today's lesson is designed to help your class explore the nature of Christian family life. More specifically, the learning goals are (1) to identify the characteristics of a Christian marriage and a Christian family, (2) to examine ways in which parents and children are to relate in love, and (3) to resolve to become a caring, loving member of one's family.

Use the following lesson outline:

    I.   Identify characteristics of Christian family life.
    II. Examine scripture on Christian family relationships.
    III. Discuss case studies.

Read carefully "The Scripture and the Main Question" and "As You Read the Scripture." These form the heart of the lesson. The ideas, insights, and suggestions in these sections should be reflected continually in your lesson plan.

As you use the suggested outline, you may want to either quote or paraphrase ideas. You might like to jot in the margin of your outline the page number and paragraph being referred to. For example, you could write a reference to page 65, paragraph 3, as 65-3.

Read carefully the comments by Dr. Willimon and Dr. Decker on the preceding pages. These form the heart of the lesson. If you have access to a Bible commentary on Ephesians, read through the exposition on today's scripture, Ephesians 5:21–6:4.

Be sure a chalkboard or sheets of newsprint are available in the classroom. Also prepare beforehand copies of the case studies given in "Helping Class Members Act." They should be written or typed on individual pieces of paper for distribution to the class.

Introducing the Main Question

I. Identify characteristics of Christian family life.

Read or rephrase in your own words Dr. Willimon's comments in the section "The Main Question." He speaks of Christian marriage and Christian family life. What are the characteristics of each?

Divide your class into two sections and each section into groups of three or four. Ask the groups in the first section to list the characteristics of a Christian marriage. That is, what kind of relationship should a Christian husband and wife have? How should each act toward the other? Ask the other groups to discuss what a Christian family should be like. Have them list the attributes and actions that ought to characterize the relationship between parents and children.

Allow about ten minutes for the groups to make and discuss their lists. Then have each group report its findings. On the chalkboard or newsprint write down the responses under the headings "Christian Marriage" and "Christian Family." Note any characteristics that appear on both lists.

Developing the Lesson

II. Examine scripture on Christian family relationships.

Turn to today's scripture, Ephesians 5:21–6:4, to see what the apostle Paul says about marital and family relationships. Read the passage aloud, then ask the class what words or ideas jump out at them. Would Paul agree with the characteristics on the lists the members just made?

Examine the passage in greater detail, focusing on three concepts.

Subjection, submission (5:21-24). Refer to the comments by Dr. Willimon and Dr. Decker. The concept of mutuality should be emphasized. Christ is the example to follow, because he subjected himself to the world as an act of love for the world.

Love (5:25-33). Paul ties the concept of marital love to the image of Christ's love for his church. Here is a merging of doctrine and practice. The unity expressed in the marriage relationship is a type of the mystic unity between Christ and his church. With this image in mind, the words "cherish" and "respect" take on an added dimension.

Obedience, discipline (6:1-4). Instruction and discipline are essential in a Christian home. And while children are enjoined to obey their parents, parents are told not to give their children cause to disobey them. Fairness and love should mark the relationship between parents and children. When children honor their parents, they are, in effect, honoring God. This places a high responsibility on the parents, who represent God to their children. This representation is usually the first way that children come to know God.

Helping Class Members Act

III. Discuss case studies.

Allow enough time in the session for class members to grapple with some real-life situations. Ask the small groups that met earlier in the session to re-form. Give each group one of the following case studies to discuss.

1. One day, while putting away the laundry, you find a half-used container of birth control pills hidden in your fifteen-year-old daughter's bureau drawer. What should you do?

2. Your husband and seventeen-year-old son just can't seem to get along. Their arguments have become increasingly bitter. Finally, one night your son hits your husband. The boy leaves in a rage but returns later. What should you do? If you were the father, what would you do?

3. You have two very successful, achievement-oriented children, but the third is not doing well in school. She is sixteen and lately has become very secretive. You are doubly alarmed because she has been going out with an unkempt, motorcycle-riding dropout. How would you handle the situation?

4. Your son is behaving erratically. He is fourteen and, you suspect, has become involved with a group of kids at school who take drugs. You have no direct evidence that he is doing drugs, and he never talks about his friends. Do you wait until you have solid evidence that your son is involved with drugs before you bring it up? What should you do?

5. Your nineteen-year-old daughter comes home from college with a girlfriend whom you sense is a religious fanatic. She belongs to a "holiness" sect that speaks in tongues, has rigid rules about conduct, and makes self-righteous judgments about people whom it feels are not saved. How would you handle the visit, and would you do anything later, such as urge your daughter to break up the friendship?

6. It is 1:00 A.M. You get a call from the police. Your sixteen-year-old son was picked up with a carload of kids. There were several empty liquor bottles and some marijuana cigarettes in the car. He is at the station house. What should you do?

There probably will not be time to have the groups report back on each of their case studies. You might ask them to share general approaches they would take or Christian principles they would follow. Of course, there are no easy answers, and there are many variables preventing one from prescribing the "right" course of action to take. But the exercise might get class members to think about what effect a Christian approach to family problems might have, as opposed to dealing with them without the Christian perspective.

Close the session by challenging your class members to become caring, loving members of their families. Encourage them to resolve to work for better family relationships at home.

Planning for Next Sunday

A new course of study begins next week. The background scripture will be Joshua 1–4.

FOURTH QUARTER
Conquest and Challenge

UNIT I: JOSHUA—A TIME OF CONQUEST AND SETTLEMENT
Horace R. Weaver

FOUR LESSONS   **JUNE 4–25**

This fourth quarter's lessons are based on studies from Joshua, Judges, and Ruth. The course offers an overview of the period in Hebrew history beginning with the Hebrews' entrance into the Promised Land and encompassing a time of turmoil that ended in the establishment of the monarchy. There are three units in this course: unit I: "Joshua—A Time of Conquest and Settlement"; unit II: "Judges—A Time of Conflict and Adjustment"; unit III: "Ruth—A Record of Committment and Hope."

Unit I, "Joshua—A Time of Conquest and Settlement," consists of four lessons. The memorializing of the crossing of Jordan by the setting up of twelve stones in the middle of the river begins the study. The battle that led to the fall of Jericho is singled out as representative of the many battles fought for the conquest of the land. This victory was the key that opened the way into the land of Canaan. The division of the land among the tribes and their settlement in the land is the topic of one lesson. The conquest, however, was never finished, since the Hebrews failed to completely drive out the people who occupied the land. The fact that the Canaanites remained in the land led Joshua to issue his final challenge to the Hebrews to choose where their loyalties would be placed. The people responded by affirming their loyalty to God.

The first unit has four lessons. June 4, "Stones for Remembering," asks how we can find the resources to both triumph over our hurts and handle unexpected blessings. June 11, "God Gives Victory," raises the question, Where does our security lie? June 18, "Settlement of the Promised Land," challenges adults to rest from time to time from their labors and to remember how they came to be where they are. June 25, "Life Is Shaped by Choices," asks the basic question, Have you made up your mind whether or not you belong to God?

Contributors to the fourth quarter:

Pat McGeachy, associate pastor, Downtown Presbyterian Church, Nashville, Tennessee.

John Steen, assistant editor for *International Christian Digest*; conductor of Christian writers' conferences, Nashville, Tennessee.

Harold Reid Weaver, retired pastor of West Bend United Methodist Church, West Bend, Wisconsin.

Horace R. Weaver

Stones for Remembering

Background Scripture: Joshua 1–4

The Main Question—Pat McGeachy

One of the most important roles that the church plays is that of helping us through life's passages. We are always crossing over some Jordan. The two most traumatic passages are the first and the last: birth and death. When we are born, the church celebrates with our parents; we are baptized and welcomed into the family of God. When we die, the church gathers to mourn, to thank God for our lives, and to wish us well on that passage through the final Jordan.

But there are many other crossings in our lives, and sometimes well, sometimes poorly, the church offers rites of passage to help us through them.

Puberty is one. Then the church provides for us an opportunity to say, "Now I am grown up," as we confirm the promises made for us when we were baptized.

Another is graduation from school, and perhaps leaving home to go off to another school or to enter into a new life with a job away from home. Often the church will recognize these times with a gift and sent us on our way with the prayers of our friends.

Another is marriage, when both church and state unite to celebrate the importance of the family, to hear our promises to each other, and to ask the blessing of God on our new families.

There are many other transitions, some fun, some frightening: birth of children, illness, moving, changing jobs, getting a divorce. How do we find the resources to triumph over the hurt and handle the blessings of such events?

This is the main question of this lesson: Can we, like Joshua and his friends, mark our Jordan crossings in such a way that we will remember God in life's passages and be able to pass on to future generations the same source of strength, so that we may say to one another, as did God to Joshua, "Be strong and of good courage, for the Lord your God is with you wherever you go" (Joshua 1:9).

Selected Scripture

King James Version	Revised Standard Version
Joshua 4:1-3, 8, 15-24	*Joshua 4:1-3, 8, 15-24*
1 And it came to pass, when all the people were clean passed over Jordan, that the Lord spake unto Joshua, saying,	1 When all the nation had finished passing over the Jordan, the Lord said to Joshua, 2 "Take twelve men from the people, from each tribe a man, 3 and command them,
2 Take you twelve men out of the people, out of every tribe a man,	'Take twelve stones from here out of

3 And command ye them, saying, Take you hence out of the midst of Jordan, out of the place where the priests' feet stood firm, twelve stones, and ye shall carry them over with you, and leave them in the lodging place, where ye shall lodge this night.

....

8 And the children of Israel did so as Joshua commanded, and took up twelve stones out of the midst of Jordan, as the Lord spake unto Joshua, according to the number of the tribes of the children of Israel, and carried them over with them unto the place where they lodged, and laid them down there.

....

15 And the Lord spake unto Joshua, saying,

16 Command the priests that bear the ark of the testimony, that they come up out of Jordan.

17 Joshua therefore commanded the priests, saying, Come ye up out of Jordan.

18 And it came to pass, when the priests that bare the ark of the covenant of the Lord were come up out of the midst of Jordan, *and* the soles of the priests' feet were lifted up unto the dry land, that the waters of Jordan returned unto their place, and flowed over all his banks, as *they did* before.

19 And the people came up out of Jordan on the tenth *day* of the first month, and encamped in Gilgal, in the east border of Jericho.

20 And those twelve stones, which they took out of Jordan, did Joshua pitch in Gilgal.

21 And he spake unto the children of Israel, saying, When your children shall ask their fathers in time to come, saying, What *mean* these stones?

22 Then ye shall let your children know, saying, Israel came over this Jordan on dry land.

23 For the Lord your God dried

the midst of the Jordan, from the very place where the priests' feet stood, and carry them over with you, and lay them down in the place where you lodge tonight.'"

....

8 And the men of Israel did as Joshua commanded, and took up twelve stones of the midst of the Jordan, according to the number of the tribes of the people of Israel, as the Lord told Joshua; and they carried them over with them to the place where they lodged, and laid them down there.

....

15 And the Lord said to Joshua, 16 "Command the priests who bear the ark of the testimony to come up out of the Jordan." 17 Joshua therefore commanded the priests, "Come up out of the Jordan." 18 And when the priests bearing the ark of the covenant of the Lord came up from the midst of the Jordan, and the soles of the priests' feet were lifted up on dry ground, the waters of the Jordan returned to their place and overflowed all its banks, as before.

19 The people came up out of the Jordan on the tenth day of the first month, and they encamped in Gilgal on the east border of Jericho. 20 And those twelve stones, which they took out of the Jordan, Joshua set up in Gilgal. 21 And he said to the people of Israel, "When your children ask their fathers in time to come, 'What do these stones mean?' 22 then you shall let your children know, 'Israel passed over this Jordan on dry ground.' 23 For the Lord your God dried up the waters of the Jordan for you until you passed over, as the Lord your God did to

up the waters of Jordan from before you, until ye were passed over, as the Lord your God did to the Red sea, which he dried up from before us, until we were gone over:

24 That all the people of the earth might know the hand of the Lord, that it *is* mighty: that ye might fear the Lord your God for ever.

the Red Sea, which he dried up for us until we passed over, 24 so that all the peoples of the earth may know that the hand of the Lord is mighty; that you may fear the Lord your God for ever."

Key Verse: **When your children shall ask their fathers in time to come, saying, What mean these stones? Then ye shall let your children know. (Joshua 4:21-22)**

Key Verse: **"When your children ask their fathers in time to come, 'What do these stones mean?' then you shall let your children know. (Joshua 4:21-22)**

As You Read the Scripture—Harold Reid Weaver

The book of Joshua begins with the death of the beloved leader, Moses. Before his death, that stalwart man of God had named Joshua the new leader of the people (Deuteronomy 31:7). Joshua was a man of heroic proportions, well trained, disciplined, a man of faith and a man of action.

The book of Joshua tells the exciting history of the nation of Israel from around 1250 to 1225 B.C. It was not written by Joshua, any more than were the books of Samuel written by Samuel. The unknown writer wrote the history of that period sometime between 626 and 600 B.C.

The writer was convinced that if Israel was to prosper it must necessarily be faithful to Yahweh. That was the new name for God given by God to Moses (Exodus 3:14). The people now had the laws of Yahweh, and they had pledged themselves in covenant relation with him. If that covenant was not kept, the people could not receive the blessing of the God who requires fidelity in life.

One promise was given by God to Joshua and his people, which is most noteworthy: "As I was with Moses, so I will be with you; I will not fail you or forsake you" (Joshua 1:5*b*). No greater gift could have been bestowed on the people than that. It was what made Moses the great man he was, for God was with him to challenge and guide him.

A major event took place when the order was given by Joshua to move at once across the Jordan. The flowing waters of the Jordan were dammed up on the north side, thus allowing the people to cross over the Jordan on "dry" land. The great event was comparable to the crossing of the Red Sea, when the slaves fled Egypt under Moses' leadership. The Canaanites heard of the event and were in a state of terror, fearing the power and wisdom of Yahweh. What happened? We do not know for sure, of course. But would it detract from the greatness of God's action in history, to believe that natural forces may be used by God for his purposes? It is worth noting that earthquake shocks have been known in Palestine not only in the distant past but in modern history as well. In 1927, such a tremor caused the damming of the Jordan River for twenty-one hours. God, who knows all about geological matters, would of course know that an earthquake was already in the making when Joshua assumed leadership of his people. If God could find a human mind sensitive to the Divine Mind, perhaps such openness might be receptive to the message: "Cross the Jordan River at once!" And cross at once they did.

Joshua 4:1-3. Joshua directed one man from each of the twelve tribes to pick up a heavy stone when passing over the dry riverbed. The stones were carried some distance and used to establish a memorial in Gilgal celebrating the action of God in their behalf.

Joshua 4:21-22. "What do these stones mean?" the children would ask in the future. Joshua knew the importance of remembrance and told his people, "You shall let your children know, 'Israel passed over this Jordan on dry ground.'"

Provocative thought: What stones have we picked up as reminders of our past? Plymouth Rock is one. The bust of Martin Luther King, Jr., as well as the stone statues of Lincoln and Washington help bring grateful thoughts to our minds. These "stones of remembrance" are of immense value, inspiring millions of people.

The Scripture and the Main Question—Pat McGeachy

The Certainty of Change

The one thing you can be certain of in this life is uncertainty. We have heard the expression "the times are a-changing" often enough to think of it almost as a boring truism. And the notion goes back into antiquity; Parmenides said it: "No one steps into the same river twice."

Of course, not all change is good, as some evolutionists insist. (C. S. Lewis said once, "When we encounter change in an egg we call it going bad.") The fittest may ordinarily survive, but sometimes it is the meanest rather than the best. What God's people want is not merely change but *good* change, that is, God's change: the changes that come into our lives with the blessing of God and through which we mature. It requires little or no effort to grow in stature (and you can't hurry it—see Matthew 6:27), but it is a challenge to grow also "in wisdom . . . and in favor with God and humankind" (Luke 2:52; the last Greek word is *anthropois*, the generic term for man).

Sometimes we adults believe that since we have grown up we are through changing, but nothing could be further from the truth. I have heard it suggested that no one should make a final career choice before reaching the age of thirty or so, because one's understanding of life is bound to change. I myself made a radical career change at forty-three and have been grateful ever since, but if you had asked me to predict the future when I was thirty, I would never have guessed where I would be today. (Moreover, certain creaks in my joints are suggesting very strongly that other changes are coming soon.)

I wonder if Joshua and his friends, a few years before our lesson's events, ever speculated about what it would be like when they got to the Promised Land. Joshua already knew a good bit about it, having been one of twelve sent to spy out the country (see Numbers 13–14), but things never turn out exactly the way you think they are going to. I doubt if anyone would have predicted this dramatic river crossing.

Change, even good change, is frightening and makes us uneasy. Psychologists warn us that we can expect emotional difficulty when it happens. If this is true for adults, then anxiety surely trickles down to the children and even the animals in a household. Have you noticed how the family dog can always tell when you are getting ready to go on a trip? Remind me to tell you some time about our dachshund, and how she reacted when we began to make preparations to move to another house!

God and Change

When we remember that God is with us in and through life's passages, we are able to see them in perspective, to rejoice in the good ones, to have strength to endure the tough ones, and in both cases to grow in grace. It helps me to remember that in Hebrew, Joshua's name (which is the same as the Greek name Jesus and a very common one in the Bible) means "God is salvation." When we are in deep waters, it is God who pulls us out. Sometimes it may be that God leads us into such waters with a purpose, as with Joshua. But if we can remember who walks with us through the valley of the shadow and whose rod and staff are there to comfort us, we can face such evils without fear (Psalm 23:3-4; Isaiah 43:1-3).

Rites of Passage

That strange business about the twelve stones at Gilgal (Gilgal means "circle of stones") was what we would call today a rite of passage, that is, a ritual act done as a reminder both to the people themselves and to their descendants. If it seems strange to us, remember that this was before the days of writing, so a rock might be a readier instrument than a pen. Today we might write a song or build a monument to commemorate a transition (I'm thinking of the Vietnam War memorial in Washington as a contemporary example of something put up to help a nation understand its history and deal with its feelings). But in those days, stones seemed to be a common way to memorialize a thing. Do you remember these strange words, all of which have to do with stone monuments?

Bethel (Genesis 28:18-19)
Mizpah (Genesis 33:46-49)
Ebenezer (I Samuel 7:12)

If you check them out, I think you will agree that they all have to do with rites of passage.

We need such rites in our own lives, to give us perspective and keep us honest. Here is a list of secular monuments that have been built or preserved to help the world remember events that have shaped our destiny: any cemetery, with its gravestones; military cemeteries; the battleship Arizona at Pearl Harbor; the Hiroshima memorial; the Wright brothers' monument at Kitty Hawk, N.C.; Mount Rushmore; the Statue of Liberty. What other ones come to your mind?

Some rites of passages do not require a monument to remember them by: birthdays, anniversaries, Mother's Day, Independence Day.

But what about specifically Christian rites of passage? In addition to those mentioned in "The Main Question," you will identify many others: Christmas, Easter, Reformation Sunday, Church School promotion events. Since baptism only occurs once, and often when we are too small to remember it, some churches have begun to follow the practice of having, from time to time, a service of the renewal of baptismal vows, when we remind each other once again how God has brought us (through the water) into a new land and a new life. This is a sort of Gilgal for us, and the baptismal fonts in our churches serve, like the circle of stones, as constant reminders.

But not all rites of passage take place at church. Sometimes the very best are those we do alone or with our families. Let me close by sharing one with you. When I was little, I hated it. Whenever anyone in our family went on a journey, we would all gather at the opened front door, kneel down amid the luggage, and say Psalm 121, because of its closing lines: "The Lord will keep your going out and your coming in from this time forth and for evermore."

I hated it because it was always our father who was going away, because I had to kneel on the cold floor in short pants, and because the neighbors could look in from across the street and see that we were being religious. But then came a day when my bags were packed, and I was on my way, never to return (I was going off to college, and in a way, I never did come back). Again we knelt in the hall and said the old prayer, but this time I understood it: My family was giving me over to God, placing me in the everlasting arms, as if to say, "Lord, we have done all we can do with this young man, now you must take care of him." They were sending me over the Jordan, knowing that the God who was with Moses and Joshua would also be with me.

If you and your family have recently crossed a Jordan or are about to do so, consider creating a rite of passage to help yourselves deal with it. If it is a very significant change you may want to ask the whole congregation or perhaps your pastor to help you plan and carry it out. But in any event, remember that we need ritual in our lives. (If you have ever read a story to a little child and gotten a line wrong, you will know how children want it repeated just so.) And remember the words of the old hymn:

> When through the deep waters I call thee to go,
> The rivers of woe shall not thee overflow;
> For I will be with thee, thy troubles to bless,
> And sanctify to thee thy deepest distress.
> The soul that on Jesus hath leaned for repose,
> I will not, I will not desert to his foes;
> That soul, though all hell should endeavor to shake,
> I'll never, no never, no never forsake.
>   ("How Firm a Foundation")

Helping Adults Become Involved—John Warren Steen

Preparing to Teach

As you begin this thirteen-week study of Joshua, Judges, and Ruth, get an overall view of the quarter's theme. One way to do this is to look up this book's table of contents and glance at the lesson titles and the scriptures covered.

You will do your best study and preparation if you approach your work with a plan for continuity. I suggest that you (1) develop a teaching goal for the quarter, (2) develop a purpose for each unit, and (3) develop an aim for every lesson. If this seems like extra work, think of the alternative: stumbling around without a direction and spending longer at the unorganized job.

FOURTH QUARTER

Consider adopting the following goal for the quarter or develop one of your own: to help class members improve their devotion to God by coming to a new understanding of these Bible accounts of conquest, conflict, and commitment, and from these to discover new ways to show others God's guiding love.

Note that the quarter has three units. Three suggested unit purposes are unit 1 ("Joshua—A Time of Conquest and Settlement")—to help members discover God's gracious leadership and determine to obey his will; unit 2 ("Judges—A Time of Conflict and Adjustment")—to lead members to view their Christian commitment as a response to divine leadership; unit 3 ("Ruth—A Record of Commitment and Hope")—to help class members make a personal commitment to serve God and his children.

Now that you have looked over the suggested goals and unit purposes, move on to the weekly lesson aims. As you move from week to week, consider each suggested aim. If it meets your need, build the lesson around it. If it doesn't meet your specific need, develop an aim of your own. This procedure will help you and the class members to make the best use of discussion time. When they see that the lesson is guided by an aim, they will not want to stray off onto less important subjects.

Most of the lesson aims will encourage a change of attitudes, but three aims (for June 25, August 6, and August 20) will stress a conduct response. Start considering ways to make the action aims understandable and challenging.

My aim for this first lesson is this: to lead members to discover the value of traditions and to find new ways to utilize them. Since this is the first lesson of the quarter, spend some time giving an overall view, as if you were a tour guide telling travelers what to expect in a foreign country.

Try to have a large map showing the route of conquest followed by the newly freed slaves.

Use the following outline:

      I.   Command for memorial given (4:1-3)
     II.   Command for memorial obeyed (4:8, 14-24)
         A. Tribes took stones
         B. Ark moved from Jordan
         C. Stones served purpose

Read carefully "The Scripture and the Main Question" and "As You Read the Scripture." These form the heart of the lesson. The ideas, insights, and suggestions in these sections should be reflected continually in your lesson plan.

As you use the suggested outline, you may want to either quote or paraphrase ideas. You might like to jot in the margin of your outline the page number and paragraph being referred to. For example, you could write a reference to page 65, paragraph 3, as 65-3.

Encourage each person to bring a Bible, to study it during class, and to mark it for furthur study.

Introducing the Main Question

Basic and helpful ideas are presented in the section "The Main Question." These ideas are essential in helping to identify the purpose of the lesson.

To get to the main point about thankfulness for God's guidance, ask: What do you think when you see the words "in remembrance of me"? I was once showing a person through a church, and he saw those words on the communion table and remarked, "A wealthy person must have given this table and wanted to be remembered for it." In a way, he was right. Jesus asked to be remembered for his sacrifice, and he passed along to us a beautiful tradition of remembrance, the Lord's Supper.

Get class members to discuss the word "tradition" and how it has such negative connotations for the young.

Recall the musical *Fiddler on the Roof*. One of its opening songs is about traditions. Every part of village life is governed by traditions, special ways of doing things. These customs have been passed along from one generation to the next without question and are expected to be followed. The whole story revolves around challenges to those customs, when the daughters want to marry.

Traditions can be severe or liberating. They are supposed to make life easier or more godly.

Now come to the main question: Can we remember our victories (as Joshua did in the Jordan crossing) and pass along the insights?

Developing the Lesson

Use Reid Weaver's exegesis to summarize the story up to this point: the appointment of Joshua to take Moses' place and the contents of God's promise (read Joshua 1:5b). After years of wilderness wanderings, it was time for the ex-slaves of Egypt to move into the land that had been promised them.

I. Command for memorial given (4:1-3)

Have someone read 3:15-17, which describes the flooding river turning dry—an echo of the crossing of the Reed Sea some forty years previously. Ask members to comment on the emotions of the participants.

II. Command for memorial obeyed (4:8, 14-24)

A. Tribes took stones

God's command, issued through Joshua, was obeyed. Representatives of each tribe picked up stones and carried them to the place where they encamped. Discuss their anxiety and confidence. The people were armed for battle. They didn't know what they were facing. Their morale strengthened by the crossing, they were ready to ward off the enemy. Invite someone to read verse 14 and to comment on the willingness of the people to follow their leader.

B. Ark moved from Jordan

When the ark left the Jordan, the river returned. Ask: Was the ark magic? No, it represented God's powerful presence.

C. Stones served purpose

The purpose of the stones was a memorial, a reminder. The stones provided a name for the place: Gilgal, "circle of stones."

Leave time for discussion of verse 24. It is important because it sums up the lesson. The verse gives two reasons why God blessed the people with the miracle of the crossing: (1) everyone would recognize the power of God, and (2) God's people would respond "for ever" with reverence to the power of the Almighty.

341

Ask: Do the words "for ever" remind you of words used at the Lord's Supper?

Helping Class Members Act

Divide into groups of twos for the next activity. (Many people will express their opinions to another but not to a group. But if you keep the class together, the activity will still be helpful.) Have members share traditions from their families that would help to remind children and youth of God's goodness. During the discussion, tell of Dr. McGeachy's touching family ritual of placing a departing one in the hands of God. If the rituals center on holiday traditions, bring the discussion back to establishing some new traditions for the rest of the year. List ideas on the chalkboard. Encourage participants to choose three ideas from the list to use in their own homes.

Planning for Next Sunday

Ask for a volunteer to bring the words of the old spiritual "Joshua Fit the Battle of Jericho" to class and to sing or read them. Tell them that even though the next lesson is about Jericho, you plan to deal with the Beatitudes also. Ask members to bring any devotional book they may possess that describes the Beatitudes, and also their Bibles.

LESSON 2   JUNE 11

God Gives Victory

Background Scripture: Joshua 6

The Main Question—Pat McGeachy

Jericho is the oldest fortified city in the world, but it fell, as everyone knows, to a little band of Israelites armed principally with rams' horns. There is no doubt from the clear word of God to Joshua in verse 2 that the success of the enterprise was due to divine, not human, intervention.

Ten years ago, when I accepted a job as urban minister to a large metropolitan area, a friend of mine on the occasion of my installation offered me Joshua 6:16 as a biblical springboard to hope and celebration: "Shout; for the Lord has given you the city!" Whether or not celebration was in order, what has been accomplished in the past decade in this ministry has clearly been brought about by the action of God, not by me or by my friends in ministry. Doors that we would not have thought of have been opened, and avenues of service have surprised us like trumpet blasts, and believe it or not, a few walls have come tumbling down.

Just as God has brought Joshua and his people through the Jordan without their aid, they are now to be given a great victory, simply by obeying their marching orders. The whole story is unlikely. Rahab the harlot is its improbable heroine, and the city's destruction is accomplished "not by might, nor by power, but by my Spirit, says the Lord of hosts" (Zechariah 4:6).

The main question is a simple one, but one that is very hard for most of us to answer with honesty: Where does my security lie? Do I depend upon God for the survival of my nation, or upon technology? Do I put my trust in the Spirit of God or in the spirit of this age? Or, what is perhaps most dangerous of all, am I confusing the two and follow a kind of "praise the Lord and pass the ammunition" path?

To put it in very bald personal terms, which would make you feel more secure, reading the Twenty-third Psalm or reading a bank statement that says you have $10,000 in the bank?

Selected Scripture

King James Version	Revised Standard Version
Joshua 6:1-4, 15-21	*Joshua 6:1-4, 15-21*
1 Now Jericho was straitly shut up because of the children of Israel: none went out, and none came in.	1 Now Jericho was shut up from within and from without because of the people of Israel; none went out, and none came in. 2 And the Lord said to Joshua, "See, I have given into your hand Jericho, with its king and mighty men of valor. 3 You shall march around the city, all the men of war going around the city once. Thus shall you do for six days. 4 And seven priests shall bear seven trumpets of rams' horns before the ark; and on the seventh day you shall march around the city seven times, the priests blowing the trumpets."
2 And the Lord said unto Joshua, See, I have given into thine hand, Jericho, and the king thereof, *and* the mighty men of valour.	
3 And ye shall compass the city, all *ye* men of war, *and* go round about the city once. Thus shalt thou do six days.	
4 And seven priests shall bear before the ark seven trumpets of rams' horns: and the seventh day ye shall compass the city seven times, and the priests shall blow with the trumpets.	
....	....
15 And it came to pass on the seventh day, that they rose early about the dawning of the day, and compassed the city after the same manner seven times: only on that day they compassed the city seven times.	15 On the seventh day they rose early at the dawn of day, and marched around the city in the same manner seven times: it was only on that day they marched around the city seven times. 16 And at the seventh time, when the priests had blown the trumpets, Joshua said to the people, "Shout; for the Lord has given you the city. 17 And the city and all that is within it shall be devoted to the Lord for destruction; only Rahab the harlot and all who are with her in her house shall live,
16 And it came to pass at the seventh time, when the priests blew with the trumpets, Joshua said unto the people, Shout; for the Lord hath given you the city.	
17 And the city shall be accursed, *even* it, and all that *are* therein, to the	

Lord: only Rahab the harlot shall live, she and all that *are* with her in the house, because she hid the messengers that we sent.

18 And ye, in any wise, keep *yourselves* from the accursed thing, lest ye make *yourselves* accursed, when ye take of the accursed thing, and make the camp of Israel a curse, and trouble it.

19 But all the silver, and gold, and vessels of brass and iron, *are* consecrated unto the Lord: they shall come into the treasury of the Lord.

20 So the people shouted when *the priests* blew with the trumpets: and it came to pass, when the people heard the sound of the trumpet, and the people shouted with a great shout, that the wall fell down flat, so that the people went up into the city, every man straight before him, and they took the city.

21 And they utterly destroyed all that *was* in the city, both man and woman, young and old, and ox, and sheep, and ass, with the edge of the sword.

because she hid the messengers that we sent. 18 But you, keep yourselves from the things devoted to destruction, lest when you have devoted them you take any of the devoted things and make the camp of Israel a thing for destruction, and bring trouble upon it. 19 But all silver and gold, and vessels of bronze and iron, are sacred to the Lord; they shall go into the treasury of the Lord." 20 So the people shouted, and the trumpets were blown. As soon as the people heard the sound of the trumpet, the people raised a great shout, and the wall fell down flat, so that the people went up into the city, every man straight before him, and they took the city. 21 Then they utterly destroyed all in the city, both men and women, young and old, oxen, sheep, and asses, with the edge of the sword.

Key Verse: **The Lord said unto Joshua, See, I have given into thine hand Jericho, and the King thereof, and the mighty men of valour. (Joshua 6:2)**

Key Verse: **The Lord said to Joshua, "See, I have given into your hand Jericho, with its king and mighty men of valor." (Joshua 6:2)**

As You Read the Scripture—Harold Reid Weaver

Jericho was the first city to be captured by Israel as it moved westward beyond the Jordan. The city's double walls securely guarded the harvest that had been stored within. The cisterns had been filled with water. The city was ready, and yet it was not ready. Fear, near panic, was crippling its psychological readiness for battle. What kind of a God is this Yahweh, who can dam a river so his people can cross over safely?

Joshua waited a few days before leading the people into battle. During that time the first Passover in Canaan was celebrated. A feeling of great joy must have bloomed among the people as they took the unleavened bread (Joshua 5:10-12) and thanked Yahweh that their fathers and grandfathers had been chosen to gain freedom from slavery in Egypt. Now they were actually in the Promised Land—or at least, at a bridgehead.

Joshua 6:6-14. Joshua called the priests together and advised them about battle procedures. All Jews would walk around the city of Jericho just once, on the first day, then return to the camp. The ordinary people would not walk as a noisy, undisciplined rabble, but in silence. They would follow behind the priests, who would carry the ark of God's presence, and seven of them would blow ram's horns as they walked. In front of the priests would be a vanguard of fighting men. Behind the people would follow a protective rear guard of soldiers. This pattern maneuver was performed for six days.

Joshua 6:16-21. On the seventh day Joshua issued a new directive. Everyone walked around the city seven times. The ram's horns were blown by the seven priests, as usual. The military marched in vanguard and rear-guard, as before. On the seventh circuit, Joshua cried out to the people, "Shout, for the Lord has given you the city" (verse 16). Having kept silence for seven days, at the word from Joshua they roared, and the walls came tumbling down (verse 20).

Archeological excavations have verified that Jericho was leveled around 1225 B.C. The outer walls fell downward on the slope of the hill of the city, while the inner, stronger wall crumbled. It was as though another earthquake had leveled the walls and made it possible for the Hebrews to overrun the city.

Verses 17-18. Joshua told the people that the "spoils of war" should be dealt with in a special way. Rahab the harlot and her family were not to be harmed, but all other living things were to be destroyed.

Most of us feel uneasy with the total destruction of Jericho's inhabitants and buildings. Such violence jolts a Christian conscience. The word "devotion" meant one thing three thousand years ago, but something else to us. We speak of devoted persons as dedicated, loyal, faithful in loving service to God and his people. Devotion in Joshua's time meant a special way of giving everything to God and keeping nothing back. Devotion meant total destruction of the city and the murder of all its creatures.

It is necessary for us to see the limitations within which the Hebrews lived at that time. Hosea had not yet spoken about forgiving love, nor Jeremiah about a new covenant of the heart. Joshua and his soldiers did what they thought at that time was the will of God. It is fruitless to wish they might have had the correction of later biblical writers and especially the admonitions of Jesus to love. It would be centuries before the words would come, "Thou shalt love thine enemies."

The Scripture and the Main Question—Pat McGeachy

True Security

We are always pursuing happiness, as is our constitutional right, but we often look for it in the wrong places. Jesus taught clearly that the world's notion of where to find security is upside down. The world says that you must cling to your life with every ounce of your energy, but Jesus says that you are to turn loose of it (Luke 9:24-25)! In his famous list of rules for happiness, which we call the Beatitudes (Matthew 5:1-12), there is a clear contrast between what the world believes and what Jesus teaches:

The World	Jesus
Happy are those who believe in themselves.	Happy are the poor in spirit.

FOURTH QUARTER

Happy are those who laugh.	Happy are those who mourn.
Happy are those who toot their own horn.	Happy are the meek.
Happy are the well fed and satisfied.	Happy are those who hunger and thirst for righteousness.
Happy are those who give people what they deserve.	Happy are the merciful.
Happy are those who look the part.	Happy are the pure in heart.
Happy are those with plenty of ammunition.	Happy are the peacemakers.
Happy are those who are comfortable.	Happy are the persecuted.
Happy are those who are spoken well of.	Happy are those who are reviled.

I can't speak for anybody but myself, but I am honestly afraid that much of the time I go through life as though the list on the left were the one to be followed. I *feel better* knowing that I have some money in an IRA. It makes me glad to be well fed and prosperous. I have a hard time taking Jesus' upside-down view of the world seriously. But do I dare do otherwise?

Do you remember an old joke, popular during World War II, about Moses and the Red Sea? It seems that a little boy was asked by his mother to tell what he had learned in Sunday School. He related how the children of Israel were fleeing the Pharaoh's hosts and found themselves trapped on the bank of the Red Sea. "But," he related, "Moses called for the Seabees and they put up a pontoon bridge. Then, as soon as they were across, he called out the Air Force and they bombed the bridge, and the Egyptians who were trying to cross on it were all drowned."

"Are you sure," asked the mother, "that is what you were told?"

"Well," he replied, "maybe not exactly, but if I told you what they really told me you never would have believed me."

Quite so. And most of us, given a thoughtful military appraisal of the situation, have a hard time believing the story of the fabled walls of Jericho. Could they really have been brought down by seven days of marching feet, a shout, and the sound of a few trumpets?

But do not forget that there was one additional item in the parade, above and beyond the marchers with their horns: the ark of the covenant (Joshua 6:6-9). The word "ark" simply means "a box" or "a container." (Noah's boat was called an ark because it was built like a box.) It contained the stone tablets of the Law (the Ten Commandments). It was, in other words, the symbol of the presence of an ethical God in the midst of God's people. There was nothing magical about the ark. The secret of its power can be said in plain language: "Trust God and put the Law of God first, and you will be victorious." Or, if you prefer Jesus' words, "Seek first [God's] kingdom and

346

[God's] righteousness and all these things shall be yours as well" (Matthew 6:33).

Christian Aggression

In spite of some recent controversy over the militarism in some of our best-loved hymns, the truth is that "spiritual warfare" is a fairly common biblical metaphor for the Christian life. See, for instance, Hebrewq 11:33; Ephesians 6:10-17 (note that this verse speaks of a *spiritual* conflict, not a physical one); I Timothy 6:12. My favorite image of the Christian at war with the powers of darkness is Matthew 16:18. Immediately after Peter's great confession of faith, Jesus announces that he will build a church and says (KJV) that "the gates of hell shall not prevail against it." For some reason, when I first heard those words (as a boy) I heard them backwards (just as any child of the world hears Jesus upside-down). I thought that the Lord was picturing an attack on heaven or the human soul, and that we, having the keys, could lock the demons out so that they would never prevail against us. But it says the opposite! It is hell that is under attack in Jesus' image! We are to sally forth from the pearly gates and, secure in our confidence in Christ, are to go after the powers of darkness with the expectation that we will win!

When Christian (the hero in Bunyan's *Pilgrim's Progress*) is armed for battle against Appolyon (the devil), his armor is only on the front, not the back; he is to march bravely forth to meet the foe, but never to turn and run. Thus we are aggressively to attack Jericho! We are to lay hold of life with gusto and expectation. We are not to be pacifists in the sense of being passive. Rather, we are to be peacemakers, lovers of peace, those who stand up for the right and shout because the Lord has given us the city to conquer in the Divine Name.

We are boldly to rescue Rahab the harlot and discover that she is to become part of the divine lineage of the Christ (Matthew 1:5; check also the reputations of the next four women in that list!) We are to go forth into spiritual combat, with our equivalent of the ark of the covenant, that is, the cross of Jesus, going on before. We are to sound the trumpets in the audacious expectation that the walls will come down.

The Dividing Wall

And indeed the walls have come down. For Christ is "our peace, who has made us both one, and has broken down the dividing wall of hostility" (Ephesians 2:14). That wall is the one separating Jew and Gentile, the old enmity that predates the battle of Jericho and continues in the Middle East in our time. It is also the wall separating liberal and conservative, heart-centered and head-centered Christians, high church and low. The wall is already down—no wonder all it takes is a trumpet to make that obvious!

The task, in other words, of the contemporary Joshua is to go boldly against the gates of darkness, to shout gladly that the walls are already down, and to begin to treat everyone as one for whom Christ has died and with whom he has become forever reconciled. We are to live by those weird, unworldly rules called the Beatitudes, to blow not out own horns but the trumpets of God, and to live in relationship with all the world as though the victory had already been won.

Because, of course, it has (see I Corinthians 15:57). It only remains for the world to recognize this fact. The walls (security) that the world raises are an illusion at best, and a false god that destroys at worst. Our walls, our arms, our money, our prestige cannot save us, but they do possess the power to lead us astray, and in the end to do us in. The walls, if we trust in them, will fall on us.

But if we trust in God and in the might of the divine arm (Isaiah 63:5; Psalm 98:1), then our money, our power, our strength, even our nuclear might, can be turned into power for changing the shape of the earth, if not the universe. All of us together in our own strength are lost; but God plus one constitutes a majority. That one is Jesus, the latterday Joshua, whose name, whose teachings, and whose life all congruently proclaim that God is salvation, and there is no other.

But it is so tempting to hide behind the might of America or of Jericho and to believe that we are secure. It is hard to be a patriotic Christian without confusing faith in God with faith in the motherland. But that is the way with false gods; the closer they are to being right, the more dangerous they become. May God give us the humility of Joshua, that we may choose ultimately to serve not the false but the true.

Helping Adults Become Involved—John Warren Steen

Preparing to Teach

This is a difficult lesson, and you will need an extra amount of preparation time. The lesson raises questions about violence in Old Testament times that you and your students will need to understand.

Prepare to center your lesson on a debate about Joshua and the destruction of Jericho. Prepare yourself to offer help to either side. Ask for volunteers for the debate at the beginning of class.

Before Sunday, duplicate the two-column list of Beatitudes in Dr. McGeachy's "The Scripture and the Main Question." Look up recent books on the Beatitudes and bring your own report on them.

Consider using the following teaching aim: The class will be able to list three reasons for the Jericho account being included in the Bible, and will understand where security truly lies.

Use the following outline:

     I. Preparing for victory (6:1-4).
       A. Jericho besieged.
       B. God gives a plan.
    II. Achieving the victory (6:15-21).
       A. Seven times, seven days.
       B. Destruction except for Rahab.

Read carefully "The Scripture and the Main Question" and "As You Read the Scripture." These form the heart of the lesson. The ideas, insights, and suggestions in these sections should be reflected continually in your lesson plan.

As you use the suggested outline, you may want to either quote or paraphrase ideas. You might like to jot in the margin of your outline the page number and paragraph being referred to. For example, you could write a reference to page 65, paragraph 3, as 65-3.

Introducing the Main Question

Basic and helpful ideas are presented in the section "The Main Question." These ideas are essential in helping to identify the purpose of the lesson.

Ask the question posed by Dr. McGeachy: What would give you more security, to read a statement on your bank account or to read Psalm 23?

Developing the Lesson

Last Sunday you dealt with the crossing of the Jordan. Build a bridge of continuity to the present study by asking: How did the migrating Hebrews begin their life in the new land? Review Joshua 5: The people circumcise their men again to show their dedication to following God's will (verses 1-9). Passover is observed (verse 10); manna ceases to fall, since there is no need of miraculous feeding in the Promised Land (verses 11-12); and Joshua has a vision (verse 13).

The Hebrews reinstituted the ceremony of circumcision, which had neither been possible nor seemed necessary in the wilderness wanderings. They kept the Passover, recalling the story of their slavery, release, and gratitude. They were ready to settle down, but all the fortified hilltops and places with a water supply had already been taken. They believed it was God's will for them to seize towns from their enemies.

Have two people debate about the destruction of Jericho. Bring out this point: the command to wage war seemed to come from God; but innocent people were to be killed.

Ask last week's volunteer to read or sing the words of the spiritual, "Joshua Fit the Battle of Jericho." Ask how the song helped the people who sang it.

Bring out points about the Bible lesson expressed below that add to the points made during the debate and the discussion of the song.

I. Preparing for victory (6:1-4).
  A. Jericho besieged.
Note the setting of the story. Ask what emotions the inhabitants of Jericho would have experienced after learning of the miraculous crossing of the Jordan and the invasion of the migrating people.

The citizens sought security behind their walls. They probably had a secret water supply and had laid in stores of food to endure a siege.
  B. God gives a plan.
Instructions were to march around the city walls once each day for six days. The Hebrews' quietness and discipline would further terrify the inhabitants of the town.

Have someone read 6:4, emphasizing the word "seven," which occurs four times. That number was sacred to the people of Israel. It emphasized the completion of creation and the perfection of all things connected with it.

II. Achieving the victory (6:15-21).
  A. Seven times, seven days.
Then, on the seventh day and the seventh circuit, the priests with the rams' horns (shofars) blew them. The silent people, like the hungry craving a feast, expressed themselves in a shout of victory. The noise and the celebration brought the walls of the fortified city down.

God had given the people an unusual procedure, used nowhere else. This was not a technique for conquering every city but a lesson in trusting their Deliverer, even in unlikely circumstances.

B. Destruction except for Rahab.

Total destruction took place because God commanded that no spoils were to be taken. All was to be devoted to God (Yahweh), who had given the victory. Only Rahab and her household were spared.

Have someone read Joshua 6:27. Help the class to see that the effect of the miracle was to demoralize the inhabitants of Canaan. Such an advantage made much of the conquest less difficult.

On the chalkboard, list some reasons for including this account in the Bible: (1) to show how the people depended on God for security, (2) to understand how Rahab the harlot became a part of the divine lineage of the Savior (Matthew 1:5), and (3) to observe the reality of progressive revelation (recalling that Joshua's people didn't have the ethical teaching of the prophets or the divine teachings of Jesus; they did what they thought was God's will).

Helping Class Members Act

Ask about the dilemma of people in Third World countries today, struggling for their freedom. Although some of their leaders encourage nonviolence, many say that nonviolence will never bring freedom. Ask class members to recall the American Revolution and to contemplate what decisions they would have made then about bearing arms to secure freedom.

Point out the ambiguities of war, recalling the statement Reinhold Niebuhr made during World War II, that the Christian church could never be pacifistic. America and the allies chose the lesser of two evils; fighting in the war seemed less serious than allowing the free world to be conquered.

Distribute copies of the parallel list of Beatitudes appearing in "The Scripture and the Main Question," or write them on the chalkboard. Discuss them one by one. Ask for examples from both columns. Show how the first column's attitudes fit in with the "'me' generation" idea. Show how Jesus' words might seem ridiculous on the surface but can bring lasting peace.

Conclude with this example from nature: Sometimes when a hawk is attacked by smaller birds, it will not fight back. Its superior wings give it the confidence to circle higher and fly beyond the range of the pestering birds. In a similar way, the Christian does not have to retaliate when attacked. The believer can mount up on wings of patience and love, discovering God's security, which far surpasses the worlds cherished weapons and money.

Planning for Next Sunday

Next week's lesson, "Settlement of the Promised Land," will discuss the demands of freedom in the Promised Land. Bring present-day illustrations of people faced with the demands of maintaining freedom.

Settlement of the Promised Land

Background Scripture: Joshua 18:1-10; 21:43—22:6

The Main Question—Pat McGeachy

I live on a farm. It is not a very productive farm (mostly I raise rocks and cedar trees), but it is not the same piece of deserted land that it was a few years ago. There's a thousand-foot well, a road, a willow tree, some spruces at the top of the drive, and a house with a new deck on it. Frankly, it has been a lot of trouble, most of which my children know nothing about. But it has been worth it! And as I rest, sassy and fat, looking back, I am tempted to say, "Look what I have done!" My children, who did none of the work involved, may, if they are not thoughtful or if I do not remind them, tend to think that this is just "the way things are." But I and my family must all remember the main question and its answer: How did we come to be where we are?

God gave us this land. Americans live in a land not of our own making. Like the Promised Land, it used to belong to someone else. It has always belonged to God (Psalm 24:1). Our presence here is a gift, and from time to time, we must rest from our labors and remember how we came to be where we are.

Of course, we *have* done a lot of the work ourselves! As the old farmer said, "You ought to have seen this land when the Lord had it all by himself!" There is a rightful pride to be taken in a job well done, and there are times when we ought to rest and rejoice. But we must never forget our heritage, on pain of losing it.

Everyone who lives in freedom must be prepared to accept the responsibilities that freedom demands. The land must be properly apportioned, we must share the duties and the responsibilities, and we must be vigilant to defend our freedoms. But not "eternally" vigilant—God alone is eternal, and from time to time, all we need to do is enjoy our hard-earned heritage. But let us never forget that, hard-earned though it may be, it is a heritage, a gift, from God.

Selected Scripture

King James Version

Revised Standard Version

Joshua 21:43-45

43 And the Lord gave unto Israel all the land which he sware to give unto their fathers; and they possessed it, and dwelt therein.

44 And the Lord gave them rest round about, according to all that he sware unto their fathers: and there stood not a man of all their enemies before them; the Lord delivered all their enemies unto their hand.

Joshua 21:43-45

43 Thus the Lord gave to Israel all the land which he swore to give to their fathers; and having taken possession of it, they settled there. 44 And the Lord gave them rest on every side just as he had sworn to their fathers; not one of all their enemies had withstood them, for the Lord had given all their enemies into their hands. 45 Not one of all

45 There failed not ought of any good thing which the Lord had spoken unto the house of Israel; all came to pass.

Joshua 22:1-6

1 Then Joshua called the Reubenites, and the Gadites, and the half tribe of Ma-nas'-seh,

2 And said unto them, Ye have kept all that Moses the servant of the Lord commanded you, and have obeyed my voice in all that I commanded you:

3 Ye have not left your brethren these many days unto this day, but have kept the charge of the commandment of the Lord your God.

4 And now the Lord your God hath given rest unto your brethren, as he promised them: therefore now return ye, and get you unto your tents, *and* unto the land of your possession, which Moses the servant of the Lord gave you on the other side of Jordan.

5 But take diligent heed to do the commandment and the law, which Moses the servant of the Lord charged you, to love the Lord your God, and to walk in all his ways, and to keep his commandments, and to cleave unto him, and to serve him with all your heart and with all your soul.

6 So Joshua blessed them, and sent them away: and they went unto their tents.

Key Verse: And the Lord gave unto Israel all the land which he sware to give unto their fathers; and they possessed it, and dwelt therein. (Joshua 21:43)

the good promises which the Lord had made to the house of Israel had failed; all came to pass.

Joshua 22:1-6

1 Then Joshua summoned the Reubenites, and the Gadites, and the half-tribe of Manas'seh, 2 and said to them, "You have kept all that Moses the servant of the Lord commanded you, and have obeyed my voice in all that I have commanded you; 3 you have not forsaken your brethren these many days, down to this day, but have been careful to keep the charge of the Lord your God. 4 And now the Lord your God has given rest to your brethren, as he promised them; therefore turn and go to your home in the land where your possession lies, which Moses the servant of the Lord gave you on the other side of the Jordan. 5 Take good care to observe the commandment and the law which Moses the servant of the Lord commanded you, to love the Lord your God, and to walk in all his ways, and to keep his commandments, and to cleave to him, and to serve him with all your heart and with all your soul." 6 So Joshua blessed them, and sent them away; and they went to their homes.

Key Verse: Thus the Lord gave to Israel all the land which he swore to give to their fathers; and having taken possession of it, they settled there. (Joshua 21:43)

As You Read the Scripture—Harold Reid Weaver

Our last lesson dealt with the capture of Jericho. This lesson takes place forty-five years later. Much of the Promised Land has now been taken by military force. Thousands of people have been killed, towns looted, and property destroyed. Gold and silver, as well as sheep, goats, and cattle, have been confiscated by the Hebrews. The people are called by Joshua to settle down, build homes, farm the land around the towns which Joshua assigned to the tribes, and learn to live a new life-style. The Hebrews are to remain the faithful, covenanted people of the Lord.

Joshua 21:43. This verse is a bit optimistic, for it says, "The Lord gave to Israel all the land which he swore to give to their fathers; and having taken possession of it, they settled there." Actually, not all of the land had been captured. Note the words the Lord had said to Joshua, "You are old and advanced in years, and there remains yet very much to be possessed" (13:1); there follows an awesome list of lands yet to be conquered. But the writer of Joshua sees with the eyes of faith that the land will be captured in the future, and counts it as actualized in the present.

Joshua 22:1-6. Joshua calls the tribes (Reubenites, Gadites, and the half-tribe of Manasseh) together and assigns them to their share of land, on the eastern side of the Jordan. It had already been given to these tribes by Moses (Deuteronomy 3:12-20). Moses had ordered their fighting men to leave their wives, children, and cattle and follow Joshua when he crossed the Jordan with the Israelites. Joshua now thanks the two and a half tribes for their faithful obedience and sacrifices over the many years. "You have not forsaken your brethren these many days, down to this day [which, we might note in parenthesis, was an incredible forty-five years later] but have been careful to keep the charge of the Lord your God" (verse 3). Joshua exhorts them to live faithful lives.

Verses 5-6 are as beautiful a summary of the faith as could have been expressed in those days. Joshua admonished them "to love the Lord your God, and to walk in all his ways, and to keep his commandments, and to cleave to him, and to serve him with all your heart and all your soul." These words echo Jesus' answer to the question, What is the greatest commandment? "Hear, O Israel: The Lord our God, the Lord is one; and you shall love the Lord your God with all your heart, and with all your soul, and with all your mind, and with all your strength" (Mark 12:29-30).

And then Jesus added the words, "You shall love your neighbor as yourself" (Mark 12:31). With these words Jesus disclosed the highest revelation of God's will. It is not in killing others in order to get ahead that we find the will of God, but in loving God and all our neighbors as we love ourselves. Love is the key. Now, its an open secret that the name "Joshua" is equivalent to "Jesus." Which Jesus are we called to follow? The one who slaughtered his enemies or the one who gave himself in self-giving love? Jesus took Joshua's sword and, figuratively, plunged the blade in the ground, leaving only the crosslike hilt to be seen. Then allowed himself to be killed on that cross, that others might live. Joshua himself will say in our next lesson, "Choose ye this day which ye will serve."

The Scripture and the Main Question—Pat McGeachy

Apportioning the Land

Things don't just "happen." I had a bit part once in an amateur play production whose director had had only modest experience in teaching people how to act. Whenever a bunch of us on stage were supposed to move to a new location, or change our stance to look at the focus of the action from a new perspective, she did not know how to tell us what to do. She would simply shout at us, "Adjust! Adjust!" Well, life isn't like that. Maybe professional actors know how to adjust, but most of us need to be told: "You go stand there on that X."

And when a nation of people settle into a new country, a lot of work has to be done. There are borders to be drawn, and "turf" needs to be identified. There is nothing fancy about this. It is no more than occupying "room assignments" on the first day of school, or on moving into a new home. But it has to be done. All human institutions require administration. I think we wish they didn't. We'd like to do without government telling us to fasten our seat belts, or otherwise infringing on our liberties. But liberty means, in this world at least, living in a kind of relationship with others, meshed like gears so that the job can get done. A wonderful description of the church made in Ephesians 4:15-16: "Speaking the truth in love, we are to grow up in every way into him who is the head, into Christ, from whom the whole body, joined and knit together by every joint with which it is supplied, when each part is working properly, makes bodily growth and upbuilds itself in love."

I'm not a very good administrator. I often wish people would just "adjust." Sometimes, things do sort of come out in the wash. But my farm didn't get to look like it does merely by "adjusting." Planning and hard work went into it, as it does in every worthwhile human endeavor.

Some parts of the Bible (like all administrative tasks) seem very dull. It's not very interesting to read Joshua 18–21, with its dry statistics and its long list of unpronounceable names. I felt that way about history books when I was going formally (formerly) to school. But today, as I look back on the history of the world in general, and my country in particular, I know that it was not merely a collection of dull facts; it was a living, breathing *happening*. You might as well say that breathing in and out is boring, as to say that history is dull. This very moment is history, and precious; let's not pass by it without stopping to smell the flowers.

Here's one of the flowers: A committee of twenty-one was formed from the seven tribes that had not yet received their assignment of land (see 18:4). One of the first things you have to do in a new country is "take stock" of things. There is an old carpenter's adage: Figure three times; measure twice; cut once. We could overcome a lot of grief if we did a better job of drawing plans and laying things out. Wasn't George Washington a surveyor?

A vision both of unity and diversity is necessary if a nation is not to perish from the earth. Think of your own family's history. Do you know of any plans made by your forebears which affect your life today? Did somebody sail from a foreign shore? One of my ancestors left the grubby soil of Argyleshire, which would no longer support all the members of his parents' family, and built the first plank house in a new county in North Carolina. A few months ago I stood at his grave on the old place and wondered at his courage and vision.

Take Five

Fortunately, we are not required to spend all our time drawing plans and sharpening pencils. History consists not merely of planning but of living! It has been said that planning the journey is more fun than getting there. But if that were true (and known to be true), why would we ever go anywhere? We'd just sit around and plan. There comes a time when we are to quit planning and just rest. Read again Joshua 22:1-6.

Note that this is not to be *irresponsible* rest. We are to "take good care to observe the commandment and the law which Moses" ordered (22:5), to "love God and walk in his ways," and to serve God with our whole being. But we are also meant to enjoy the land.

Perhaps it is the fault of my Scottish ancestry, but I'm afraid not all the planning that went into my history was wholesome. I was taught so much about the importance of the work ethic and of sound business sense that I have a hard time relaxing and enjoying the world that my stewardship (and the Lord's and my forebears') has brought into being. I hope you are not so afflicted. As a hopeless workaholic, I long for a tenth Beatitude: "Blessed are they that don't take their job too seriously, for they will occasionally get a vacation."

Breathing

As I look back on the two things we have just emphasized, I see clearly that they are almost opposites:
— Plan carefully and work hard to preserve your liberty.
— Relax and enjoy what you have been given.
But they are not really opposites, they are two sides of a healthy life, a breathing in and a breathing out. I might extend this comparison in parallel columns to drive home the point:

The land is the free gift of God.	I have to work hard to maintain it.
We must plan carefully.	But some things will be decided for us (by lot? Joshua 18:6).
Everybody must take a fair share of the inheritance.	But we must look out for those who have nothing, like the Levites (Joshua 18:7).
We must not be slack, but get to work (Joshua 18:3).	Be sure to stop and get some rest (Joshua 22:4).
Enjoy!	Don't forget God's rules (Joshua 22:5).
Don't forget that God gave you this land (Joshua 21:43).	But you can't stay in church all week. Go home! (Joshua 22:6).

All this healthy inhaling and exhaling is possible because God's grace surrounds us with love; God is the eternal keeper of promises (Joshua 21:45). We should make joyful noises because the divine love and mercy lasts forever. The favor of God is to all generations (Psalm 100). Would it be appropriate for your family, your church, and your nation to say this from time to time? In my church we try to say it to each other every Lord's day, in the hopes that the healthy rhythm of the spiritual life, like that of nature—seedtime and harvest (Genesis 8:22)—shall not cease.

Helping Adults Become Involved—John Warren Steen

Preparing to Teach

This Sunday you will deal with case histories, quotations, and a penetrating opening question. These should lend variety to your Bible study. Work in advance to make these various parts come together in a unified whole.

Write out on separate slips of paper the following seven quotations on success. You will be using them as topics of discussions.

1. "Success, remember, is the reward of toil." —Sophocles

2. "If you want to succeed you should strike out on new paths rather than travel the worn paths of accepted success."—Rockefeller

3. "I believe the true road to pre-eminent success in any line is to make yourself master of that line."—Andrew Carnegie

4. "If you wish to succeed, consult three old people."—Chinese adage

5. "It is wise to keep in mind that neither success nor failure is ever final."—Roger Babson

6. "Six essential qualities that are the key to success: sincerity, personal integrity, humility, courtesy, wisdom, charity."—Dr William Menninger

Being modern, class members should have little trouble identifying with people who have struggled up the hill of success and are then tempted to coast down the other side. Some may have lived through the Depression. Others may have had to struggle through college or graduate school. Still others might still be struggling with a meager job and salary.

Consider using the following teaching aim: Class members will be able to articulate their own definitions of Christian success.

Use the following outline:

    I.   Remaining territory surveyed and divided (18:1-10)
   II. Conquest concluded (21:43-45)
  III. Tribes blessed and dismissed (22:1-6)
       A. Faithfulness recognized
       B. Reward of rest and home
       C. Advised to keep the Law
       D. Dismissed

Read carefully "The Scripture and the Main Question" and "As You Read the Scripture." These form the heart of the lesson. The ideas, insights, and suggestions in these sections should be reflected continually in your lesson plan.

As you use the suggested outline, you may want to either quote or paraphrase ideas. You might like to jot in the margin of your outline the

page number and paragraph being referred to. For example, you could write a reference to page 65, paragraph 3, as 65-3.

Introducing the Main Question

Basic and helpful ideas are presented in the section "The Main Question." These ideas are essential in helping to identify the purpose of the lesson.

The main question is this: How did we come to be where we are? Of course, the question implies that we have not accomplished our present positions by our own talents or by getting what we deserve. Actually, the question suggests God's providence and grace. Ask the class members if they agree.

Ask: How did we get here today? Some might answer, by family car or by the church van. Others might take a more philosophical approach and talk about ancestors or receiving the land from immigrant forebears. The important idea is to see that people feel helpless when they have no land, but they feel an importance and a stability when they have some property to call their own. Minority groups feel this way today; most of them resent renting and look forward to the time when they can own a piece of property.

Developing the Lesson

I. Remaining territory surveyed and divided (18:1-10)

The ancient Hebrew people felt the same way. Coming out of slavery, they yearned for a land of their own—a land to cultivate, a land to give them stability and to supplant their nomadic way of life, a land to pass along to their progeny.

Have members recall the movie scene where Scarlett O'Hara returned to Tara and knelt down and ate some of the dirt in gratitude. A feeling of belonging is an integral part of success.

Summarize the background passage, Joshua 18:1-10. Tell how the tribes gathered at Shiloh (in the central hill country about ten miles north of Bethel). Joshua scolded them for not taking possession of what God had given. He sent out three surveyors from each tribe to describe the land for the final division. Notice the use of sacred lots to apportion the land.

II. Conquest concluded (21:43-45)

Remind the class that this scene takes place some four and a half decades after the conquest of Jericho.

Have someone read Deuteronomy 3:12-20. Moses had apportioned the land and had ordered fighting men to leave their families to follow Joshua. They had obeyed.

Have the class read in unison the beautiful words of 21:45 about all the good promise coming to pass.

III. Tribes blessed and dismissed (22:1-6).

A. Faithfulness recognized

Ask the effect on the tribes of Joshua's complimentary words in 22:2-3. Wouldn't any soldier burst with pride to hear such a compliment from his general?

B. *Reward of rest and home*

The result of all these years of hard work is rest in a new home. The two words "rest" and "home" are beautiful in other languages as well.

C. *Advised to keep the Law*

Then a word of advice was necessary. Ask the class to evaluate whether the advice was legalistic or loving.

Verse 5 ends with the challenge "Serve him with all your heart and with all your soul." Ask the class if they can remember whether similar words can be found in the New Testament. They are quite similar to Jesus' challenging command in Mark 12:29-30. Have this place marked in your Bible so that you can read it aloud with feeling. Point out the similarities between Joshua and Jesus, starting with their having the same name (although it looks different in English).

D. *Dismissed*

Point out on a map the destinations of the tribes on the eastern side of the Jordan.

Helping Class Members Act

Divide the class into groups and distribute to them one or more of the quotations on success that you have written down. Ask the class to discuss their adequacy as guides for Christians. Have members suggest their own success mottos. List them on the chalkboard.

Someone once asked a cook how he made such good pound cake. He answered, "Put plenty in it." This recipe also applies to life. The people who work hard to help others seem happier than the ones who are interested in getting what they can out of life.

The most dangerous time in life, many people claim, is when they have achieved success. Ask why. Isn't it because people tend to congratulate themselves in a self-centered fashion and forget about God's guiding providence? Isn't it also because they tend to slow down, to rest on their laurels?

Ask members what is behind the advertising campaign of the car rental people who claim they are Number Two. Does it suggest that they try harder than the one that is in first position? Ask if they know individuals or churches that have reached success and then quit trying.

In a time of dedication, invite class members to bow their heads and thank God for guidance and blessings. Invite them to pledge their allegiance to God's will.

Planning for Next Sunday

Ask the class to start thinking of any false gods they worship.

If there is time left, invite some discussion on the idea of choices. Promise to complete the discussion at the next class session.

Life Is Shaped by Choices

Background Scripture: Joshua 24

The Main Question—Pat McGeachy

"Not to decide is to decide." I think it was Albert Camus who said that, but Joshua put it to his people long before that. We have to make up our minds. If there is anything that makes God sick to the stomach, it is indecisive, dishwater Christians. (If that seems an offensive way to put it, check Revelation 3:16.) To put it more gently, think of the Old Sailor, a lovable character in one of A. A. Milne's poems. He could never decide what to do next for survival,

> And so in the end he did nothing at all,
> But basked on the shingle wrapped up in a shawl.
> And I think it was dreadful the way he behaved—
> He did nothing but basking until he was saved!

For many of us, life is like that. We bounce from one preoccupation to another, without any real sense of purpose to what we do, *re*-acting rather than acting.

Joshua challenged the young nation to make a faith decision. "Choose this day whom you will serve!" he cried, demanding that they either become honest pagans and go after the Canaanite gods with which they had been flirting, or take a moral and ethical stance with the God of Mount Sinai and the Ten Commandments.

"Sin boldly," Martin Luther once wrote, because he knew that one who faced the honest truth about him- or herself would be more likely to boldly choose the moral route. The supreme example of this in the New Testament is Saul of Tarsus, raging against Christ with every fiber of his being until he was struck down on the Damascus highway. There God took his bold enmity and transformed it into missionary zeal.

This main question is as clear as any in the Bible: Make up your mind—do you belong to God or not? The way in which you and I answer this question will shape our lives and the life of the community around us for all the years to come.

Selected Scripture

King James Version

Joshua 24:14-22, 26-27

14 Now therefore fear the Lord, and serve him in sincerity and in truth: and put away the gods which your fathers served on the other side of the flood, and in Egypt; and serve ye the Lord.

15 And if it seem evil unto you to

Revised Standard Version

Joshua 24:14-22, 26-27

14 "Now therefore fear the Lord, and serve him in sincerity and in faithfulness; put away the gods which your fathers served beyond the River, and in Egypt, and serve the Lord. 15 And if you be unwilling to serve the Lord, choose this day

serve the Lord, choose you this day whom ye will serve; whether the gods which your fathers served that *were* on the other side of the flood, or the gods of the Amorites, in whose land ye dwell; but as for me and my house, we will serve the Lord.

16 And the people answered and said, God forbid that we should forsake the Lord, to serve other gods;

17 For the Lord our God, he *it is* that brought us up and our fathers out of the land of Egypt, from the house of bondage, and which did those great signs in our sight, and preserved us in all the way wherein we went, and among all the people through whom we passed:

18 And the Lord drave out from before us all the people, even the Amorites which dwelt in the land: *therefore* will we also serve the Lord; for he *is* our God.

19 And Joshua said unto the people, Ye cannot serve the Lord: for he *is* an holy God; he *is* a jealous God; he will not forgive your transgressions nor your sins.

20 If ye forsake the Lord, and serve strange gods, then he will turn and do you hurt, and consume you, after that he hath done you good.

21 And the people said unto Joshua, Nay; but we will serve the the Lord.

22 And Joshua said unto the people, Ye *are* witnesses against yourselves that ye have chosen you the Lord, to serve him. And they said, *We are* witnesses.

. . . .

26 And Joshua wrote these words in the book of the law of God, and took a great stone, and set it up there under an oak, that *was* by the sanctuary of the Lord.

27 And Joshua said unto all the people, Behold, this stone shall be a witness unto us; for it hath heard all the words of the Lord which he

whom you will serve, whether the gods your fathers served in the region beyond the River, or the gods of the Amorites in whose land you dwell; but as for me and my house, we will serve the Lord."

16 Then the people answered, "Far be it from us that we should forsake the Lord, to serve other gods; 17 for it is the Lord our God who brought us and our fathers up from the land of Egypt, out of the house of bondage, and who did those great signs in our sight, and preserved us in all the way that we went, and among all the peoples through whom we passed; 18 and the Lord drove out before us all the peoples, the Amorites who lived in the land; therefore we also will serve the Lord, for he is our God."

19 But Joshua said to the people, "You cannot serve the Lord; for he is a holy God; he is a jealous God; he will not forgive your transgressions or your sins. 20 If you forsake the Lord and serve foreign gods, then he will turn and do you harm, and consume you, after having done you good." 21 And the people said to Joshua, "Nay; but we will serve the Lord." 22 Then Joshua said to the people, "You are witnesses against yourselves that you have chosen the Lord, to serve him." And they said, "We are witnesses."

. . . .

26 And Joshua wrote these words in the book of the law of God; and he took a great stone, and set it up there under the oak in the sanctuary of the Lord. 27 And Joshua said to all the people, "Behold, this stone shall be a witness against us; for it has heard all the words of the Lord which he spoke to us; therefore it

spake unto us: it shall be therefore a witness unto you, lest ye deny your God.

Key Verse: **If it seem evil unto you to serve the Lord, choose you this day whom ye will serve; whether the gods which your fathers served that were on the other side of the flood, or the gods of the Amorites, in whose land ye dwell: but as for me and my house, we will serve the Lord. (Joshua 24:15)**

shall be a witness against you, lest you deal falsely with your God."

Key Verse: **If you be unwilling to serve the Lord, choose this day whom you will serve, whether the gods your father served in the region beyond the River, or the gods of the Amorites in whose land you dwell; but as for me and my house, we will serve the Lord. (Joshua 24:15)**

As You Read the Scripture—Harold Reid Weaver

Joshua 24:1-13. Joshua, an old man, recognizes his death is near. He calls all the tribes together for a final word of impassioned challenge. He reminds them that Abraham was called from the other side of the flood, which meant on the eastern side of the Euphrates River. Later, the Lord called the Israelites from Egypt.

Verse 14. They are to put away their gods. Note the plural here: not one God but the gods "which your fathers served." Joshua refers also to the gods the Israelites worshiped in Egypt. The Hebrews had continued their ancient practice of worshiping the gods of the lands in which they found themselves by adopting those of Canaan.

Verse 15. After all, what god knows about fertility of fields, or cattle, or the life of city people? The local god, of course! What would the God of Moses, Yahweh, know about such things? Verse 15 catches the demand in the mind of Joshua. If you want to worship pagan gods, then do it. Be honest about it. Give up the Lord, who brought you to this land of promise. "But," he thundered, "as for me and my house, we will serve the Lord." To reject him is to accept eventual national collapse and disintegration. To accept him is to find the source of strength, human dignity, justice, and mercy.

Note that by this time in the history of Israel there were many people who had only lately been assimilated into the tribes, folk who had not been slaves in Egypt. They were descendents of the eleven brothers of Joseph who returned from Egypt to the lands Abraham had first settled. They had had their own "gods," and Yahweh was a new God for them. It was a difficult thing for them to "choose, now" between their gods and Joshua's God, the God of Moses. No more dillydallying, no more fence-straddling. Make up your minds. Now.

Verses 16-19. They voted yes for the Lord, but Joshua knew they had not yet voted with their lives. Joshua states they cannot worship the holy God, the jealous God. He considers them, for the moment, incapable of a high, religious life. He challenges their integrity with that statement.

Holy? That word grows new meanings as the centuries pass. It once meant God was too awesome to be seen. People should be abased, fall to the ground, cover their eyes. No one could see God and live! But as their spiritual vision cleared, the Israelites came to see the Holy God as the Spirit in whom is no evil. He is the Spirit of truth, of righteousness, who desires justice and mercy. And they who worship him must seek to develop those godly qualities.

Is God jealous? Is he fearful of losing his people? That is a very human interpretation. A deeper understanding of this concept is that God calls us to be faithful to given principles, to loyalty to persons, and to refusal to shift at whim from truth to untruth, from holy living to unholy living, from life to destruction.

Joshua announces an ultimatum: not "both this and also that," but "either this God or that god." One way leads to life, the other to death.

Verses 25-26. The covenant is made. A stone is placed under a sacred oak that is part of the shrine at Shechem. It is the witness not to be forgotten of this major decision of the united tribes.

The Scripture and the Main Question—Pat McGeachy

Choices

A friend of mine who teaches creative writing in high school hit upon the following delightful experiment. She asked each student in her class to write the opening chapter of an adventure story, ending it with a decision to be made. The class voted on them all for the one that would serve as the beginning of their joint project. The class then divided into two groups: those who answered the decision one way, and those who answered it another. From there on, the process got complicated, but the end result was a story with thirty different endings, based on the pyramid of choices that began with the one decision made at the end of chapter one. The chapters were delightfully arranged so that the reader sort of creates the book by choosing among the plot options along the way, ultimately selecting a final ending.

I commend to you that class project as a way of describing the real world in which we live. Every decision we make reveals two or more roads down which we might walk, and each of them branches into more and more. But we are always at the moment of decision.

Here is another way of looking at it, if that one was too complex: Imagine that life is a movie film. The past is over and done with, wound up on the take-up reel. The future is still on the other reel, not having yet passed through the bright frame of the present. Life is lived in the flashing instant of projection. But the future is not static and rigid like the past. It is as though the future film has not even been exposed yet, but waits in the camera to see what choices we make and develops itself accordingly.

Perhaps you can come up with a better way of thinking about it, but for me, life can be visualized in just this way: The past is memory; the future is anticipation; the present (real life) is the moment of choosing. In other words, to be really alive is to be in constant touch with the great questions of life and continually choosing between false gods and true. "Now," said Paul (II Corinthians 6:2), "is the acceptable time; behold, now is the day of salvation." "The time is fulfilled," said Jesus (Mark 1:15), "and the kingdom of God is at hand; repend; and believe in the gospel."

Honesty

Joshua seems almost willing to let his people go away after the Canaanite gods, if they truly wish to do so. The point is that they are trying to have their cake and eat it, too. They are attempting to display the outward signs of following the moral and ethical God that Moses taught them to worship and at the same time enjoy the tempting fruits of the fertility cults of the people of Canaan. Bear in mind that the choice we have here was not merely a minor cultural choice, like deciding whether to be a Methodist or a Presbyterian. (That may be a bigger choice than I suppose, but at least it means choosing within the framework of Bible-centered Protestant Christianity.) This was a choice between cultic practices built around obedience to the moral law and those built around temple prostitution.

To put it in modern perspective, it would be like a Christian who tried to enjoy all the benefits of church membership, sat proudly in the pew on Sunday morning, but by night frequented those places where good Christians are not ordinarily seen, and who called that behavior faithful, too. The strong command of Joshua comes to us, demanding that we choose this very day which side we are on. If we do not, we are fooling no one but ourselves. Like the addict who in self delusion believes that "one more won't hurt," we have rationalized our life-styles until we have learned to pretend that all sorts of "little" sins are really Christ-like behavior.

I want to be careful not to nag here, because I believe in grace before works, but at the risk of that danger, consider making a list of things that in your heart you know are wrong but which have become a part of your everyday life. What about the language you use? The sort of television shows you watch? The sexual habits you (and your children) have gotten into? The white lies you tell? Do you always keep your promises? How about the hatreds, jealousies, and envies you nurture in your heart (see Matthew 5:21-24)?

Even if, by some miraculous doings on your part, you manage to have a perfect score on your personal morality, what about the society of which you are a part? Simply by being a member of a community that is peopled with drug abusers, criminals, cruel landlords, and those who rip off the welfare system, you are partially responsible. I may be a lover of peace, but some of my tax dollars go to stockpile weapons of death.

I'm not trying to call names here; I'm trying to do what Joshua demanded of his people: to be honest about who we are, before God and the world, and to choose. Do I know "whom" I have believed? Do I belong to Christ or to the world? Am I trying to have it both ways?

False Gods

Am I wrong? I suspect that we tend to dismiss much of the Old Testament because it talks about going off after "idols." I certainly don't make graven images and bow down before them. I don't go to the "high places" and perform silly, steamy ceremonies. I don't believe in Baal or Zeus or any of those pagan superstitions. Of *course* when Joshua says, "Do you choose God?" I answer yes.

But let us take extra care here. It may be that we are in *worse* shape than our primitive ancestors, simply because the false gods we worship are so well hidden. Let's define our terms: A god is anything (or anybody) to which we give our ultimate allegiance. There is a country music song that contains the line, "I don't care what's right or wrong." It says, in effect, "I don't care what God thinks; I'm going to do what I think." In this case, the god in question is sexual pleasure. But there are others, and we build temples to them. Maybe we ought to give them names, so that they will be just as obvious as the gods of the Amorites:

—Mammon, whose temple is the bank.

—Venus, whose temple is the Playboy mansion.

—Hero, whose temple is the football stadium or the movie palace.

—Pride, whose temple could be everything from the hairdressers' to the department store.

You get the idea. These are not evil things if we don't worship them, but when we do, they can destroy us.

The better and nobler the thing we admire, the more danger there is of its being made into a god. For that reason we can make a god out of the Bible by glorifying its words and ignoring its commandments. We can worship the church or the building where it meets. Perhaps the single most dangerous god in our day is Nation, whose temple is the statehouse and whose symbols are seen everywhere. Because national security is so important and because of our fears of other gods (Communism, Naziism, etc.), we throw up Nation and, forgetting where our true security comes from (see lesson 2), bow down before our own patriotism. But no nation can survive unless it is (as our pledge reminds us) "under God." A nation that becomes a god becomes a destroyer, as do all false gods.

But when we chose God first, then the false gods fall into their proper place: sex, money, pride, and patriotism all have their wholesome roles. Seek first the kingdom and the righteousness, and all these things shall be yours as well (see Matthew 6:33). But make up your minds—right now!

Helping Adults Become Involved—John Warren Steen

Preparing to Teach

This is the first lesson in this quarter with an action aim.

Be ready to discuss the life and career of Joshua.

Consider using the following teaching aim: to enable students, when they are confronted with choices during the following week, to make a decision in keeping with God's will.

Use the following outline:

> I. Joshua told tribes to serve God (24:14-22).
> II. Israel declared allegiance to God (24:26-27).

Read carefully "The Scripture and the Main Question" and "As You Read the Scripture." These form the heart of the lesson. The ideas, insights, and suggestions in these sections should be reflected continually in your lesson plan.

As you use the suggested outline, you may want to either quote or paraphrase ideas. You might like to jot in the margin of your outline the page number and paragraph being referred to. For example, you could write a reference to page 65, paragraph 3, as 65-3.

Introducing the Main Question

Basic and helpful ideas are presented in the section "The Main Question." These ideas are essential in helping to identify the purpose of the lesson.

Ask: Are decisions influenced more by emotion than by reason? Then ask what the greatest decisions of life are. Many Christians would say (in order of importance) the decision to accept Christ as Savior, the decision of one's mate in life, and the decision of one's vocation. Ask the class to analyze the important features of these three.

Now introduce the main question: Do you belong to God or not? Another way of stating the main question is this: Have your sworn allegiance to God? Remind members that some (if not many) have reached a time in their moral lives when making right decisions should be almost automatic (i.e., an act of moral spontaneity), and a time when they need to be setting a Christian example for younger people to follow.

Not many people are put on the spot, so to speak, to make a decision, as were Joshua's people. Paint the background of the occasion. Ask: Did Joshua have a role model for a farewell to his people? Yes, he had followed Moses, seen him grow older, and listened as he spoke his final words to Israel. Now Joshua, too, has grown old. Examine his motives. Ask if Joshua just wants some personal approval at the end of his career, or if he is truly interested in the new and in subsequent generations?

Developing the Lesson

I. Joshua told tribes to serve God (24:14-22).

The covenant Joshua wanted to make at that occasion was not too different in form from the pledges of other ancient Near Eastern people of that time. According to Hittite texts dating from 1450–1200 B.C., five elements were typical in a treaty text: (1) identification of the great king and author of the covenant, (2) narration of the gracious acts of the king, (3) covenant obligations of the vassal, (4) instructions for depositing the document in the sanctuary for regular public reading, and (5) blessings accompanying fidelity and curses invoked for violations. Each of these ideas is reflected in Joshua 24. A sixth point of ancient treaties does not appear in this one: Deities of the covenanting parties were invoked as witnesses.

Verses 24:1-13 recite God's providence in dealing with Israel. Have someone read verses 14 and 15, stating the covenant obligations of the people who have received his blessings.

The aging leader challenged his people to make a decision. He commanded them to decide whether they would serve the living God of history or the gods of pagan neighbors. Then Joshua announced that he and his household would make their decision in God's favor. Ask what sacrifices this decision caused him to endure. Ask: Could Joshua have been more popular if he had allowed people to serve any god they chose? Does a choice of one God today cause people to endure any hardship, misunderstanding, or sacrifice?

II. Israel declared allegiance to God (24:26-27).

The people said they were willing. Do you think they realized what they were pledging? Apparently, from Joshua's response, he didn't think they completely comprehended.

Have someone read verses 19-22, in which Joshua reminds the people of the kind of God they are dedicating themselves to. This one is a holy and a jealous God.

Refer to Reid Weaver's exegesis on "holy." Read or extemporize on his statement. Then ask: When do people feel the most reverent, at a funeral, a wedding, a communion service, an Easter service, or in personal Bible study and contemplation? How can we foster such feelings?

The word "jealousy" is related to the words for zeal and fury. God's jealously breaks forth when his people depart from the covenant. Divine jealousy is the principle of God's protecting the covenant people. The Almighty expects absolute and exclusive allegiance.

A person in India said to a missionary, "I will be glad to accept your Christ as another god in addition to the others I honor." When the missionary said that was impossible, the Indian said, "But why must your God be so exclusive?"

The answer came back. "In marriage, a husband or wife wants the exclusive devotion of the other person. That is the nature of monogamous marriage. We worship a jealous divinity. That is the nature of our God."

Ask class members if they see any similarity in the great stone of verses 26-27 and the twelve stones of the memorial, discussed in the first lesson of this quarter. Is there any similarity between this stone and the kind of war memorials we have erected in this century?

Both sacred pillars and sacred trees were common cultic features of ancient sanctuaries. Because of their abuse as objects of superstition and veneration, they were later prohibited (see Deuteronomy 16:21-22).

Helping Class Members Act

Distribute paper and pencils following Dr. McGeachy's lead, have class members make a list of things that they know are wrong which have become a part of their everyday lives. Examples are bad language, certain television programs, white lies and other fibs, gossip, jealousy, contempt, feelings of revenge, and so forth. Start with your own confession of one wrong you want to remove from your life. Allow others to also confess, if they wish.

Mention some times in life when decisions must be made, such as leaving a comfortable situation for work in another location, voting a certain way on a church building program, helping in volunteer work for a community project, and so forth. Everytime a person says yes to one activity it means saying no to another.

In a time of quiet dedication, ask members to think of some decision in their lives that needs to be made at this very moment. It could be a new insight about the lessons of this quarter, or it might be some ethical or theological question that has been nagging at their consciences. Give them an opportunity to pledging allegiance to God in prayer.

Planning for Next Sunday

Ask members to watch television or the newspapers during the coming week for examples of patriotism taken to an extreme.

UNIT II: JUDGES—A TIME OF CONFLICT AND ADJUSTMENT

Horace R. Weaver

SIX LESSONS   JULY 2–AUGUST 6

This unit, consisting of six lessons, surveys the period of turmoil that followed the Hebrew tribes' settlement in the land of Canaan. Lesson 1 deals with the recurring cycle observed throughout the book of Judges: apostasy, oppression, repentance, deliverance. Then two lessons show how God used various judges as local leaders to deliver the Hebrews from their oppression. A lesson on Abimelech's seizure of power through violence provides an example of corrupt leadership. The tragedy of unfulfilled potential is illustrated in the story of Samson.

The concluding "time of conflict and adjustment" focuses on the relocation of the tribe of Dan, necessitated because it never completely settled its allotted portion of land. The tribe of Dan's difficulties underscored the need for a strong national leadership among the Hebrews.

The six lessons are as follows: July 2, "Dealing with a Nation's Sins," asks, Can we as a people turn from our disobedience, and will God send us leadership? July 9, "Working Together for Justice," challenges us: Will we seek God's will and live by it? July 16, "Gideon: Reluctant Leader," deals with how we decide what God's will is for us. July 23, "Gideon: Relying on God's Power," helps us think about not only how we know God, but also how to respond with loyalty. July 30, "Choosing Trustworthy Leaders," asks, How do we distinguish between a genuine call to lead and a neurotic desire to rule? August 6, "Samson: Man of Weakness and Strength," asks, How can we avoid Samson's faults and emulate his virtues?

LESSON 5   JULY 2

Dealing with a Nation's Sins

Background Scripture: Judges 1–2

The Main Question—Pat McGeachy

Life seems to follow wave-like cycles. There is the manic-depressive cycle that we are all familiar with; we say jokingly, "I'm like an elevator operator; I have my ups and downs." The economy seems to vacillate between bullish and bearish times. And we seem to go from times of international tension to times of relative peace. Apparently there is also such a pattern in our moral and spiritual lives. In Judges 2:11 we read that "the people of Israel did what was evil in the sight of the Lord." This establishes a pattern that is to occur again and again (see 3:7, 12; 4:1; 6:1. And the opposite theme of

FOURTH QUARTER

Judges is God's continual reaching down to help the Israelites (2:16) by raising up judges to save them.

The pattern repeats throughout the book: disobedience—judgment—deliverance. Will they (we) never learn?

The institution of judicial leadership was established by Moses before his death (see Deuteronomy 16:18-20) to decide controversies and to give leadership to the people in doing what is right. But when the people insist on doing "what is evil in the Lord's sight," there is not much that any human institution can do. Only genuine national repentance can make possible the recovery of the moral life of a people; and gifted leadership is needed to make this happen.

What do you think? Are we in a moral decline in our time? If so, what can be done about it? The people of Israel did plenty of weeping (2:4-5) and plenty of groaning (2:18). The main question for us is: Can we as a people turn from our disobedience, and will God send us leadership? It's a kind of chicken-and-egg question: We need leaders to rescue us, but we need repentance to open the way for leadership. In the time of the judges it seemed clear that it was God who made both of these things possible. Can it happen for us?

Selected Scripture

King James Version

Judges 2:11-19

11 And the children of Israel did evil in the sight of the Lord and served Ba'-al-im:

12 And they forsook the Lord God of their fathers, which brought them out of the land of Egypt, and followed other gods, of the gods of the people that *were* round about them, and bowed themselves unto them, and provoked the Lord to anger.

13 And they forsook the Lord, and served Ba'al and Ash'-ta-roth.

14 And the anger of the Lord was hot against Israel, and he delivered them into the hands of spoilers that spoiled them, and he sold them into the hands of their enemies round about, so that they could not any longer stand before their enemies.

15 Whithersoever they went out, the hand of the Lord was against them for evil, as the Lord had said, and as the Lord had sworn unto them: and they were greatly distressed.

16 Nevertheless the Lord raised up judges, which delivered them

Revised Standard Version

Judges 2:11-19

11 And the people of Israel did what was evil in the sight of the Lord and served the Ba'als; 12 and they forsook the Lord, the God of their fathers, who had brought them out of the land of Egypt; they went after other gods, from among the gods of the peoples who were round about them, and bowed down to them; and they provoked the Lord to anger. 13 They forsook the Lord, and served the Ba'als and the Ash'taroth. 14 So the anger of the Lord was kindled against Israel, and he gave them over to plunderers, who plundered them; and he sold them into the power of their enemies round about, so that they could no longer withstand their enemies. 15 Whenever they marched out, the hand of the Lord was against them for evil, as the Lord had warned, and as the Lord has sworn to them; and they were in sore straits.

16 Then the Lord raised up judges, who saved them out of the

368

out of the hand of those that spoiled them.

17 And yet they would not hearken unto their judges, but they went a whoring after other gods, and bowed themselves unto them: they turned quickly out of the way which their fathers walked in, obeying the commandments of the Lord; *but* they did not so.

18 And when the Lord raised them up judges, then the Lord was with the judge, and delivered them out of the hand of their enemies all the days of the judge: for it repented the Lord because of their groanings by reason of them that oppressed them and vexed them.

19 And it came to pass, when the judge was dead, *that* they returned, and corrupted *themselves* more than their fathers, in following other gods to serve them, and to bow down unto them; they ceased not from their own doings, nor from their stubborn way.

power of those who plundered them. 17 And yet they did not listen to their judges; for they played the harlot after other gods and bowed down to them; they soon turned aside from the way in which their fathers had walked, who had obeyed the commandments of the Lord and they did not do so. 18 Whenever the Lord raised up judges for them, the Lord was with the judge, and he saved them from the hand of their enemies all the days of the judge; for the Lord was moved to pity by their groaning because of those who afflicted and oppressed them. 19 But whenever the judge died, they turned back and behaved worse than their fathers, going after other gods, serving them and bowing down to them; they did not drop any of their practices or their stubborn ways.

Key Verse: **When the Lord raised them up judges, then the Lord was with the judge, and delivered them out of the hand of their enemies all the days of the judge. (Judges 2:18)**

Key Verse: **Whenever the Lord raised up judges for them, the Lord was with the judge, and he saved them from the hand of their enemies all the days of the judge. (Judges 2:18)**

As You Read the Scripture—Harold Reid Weaver

Deuteronomy ended with the story of the death of Moses. The book of Joshua told of the life and death of Joshua. Judges briefly recounts the closing days of Joshua and then adds stories of the valiant Israelite leaders called judges. In the absence of the great Moses and the faithful, energetic Joshua, individuals arose here and there in response to immediate leadership needs. These "judges" were often distinguished soldiers or civic leaders.

It is essential to know that the writer of Judges sets forth a specific belief about God and his people: Obey God and you will be a prosperous and successful people; disobey God and you will be punished. The punishment may be seen in famines, diseases, wars, or social disintegration.

Judges 2:11. This verse states, "And the people of Israel did what was evil in the sight of the Lord and served the Baals." The Baals were fertility gods worshiped by the Canaanites.

Verse 13. The people also adopted Ashtaroth, the Canaanite goddess of war and fertility, whose worship involved the public glorification of sex. This was in sharp violation of the covenant with Yahweh. Therefore, evil could be expected directly from the hand of God.

Verses 14-15. The Lord was angry and "sold" his unfaithful people to plunderers. "The Lord was against them for evil," so that they lost their battles to the enemies around them.

What is being taught here is that God uses the so-called "principle of retaliation." If people do evil things, then they will be punished. It is also called the "law of retribution," or "getting even." Jesus knew about this law and denounced it as inadequate. "You have heard that it was said, 'An eye for an eye and a tooth for a tooth'" (Matthew 5:38). Then he goes on to say, "But I say to you, love your enemies and pray for those who persecute you" (Matthew 5:43).

Christians must always check any ethical standard in the light of the message of Jesus. When we do so, we see the inadequacy of the old "eye for an eye" ethic. It is not only to be rejected as an ethic for human relations with other humans, but more importantly as the governing relationship between God and humanity.

Verses 16-19. "The Lord raised up judges who saved them," but the reign of justice never lasted very long, for as soon as a judge would die, apostasy would start all over again. The missing ingredients in this cycle of deliverance and disobedience are love, forgiveness, and growth in learning to be faithful witnesses of that divine gift. Through divine love we find the means of salvation from both personal and social decay.

The Scripture and the Main Question—Pat McGeachy

Charismatic Leadership

Sometimes thoughtful Americans ask, "Whatever happened to heroes?" When our nation was young there seemed to be giants in the land: Patrick Henry, Thomas Jefferson, Benjamin Franklin, George Washington, John Adams, Alexander Hamilton. The list goes on and on. They were political and intellectual geniuses. And in such a small nation! Now, in our many millions, we don't seem to have such heroes any more. Where have all the heroes gone?

Some would answer by saying that we still have such leaders, only they don't come to the surface as readily in our day. Others would say that God raised those people up to bless the young nation, and that our own willful ways are not being blessed by God. I suspect that both of these things may be true. We do need leadership, and if we would seek it in genuine repentance, God would bring it to the surface.

The word "charismatic" is a powerful, somewhat frightening word. It means "gifted," not merely with spiritual qualities but with any of the gifts (see for example the list in I Corinthians 12:4-11, 28) found in people of talent. There can be negative charisma as well as positive; an Adolph Hitler has the power to sway people in demonic ways. It may help you to use the word "charismatic" properly by thinking of its sister word, "charity," which comes from the same Greek root (so does "care") and reminds us that God's grace is to the undeserving (see Ephesians 2:8).

How do we get such leaders? Well, we don't get them by Madison Avenue image-making techniques, or by building a powerful political machine.

They come, the book of Judges tells us, to people who, in the grip of their own self-destructive ways, finally turn to God and ask for help. Repentance, we call it; that is, not merely feeling sorry for ourselves, but genuinely attempting to turn our lives around. And the first step in this process, our friends at Alcoholics Anonymous tell us, is to become convinced that we are powerless, that we must put our trust in one greater than ourselves. We must, in other words, return to God (see Isaiah 55:6-7) and ask for a gift.

Judges

The judges were strange political animals. Not exactly priests and not exactly kings, they possessed both spiritual and political authority. They seemed almost to spring up as needed, when things got bad enough. The period of the judges was politically very unsettled. Apparently the tribes of Israel were a pretty loose confederation and did not get along very well even with each other. In that sense they were much like the early colonies in America. Before, when they were fresh out of slavery, they had been whipped into line by Moses and Joshua, themselves gifted leaders, who established strong structures and vigorously enforced them. Later, in the period of the kings, there would be a strong central military government (it would have troubles of a different sort) that could call the tribes together for action. (Note that the first kings, Saul and David, were chosen very much like the judges for their charismatic gifts. It is not until we get to Solomon that the kingship becomes a kind of inheritance, and after that there seems to be nothing but a great deal of trouble for the nation.) But during the period of the judges, the people were sort of "turned loose" on their own recognizance, to live as they should. And they insisted on doing what was evil in the Lord's sight.

Original Sin

William Golding's book *The Lord of the Flies* is a pessimistic novel about human depravity. It is the story of a group of boys shipwrecked on a desert island. Without supervision, they resort to beastly behavior, even to murder. When at last they are rescued, it is by a military vessel, whose presence seems to argue that adults are the same way: doomed to do that which is evil in God's sight, to kill and misuse one another and to behave cruelly and selfishly.

What do you think of Golding's vision of humanity? Are we really like that? When a baby is born, do you think of that infant as innocent? Probably so—it is built into our vocabulary: as innocent as a babe. But consider: Have you ever met an unselfish baby? Did you ever hear of an infant saying, "Mother, I know you are tired tonight. Why not just rest awhile before you change and feed me?" No, a baby is the center of the universe. It cries and the world jumps to meet its needs. It is only as the infant grows older and is taught, sometimes with great difficulty, how to share, that the virtues of charity, patience, and unselfishness are to some extent displayed.

Then why does God turn us loose? Why weren't the children of Israel forced to toe the mark, morally and spiritually? It looks as though God built them up, through Moses and Joshua and the Law, and then just let them slip right back into their old pagan ways. Is God that sloppy an administrator?

Apparently God values freedom more than security! The divine favor would rather see us set free to fail than force us to dance like puppets on the strings of righteousness. We are given the opportunity to fall from grace; God turns us loose, with only an occasional charismatic leader to bail us out when things get too bad. Evidently when we are told in lesson 4 of this quarter that God wants us to "choose this day whom you will serve," that choice is meant to be a real one. It's up to us. God wants us to love justice and mercy and truth and righteousness, not because the stars demand it, or because we are afraid of punishment, or because we want to go to heaven, but because we want the same things that God wants for us.

And even when we choose the wrong thing, God sends judges to set us back on the right track. Over and over again, in the cycle of our disobedience, we are called once more to repentance by the saviors whom God sends. Think of them throughout history: Abraham, Moses, Joshua, David, Elijah, Isaiah, Jeremiah—and in the fullness of time, the one who is Judge and Redeemer of all: Jesus, whom we call Christ. (That name means the anointed one, the one chosen by God, appointed to the task of delivering us from our sins.)

Even after the one true Judge was taken up into heaven, we were still permitted to slip back into trouble. And God has not ceased to send us charismatic leaders: Paul, Augustine, Francis of Assisi, Aquinas, Luther, Calvin, Wesley . . . continue the list down to the present time and think of your personal heroes. God comes down into our not-so-original sinfulness and delivers us once more.

What Hope Have We

In our day, times being what they are, will God give up on us? (See Hosea 11:8.) When we get utterly discouraged, have we any hope for delivery from our moral and religious depression? (See Exekiel 37:11-14—words spoken during the time of Israel's Babylonian captivity.) The promise of Scripture is that God does not change (see Judges 2:1-2); rather it is we who have departed from the will of God.

If we truly repent, will God take us back? Turn once again to the parable of the waiting father in Luke 15 and answer the question in that light. And if you believe in that sort of God, then join with me in praying, "Let there be heroes once again on the face of the land, O God! Send us a deliverer!" When I find myself crying such pleas in my place of Bochim (Judges 2:4-5), I seem to hear God answering, "All right, let's set things right again. Let's return to morality and obedience and moral prosperity. And let's start with you. *You* be a hero! You begin to live as you should, and let us see what sort of benign infection will spread from you to the rest of the world."

Helping Adults Become Involved—John Warren Steen

Preparing to Teach

Prepare slips of paper with one of the following words on each: "idolatry," "Baal," "Ashtaroth," "anger of God." Provide some Bible dictionaries and other resources for class members to use. Prepare an interest center, with patriotic items or photos.

Consider using the following teaching aim: to seek ways to influence local and national policies, and to help class members develop a patriotism that is informed and God-related.

Use the following outline:

I.   Defection of Israel (2:11-13).
     A. They left God, their Deliverer.
     B. They served Baals and Ashtaroth.
II. Divine retribution (2:14-19).
     A. God sent plunderers and warriors.
     B. God gave judges as leaders.

Read carefully "The Scripture and the Main Question" and "As You Read the Scripture." These form the heart of the lesson. The ideas, insights, and suggestions in these sections should be reflected continually in your lesson plan.

As you use the suggested outline, you may want to either quote or paraphrase ideas. You might like to jot in the margin of your outline the page number and paragraph being referred to. For example, you could write a reference to page 65, paragraph 3, as 65-3.

Introducing the Main Question

Basic and helpful ideas are presented in the section "The Main Question." These ideas are essential in helping to identify the purpose of the lesson.

The main question is: Can we as a people turn from our disobedience, and will God send us leadership?

Ask: What has resulted from the act of Congress that added the words, "One nation under God" to the Pledge of Allegiance to the flag? Some may say that we are further from God than ever, and others might say that we are constantly reminded of God's providence in forming and guiding our fortunate nation. There is no correct answer; the purpose of the question is to get the class to think about the effect of religious ideas on the nation today. Help the class to see the need for stronger Christian influence on local and national policies.

Add a word of caution. In the early part of this decade significant emphasis was put on religion and government, with people on the far right in both areas joining forces. Ask if these alliances brought about a better understanding of God and the divine will. Or did all the speeches about religion and faith remain merely words, failing to penetrate the lives of the proponents or change the nature of the government and its policies?

Developing the Lesson

Give out the slips of paper and ask the class to give definitions of the words. Allow time for members to use the resources, then call for reports.

I. Defection of Israel (2:11-13).
  A. They left God, their Deliverer.
The simple formula used here and throughout the book of Judges carries many overtones of drama and tragedy. Just as the old, simple words "boy

meets girl" cannot portray all the emotions of falling in love, the words of these verses can only give the briefest outline of history.

Notice that it was the Israelites who deserted God, not the other way around. They repudiated their covenant religion, ungrateful for the Exodus and the conquest of the Promised Land.

B. *They served Baals and Ashtaroth.*

Instead, they served the Canaanite Baals ("masters") and Ashtaroth (fertility deities). In the ancient Ras Shamra texts, Ashtorah is a goddess who is the ally of Baal in his conflict with sea and river. Both goddess and god were association with fertility of the land and the people. As the giver of life, Ashtorah was believed to have the power of healing.

Ask: Why was monotheism so hard to maintain in the ancient world? Because of the influence of powerful and successful polytheistic nations and the dullness of monotheism in contrast to the elaborate myths and wild worship activities connected with fertility rites.

II. Divine retribution (2:14-19).

A. *God sent plunderers and warriors.*

Divine wrath came through human action. God let the people become the victims of plunderers. God had warned of this; have someone read Leviticus 26:17, 36-39. The people had brought judgment upon themselves.

Ask at what point the people turned to God. They had to hit the bottom before they could bounce back up. They had to feel hopeless before they would turn to the giver of supreme hope.

B. *God gave judges as leaders.*

Have someone read Judges 2:18. What do class members think of when they hear the word "judges"? These ancient Israelite leaders were very different from legal authorities of today. The judges were charismatic leaders who spoke for God and gave dramatic guidance to the people.

Note in verse 18 that the Lord was moved with pity. Just as God was impressed by the suffering of the slaves in Egypt, God again cared when the Chosen People were mistreated and oppressed. Point out that people who call the God of the Old Testament one of anger and judgment must not be familiar with the many accounts of loving-kindness found in the Exodus account and in the pronouncements of the prophets. Help the class to get an overall view of the liberating God who cares for people in trouble and offers them divine help.

Helping Class Members Act

Let class members share ideas for celebrating Independence Day. Put the ideas on the chalkboard. Encourage interesting and unusual celebrations, especially if they emphasize the spiritual meaning of independence, freedom, and liberty.

In conclusion, ask for examples of ways that each person can have a part in government. Tell the following story. According to an old account, it was a small boy who helped send out the message of liberty on July 4, 1776. On that morning, the old bell ringer of the state house in Philadelphia went up to the steeple to ring the bell. He wanted to wait, though, until Congress had adopted the Declaration of Independence. He asked a boy to wait at the door downstairs and let him know the news.

374

Hours went by with no news. The bell ringer said, "They will never do it."

Suddenly, he heard a shout. The boy was standing down below clapping his hands and yelling, "Ring! Ring!" With the boy's help, the bell lived up to the motto that had been engraved on it more that twenty years before: "Proclaim liberty throughout all the land and to the inhabitants thereof."

Ask the class to read together the inspiring words of Proverbs 14:34: "Righteousness exalts a nation, but sin is a reproach to any people."

Planning for Next Sunday

Ask members to read a few magazine or newspaper articles about women in positions of leadership. Ask them to particularly examine the controversy about the ordination of women.

Ask for a volunteer to take the part of Deborah in a mock television interview with the press. This person should prepare by studying the life of Deborah and the conditions of her time and be ready to answer questions in such a way as to present Deborah's story in Judges.

Working Together for Justice

Background Scripture: Judges 4–5

The Main Question—Pat McGeachy

This story has a sting to it: Deborah means in Hebrew "a bee," and her memory causes a buzz to this day among those who are struggling with the role of women in our society and the place of prophecy in the political world (or the relationship between church and state). The story also contains one of the oldest songs known, a strange song of victory and violence celebrating Deborah and another woman, Jael. This ancient tale and its song bring us smack up against the sharp pain of our humanity and our need for divine assistance in the never-ending struggle for justice.

It is hard for a modern day Christian to identify with the primitive and violent era of the judges. We are appalled by the horror (read 5:26-27 aloud and see what sort of feelings it arouses in you), and we are left uneasy by the suggestion of sorcery in the ancient role of the prophetess. But let us look for the theology that informs the text. Lying behind this strange story, with its customs unfamiliar to our ears, is a clear message that need not be confusing: (1) God speaks through people who, like Deborah, the bee, attune themselves to the divine will. (2) When such prophets, together with the faithful servants of the secular order, like Barak, lead the people forth, great injustices can be overcome. (3) Every housewife (like Jael) can have a part in the battle. The truth will triumph.

FOURTH QUARTER

Even though there are troublesome things in this ancient tale, the main question is clear: Will we seek God's will and live by it? If so, we can expect victory. It will not come without cost (see Luke 12:29-53), but it will come. We need that great combination in our time: the voice of one who understands the will of God, the hand of the brave warrior, and the commitment of the common people.

Selected Scripture

King James Version

Revised Standard Version

Judges 4:1-9, 14-15

1 And the children of Israel again did evil in the sight of the Lord, when E'-hud was dead.

2 And the Lord sold them into the hand of Ja'-bin king of Canaan, that reigned in Ha'-zor; the captain of whose host *was* Sis'-e-ra, which dwelt in Ha-ro'-sheth of the Gentiles.

3 And the children of Israel cried unto the Lord: for he had nine hundred chariots of iron; and twenty years he mightily oppressed the children of Israel.

4 And Deb'-o-rah, a prophetess, the wife of Lap'-i-doth, she judged Israel at that time.

5 And she dwelt under the palm tree of Deb'-o-rah between Ra'-mah and Beth-el in mount E'-phra-im: and the children of Israel came up to her for judgment.

6 And she sent and called Ba'-rak the son of A-bin'-o-am out of Ke'-desh-naph'-ta-li, and said unto him, Hath not the Lord God of Israel commanded, *saying*, Go and draw toward mount Ta'-bor, and take with thee ten thousand men of the children of Naph'-ta-li and of the children of Zeb'-u-lun?

7 And I will draw unto thee to the river Ki'-shon Sis'-e-ra, the captain of Ja'-bin's army, with his chariots and his multitude; and I will deliver him into thine hand.

8 And Ba'-rak said unto her, If thou wilt go with me, then I will go: but if thou wilt not go with me, *then* I will not go.

Judges 4:1-9, 14-15

1 And the people of Israel again did what was evil in the sight of the Lord, after Ehud died. 2 And the Lord sold them into the hand of Jabin king of Canaan, who reigned in Hazor; the commander of his army was Sis'era, who dwelt in Haro'sheth-ha-goiim. 3 Then the people of Israel cried to the Lord for help; for he had nine hundred chariots of iron, and oppressed the people of Israel cruelly for twenty years.

4 Now Deb'orah, a prophetess, the wife of Lapp'idoth, was judging Israel at that time. 5 She used to sit under the palm of Deb'orah between Ramah and Bethel in the hill country of E'phraim; and the people of Israel came up to her for judgment. 6 She sent and summoned Barak the son of Abin'o-am from Kedesh in Naph'tali, and said to him, "The Lord, the God of Israel, commands you, 'Go gather your men at Mount Tabor, taking ten thousand from the tribe of Naph'tali and the tribe of Zeb'ulun. 7 And I will draw out Sis'era, the general of Jabin's army, to meet you by the river Kishon with his chariots and his troops; and I will give him into your hand.'" 8 Barak said to her, "If you will go with me, I will go; but if you will not go with me, I will not go." 9 And she said, "I will surely go with you; nevertheless, the road on which you are going will not lead to your glory, for the Lord will

9 And she said, I will surely go with thee: notwithstanding the journey that thou takest shall not be for thine honour; for the Lord shall sell Sis'-e-ra into the hand of a woman. And Deb'-o-rah arose, and went with Ba'-rak to Ke'-desh.

....

14 And Deb'-o-rah said unto Ba'-rak, Up; for this *is* the day in which the Lord hath delivered Sis'-e-ra into thine hand: is not the Lord gone out before thee? So Ba'-rak went down from mount Ta'-bor, and ten thousand men after him.

15 And the Lord discomfited Sis'-e-ra, and all *his* chariots, and all *his* host, with the edge of the sword before Ba'-rak; so that Sis'-e-ra lighted down off *his* chariot, and fled away on his feet.

Key Verse: Ba'-rak said unto her, if thou wilt go with me, then I will go: but if thou wilt not go with me, then I will not go. (Judges 4:8)

sell Sis'era into the hand of a woman." Then Deb'orah arose and went with Barak to Kedesh.

....

14 And Deb'orah said to Barak, "Up! For this is the day in which the Lord has given Sis'era into your hand. Does not the Lord go out before you?" So Barak went down from Mount Tabor with ten thousand men following him. 15 And the Lord routed Sis'era and all his chariots and all his army before Barak at the edge of the sword; and Sis'era alighted from his chariot and fled away on foot.

Key Verse: Barak said to her, "If you will go with me, I will go; but if you will not go with me, I will not go." (Judges 4:8)

As You Read the Scripture—Harold Reid Weaver

In this lesson, a charismatic leader is called to the leadership of Israel—a woman named Deborah. A wise judge, she aided her people when help was needed in personal decision-making. She called for decisive action on the part of an Israelite named Barak, urging him to lead the battle against the commander of the military forces of Canaan. Their commander, Sisera, had nine hundred chariots of iron, which were the latest and most feared instruments of war at that time. Who could stand against him? Barak! Barak and the Lord! Also Deborah, for Barak would not fight without her.

Judges 4:1. This verse tells of the death of Ehud. Ehud had used deceit to get to Eglon, king of the Moabites (Judges 3:15-30). Telling him he had a secret message from God, Ehud got rid of the king's guard and drew near to the king so he could whisper in his ear. Ehud delivered the message: the fatal thrust of his two-edged sword into the body of the king. Ehud was considered a heroic figure. It was said that peace came for eighty years, after that. However, once he died, the people rebelled against God.

Verse 2. This verse creates a problem: Jabin is called the king of Canaan, who ruled in Hazor. Sisera is called the commander of his army. Joshua 11 states that Jabin was king of Hazor, a small area of Canaan, but that he was not king of all Canaan. Sisera was known as king of his small area, Harosheth-ha-goiim, but was not under Jabin as leader of that man's army. No doubt Sisera was named commander of a larger gathering of Canaanite warriors, which included Jabin. (See *The Interpreter's Bible*, vol. 2, p. 712, for a more detailed account.)

Verse 8. Barak accepts Deborah's challenge to become leader of the war against Sisera, but only if Deborah will go with him. Barak was not asking merely for Deborah's presence but for the Lord's presence, who had made her what she was!

Verse 9. Barak is told that the glory of victory will not be his, but a woman's. This woman is not Deborah but Jael, who drives a tent peg through the skull of Sisera (verses 18-22).

Judges 5. Deborah's vision of victory proved correct. According to Deborah's poetic account of the event, the battle took place in the valley at the foot of Mount Tabor. The nine hundred iron chariots drawn by warhorses would have won the day, except that the River Kishon flooded during an unexpected heavy rain. Instead of an advantage, the chariots became the cause of disaster, when they became mired in the mud of the valley. The warhorses floundered in the muck, broke loose from their harnesses, and galloped madly in the maelstrom. Canaanite drivers and the warriors in the iron chariots were slain by the ten thousand Israelites who rushed down the mountain side, swords slashing.

It was from this scene of carnage that Sisera escaped on foot and sought aid from the woman, Jael. She would be immortalized as the woman who offered aid and comfort to a weary commander and then killed him.

Deborah felt inspired by God to call for this battle, doing it in good faith. Her position must be viewed in the light of her day if we are to understand it. The "God of war" of that day must be contrasted to the "God of peace" of later centuries.

The Scripture and the Main Question—Pat McGeachy

What Is a Prophetess?

The word "prophet" in English comes from a Greek word that means, roughly, "interpreter." It means "one who knows God's will and can interpret it to others." It does not, except indirectly, mean a person who can see into the future, though that is its popular meaning. To some extent, of course, anyone who knows the will of God can see what will happen down the road, because the will of God causes certain things to happen. A prophet can predict that certain behavior will lead to certain results: "You keep on drinking like that and it will kill you," or, "If we don't take care of natural resources, our children will suffer." Consider this parable: Among the mountains of Aris there is almost no water. The people there never take baths, and they would die of thirst if it were not for the juice of the hydro plant, a huge desert cactus that draws up water from the earth and stores it in its arms. But it came to pass in the fullness of time that an underground spring burst forth on the side of a great hill. The people gathered around it in great fear and curiosity. They watched as the water spread and dripped among the rocks and down the roadways. "Let us stop it," they cried, "or it will flow into our villages and drown us all!" Now it so happened that there came along just then a hydraulics engineer, who understood all about the nature of water. "You may direct and alter its flow," she told them, "but you cannot stop it. I predict that it will keep on flowing until one day it reaches the sea."

"Nonsense," they said. "We will build a dam."

"You will see," said the engineer. And sure enough, no matter how high they built it, the water eventually flowed over the dam and continued its course to sea, seeking, as we say, its own level. At last it reached the ocean, and from then on, the engineer was hailed as a prophetess. "You can predict the future," they cried. "You can see into tomorrow." "No," she replied, "but I do understand about water."

Just so, a prophet in the Bible understands about God and can predict what will happen if our human behavior insists on departing from God's will.

Deborah is not the only prophetess in the Bible. Perhaps even more celebrated than she was Miriam, the sister of Moses (see Exodus 15:20-21). It is not a coincidence that she is also remembered for her song, which like the song of Deborah is one of the oldest known in the world. Don't you wish we knew the tune to it!

Church and State

We don't know much about Barak. As Deborah predicted (4:9), he did not become as famous as the two women in the story. But he was an essential part of the pattern. Barak means "lightning" in Hebrew. As electricity when properly harnessed is a useful servant, so the church and the state when properly aligned can accomplish many things in the struggle for justice in the world. When one seeks to dictate to the other, the results can be tragic; they dare not ignore each other. In Germany, prior to World War II, good people continued to attend church while they allowed their consciences to become dulled in their obedience to the Third Reich. If they had listened to the few prophetic voices of that day, things might have turned out differently for the world.

In our case here, Barak listened to Deborah (partly because what she had to say was hopeful news; that makes it easier for the state to listen), and together they went forth to do battle against the enemy. Can you think of an example in our time of church and state working hand in hand? The first that comes to my mind is a wedding service. Both church and state have a vested interest in families as the basic building-blocks of society, and both have rules concerning marriage. A minister who performs a wedding is simultaneously an agent of the church and the state. Would that we could do more things together without getting on each other's constitutional nerves!

I'm Just a Housewife

Jael was a very ordinary woman (her husband's name actually means "smith" in Hebrew!), but like Mrs. Miniver in the famous World War II story, she rose to heroic heights. It is too bad that the role of "housewife" is sometimes looked down upon. You shouldn't say, "I'm only a housewife," any more than you should say, "I'm only a layperson." Everyone, regardless of role, is of infinite importance in the eyes of God, and the woman who is a homemaker belongs near the top of a list of important functions in a well-ordered society.

But every one of us can be at any moment thrust on the stage. You never know when a great enemy like Sisera may knock at your door, or an angel unawares appear in the guise of a stranger (Hebrews 13:2). Whoever we are, we have our parts to play in the great battle of life.

As a Christian, I am bothered by the R-rated violence in this story, but I think we must see beyond that to the dedication and courage of Jael. She lived in a more primitive society than ours. Who knows when we might be called upon to do something equally unnerving? The point is that she did what she thought was right and did it well. So with the combination of the three—prophet, soldier, and woman—the battle is given into the hands of Israel. But let us not forget that ultimately it was God who gave the victory (4:23).

The Song

I think you will agree with me that this song falls strangely on modern ears. But then, so do a good many of the songs I hear nowadays. Note, first of all, that it was a duet. Though it is usually called "The Song of Deborah," it was sung by her and Barak. You might call it, "The Song of the Bee and the Lightning."

It sounds as though it might have been sung spontaneously, like Moses' and Miriam's songs in Exodus 15, but then how did the words get recorded? (There was very little writing in that ancient time.) Read once again, perhaps aloud and in a chanting voice, the part about Jael in 5:24-27. They sound sort of like the lyrics to contemporary rock songs that you sometimes find printed in the newspaper:

> He sank, he fell,
>   he lay still at her feet;
> at her feet he sank, he fell;
>   where he sank, there he fell dead.

Is that not strange to the ear?

I also find strange the gloating in the last stanza (verses 28-30), which describes the grief and disappointment that Sisera's mother must have felt when her son's glory turned to tragedy. We have perhaps learned something from Jesus about how to feel about enemies. (See Matthew 5:43-44 and Romans 12:20. But this idea is not exclusive to the New Testament; see also Proverbs 25:21-22.)

It would perhaps be good to live in a world where all the good guys wear white and all the bad guys black. But in the real world we know that there is a little of the bad guy in all of us. There is none righteous, no, not one. And while we rejoice at the courage of Jael, let's not forget that sometimes courage takes other forms than violent acts with a tent peg and mallet.

The song ends with the pious wish that God's enemies should all perish and God's friends be like the sunrise. Perhaps this is not so different from the prayer of Paul for the coming of the time when "every knee should bow . . . and every tongue confess that Jesus Christ is Lord" (Philippians 2:10-11), or the longing of Amos for the time when the world will see "justice roll down like waters" (Amos 5:24).

Helping Adults Become Involved—John Warren Steen

Preparing to Teach

When Sandra Day O'Connor was appointed to the Supreme Court, an artist friend of mind did a picture of the judges in a formal pose, to present to the new justice. The artist took a photograph of the court and, leaving all the male justices in black and white, tinted the picture of the new female judge in bright colors. The picture shows the artist's expectation that the first woman to sit on the Supreme Court will bring color and unique qualities of leadership to that position. Justice O'Connor's appointment is emblematic of the new positions of leadership now occupied by American women. We can rely upon them to use their unique talents to wisely guide the nation.

A study of Deborah will help in understanding the Bible's attitude toward women as leaders.

The mock television interview that class members will be presenting will help bring out the important facts of today's lesson. If you do not have a class member play Deborah, plan to do it yourself, whether you are male or female, and try to get at the emotions of Judge Deborah. Try to complete the Bible study before getting off on any controversial topics, such as the ordination of women. Create an atmosphere that will permit differing viewpoints to be expressed.

Consider using the following teaching aim: to develop the conviction in the class that with proper leaders God can bring blessings to a people.

Use the following outline:

      I.   Sin and punishment (4:1-3)
     II. A commission for battle (4:4-9)
   III. Victory at Mount Tabor (4:14-15)

Read carefully "The Scripture and the Main Question" and "As You Read the Scripture." These form the heart of the lesson. The ideas, insights, and suggestions in these sections should be reflected continually in your lesson plan.

As you use the suggested outline, you may want to either quote or paraphrase ideas. You might like to jot in the margin of your outline the page number and paragraph being referred to. For example, you could write a reference to page 65, paragraph 3, as 65-3.

Introducing the Main Question

Basic and helpful ideas are presented in the section "The Main Question." These ideas are essential in helping to identify the purpose of the lesson.

The main question is, Will we seek God's will and live by it?

Ask members what they think about women as leaders in government and in churches. Then ask how one can ascertain whether or not a leader is being led by God.

Present the mock television interview with Deborah. Let the class ask the person taking Deborah's part any questions they desire. Every question should be answered if at all possible—use imagination.

Developing the Lesson

Write on the chalkboard the names Deborah and Barak. They mean "bee" and "lightning." Ask what their parents must have had in mind when they gave them those names. Then ask what the children of Israel must have thought when they heard them, at the beginning of today's episode (before the battle at Mount Tabor).

I. Sin and punishment (4:1-3)

Ask what a formula story or television sitcom is. They are shows in which the same type of actions predictably occur in each episode. People who want a happy ending to a story will not be disappointed by the typical television family comedy.

Ask: What is the formula used in the book of Judges? The people sin and bring bondage or destruction on themselves; they cry out to God, who raises up a leader to bring deliverance.

Have someone read Judges 4:1 and discuss what the "evil" might be and the appropriateness of the punishment.

Read verses 2 and 3, commenting on the type of weapons available in that time. Discuss the superiority of the iron chariot on the battlefield, emphasizing its maneuverability, height advantage, sturdy protection, and so forth.

II. A commission for battle (4:3-9)

Ask: How did the palm of Deborah get its name? She held her court under the tree, and her popularity gave her name to the tree and the place. Why was Deborah a good judge? She was also a prophet, speaking out for God. How did she know to summon Barak? Even though his military skills might have been common knowledge, she had felt led by God to call him and to send him forth with a divine assurance of victory.)

Ask someone to read Barak's response (verse 8) in several ways: like a pouting child, like a frightened draftee, and so on. See if you can agree on the reasons for his reluctance.

Have someone read verse 9, Deborah's answer, in as many ways as possible. Why did she seem disappointed and irritated? Because she thought it showed a lack of faith on his part, but she was willing to go and give inspired advice and to help build morale among the troops.

III. Victory at Mount Tabor (4:14-15)

Have someone read two verses from Deborah's song, Judges 5:4-5. Describe the setting of the battle. Sisera had deployed his forces at the river Kishon, with a division of nine hundred iron-framed chariots. The rains caused the chariots to bog down in the plain of Megiddo and become useless. The commander, Sisera, fled away on foot and was killed by a Hebrew woman.

Note the details in Deborah's song, Judges 5:24-31. Another woman, Jael, carried out the execution of the once-feared general. Then, Deborah imagined the mother of Sisera watching out her window for her son's return from battle—a poignant image.

The words in both chapters 4 and 5 ascribe the victory to God's leadership.

Helping Class Members Act

Since 1927, *Time* magazine has been selecting a Man of the Year for its cover story. In 1936, the choice was a woman, Wallis Simpson, for whom King Edward VIII abdicated his throne; she later became the Duchess of

Windsor. In 1952, Queen Elizabeth was the Woman of the Year. In 1987, the selection went to Corazon Aquino, the president of the Philippines.

The *Time* correspondent who wrote the story on President Aquino made this statement: "She is one of the rare world leaders whose appeal crosses every barrier of ideology and geography. All the world can rejoice in her rise."

List on the chalkboard some qualities of a God-directed leader. Be sure to include integrity (a good leader must be sincere and trustworthy), ability to inspire (to give people hope), an adequate understanding of events and skill at problem solving, and attention to the divine will (which affects all the other qualities).

Ask members to keep their minds open for new insights about leaders.

If time permits, have a brief discussion about church and state separation. Point out that in the United States there is a complete separation, guaranteed by the Constitution and upheld by the Supreme Court. Yet there are areas where the interests of church and state combine. Ask the class to name some. Don't overlook the chaplaincy in the military forces; in veterans' hospitals, state mental hospitals, and prisons; and in the Congress and state legislatures. Church and state have a common interest in the stability of the family and in a healthy, safe community.

Planning for Next Sunday

Ask members to be thinking about the word "loyalty" and particularly on what it means to be loyal to a pastor, to a church, and to God. Tell them to anticipate an interesting discussion on the ideas of loyalty and reluctance.

———————————

LESSON 7   JULY 16

Gideon: Reluctant Leader

Background Scripture: Judges 6

The Main Question—Pat McGeachy

Sometimes I hear people say, "If only I knew exactly what God wanted me to do, I would gladly do it." And then, at other times, "I know what I ought to be doing; I just don't seem to have the will to do it." We plead either ignorance or weakness. In the case of Gideon, we have a man whose excuse is uncertainty. Once he has been given a clear, visible sign, he fearfully goes about the task to which he has been appointed. The main question for me in this chapter is, How do we decide what God's will is?

Gideon, like the other judges, was chosen by the Spirit of God to fill a position of leadership in a time of great need. The Lord's messenger sought him out to fight the cruel banditry of the Midianites, desert people from southern Arabia. As we can see from 6:1, the children of Israel had brought plague on themselves.

Gideon was at first reluctant to respond. Like most of us, he was a combination of courage and caution. But in the end, after testing God in a number of ways, he did his duty and was successful. Many other saints of the Bible had to be dragged into their positions of responsibility. Consider the calls of Moses (Exodus 4:1, 10), Jeremiah (Jeremiah 1:6, 20:9), and, perhaps most striking of all, Paul (Acts 9:1-20). Reluctance is apparently not always bad. Indeed, it is a virtue not to seek glory for one's self.

Nevertheless, sooner or later reluctance has to be overcome. We need to make up our minds what to do and get on with it. Though subject to the human frailties of uncertainty, fear, and pride, Gideon eventually did what God asked, and in the end gave credit to God for his successes. The question for us is, How do we do the same? Shall we wait for a pot of stew to catch on fire, or a dry fleece to turn up wet when all the morning grass is dry? Or are there other signs all around us, which if we were willing to see them could help us make up our minds?

Selected Scripture

King James Version

Revised Standard Version

Judges 6:11-16, 25-29, 32

11 And there came an angel of the Lord, and sat under an oak which *was* in Oph'-rah, that *pertained* unto Jo'-ash the A'-bi-ez'-rite: and his son Gideon threshed wheat by the winepress, to hide *it* from the Mid'-i-an-ites.

12 And the angel of the Lord appeared unto him, and said unto him, The Lord *is* with thee, thou mighty man of valour.

13 And Gideon said unto him, Oh my Lord, if the Lord be with us, why then is all this befallen us? and where *be* all his miracles which our fathers told us of, saying, Did not the Lord bring us up from Egypt? but now the Lord hath forsaken us, and delivered us into the hands of the Mid'-i-an-ites.

14 And the Lord looked upon him, and said, Go in this thy might, and thou shalt save Israel from the hand of the Mid'-i-an-ites: have not I sent thee?

15 And he said unto him, Oh my Lord, wherewith shall I save Israel? behold, my family *is* poor in Ma-

Judges 6:11-16, 25-29, 32

11 Now the angel of the Lord came and sat under the oak at Ophrah, which belonged to Jo'ash the Abiez'rite, as his son Gideon was beating out wheat in the wine press, to hide it from the Mid'ianites. 12 And the angel of the Lord appeared to him and said to him, "The Lord is with you, you mighty man of valor." 13 And Gideon said to him, "Pray, sir, if the Lord is with us, why then has all this befallen us? And where are all his wonderful deeds which our fathers recounted to us, saying, 'Did not the Lord bring us up from Egypt?' But now the Lord has cast us off, and given us into the hand of Mid'-ian." 14 And the Lord turned to him and said, "Go in this might of yours and deliver Israel from the hand of Mid'-ian; do not I send you?" 15 And he said to him, "Pray, Lord, how can I deliver Israel? Behold, my clan is the weakest in Manas'seh, and I am the least in my family." 16 And the Lord said to him, "But I will be with you, and you shall smite the Midianites as one man."

nas'-seh, and I *am* the least in my father's house.

16 And the Lord said unto him, Surely I will be with thee, and thou shalt smite the Mid'-i-an-ites as one man.

....

25 And it came to pass the same night, that the Lord said unto him, Take thy father's young bullock, even the second bullock of seven years old, and throw down the altar of Ba'-al that thy father hath, and cut down the grove that *is* by it:

26 And build an altar unto the Lord thy God upon the top of this rock, in the ordered place, and take the second bullock, and offer a burnt sacrifice with the wood of the grove which thou shalt cut down.

27 Then Gideon took ten men of his servants, and did as the Lord had said unto him: and *so* it was, because he feared his father's household, and the men of the city, that he could not do *it* by day, that he did *it* by night.

28 And when the men of the city arose early in the morning, behold, the altar of Ba'-al was cast down, and the grove was cut down that *was* by it, and the second bullock was offered upon the altar *that was* built.

29 And they said one to another, Who hath done this thing? And when they enquired and asked, they said, Gideon the son of Jo'-ash hath done this thing.

....

32 Therefore on that day he called him Je-rub'-ba-al, saying, Let Ba'-al plead against him, because he hath thrown down his altar.

Key Verse: **The angel of the Lord appeared unto him, and said unto him, the Lord is with thee, thou mighty man of valour. (Judges 6:12)**

....

25 That night the Lord said to him, "Take your father's bull, the second bull seven years old, and pull down the altar of Ba'al which your father has, and cut down the Ashe'-rah that is beside it; 26 and build an altar to the Lord your God on the top of the stronghold here, with stones laid in due order; then take the second bull, and offer it as a burnt offering with the wood of the Ashe'rah which you shall cut down." 27 So Gideon took ten men of his servants, and did as the Lord had told him; but because he was too afraid of his family and the men of the town to do it by day, he did it by night.

28 When the men of the town rose early in the morning, behold, the altar of Ba'al was broken down, and the Ashe'rah beside it was cut down, and the second bull was offered upon the altar which had been built. 29 And they said to one another, "Who has done this thing?" And after they had made search and inquired, they said, "Gideon the son of Jo'ash has done this thing."

....

32 Therefore on that day he was called Jerubba'al, that is to say, "Let Ba'al contend against him," because he pulled down his altar.

Key Verse: **The angel of the Lord appeared to him and said to him, "The Lord is with you, you mighty man of valor." (Judges 6:12)**

As You Read the Scripture—Harold Reid Weaver

Judges 6:1-5. The Midianites have been murdering, raping, and stealing from the Israelites (and other nearby peoples) for many years. The Midianite raids were called *mazzias*, and were swift, ruthless, and merciless. The Midianites lived in the Arabian Desert, east and southeast of the Dead Sea. They were nomads, as the Israelites had been, and in fact were considered part of the descendents of Abraham through one of his concubines (see Genesis 25:1-6). The Israelites feared the lightning-swift strikes of the Midianites and hid in dens, caves carved in the mountains, and in strongholds they had built.

Verses 11-13. Gideon is furtively threshing his wheat in his wine press. If the Midianites had come, he would have been powerless to defend himself and his property. But an angel of the Lord appears. This is "an expression designating the divine presence which had accompanied Israel from the Red Sea through the wilderness wanderings" (*The Interpreter's Bible*, vol. 2 pp. 698-99). This visitor says to Gideon, "The Lord is with you, you mighty man of valor" (verse 12). Gideon seems annoyed. With a touch of defiance, mingled with shame, he replies, in effect, "Who, me? A man of valor? Are you kidding? I am afraid, hiding away like a scared rabbit, and you call me a man of valor!"

Gideon is also a bit annoyed by the angel's "The Lord is with you" comment. If he is with me, then why doesn't he do something? "Where have you been when we needed you most?" is the charge. Prove that you are with me!

Verses 19-24. The reluctant Gideon asks for and receives a sign, which convinces him to go ahead.

Verses 25-29. The people have strayed very far from Yahweh. Gideon is ordered by God to tear down the altar of Baal and to cut down the Asherah (a phallic symbol of the gods of fertility). Gideon performs the deed under cover of night. He feared his own family and his townsmen. This reveals, too, the extent of the acceptance of Baal worship. Gideon's own people would punish him for destroying Baal's altars! When morning breaks, the men of the city find their beloved Baal altars destroyed, and identify Gideon and ten of his friends as the culprits.

Verses 30-32. Furious, they turn to Joash, the father of Gideon, and demand that the son be turned over to them "that he may die." But Joash rises to the occasion, backing the destruction of the pagan altars. Joash bases his defense on the idea that if Baal is god, then he should fight his own battles. "If he is a god, let him contend for himself, because his altar has been pulled down."

From that time forth, Gideon would be referred to as Jerubbaal, which means "let Baal fight his own battle against him."

The rest of the story of Gideon immediately follows. The reluctant leader goes forth as the reluctant Moses did, to fight manfully for what he believes is the will of God.

The Scripture and the Main Question—Pat McGeachy

Gideon the Skeptic

When we first meet Gideon (Judges 6:11), he is not a soldier but a farmer, the least important member of a small clan (verse 15). We find him threshing wheat in a winepress, of all places, so that he won't be discovered by the Midianites. There he is discovered by God's messenger (the word "angel" means "messenger"; can you see it hiding in the word "evangelist"?), who salutes him with, "The Lord is with you." But the skeptical Gideon says, in effect (verse 13), "If that's so, then why are we in such a fix? Where is the great God of Moses' day that we have all heard about?"

Then the Lord (it is sometimes difficult to distinguish between God and images or appearances of God) says, "I personally send you; go and deliver Israel" (verse 14). But still Gideon is reluctant. "I'm a weak man from a weak people," he whines (reminds us of Isaiah 6:5). "Yes," says the Lord, "but I will be with you." This ought to be enough, but no, Gideon asks for a sign (verse 17).

The Lord shows remarkable patience through all this and waits (verse 18) for Gideon to make up his mind, and even goes to the length of doing a trick, setting some cakes and meat on fire as a sign. This makes me think of a number of other signs performed in the Bible for the purpose of helping people believe. My list would include Moses' rod (Exodus 7:9), Elijah's fire (I Kings 18:30-40), and Jesus' wine (John 2:1-11). God uses many and various means to convince the most skeptical, from enemies like Pharaoh and the prophets of Baal, to uncertain friends, like Jesus' disciples and Gideon.

What Will Convince Us?

A person once said to me, "If God really wanted to prove that religion is real, why aren't the stars arranged in the sky to spell out a clear message, such as, 'I AM GOD, BELIEVE IN ME'?" I pondered that quite a while, and apart from some trivial objections (such as, what language would God write the message in, and toward which civilization in the universe should the sign be oriented?), I think I know the answer. Apparently God wants us to believe not because things are obvious but because the truth is the truth. For one thing, the Bible says that the stars *do* spell out the truth about God (see Psalm 19:1-4 and Romans 1:20). And, though tempted by the devil to do some dramatic things (Luke 4:1-12), Jesus consistently avoided the dramatic in his ministry; instead, most of the time when he healed people he would ask them to be quiet about it (see Luke 4:41, 5:14, etc.). God wants us to believe by free choice, not to be bullied into it by a heavenly advertising campaign.

In fact, you and I have plenty of signs to show us the way:

1. The Bible itself is a sign, handed down by generations, a faithful guide to all we need to know about belief and behavior.

2. Jesus is a sign. If we have seen Jesus, we know what God is like (John 14:9), and we know the way in which we are to walk (John 14:6).

3. The traditions of the church are signs. The wisdom of generations of Christians, collected in the stories of our spiritual ancestors, is available for us by way of example, and their writings and teachings guide us as well.

4. The presence of Christian friends is a sign for us today. We are not alone and without guidance; the church, past and present, surrounds us with example and counsel.

5. The God-given intelligence and talents with which we have been blessed are signs. Most of life's questions can be answered by looking at the

gifts we have and using our common sense to decide what to do with them.

6. The Holy Spirit speaks to us in our hearts and consciences, giving us an inner sign, so that "deep down" we often know from within what we ought to be doing.

This great "crowd of witnesses" is usually all the evidence we need to decide on proper courses of action in our lives. And if we have exhausted them all and still are not sure, we may cry out to God to make it clearer to us. Even then, we may not always get an obvious answer. Sometimes God prefers for the decision to be left entirely up to us, saying, in effect, "I trust you. You know what is right, now do it."

Get On with It!

In the end, though, the great question is not so much, Can I prove that this is really God? but, Can I prove that I am really God's faithful disciple? When all is said and done, I need to get up and get started.

There is an old World War II story about a lieutenant drilling a contingent of Marines on the deck of an aircraft carrier. The platoon was marching closer and closer to the edge of the flight deck, but the young officer, in panic, had drawn a blank and couldn't remember the command to halt or "to the rear, march!" Looking down from the bridge above, a grizzled Navy chief watched the affair with wonder and finally cried out, "For heaven's sake, mister, say *something*, even if it's only, 'Goodbye!'"

As Elijah has sarcastically asked us, "How long will you go limping along with two different opinions?" (I Kings 18:21). It is better to be wrong than lukewarm (Revelation 3:16). Thus, Martin Luther enjoined us to "sin boldly." He did not mean that we should be bold libertines, but that, knowing we are sinners, we should live life heroically, trusting in God for the consequences. The most dramatic example of this that I can think of is Dietrich Bonhoeffer, the minister who took part in the underground against Hitler and was eventually executed as a traitor. He found himself caught in a dilemma: "If I take part in an attempt to assassinate Hitler, I am clearly in violation of my Christian ethics, but if I do not try to stop him, I will be responsible for the deaths of millions." In the end, he chose to act, telling his friends that it is no harder for God to forgive our evil deeds than it is to forgive what we believe to be our good deeds!

In Gideon's case, the action consisted of tearing down an altar to Baal and erecting an altar to God. He burned the Asherah (a kind of fertility rite totem pole) in a sacrifice to the Lord. This whole thing was done rather fearfully by night, for Gideon was still not all that convinced. He has yet to ask for still another sign, the familiar one about the wet and dry fleeces. But the fact is, he did it! Timidly and hesitantly he did it, and it must have felt wonderful. He must have felt like Willie Keith did in *The Caine Mutiny*, when he finally got the courage to tell the truth about the way he felt about Captain Queeg's cowardice. It was at once terrifying and satisfying, "like punching a fist through a glass door."

True, it stirred up the Midianites to a bigger fight (sometimes doing the right thing makes things worse at first), but it also seemed to electrify Gideon himself and to give him strength. For this second go-round he was powerfully filled with the Spirit (Judges 6:34) and was able to rally the troops around him. True also, he wasn't fully courageous or entirely convinced yet. The fleece business was yet to come (verses 36-40), but

Gideon was on his way at last, and as we shall see in the next lesson, a greater victory was still to come.

Gideon is in some ways easier for most of us to identify with than Samson. They both had faults, but Gideon's are more universal. Samson was a rare man, an almost superhuman character. But Gideon could be any one of us: eager but uncertain, brave but frightened, ready to serve God but not quite yet. If God can take a person like that and turn him into a famous judge, a name in the list of divine heroes (Hebrews 11:32), is it not possible that the same thing could happen to you or me?

Helping Adults Become Involved—John Warren Steen

Preparing to Teach

Be careful not to approach this lesson with a judgmental attitude. Recall your own reluctance when you were called to teach (or perhaps when you were first called to Christ). Remain sympathetic about the difficulties of changing, while you challenge the class to develop new attitudes of devotion.

Consider using the following teaching aim: to assist the class to develop an attitude of loyal waiting for God's leadership and direction.

Use the following outline:

> I. The call of Gideon (Judges 6:11-17)
>   A. Confrontation
>   B. Introductory word
>   C. Commission
>   D. Objection
>   E. Reassurance
>   F. Sign
> II. The response of Gideon (6:25-32)
>   A. Destruction of the Altar of Baal
>   B. Reaction of town: from anger to awe

Read carefully "The Scripture and the Main Question" and "As You Read the Scripture." These form the heart of the lesson. The ideas, insights, and suggestions in these sections should be reflected continually in your lesson plan.

As you use the suggested outline, you may want to either quote or paraphrase ideas. You might like to jot in the margin of your outline the page number and paragraph being referred to. For example, you could write a reference to page 65, paragraph 3, as 65-3.

Introducing the Main Question

Basic and helpful ideas are presented in the section "The Main Question." These ideas are essential in helping to identify the purpose of the lesson.

The main question, which I have slightly reworded, is, How can I know God and respond with loyalty?

Relate Dr. McGeachy's account of his friend's question about why God doesn't arrange the stars to dispel all doubts about God's reality. Discuss this seemingly simple request of the Almighty. Then have a member read Psalm 19:1-4, and discuss how God has already done this. Next, have someone read Luke 4:9-12 and note how Jesus avoided using the spectacular to convince people.

Ask: Are any of us truly loyal? The students will probably answer in the negative. Relate to the class the statement of the distinguished minister Dr. S. Parkes Cadman, in his seventh decade of life, about what was wrong with his church. He said, "My church is slipping. Do you know what is wrong with my church? My people like me, but they don't love God."

Ask: Is it easier to be loyal to a pastor than to the Redeemer who called the pastor? Is it easier to be loyal to a college or a church than to the Christ who inspired the institution? Most will agree we need to know God better in order to be more loyal. They will likely add that we need to fully express our loyalty. Ask the class to evaluate Dr. McGeachy's comment that we usually plead either ignorance or weakness, in not showing loyalty to God.

Developing the Lesson

I. The call of Gideon (Judges 6:11-17)

Point to the situation described in Judges 6:1, which reiterates the story of the people sinning and the Lord giving them over to an enemy. In this case the enemy is the neighboring Midianites, who come at harvest time to steal the provisions of the Israelites. Discuss the statement that the marauders were "like locusts" (6:5). In some ways they were worse than locusts, who simply follow the instincts of nature to feed. These people do not seem to have farmed, but fed themselves by raiding others' crops. Their kind of stealing is reprehensible.

A. Confrontation

God called a judge to help. In this case, the potential judge was reluctant. The call of Gideon, like the call of Moses, Jeremiah, and Ezekiel, can be divided into six parts: confrontation, introductory word, commission, objection, reassurance, sign, and action.

B. Introductory word

The angel or messenger found Gideon not out in the fields threshing but hidden in a wine press, which was carved out of rock. Do you think Gideon smiled when the angel called him "mighty man of valor" (6:12)?

Note Gideon's doubt, taking the angel's words, "the Lord is with you," and putting an "if" in front of them. He goes on to express doubt about one of the most treasured facts of Hebrew history—the Exodus. He contrasted a glorious past with a miserable present.

C. Commission

Gideon's commission is to use his might (perhaps demonstrated by the zeal with which he threshed his wheat) and to deliver his people, in the knowledge that he is sent by God.

D. Objection

Note his humility in verse 15. His family's reputation and his own record are not sufficient qualifications for him to be a deliverer and judge.

E. Reassurance

The reassurance offered him sounds like the New Testament promise of the visitation of the Holy Spirit, which offers comfort and leadership. Read John 14 and note similarities.

F. Sign

The sign consisted of the meal (prepared by Gideon) of meat, broth, and cakes. The gift was burned up by a fire of unknown origin, and the angel disappeared. Gideon's belief in the divine nature of the call was affirmed.

II. The response of Gideon (6:25-32)

A. Destruction of the altar of Baal

Note that the father of Gideon had a shrine to Baal for the whole community. People sometimes say, "Judgment must start at home." With Gideon, this was literally true.

Ask why Gideon needed ten helpers. Answer: The shrine must have been of considerable size and complexity. It took eleven people to remove it.

Note that they worked by night. Why? They didn't want to be stopped. The next morning, everyone knew what had happened. They discovered a newly constructed altar with a sacrificed bull on it.

B. Reaction of town: from anger to awe

Why were the citizens so concerned about the destruction? They had likely invested some time and expensive materials in it. But even more importantly, they were afraid of the wrath of the storm and fertility gods.

Note the answer that Gideon's father gave the people. He told them that anyone who sought revenge for Baal was meddling in Baal's business, then interjected the doubt, "if he is a god." Events showed the false god to be powerless.

Jerubaal, "let Baal be content," became a nickname that Gideon wore proudly.

Helping Class Members Act

Look again at the word "reluctant." Ask members to be ready to act with boldness in right causes, assured that God will be with them.

Say (or sing) together the words of a hymn of dedication, such as "The Master Hath Come, and He Calls Us to Follow."

Planning for Next Sunday

Ask members to watch for evidence of new trends in society. Ask them to bring examples from a public opinion poll.

Encourage members to reach out beyond the regular attenders and bring in a new person for Bible study.

Gideon: Relying on God's Power

Background Scripture: Judges 7

The Main Question—Pat McGeachy

It is almost impossible not to celebrate bigness. The questions we ask of people are almost always quantitative, like, "How many children does she have?" "How much money?" "How many people work for him?" "What does he weigh?" I know this because almost without exception, when I meet a stranger, after they learn my name and that I am a pastor, the next question is, "How big is your church?" Now it happens that I prefer small churches, but it always gets me just a little to admit how few members we have. Even though I sought this appointment for the very reason that it is small and dedicated, and even though I believe in my heart that small is beautiful, I am just as size-conscious as everybody else. The last time anybody asked me, "How big is your church?" I said, "Oh, they vary from about twenty-one inches to around six feet four inches". But I was ashamed of myself afterward.

But the questions of God are "qualitative." God accomplishes things "not by might, nor by power, but by my Spirit, says the Lord of hosts" (Zechariah 4:6). And you remember the lady who put a penny in the collection plate and it turned out to be worth more than the contributions of all the big givers put together? (Mark 12:41-44). We are far from the truth when we put our trust in human resources, however powerful (Psalm 146:3). The story of Gideon forces us to look at the question, In what do we trust? God made Gideon pare down the troops until they were so few in number that it would be obvious that it was a divine, not a human victory. So said Paul of the human body: "We have this treasure in earthen vessels, to show that the transcendent power belongs to God and not to us" (II Corinthians 4:7).

There is no more difficult lesson for people to learn than to trust an invisible God more than a visible human army. It is for this reason that only a few get into the kingdom (Luke 22:24); it is a narrow door. But it is the only door there is, so we must find the courage to believe in the impossible.

Selected Scripture

King James Version

Judges 7:2-7, 19-21
2 And the Lord said unto Gideon, The people that *are* with thee *are* too many for me to give the Mid'-i-an-ites into their hands, lest Israel vaunt themselves against me, saying, Mine own hand hath saved me.

3 Now therefore go to, proclaim in the ears of the people, saying, Whosoever *is* fearful and afraid, let

Revised Standard Version

Judges 7:2-7, 19-21
2 The Lord said to Gideon, "The people with you are too many for me to give the Mid'ianites into their hand, lest Israel vaunt themselves against me, saying, 'My own hand has delivered me.' 3 Now therefore proclaim in the ears of the people, saying, 'Whoever is fearful and trembling, let him return home.'"

him return and depart early from mount Gilead. And there returned of the people twenty and two thousand; and there remained ten thousand.

4 And the Lord said unto Gideon, The people *are* yet *too* many; bring them down unto the water, and I will try them for thee there: and it shall be *that* of whom I say unto thee, This shall go with thee, the same shall go with thee; and of whomsoever I say unto thee, This shall not go with thee, the same shall not go.

5 So he brought down the people unto the water: and the Lord said unto Gideon, Every one that lappeth of the water with his tongue, as a dog lappeth, him shalt thou set by himself; likewise every one that boweth down upon his knees to drink.

6 And the number of them that lapped, *putting* their hand to their mouth, were three hundred men: but all the rest of the people bowed down upon their knees to drink water.

7 And the Lord said unto Gideon, By the three hundred men that lapped will I save you, and deliver the Mid'-i-an-ites into thine hand: and let all the *other* people go every man unto his place.

....

19 So Gideon, and the hundred men that *were* with him, came unto the outside of the camp in the beginning of the middle watch; and they had but newly set the watch: and they blew the trumpets, and brake the pitchers that *were* in their hands.

20 And the three companies blew the trumpets, and brake the pitchers, and held the lamps in their left hands, and the trumpets in their right hands to blow *withal*: and they cried, The sword of the Lord, and of Gideon.

21 And they stood every man in his place round about the camp: and

And Gideon tested them; twenty-two thousand returned, and ten thousand remained.

4 And the Lord said to Gideon, "The people are still too many; take them down to the water and I will test them for you there; and he of whom I say to you, 'This man shall go with you,' shall go with you; and any of whom I say to you, 'This man shall not go with you,' shall not go."

5 So he brought the people down to the water; and the Lord said to Gideon, "Every one that laps the water with his tongue, as a dog laps, you shall set by himself; likewise every one that kneels down to drink." 6 And the number of those that lapped, putting their hands to their mouths, was three hundred men; but all the rest of the people knelt down to drink water. 7 And the Lord said to Gideon, "With the three hundred men that lapped I will deliver you, and give the Mid'ianites into your hand; and let all the others go every man to his home."

....

19 So Gideon and the hundred men who were with him came to the outskirts of the camp at the beginning of the middle watch, when they had just set the watch; and they blew the trumpets and smashed the jars that were in their hands. 20 And the three companies blew the trumpets and broke the jars, holding in their left hands the torches, and in their right hands the trumpets to blow; and they cried, "A sword for the Lord and for Gideon!" 21 They stood every man in his place round about the camp, and all the army ran; they cried out and fled."

all the host ran, and cried, and fled.

As You Read the Scripture—Harold Reid Weaver

A major battle is to take place between the forces of Gideon and those of the Midianites. The forces of Gideon include the unseen power of the Lord. Yahweh seeks to minimize Gideon's role, in order that the Israelites may see the superior power of the Almighty.

Judges 7:2. God tells Gideon that he has too many fighting men. As a matter of fact, he has thirty-two thousand of them, an awesome body of warriors. If they won the battle, they might glory in their own strength and give relatively little recognition to the God who leads and inspires them.

Verse 3. Gideon asks the men how many of them are afraid, at God's command, and twenty-two thousand admit it. Gideon tells those men to go home. Neither he nor God can use men without backbone.

Verses 4-7. The Lord asks Gideon to reduce his forces even more. At God's behest, Gideon brings his army to the water and watches how they drink it. Many thirstily throw themselves to the ground and drink. Others lift the water in their hands to their mouths and drink, so they can keep a watch for enemies at the same time. God tells Gideon to keep the three hundred careful men and to send the rest of the soldiers away. The Lord states he will give Gideon the victory through these men.

Verses 16-20. Gideon divides the men into three companies of one hundred each, so that they can attack from three sides simultaneously. He arms them with trumpets and clay jars with torches inside. Gideon and his men sneak up to the outskirts of the camp at the beginning of the middle watch. The middle watch refers to the custom of dividing the night into three equal segments of four hours each. (The Roman custom in Jesus' day was to have four watches during the night.) At Gideon's signal, first the one hundred who were with him, then those surrounding the camp, blew on their trumpets, smashed the clay pitchers, and lifted the torches hidden inside.

Verses 21-22. Panic took possession of the Midianites. They were awakened in darkness with the blasting of trumpets all about them, and the Israelites screaming, "A sword for the Lord and for Gideon!" Where to go? What to do? Who to follow? No one knew. Bedlam took the place of order. Flight replaced fight. In their panic, they turned their weapons on each other, stumbling and hacking away, seeking to find escape from Gideon, his men, and his God.

Later in the chapter, we find the Midianites plunging headlong down the eastern slope. This first battle had been won, but not the war. In fact, Gideon calls for help from the nearby tribe of Ephraim.

The key verse points out, "That same night the Lord said to [Gideon] 'Arise, go down against the camp; for I have given it into your hand'" (Judges 7:9). It was the Lord, the unseen presence, but it was also the three hundred men following their intrepid leader, Gideon.

Perhaps it would be helpful to note that Gideon made such an impression on his people that they wanted him to become king. "Rule over us, you and your son and your grandson also; for you have delivered us out of the hand of Midian" (Judges 8:22). They were ready to establish the dynasty of Gideon. But the man had the wisdom to say no. He wanted the rule of God, not the rule of a man. It was the first attempt by the Israelites to establish a monarchy. Gideon wanted instead a theocracy, that is, a kingdom ruled by God. He was faithful in his belief that his people had been delivered by God's power.

The Scripture and the Main Question—Pat McGeachy

Stripping for Action

When you get ready to fight, you take off your coat; when you get ready to rescue someone drowning, you may take off everything. Usually when we think of going into battle, we think of putting armor on (Ephesians 6:11), but in this case we are to reduce things to their absolute essentials. God does not play the numbers game. Chapter 7 begins with the paring down of Gideon's forces, first by sending home the reluctant (verse 3), and then by sending those who knelt down to drink (verses 4-7). Apparently those who lapped the water like dogs were considered the more wary warriors. Furthermore, comforted by a visit to the enemy camp, where he hears an encouraging conversation about a dream (verses 9-14), Gideon divides the small army, now only three hundred, into three still smaller companies and sends them to surround the Midianites in the dark, armed with trumpets and concealed lamps. On signal, the lamps are revealed, the trumpets blown, and the cry raised, "For the Lord and for Gideon!" The enemy camp is thrown into utter confusion, and in the resulting rout, with the help of the Ephraimites (verses 24-25) their princes are captured.

On the surface, it looks as though we have evidence here that the Lord prefers to do things by trickery, by using clever stunts rather than overwhelming might. But it is deeper than that. It is something like jiu jitsu, which, I am told, means in Japanese "the gentle art." The enemy is overcome by employing his own momentum on your behalf. The leverage of your action uses his charge against him, and you pitch him over your shoulder. The point is that God chooses to work through unexpected and small things, like the flick of a wrist or the turn of a knee.

This is best illustrated for the Christian by remembering the most powerful thing God has done. Jesus Christ came into the world, born in a stranger's barn in a tiny, obscure country near one end of the Roman Empire. He chose the way not of power and prestige but of quiet truth and vulnerability (Luke 4:1-12). His followers were rude, uneducated fishermen, few in number. In the end, they forsook him and fled. He never wrote a book or traveled very far from the place of his birth. He had no army, no money, not even a house to lie down in. And he died the death of a common criminal, between two thieves, after an active ministry of less than three years. Today, that Roman Empire is in ruins, a dozen great civilizations have risen and fallen since, but still the world numbers its years from the date of Jesus' birth, and the number of his followers, now in the billions, continues to grow, spreading his gospel around the world.

It is as though God, going into battle against the dark forces of this world, first stripped for action. Paul says in Philippians 2:7-8 that Christ "emptied himself, taking the form of a servant, being born in the likeness of men. And being found in human form, he humbled himself and became obedient unto death, even death on a cross." But this emptying resulted in the overthrow of the dark powers, just as Gideon's tiny army overcame the Midianites.

In terms of your life and mine, we are enjoined to give ourselves not to statistics or to the worship of quantitative things but to the worship of God, who moves in Spirit to accomplish great deeds that the powers of darkness dare not attempt. What does all this say to our preoccupation with enormous defense budgets and nuclear arsenals? What does it say to our frantic preoccupation with home security devices and retirement funds?

We are not advocating, here at least, complete pacifism or utter disdain for practical realities. There does need to be a small, carefully chosen army. We do need to make plans for our defense. We even need, when the time is right and the moral issues are clear, to attack the enemy in his camp. But the question is, In what, or more properly, in *whom* do we trust? And whose orders do we obey?

Self-Made Men and Women

Opposite to Gideon's trust (however slow in coming) and his obedience to God is the popular notion that we are obedient only to Number One. I saw an ad for a certain brand of Scotch whiskey not long ago, which consisted simply of a pure black page with a small bottle of the liquor in question on it, and underneath the two words: "Honor Thyself." That seems to me to sum up the "me" generation.

Now, to honor one's family or one's church or one's nation is to take this loyalty a step further. Instead of being selfishly interested in myself, I become unselfishly a faithful parent, a mate, a church member, a patriotic citizen. But have a care here! These are secondary loyalties, however noble: false gods at worst, servants of the true God at best. I may be a moral man in an immoral society! I may pay my taxes faithfully, but my country may use that money to stockpile bombs and overthrow governments! I may give faithfully to the church, and the religious leaders may use my tithe unwisely, for frivolous or unworthy expenses. I may remain loyal to my family, and my family may be far from righteous.

So, if I cannot be a righteous individual and I belong to an unrighteous society (remember what Gideon said in Judges 6:15), what possible hope is there for me? Ah, now I have arrived at the point where I am able, if willing, to pass through that narrow gate. I have come to the realization that by my own efforts I can never be saved; I must turn to the promise summarized in Ephesians 2:8-9: "For by grace you have been saved through faith; and this is not your own doing, it is the gift of God, not because of works, lest any man should boast." That is why God made Gideon pare his army down to a minimum—to win a clever victory, yes, but more than that, to force the people to understand that it was by God alone that their salvation came.

Patriotism

It is very very difficult, indeed, it is almost impossible to be a patriotic citizen of an earthly country and at the same time a faithful citizen of the kingdom of God. Jesus might well have used the illustration of the camel and the needle's eye to describe the patriot as well as the rich man, for the nation is, after all the most wonderful possession anyone can have, the poor as well as the rich.

The temptation is to wriggle out of this dilemma by identifying national interests with those of God. Here again, if we are to manage the difficult step, it will be done only if, like Gideon, we remember that our first loyalty is to the Lord; we must be, as the pledge of allegiance to our flag says, "one nation under God." But even in America, where we have done a fairly good job of keeping church and state separate, there are always those who think (and times when most of us think) that surely God loves our nation more than all the others in the world.

In one sense, this is true. At any rate, we are certainly blessed among the world's nations. But just because America is "my country right or wrong," that does not make her always right. And when America is wrong, we must stand up for the right and seek (as Stephen Decatur urged in his quote) that "she may ever be right." We can learn here from Gideon, the reluctant warrior, who will (as we shall see in the next lesson) refused to be crowned king. We can be, as we should be, very slow to assume righteousness for our cause. We should wait as long as we dare before taking the tragic step of making war to keep the peace. Sometimes it has to be done, but we needn't be in a hurry, nor build our standing army too large.

Helping Adults Become Involved—John Warren Steen

Preparing to Teach

Consider using the following teaching aim: to lead the class to see that numbers are not important for measuring success in God's work.

Use the following outline:

      I.   Reducing the numbers (Judges 7:2-7).
          A. Gideon released 22,000 fearful men.
          B. Gideon released 9,700 careless men.
     II. Defeating the enemy (2:19-21).
          A. Gideon used a stratagem.
          B. Midianites fled in panic.

Read carefully "The Scripture and the Main Question" and "As You Read the Scripture." These form the heart of the lesson. The ideas, insights, and suggestions in these sections should be reflected continually in your lesson plan.

As you use the suggested outline, you may want to either quote or paraphrase ideas. You might like to jot in the margin of your outline the page number and paragraph being referred to. For example, you could write a reference to page 65, paragraph 3, as 65-3.

Introducing the Main Question

Basic and helpful ideas are presented in the section "The Main Question." These ideas are essential in helping to identify the purpose of the lesson.

Ask about the significance of the Gallup Poll, the Harris Poll, and other political and entertainment rating systems. Ask for examples of people following a trend.

Point out that the fashion industry seems to be based on introducing new styles. In magazines and on television, fashion commentators announce, "This is what everybody will be wearing next fall." Thus, an appeal is made to the 10 to 20 percent of the population who are trendsetters, in the hopes that the remaining sector will pick up the trend within the next year or two.

Pause to ask if this is just amusing or if it is dangerous. Then move to the area of religion and morals and ask the same question. Also ask if we are just as guilty as teenagers who justify their actions with the expression, "Everybody's doing it."

Now come to the main question: In what or in whom do we put our trust?

Developing the Lesson

I. Reducing the numbers (Judges 7:2-7).
   A. Gideon released 22,000 fearful men.
Give the background from Judges 6:33, which explains about the annual raids at the time of the wheat harvest. The Valley of Jezreel was a rich agricultural section. Gideon took his volunteer troops to the valley to meet them and encamped at the spring of Harod at the foot of Mount Gilboa.

Have a member read Judges 7:2 and comment on it. Explore the reasons for cutting down on the sizeable army. What would be wrong with people taking pride in an army's accomplishments in delivering them from a marauding enemy? Answer: Their pride could lead them away from dependence on God their leader and protector; they would tend to exalt themselves and make their own rules.
   B. Gideon released 9,700 careless men.
Discuss the technique described in verses 5 and 6 of weeding out the 9,700 who were not alert. They put their heads down to the water in order to drink, but the cautious men brought the water up in their hands while keeping a sharp lookout for the enemy.

II. Defeating the enemy (2:19-21).
   A. Gideon used a stratagem.
Now move quickly to the battle and the stratagem Gideon employed. Note that the three hundred were divided into three patrols of one hundred each.

Have class members explain the how the surprise raid must have looked and sounded to the sleeping Midianite soldiers: the surprise of a night raid, the noise of the trumpets, and the sight of torches surrounding the camp on every side.
   B. Midianites fled in panic.
Have class members visualize the effect on the Midianites. They fled screaming. Of course, all of them were not killed by the three hundred. But the tribes of Naphtali, Asher, and Manasseh had been summoned, and they pursued the fleeing invaders. God gave them a mighty victory.

If you have time, you might note two unexpected effects of the victory: (1) the wounded feelings of Ephraim (8:1) and Gideon's tactful and humble reconciliation, and (2) the move to acclaim Gideon as king (8:20), which he wisely refused, pointing people to the rule of God.

Helping Class Members Act

Repeat the main question: In what or in whom do we trust? Ask members to discuss and make new commitments in measuring success.

The next time somebody asks you the size of your church, you might want to have a ready answer that would not emphasize the number of members and the size of the building. Have members think of some more appropriate responses. They might say, "It is small enough to know everybody but large enough to include anybody who wants to join." Or maybe this: "We are pleased with our increasing membership, but we are trying to give God the glory."

Read (or have someone with a good voice read) these words of a venerable Southern Baptist preacher, Vance Havner, commenting on his demonination's size:

We seem to have the notion that if we had more church members, bigger churches, more money, and finer programs, we could win the world. God does not work that way. He can do more with a dedicated few than with an indifferent multitude. We have been counting numbers, but we have not been making the numbers count.

God is in the remnant business and always has been. He has wrought with the Faithful Few. Consider Noah and his family, Gideon and his band, Elijah and the seven thousand who had not bowed to Baal, and Isaiah and the small remnant of his day (6:12-13).

He is not marshaling a mixed multitude. He is making up his Master's minority.

We have "mob-ilized" instead of mobilized an unwieldy multitude and our size is now our greatest embarrassment. We cannot reach our goal for stumbling over our own team. We furnish our own greatest interference.

God magnifies the few. Where two or three gather in the Lord's name, he is present. If two shall agree in prayer, it shall be done for them. One shall chase a thousand, and two shall put ten thousand to flight. Many are called but few are chosen. We magnify the many. God does not move the world with statistics but with saints.

After the reading, evaluate these words. Do they apply to your church and your denomination? What can you do to keep the emphasis where it ought to be?

Planning for Next Sunday

Ask class members to bring information about the careers of Adolph Hitler and other dictators. Tell them to look for similarities with a biblical character most people don't know, Abimelech.

Ask them to be thinking of the qualities of great leadership.

Choosing Trustworthy Leaders

Background Scripture: Judges 8:22–9

The Main Question—Pat McGeachy

I don't like Abimelech. Although none of them was perfect, I have a certain pleasure in thinking of the lives of the other judges. But I just don't like Abimelech. Maybe it has something to do with the fact that when I was a little kid learning to play "Hearts and Flowers," that old piano piece that everybody knows, I used to sing his name to the bass line: "Bimalecka, Bimalecka, Bimalecka, Bimalecka," over and over monotonously. But mainly, I think it is because he flies in the face of everything I have ever been taught about the meaining and purpose of my faith.

Christ calls us to obedience; Abimelech proclaimed himself ruler.

Christ calls us to be peacemakers; Abimelech murdered seventy of his brothers. (He makes Cain look like Mother Theresa!)

Christ calls us to meekness; Abimelech was an arrogant so and so.

And I could go on. I suppose one of the natural penalties of polygamy is that it tends to produce quarrels among the offspring (of course that happens a good bit among the children of monogamous marriages, too). But the main problem with Abimelech is that he wanted to be a big shot. But there is a catch to this. Do we want a leader who has no ambition? Where do we draw the line between a genuine call to lead and a neurotic desire to lord it over others? Perhaps in looking closely at Abimelech we can approach an answer to this question, which will help us to seek dependable, capable leaders, as well as to avoid being misled by the clever and deceptive.

I think I would even rather have that old bully Samson or the scaredy-cat Gideon than Abimelech. Secretly, who I *really* would like is George Washington, but we will have more to say about that later. (By the way, Abimelech wasn't really one of the twelve judges. I prefer to think of him as a petty king. Very petty.)

Selected Scripture

King James Version	Revised Standard Version
Judges 9:1-2, 4-15	*Judges 9:1-2, 4-15*
1 And A-bim'-e-lech the son of Je-rub'-ba-al went to She'-chem unto his mother's brethren, and communed with them, and with all the family of the house of his mother's father, saying,	1 Now Abim'elech the son of Jerubba'al went to Shechem to his mother's kinsmen and said to them and to the whole clan of his mother's family, 2 "Say in the ears of all the citizens of Shechem, 'Which is better for you, that all seventy of the sons of Jerubba'al rule over you, or that one rule over you?' Remember also that I am your bone and your flesh."
2 Speak, I pray you, in the ears of all the men of She'-chem, Whether *is* better for you, either that all the sons of Je-rub'-ba-al, *which are* threescore and ten persons, reign	

over you, or that one reign over you? remember also that I *am* your bone and your flesh.

....

4 And they gave him threescore and ten *pieces* of silver out of the house of Ba'-al-be'-rith, wherewith A-bim'-e-lech hired vain and light persons, which followed him.

5 And he went unto his father's house at Oph'-rah, and slew his brethren the sons of Je-rub'-ba-al, *being* threescore and ten persons, upon one stone: notwithstanding yet Jo'-tham the youngest son of Je-rub'-ba-al was left; for he hid himself.

6 And all the men of She'-chem gathered together, and all the house of Mil'-lo, and went, and made A-bim'-e-lech king, by the plain of the pillar that *was* in She'-chem.

7 And when they told *it* to Jo'-tham, he went and stood in the top of mount Ger'-i-zim, and lifted up his voice, and cried, and said unto them, Hearken unto me, ye men of She'-chem, that God may hearken unto you.

8 The trees went forth *on a time* to anoint a king over them; and they said unto the olive tree, Reign thou over us.

9 But the olive tree said unto them, Should I leave my fatness, wherewith by me they honour God and man, and go to be promoted over the trees?

10 And the trees said to the fig tree, Come thou, *and* reign over us.

11 But the fig tree said unto them, Should I forsake my sweetness, and my good fruit, and go to be promoted over the trees?

12 Then said the trees unto the vine, Come thou, *and* reign over us.

13 And the vine said unto them, Should I leave my wine, which cheereth God and man, and go to be promoted over the trees?

14 Then said all the trees unto the bramble, Come thou, *and* reign

....

4 And they gave him seventy pieces of silver out of the house of Ba'al-be'-rith with which Abim'elech hired worthless and reckless fellows, who followed him. 5 And he went to his father's house at Ophrah, and slew his brothers the sons of Jerubba'al, seventy men, upon one stone; but Jotham the youngest son of Jerubba'al was left, for he hid himself. 6 And all the citizens of Shechem came together, and all Beth-millo, and they went and made Abim'elech king, by the oak of the pillar at Shechem.

7 When it was told to Jotham, he went and stood on the top of Mount Ger'izim, and cried aloud and said to them, "Listen to me, you men of Shechem, that God may listen to you. 8 The trees once went forth to anoint a king over them; and they said to the olive tree, 'Reign over us.' 9 But the olive tree said to them, 'Shall I leave my fatness, by which gods and men are honored, and go to sway over the trees?' 10 And the trees said to the fig tree, 'Come you, and reign over us.' 11 But the fig tree said to them, 'Shall I leave my sweetness and my good fruit, and go to sway over the trees?' 12 And the trees said to the vine, 'Come you, and reign over us.' 13 But the vine said to them, 'Shall I leave my vine which cheers gods and men, and go to sway over the trees?' 14 Then all the trees said to the bramble, 'Come you, and reign over us.' 15 And the bramble said to the trees, 'If in good faith you are anointing me king over you, then come and take refuge in my shade; but if not, let fire come out of the bramble and devour the cedars of Lebanon.'"

over us.

15 And the bramble said unto the trees, If in truth ye anoint me king over you, *then* come *and* put your trust in my shadow: and if not, let fire come out of the bramble, and devour the cedars of Lebanon.

Key Verse: **Pride goeth before destruction, and a haughty spirit before a fall. (Proverbs 16:18)**

Key Verse: **Pride goes before destruction, and a haughty spirit before a fall. (Proverbs 16:18)**

As You Read the Scripture—Harold Reid Weaver

Judges 9:1-2. After Gideon's death, his son Abimelech decided he would like to be king of Shechem. Two things favored him: (1) He was the son of a Canaanite woman; (2) he was the son of Gideon. Actually, the woman who bore him was Gideon's concubine, not his wife. Nevertheless, it made a valuable bit of informaton with which to garner votes. Remember, he would say, "I am your bone and flesh. Vote for me!" Also, his mother's relatives put it "in the ears of all the men of Shechem; and their hearts inclined to follow Abimelech."

Judges 9:1 used the name "Jerubbaal" for Gideon because he had destroyed the Baal altar as a youth. (See Judges 6:32.) Now Abimelech uses his father's good name to help his cause, but does not call for the return to Yahweh. He was an ambitious, self-centered pagan, seeking the kingship that his father had refused.

Verses 4-5. Abimelech's followers give him silver taken from the shrine of Baalberith, the Canaanite "god of the covenant." Blasphemy was thus involved, for the people not only worshiped Baal but used a term which should have been reserved for Yahweh alone: the God of the Covenant.

Abimelech used the silver to buy the sevices of "worthless and reckless fellows." Their task? To heartlessly kill all the other sons of Gideon. But one escaped them—Jotham.

Verses 6-7. Plans were made for the coronation of Abimelech as king in Shechem, where Joshua had delivered his farewell speech to Israel (Joshua 24:1, 25). On coronation day, Jotham appeared on the top of Mount Gerizim. People listened to this son of Gideon as he spoke from the mount.

Verses 8-15, 21. He offered a fable. Which of several trees shall be selected as king over the others? The olive gets first choice but refuses the honor on the grounds that it should continue producing the olive oil used to anoint both gods and honorable men. The fig tree refuses because of the value of its appetizing fruit. The vine's sweet juice is cherished by both god and man. Only the bramble, a fruitless, unproductive weed, would accept the honor. Jotham pointed out that no tree could find shelter or shade under the bramble. It was worthless. In fact, fires could start within the bramble and destroy the other trees.

Jotham's message was clear: Abimelech is a worthless fellow without honor, who will give no one comfort and who can create a destructive fire to destroy the nation. In fact, he has already killed all the other sons of Gideons. With that, Jotham runs for his life, lest Abimelech capture and kill him.

Later in this chapter (Judges 9:54), the dishonorable death of Abimelech is described. Such was the fate of this self-appointed leader, who revealed no sense of integrity, honor, or faithfulness to Yahweh. He seems totally devoid of spiritual depth, and one may wonder why he was included in the biblical account of judges of that period. Perhaps it was to show what can happen to a man, as well as a nation, who says no to Yahweh.

The Scripture and the Main Question—Pat McGeachy

We Don't Need a King

Before we say farewell to our friend Gideon, the hero of the last two lessons, we should notice a little-remembered fact about him. We all know about his testing God with the fleece and his remarkable victory with the tiny army, but we may not recall that when the war was over, he refused to accede to the flattery of the crowds who welcomed him as a conquering hero and wanted to make him king (look now at Judges 8:22-23).

Unlike his son Abimelech, who forgot the lesson of his father, Gideon has remembered that it is God alone who has the right to be sovereign. He knows that people should not put their ultimate trust in political structures. If three hundred can defeat an army of thousands, then a permanent military establishment is not necessary. So he refuses their request. In this he is anticipating the reluctance of Samuel, the prophet/judge who is to come, to give Israel their first king (see I Samuel 8:4-22). His is also an early type of the attitude that historians tell us George Washington had. Our first president, fearful of the excesses that he saw in the English royalty, fought hard to keep the American people from making his presidency a kind of royal office. It was for this reason that, though he was the only president ever to be elected unanimously to that office, he refused to run for a third term. This was no doubt due in part to his own humility and to his wisdom in knowing what would be ultimately best for the young nation.

But Abimelech had no such reluctance. (I am beginning to appreciate Gideon's tentativeness a whole lot more as I get to know Abimelech.) His name means "my father is king," which shows that his very nature has missed the point. His father was not the king. (As a matter of fact, though Gideon is usually counted among the twelve judges, I think you will find that nowhere is he referred to as a judge in this book. But it is surely implied.) Abimelech was the child not of one of Gideon's many wives but of his concubine, a woman of Shechem. (A concubine was a sort of associate wife. Gideon by no means held the record. For that, see I Kings 11:3.) And he was a bloodthirsty man, very likely jealous of his half-brothers for their more legitimate status. At any rate, he showed no reluctance to slay them all, in his mad quest for power.

Actually Abimelech never really became king, not of Israel at any rate. I know 9:22 says that he ruled Israel for a little while, but it was really only because of his influence in the fortified city of Shechem, an important but not mighty town. It was there that the kingdom of Israel would ultimately be split in half (I Kings 12:1-19), and it would one day become the chief city of the Samaritans. But he did make it to the office of petty tyrant, and he caused considerable bloodshed. I don't like him.

FOURTH QUARTER

Why Do We Choose Bad Leaders?

Ever since the horrible business at Jonestown, in Guyana, we have been asking ourselves, How could people have fallen for a madman like that? (It has also been said by some about nearly every president we have ever had.) We all identify with young Jotham's parable of the trees, in which the better trees refuse to be king. Finally the trees select the poorest choice, the briar. This parable suggests two things to me: one, that we need more competent people of integrity to agree to go into politics, and two, that we need to use far more discernment in electing our leaders.

I remember my first introduction to politics. (I grew up when Roosevelt was president for most of four terms, and it seemed strange at the time to be talking about anyone else in that office.) Mr. Truman ran against Thomas E. Dewey, and I remember hearing one of the older members of my church say to another, "You know, I've always been a Republican, but I just don't like that fellow Dewey's moustache." It began to slowly dawn on me that if the electorate has no more judgment than that, then we are in serious trouble as a nation. People clutch at straws, vote for those who are glib rather than profound, popular rather than moral, and we even like ambitious men like Abimelech!

In fact, it seems if a person isn't somewhat ambitious, we are suspicious of him. Once when I tried to move to a smaller church, for what I thought were very fine reasons, I was viewed with suspicion. "Nobody goes *down* the ladder on purpose," they said. But Jesus did. And Paul has warned us, saying, "I bid every one among you not to think of himself more highly than he ought to think, but to think with sober judgment, each according to the measure of faith which God has assigned him" (Romans 12:3).

One final point: Hidden in Paul's warning is our need to admit our strengths as well as our weaknesses. We are not to think of ourselves more *lowly* than we ought to think, either. Let's not have our political process degenerate into a kind of passive-aggressive battle between two politicians playing a kind of Alphonse and Gaston routine of "After you." Let's have good people running and let's use good judgment in electing them.

How to Spot a Phony

"Beware of false prophets," we are told by Jesus (Matthew 7:15). But how are we to recognize them? Perhaps you have, as I do, a list of questions that you use to help determine the answer to this one. Things like, How much do they charge? If the answer is anything at all, I figure they are in it for the money. The prophetic word is free (see Isaiah 55:1), and if ever anybody tries to sell you the secret, that one is false.

But what can we learn about this from Abimelech? At the risk of being simplistic, here are a few suggestions:

1. Don't elect a king who can't get along with his family (see I Timothy 3:4). Abimelech was one of the worst family men in history.

2. Don't elect a queen who's more concerned with her image than with what she accomplishes. Note from the strange manner of his death (9:54) that Abimelech was utterly preoccupied with his reputation.

3. Don't elect a king who's way of dealing with his enemies is ambushing them (9:34, 43). What we need are straightforward leaders who will meet us

404

head-on with the issues and who are more concerned with doing what is right than with winning.

4. Don't elect a queen who has to pay people to be her friends (see 9:4). Abimelech had to play on kinship and cash to win his way into power. What do you think about the cost of election campaigns?

Of, by, and for the People

I am told that when Mr. Lincoln gave the Gettysburg Address, he emphasized its famous opening words differently from the way we usually do when we quote them: He said that government "of the *people*, by the *people*, and for the *people*, should not perish from the earth." Yes, and he also said, I am told, that while you can fool some of the people all of the time, and all of the people some of the time, you cannot expect to fool all of the people all of the time. So we, the people, ought most of the time to be choosing the best leaders. And yet we don't seem to. Is there any hope for us?

I believe that the lesson of Abimelech can bring us once again to the realization, seen by Gideon, Joshua, and other legitimate judges, that it is God and God alone who gives the true authority to the leadership of the nation. Of course we do not want a theocracy, a government of people who think they have somehow been divinely appointed. Hitler was such a leader. Theocrats can never be disagreed with; they always think they are doing God's will, and nothing can stop them.

No, what we want is a leader who says, "God, I don't want to be in charge, but if somebody has to, I will do it, and I will do my best to say, 'Lord, not my will, but thine, be done.'" There was such a leader once, and we killed him. Let us pray for his return soon.

Helping Adults Become Involved—John Warren Steen

Preparing to Teach

Bring information about the strange career of Adoph Hitler. Be able to show comparisons between his career and that of Abimelech.

Consider ways to get members involved in a discussion about ambition and leadership. Type up or write out the following statements to pass out to the class.

1. "Ambition is so powerful a passion in the human breast that however high we reach we are never satisfied."—Machiavelli
2. "Ambition and love are the wings to great deeds."—Goethe
3. "Great ambition is the passion of a great character. He who is endowed with it may perform very good or very bad actions; all depends upon the principles which direct him."—Napoleon
4. "There is a loftier ambition than merely to stand high in the world. It is to stoop down and lift mankind a little higher."—Henry van Dyke

Consider using the following teaching aim: to help class members to identify the qualities of great leadership.

Use the following outline:

      I.   Abimelech's rise to power (9:1-2).
          A. His appeal to civic pride.
          B. His appeal to fear.

        C. His appeal to kinship.
   II.   Abimelech is crowned king (9:4-6).
  III. Jotham's fable (9:7-15).

Read carefully "The Scripture and the Main Question" and "As You Read the Scripture." These form the heart of the lesson. The ideas, insights, and suggestions in these sections should be reflected continually in your lesson plan.

As you use the suggested outline, you may want to either quote or paraphrase ideas. You might like to jot in the margin of your outline the page number and paragraph being referred to. For example, you could write a reference to page 65, paragraph 3, as 65-3.

Introducing the Main Question

Basic and helpful ideas are presented in the section "The Main Question." These ideas are essential in helping to identify the purpose of the lesson.

This is the main question: How do we distinguish between a genuine call to lead and a neurotic desire to rule?

Write the word "ambition" on the chalkboard. Ask for reactions to it from class members. What emotions do they feel? Explain that the root meaning of the word is to go around to get votes.

Pass out the duplicated sheets of quotations to the class. Get someone to read the quote from Machiavelli, about ambition being a powerful passion.

Now spend a few minutes recounting the highlights of Adolph Hitler's life. Show his similarity to Abimelech: Both possessed a burning ambition to rule their countries. Be sure to point out how many people lost their lives because of Hitler's ambition.

Developing the Lesson

I. Abimelech's rise to power (9:1-2).

Begin with the background of this strange man. Have someone read 8:22-23, concerning Gideon's refusal to be king. Then have someone read 8:30-31, a passage that tells about Gideon's many wives, their sons, and the concubine and her son.

Remind the class that polygamy and concubinage were common institutions of the day (compare I Chronicles 2:46, 48; Judges 19). Gideon, a worthy leader, did not have the same outlook that we do today, since we have the words of the prophets and the New Testament.

Ask members to be ready to evaluate Dr. Reid Weaver's description of Abimelech: an "ambitious, self-centered pagan, seeking the kingship which his father had refused." Add "murderer."

A. His appeal to civic pride.

The concubine had possession of the child in Shechem, but the seventy sons lived in the ancestral home of Ophrah, thirty miles away. The main character of this lesson went to Shechem and appealed to their civic honor and their local pride.

B. His appeal to fear.

Then Abimelech asked how they would like to be ruled over by the seventy sons. They didn't really know, but they probably feared it would cause confusion. He appealed to that fear.

   C. His appeal to kinship.

Then he reminded them that he was their bone and flesh, in the same spirit as the old saying, "Blood is thicker than water."

II. Abimelech is crowned king (9:4-6).

Ask your students to note who financed his expedition: the shrine of Baal-berith—evil money paid for an evil deed, the murder of sixty-nine sons of Gideon. The coronation took place, with the citizens of the nearby town Beth-millo participating.

III. Jotham's fable (9:7-15).

Ask if class members are familiar with Aesop's fables. See if they can explain how fables differ from short stories. Fables are stories in which plants or animals behave like people. This is one of only two fables in the Bible, the other appearing in II Kings 14:9.

Jotham, the only survivor of the seventy sons, went and stood on Mount Gerizim. He told the assembled people an interesting fable and then fled for his life. The story was one of ambition. When the trees wanted to appoint a king, they went to the best specimens: the olive tree, the fig tree, and the grapevine. All of these refused. No doubt the people thought of Gideon's refusal to be king (Judges 8:22-23).

Then the fable teller moved on to the invitation to the bramble, a plant worthless except for burning. The story ends with a curse: "Let fire come out of the bramble and devour the cedars of Lebanon" (9:15). The worthless bramble could cause destruction of the mighty and useful cedars of Lebanon. Ask class members to recall the destruction that Hitler caused. Think of other dictators whose love for power ruined their countries and took many lives.

Helping Class Members Act

Ask the class to go back to the main question and try to answer it.

Have someone read the quote from Goethe: "Ambition and love are the wings to great deeds." Compare this to the wings of ambition and lovelessness, whose creature can soar high and cause destruction.

Now have another person read the quote from Napoleon. Let the class discuss the statement.

Now move on to the third quotation from Henry van Dyke. Discuss ambition in the light of this statement. Describe the ambition of the apostle Paul, who channeled his desires for greatness into work for Christ. Read Galatians 6:14 in the King James Version: "God forbid that I should glory, save in the cross of our Lord Jesus Christ, by whom the world is crucified unto me, and I unto the world."

Ask if Jesus had any ambition, and discuss the answers.

Remind the class that in lesson 6 on Deborah you listed qualities of leadership. Ask if you should have included the ability to get along with one's family.

Conclude with this story: A group of politicians met in a church to discuss their platforms. Waiting for the meeting to start, they sat on the front row. In the quiet of the church, they all looked up to a painting of Jesus on the cross. He was not dead, and his eyes were not closed. His eyes were full of pity and love. In the solemn silence, one of them could keep quiet no longer and said, "I love him." The woman next to him said, "I love him, too." The politicians were overcome with a feeling of being in the presence of one who had a burning ambition to save sinners but who was willing to give himself in that determination. From that moment on, their campaign was waged on a higher plane.

Planning for Next Sunday

Explain that next week's lesson is about Samson, a person who had great abilities and misused them. Ask class members to watch the newspapers this week for articles about young people who have either used or misused a special talent they possess. Invite a class member who is interested in dramatics to portray Samson in a dramatic monologue.

LESSON 10   AUGUST 6

Samson: Man of Weakness and Strength

Background Scripture: Judges 16

The Main Question—Pat McGeachy

I've always liked Samson. When I was young and a hero-worshiper, it was because of his super powers and his clever trickery. But as an adult with responsibility for leadership, and being very conscious of my own weaknesses, I like Samson for almost the opposite reason: He was a weakling! O yes, he was physically strong and quite bright, but he didn't have very much common sense; he was a bully and a tease, and he let his mates use him. Then why do I admire him? Because, confronted with his failure, he repented, and with divine help made good as a member of the list of God's heroes (see Hebrews 11:32).

In this respect, Samson is like other heroes of the Bible: Moses, David, Peter, and the rest, who had plenty of failures but who managed to win the day. And both he and they give me hope. It is hopeful for me (and I trust for you) because it enables me to come to terms with the inconsistencies in myself, and thus to go on with the difficult task of living the Christian life. If I couldn't accept this, my faults would burden me and prevent me from accomplishing anything. As it is, Samson helps me to know that God can use an imperfect person as part of the great plan.

And he was such an *interesting* imperfect person! A male chauvinist, I think (and therefore one who allowed himself to be fooled by women), Samson continually found himself in situations where he felt that he had to resort to meanness to accomplish his ends (read his exploits in Judges 14 and 15, in particular). All this makes for good press, and he is a favorite of many. But for me he is a favorite just because of his faults. If Samson can make it to God's list of heroes, then so can you and I.

The main question, then, goes like this: How can we do the best possible job of avoiding Samson's faults and emulating his virtues? But, beyond that, given our inevitable failings as humans beings, how can we use all our potential strength to win for God?

Selected Scripture

King James Version

Judges 16:23-31

23 Then the lords of the Philistines gathered them together for to offer a great sacrifice unto Da'-gon their god, and to rejoice: for they said, Our god hath delivered Samson our enemy into our hand.

24 And when the people saw him, they praised their god: for they said, Our god hath delivered into our hands our enemy, and the destroyer of our country, which slew many of us.

25 And it came to pass, when their hearts were merry, that they said, Call for Samson, that he may make us sport. And they called for Samson out of the prison house; and he made them sport: and they set him between the pillars.

26 And Samson said unto the lad that held him by the hand, Suffer me that I may feel the pillars whereupon the house standeth, that I may lean upon them.

27 Now the house was full of men and women; and all the lords of the Philistines *were* there; and *there were* upon the roof about three thousand men and women, that beheld while Samson made sport.

28 And Samson called unto the Lord, and said, O Lord God, remember me, I pray thee, and strengthen me, I pray thee, only this once, O God, that I may be at once avenged of the Philistines for my two eyes.

29 And Samson took hold of the two middle pillars upon which the house stood, and on which it was

Revised Standard Version

Judges 16:23-31

23 Now the lords of the Philistines gathered to offer a great sacrifice to Dagon their god, and to rejoice; for they said, "Our god has given Samson our enemy into our hand."

24 And when the people saw him, they praised their god; for they said, "Our god has given our enemy into our hand, the ravager of our country, who has slain many of us." 25 And when their hearts were merry, they said, "Call Samson, that he may make sport for us." So they called Samson out of the prison, and he made sport before them. They made him stand between the pillars; 26 and Samson said to the lad who held him by the hand, "Let me feel the pillars on which the house rests, that I may lean against them." 27 Now the house was full of men and women; all the lords of the Philistines were there, and on the roof there were about three thousand men and women, who looked on while Samson made sport.

28 Then Samson called to the Lord and said, "O Lord God, remember me, I pray thee, and strengthen me, I pray thee, only this once, O God, that I may be avenged upon the Philistines for one of my two eyes." 29 And Samson grasped the two middle pillars upon which the house rested, and he leaned his weight upon them, his right hand

borne up, of the one with his right hand, and of the other with his left.

30 And Samson said, Let me die with the Philistines. And he bowed himself with *all his* might; and the house fell upon the lords, and upon all the people that *were* therein. So the dead which he slew at his death were more than *they* which he slew in his life.

31 Then his brethren and all the house of his father came down, and took him, and brought *him* up, and buried him between Zo'-rah and Esh'-ta-ol in the buryingplace of Ma-no'-ah his father. And he judged Israel twenty years.

on the one and his left hand on the other. 30 And Samson said, "Let me die with the Philistines." Then he bowed with all his might; and the house fell upon the lords and upon all the people that were in it. So the dead whom he slew at his death were more than those whom he had slain during his life. 31 Then his brothers and all his family came down and took him and brought him up and buried him between Zorah and Esh'ta-ol in the tomb of Manoah his father. He had judged Israel twenty years.

Key Verse: **Samson called unto the Lord, and said, O Lord God, remember me, I pray thee, and strengthen me, I pray thee, only this once, O God, that I may be at once avenged of the Philistines for my two eyes. (Judges 16:28)**

Key Verse: **Then Samson called to the Lord and said, "O Lord God, remember me, I pray thee, and strengthen me, I pray thee, only this once, O God, that I may be avenged upon the Philistines for one of my two eyes." (Judges 16:28)**

As You Read the Scripture—Harold Reid Weaver

Samson seems the perfect product of a successful physical fitness program, a person of enormous physical strength and boundless energy. He could grab a young lion that roared against him and destroy it with his own hands (14:5-6). He could take the jawbone of a dead donkey and slay a thousand men with it (15:15).

His birth story appears in Judges 13:2-5. Before his birth, he was committed by his parents to be a Nazirite. That meant he would not imbibe alcoholic drinks, would not cut his hair, and would not handle dead bodies (see Numbers 6:1-21). His parents believed he would be something special! He would be in some way a deliverer of Israel from the hand of the Philistines.

Judges 16:4-5. The mighty Samson had a fatal weakness for women, as the famous story of his love affair with Delilah reveals. The lords of the Philistines offered Delilah a fortune in silver if she would discover for them the secret of Samson's strength.

Verses 6-14. Three times Samson lied to her about how his strength could be reduced. Each time she would perform the act that he said would destroy his strength and then summon the Philistines, who would only find out that he was as strong as ever.

Verses 15-22. Delilah's pleading finally got to Samson, and he told her that his strength lay in his long hair, a Jewish belief related to the fact that the hair grows more quickly than other parts of the body and thus expresses the lifegiving energies of God in human life. When he fell asleep, head in

Delilah's lap, she had his hair cut. The Philistines thus captured him, bound him, gouged out his eyes, and took him to prison, where he was set to hard labor, grinding grain.

Verses 23-24. The lords of the Philistines gathered to celebrate. They offered thanks to Dagon, their god, for the victory over Samson. Dagon was the father of Baal and a very old Mesopotamian deity, worshiped as long as 2500 B.C. The lords and ladies made merry, poking fun at Samson and his God.

Verses 25-30. Thousands of people watched as Samson was positioned between two main pillars of the temple. While they scorned him, he prayed for strength to push the pillars apart. His hair had grown long again, suggesting how long he had been in prison, and his strength was renewed. The temple collapsed. In his death Samson killed more men than he had killed in his lifetime.

Only two prayers are mentioned regarding Samson: the prayer for revenge in the temple (16:28), and the prayer for water when he was thirsty (15:18). We can see physical strength in the Hebrew hero, but little to admire in the way of morality and commitment to God. He was a man of his time, to be sure.

Verse 31. His body was buried by his brothers in his father's tomb, near Zorah.

The Scripture and the Main Question—Pat McGeachy

Flawed Heroes

From the beginnings of the history of drama, the Greeks recognized that tragedy hinges on a character flaw in an otherwise noble person. For Oedipus, it was his sexual confusion; for Macbeth, his ambition. (Note that in the case of both of those characters, as well as for our hero, Samson, there was a questionable wife involved.) What was Samson's tragic flaw? I'm suggesting that it was pure machismo, his need to be a big shot. But you may have another idea after looking over his whole story in Judges 13–16.

Samson has long reminded me of another folk hero—John Henry, the steel-driving man. Like Samson, John Henry was a member of a minority group, and he did battle against the mechanized steam drill that threatened to put his fellow hand-drillers out of work. Samson did battle against the highly mechanized Philistines [who brought the iron age to Israel], who threatened the security of his people. Both men died in the achievement of their tasks, and both have been celebrated in the legends of their people as men of great strength. Moreover (if you come to know the John Henry saga through the songs sung about him, you will see this), they were both womanizers who continually got into trouble through their marital relationships.

A word of warning to all young men and women who desire to become folk heroes: It is a costly process. Look at the number of heroes who have died tragically in the last ten or so years: the Kennedy brothers, Martin Luther King, Elvis Presley, John Lennon, and others from entertainment, sports, and all walks of life. Do heroes *have* to make bad marriages, or mess with drugs, or be assassinated by their enemies? It sometimes looks that way, but we need to remember that there are many heroes with good marriages, long lives, and fruitful missions (Pablo Casals, Winston Churchill, Helen Hayes—you make your own list).

FOURTH QUARTER

Here's to the Samsons of the world—those who manage to be heroes in spite of themselves!

Delilah

Delilah was not Samson's first wife. He seems to have done rather badly by marriage in general, I suspect because he went into it for the wrong reasons. He married outside of his own cultural circles, which is not necessarily fatal but which needs a strong basis on which to survive. Superficial sexual attraction simply won't bring it off. A truly Christian marriage must be based on "charity," that is, the *agape* love that Paul celebrates in I Corinthians 13, which builds on trust, patience, and faithfulness and keeps on keeping on in the midst of troubles.

Delilah may have been very beautiful (she has certainly been so portrayed by Hollywood), but she couldn't be trusted. Why do men like Samson so often marry women just like themselves? Perhaps it is that they (we) are searching for the wrong things from the very beginning. If you are seeking to be a superficial hero, you may want a wife or husband suitable for the role: Somebody who looks the part, regardless of how deep they may run. If, on the other hand, you are following Jesus' good counsel about losing one's life, you don't need a wife or husband that you can show off. (Jesus didn't get married at all!) You need a person who shares your own aspirations and is willing humbly to work with you to achieve them. Together you may become heroes in the eyes of the world, or you may not, but you will achieve something far greater than worldly fame.

The Downfall of the Great

Mahatma Gandhi used to take comfort in the fact that all the tyrants in the history of the world have eventually failed. It is certainly a truism that "pride goes before destruction" (Proverbs 16:18). And, as we say with Newtonian wisdom, "What goes up must come down." Sooner or later, those who disregard the humble laws of nature (or the natural laws of humility) will find that their feet have been set in slippery places (Psalm 73:18) and that their ruin is inevitable

We can get away with a little bullying, a little meanness, a little "I did it my way," and perhaps survive. But that is like saying, "a little more eating or drinking, or a few more hours in bed, or another round of self-indulgence won't hurt." Eventually we wake up fat, sick, or dead. Samson ended up "eyeless, in Gaza, at the mill, with slaves" (a quote from Milton's poem "Samson Agonistes," which has been called the saddest line in all of literature; I would vote, however for Ephesians 2:12).

Phoenix from the Ashes

Buried deep in the heart of Samson the self-indulgent bully, the womanizing tease, and the iron-pumping show-off, there was a truly tough seed of spiritual reality that would not be denied. Even though we find him blind at the mill, we do not find him without inner resources. I have always suspected that the promise of the angel at the announcement of his birth (Judges 13:4-5) is involved here. The boy had been committed to the vows of a Nazirite before he was old enough to know what that meant.

412

For further insight into the meaning of Naziritic vows, read Numbers 6:1-21. There are other famous Nazirites besides Samson, notably John the Baptist (Luke 1:15) and possibly the apostle Paul (Acts 21:20-26). The three standard vows of the Nazirite (the word means "consecrated") were no razor, no alcohol, no corpses. So apparently the length of Samson's hair really *was* the secret of his strength, for it was the symbol of his special set-apartness, his commitment to God. But just as he violated the haircut moratorium, so also he flouted a number of other laws and customs, and the dictates of refinement. In marrying a Philistine in the first place Samson had displayed a flippant attitude toward the traditions of his ancestors. The doom of Samson was sealed long before he met Delilah, by his disrespect for the traditions that were rightfully both his privilege and his responsibility.

I have seen this happen to me and to other Christians. I was set apart for Christ before I was born and, like Samson, trained from childhood to live by certain customs and laws not of my own making. As an adolescent I rebelled against many of these rules, which I considered arbitrary and parental, and as a result my life was the less. But when I came to myself (Luke 15:17), as Samson did in the temple of Dagon, new strength was given to me and the promise of a hopeful ending was renewed.

In the depths of his despair, Samson prayed, a prayer of vengeance perhaps but not of self-pity, an honest open confession that he had forgotten God along the way but that he hoped God had not forgotten him. Like the returning prodigal, he asked not for glory and sonship but just for "one more chance." And the answer comes. In what may be one of the most dramatic scenes in all of literature (I can still see Victor Mature straining at the styrofoam stones in de Mille's movie), Samson puts his muscle to work against the load-bearing pillars of the temple and destroys himself along with three thousand of the enemy.

In his death, Samson was almost Christ-like, in the sense that his noblest deed was performed on the last day of his physical life. In like manner, you and I may still rise out of the dust of our failures, armed with renewed vows to God to break down demonic temples and dividing walls, and play a role in the ancient fight for justice and peace. But if we could do that at the last minute, saved by the bell, in a cloud of dust and doom, destroying ourselves and those around us, how much more could we accomplish if all our lives we would keep God's law and live as Christ's sisters and brothers! We might never become celebrated in history like Samson, but our names would be written in the Lamb's book of life, in the immortality of what Wordsworth called the best portion of a good person's life: "those little, nameless, unremembered acts of kindness and of love."

Helping Adults Become Involved—John Warren Steen

Preparing to Teach

Look up the definitions of three words you will use in the lesson: Philistines, Nazirites, and Dagon.

Consider using the following teaching aim: to help members determine to build their lives on morality and trust, not sensuality and egotism, as Samson did, and to learn from his mistakes.

Use the following outline:

    I.   A pagan celebration (Judges 16:23-25)
   II.   A godly request (16:26-30)
 III.   A reverent memory (16:31)

Read carefully "The Scripture and the Main Question" and "As You Read the Scripture." These form the heart of the lesson. The ideas, insights, and suggestions in these sections should be reflected continually in your lesson plan.

As you use the suggested outline, you may want to either quote or paraphrase ideas. You might like to jot in the margin of your outline the page number and paragraph being referred to. For example, you could write a reference to page 65, paragraph 3, as 65-3.

Introducing the Main Question

Basic and helpful ideas are presented in the section "The Main Question." These ideas are essential in helping to identify the purpose of the lesson.

The main question, according to Dr. McGeachy, in this: How can we open ourselves to the potential to win for God? I have reworded it, How can we find the strength to avoid Samson's faults and emulate his virtues?

Here are two alternate beginnings for the lesson:

1. Start with this story: A gifted preacher was preaching on Samson. His mind was so preoccupied with the strength and prowess of the man, he did not realize he had called him "Tarzan" at the beginning of the message. Then he kept repeating the name and wondering why the congregation was smiling.

Discuss this incident. It was an easy mistake. Yet the preacher did not call the strong man by an actual person's name but the name of a movie hero. Our trouble is similar—making the connection between the biblical hero and today's people. We need to learn lessons from his story that will apply to our lives.

2. Or, ask: If two of your close friends and neighbors suffered a death in the family, which one would need your visit the most—one who lost an eighty-five year-old mother or one who lost a teenage son? Why?

Ask if anyone brought in newspaper clippings about promising young people. Talk about writers, sports figures, artists, or musicians who never seem to use all their God-given potentialities. Then ask: Even though you might not be a ten-talent person, what can you do to live up to your potential?

Write the main question on the chalkboard along with "Philistines," "Nazirites," and "Dagon." Tell the class the definition for these words. Consider putting the outline on the board, also.

Developing the Lesson

I. A pagan celebration (Judges 16:23-25)

The printed passage involves the final scene in the life of Samson. In order for this to make sense, you will need to give a brief summary of the life of the strongman. If you can get a member to give a dramatic monologue of the adventures leading up to his capture, this will add variety to the Bible study and help members feel a kinship with the emotions Samson experienced. The idea is to get Samson into the area of reality and believability, in order that we might learn lessons from his life. Most people will remember the name Delilah. Have someone recount the way she extracted information from him. Notice Judges 16:20-21. The promise had been made that his hair would never be cut; his consecrated locks were associated with the spirit of the Lord. His fate was punishment—to do the work of a farm animal.

Then move on to the passage in Judges 16:23-31. Tell the students you can imagine that in the darkness of his blindness, Samson had no doubt gone over the details of his adventuresome life and tragic capture. He likely recognized his self-centeredness. He saw times when he should have exalted God instead of himself, times when he should have encouraged the people he judged and should have set an example for them. In those long, dark days, his hair continued to grow.

The Philistines were sea people of Aegean origin who migrated into southern Canaan about 12 B.C., perhaps by way of Crete (Caphtor—see Jeremiah 47:4; Amos 9:7; compare Deuteronomy 2:23). The Greeks gave the names of these people to the entire area, coming into the English language as "Palestine." They had a monopoly on smelting iron and seemed, with their weapons, to be invincible in battle. The five lords of their five cities gathered to celebrate a national festival honoring their god Dagon. Dagon was a Semitic deity associated with Baal and recognized in Mesopotamian religion quite early. He was worshiped at Ugarit by Canaanites. The Philistines made him their chief god.

Sometimes you hear the expression "party animals." The Philistines were party animals; they called for their enemy, Samson, to be paraded before them in his weakness and blindness. The revelers gave their god Dagon thanks for the capture of Samson. None of them seemed to notice that his hair had continued to grow. His captors were more interested in poking fun at the pitiful enemy (and perhaps at his powerless God, too) than in recalling what had made him strong.

II. A godly request (16:26-30)

Ask: What were the emotions going through the blind man's mind at this time? Repentance for his mistakes, no doubt. What other biblical characters did he resemble in his remorse? Moses, David, Peter, but perhaps most all the prodigal son.

Ask: What request did the tormented Samson make of the young man who guided him? Read Judges 16:26. Ask: What two requests did the repentant judge make of God? Read Judges 16:28-30 for the answers.

III. A reverent memory (16:31)

Read this verse and think of its depth of meaning.

Some people have questioned the advisability of displaying the Nazi concentration camps, where myriads of people were exterminated. It offends human sensibilities to see cages, ovens, and photographs of shocking horror. But the reasoning behind the display is this: If people are properly informed about what happened before, they will be more careful never to let such atrocities occur again.

The life and exploits of Samson should be studied for the same reasons: so that we can learn lessons in moral guidance, love for the home, and dedication of talents, which will prevent this story from being repeated. Ask for some warning signs that we are not heeding the lessons of Samson's life.

Helping Class Members Act

Ask your students to discuss Dr. McGeachy's statement: God can use an imperfect person as part of the great divine plan.

Ask how we can get more of the prodigal son attitude into our lives. Is it possible we do not want to forgive ourselves and so keep living in guilt?

Planning for Next Sunday

Enlist a member of your class (or of another class) to enact the part of Ruth. Ask her to prepare herself to answer questions from the class by reading about Ruth in the Bible and in either *The Interpreter's Bible* or a Bible dictionary.

Have people look back through magazines or books to find pictures of the recent royal weddings in England. Lead up to the lesson on Ruth's marriage, helping the members to anticipate the romance and the deeper spiritual lessons involved.

UNIT III: RUTH—A RECORD OF COMMITMENT AND HOPE

Horace R. Weaver

THREE LESSONS   **AUGUST 13–27**

"Ruth—A Record of Commitment and Hope" in three lessons pictures Hebrew family life during a period of anarchy and turmoil. The first lesson highlights the strong commitment of Ruth to her mother-in-law, Naomi. The second lesson describes the meeting of Ruth and Boaz, and its outcome. The final lesson deals with the marrriage of Ruth and Boaz, the birth of their son, and the rejoicing of Naomi and her friends at the fulfillment of Naomi's dreams.

The lessons are as follows: August 13, "Courageous Choices," asks: As we struggle to find direction for living and wise choices, what can Ruth's commitment offer to us? August 20, "The Compassion of Boaz," raises the significant question, What constitutes a good person? August 27, "The Fulfillment of Hope," helps answer the question of whether there is any point in hanging on to the morality, faith, and hope of our parents.

Courageous Choices

Background Scripture: Ruth 1

The Main Question—Pat McGeachy

It would be nice, I suppose, if the world were really like "Father Knows Best" or "Leave It to Beaver"—if all couples got married, had 2.4 children, lived for fifty years on Oak Street, and died within two days of each other, full of years and happy memories. But it doesn't work that way. Families, like Elimelech's and Naomi's, sometimes have to move to strange places. Men die before their families are ready for it, just like Elimelech. Widows, like Naomi have a difficult time in the struggle to survive. And young adults, like Ruth and Orpah, have to make tough choices.

This well known and beloved tale, set in the world of Israel under the judges, is a love story that gives us a rare picture of life in that pastoral time and raises some fundamental questions about life and loyalty, which will help us in our own struggles to find meaningful lives in our day.

The famous quote, "Whither thou goest . . ." (KJV) has been recited at many weddings (almost as much as certain Kahlil Gibran poems), but it has little to do with wedding services; it is a promise made between in-laws. It is a courageous affirmation of faith on the part of a single foreign woman (those three words would all be considered strikes against a person, in that day) to pursue life in another land with her mother-in-law, in poverty and obscurity. What made her do it? What sort of commitment was this? Could she have guessed that her decision that day would lead to her installment in the lineage of David, and of Jesus the Messiah?

In the troubling times of life, when we struggle to keep our heads above water, to find direction for living, and to make wise choices, what can Ruth's commitment offer to us? Do we have the will and the wisdom to make such commitments ourselves? To whom should we make them? Where do our loyalties lie? To whom should we say, "Where you go, I will go . . . , your people shall be my people, and your God, mine"?

Selected Scripture

King James Version	Revised Standard Version
Ruth 1:1-8, 16-18	*Ruth 1:1-8, 16-18*
1 Now it came to pass in the days when the judges ruled, that there was a famine in the land. And a certain man of Beth-le-hem-judah went to sojourn in the country of Moab, he, and his wife, and his two sons.	1 In the days when the judges ruled there was a famine in the land, and a certain man of Bethlehem in Judah went to sojourn in the country of Moab, he and his wife and his two sons. 2 The name of the man was Elim′elech and the name of his wife Na′omi, and the names of his two sons were Mahlon and Chil′ion; they were Eph′rathites from Bethlehem in Judah. They went into the country of Moab and remained
2 And the name of the man *was* E-lim′-e-lech, and the name of his wife Naomi, and the name of his two sons Mah′-lon and Chil′-i-on, Eph′-rath-ites of Beth-lehem-judah. And	

417

they came into the country of Moab, and continued there.

3 And E-lim'-e-lech Naomi's husband died; and she was left, and her two sons.

4 And they took them wives of the women of Moab; the name of the one *was* Or'-pah, and the name of the other Ruth: and they dwelled there about ten years.

5 And Mah'-lon and Chil'-i-on died also both of them; and the woman was left of her two sons and her husband.

6 Then she arose with her daughters in law, that she might return from the country of Moab: for she had heard in the country of Moab how that the Lord had visited his people in giving them bread.

7 Wherefore she went forth out of the place where she was, and her two daughters in law with her; and they went on the way to return unto the land of Judah.

8 And Naomi said unto her two daughters in law, Go, return each to her mother's house: the Lord deal kindly with you, as ye have dealt with the dead, and with me.

....

16 And Ruth said, Intreat me not to leave thee, *or* to return from following after thee: for whither thou goest, I will go; and where thou lodgest, I will lodge: thy people *shall be* my people, and thy God my God:

17 Where thou diest, will I die, and there will I be buried: the Lord do so to me, and more also, *if ought* but death part thee and me.

18 When she saw that she was stedfastly minded to go with her, then she left speaking unto her.

Key Verse: Intreat me not to leave thee, or to return from following after thee: for whither thou goest, I will go; and where thou lodgest, I will lodge: thy people shall be my people, and thy God my God. (Ruth 1:16)

there. 3 But Elim'elech, the husband of Na'omi, died, and she was left with her two sons. 4 These took Moabite wives; the name of the one was Orpah and the name of the other Ruth. They lived there about ten years; 5 and both Mahlon and Chil'ion died, so that the woman was bereft of her two sons and her husband.

6 Then she started with her daughters-in-law to return from the country of Moab, for she had heard in the country of Moab that the Lord had visited his people and given them food. 7 So she set out from the place where she was, with her two daughters-in-law, and they went on the way to return to the land of Judah. 8 But Na'omi said to her two daughters-in-law, "Go, return each of you to her mother's house. May the Lord deal kindly with you, as you have dealt with the dead and with me."

....

16 But Ruth said, "Entreat me not to leave you or to return from following you; for where you go I will go, and where you lodge I will lodge; your people shall be my people, and your God my God; 17 where you die I will die, and there will I be buried. May the Lord do so to me and more also if even death parts me from you." 18 And when Na'omi saw that she was determined to go with her, she said no more.

Key Verse: Entreat me not to leave you or to return from following you; for where you go I will go, and where you lodge I will lodge; your people shall be my people, and your God my God. (Ruth 1:16)

As You Read the Scripture—Harold Reid Weaver

This beautiful story of love and commitment was written by an unknown Jew around 450 B.C. The story is a gem and worthy of a place in the Bible. But its writer had something more in mind than mere entertainment. Hidden in the book of Ruth is a protest message, making this work a kind of "tract for the times."

The book was written at the point in history when Nehemiah was permitted to leave the court of the Persian king, Artaxerxes, and go back to Jerusalem. His intent was to rebuild the walls of the city, which had been destroyed in 586 B.C. by the Babylonians. (See Nehemiah 1 and 2.)

Nehemiah, a layman, would not tolerate the marriage of Jewish men to foreign women. "Shall we . . . act treacherously against our God by marrying foreign women?" he asked (Nehemiah 13:27). Foreign women, he pointed out, had led Solomon astray. Nehemiah made the harsh rule that there would be no more marriages between Jews and foreigners.

An unknown writer picked up his pen and wrote the book of Ruth in protest. It is a lovely story of the loving faithfulness of the foreign-born Ruth to Naomi, a Jew, and an account of the marriage of Ruth and Boaz. From this marriage of a Jew a foreigner came Obed, whose sons was Jesse, whose son was David, the greatest of the kings of Israel. The message was clear: David had foreign blood in him! (And not only David, but the great "son of David" who would be born a thousand years later in Bethlehem and whose name would be Jesus.) It was a statement of vital importance for the time of Nehemiah, needed as a corrective to gross racial arrogance.

All of that constitutes the larger context of the book of Ruth, to which we now turn for closer examination.

Ruth 1:1-3. The "judges" were not settlers of disputes in courts of law, but rulers of tribes before the kings arrived in Jewish history. Note that famines were not unusual. It was often necessary for the sake of survival to go to other lands to find food. Naomi and her husband "sojourned" in Moab, meaning they lived as aliens, forfeiting all legal rights in the new country.

Verses 4-5. Naomi's husband and two sons died within ten years, leaving Naomi with two Moabite daughters-in-law. Naomi had no means of support for herself and certainly could not house and feed two daughters-in-law. Tearfully she had to tell them good-bye. She would return to Bethlehem, and they must return to their homes and gods in Moab.

Verse 6. "Visited" means God had been gracious and brought food again to Bethlehem, Naomi's homeland.

Verses 16-18. This beautiful confession of tender loving care for a mother-in-law is almost unsurpassed in literature. Ruth uses the word "Yahweh" for God, meaning she has accepted the religion of Naomi and wants to go with her to Judah. Couples have used these words in weddings across the centuries to declare their devotion, love, and undying commitment to a special loved one.

The picture sketched by the unknown writer portrays Ruth as a positive, committed, affirming person. She faces a new country, a new language, and a new religion, with no friends save Naomi. She cannot leave her mother-in-law to face a tough world alone. They move forward, facing the future, with faith and hope.

The Scripture and the Main Question—Pat McGeachy

Vicissitudes

I want you to picture the setting of this story. Outside of the town of Bethlehem there is a lovely hillside known as the Fields of Boaz. Sheep graze there now, where barley was once harvested; by tradition, it is that same field where the Christmas shepherds lay watching their flocks. (A church has been built there to commemorate the events.) By contrast, the land that was once Moab, on the other side of the Jordan, is today very arid, a volcanic desert. But in the time of Ruth, briefly at least, they were opposite: there was famine in Judah and plenty in Moab.

Most Americans would find it hard to make a living in that country, for we are people of the town and city. Even if we are farmers, we'd have difficulty managing with wooden threshing forks and ox-drawn plows. Try to imagine what it would be like to be a widow in such a time and place. I can imagine that the land would be precious to Naomi, and that she would want to return to the well remembered pastoral setting of her young-woman-hood, where there might be a chance for survival. As a widow in Moab she would be doomed to a beggar's existence, but back with her family—that would be a different story.

Maybe. You can't go home again, as Thomas Wolfe reminded us. She'll still be "only a woman." In those days that phrase had even more unpleasant implications than it does today: Women were not allowed to own property or to have any say in the life and economy of the community. It was a society dominated by men, and the only hope for a widow with no male offspring was to be cared for by the family of her late husband. The curious phenomenon known as the levirate marriage (from the Hebrew *levir*, meaning "brother-in-law"; see Deuteronomy 25:5-10 and Matthew 22:23-33) was designed to protect the widow by making it possible for her to become her brother-in-law's wife. But this would not necessarily happen, nor always be pleasant. In short, such a woman had a hard row to hoe.

I have said that it would be hard for us moderns to identify with Naomi and Ruth, and in some ways that must be so. But, on the other hand, the plight of single women in our society today is a problem. They far outnumber single men (the opposite was true in Naomi's time), and many are electing, some by choice and some by necessity, a solitary life. Jobs are available for some of them, but the YWCA has found it necessary in recent years to offer workshops for "displaced homemakers" who have suddenly become breadwinners and are unfamiliar with the job market or are unaware that they possess marketable skills. Maybe things are not so different after all. Perhaps we *can* feel a kinship with Naomi and Ruth, in their ups and downs.

Commitment

What do you suppose bound Ruth to Naomi? We can only speculate, but because of the nature of the wonderful vow she made, our guesses can have some assurance to them. Listen to it again: "Entreat me not to leave you or to return from following you; for where you go I will go, and where you lodge I will lodge; your people shall be my people, and your God my God; where you die I will die, and there will I be buried." It is a dramatic statement, and we can infer from it a number of things.

First of all, Ruth must have learned, during the ten years of her marriage to Naomi's son, something about family and loyalty that she liked. The people of Moab were desert folk; the children of Israel were a newly emerging agrarian society, and Ruth must have said to herself something like what I have occasionally overheard in my own society: "You know, those country folk have a way of life and a sense of community that I could really go for."

In addition, Ruth must have learned some theology from her adopted family. We don't know much about the gods of Moab (their principal deity was Chemost [see I Kings 11:7] who was worshiped in part by the sacrificing of children) but what we do know indicates that it was a fearful and superstitious faith, probably associated with religious protitution. The ethical monotheism of her new family must have been refreshing to her. I can imagine her thinking, "It is wonderful to believe in one God alone, and not only that, but to believe that that God desires a life that fulfills the ten commandments."

Such decisions are often made at levels below (or above) conscious thought. We decide "on the gut level" (a good biblical phrase) that something is right for us. Something (someone?) told Ruth that this was the best course for her life. There is an old song that says, "I'd rather be blue with someone like you, Than be happy with somebody else." Ruth is saying to Naomi, I'll take my chances with you. In a way it *is* almost a marriage vow, a promise to stay with someone through thick and thin. It's the best deal Ruth could have made, and as it turns out, it blossoms into a love story.

To Whom Do You Turn?

Now what about you and me? Suppose you were (and many of us are) a stranger in your community. With whom would you link up? I have been a pastor all of my adult life, so my church relationships have largely been decided for me by individuals' choice of my church. But on occasion I have been close enough to lay people in their decisions to think that if I were alone in a strange city, I would start going to churches until I found one where I could say, "You are my kind of people, and your God is my God." Then I would settle in.

These people wouldn't have to look like me. They could be foreigners, Moabites. They wouldn't have to have been raised in my cultural traditions. But there would be something about them that I could identify with. It might take me a while to make up my mind (Ruth had known Naomi for ten years or so before making her commitment), but sooner or later I would need to act. For, you see, none of us can survive alone. It's not just foreign widows who have need for community; it's every one of us. Some of us are forced by circumstances—economic, political, or personal—to forsake the place of our birth, and we don't always get to return. We are always having to make choices of jobs, roommates, friends, relationships, and marriages, which will have significant effect on the rest of our lives. Most of us will pass through the difficult time of the death of a spouse, other family members, or dear friends. Our marriages run on rugged rocks. If we are single, we have another set of difficult adjustments. In all these situations we must be capable of making lasting commitments to other persons, if we are to survive.

From Ruth's story we can draw certain conclusions about such commitments.

1. They should be based on deeply felt religious and emotional commitments.

2. We should choose relationships that will be strengthening, not debilitating. (Do we need to remind ourselves how many people make commitments that end up being destructive?)

3. Once we have made such commitments, we should stick to them as Ruth promised, "until death us do part." (I am glad to say that the questionable wedding vow "as long as we both shall love" is no longer in vogue.) This does not mean that there is no escape from mistaken commitments, but that it is God's intention that we should be faithful to one another.

Our commitments should be modeled on God's faithfulness to us. It must have been an awareness of this that caused Ruth to go with Naomi. For the two of them, the story turned out well. And that is the promise to us: A happy ending is in store for those who commit themselves to God in Christ. Things may not always be easy for us, but that will not prevent the story from turning out well. Nothing, not death or life or time or space or the powerful forces of this world, will be able to separate us from the love of God in Jesus (see Romans 8:38-39).

Helping Adults Become Involved—John Warren Steen

Preparing to Teach

As you come to the last unit of this quarter, think of how these final lessons pull together the insights of the whole quarter. Begin to bring in elements of a summary now and next Sunday, but leave most of the summary for August 27, the final session. For this Sunday's lesson, concentrate on the romantic story of Ruth and Boaz.

Have a map available to point out the locations of Bethlehem and Moab.

Consider using the following teaching aim: to help class members understand the basis of real commitment.

Use the following outline:

    I. A family in exile (1:1-8).
        A. Naomi's loses her husband and sons.
        B. Naomi plans to return.
    II. A commitment of devotion (1:16-18).
        A. Ruth pledges undying devotion to Naomi and her God.
        B. Naomi recognizes Ruth's loyalty.

Read carefully "The Scripture and the Main Question" and "As You Read the Scripture." These form the heart of the lesson. The ideas, insights, and suggestions in these sections should be reflected continually in your lesson plan.

As you use the suggested outline, you may want to either quote or paraphrase ideas. You might like to jot in the margin of your outline the page number and paragraph being referred to. For example, you could write a reference to page 65, paragraph 3, as 65-3.

Introducing the Main Question

Basic and helpful ideas are presented in the section "The Main Question." These ideas are essential in helping to identify the main purpose of the lesson.

The main question is this: As we struggle to find direction for living and to make wise choices, what can Ruth's commitment offer to us?

Ask why so many people today feel that commitments are shallow and friendships are trivial. Perhaps out of selfishness, people are afraid of giving up too much in a commitment of friendship or love. Ask your students to think of ways to overcome this weakness in modern life.

Introduce the book of Ruth—a charming, short story. It has striking imagery, good characterization, a plot that progresses, and enough details to make it understandable.

Developing the Lesson

I. A family in exile (1:1-8).

A. Naomi loses her husband and sons.

Buddha taught "Four Noble Truths." The first one was "Existence is suffering." Isn't this thought similar to the one expressed about the suffering of Job: "Man is born to trouble as the sparks fly upward" (Job 5:7). Discuss the temptation to develop a pessimistic view of life, to become a grumpy person. Show how Naomi faced her problems, admitted them, and did something good about them.

Before someone reads verses 1-5, suggest that Naomi had three strikes against her. Get the class to listen for them.

Center on verse 1, and get the setting for the story. The time is near the close of the period of judges, a turbulent period just before the establishment of the monarchy. Bethlehem is just five miles southwest of Jerusalem, in the land of Judah. It was in the Fields of Boaz that the shepherds heard the angels' announcement of the Messiah's birth in Bethlehem.

Moab was the high country east of the Dead Sea and south of the Arnon River, in the area now known as Transjordan.

Get the class to identify the characters by name. Elimelech, whose name meant "my God is king," took his family to a place where there would be enough food. He had a wife, Naomi, and two sons, Mahlon and Chilion.

In the land of Moab, Elimelech died. His two sons married Orpah and Ruth, Moabite women. According to Genesis 19:36-37, Moabites were considered the descendents of Lot. Apparently, there was no law at this time to prohibit such unions. Within a ten-year period, the father and both sons died.

Now come back to the question about the three strikes against Naomi. One, she was a woman, a distinct disadvantage in that time. Two, she was a foreign woman. She had no close relatives in Moab to watch out for her welfare. Three, she was a single woman. A widow in that time couldn't go out and apply for a nine-to-five job. There was no welfare system to provide help. Her support came from her father, or if she was married, from her husband. Once her husband was dead, a widow looked to her sons to support her. This woman, emotionally grieved over her losses, had no one but foreign daughters-in-law to look to.

B. Naomi plans to return.

What news did Naomi receive about home? See verse 6. She and her daughters-in-law started the trip back to Bethlehem of Judah. Perhaps there, relatives would share food with her. Along the way, Naomi began to think of what would be best for the two younger women. Read or summarize verses 8-14, and ask for a comment on the emotions of the women.

II. A commitment of devotion (1:16-18).
  A. Ruth pledges undying devotion to Naomi and her God.

Even though Orpah turned back to Moab, Ruth clung to her dear mother-in-law. Then she uttered some of the most heartwarming words of loyalty ever written. Have someone read verses 16-17. At that time, many people identified God as being restricted to a certain area. (Read about Jacob's surprise that God existed at Bethel in Genesis 28:16.)

Note the loyalty in her commitment: companionship wherever Naomi went until she died, family loyalty to relatives she had not even met, and a loyalty to the one true God she had come to know over her ten-year period of association with Naomi. Ask the class what kind of personality Naomi must have radiated in order to elicit such devotion as Ruth exhibited.

Ask members to notice that Ruth's choice of words for God was *Yahweh*, the Hebrews' covenant name for God, revealed to Moses.

Ask: Was Ruth's understanding of God limited by geographical borders? No. Ask: Was Ruth's loyalty influenced by racial prejudice? No. From the words of the two women, you can tell about the character of each. Try to describe them.

  B. Naomi recognizes Ruth's loyalty.

When Naomi saw that Ruth was determined, she did not try to stop her. Ask what effect the statement must have had on the mother-in-law. She must have been overcome by the generous outpouring of love and loyalty, and more determined than ever to be of any help she could to her loyal daughter-in-law.

Helping Class Members Act

Note that Dr. McGeachy points out that our commitments should be modeled on God's faithfulness to us. Ask class members if they agree, and why. Ask if it is possible for persons to be kind if they have never received kindness themselves. Do children respond to other children outside the home in the same way their parents have treated them? Ruth must have observed and learned compassion from Naomi.

Recalling your teaching aim, ask about the basis of real commitment. Read the words of a poem or a hymn of commitment.

Planning for Next Sunday

Ask for a volunteer to bring a report on the regulations about gleaning as set down in Deuteronomy 24:19-21, using a Bible dictionary if possible.

The Compassion of Boaz

Background Scripture: Ruth 2–3; Deuteronomy 24:19-21

The Main Question—Pat McGeachy

It is a wonderful thing to discover in this world, as from time to time, thank God, we do, a truly *good* person. That there are such, even in our sinful world, is a rare and pleasant surprise. I have known a few who treat everyone they meet with gentleness, fair-mindedness, and cheerful, loving acceptance. Even in the Bible there are not many: Jesus (of course), Leah (maybe), Josiah, Andrew, Barnabas (Acts 11:24)—you will have your choices. But Boaz was certainly one of them.

His compassionate acts in accepting Ruth the Moabitess as a gleaner among his people (2:8-13) and in honoring with dignity her offer of herself to him on the threshing floor (3:7-11) testify both to his honor and his integrity.

A friend of mine, when asked on the occasion of his retirement, "Well, what are you going to do now?" replied, "I'm just going to try to be a good man." It is a full-time occupation. Jesus went about doing good, we are told by Peter (Acts 10:38), and in this "me generation" in which they say we are now living, it would behoove us all to do the same.

The main question then, of this lesson, is, what constitutes a good person? Let us think of Boaz as a model for the improving of our own standard of behavior, and see what rules we can devise by watching him operate. He is a good example of the kind of light Jesus meant (Matthew 5:16) for us to be, shining before the world so that others may, seeing the good in us, glorify God. I said a few lessons back that I did not like Abimelech. Well, I do like Boaz. I would like to be like him, too. The heroes of the Bible serve often as negative examples; we have already seen how God can use a bully like Samson, or a wishy-washy person like Gideon. But I can't find a thing that I don't like about Boaz. When I stood, a good many years ago, outside of Bethlehem, looking over the fields named after him, where he may have lived, I wished he were still among us. Perhaps he is.

Selected Scripture

King James Version	Revised Standard Version
Ruth 2:5-12, 19-20	*Ruth 2:5-12, 19-20*
5 Then said Bo'-az unto his servant that was set over the reapers, Whose damsel *is* this?	5 Then Bo'az said to his servant who was in charge of the reapers, "Whose maiden is this?" 6 And the servant who was in charge of the reapers answered, "It is the Moabite maiden, who came back with Na'omi from the country of Moab. 7
6 And the servant that was set over the reapers answered and said, It *is* the Moabitish damsel that came back with Naomi out of the country of Moab:	She said, 'Pray, let me glean and gather among the sheaves after the reapers.' So she came, and she has
7 And she said, I pray you, let me glean and gather after the reapers	

425

among the sheaves: so she came, and hath continued even from the morning until now, that she tarried a little in the house.

8 Then said Bo'-az unto Ruth, Hearest thou not, my daughter? Go not to glean in another field, neither go from hence, but abide here fast by my maidens:

9 *Let* thine eyes *be* on the field that they do reap, and go thou after them: have I not charged the young men that they shall not touch thee? and when thou art athirst, go unto the vessels, and drink of *that* which the young men have drawn.

10 Then she fell on her face, and bowed herself to the ground, and said unto him, Why have I found grace in thine eyes, that thou shouldest take knowledge of me, seeing I *am* a stranger?

11 And Bo'-az answered and said unto her, It hath fully been shewed me, all that thou hast done unto thy mother in law since the death of thine husband: and *how* thou hast left thy father and thy mother, and the land of thy nativity, and art come unto a people which thou knewest not heretofore.

12 The Lord recompense thy work, and a full reward be given thee of the Lord God of Israel, under whose wings thou art come to trust.

....

19 And her mother in law said unto her, Where hast thou gleaned to day? and where wroughtest thou? blessed be he that did take knowledge of thee. And she shewed her mother in law with whom she had wrought, and said, The man's name with whom I wrought to day *is* Bo'-az.

20 And Naomi said unto her daughter in law, Blessed *be* he of the Lord, who hath not left off his kindness to the living and to the dead. And Naomi said unto her, The man *is* near of kin unto us, one

continued from early morning until now, without resting even for a moment."

8 Then Bo'az said to Ruth, "Now, listen, my daughter, do not go to glean in another field or leave this one, but keep close to my maidens. 9 Let your eyes be upon the field which they are reaping, and go after them. Have I not charged the young men not to molest you? And when you are thirsty, go to the vessels and drink what the young men have drawn." 10 Then she fell on her face, bowing to the ground, and said to him, "Why have I found favor in your eyes, that you should take notice of me, when I am a foreigner?" 11 But Bo'az answered her, "All that you have done for your mother-in-law since the death of your husband has been fully told me, and how you left your father and mother and your native land and came to a people that you did not know before. 12 The Lord recompense you for what you have done, and a full reward be given you by the Lord, the God of Israel, under whose wings you have come to take refuge!"

....

19 And her mother-in-law said to her, "Where did you glean today? And where have you worked? Blessed be the man who took notice of you." So she told her mother-in-law with whom she had worked, and said, "The man's name with whom I worked today is Bo'az." 20 And Na'omi said to her daughter-in-law, "Blessed be he by the Lord, whose kindness has not forsaken the living or the dead!" Na'omi also said to her, "The man is a relative of ours, one of our nearest kin."

of our next kinsmen.

Key Verse: **Why have I found grace in thine eyes, that thou shouldest take knowledge of me, seeing I am a stranger? (Ruth 2:10)**

Key Verse: **Why have I found favor in your eyes, that you should take notice of me, when I am a foreigner? (Ruth 2:10)**

As You Read the Scripture—Harold Reid Weaver

Ruth 2:1. Boaz was a relative of Naomi, a wealthy "country gentleman" type who ran a farm and directed the work of both men and women in the fields. The Hebrew word for "kinsman" also carried the meaning of "honorable" and "distinguished."

Verse 4. The character of Boaz might have been attested by his words of greeting to the reapers in the fields: "The Lord be with you." The reapers replied using words found in Psalm 129:8, "The Lord bless you." They may have been casual words uttered with no special meaning, but on the other hand they might have revealed the depth of Boaz' spiritual life. They could indicate his concern for his workers, not only that they work industriously but that they have a feeling for God and that their work has meaning in the eyes of their creator.

The Law, expressed in Deuteronomy, has something good to say about gleaners, and Ruth was now in that category: "When you reap your harvest in your field, and have forgotten a sheaf in the field, you shall not go back to get it; it shall be for the sojourner, the fatherless, and the widow; that the Lord your God may bless you in all the work of your hands" (Deuteronomy 24:19).

Verses 5-6. Boaz recognizes the stranger in their midst, a young woman. He asks a servant about her and is informed that she is the foreigner from Moab who came back with Naomi.

Verse 7. As a foreigner, Ruth would not be able to claim the right to glean in the fields with Jewish widows and orphans. That is why she had come to the fields early in the morning, seeking permission from the person in charge of the field. She wanted to follow after the workers and pick up what they accidentally or purposefully missed.

Verse 8. Boaz listens to the servant speak of Ruth and then speaks gently to her. Calling her "my daughter," he invites her to continue to glean. He adds that he already knows about her and honors her for staying with Naomi, her mother-in-law, in her time of special need. He tells her he has ordered the men in the field not to molest her—something Naomi might have feared would happen to Ruth as a single, foreign girl.

Verse 9. Ruth is graciously invited to drink from the water provided by the young male workers, water which had been carried from the village well to the field. The jars of water were not available to all gleaners, so a special invitation had been offered to Ruth by the thoughtful and kindly Boaz. Here again is seen the generosity of a "distinguished" human being in offering the common, foreign, female gleaner some gracious concessions.

Verses 10-12. In humility, Ruth "falls on her face." That is, she is humbled and honored and grateful. Why has Boaz done all this? He knows she has left her native country, her own people, even her gods, to come to a new land in order to help Naomi. Boaz is deeply touched that she has come to the Lord, "the God of Israel, under whose wings [she has] come to take refuge."

The Scripture and the Main Question—Pat McGeachy

A Good Man

"There is none righteous, no not one." So say the Psalms (14:3, 53:3) and Paul (Romans 3:10), and of course they are right. Not even Jesus would let the young man call him good. "No one is good but God alone," he cautioned (Mark 10:18). Which makes goodness, when we find it, all the more remarkable and a certain sign of the grace of God. There are five women identified by Matthew in the genealogy he gives in the first chapter of his Gospel: Tamar, Rahab, Ruth, Bathsheba, and Mary. It is a source of astonishment to me to remember that every one of them, at one time or another, was in a questionable situation with respect to their reputation. Tamar played the harlot (Genesis 38:6-30), Rahab *was* a harlot (Joshua 6:22-25), Bathsheba was an adulteress (II Samuel 11-12), and Mary was suspected by Joseph before he understood the remarkable nature of her pregnancy (Matthew 1:18-21). As for Ruth, we are coming to that.

God used all of these women, as well as an even larger list of men with reputations even worse, as heroines and heroes of the faith. And so, great is the comfort, can you and I be used. But it is a pleasure to discover in the midst of these folk a man like Boaz. I could spend this entire section making a list of the evidence of his virtue. Let's make do with the following, by way of example:

When we first meet Boaz we like him from the way he says, "Hello." His greeting (2:4) is, "The Lord be with you!" to which his field-hands reply: "The Lord bless you." What a wonderful way for boss and employees to be talking!

Boaz is interested in the stranger in his fields (2:5).

He immediately makes her feel at home and looks out for her welfare (2:10).

He does not take advantage of Ruth's offer of herself (3:9), although he could have, but shows himself to be a thoroughly moral person who wishes to protect her reputation (3:14).

He does all that is legally necessary to carry out his duties, always keeping Ruth's interests at heart (4:1-6).

Oh, I know that some will find fault with him. He drank too much sometimes; he used a little trickery; he was an old man flattered by the attentions of a younger woman . . . OK, so he wasn't perfect. But he was a good man, all the same. I wish you and I were that good.

The Proposal

Ruth's journey by night to the threshing floor of Boaz is an incredible story! A modern writer would have to tell it with innuendoes or even overt sexual descriptions, with much panting and groaning. But the Bible story is as pure as snow. It is plain that Ruth was taking a considerable risk. Perhaps it was not so great because both she and Naomi clearly knew the character of Boaz and had good reason to believe that he would do the honorable thing. But it was a risk all the same. In modern terms, she was offering herself to him, putting herself at his mercy. It was, in other words, a dramatic proposal of marriage, not ordinarily done by the woman in those days, let alone a foreign one.

Let me tread very carefully here, for I have no wish to spoil the pure and tender story of Ruth and Boaz, but it needs to be pointed out that her action was one that put her in a very compromising position. It was women who were usually accused of adultery in those days; the men seemed to be able to get by without much criticism. Apart from the story of David and Bathsheba, can you think of a Bible story about a *man* taken in adultery? The writer says that Ruth uncovered the feet of Boaz and lay down there (3:7). In some cases in the Hebrew Bible, the word "feet" is clearly employed as a euphemism for the private parts. See, for instance, Isaiah 6:2 and 7:20, and possibly II Chronicles 16:12. Whether so blatant an act is intended here, I do not know, but it is certain that this was a sexually explicit overture, which said in effect, "I am at your mercy; you are my father-in-law's kinsman; do what you will for my honor and that of Naomi."

And Boaz kept her there all night, in all innocence, and let her go before daybreak, giving her a load of grain to carry, not only as a much needed gift but so that if she got stopped she could say that that had been the purpose of her errand. He had, in effect, accepted her proposal, but he intended to do it according to the proper rules, and that would have to wait until morning.

Taking Care of One Another

What does being a good person mean? Certainly one of the hallmarks of goodness is charity, or caring. Charity has become a sort of dirty word in our day. People say, "I don't want your charity." Other people look down on those who accept welfare (another beautiful word that has become negative to some), as though they do not believe there is such a thing as legitimate poverty. But Ruth and Naomi were truly and legitimately poor, whatever that means. And charity is always in order, even for our enemies (Romans 11:20); how much more so for our friends? "Charity" (and caring) come from the same root as "charismatic," meaning "gifted." It means simply that if it has been given to us, we are to give it.

Boaz's charity begins in small ways: allowing Ruth to glean, that is, pick up in the corners of the field that which the reapers leave behind; seeing to her security, that she not be molested by some less charitable farmers in the region. It ends with his taking care of her in the night on the threshing floor, in an act that combines both "caritas" (agape) and "eros." He was evidently moved to love her in the romantic sense, but he expressed it in the sense of I Corinthians 13.

I serve an inner city congregation which is daily besieged by the poor. For years I agonized over whether I should help certain people. If I give them money (I rarely do), will they use it wisely? Will they trade their bus or meal tickets for cash and spend it on booze? Are they really looking for work, or are they just trying to live off of the charity of suckers like me? And then one day, largely through the help of some wiser theologians than myself, the truth began to dawn. The question is not, "Is this a worthy person?" (Don't forget that no one is righteous!) The question is a much easier one to answer: "Have I got anything to give?" And that one has to do with me. Jesus did not say, "If he seems worthy, help him out." Rather, our Lord said, "Give to him who begs from you, and do not refuse him who would borrow from you." In short, "If you've got it, give it." Often for the Christian it is not money (Acts 3:6)that we have but something better. And even in the case of Boaz something more than money was at stake. Boaz gave that which everyone of us, rich or poor, can give. That is our friendship.

Boaz, the good farmer of Bethlehem, had translated the ethics of Moses, born in the desert, into the life of a loving, caring, "good" man. We will do well to emulate him. Like Boaz, we need to build on the culture and traditions that are ours and to live as those who care for the needy, protect the poor, and stand morally square. Like Boaz, we need to recognize the genuine needs of those around us and share our goods with them. In our day, this is becoming increasingly essential. There is starvation in the far places, yes, but there is hunger here at home, too. The increasing cut-back of government funds is making the plight of the poor even more desperate than before. I don't know about you, but one of the things I intend to do about it is be more like Boaz. I think I will sharpen my skills at being a good person. Jesus would like that, I think. As you show charity to the poor, the homeless, the hungry and the imprisoned, he said, "you [do] it to me" (Matthew 25:40).

Helping Adults Become Involved—John Warren Steen

Preparing to Teach

Look up some information on gleaning, in case the person assigned the topic is not able to make the report. Prepare an interest table with copies of *National Geographic* and *International Christian Digest* for early arrivals to look over.

Prepare the following true-false test to pass out, for members to see how much they know about the love story and to stimulate them to learn more.

1. Boaz was a poor man and no relation to Naomi.
2. Gleaning was gathering the grain overlooked or dropped by the harvesters.
3. Ruth started gleaning early in the morning and worked without stopping.
4. Boaz said, "Why don't you do your grain picking in somebody else's fields?"
5. Ruth was surprised Boaz had taken notice of her and had been kind to her, a foreigner.
6. Boaz told Ruth he was grateful for the way she had taken care of her mother-in-law.
7. Boaz gave instructions that extra attention be paid to Ruth, including privileges to the drinking water and protection.
8. Ruth took her grain to a mill to be ground.

Answers: Numbers 1, 4, and 8 are false. All the rest are true.

Consider using the following teaching aim: to cause class members to befriend someone or to show an act of compassion during the following week.

Use the following outline:

     I.   The setting for a kind act (Ruth 2:5-12)
         A. Meeting of Ruth and Boaz
         B. Boaz's extra concern
    II. Gratitude for a kind act (2:19-20)

Read carefully "The Scripture and the Main Question" and "As You Read the Scripture." These form the heart of the lesson. The ideas, insights, and suggestions in these sections should be reflected continually in your lesson plan.

As you use the suggested outline, you may want to either quote or paraphrase ideas. You might like to jot in the margin of your outline the page number and paragraph being referred to. For example, you could write a reference to page 65, paragraph 3, as 65-3.

Introducing the Main Question

Basic and helpful ideas are presented in the section "The Main Question." These ideas are essential in helping to identify the purpose of the lesson.

The main question is this: What constitutes a good person? Name good persons in the Bible. Do not forget Barnabas, "a good man, full of the Holy Spirit and of faith" (Acts 11:24) and Tabitha (Dorcas), "full of good works and acts of charity" (Acts 9:36).

Ask for the report on gleaning or give it yourself. Then ask: What is the motivation behind this custom? (Concern for the welfare of the poor.) Ask for examples of modern concern for the poor. (Shelters for homeless people, provision for hot meals for school children and shut-ins, medical and nursing benefits for the underprivileged, shelters for abused children and spouses, treatment centers and halfway houses for addicts and the mentally ill, and many others.)

Developing the Lesson

I. The setting for a kind act (2:5-12)

Have someone read Ruth 2:1-4 in order to get the background for the rest of the story. Ask: Would the story be as interesting if Boaz had not been a wealthy man? Yes, the story does not depend on his wealth but on his generosity. When Ruth spoke about "him in whose sight I shall find favor" (verse 2), she was not implying Boaz. She was merely alluding to the fact that anyone who let a foreigner glean is a generous person.

When Boaz spoke to his helpers in the field, he greeted them with religious words, which were similar to those that the angel had used with Gideon (see Judges 6:12).

A. Meeting of Ruth and Boaz

Ask what it was about Ruth that caught Boaz's attention (perhaps her beauty or diligence. The supervisor of the workers had already noted how hard she worked, without taking a break for rest or food. He learned that Ruth was the Moabite maiden who returned from Moab with Naomi.

B. Boaz's extra concern

Ask: Was it blind chance, a deceptive plan, or God's providence that brought Ruth to this field? It certainly appears to be God's mysterious leading.

Look at the words to Ruth and call for someone to explain them. Boaz wanted her to stay in his field, to keep close to his maidens, to feel safe from molestation by the young men, and to drink with the servants, who were provided water.

Notice Ruth's response. She bowed to the ground in humility. She called herself "a foreigner." In the Hebrew, the word comes from the same root as "take notice"; both words are used in this verse.

Look at the words of Boaz in verse 12. Boaz was ready to marry a foreign (Moabite) woman, who would bless Israel with its first king—David.

II. Gratitude for a kind act (2:19-20)

After she finished gleaning, Ruth beat (fanned) away the chaff and had an ephah, or about two-thirds of a bushel. She took the prized barley to Naomi, who asked all about how she got it.

Before Naomi learned the identity of the landowner, she blessed him. When she discovered it was her husband's kinsman, she was delighted. Again she asked for blessings, but this time on one she knew. She called him the "nearest kin," which implied the family's redeemer.

Ruth's bold act in chapter 3 was in reality a proposal of marriage. Boaz upheld her honor and cherished her love, in his dealing with her.

Helping Class Members Act

Say to your class: When all is said and done about Sunday school, more is said than is done. Let this week be different. Determine now to show an act of compassion to a foreigner during the coming week, or at least to meditate on the issue of discrimination against foreigners.

Does your church sponsor or need to sponsor services in another language? Do you have a refugee committee or a missions committee? Does your church ever send young people or senior adults to another country in volunteer service? Have you thought of getting materials from your missions board about volunteering for service within your own country or in another country?

When my church learned of the plight of the boat people of Vietnam, it appointed a refugee committee to adopt a family. After waiting nine months we received a Vietnamese man and his eleven-year-old daughter, Le Tho (pronounced "lay toe"). They had caught a boat and had to leave the rest of the family behind. When they became homesick, church members contributed money to send them to see other family members who had escaped on the same boat, in Minnesota. They enjoyed their first white Christmas there and returned to Tennessee.

Le Tho, who had arrived holding a hand towel that was a security blanket for her, soon developed into an intelligent, attractive high school student. A senior adult woman in the church took an interest in her, frequently took her to Sunday dinner, and offered to pay for an evening dress when Le Tho was elected to the homecoming queen's court.

Many people in the church helped in various ways: cleaning the apartment they would move into, contributing furniture, tutoring in English, teaching them banking and grocery shopping, and finding the man a job. After several more months, the mother and remaining children were able to leave Vietnam to join the family. Again, the church members enjoyed contributing time and money in order to help a family in critical need. All members of the family learned English. Both father and mother found good jobs and purchased used cars. Soon the thrifty family was able to move out of public housing and purchase their own home. They continued to be grateful to the church. Each year at Christmas, they bring a nice present to the chairman of the refugee committee to express their thanks to the entire congregation.

Planning for Next Sunday

Remind the class that the final lesson of the quarter will call for some review and evaluation. Tell them you will be asking for lessons that individuals can take away from this quarter.

_____

The Fulfillment of Hope

Background Scripture: Ruth 4

_____

The Main Question—Pat McGeachy

There is much tragedy and pain in the world, so much so that many writers sneer at stories with happy endings, saying that they are "not realistic" or that they are "maudlin and sentimental." But such writers, I believe, are cynics, who only see a partial truth. The story of Boaz and Ruth encourages hope and promise in the midst of a troubled world and invites you and me to share that hope. It does not promise that all will go smoothly, but it does promise that ultimately all will go well.

The levirate marriage, discussed in lesson 11, has been found in other nations than ancient Israel, I am told, such as India and Latin America. But among the Hebrews it had a special purpose: It saved the property belonging to a family from being broken up and dispersed among others and prevented the extinction of the dead man's line. The ancient Hebrew had little faith in an afterlife; immortality and hope were achieved through one's offspring and, ultimately, in the coming of the promised Messiah.

The marriage of Ruth and Boaz thus fits into a purpose above and beyond the happy story of the two lovers. It is part of holy history. It is for this reason that the author concludes the book with the reminder that from this line the king is to come. Boaz, whom Matthew 1 says was the son of the reformed harlot, Rahab, because of his kindness and faithfulness is to become grandfather of the greatest of Israel's kings. And Ruth, the foreigner, for her courage and commitment will be similarly remembered.

The question for us is simply this: Does it matter how we play the game? Is there any point in hanging on to the morality and the faith of our mothers and fathers? The plain answer of this wholesome little story is yes. Love God and live as you know you should, for there is a great day coming, and if you will be faithful, like Boaz and Ruth, you will have a part in it.

Selected Scripture

King James Version

Ruth 4:9-17

9 And Bo'-az said unto the elders, and *unto* all the people, Ye *are* witnesses, this day, that I have bought all that *was* E-lim'-e-lech's, and all that *was* Chil'-i-on's and Mah'-lon's, of the hand of Naomi.

10 Moreover Ruth the Moabitess, the wife of Mah'-lon, have I purchased to be my wife, to raise up the name of the dead upon his inheritance, that the name of the dead be not cut off from among his brethren, and from the gate of his place: ye *are* witnesses this day.

11 And all the people that *were* in the gate, and the elders, said, *We are* witnesses. The Lord make the woman that is come into thine house like Rachel and like Leah, which two did build the house of Israel: and do thou worthily in Eph'-ra-tah, and be famous in Beth-lehem:

12 And let thy house be like the house of Pha'-rez, whom Ta'-mar bare unto Judah, of the seed which the Lord shall give thee of this young woman.

13 So Bo'-az took Ruth, and she was his wife; and when he went in unto her, the Lord gave her conception, and she bare a son.

14 And the women said unto Naomi, Blessed *be* the Lord, which hath not left thee this day without a kinsman, that his name may be famous in Israel.

15 And he shall be unto thee a restorer of *thy* life, and a nourisher of thine old age: for thy daughter in law, which loveth thee, which is better to thee than seven sons, hath born him.

16 And Naomi took the child, and

Revised Standard Version

Ruth 4:9-17

9 Then Bo'az said to the elders and all the people, "You are witnesses this day that I have bought from the hand of Na'omi all that belonged to Elim'-elech and all that belonged to Chil'-ion and to Mahlon. 10 Also Ruth the Moabitess, the widow of Mahlon, I have bought to be my wife, to perpetuate the name of the dead in his inheritance, that the name of the dead may not be cut off from among his brethren and from the gate of his native place; you are witnesses this day." 11 Then all the people who were at the gate, and the elders said, "We are witnesses. May the Lord make the woman, who is coming into your house, like Rachel and Leah, who together built up the house of Israel. May you prosper in Eph'rathah and be renowned in Bethlehem; 12 and may your house be like the house of Perez, whom Tamar bore to Judah, because of the children that the Lord will give you by this young woman."

13 So Bo'az took Ruth and she became his wife; and he went in to her, and the Lord gave her conception, and she bore a son. 14 Then the women said to Na'omi, "Blessed be the Lord, who has not left you this day without next of kin; and may his name be renowned in Israel! 15 He shall be to you a restorer of life and a nourisher of your old age; for your daughter-in-law who loves you, who is more to you than seven sons, has borne him." 16 Then Na'omi took the child and laid him in her bosom, and became his nurse. 17 And the

laid it in her bosom, and became nurse unto it.

17 And the women her neighbours gave it a name, saying, There is a son born to Naomi; and they called his name O'-bed: he *is* the father of Jesse, the father of David.

Key Verse: **And the women said unto Naomi, Blessed be the Lord, which hath not left thee this day without a kinsman, that his name, may be famous in Israel. (Ruth 4:14)**

women of the neighborhood gave him a name, saying, "A son has been born to Na′omi." They named him Obed; he was the father of Jesse, the father of David.

Key Verse: **Then the women said to Naomi, "Blessed be the Lord, who has not left you this day without next of kin, and may his name be renowned in Israel!" (Ruth 4:14)**

As You Read the Scripture—Harold Reid Weaver

Ruth 4:1-6. Chapter 4 tells us how Boaz made arrangements so he could marry Ruth. The procedure involves ancient customs, some of which are not clear to us today. Boaz stopped by the gate of the city until his relative came by. He asked him to sit down with him for a while. Then he stopped ten elders of the city as they approached the gate, the number required to constitute a synagogue—and to pronounce the marriage benediction!

In the presence of the ten, Boaz told his kinsman about the situation of Naomi, a childless widow. Naomi's husband, Elimelech, had once owned land, which Boaz says is now for sale. Would the kinsman like to purchase it? Yes, he would. Boaz points out that if he buys the land, the young foreigner, Ruth, will have to go with it. So it appears that Ruth was up for sale too, as part of the property. The kinsman changed his mind! Why? A jealous wife? Maybe. But also it might have been the marriage law, which stated that the firstborn son of a widow who married again would inherit the land of his natural father. Thus the ancestral lands could be kept intact. Other sons born to such a man and his wife would be legal heirs of the second husband (see *Interpreter's Bible*, vol. 2, p. 848). Boaz accepted all of that, gentleman that he was. He was now free to do this inasmuch as he had first offered it to the next of kin.

Verses 9-10. Boaz buys the land owned by Naomi's dead husband and two sons, Chilion and Mahlon. Naomi's hope and Ruth's, to be sure, now lay in the marriage of Ruth and Boaz, which took place at once.

Not only would Ruth have security in the new home with Boaz, but Naomi also would now be cared for till death. That had been Ruth's hope, and now fulfillment of it was assured.

Verses 11-12. This verse speaks of Rachel and Leah, the two wives of Jacob, around 1600 B.C. They had a total of twelve children. The elders express the hope that Boaz may have as many! (See Genesis 30 for part of that story.) That generous hope for many children is further emphasized by the words, "May your house be like the house of Perez." Perez was the firstborn of a pair of twins fathered by Judah. His line would go down through history to David and the Messiah. (See Genesis 38:29.)

The story of the birth of Perez is a most unsavory one. But it emphasizes the primary theme of the book of Ruth: Not only are foreigners acceptable in the best genealogies (since Ruth became the great-grandmother of

David), but God makes use of even the evil characters in ancestral lines to establish important families. The writer of Ruth skipped over any moral concerns about Judah's dealings with women and marriage responsibilities, mentioning Perez only because a long line of important descendants came from him.

Verses 14-17. The women of the village praise Naomi, saying, "May [your son's] name be revered in Israel." It truly was, far beyond the wildest hopes of Ruth or Naomi. From this son, Obed, came Jesse, and from him came David. A thousand years later, the boy born of David's line in Bethlehem, the son of Joseph and Mary, was born of the "stock of Jesse."

The Scripture and the Main Question—Pat McGeachy

Uncommon Hopes for Common Folk

With this lesson we conclude our visit with the people of the period of the judges. This pleasant love story of Ruth and Boaz gives us insight into the lives of ordinary men and women during that time of heroes and heroines and drives home the point that all creatures great and small are in the hands of God. We learn from the wisdom and faith of Naomi, from the courage and loyalty of Ruth, and from the generosity and competence of Boaz. It is important that we remember that these are not major characters in the Bible. Their tale takes up less than three pages in a book a thousand pages long. They are ordinary people, like you and me.

But this says something about my ordinariness and yours. It doesn't exist! Everyone is precious in the eyes of the One who numbers the falling sparrows. Is David more important than Boaz? Only in the eyes of secular historians. The Lord sees the question from a qualitative perspective (I Samuel 16:7). There is no one in the universe more important than you. You may well, like Boaz or Ruth, one day be given an award as best supporting actor or actress! God, the great playwright, has time for each character individually. For God, the plot of history turns on your personality, as a massive vault door turns on a tiny bearing. "Now is the acceptable time; behold now is the day of salvation" (II Corinthians 6:2).

But will your story turn out happily? Is there hope for us minor characters? Let's look once more at the story of Ruth and Boaz for the answer to that question.

Tension and Release

The last chapter of the story of Ruth is a well-written cliff-hanger: Will Boaz be able to settle things with the one who is closer kin to Elimelech? What if the near-kinsman has had a good look at Ruth and wants to marry her himself, with all that good property? But no, the matter is settled happily; there is a marriage, a baby, and the women's chorus concludes the musical with a glad song (4:14-15). They even named the baby after Ruth (an unusual custom): they called him Obed, which means "servant."

The little genealogy at the end serves to tie the story's actors to the genealogy of David and hence to Jesus. The list of descendants given in Matthew 1 lets us know something about Boaz's mother (Obed's grandmother): she was a foreigner too! and more than that, she was a prostitute: Rahab the harlot of Jericho (see Joshua 6:22-25). If you had looked at all this from the beginning, you might have said, "There is no way this marriage can work. Their backgrounds are too different. This sort of crosscultural matchup is bound to cause trouble." And sometimes it does. But the point is this: God can raise a phoenix from the ashes. Who would have thought that the child of Mary and Joseph the carpenter, born in a barn, would turn the world upside down?

But God has allowed this suspense to build up to make the ending all the more triumphant. As Jesus once said, it is better to start at the bottom of the ladder and work up than to start at the top and come crashing down. (Well, you can see his exact words in Luke 14:7-11.)

Can We Be Sure?

Yes, you may say, it is all well and good to claim that our present troubles may build up suspense, but that the future will be all right. Isn't that pretty silly, like the man who sat on the stove all morning because it felt so good when he got off? I can stand my troubles if I really know that it is all going to turn out OK, but can I really know?

I think that Naomi knew from the beginning that things would be all right; it was in hope that she began her long journey back to Bethlehem. I know she called herself "Bitter," for her grief was great. But it is also clear that she was full of hope. Notice how she advises Ruth all along with little words of comfort (2:20; 3:1, etc.). It is the faith of Naomi that keeps the story alive and makes the happy ending come true.

It is also the faith of Boaz, who sees in Ruth a sign of hope and who promises her (4:11-13) that things will work out. And it is the faith of Ruth, clinging to what she has seen in Naomi and bravely fitting in to the customs of this strange people.

You mean faith makes it come out all right? No, I mean the promise of God is that it *will* come out all right, and faith is belief in that promise. "Faith is the assurance of things hoped for, the conviction of things not seen" (Hebrews 11:1). It is the faith of that roll-call of the heroes (Hebrews 11:1-40) we have been studying all this quarter that keeps us going:

By faith, Joshua . . .
By faith, Rahab . . .
By faith, Deborah . . .
By faith, Barak . . .
By faith, Jael . . .
By faith, Gideon . . .
By faith, Samson . . .
By faith, Naomi . . .
By faith, Ruth . . .
By faith, Boaz . . .

God is working on a happy ending for all these, which has not yet been fully realized (Hebrews 11:39-40). Therefore it is up to us "Since we are surrounded by so great a cloud of witnesses" to "lay aside every weight and . . . run with perseverance the race that is set before us, looking to Jesus the pioneer and perfector of our faith" (Hebrews 12:1-2).

You and I are to be faithful like Naomi, daring like Ruth, gracious like Boaz, and in all things, to be like Jesus, living in the assurance of a happy ending.

You see, we are witnesses to an event far more radical than Joshua's conquest of Canaan, far more astonishing than the Exodus and the coming of the Law, far more amazing even than the acts of the kings and the prophets. We believe that there came a time, there in the same Fields of Boaz near Bethlehem, that the Author of history became himself a character in the play. He looked back with gratitude to the same Law and forward with the same hope. And he has invited us to walk with him on the journey. It is one thing to associate with fellow actors on the stage; it is quite another to know the playwright personally. I know there are those who do not believe this tale. There were some who did not believe it even when he was present on the stage. They resented his claims, feared for their own glory in his presence, and in the end killed him.

But the characters cannot kill the Author of the play. Oh, we may manage to kill the character playing the part, but there is evidence that he will be written into the next act. As far as that goes, the plot may well change as we go along. We cannot see into tomorrow, but the Lord of history can.

Let us then leave the future in those Hands and let us, laying aside all weights, run the race here and now. Let us make choices with Joshua, stand up for the right with Deborah, trust God with Gideon, confess our sins with Samson, risk with Ruth, love with Boaz, and plan wisely with Naomi. Even if things don't turn out in history the way we think they should, that is no reason to desert the Lord of history. We have the divine promise that all will be well, therefore let us live in hope. And, as the prophet Habakkuk once sang,

> Though the fig tree do not blossom,
>   nor fruit be on the vines,
> the produce of the olive fail
>   and the fields yield no food,
> the flock be cut off from the fold
>   and there be no herd in the stalls,
> yet I will rejoice in the Lord,
>   I will joy in the God of my salvation.
> God, the Lord, is my strength;
>   he makes my feet like hinds' feet,
>   he makes me tread upon my high places.
>   (3:17-19)

Helping Adults Become Involved—John Warren Steen

Preparing to Teach

Make sure that someone brings photos of the latest British royal weddings, or bring them yourself.

Review briefly your goals for the quarter and for each of the three units. Be prepared to share your personal feelings about spiritual formation with the class. Plan to give a brief review of the quarter. Schedule adequate time to complete the story of Ruth and Boaz.

Consider using the following teaching aim: to help class members to combine the admirable character traits of the people discussed in this quarter, including Ruth's love of her family, into a composite that will serve as a goal in developing their spiritual personalities.

Use the following outline:

    I.   Ruth and Boaz are married (4:9-12).

> II.   The heir is born (4:13).
> III. Naomi shares the joy (4:14-17).

Read carefully "The Scripture and the Main Question" and "As You Read the Scripture." These form the heart of the lesson. The ideas, insights, and suggestions in these sections should be reflected continually in your lesson plan.

As you use the suggested outline, you may want to either quote or paraphrase ideas. You might like to jot in the margin of your outline the page number and paragraph being referred to. For example, you could write a reference to page 65, paragraph 3, as 65-3.

Introducing the Main Question

Basic and helpful ideas are presented in the section "The Main Question." These ideas are essential in helping to identify the purpose of the lesson.

Invite class members to share how they carried out last Sunday's commitment to be friend or show compassion to a foreigner.

Tell the class that today's lesson will summarize the entire quarter. Ask the class to list the topics for this quarter's lessons; help them as needed, and write the topics on the chalkboard. Then, with some firm answers in your own mind, ask the students: What are the main insights you would like to take with you from these lessons? List these on the chalkboard also. Tell the class you will be returning to this list later, then announce the main question for this lesson: Is there any point in hanging onto the morality, faith, and hope of our parents?

Developing the Lesson

Begin by asking members what arrangements have to be made before a wedding today. Point out the differences in ancient times.

I. Ruth and Boaz are married (4:9-12).

The village gate had a wide place where elders of the town met to discuss business. The discussion centered around property.

Boaz told the anonymous kinsman that Naomi was selling a parcel of land. The kinsman-redeemer seemed delighted to have a chance to get the land until he learned that certain obligations went with the land, namely, Ruth. Then he renounced his claim publicly, and Boaz could proceed with his plans.

After the quaint ritual of the exchange of sandals, Boaz asked the witnesses to verify that he was performing the duties of the levirate marriage. Ask if anyone can say what this meant. Point out the importance of passing along property to progeny, all the more significant because the people had no clear view of an afterlife. The elders and others acted as a voice of conscience for the community. There was rejoicing that Naomi's circumstances were improving and that Ruth would become the wife of a wealthy man.

Read verse 11 and explain that the word "son" is similar to the word meaning "to build." Like Rachel and Leah, the wives of Jacob, she could aspire to having many children. They hoped that Boaz would prosper financially and achieve renown for his large family.

Refer to what Dr. Reid Weaver says about Perez, and call attention to that strange inclusion in verse 12.

II. The heir is born (4:13).

Not only were the newlyweds happy in their new home, they were blessed with a baby boy. It was a cause for ecstatic celebration. The heritage of Elimelech and Mahlon would be preserved. The widow Naomi would have cause to rejoice. She would be no longer rejected but cared for; no longer without a family but the grandmother of Obed, and through him great-greatgrandmother of King David.

III. Naomi shares the joy (4:14-17).

The women clustered around Naomi. Her circumstances had changed radically. Have someone read Luke 1:48-52 and point out the similarities: "He has regarded the low estate of his handmaiden . . . all generations will call me blessed . . . he has scattered the proud . . . and exalted those of low degree." Indeed, Mary and Naomi had much in common. But Ruth and Mary even more: Both were in the lineage of a king.

Have someone read verse 15. The word "loves" is used here for the relation between two women in the Old Testament. The daughter-in-law is "more to you than seven sons," an idiomatic expression that meant a perfect family.

Helping Class Members Act

Relate the following anecdote to the class: If you visit a certain Oklahoma church, you will see a green banner featuring a cocoon, a butterfly, and the words, "Behold, I make all things new." It signifies hope. If you inquire about it, you learn the touching story behind the banner. You discover that it was made by Patty Chambers, one of the fifteen postal employees in Edmond, Oklahoma, who were killed in 1986 by a crazed gunman. The banner calls attention to her love for her fellow church members and her belief in a life after death. What a consolation it must be for her family to view that work of art, completed just days before her inexplicable murder. The banner, like her life, is a testimony to her belief in hope.

Ask the class to consider what character traits they would like to be remembered for. Point to the list of the insights of this quarter's lessons, and ask what personality changes would result from taking these insights to heart. Tell the class that now might be a good time to think about adopting character traits that can help you grow in favor with God and humankind.

Share with the class how this quarter's study has affected your life. Tell what you hope it will mean for your outlook in coming days. For example, you could say, "I want you to pray with me that I will be a more effective Christian and a more effective teacher." Lead the class in a time of quiet meditation, goal setting, and commitment.

Ask the class to join you in prayer. Here is a suggested example: O God, we are thankful for this fellowship of learning and love. Help us to learn more and to love more. As we recall our studies for this quarter, we give thanks for those whose lives encourage us to grow. Help us to make choices like Joshua, to stand up for the right like Deborah, to trust you like Gideon, to confess our sins like Samson, to make commitments like Ruth, to love generously like Boaz, and to plan faithfully and wisely like Naomi. In the spirit of Jesus our Teacher and Friend, Amen.

Planning for Next Sunday

Remind the class that next Sunday starts a new quarter. Announce that the theme is "Visions of God's Rule." Point out that the scripture passages come from parts of the Bible that many believers have abandoned to fanatics, who rave and rant about them. Ask: wouldn't you like to know more about apocalyptic literature as found in the book of Revelation, the letters to the Thessalonians, and the prophecies of Ezekiel and Daniel? Encourage class members to set some goals for themselves as they study these neglected parts of the Bible.